Foreign Exchange Markets

The International Library of Critical Writings in Financial Economics

Series Editor: Richard Roll

Allstate Professor of Economics
The Anderson School at UCLA, USA

This major series presents by field outstanding selections of the most important articles across the entire spectrum of financial economics – one of the fastest growing areas in business schools and economics departments. Each collection has been prepared by a leading specialist who has written an authoritative introduction to the literature. A full list of published and future titles in this series is printed at the end of this volume.

Wherever possible, the articles in these volumes have been reproduced as originally published using facsimile reproduction, inclusive of footnotes and pagination to facilitate ease of reference.

For a list of all Edward Elgar published titles visit our site on the World Wide Web at www.e-elgar.com

Foreign Exchange Markets

Edited by

Richard J. Sweeney

Chair in International Finance
McDonough School of Business, Georgetown University, USA

THE INTERNATIONAL LIBRARY OF CRITICAL WRITINGS IN FINANCIAL ECONOMICS

An Elgar Reference Collection
Cheltenham, UK • Northampton, MA, USA

Published by
Edward Elgar Publishing Limited
Glensanda House
Montpellier Parade
Cheltenham
Glos GL50 1UA
UK

Edward Elgar Publishing, Inc.
136 West Street
Suite 202
Northampton
Massachusetts 01060
USA

A catalogue record for this book is available from the British Library.

Library of Congress Cataloguing in Publication Data

Foreign exchange markets / edited by Richard J. Sweeney.
p. cm. — (The International library of critical writings in financial economics ; 17) (An Elgar reference collection)
Includes bibliographical references and index.
1. Foreign exchange market. I. Sweeney, Richard J. (Richard James), 1944– II. Series. III. Series: An Elgar reference collection

HG3851.F624 2005
332.4'5—dc22

2005054902

ISBN 1 84064 831 7

Printed and bound in Great Britain by MPG Books Ltd, Bodmin Cornwall.

Contents

Acknowledgements

The editor and publishers wish to thank the authors and the following publishers who have kindly given permission for the use of copyright material.

American Economic Association for article: Stanley Fischer (2001), 'Exchange Rate Regimes: Is the Bipolar View Correct?', *Journal of Economic Perspectives*, **15** (2), Spring, 3–24.

Blackwell Publishing Ltd for articles: Bettina Peiers (1997), 'Informed Traders, Intervention, and Price Leadership: A Deeper View of the Microstructure of the Foreign Exchange Market', *Journal of Finance*, **LII** (4), September, 1589–614; Torben G. Andersen and Tim Bollerslev (1998), 'Deutsche Mark–Dollar Volatility: Intraday Activity Patterns, Macroeconomic Announcements, and Longer Run Dependencies', *Journal of Finance*, **LIII** (1), February, 219–65; Andreas M. Fischer and Mathias Zurlinden (1999), 'Exchange Rate Effects of Central Bank Interventions: An Analysis of Transaction Prices', *Economic Journal*, **109** (458), October, 662–76.

Elsevier for articles: Richard A. Meese and Kenneth Rogoff (1983), 'Empirical Exchange Rate Models of the Seventies: Do They Fit Out of Sample?', *Journal of International Economics*, **14**, 3–24; Richard K. Lyons (1995), 'Tests of Microstructural Hypotheses in the Foreign Exchange Market', *Journal of Financial Economics*, **39**, 321–51; Torben G. Andersen and Tim Bollerslev (1997), 'Intraday Periodicity and Volatility Persistence in Financial Markets', *Journal of Empirical Finance*, **4**, 115–58; Richard T. Baillie and William P. Osterberg (1997), 'Why Do Central Banks Intervene?', *Journal of International Money and Finance*, **16** (6), 909–19; R.J. Sweeney (2000), 'Does the Fed Beat the Foreign-Exchange Market?', *Journal of Banking and Finance*, **24**, 665–94; Nelson C. Mark and Donggyu Sul (2001), 'Nominal Exchange Rates and Monetary Fundamentals: Evidence from a Small Post-Bretton Woods Panel', *Journal of International Economics*, **53**, 29–52; Jun Cai, Yan-Leung Cheung, Raymond S.K. Lee and Michael Melvin (2001), '"Once-in-a-Generation" Yen Volatility in 1998: Fundamentals, Intervention, and Order Flow', *Journal of International Money and Finance*, **20**, 327–47; Christopher J. Neely (2002), 'The Temporal Pattern of Trading Rule Returns and Exchange Rate Intervention: Intervention Does Not Generate Technical Trading Profits', *Journal of International Economics*, **58**, 211–32; Vicentiu Covrig and Michael Melvin (2002), 'Asymmetric Information and Price Discovery in the FX Market: Does Tokyo Know More About the Yen?', *Journal of Empirical Finance*, **9**, 271–85; Kathryn M.E. Dominguez (2003), 'The Market Microstructure of Central Bank Intervention', *Journal of International Economics*, **59**, 25–45.

Ohio State University Press for article: Rasmus Fatum and Michael Hutchison (1999), 'Is Intervention a Signal of Future Monetary Policy? Evidence from the Federal Funds Futures Market', *Journal of Money, Credit, and Banking*, **31** (1), February, 54–69.

University of Chicago Press for articles: Rudiger Dornbusch (1976), 'Expectations and Exchange Rate Dynamics', *Journal of Political Economy*, **84** (6), December, 1161–76; Martin D.D. Evans and Richard K. Lyons (2002), 'Order Flow and Exchange Rate Dynamics', *Journal of Political Economy*, **110** (1), 170–80.

Every effort has been made to trace all the copyright holders but if any have been inadvertently overlooked the publishers will be pleased to make the necessary arrangement at the first opportunity.

In addition the publishers wish to thank the Library of Indiana University at Bloomington, USA for their assistance in obtaining these articles.

Foreword

Richard Roll

By the volume of trading, the foreign exchange markets are by far the largest financial markets on earth. As such, they are highly attractive to speculators and fascinating for scholars. In addition, they are of primary importance to central banks conducting monetary policy and attempting to maintain stability in international trade.

In this volume, Professor Sweeney, a leading contributor to the literature about exchange markets, has compiled a noteworthy collection of mainly empirical papers about exchange rates. Many are acknowledged classics and others, though perhaps lesser known, have made significant improvements in empirical analysis.

Given the allure of trading profits, it is no surprise that many articles in this collection deal with exchange rate predictability. There are two well-accepted prediction methods for financial prices: fundamental and technical. In Part I of this collection, Sweeney presents articles dealing with exchange rate fundamentals; for example, macroeconomic constructs that seem likely to be candidates for predictors. Unfortunately for speculators, Sweeney finds little hope in these articles for significant profits.

For example, after discussing prediction models based monetary constructs, he concludes:

> If the monetary models had beaten the random walk, the results might have seemed satisfactory: Economic fundamentals would have explained at least some of the ups and downs of exchange rates. Still, because the fundamentals could not have been known in advance, but only noisy estimates of them, exchange rates would have remained largely unpredictable based on fundamentals.

He speculates that the failure of fundamental predictions might be attributable to the fact that much of the literature does not control for market microstructure effects.

Articles on technical analysis, the other standard prediction method, are assembled in Part III of this volume. Understandably, they are preceded by Part II containing articles on the statistical processes followed by exchange rates. The statistical results are rich and intriguing. As Sweeney emphasizes, there is much more to be learned from high frequency data (e.g., trade-to-trade observations) than from lower frequency data used in earlier articles. For instance, it is much easier to detect the effects of central bank intervention. The impact of order flow is also more transparent.

Sweeney notes that professional traders rely much more on technical than on fundamental prediction methods, so he expects to find that articles involving technical methods report better predictive power. Only one article is reprinted in Part III but the editor notes that it contains most of the important results. Technical analysis does indeed seem to bring significant trading profits, even after being adjusted for risk, but, perhaps contrary to popular belief, these profits are not derived from central bank interventions.

Central bank activity is itself the subject of articles in Part IV. Intervention is widespread, but is highly variable across countries and over time. For some countries, the data are truly excellent; the Swiss central bank, for instance, publishes details of its interventions (unlike the U.S. Federal Reserve.)

One interesting question involves the motivation for intervention. Many countries state that they are attempting to stabilize exchange rates, though why this is necessarily desirable or even effective is a good question. Indeed, it has been quite difficult to uncover the effects of intervention, which is something of a puzzle given the large amounts involved. Much work has involved improving econometric methods, such as using simultaneous equations, while other articles have purported to explain the puzzle in terms of private anticipations about central bank activities. Some articles have had better luck discerning the impact when interventions are coordinated among central banks in several countries.

The final part of this volume assembles articles dealing with exchange rate market microstructure. Throughout his introductory essay, Professor Sweeney extols the virtues of very short-term data. Part V presents several important and interesting papers using such data. As with other assets, exchange rates exhibit intra-day seasonalities such as a U-shaped pattern of volatility across the trading day. Other interesting phenomena involve curious events such as removal of a lunchtime trading ban in Japan.

The bottom line of Part V is that order flow in the market must be considered in any model. Of course, order flow itself must depend on something else, such as public or private information events, but it cannot be ignored by a successful trader or scholar.

The articles in this volume are essential reading for anyone who wants to develop an understanding of the world's largest market, foreign exchange. Professor Sweeney has provided a valuable contribution by choosing the best articles on this topic and discussing so lucidly their various contributions.

Introduction

Richard J. Sweeney

The foreign exchange market may usefully be examined from a variety of viewpoints. This book adopts one viewpoint, the behavior of exchange rates. The book focuses on shorter-term exchange rate behavior, daily or intra-day, but it also looks at some longer-term questions as background to short-term behavior.

It is a commonplace that foreign exchange traders analyze the market with fundamental analysis and with technical analysis, though it is becoming better understood that a third, complementary approach that inter-bank dealers and brokers rely on is analysis of order flow, that is, the sequence of purchases and sales of foreign exchange. As is well known, on average traders rely much more heavily on technical rather than fundamental analysis. The articles in Part I in this volume show why traders may well be skeptical of fundamental analysis: models of exchange rate behavior that rely on fundamentals work pretty poorly. In fact, fundamental models seem to work only for panels of exchange rates, and, even then, their forecasting ability is rather small, and some question this forecasting ability, as discussed below. Given this perhaps surprising inability of fundamental models to shed light on short- and medium-term exchange rate movements, Part II contains articles on statistical models of exchange rate behavior, and Part III covers technical analysis. Related to Parts II and III, an important and controversial issue is the effect on exchange rates of government intervention in foreign exchange markets; Part IV contains several articles on this topic. Finally, Part V contains articles that cover the important and basic topic of the micro structure of the foreign exchange market; to be sure, implicitly or explicitly in many of the articles in earlier parts of this volume micro structure is an important topic.

This introductory essay discusses the articles in this volume, and selectively reviews some of the literature in which these articles are landmarks. Often the articles themselves contain masterful literature reviews, but there may still be value in elaborating in places, and in tying together some of the literatures. Many of the articles in this volume are largely empirical, but almost all have solid theoretical foundations. One key issue many of these articles address is what is known about empirical regularities in exchange rate behavior. Another key issue many address is what is known about the relationship between risk and expected returns in foreign exchange markets.

One influential view of the foreign exchange markets is that they show excessive volatility, that their fluctuations bear no meaningful relationships to underlying economic fundamentals, and that their behavior cannot easily be rationalized in terms of risk and return; many central bankers hold these or closely related views. These views are sometimes used to justify proposals for greater fixity of exchange rates – either more government intervention, or pegging or even permanently fixed rates. In principle, one might agree with all of the criticisms of exchange rate behavior without believing that any plan for greater fixity would lead to better economic outcomes. Still, it is important to investigate just how the markets behave, in order to know what kind of case there is to answer about their behavior.

Predictability of foreign exchange rates offers the dangers of a rock and a hard place. On the one hand, if fundamental models offer little insight into exchange rate behavior, one can argue that there is a prima facie case in favor of government intervention or regulation, for the purpose of making the markets better reflect fundamental economic forces. On the other hand, if exchange rates contain reliably predictable movements, either from fundamentals, statistical analysis, technical analysis or order flow analysis, this predictability may indicate that the markets are inefficient in the technical sense that they offer predictable risk-adjusted profits. Thus, in the articles below that find evidence of predictability, it is important to ask whether this predictability offers the possibility of risk-adjusted profits. Surprisingly, a number of excellent, well-done articles in this volume ignore the issue of whether the predictability they detect allows risk-adjusted profits. Still, it is important to note that even further analysis suggests that traders might be able to earn risk-adjusted profits, central bank intervention aimed at offsetting such inefficiency may fail to do so or may even exacerbate problems reflected in the predictability – government failure is often as serious as market failure.

Part I Fundamentals in the Foreign Exchange Market

The behavior of a given foreign exchange rate and its theoretical relationship to fundamentals depend on the type of exchange rate regime the country follows. At one extreme is a currency union, for example, the European Monetary Union (EMU), where the 12 member countries all use the same currency, the Euro. To be sure, a member state can always in principle leave the union and reintroduce its own currency. A different version of a currency union is Panama's use of the US dollar as its currency; unlike EMU member states, which have representation at the European Central Bank, Panama is unrepresented at the Federal Reserve (Fed). A currency board is a weaker version of monetary union. Under a currency board, a country has its own currency, but commits to keeping a fairly strict relationship between the amount of its currency outstanding and central bank holdings of the currency to which the domestic currency is pegged. Similar to a currency-union member reintroducing its own currency, Of course, a country with a currency board can in principle abrogate at any time its commitment to the strict relationship to holdings of the pegging currency, as Argentina in fact did in the 1990s. At the other extreme, a country can allow its currency to float freely, in the sense that it does not intervene to influence the currency's value. Floating countries, however, virtually always adopt some degree of management through intervention, though the amount and frequency of intervention can vary widely. Between these two extremes lie various versions of the 'soft peg,' where a country pegs its rate but is not willing to tie its hands to the extent of adopting a currency union or a currency board. Stanley Fischer (Chapter 1) gave an analytical discussion of hard pegs, managed floating and soft pegs. This serves as background for the chapters that follow.

In the 1960s and 1970s, a large number of influential papers dealt with portfolio balance and monetary models of exchange rate determination. The theory started with Robert A. Mundell, many of whose articles are collected in Mundell (1968), and Marcus Fleming (1962). Related articles on the monetary approach to the balance of payments are Jacob A. Frenkel (1976),

Pentti Kouri (1976) and Richard J. Sweeney (1976). These articles dealt both with floating and fixed exchange rates. A classic in the monetary approach genre is Rudiger Dornbusch's article on overshooting of floating exchange rates in response to monetary shocks (Chapter 2). Overshooting models seemed to offer a possible explanation for the large amount of exchange-rate volatility observed under floating, an amount that surprised many observers.

A key to the acceptance of these models is that, on data up to the early and mid 1970s, they seemed to perform fairly well empirically, at least within the sample period, typically for quarterly or monthly data, for example, Jeffrey Frankel (1979). As time went on and the sample period was lengthened, these models performed less well, and various 'fixes' were tried to get them to perform, for example, adding variables such as balance-of-payments measures, such as the cumulative current account. Ultimately, these fixes provided temporary solutions that failed over longer sample periods (Paul Boothe and Debra Glassman 1987).

Richard A. Meese and Kenneth Rogoff (Chapter 3) reported devastating results: in out-of-sample forecasts, monetary models systematically under-performed compared with a random walk. Further, the monetary models under-performed even though actual data on money stocks, real incomes, and so on were used, for example, for money stocks, that could not in practice have been known when the monetary-model forecasts were made. (See also their follow-up paper, Meese and Rogoff 1988.) If the monetary models had beaten the random walk, the results might have seemed satisfactory: economic fundamentals would have explained at least some of the ups and downs of exchange rates. Still, because the fundamentals could not have been known in advance, but only noisy estimates of them, exchange rates would have remained largely unpredictable based on fundamentals. Exchange rates might still have been predictable, or more predictable, from technical analysis, and at much the same time as fundamentals were being investigated, technical analysis was also being investigated, as discussed below.

In response to Meese and Rogoff's (1983, Chapter 3, and 1988) articles, a large number of articles examined various possible explanations for the empirical failure of monetary models, including non-linearities, omitted variables, parameter instability, and more. (A useful survey is Neely and Sarno 2002.) Many of these possible explanations did little in practice to rehabilitate the monetary model. In what seemed to be an important approach, Nelson A. Mark (1995) asked whether the monetary model might work for long forecast horizons, if not for short horizons, and found evidence that the model performed for long horizons. A number of articles, however, cast doubt on Mark's long-horizon results, essentially because of non-standard econometric properties of long-horizon estimators (see the references in the next article discussed here). More recently, Nelson A. Mark and Donggyu Sul (Chapter 4), presented results for quarterly data, but using panels for 19 countries over the sample period 1973.1 to 1997.1 rather than for single equations estimated separately for each country. They succeed in finding some limited forecasting ability for their panel approaches, relative to random walks and to forecasts based on Purchasing Power Parity relationships. Because they use actual data, for example, for money stocks, which could not in practice have been known when forecasts were made, the predictability they find is still minor, even if accepted at face value. Mark and Sul's results, interesting as they are, have econometric weaknesses, however. For one thing, they assume that aside from fixed time effects (in their equation (3)) the equations' errors are uncorrelated across countries; in fact, the errors are likely to show substantial, positive correlations that are far from explained by fixed-time effects. Thus, the economic significance of their results remains unclear. (David E. Rupach and Mark E. Wohar 2001 gave a wide ranging investigation of the use of panels in fitting monetary exchange rate models, including much discussion of Mark and Sul 2001. They find good arguments on each side of the debate about using panels.) Note that Martin D.D. Evans and Richard K. Lyons (Chapter 17), and Kathryn Dominguez (Chapter 13) have suggested that one reason that monetary models might not work is that they do not take account of the micro structure of the foreign exchange market, in particular, order flow.

Part II Statistical Models of the Foreign Exchange Market

Other authors focus more on statistical analysis than on economic models of foreign exchange rates. Some of the most interesting statistical work is on shorter-term behavior, daily or intra-day data, rather than the monthly or quarterly data used in models based on fundamentals. As the observation interval rises from one day, to two days, to a week, to a month, much of the process in changes in log exchange rates becomes less and less observable. For example, parameter estimates of generalized autoregressive conditional heteroskedastic (GARCH) processes may be highly significant on daily data but much less significant on monthly data; this relates to the fact that GARCH processes are not invariant with changes in the observation interval of the data (Richard T. Baillie and Tim Bollerslev 1989; see also the later analytical work that Andersen and Bollerslev cited in Chapter 5). Thus, daily and especially intra-day data tend to offer much richer statistical processes. Further, these intra-day data offer the possibility of detecting inefficiencies that might be harder to detect in daily data; after all, foreign exchange traders typically hold their positions for only relatively short periods during the day, and often are constrained to have positions close to zero at the close of business (see Chapter 14 by Richard K. Lyons for a discussion of inter-bank dealers and their behavior). Higher-frequency data also offer the possibility of detecting government intervention effects on exchange rates that also might be harder to detect in daily data; see Chapter 13 by Kathryn Dominguez.

Intra-day data offer the possibility of within-day periodicity, or 'seasonality.' This is a likely phenomenon because of changes in market thickness and liquidity during the trading day. For example, during the New York trading day, the London market is open for several hours in the morning, during which time the world foreign exchange market is thicker and more liquid *ceteris paribus* than in New York's afternoon when London is closed or in London's morning when New York is not yet open. The greater thickness and liquidity when London and New York are both open leads to more trading *ceteris paribus*. Thus, the thickness and liquidity of the market, and the trading activity in it, are endogenous and interact with each other. Because of this endogeneity, it is to be expected that a richer and more satisfactory analysis is possible if both price and order-flow data are available. Unfortunately, few articles exist that analyze both transactions prices and order flows; in Chapters 14 and 17, respectively, Richard K. Lyons, and Martin D.D. Evans and Richard K. Lyons present important and influential evidence on order flow and price formation in foreign exchange markets.

Part II of this volume includes three key articles for understanding intra-day price behavior in exchange markets. The first two, by Andersen and Bollerslev (Chapters 5 and 6), are rich in the methods and econometrics of high-frequency data, and have served as guides to many later articles. Torben G. Andersen and Tim Bollerslev (Chapter 5) found intra-day periodicity in the *volatility* in both foreign exchange and equity markets, and also found volatility persistence – they examined the Deutsche Mark–Dollar rate and the Standard and Poor's (S&P) 500. (Related, an earlier, interesting article is Richard T. Baillie and Tim Bollerslev 1991 that documents intra-day patterns of volatility in foreign exchange markets.) They showed that uncovering the true dynamic properties of intra-day foreign exchange rates of return requires modeling of volatility that takes account of both strong periodicity in intra-day volatility and in its persistence. For example, in their period, the Deutsche Mark–Dollar exchange rate showed periodicity in volatility, larger when both New York and London were open, smaller when Tokyo was closed for lunch, as Japanese regulations required during their sample period of October 1, 1992 to September 30, 1993. (For the same period, in Chapter 15 Bettina Peiers examined price leadership among German banks in the Deutsche Mark–Dollar in responding to Bundesbank intervention. Vicentiu Covrig and Michael Melvin, in Chapter 16, examined the consequences when Japanese regulators changed the rules and allowed lunch-time trading in Tokyo.) Further, Andersen and Bollerslev (Chapter 5) found that volatility picked up when the Tokyo market was still open and Europe first opened, with persistence in volatility. Similarly, volatility increases sharply when New York opens in the European afternoon, with persistence in volatility; when Europe closes, volatility monotonically declines until Far Eastern markets start to trade. Notably, Andersen and Bollerslev showed that using GARCH models on intra-day data is inadequate and misleading.

In Andersen and Bollerslev (Chapter 6), they focused on the Deutsche Mark–Dollar market and gave an integrated analysis of intra-day and inter-day behavior, and reactions to macroeconomic announcements, that is, to announcements of fundamentals, as well as holidays, daylight savings time, and so on. They showed that the GARCH process observable in daily data is related to underlying persistence in intra-day volatility, which is superimposed on intra-day periodicity in volatility. More generally, they successfully modeled the surprise in the (five-minute) rate of return as depending on the product of (i) a term that represents effects of intra-day volatility patterns and scheduled macroeconomic announcements, (ii) ARCH components to intra-day volatility, and (iii) an independent identically distributed (i.i.d.) mean-zero, unit-variance error term.

Building on the methods Andersen and Bollerslev developed in Chapters 5 and 6, Jun Cai, Yan-Leung Cheung, Raymond S.K. Lee, and Michael Melvin (Chapter 7) used intra-day data to examine the Japanese Yen–Dollar exchange rate for the extraordinarily volatile year on 1998. As did Andersen and Bollerslev in Chapter 6, they examined fundamentals including regularly scheduled announcements, and also the crisis around the bail-out of Long-Term Capital Management. In addition, they examined the effects of central bank intervention, including joint Japan–US intervention, the first yen intervention by the Clinton Administration. Similar to Andersen and Bollerslev, they detected a distinct pattern of intra-day volatility. In an important difference with the Andersen–Bollerslev chapters, they also investigated the effects of order flow. They found that order flow plays an important role. A weakness of their analysis is that they used weekly data to proxy order flow; in contrast, Richard K. Lyons (Chapter 14) and Martin D. Evans and Richard K. Lyons (Chapter 17) used intra-day and daily data on order flow, respectively. As special cases of order flow, Andreas M. Fischer and Mathias Zurlinden (Chapter 12) and Kathryn Dominguez (Chapter 13) use central bank order flow. Thus, in a sense, Chapter 7 by Cai *et al.* serves as a transition. Cai *et al.* used weekly data to proxy order flow; articles in Parts IV and V used intra-day or daily order flow.

It should be noted that all three chapters in Part II used indicative quotes that appeared on the Reuters network (the so-called FXFX series), obtained from Olsen and Associates Limited.

These data are not transaction prices, and for some purposes are distinctly inferior to transactions prices; Richard K. Lyons (Chapter 14) discussed differences in the series on indicative quotes and transaction prices. Nevertheless, in the absence of series on transaction prices, careful use of indicative quotes can produce interesting and useful results, as a number of articles in this volume illustrate.

There are, of course, other related literatures on stochastic properties of exchange rates. A brief and partial list of some of the important literatures, along with important articles, are the following. David A. Hsieh (1989) provided an early example of attempts to model heteroskedasticity in foreign exchange rates, in this case, daily rates. Kees G. Koedijk, Marcia M.A. Schafgans and Casper G. de Vries (1990) discussed the tail index of exchange rate returns. There is an enormous literature on jump processes in exchange rates; Philippe Jorion (1988) offered an early, important contribution. Frederick G.M.C. Nieuwland, Willem F.C. Verschoor and Christian C.P. Wolff (1994) examined European Monetary System exchange rates for stochastic trends and in particular jumps in these rates. In a well-known and influential article, Charles M. Engel and James D. Hamilton (1990) investigated 'long swings' in the dollar exchange rate using Markov changes in the mean of the appreciation rate. Yin-Wong Cheung (1993) gave an early report on 'long memory' in foreign exchange rates due to fractional integration. Michael M. Dacorogna, Ulrich A. Muller, Robert J. Nagler, Richard B. Olsen, and Olivier V. Pictet (1993) discussed a 'geographical' model of daily and weekly seasonal volatility in the foreign exchange market.

Part III Technical Analysis of Foreign Exchange Markets

As noted above, on average foreign exchange traders rely much more heavily on technical than fundamental analysis. Soon after the world moved to managed floating in March, 1973, authors began to investigate whether technical analysis might allow the trader to predict exchange rate movements well enough to make risk-adjusted profits. Early articles reported evidence that technical trading rules made profits (for example, Michael P. Dooly and Jeffry Shafer 1976, W. Bradford Cornell and J. Kimball Dietrich 1978, and Dennis E. Logue, Richard J. Sweeney and Thomas D. Willett 1978), but these articles usually did not adjust their estimated speculative profits for risk, and did not present tests of the statistical significance of profits. Later articles, however, presented estimates of risk-adjusted profits and gave tests of statistical significance. For example, Richard J. Sweeney (1986) and Patchara Surajaras and Richard J. Sweeney (1992) presented evidence that well-chosen technical trading rules yielded out-of-sample risk-adjusted profits on a consistent basis, and that these profits were statistically significant. They argued that these profits might arise from a number of sources. There might be an insufficient amount of stabilizing speculation in foreign exchange markets, including profit-making central bank intervention (see the discussion below), allowing profits for the marginal speculator. There might be destabilizing speculation, allowing profits for stabilizing speculators. Or central banks may intervene in ways that add inefficiencies from which stabilizing speculators can profit; one possibility, for example, is that central banks lean against the wind, with speculators profiting by betting against central bank intervention.

Part III on the profits from technical trading rules contains a single chapter by Christopher J. Neely (Chapter 8), which fits in nicely with these considerations. Neely's work was motivated by Blake LeBaron's (1999) earlier article (as well as Stephen Sapp 1999, Peter Saacke 2002 and Andrew C. Szakmary and Ike Mathur 1997). LeBaron presented evidence that suggested that profits from speculation based on technical trading rules arose from central bank intervention. Neely gave a more extensive analysis in which he found that speculators can profit from technical trading rules, but that central bank intervention plays little role in these profits. Neely used intra-day exchange rate series and Dollar intervention series by the central banks for Australia, Germany and Switzerland, and also used Deutsche Mark and Japanese Yen intervention series by the Fed. Similar to Kathryn Dominguez (Chapter 13), he had to use approximations for the timing of central bank interventions. He found that profits from technical trading typically preceded, rather than followed, central bank interventions. Evidently, both private speculative trading and central bank intervention were motivated by the same trends in exchange rates, with speculators acting in advance of the central banks.

Neely made a number of attempts to risk-adjust the measured speculative profits he detected, and reported that the risk adjustment had no important effect. Of course, risk adjustment is crucial for judging the meaning of persistence and seasonality in intra-day data, as well as the effects of intervention and order flow. Richard J. Sweeney (Chapter 11) also made attempts to risk-adjust Fed profits from intervention which he found using daily data; he reported that by and large the Fed profits remained. Other chapters in this volume did not attempt to provide risk adjustment and thus it is more difficult to interpret their results.

As discussed above, however, Andersen and Bollerslev (Chapter 6) reported that the surprise in intra-day Deutsche Mark appreciation rates could be modeled as the product of (i) a term capturing patterns of persistence and seasonality, (ii) a term capturing standard ARCH effects, and (iii) a mean-zero, unit-variance error term. If the error term is interpreted as capturing a combination of the surprise in underlying, systematic risk factors plus an idiosyncratic component, then the product of the first two terms in their explanation of the surprise in appreciation can be interpreted as reflecting in part the loadings of appreciation on the surprises in the risk factors. Their modeling, then, suggests a preliminary approach that might usefully be modified to allow risk adjustment of results in a number of chapters in this volume. Using their approach to find the risk-adjusted rate of return requires decomposing the error term into systematic and non-systematic components.

In addition to its intrinsic interest, Neely's chapter on private speculative profits and government intervention serves as a transition to Part IV's chapters, which deal with the effects of government intervention in foreign exchange markets.

Part IV Central Bank Intervention in the Foreign Exchange Market

The chapters in this section deal in a number of complementary ways with central bank intervention, starting with the issue of how and when central banks choose to intervene. The current exchange-rate regime of generalized managed floating began in mid March, 1973; since then, some central banks have intervened heavily, others have intervened relatively little, and some have intervened in some periods but not in others (see Chapter 1 by Stanley Fischer). For a country with a fixed but adjustable rate, or managing a target zone, intervention is generally a reaction to market pressure on its exchange rate, and can occur frequently. (Geert Bekaert and Stephen F. Gray 1998 presented an excellent discussion of target zones. Karen K. Lewis

1995a provided an innovative approach to special cases of target zone interventions, around the Plaza and Louvre Accords. Christopher J. Neely 1999 also offered an interesting approach to target zones.) Managed-floating countries intervene in some cases but not in others, sometimes heavily but sometimes only to a limited extent. For these countries, it is much less clear how they decide on their interventions.

Many central banks state that they intervene in order to stabilize exchange rates in the sense of reducing the volatility of the rates, rather than aiming at particular exchange rate targets. Richard T. Baillie and William P. Osterberg (Chapter 9) investigated issues concerning the motives for central bank intervention. (An interesting related article is Richard T. Baillie and William P. Osterberg 1997.) They found that the Bundesbank and the Fed were more likely to intervene the larger were the deviations of the bilateral Deutsche Mark–Dollar exchange rate from targets agreed by the Group of Seven (Canada, France, Germany, Italy, Japan, the United Kingdom and the United States) and the larger was the current volatility of exchange rates.

Many observers doubt that central bank intervention has major or long-lasting effects on exchange rates. Consistent with this view, many articles report tests of intervention effects on expected appreciation in portfolio balance and signaling models, in which intervention effects are small or statistically weak relationships – though other articles find stronger relationships (Michael P. Dooley and Peter Isard 1982, 1983; Jeffrey A. Frankel 1982a,b; Jeffrey A. Frankel and Charles M. Engel 1984; Kenneth Rogoff 1984; Charles M. Engel and Anthony P. Rodrigues 1989; Alberto Giovannini and Philippe Jorion 1989; Atish R. Ghosh 1992; Hali Edison 1993 surveys earlier work; Lucio Sarno and Mark P. Taylor 2001 survey more recent work). In one view, these weak results arose because the Fed's stated policy is to sterilize its intervention, and many observers doubt that sterilized intervention importantly affects appreciation. Data problems may also play a role: these studies used quarterly, monthly or weekly instead of daily data, and typically use outside assets or international reserves rather than intervention. More recent studies have used daily intervention data; a number of articles used intra-day data, as did Kathryn Dominguez (Chapter 13) and Andreas Fischer and Mathias Zurlinden (Chapter 12).

Daily intervention and appreciation are significantly associated in single-equation regressions in a number of studies. Some regressed appreciation on contemporaneous intervention, others on lagged intervention. Regressions of appreciation on contemporaneous intervention (Bonnie Loopesko 1984, table 1; Pietro Catte, Giampaolo Galli and Salvatore Rebecchini 1992; Kathryn Dominguez and Jeffrey A. Frankel 1993a, tables 7.1–7.7) are subject to simultaneous equations bias, where significant estimates may arise even if intervention does not affect appreciation; indeed, some cite this bias as a partial explanation of why their estimated slopes often have theoretically incorrect signs (Dominguez and Frankel 1993a, pp. 114–15). Other studies attempted to mitigate simultaneous equations bias by regressing appreciation on predetermined intervention (Kathryn Dominguez 1990, Kathryn Dominguez and Jeffrey A. Frankel 1993b, and Richard T. Baillie and William P. Osterberg 2000). Use of predetermined intervention is not a panacea for bias, however. First, predetermined intervention may be correlated with the estimating equation error, unless the exchange market is strong-form efficient relative to intervention; many observers are skeptical of this strong-form efficiency. Second, if the true relationship is between appreciation and current intervention, then use of predetermined intervention may cause bias from mis-specification. Of course these qualifications regarding estimates that use daily intervention also hold for the less frequent studies that use intra-day intervention.

Two important studies that used intra-day intervention to study the effects of central bank intervention, by Andreas M. Fischer and Mathias Zurlinden (Chapter 12) and Kathryn Dominguez (Chapter 13), are included in this book. (Charles A.E. Goodhart and Thomas Hesse 1993 presented an interesting earlier investigation with intra-day data. See also Yuanchen Chang and Stephen J. Taylor's 1998 article on intra-day effects of Bank of Japan intervention.)

Andreas M. Fischer and Mathias Zurlinden (Chapter 12) examined the exchange-rate effects of Swiss central bank intervention by analyzing transaction-price data over the period 1986–1994. Much less attention has been paid to Swiss central bank intervention as opposed to Fed and Bundesbank intervention. (In Chapter 8, Christopher H. Neely also used Swiss central bank intervention data, and Dominguez and Frankel 1993a,b examined the effects of Swiss central bank intervention.) Further, the Swiss central bank announced all of its interventions over this period, though the Fed and Bundesbank do not announce some of theirs. Like the Fed and Bundesbank, the Swiss central bank sterilized all of its interventions. It is interesting to note that Fischer and Mathias Zurlinden typically find coefficients have the 'right' sign, in the sense that Swiss central bank sales of Dollars for Swiss francs strengthen the franc, as opposed to the results in many studies using daily data. Further, Fischer and Zurlinden noted that all Swiss central bank interventions were coordinated in the sense that the Fed or the Bundesbank intervened in the same direction that day.

Kathryn Dominguez in a related article (Chapter 13) investigated the micro structure of central bank intervention by examining the effects of intra-day intervention in the Deutsche Mark–Dollar and Japanese Yen–Dollar foreign exchange markets. She used a unique data set that contained intra-day interventions by the Fed, the Bundesbank and the Bank of Japan; further, she uses data for each day that the Fed intervened from 1987 through 1995, a much longer span than other studies. A particular focus of her study is on how traders learn about these central banks' interventions and the extent to which these interventions' effects depend on intra-day market conditions. Related to the Andersen and Bollerslev (Chapters 5 and 6), Dominguez found that that interventions during heavy trading volume are more likely to have large effects than at other times, and that interventions close to scheduled macro-variable announcements are more likely to have large effects on price. Related to Chapter 12 by Fischer and Zurlinden, Dominguez found that the largest effects on price occur when interventions are coordinated. Two drawbacks to her analysis are that the price data she used were indicative quotes (the Reuters FXFX quotes) rather than transactions data, which can be different in important ways (see Lyons, Chapter 14), and that no associated volume data were available. A further problem was that the Fed kept time-stamped intervention data only for the last two years of the sample; Dominguez thus used Reuters' reports on Fed intervention to establish the time of intervention (unfortunately, Reuters missed a significant fraction of Fed interventions). Because of this, as she noted, it is likely that some foreign exchange dealers knew of the intervention before the Reuters report went out, and some or most of the price effect might lead the report – and this is what she found on average. (In Chapter 15 on Bundesbank intervention, Bettina Peiers 1997 also found that foreign exchange dealers evidently knew that intervention had occurred before it was reported.) Further, Dominguez found that both leading and lagging interventions are importantly related to appreciation.

One way around some of the econometric problems discussed above is to focus on the information content of central bank intervention. Rasmus Fatum and Michael Hutchison (Chapter 10) provided an interesting example of this approach. They examined whether government intervention is a signal of future monetary policy, by examining the relationship between intervention and movements in the federal funds futures market. They detected no relationship. To the extent that intervention works by signaling, the lack of any detectable signaling effect suggests that intervention does not succeed in moving the exchange market. (Among other studies looking for evidence that intervention provides a signal for coming monetary policy, Karen K. Lewis 1995b and Gabriela Kaminsky and Karen K. Lewis 1996 provided interesting results regarding intervention and coming monetary changes.)

Milton Friedman (1953) suggested another approach to evaluating the effectiveness of central bank intervention. He argued that central bank intervention is stabilizing if and only if the bank makes profits from its interventions. After much discussion, the consensus is that central bank profits are neither necessary nor sufficient for intervention to be effective in stabilizing exchange rates. Nevertheless, the question of central bank profits or losses on its intervention is still of some interest. This volume includes a article by Richard J. Sweeney (Chapter 11) on whether the Fed beats the foreign exchange market. He presented results that showed that the Fed's risk-adjusted intervention profits were not negative and may have been positive; the results depended on the time period examined and the risk model used to adjust profits. Nevertheless, this evidence suggested that that Fed intervention may indeed have exchange-rate effects. (Richard J. Sweeney 1997 and Boo Sjöö and Richard J. Sweeney 2000, 2001 presented related evidence on the profitability of both Fed intervention and Swedish central bank intervention. As in Sweeney (Chapter 11), they found that risk-adjusted Fed profits were not negative and may have been positive, depending on the sample period and risk model; they found that the Swedish central bank did not make losses, but that the evidence for profits were weaker than for the Fed. These comparative results are of some interest because of the different exchange-rate regimes the two central banks faced. The Swedish central bank in the sample period they examined aimed to stabilize the Swedish crown relative to a basket of currencies within a target zone, and hence the market often constrained it to intervene. In contrast, the Fed ran a managed float and often went long periods without intervening, on occasion more than an entire calendar year.)

Part V Micro Structure of the Foreign Exchange Market

A theme of this volume, exemplified by chapters in Parts II to IV, is that use of intra-day data can provide valuable information that is not available when longer observation intervals are used. When intra-day data are used, a key issue is the micro structure of the foreign exchange market, and its effects on the behavior of exchange rates. The Fischer and Zurlinden (Chapter 12) and Dominguez (Chapter 13) chapters in Part IV dealt with intra-day data on central bank interventions and the micro structure of central bank interventions. Beyond the issues Fischer and Zurlinden and Dominguez examined in these chapters, a key issue is the effect of private-transactors' order flow on price and volume.

Richard K. Lyons (Chapter 14) provided an early, influential discussion of micro structure issues in the Deutsch Mark–Dollar market, focusing on order flow, and investigating a number of key results from standard microstructure models. (See also Richard K. Lyons 1998, and his 2001 book.) In particular, standard micro structure theory focuses on effects through two channels: (i) an inventory control channel – dealers adjust price to control inventory fluctuations that arise because of order flow; and (ii) an information channel—dealers adjust price in response to order flow because of the information that the order flow may contain. Lyons used a data set for the trading activity of a spot Deutsche Mark–Dollar inter-bank dealer at a major New York bank over a single five-day trading week. Time stamps on the dealer's quotes and trades are computer assigned without a lag (compare this with the time-stamp problems faced by Dominguez 2002 in Chapter 13). Thus, for trades Lyons had the dealer's transactions prices and volumes; in particular, he did not have to rely on indicative quotes (for example, Reuters FXFX). Further, he had records for one of the four or five inter-dealer brokers for this same week. After disentangling the channels, Lyons found that both the inventory and information channels were significant in the Deutsche Mark–Dollar market. For the inventory channel the dealer set price about three-quarters of a pip lower for every $10 million of net open position, and for the information channel, incoming sell order flow reduced price by about one pip for every $10 million.

The next two chapters made do with lower quality data than in the Lyons study just discussed, but illustrate that useful results can be obtained even in the absence of top-quality data. In Chapter 15, Bettina Peiers discussed the micro structure of the foreign exchange market, taking particular account of price leadership based on superior information about central bank intervention. She used publicly available information on indicative quotes (FXFX) to test the price leadership hypothesis. On the one hand, this approach is replicable; the data include bid and ask quotes, and the banks making the quotes. On the other hand, indicative quotes are inferior to transactions data, sometimes quite inferior; see the discussion in Richard K. Lyons (Chapter 14). From her results, information on Bundesbank intervention appeared to be revealed to the market well before a public announcement during the October 1, 1992–September 30, 1993 period (the same period Andersen and Bolleslev examined for the Deutsche Mark–Dollar in Chapters 5 and 6). Further, Deutsche Bank appeared to be the price leader for between 60 and 25 minutes prior to Bundesbank reports, with less favored banks learning about the intervention from the informed trader's order flows; after this period of leadership, less favored banks seemed to have caught on and to engage in strategic quote interactions of the type that is standard in micro structure models.

Vicentiu Covrig and Michael Melvin (Chapter 16) made creative use of an institutional change in the Tokyo foreign exchange market. On December 22, 1994, the restriction on trading during the lunch break, 12.00–1.30, Tokyo time, was removed. The U-shaped pattern in volatility previously detected during the lunch hour in a number of papers disappeared with the lifting of the restriction. (This pattern corresponded to the U-shaped pattern in absolute returns, a measure of volatility, during the lunch hour detected by Andersen and Bollerslev in Chapters 5 and 6 for the period October 1, 1992–September 30, 1993.) Covrig and Melvin argued that while the ban on lunch-time trading was in force, the morning hours in advance of the noon closing were richer in informed trading than the same hours after the lunch-time closing was removed; in particular, from 10.30–12.00, as the lunch-time close approached, they thought there should be a larger amount of informed trading. They hypothesized that the richer the informed trading, the faster the speed of adjustment of the exchange rates to their 'full-information level.' They also adopted the hypothesis that Japanese traders had an information advantage regarding the Japanese Yen–Dollar exchange rate as compared to non-Japanese traders; they noted that this advantage was commonly believed to exist and they offered a number of possible reasons for this assumed advantage. They supposed that before December 22, 1994, Japanese bank quotes caused non-Japanese quotes in the 10.30–12.00 time period, but that this uni-directional causality would disappear from the data after the lunch-time restriction was lifted. They used Reuters' FXFX data to test their hypotheses. They detected evidence of price leadership in Tokyo in the period when the lunch-time restriction was in place, as they predicted, but that bi-directional causality arose after the restriction was removed, again as predicted.

This book begins with studies on fundamentals, in particular, monetary models of the foreign exchange market. As was noted above, it has been difficult to make these models perform well. The book closes with a new approach that holds promise for greatly improving performance. Martin D.D. Evans and Richard K. Lyons (Chapter 17) noted that macro models of exchange-rate behavior perform quite poorly, as is discussed above. They proposed to add a micro structure variable, order flow, to the typical macro model. Further, rather than examining intra-day data as in micro structure models, or monthly or quarterly data as in monetary models, they examined daily data. They argued their model provided a link between micro structure phenomena and macro model phenomena. They explained the continuously compounded percentage appreciation of the Deutsche Mark–Dollar and Japanese Yen–Dollar exchange rates by using two variables: the change in the interest-rate differential (or in alternative specifications, the level of the interest-rate differential) and the cumulative, worldwide order flow. As is typical, the interest-rate differential variables were not significant at the 5 percent level. The order flow variable, however, was highly significant, with t-values above 5.0, and with the theoretically correct sign. R^2 values are about 60 percent for the Deutsche Mark and about 40 percent for the Japanese Yen.

References

Baillie, Richard T. and Tim Bollerslev (1989), 'The message in daily exchange rates: a conditional variance tale', *Journal of Business and Economic Statistics*, **7**, 297–305.

Baillie, Richard T. and Tim Bollerslev (1991), 'Intra-day and inter-market volatility in foreign exchange rates', *Review of Economic Studies*, **58**, 525–42.

Baillie, Richard T. and William P. Osterberg (1997), 'Central bank intervention and risk in the forward market', *Journal of International Economics*, **43**, 483–97.

Baillie, Richard T. and William P. Osterberg (2000), 'Deviations from daily uncovered interest rate parity and the role of intervention', *Journal of International Financial Markets, Institutions and Money*, **10**, 363–79.

Bekaert, Geert and Stephen F. Gray (1998), 'Target zones and exchange rates: an empirical investigation', *Journal of International Economics*, **45**, 1–35.

Boothe, Paul and Debra Glassman (1987), 'Off the mark: lessons for exchange rate modeling', *Oxford Economic Papers*, **39**, 443–57.

Catte, Pietro, Giampaolo Galli and Salvatore Rebecchini (1992), 'Exchange markets can be managed!' *International Economic Insights*, September–October, 17–21.

Chang, Yuanchen and Stephen J. Taylor (1998), 'Intraday effects of foreign exchange intervention by the Bank of Japan', *Journal of International Money and Finance*, **18**, 191–210.

Cheung, Yin-Wong (1993), 'Long memory in foreign-exchange rates', *Journal of Business and Economic Statistics*, **11**, 93–101.

Cornell, W. Bradford and J. Kimball Dietrich (1978), 'The efficiency of markets for foreign exchange', *Review of Economics and Statistics*, **60**, 111–20.

Dacorogna, Michael M., Ulrich A. Muller, Robert J. Nagler, Richard B. Olsen, and Olivier V. Pictet (1993), 'A geographical model for the daily and weekly seasonal volatility in the foreign exchange market', *Journal of International Money and Finance*, **12**, 413–38.

Dominguez, Kathryn M. (1990), 'Market responses to coordinated central bank intervention', *Carnegie-Rochester Series on Public Policy*, **32**, 121–63.
Dominguez, Kathryn M. and Jeffrey A. Frankel (1993a), *Does Foreign Exchange Intervention Work?* Washington, DC: Institute for International Economics.
Dominguez, Kathryn M. and Jeffrey A. Frankel (1993b), 'Does foreign-exchange intervention matter? The portfolio effect', *American Economic Review*, **83**, 1356–69.
Dooley, Michael P. and Peter Isard (1982), 'A portfolio-balance rational-expectations model of the Dollar–Mark rate', *Journal of International Economics*, **12**, 257–76.
Dooley, Michael P. and Peter Isard (1983), 'The portfolio balance model of exchange rates and some structural estimates of the risk premium', *IMF Staff Papers*, 1983, 683–702.
Dooley, Michael P. and Jeffry Shafer (1976), *Analysis of Short-Run Exchange Rate Behavior: March 1973 to September 1975*. Washington, DC: Working Paper, Board of Governors of the Federal Reserve System.
Edison, Hali J. (1993), *The Effectiveness of Central-Bank Intervention: A Survey of the Literature After1982*. Princeton, NJ.: Special Papers in International Economics, International Finance Section, Department of Economics, Princeton University.
Engel, Charles M. and James D. Hamilton (1990), 'Long swings in the dollar: are they in the data and do the markets know it?' *American Economic Review*, **80**, 689–713.
Engel, Charles M. and Anthony P. Rodrigues (1989), 'Tests of the international CAPM with time-varying covariances', *Journal of Applied Econometrics*, 119–38.
Fleming, Marcus (1962), 'Domestic financial policies under fixed and floating exchange rates', *IMF Staff Papers*, **9**, 369–79.
Frankel, Jeffrey A. (1979), 'On the mark: theory of floating exchange rates based on real interest rate differentials', *American Economic Review*, **69**, 610–22.
Frankel, Jeffrey A. (1982a), 'A test of perfect substitutability in the foreign exchange market', *Southern Economic Journal*, **46**, April, 406–16.
Frankel, Jeffrey A. (1982b), 'In search of the exchange rate risk premium: a six-currency test assuming mean–variance optimization', *Journal of International Money and Finance*, **1**, 255–74.
Frankel, Jeffrey A. and Charles Engel (1984), 'Do asset demand functions optimize over the mean and variance of real returns? A six-currency test', *Journal of International Economics*, **17**, 309–23.
Frenkel, Jacob A. (1976), 'A monetary approach to the exchange rate', *Scandinavian Journal of Economics*, **2**, 200–221.
Friedman, Milton (1953), 'The case for flexible exchange rates', *Essays in Positive Economics*, Chicago: University of Chicago Press.
Ghosh, Atish R. (1992), 'Is it signalling? Exchange intervention and the Dollar–Deutschemark rate', *Journal of International Economics*, **32**, 201–20.
Giovannini, Alberto and Philippe Jorion (1989), 'The time-variation of risk and return in the foreign exchange and stock markets', *Journal of Finance*, **44**, 307–24.
Goodhart, Charles A.E. and Thomas Hesse (1993), 'Central bank forex intervention assessed in continuous time', *Journal of International Money and Finance*, **12**, 368–89.
Hsieh, David A. (1989), 'Modeling heteroskedasticity in daily foreign exchange rates', *Journal of Business and Economic Statistics*, **7**, 307–17.
Jorion, Philippe (1988), 'On jump processes in the foreign exchange and stock markets', *Review of Financial Studies*, **1**, 427–45.
Kaminsky, Gabriella and Karen K. Lewis (1996), 'Does foreign exchange intervention signal future monetary policy?' *Journal of Monetary Economics*, **37**, 285–312.
Koedijk, Kees G., Marcia M.A. Schafgans and Casper G. de Vries (1990), 'The tail index of exchange rate returns', *Journal of International Economics*, **29**, 93–108.
Kouri, Pentti (1976), 'The exchange rate and the balance of payments in the short run and in the long run', *Scandinavian Journal of Economics*, **2**, 280–304.
LeBaron, Blake (1999), 'Technical trading rule profitability and foreign exchange intervention', *Journal of International Economics*, **49**, 125–43.
Lewis, Karen K. (1995a), 'Occasional interventions to target zones', *American Economic Review*, **103**, 691–715.

Lewis, Karen K. (1995b), 'Are foreign exchange intervention and monetary policy related, and does it really matter?' *Journal of Business*, **68**, 185–214.
Logue, Dennis E., Richard J. Sweeney and Thomas D. Willett (1978), 'Speculative behavior of foreign exchange rates during the current float', *Journal of Business Research*, **6**, 159–74.
Loopesko, Bonnie (1984), 'Relationships among exchange rates, intervention, and interest rates: an empirical investigation', *Journal of International Money and Finance*, **3**, 257–77.
Lyons, Richard K. (1998), 'Profits and position control: a week of FX dealing', *Journal of International Money and Finance*, **17**, 97–115.
Lyons, Richard K. (2001), *The Microstructure Approach to Exchange Rates*, Cambridge, MA: MIT Press.
Mark, Nelson C. (1995), 'Exchange rates and fundamentals: evidence of long-horizon prediction', *American Economic Review*, **85**, 201–18.
Meese, Richard A. and Kenneth Rogoff (1988), 'Was it real? The exchange rate-interest differential relation over the modern floating rate period', *Journal of Finance*, **43**, 933–48.
Mundell, Robert A. (1968), *International Economics*. New York: Macmillan.
Neely, Christopher J. (1999), 'Target zones and conditional volatility: the role of realignments', *Journal of Empirical Finance*, **6**, 177–92.
Neely, Christopher J. and Lucio Sarno (2002), 'How well do monetary fundamentals forecast exchange rates?' *Review, Federal Reserve Bank of St. Louis*, 2002, 51–74.
Nieuwland, Frederick G.M.C., Willem F.C. Verschoor and Christian C.P. Wolff (1994), 'Stochastic trends and jumps in EMS exchange rates', *Journal of International Money and Finance*, **13**, 699–727.
Rogoff, Kenneth (1984), 'On the effects of sterilized intervention: an analysis of weekly data', *Journal of Monetary Economics*, **14**, 133–50.
Rupach, David E. and Mark E. Wohar (2001), 'Testing the monetary model of exchange rate determination: a closer look at panels'. Working Paper.
Saacke, Peter (2002), 'Technical analysis and the effectiveness of central bank intervention', *Journal of International Money and Finance*, **21**, 459–79.
Sapp, Stephen (1999), *The Role of Central Bank Intervention in the Profitability of Technical Analysis in the Foreign Exchange Market*, London, Ontario: Working Paper, University of Western Ontario.
Sarno, Lucio and Mark P. Taylor (2001), 'Official intervention in the foreign exchange market: is it effective and if so, how does it work?' *Journal of Economic Literature*, **39**, 839–68.
Sjöö, Boo and Richard J. Sweeney (2000), 'Time-varying foreign-exchange risk and central bank intervention: estimating profits from intervention and speculation', *Journal of International Financial Markets, Institutions and Money*, **10**, 275–86.
Sjöö, Boo and Richard J. Sweeney (2001), 'The foreign-exchange costs of central bank intervention: evidence from Sweden', *Journal of International Money and Finance*, **20**, 219–47.
Surajaras, Patchara and Richard J. Sweeney (1992), *Profit-Making Speculation in Foreign-Exchange Markets*, Boulder, CO: Westview Press.
Sweeney, Richard J. (1976), 'Inflation, the balance of trade, and the effects of exchange rate adjustments', in *The Effects of Exchange Rate Adjustments*, Peter Clarke, Dennis E. Logue and Richard J. Sweeney (eds), Washington, DC: Office of the Assistant Secretary for International Affairs, US Treasury Department.
Sweeney, Richard J. (1986), 'Beating the foreign exchange market', *Journal of Finance*, **41**, 163–82.
Sweeney, Richard J. (1997), 'Do central banks lose on foreign-exchange intervention? A review article', *Journal of Banking and Finance*, **21**, 1667–84.
Szakmary, Andrew C. and Ike Mathur (1997), 'Central bank intervention and trading rule profits in foreign exchange markets', *Journal of International Money and Finance*, **16**, 513–35.

Part I
Fundamentals in the Foreign Exchange Market

[1]

Journal of Economic Perspectives—Volume 15, Number 2—Spring 2001—Pages 3–24

Exchange Rate Regimes: Is the Bipolar View Correct?

Stanley Fischer

Each of the major international capital market-related crises since 1994—Mexico, in 1994, Thailand, Indonesia and Korea in 1997, Russia and Brazil in 1998, and Argentina and Turkey in 2000—has in some way involved a fixed or pegged exchange rate regime. At the same time, countries that did not have pegged rates—among them South Africa, Israel in 1998, Mexico in 1998, and Turkey in 1998—avoided crises of the type that afflicted emerging market countries with pegged rates.

Little wonder, then, that policymakers involved in dealing with these crises have warned strongly against the use of adjustable peg and other soft peg exchange rate regimes for countries open to international capital flows. That warning has tended to take the form of the bipolar, or corner solution, view, which is that countries need to choose either to peg their currencies hard (for instance, as in a currency board), or to allow their currencies to float, but that intermediate policy regimes between hard pegs and floating are not sustainable.[1]

Figure 1 shows the change in the distribution of exchange rate arrangements of the IMF's member countries between 1991 and 1999. The three categories shown are derived from a more detailed classification of de facto exchange regimes that is presented in the *Annual Report 2000* of the International Monetary Fund

[1] Exchange rate regimes will be defined more precisely below: soft pegs are exchange rates that are currently fixed in value (or a narrow range of values) to some other currency or basket of currencies, with some commitment by the authorities to defend the peg, but with the value likely to change if the exchange rate comes under significant pressure. The adjustable peg exchange rates of the Bretton Woods regime were typically soft pegs.

■ *Stanley Fischer is First Deputy Managing Director, International Monetary Fund, Washington, D.C.*

Figure 1
All Countries: Exchange Rate Regimes, 1991 and 1999

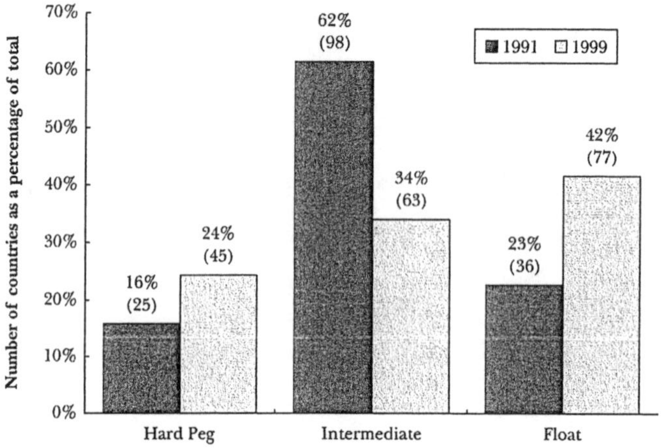

Source: IMF.
Note: The number of countries is in parenthesis.

(pp. 141–143).[2] The arrangements described as "hard pegs" in Figure 1 include currency boards and situations where countries have no national currency, either because they are in a currency union or because they have dollarized by formally adopting the currency of some other country. The floating group contains economies whose systems are described either as independently floating, or as a "managed float," which means that while the central bank may intervene in the exchange market, it has not committed itself to trying to bring about a particular exchange rate or exchange rate range. The "intermediate" group consists of economies with a variety of soft peg currency arrangements: these include a conventional fixed exchange rate peg; a crawling peg, in which the peg is allowed to shift gradually over time; an exchange rate band, in which the central bank is committed to

[2] Until recently the IMF's categorization of exchange rate regimes was based on self-descriptions by member countries, which are presented in the IMF's *Exchange Arrangements and Exchange Restrictions* (EAER) publication. The categorization used in this paper, taken from the *Annual Report 2000*, is based on the IMF staff's evaluation of the de facto arrangements actually in place, rather than what the authorities say the regime is. Several authors, including Ghosh et al. (1997) and Levy-Yeyati and Sturzenegger (2000), have wrestled with the difficulty that the authorities' own description of exchange rate regimes in *EAER* is patently inaccurate for some countries, and Levy-Yeyati and Sturzenegger have developed their own categorization, based on aspects of exchange rate and reserve variability. The staff of the IMF is currently developing data for earlier years on de facto exchange rate regimes corresponding to the information provided in the *Annual Report 2000.*

keeping the exchange rate within a specified range; and a crawling band, which allows the exchange rate band itself to move over time.[3]

As Figure 1 shows, there has since 1991 been a thinning out of the middle or intermediate range, and increases in the percentage of countries having either hard pegs or floating.[4] The percentage of countries with hard pegs increased from 16 to 24 percent; the percentage with floating rate regimes increased from 23 to 42 percent. Correspondingly, whereas 62 percent of economies had intermediate regimes in 1991, only 34 percent did in 1999. Thus, it does appear that during the 1990s, countries were moving away from the intermediate arrangements and toward either hard pegs or floating exchange rate regimes. But the significance of this movement and the specific conditions under which it makes economic sense need to be spelled out and refined.

In seeking to refine the analysis, I will argue that proponents of what is now known as the bipolar view—myself included—probably have exaggerated their point for dramatic effect. The right statement is that *for countries open to international capital flows*: (i) soft exchange rate pegs are not sustainable; but (ii) a wide variety of flexible rate arrangements remain possible; and (iii) it is to be expected that policy in most countries will not be indifferent to exchange rate movements. To put the point graphically, if exchange rate arrangements lie along a line connecting hard pegs like currency unions, currency boards, and dollarization on the left, with free floating on the right, the intent of the bipolar view is not to rule out everything but the two corners, but rather to pronounce as unsustainable a segment of that line representing a variety of soft pegging exchange rate arrangements.[5]

This version of the bipolar argument accepts that countries are likely to be concerned about the level of their exchange rate. In particular, countries will often have what Calvo and Reinhart (2000) term a "fear of floating," because they are not willing to accept the extent of exchange rate fluctuations generated by a totally free float of the exchange rate. In this case, monetary policy and possibly foreign exchange intervention policy will respond to exchange market pressures.[6] The formulation also leaves open a variety of exchange rate arrangements. For countries open to international capital flows, it includes as sustainable regimes both very hard pegs and a variety of floating rate arrangements, including managed floats.

[3] Classification of the exchange rate regime may be difficult in marginal cases; for instance, whether a very broad exchange rate band should be classified as a soft peg or a managed float.

[4] The exchange rate classifications for 1991 used in Figure 1 were provided by the staff of the IMF, on the same basis as those for 1999—that is, using their judgment of the de facto exchange rate arrangements actually in place in member countries.

[5] For analyses of exchange rate systems, see Mussa et al. (2000), Calvo and Reinhart (2000), Edwards (2000), Frankel (1999), Summers (2000), and Velasco (2000).

[6] Several colleagues who commented on the first draft of this paper emphasized that monetary and exchange rate policy should not be regarded as separate, and that the key issue in choosing an exchange rate policy is the consistency of the overall macroeconomic policy framework. This perspective is of course correct, but for expositional reasons I focus more narrowly on the choice of exchange rate regime, taking it for granted that no exchange rate regime can be sustained if it is inconsistent with overall macroeconomic policy.

For countries not as yet open to international capital flows, it includes the full gamut of exchange rate arrangements.

The question that then arises is what exchange rate arrangements are excluded by the bipolar view. The answer is: for countries open to international capital flows, exchange rate systems in which the government is viewed as being committed to defending a particular value of the exchange rate, or a narrow range of exchange rates, but has not made the institutional commitments that both constrain and enable monetary policy to be devoted to the sole goal of defending the parity. In essence, the excluded arrangements are fixed exchange rate pegs, adjustable exchange rate pegs, and narrow band exchange rate systems.

I will start this paper by focusing on the critical point that for developed and emerging market countries, adjustable peg exchange rate systems have not proved to be viable for the long term, and should not be expected to be viable. I will then take up a set of other issues: the "fear of floating" argument, and monetary policy under floating rate regimes; the nature of the hard peg arrangements that may be expected to be viable; the use of the exchange rate as a nominal anchor in disinflation; the behavior of exchange rates among the United States, Europe, and Japan; and what can be said about exchange rate arrangements for developing countries that are not open to international capital flows.

Exchange Rate Regimes for Developed and Emerging Market Countries

The fresh thinking about exchange rate regimes that has followed the crises of the last seven years centers on exchange rate systems for countries integrated or integrating into global capital markets.

Two groups of countries can be considered as integrated or integrating into international capital markets: the advanced countries, and emerging market countries. For the advanced countries, I draw on the list of "developed market" economies produced by Morgan Stanley Capital International (MSCI). This contains 22 economies, listed in Table 1. The emerging market group is defined as the 33 economies contained in the union of the 27 economies that are in the MSCI emerging markets index and the 17 economies that are in the Emerging Markets Bond Index Plus (EMBI+), which is from J.P. Morgan. These are listed in Table 2. Tables 1 and 2 also list exchange rate arrangements in place at the end of 1999.[7]

Figure 2 shows the development of exchange rate regimes among the devel-

[7] For further information on indexes from Morgan Stanley Capital International, see ⟨http://www.msci.com⟩. For a general discussion of EMBI+, which tracks total returns for traded external debt instruments in the emerging markets, see ⟨http://www.jpmorgan.com/MarketDataInd/EMBI/embi.html⟩. The MSCI list of developed market economies excludes six that are included in the IMF listing of "Advanced Economies": Greece, Iceland, Israel, Korea, Luxembourg, and Taiwan POC. Except for Iceland and Luxembourg, these are included in the emerging market economies listed in Table 1. The description of the exchange rate regime for Taiwan POC, which is not listed in the original source, is provided by the author.

Table 1
Developed Market Economies
(as of December 31, 1999)

Euro Area		*Other*	
	Exchange Arrangement		*Exchange Arrangement*
Austria	No separate legal tender	Australia	Independent float
Belgium	No separate legal tender	Canada	Independent float
Finland	No separate legal tender	Denmark	Pegged rate in horizontal band
France	No separate legal tender	Hong Kong SAR	Currency board
Germany	No separate legal tender	Japan	Independent float
Ireland	No separate legal tender	New Zealand	Independent float
Italy	No separate legal tender	Norway	Managed float
Netherlands	No separate legal tender	Singapore	Managed float
Portugal	No separate legal tender	Sweden	Independent float
Spain	No separate legal tender	Switzerland	Independent float
		United Kingdom	Independent float
		United States	Independent float

Source: IMF, Annual Report 2000.
Note: Economies listed in the MSCI Developed Markets index.

oped and emerging market countries listed in Tables 1 and 2. In these cases, too, there has been a shift in the bipolar direction, away from the soft peg center, towards harder pegs on one side, and floating arrangements on the other.

Of the 22 developed market economies in Table 1, all of which have complete or nearly complete capital mobility, 10 are in the euro area and are listed as having no separate legal tender.[8] Another 10 countries are listed as having floating rates, either independently floating or managed floating. The other two countries are Hong Kong SAR, with a currency board arrangement, and Denmark, which has not agreed to join the euro zone but is officially still pegging its exchange rate within a band to the other European currencies. *Thus, among the developed economies listed in Table 1, and depending on how the euro zone countries are regarded, half the economies have established very hard pegs, and nearly half the countries float.*

A decade ago, Table 1 would have looked quite similar for the non-euro area countries. However, the European countries were at that time operating under the European Monetary System (EMS), a set of adjustable exchange rate pegs operating within horizontal bands. Part of the belief in the nonrobustness of adjustable pegs derives from the manner in which EMS currencies were attacked in 1992 and 1993. It proved impossible to hold the adjustable pegs within the EMS after the rise in German interest rates necessitated by Germany's unification had imposed a domestically inappropriate monetary policy on the other EMS members. This example is particularly telling since the attack on the EMS was successful despite

[8] Technically, the national currencies for the euro area countries are scheduled to continue as legal tender within each country until the first half of 2002.

Table 2
Emerging Market Countries Grouped by Exchange Rate Arrangement
(as of December 31, 1999)

Exchange Rate Regime (Number of Countries)	*Countries*
No separate legal tender/ Currency board (3) (*3)	*Argentina, *Bulgaria, *Panama
Other fixed pegs (7) (*2)	*China, Egypt, Jordan, *Malaysia, Morocco, Pakistan, Qatar
Pegged rate in horizontal band (1) (*1)	*Greece
Crawling peg (1)	Turkey
Rates within crawling bands (5) (*2)	Hungary, *Israel, Poland, Sri Lanka, *Venezuela
Managed float (3) (*1)	Czech Republic, Nigeria, *Taiwan POC
Independent float (13) (*7)	*Brazil, *Chile, Colombia, Ecuador, *India, Indonesia, *Korea, *Mexico, Peru, *Philippines, Russia, *South Africa, Thailand

Source: IMF, Annual Report 2000.
Note: *indicates country whose weight in either the EMBI+ or MSCI index is 2% or greater. Numbers in parenthesis indicate number of countries in each group; asterisked numbers are self-explanatory.

the political commitment to it by the system's members, who saw the adjustable peg system within the EMS as a stepping-stone towards the goal of monetary union. Part of the empirical support for the view that countries will move away from soft peg exchange rate mechanisms to hard pegs or fixed exchange rate mechanisms is based on the creation of the euro as a single currency for Europe.

The 33 emerging market economies are grouped by exchange rate arrangement in Table 2. The largest group of countries (13) consists of those described as independently floating. Six of those countries (Indonesia, Korea, Thailand, Russia, Brazil and Mexico) became floaters after the major crises of the last decade, while Colombia joined the group in 1999. This is the set of transitions that has most influenced the view that soft pegs are not viable for sustained periods—and it includes many of the largest emerging market economies. Three economies are described as having managed floats. Thus, half the emerging market group of countries has some form of floating rate arrangement. While there is room for judgment over whether these countries should be listed in the "managed" or "independent" floating group, there should be no dispute that all 16 belong in one or other of those categories. Furthermore, there has during the last decade been a significant shift among these emerging market economies from various forms of pegged arrangements towards floating.

Of the remaining 17 countries listed in Table 2, at the end of 1999 three either had currency boards or no independent legal tender. Ecuador and Greece have subsequently joined this group: Ecuador (an independent floater in December 1999) by dollarizing and Greece by joining the European Monetary Union. Eight countries had fixed or adjustable pegs at the end of 1999. Turkey had just instituted a crawling peg regime, which has now given way to a float. Five countries—Hungary, Israel, Poland, Sri Lanka and Venezuela—had crawling bands, which in

Figure 2

Developed and Emerging Market Countries: Exchange Rate Regimes, 1991 and 1999

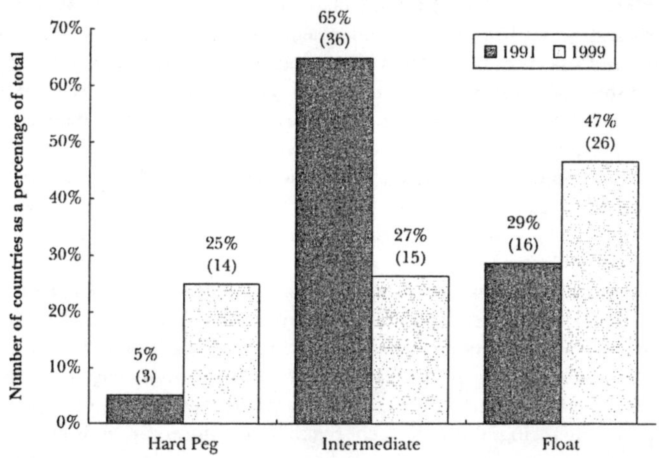

Source: IMF.
Note: The number of countries is in parenthesis.

the cases of both Israel and Poland have been widening over the years, to the point of considerable flexibility.

The pattern is similar if one looks at the 16 larger emerging market economies, which are identified with asterisks in Table 2. Half of these larger emerging market economies are floaters. Three have hard pegs, a number that by now has risen to four. Two have crawling bands. Only two of the countries in this group of larger emerging market economies have soft pegs: China and Malaysia.

Within the emerging market economies, the number of intermediate exchange rate arrangements declined in the 1990s and the number of floating and fixed regimes has increased.[9] This shift appears likely to continue. Looking ahead from the end of 1999, Greece has joined the euro zone, and Hungary and Poland are likely to. Israel is likely to move to an independently floating rate regime; Turkey is scheduled to move in that direction too, with possible membership in the euro zone a more distant prospect.

It is thus reasonable to say that economies open to international capital flows have been and are in the process of moving away from adjustable peg exchange rate systems, some towards harder pegs and more fixed exchange rates (especially in the creation of the euro zone), more towards systems with greater exchange rate flexibility. But why? *The reason is that soft peg systems have not proved viable over any*

[9] Fischer and Sahay (2000) document a very similar pattern over time among the transition economies in the 1990s.

lengthy period, especially for countries integrated or integrating into the international capital markets. The fact that pegged exchange rates have a short life expectancy whether the economy is open to international capital flows or not was emphasized by Obstfeld and Rogoff (1995). But the collapse of the Bretton Woods system in the late 1960s and early 1970s, the repeated crises of the European Monetary System in the 1980s and the successful attacks on currencies within the system in 1992 and 1993, and the emerging market crises of 1994–2000 all drive home the lesson that this problem is especially intense for countries that are more open to international flows of capital.[10]

In several countries, extensive economic damage has been caused by the collapses of pegged rate regimes that had lasted for a few years. After a few years of exchange rate stability under a pegged regime, a belief gradually arises that the exchange rate will never change, which reduces perceptions of the risk of borrowing in foreign currencies and removes the need to hedge. Then, when an exchange rate crisis does strike, it is exceptionally damaging in its effects on banking systems, corporations, and government finances. In principle, it should be possible to reduce the potential damage through prudential regulations that limit the open foreign exchange positions of banks. But it is harder to control corporate sector international financing through such regulations. Moreover, it is in any case probably unwise to rely too heavily on regulatory supervision to prevent transactions that would otherwise be highly profitable.[11]

The concept of the "impossible trinity" points out that no economy can simultaneously have a fixed exchange rate, capital mobility, and a monetary policy dedicated to domestic goals. The major explanation for the nonviability of soft pegs is that they are an attempt by a country open to international capital flows to have both a fixed exchange rate and a monetary policy directed at domestic goals—and sooner or later, an irreconcilable conflict arises between these goals. But this insight leaves open three questions. First, if the impossible trinity is correct, why did soft peg arrangements survive for so long, and why did their vulnerability become so much more apparent only in the 1990s? The second question is one of political economy: Why can't domestic monetary policy be directed credibly solely towards maintenance of the soft peg exchange rate? The third question is whether to seek to combine a fixed exchange rate and a domestically-oriented monetary policy by using capital controls to limit the mobility of foreign capital.

The evidence shown in Figures 1 and 2 raises the question of what happened in the 1990s to cause exchange rate arrangements to shift in a bipolar direction. The beginnings of that move can be dated much earlier, to the breakup of the Bretton Woods system in the early 1970s. In the 1990s, the creation of the European Monetary Union accounts for much of the shift towards hard pegs. Among emerging market countries, the growing openness of capital accounts, combined with the associated development of private sector capital flows towards the emerging mar-

[10] John Williamson (2000) offers an alternate argument for the movement away from soft pegs, suggesting that it is because of pressure from the IMF and U.S. Treasury.

[11] I return to a closely related point below in discussing the potential use of capital controls.

kets, made the force of the inconsistency expressed in the impossible trinity much more apparent and led to the collapse of several important soft pegged exchange rate arrangements in major crises.

The answer to the second question, the political economy question of why it is difficult for macroeconomic policy to protect a soft peg, must be that if the option of changing the exchange rate is open to the political system, then at a time when the short-run benefits of doing so appear to outweigh the costs, that option is likely to be chosen. Both foreign and domestic economic shocks (including policy actions) may move the equilibrium nominal exchange rate away from the official rate. If the official or pegged exchange rate is overvalued, then a government that wishes to prevent a devaluation typically has to raise interest rates. As long as the extent of the disequilibrium is small, and the requisite policy actions are taken in time, they can be expected to stabilize the situation. But if the disequilibrium has become large, either because policy was slow to react or because the country has been hit by a strong and long-lasting shock, the required high interest rates may not be viable—either for political reasons or because of the damage they will inflict on the banking system or aggregate demand. Under those circumstances, speculators can be expected to attack the currency, selling it in the anticipation that the government will be forced to devalue. If the disequilibrium is large, such a speculative attack on the exchange rate is likely to succeed.

Third, why not impose capital controls to protect the exchange rate from the effects of unwanted capital flows?[12] Among the 16 larger emerging market economies identified in Table 2, China successfully maintained its pegged exchange rate through the Asian crisis with the assistance of long-standing capital controls, providing an important element of stability in the regional and global economies. Malaysia's imposition of capital controls and pegging of the exchange rate in September 1998 has attracted more attention. However, evaluation of the effects of the Malaysian controls has been difficult since they were imposed after most of the turbulence of the first part of the Asian crisis was over—that is, after most of the capital that wanted to leave had done so—and when regional exchange rates were beginning to appreciate.[13]

In discussing capital controls, I shall assume that countries will in the course of their development want to liberalize the capital account and integrate into global capital markets. This view is based in part on the fact that the most advanced economies all have open capital accounts, which suggests that this is an appropriate goal for emerging market economies. It is also based on the view that the potential benefits of integration into the global capital markets—importantly including the benefits obtained by allowing foreign competition in the financial sector—outweigh the costs.[14]

[12] This question is examined by Edwards (2000), Mussa et al. (2000) and Williamson (2000). For more detailed discussion of experience with capital controls, see Ariyoshi et al. (2000).
[13] See Kaplan and Rodrik (2000) for a relatively positive appraisal of the Malaysian controls.
[14] The argument is developed at greater length in Fischer (1998). The point has been much disputed, including by Jagdish Bhagwati (1998).

It is necessary to distinguish between capital controls on outflows and on inflows. For controls on capital outflows to succeed, they need to be quite extensive, to cover potential loopholes. Even so, experience shows that controls on capital outflows cannot prevent a devaluation of the currency if domestic policies are fundamentally inconsistent with maintenance of the pegged exchange rate. Some countries have attempted to impose controls on outflows once a foreign exchange crisis is already underway. It is generally believed that this use of controls has been ineffective (Ariyoshi et al., 2000, pp. 18–29; Edwards, 1999, pp. 68–71). In addition, the imposition of controls on capital outflows is likely to have an effect on capital inflows to the country, since investors who are concerned about not being able to withdraw their capital from a country may respond by not sending it there in the first place.

Moreover, as an economy develops and experiences a growing range of contacts with foreign economies, controls on capital outflows are likely to become both more distorting and less effective. At some point the controls will need to be removed. Where controls on capital outflows are reasonably effective, they would need to be removed gradually, at a time when the exchange rate is not under pressure. The removal of controls on outflows sometimes results in a capital inflow, a result of either foreigners and/or domestic residents bringing capital into the country in light of the greater assurance it can be removed when desired. If the country is moving from a fixed exchange rate regime with controls on capital outflows to floating exchange rates, it is desirable to begin allowing some flexibility of exchange rates as the controls are gradually eased. Moreover, prudential controls that should be put in place for the efficient operation of the financial system often have a similar effect to some capital controls—for instance, limits on foreign exchange positions taken by domestic institutions. More generally, to reduce the economy's vulnerability to crises, a strong domestic financial system should be in place when capital controls are removed.

The IMF has supported the use of market-based capital inflow controls: for example, those that impose a tax on capital inflows. The typical instance occurs when a country is trying to reduce inflation using an exchange rate anchor. For anti-inflationary purposes, the country needs interest rates higher than those implied by the sum of foreign interest rates and the expected rate of currency depreciation. In such circumstances, the high interest rate will attract an inflow of foreign capital, which will tend to cause an exchange rate appreciation; alternatively, the country can permit the inflows and try to sterilize their monetary impact, but this typically becomes costly. A tax on capital inflows can in principle help a country maintain a high domestic interest rate without experiencing a substantial inflow of capital. In addition, by taxing short-term capital inflows more than longer-term inflows, capital inflow controls can also in principle influence the composition of inflows.

Evidence from the Chilean experience with controls on capital inflows suggests that controls on capital inflows were for a time successful in allowing some monetary policy independence, and also in shifting the composition of capital inflows towards longer-term investment. However, the Chilean controls eventually seemed to lose their effectiveness (Edwards, 2000), and they have recently been removed.

Direct controls on inflows are also used by some countries. These may be aimed at specific types of inflows, for instance, short-term (hot money) flows, or sometimes foreign direct investment. Direct investment inflows are typically quite stable, and indeed at the aggregate level continued rising even during the Asian crisis; they also bring advantages in the form of new technology. Most countries that seek to control inflows prefer long-term direct investment to short-term inflows. Nonetheless, some countries have liberalized short-term flows, while seeking to keep long-term flows out, thereby exacerbating the volatility of short-term capital flows as market uncertainties increased.

There is little question that capital controls—whether on outflows or inflows—can for some time help a country sustain a soft peg exchange rate regime. Nonetheless, such controls tend to lose their effectiveness over time. Moreover, as countries develop, they are likely to want to integrate further into global capital markets. Countries in these circumstances would be well advised to move away from a soft peg exchange rate, typically towards a more flexible exchange rate regime.

Fear of Floating

Many countries that claim to have floating exchange rates do not allow the exchange rate to float freely, but rather deploy interest rates and intervention policy to affect its behavior. As long as such interventions are not undertaken to defend a particular exchange rate, or narrow range of exchange rates, this paper has categorized such behavior as a managed float. But such fear of floating behavior has been described as demonstrating that many—particularly emerging market—countries are not willing to allow their exchange rates to float.

It is hardly a surprise that most policymakers in most countries are concerned with the behavior of the nominal and the real exchange rates. Changes in the nominal exchange rate are likely to affect the inflation rate. Changes in the real exchange rate may have a powerful effect on the wealth of domestic citizens, and on the allocation of resources, which may have not only economic but also political effects—especially in the case of currency appreciations, in countries where exporters matter.

Thus in most countries, even those with floating exchange rate regimes, monetary policy is likely to respond to some extent to movements of the exchange rate. The United States is one of the few examples of a country that largely ignores its exchange rate in the conduct of monetary policy. But most of the other G-7 countries (Canada, France, Germany, Italy, Japan, and the United Kingdom) and emerging market economies do pay attention to exchange rates in the conduct of monetary policy. Canada, for example, until recently used a monetary conditions index to guide monetary policy, which was based on movements in both the exchange rate and the interest rate.

Many of the recent converts to floating exchange rates (several of whom were forcibly converted) have opted for inflation targeting, and that system seems to be working well and has much to commend it. With the inflation targeting approach to monetary policy, movements in the exchange rate will be taken into account indirectly in setting monetary policy, because the exchange rate affects price behavior. This will generally produce a pattern of monetary tightening when the exchange rate depreciates, a response similar, but not necessarily of the same magnitude, to that which would be undertaken if the exchange rate were being targeted directly.

Why should monetary policy not target both the nominal exchange rate and the inflation rate? Central banks may face this issue with particular force in a situation with an appreciated real exchange rate and the current account in large deficit. The first answer must be that monetary policy fundamentally affects the nominal exchange rate and not the real exchange rate, and that if any part of macroeconomic policy should take care of the current account balance by redressing an imbalance between domestic savings and investment, it is fiscal policy.

However, there is an unresolved issue about whether monetary policy in a floating rate system should be used in the short run to affect the real exchange rate. If the nominal exchange rate moves faster than the real exchange rate, then monetary policy can influence the real exchange rate in the short run. In many respects, this issue is similar to that of how monetary policy in an inflation-targeting framework should respond to movements in output and unemployment. There is almost certainly a short-run tradeoff between the real exchange rate and inflation, analogous to the Phillips curve, although it has not received much empirical attention.[15] This is not the place to pursue the issue, but just as answers have been developed to how to deal with the short-run Phillips curve in an inflation-targeting framework, so that a central bank can take into account the short-run impact of its actions on output and unemployment while recognizing that the long-run effects are negligible, it remains necessary to answer the question of how to deal with the short-run tradeoff between the real exchange rate and inflation, recognizing that in the long run greater inflation will not affect the real exchange rate.

Beyond the use of interest rates, some countries intervene directly from time to time in the foreign exchange markets to try to stabilize the exchange rate. So long as they are not perceived as trying to defend a particular rate, such interventions can be useful in reducing the degree of volatility in exchange rate markets. This is one of the remaining areas in which central bankers place considerable emphasis on the touch and feel of the market, and where systematic policy rules are not yet common. There is of course controversy over whether exchange rate intervention works at all—and even if it does, whether it is wise to use it. The Banco de Mexico has developed a method of more-or-less automatic intervention designed to reduce day-to-day movements in exchange rates, which could provide lessons in this area.

Recognizing the difficulty for an emerging market country of defending a

[15] Cushman and Zha (1997) contain vector autoregressions from which the implied tradeoff can be calculated in the Canadian case. See also Calvo, Reinhart and Végh (1995).

narrow range of exchange rates, John Williamson (2000) proposes alternative regimes. He calls these BBC arrangements: basket (that is, a peg to a basket of currencies rather than a single currency), band, and crawl. He also recommends that countries if necessary allow the exchange rate to move temporarily outside the band, so that speculators cannot predict with certainty when the central bank is going to intervene. In these circumstances, a moving and elastic band would be serving as a weak nominal anchor for the exchange rate, but it is not at all clear why such a system is preferable to an inflation-targeting framework. Possibly the exchange rate band could be thought of as a supplement to an inflation-targeting framework, but it would need to be demonstrated what benefits that brings, if any. One possibility—which is not very plausible—is that by committing weakly to some range of exchange rates, the authorities make it more likely that fiscal policy will be brought into play if the real exchange rate moves too far from equilibrium.

Viable Hard Pegs

At the end of 1999, 45 of the IMF's then-182 members had hard peg exchange rate systems, either with no independent legal tender, or a currency board. Except for the 11 countries in Europe, all of the 37 economies with no independent legal tender were small. But the exception of the European single currency, the euro, is a very big one. Argentina and Hong Kong SAR are the biggest economies with currency boards. Since the end of 1999, Ecuador and El Salvador have dollarized, so that over a quarter of the IMF's 183 members have very hard pegs; the proportion in terms of GDP is similar.

At the end of 1990, plans for a single European currency did not yet exist, and there were only three currency board economies. The appraisal of the performance of currency boards, once regarded as a historical curiosity, has undoubtedly changed, as a result of several factors: the tireless proselytizing by Steve Hanke and others (for instance, Hanke and Schuler, 1994); examination of their historical record; and their performance in a number of economies, including Hong Kong SAR, Argentina, and the transition economies of Estonia, Lithuania, Bulgaria, and Bosnia-Herzegovina. Ghosh, Gulde and Wolf (2000, p. 270) provide a balanced summary:

> First, the historical track record of currency boards is sterling . . . Countries that did exit . . . did so mainly for political, rather than economic reasons, and such exits were usually uneventful. . . . Second, modern currency boards have often been instituted to gain credibility following a period of high or hyperinflation, and in this regard have been remarkably successful. Countries with currency boards experienced lower inflation and higher (if more volatile) GDP growth compared to both floating regimes and simple pegs. . . . The GDP growth effect is significant, but may simply reflect a rebound from depressed levels. Third, . . . the successful introduction of a currency board

> ... [is] far from trivial ... Moreover, there are thorny issues, as yet untested, regarding possible exits from a currency board ...

The great strength of the currency board arrangement, the virtual removal of the nominal exchange rate as a means of adjustment, is also its principal weakness. In the case of an internal or external macroeconomic shock, the economy can adjust via a change either in exchange rates or domestic prices and wages. The nominal exchange rate adjustment is typically much quicker, and that via wages and prices more prolonged and, certainly in the case of the need for a decline in the real exchange rate, more difficult. In late 2000, this difficulty was evident in Argentina, where a currency board arrangement prevents the nominal exchange rate from moving, but even in Argentina, the adjustment *is* taking place as domestic prices and costs decline relative to foreign prices and costs.

It is difficult to make a general evaluation of the benefits and costs of the constraints imposed by the commitment to a currency board. For a country with a history of extreme monetary disorder, a currency board appears to be a means of obtaining credibility for a low-inflation monetary policy more rapidly and at lower cost than appears possible any other way. For a country like Argentina, with a long and unhappy inflationary history, the society may be willing to accept the occasional short-run costs of doing without the exchange rate as a means of adjustment in exchange for lower inflation, just as the memory of the German hyperinflation in the 1920s has colored German attitudes to inflation ever since.

The extensive discussion leading up to the European single currency emphasized how member countries, when deprived of exchange rate flexibility, would need to adjust to shocks with wage and price flexibility, the mobility of labor and capital, and fiscal compensation. A currency board country is unlikely to have access to fiscal compensatory measures from abroad, and nor is its labor likely to be as mobile internationally as that in the European Union will be—but we should not exaggerate the role of geographical labor mobility as a means of short-run adjustment to shocks even in large national economies. For such a country, the emphasis has to be on wage and price flexibility as well as internal labor market mobility. Domestic fiscal policy can play a countercyclical role in a currency board economy, provided the fiscal situation is strong enough in normal times for fiscal easing during a recession not to raise any questions about long-term fiscal sustainability.

Policies to this end—to encourage internal factor mobility, wage and price flexibility, and fiscal prudence in normal times—are entirely possible, and can help ensure the sustainability of a currency board over time. Such policies are of course generally desirable in *any* economy, but the need for them is greater if the exchange rate is not available as a tool of adjustment.

Another disadvantage sometimes cited for a currency board arrangement is that since the central bank cannot create money, it may not be able to act as lender of last resort. However, the circumstance envisaged by the classic argument for lender of last resort—a pure panic-based run on banks into currency—is rare. Most often financial crises have a real basis, and take real resources to resolve, as Goodhart and Schoenmaker (1995) have shown. One way or another, these resources come from the fiscal authority. The absence of a central bank capable of acting as lender of last resort can be compensated for in various ways: by the creation, typically with fiscal resources, of a banking sector stabilization fund (as has been done in Bulgaria); by setting up a deposit insurance scheme, financed by the banks and if necessary in the final resort by the treasury; by strengthening financial sector supervision and prudential controls; by allowing foreign banks to operate in the economy; and by lining up contingency credits for the banking system.

The discussion so far has implicitly centered on how the goods and factor market and the current account would adjust in world of floating or fixed exchange rates. Those who strongly favor hard pegs, such as Calvo and Reinhart (2000) or Eichengreen and Hausmann (2000), tend to focus on international flows of capital and on asset markets. Their argument is that with respect to asset markets, a country obtains essentially no benefit—seigniorage aside—from exchange rate flexibility. For example, emerging market economies cannot borrow abroad in their own currencies, and so the exchange rate creates a source of additional risk and higher interest rates for all foreign borrowing. Given this, they argue for going beyond currency boards to dollarization and perhaps in the longer run to wider currency unions.

If a country intends never to use the exchange rate as a mechanism of adjustment, then retaining exchange rate flexibility is clearly counterproductive. Hence the argument for dollarization relative to a currency board must turn on an appraisal of the gains from dollarization that would be obtained in the capital markets, for example in the reduction of spreads between domestic and foreign interest rates and by the strengthening of the financial system, versus the losses implied by forgoing both seigniorage and the option of changing the exchange rate in extremis by giving up a national currency. The balance of the argument would be tilted if a politically acceptable means could be found of transferring seigniorage to dollarizing countries; the Mack bill in the previous Congress would have done that, suggesting that, at least in the case of the dollar, some means of transferring seigniorage from the use of the dollar could eventually become politically feasible.

Both Ecuador and El Salvador dollarized in 2000, but under very different circumstances. Ecuador's decision was essentially one of desperation (Fischer, 2000); El Salvador's was based on careful consideration. The Ecuadorian case provides much food for thought about what it takes for dollarization to succeed. It was implemented without many of what were thought of as the prerequisites for success, such as a strong banking system, being in place. Much work remains to be done, particularly in the banking sector, to ensure the long-term success of Ecuador's dollarization. But at least in its first year, it has worked reasonably well.

Hard peg exchange rate systems have become more attractive than had been thought some years ago. For a small economy, heavily dependent in its trade and capital account transactions on a particular large economy, it *may* make sense to adopt the currency of that country, particularly if provision can be made for the transfer of seigniorage. While the requirements for the effective operation of such a system are demanding, in terms of the strength of the financial system and fiscal soundness, meeting those requirements is good for the economy in any case. To be sure, careful consideration needs to be given to the nature of the shocks affecting the economy. For example, even though the Canadian economy is closely connected to the U.S. economy, Canadian policymakers regard their country as benefitting from the shock-absorber role of the floating exchange rate with the U.S. dollar. But there is clearly a trend, which can be expected to accelerate if the euro zone succeeds, in the direction of hard pegged exchange rate regimes. This trend is already reducing the number of currencies in existence, and further reductions should be expected in future.

The Exchange Rate as a Nominal Anchor for Disinflation

The benefits and risks of using the exchange rate as a nominal anchor to disinflate from triple-digit inflation, as well as the real dynamics associated with such stabilizations, have been extensively studied (for a summary, see Mussa et al., 2000, Appendix III, pp. 44–47; Calvo and Végh, 1999). There are few instances in which a successful disinflation from triple-digit inflation has taken place without the use of an exchange rate anchor, particularly in countries that have suffered from chronic monetary instability. The exchange rate anchor in such disinflations sometimes takes the form of a very hard peg, for instance a currency board, but is more often a softer peg, often a crawling peg regime.

Of the eleven major exchange rate-based stabilizations since the late 1980s studied in Mussa et al. (2000), four of them—Argentina in 1991, Estonia in 1992, Lithuania in 1994 and Bulgaria in 1997—entered currency boards and disinflated successfully. The other seven countries (and Israel in 1985 could be added to this sample) generally either undertook exchange rate devaluations a step at a time, or introduced crawling exchange rate bands, which in many cases have widened over time. The disinflations of three countries—Mexico in 1994, Russia in 1998 and Brazil in 1999—ended in a currency crash, though in each case low inflation was preserved or rapidly regained following the crisis.

Countries which disinflate using a soft peg exchange rate strategy must consider their exit strategy from the pegged arrangement. An IMF study of exit strategies in this case showed that exit is best undertaken when the currency is strong, something which is quite likely to happen as the stabilization gains credibility and capital inflows expand (Eichengreen et al., 1998). This was the pattern for instance in Poland and Israel, where the band was widened as pressure for appreciation mounted. However, the political economy of moving away from a peg is complicated, even in this case. When the currency is strong, the authorities generally see no reason to move off the peg; when it is weak, they argue that devaluation or a widening of the band under pressure would be counterproductive. But the longer the peg continues, the more the dangers associated with soft pegs grow. In some cases in which the currencies of disinflating countries crashed, the IMF had been pushing unsuccessfully for greater exchange rate flexibility.

The need to move away from a soft peg is one of the reasons an exit mechanism was built into the Turkish stabilization and reform program that began in December 1999. Nonetheless, as a result of unresolved banking sector problems, the failure to undertake corrective fiscal actions when the current account widened, and political difficulties, the crawling peg failed to hold and in February 2001, Turkey was forced to float its exchange rate.

Big Three Exchange Rates

The remarkable instability of exchange rates among the major currencies is a perennial topic of concern and discussion. Movements in exchange rates among the big three—the United States, Europe, and Japan—can create difficulties for other countries, particularly for those that peg to one of those currencies. Thus the exports of east Asian countries were adversely affected by the appreciation of the dollar that began in 1995, and the strengthening of the dollar was also a factor in the difficulties faced by Argentina and Turkey in 2000.

There have been frequent proposals for target exchange rate zones among the dollar, the euro and the yen. If the target zones were to be narrow, monetary policy in each currency area would have to be dedicated to maintenance of the exchange rate commitment. There is no political support for a commitment to narrow target zones; it is not clear that monetary policy could maintain the desired exchange rate commitment; and there is not a persuasive case that the gains from maintaining a narrow commitment would be large. But given the extent of exchange rate movements among the major currencies, even wide target zones could be stabilizing.

In practice, something akin to such a system appears to operate, informally and loosely. When exchange rates get far out of line with fundamentals, two or three countries of the big three agree to intervene in the currency markets. This happened in mid-1995 when the yen-dollar exchange rate reached 80, implying a yen that was significantly appreciated relative to estimates of its equilibrium value, and in the fall of 2000, when the euro was significantly depreciated relative to its estimated equilibrium value.[16]

This informal system differs from a formal target zone system in three important ways. First, there are no preannounced target zones, and so no commitment to intervene at any particular level of exchange rates. This removes the possibility of one-way bets for speculators, but of course also removes the certainty about future exchange rates that a credible target zone system would provide—if such a system were possible. Second, the informal system operates more through coordinated interventions in the foreign exchange market than through coordinated monetary policy actions. While exchange rate movements may influence interest rates in the big three, both through their implications for inflation, and probably more directly

[16] For the IMF's methodology for estimating equilibrium exchange rates, see Isard and Faruqee (1998). These estimates come with a wide confidence interval, but from time to time discrepancies between actual and estimated equilibrium exchange rates can be clearly identified. Several private sector financial institutions also estimate equilibrium exchange rates; see Edwards (2000) for discussion of the methodologies and the range of estimates provided by different sources.

Figure 3
All Other Countries: Exchange Rate Regimes, 1991 and 1999

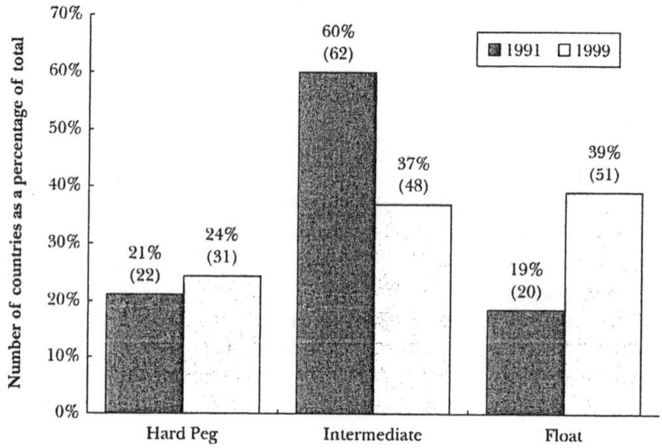

Source: IMF.
Note: The number of countries is in parenthesis.

in the cases of the Bank of Japan and the European Central Bank, coordinated interest rate changes with the sole purpose of affecting exchange rates do not appear to be on the current agenda. Third, such interventions are rare.

All of which is to say that the system is indeed informal and loose. Nonetheless it provides some bounds on the extent to which exchange rates among the United States, Europe and Japan are likely to diverge from equilibrium.

Exchange Rate Regimes for Other Countries

I have focused so far on exchange rate regimes for 55 developed and emerging market economies, which account for the bulk of global GDP, trade, and international capital flows. Figure 3 shows the distribution of exchange rate arrangements among the other members of the IMF as of end-1999 and end-1991, respectively. Table 3 groups these countries by their exchange rate regime at the end of 1999. The pattern is a familiar one: There has been a mild shift towards hard pegs on one side and a stronger shift to more flexible exchange rate regimes on the other.

These countries represented in Figure 3 are developing economies that are not classified as emerging market, which means that they typically have low per capita incomes. Many of them are also small economies and not very well integrated into the world economy. Such countries will display a wide range of situations and experiences, which makes it hard to make any definite recommendations on what

Table 3

All Other Countries Grouped by Exchange Rate Arrangements

(as of December 31, 1999)

Exchange Rate Regime (Number of countries)	*Countries*
No separate legal tender/Currency board (31)	Antigua and Barbuda, Benin, Bosnia and Herzegovina, Brunei Darussalam, Burkina Faso, Cameroon, Central African Rep., Chad, Congo (Rep. of), Côte d'Ivoire, Djibouti, Dominica, Equatorial Guinea, Estonia, Gabon, Grenada, Guinea-Bissau, Kiribati, Lithuania, Luxembourg, Mali, Marshall Islands, Micronesia, Niger, Palau, San Marino, Senegal, St. Kitts and Nevis, St. Lucia, St. Vincent and the Grenadines, Togo
Other fixed pegs (38)	Aruba, Bahamas, Bahrain, Bangladesh, Barbados, Belize, Bhutan, Botswana, Cape Verde, Comoros, El Salvador, Fiji, Iran, Iraq, Kuwait, Latvia, Lebanon, Lesotho, Macedonia FYR, Maldives, Malta, Myanmar, Namibia, Nepal, Netherlands Antilles, Oman, Samoa, Saudi Arabia, Seychelles, Solomon Islands, Swaziland, Syrian Arab Republic, Tonga, Trinidad and Tobago, Turkmenistan, United Arab Emirates, Vanuatu, Zimbabwe
Pegged rate in horizontal band (4)	Cyprus, Iceland, Libya, Vietnam
Crawling peg (4)	Bolivia, Costa Rica, Nicaragua, Tunisia
Rates within crawling bands (2)	Honduras, Uruguay
Managed float (23)	Algeria, Azerbaijan, Belarus, Burundi, Cambodia, Croatia, Dominican Rep., Ethiopia, Guatemala, Jamaica, Kenya, Kyrgyz Republic, Lao PDR, Malawi, Mauritania, Paraguay, Romania, Slovak Rep., Slovenia, Suriname, Tajikistan, Ukraine, Uzbekistan
Independent float (29)	Afghanistan, Albania, Angola, Armenia, Congo (Dem. Rep.), Eritrea, Gambia, Georgia, Ghana, Guinea, Guyana, Haiti, Kazakhstan, Liberia, Madagascar, Mauritius, Moldova, Mongolia, Mozambique, Papua New Guinea, Rwanda, São Tome and Príncipe, Sierra Leone, Somalia, Sudan, Tanzania, Uganda, Yemen, Zambia

Source: IMF, Annual Report 2000.

exchange rate regimes would work best for countries in this group. In a review of exchange rate arrangements in these economies, Mussa et al. (2000, p. 31) state:

> Reflecting wide differences in levels of economic and financial development and in other aspects of their economic situations, no single exchange rate regime is most appropriate for all such countries, and the regime that is appropriate for a particular country may change over time.[17] Because of their limited involvement with modern global financial markets, some form of exchange rate peg or band or highly managed float is generally more viable and more appropriate for them than for most of the emerging market countries. Even this conclusion, however, leaves a wide range of possible regimes—for a diverse range of developing and transition countries.

[17] At this point the authors note that this is the conclusion reached by Frankel (1999).

They add: "IMF advice to members . . . reflects this ambiguity and diversity. Consistent with the Articles of Agreement, the IMF generally respects the member's choice of exchange rate regime and advises on policies needed to support that choice."

There is room for further research on the characteristics of exchange rate systems and accompanying financial sector structural policies most suited to particular types of countries that are not yet integrated into the global financial system, taking into account the likelihood that as the country develops, it will want to open up its capital account.

Summary and Conclusions

In the last decade, there has been a hollowing out of the middle of the distribution of exchange rate regimes in a bipolar direction, with the share of both hard pegs and floating gaining at the expense of soft pegs. This is true not only for economies active in international capital markets, but among all countries. A look ahead suggests this trend will continue, certainly among the emerging market countries. The main reason for this change, among countries with open capital accounts, is that soft pegs are crisis-prone and not viable over long periods.

A country's choice between a hard peg and floating depends in part on the characteristics of the economy, and in part on its inflationary history. The choice of a hard peg makes sense for countries with a long history of monetary instability, and/or for a country closely integrated in both its capital and current account transactions with another or a group of other economies. However, countries with a historical tradition of monetary stability, or no obvious subset of other countries with which to form a monetary union, or a belief that a flexible exchange rate helps their economy adjust to the sorts of macroeconomic shocks that it experiences, may be better off with a floating exchange rate.

As more countries adopt very hard exchange rate pegs of one sort or another, including dollarization and currency unions, there will in the future be fewer independent national currencies. Exchange rates among the remaining independent currencies will mostly be floating, and for all but the biggest countries, monetary policy—and occasionally exchange market intervention—will react to and sometimes seek to affect the nominal exchange rate.

In the medium term, as in recent years, as the center of the distribution of exchange rate regimes hollows out, the shift will likely be more towards the floating than the hard peg end of the spectrum. However, over the longer term, and depending on how well the euro area and dollarized economies operate, the trend could well be to move from the floating to the hard peg ends of the spectrum.

■ *This paper is an edited version of a lecture delivered to a joint session of the Society of Government Economists and the American Economic Association at the meetings of the Allied Social Science Associations in New Orleans, Louisiana, on January 6, 2001. I would like to thank Timothy Taylor for his excellent editing. I am grateful to my colleagues at the IMF for continuing discussion of these issues, and, in the preparation of this paper, particularly to Ratna Sahay and Grace Juhn for their assistance, Shogo Ishii, Barry Johnson, Nadia Malikyar, and Inci Otker for their work in classifying exchange rate regimes, and many other colleagues for further information regarding those classifications. Thanks, too, to Stanley Black, Olivier Blanchard, Robert Chote, Dan Citrin, Stijn Claessens, Brad De Long, David Goldsbrough, Taka Ito, Mohsin Khan, Louis Kuijs, Jaewoo Lee, Eduardo Levy-Yeyati, Paul Masson, Paolo Mauro, Sandy McKenzie, Jacques Polak, Dani Rodrik, Federico Sturzenegger, Gyorgy Szapary, Teresa Ter-Minassian, Michael Waldman, John Williamson, and Holger Wolf for their comments. Views expressed are those of the author, not necessarily of the International Monetary Fund.*

References

Ariyoshi, Akira, Karl Habermeier, Bernard Laurens, Inci Ötker-Robe, Jorge Iván Canales-Kriljenko and Andrei Kirilenko. 2000. *Capital Controls: Country Experiences with Their Use and Liberalization*, IMF Occasional Paper 190.

Bhagwati, Jagdish. 1998. "The Capital Myth." *Foreign Affairs.* May/June, 77:3, 7–12.

Broda, Christian. 2000. "Coping with Terms of Trade Shocks: Pegs vs. Floats," in Alberto Alesina and Robert Barro, eds. *Currency Unions*, forthcoming. Stanford: Hoover Institution Press.

Calvo, Guillermo A. 2000. "Capital Markets and the Exchange Rate, With Special Reference to the Dollarization Debate in Latin America," University of Maryland, April.

Calvo, Guillermo A. and Carmen M. Reinhart. 2000. "Fear of Floating," NBER Working Paper 7993, November.

Calvo, Guillermo A. and Carmen M. Reinhart. 2000. "Reflections on Dollarization," in Alberto Alesina and Robert Barro, eds. *Currency Unions*, forthcoming. Stanford: Hoover Institution Press.

Calvo, Guillermo A., Carmen M. Reinhart, and Carlos A. Végh. 1995. "Targeting the Real Exchange Rate: Theory and Evidence." *Journal of Development Economics*, 47, pp. 97–133.

Calvo, Guillermo A. and Carlos Végh. 1999. "Inflation Stabilization and BOP Crises in Developing Countries," NBER Working Paper 6925.

Chang, Roberto and Andres Velasco. 2000. "Exchange Rate Policy for Developing Countries." *American Economic Review, Papers and Proceedings.* May, 90:2, pp. 71–75.

Cushman, David O. and Tao Zha. 1997. "Identifying Monetary Policy in a Small Open Economy under Flexible Exchange Rates." *Journal of Monetary Economics.* 39, pp. 433–48.

Edwards, Sebastian. 1999. "How Effective are Capital Controls?" *Journal of Economic Perspectives.* Fall, 13:4, pp. 65–84.

Edwards, Sebastian. 2000. "Exchange Rate Regimes, Capital Flows and Crisis Prevention," NBER, December.

Eichengreen, Barry and Ricardo Hausmann. 1999. "Exchange Rates and Financial Fragility," NBER Working Paper 7418, November.

Eichengreen, Barry, Paul Masson, Hugh Bredenkamp, Barry Johnston, Javier Haman, Esteban Jadresic, and Inci Ötker. 1998. *Exit Strategies: Policy Options for Countries Seeking Greater Exchange Rate Flexibility*, IMF Occasional Paper 168.

Fischer, Stanley. 1998. "Capital-Account Liberalization and the Role of the IMF," in *Should the IMF Pursue Capital-Account Convertibility?* Princeton University, International Finance Section, Essays in International Finance, May, 207, pp. 1–10.

Fischer, Stanley. 2000. "Ecuador and the IMF," in Alberto Alesina and Robert Barro, eds. *Currency Unions*, forthcoming. Stanford: Hoover Institution Press.

Fischer, Stnaley and Ratna Sahay. 2000. "The Transition Economies After Ten Years," IMF Working Paper, WP/00/30, International Monetary Fund, Washington D.C., February.

Frankel, Jeffrey A. 1999. *No Single Currency Regime is Right for All Countries or At All Times.* Princeton University, International Finance Section, Essays in International Finance, August, 215.

Ghosh, Atish R., Anne-Marie Gulde, Jonathan D. Ostry and Holger C. Wolf. 1997. "Does the Nominal Exchange Rate Regime Matter?" NBER Working Paper 5874, January.

Ghosh, Atish R., Anne-Marie Gulde and Holger C. Wolf. 2000. "Currency Boards: More than a Quick Fix?" *Economic Policy.* October, 31, pp. 270–335.

Goodhart, Charles and Dirk Schoenmaker. 1995. "Should the Functions of Monetary Policy and Bank Supervisor be Separated?" *Oxford Economic Papers.* 47, pp. 539–60.

Hanke, Steve H. and Kurt Schuler. 1994. *Currency Boards for Developing Countries.* International Center for Economic Growth. San Francisco: ICS Press.

Hausmann, Ricardo, Michael Gavin, Carmen Pages-Serra and Ernesto Stein. 1999. "Financial Turmoil and the Choice of Exchange Rate Regime." Inter-American Development Bank, Working Paper 400.

International Monetary Stability Act of 2000. 106th Congress, 2nd Session, S. 2101.

Isard, Peter and Hamid Faruqee, eds. 1998. *Exchange Rate Assessment: Extensions of the Macroeconomic Balance Approach,* IMF Occasional Paper 167.

Kaplan, Ethan and Dani Rodrik. 2000. "Did the Malaysian Capital Controls Work?" Kennedy School of Government, December.

Kenen, Peter. 2000. "Currency Areas, Policy Domains, and the Institutionalization of Fixed Exchange Rates." Princeton University, April.

Levy-Yeyati, Eduardo and Federico Sturzenegger. 2000. "Exchange Rate Regimes and Economic Performance," paper presented at IMF First Annual Research Conference, November.

Mussa, Michael, Paul Masson, Alexander Swoboda, Esteban Jadresic, Paolo Mauro and Andrew Berg. 2000. *Exchange Rate Regimes in an Increasingly Integrated World Economy,* IMF Occasional Paper 193.

Obstfeld, Maurice and Kenneth Rogoff. 1995. "The Mirage of Fixed Exchange Rates." *Journal of Economic Perspectives.* Fall, 9:4, pp. 73–96.

Summers, Lawrence H. 2000. "International Financial Crises: Causes, Prevention, and Cures." *American Economic Review, Papers and Proceedings.* May, 90:2, pp. 1–16.

Velasco, Andres. 2000. "Exchange Rates in Emerging Markets: Floating Toward the Future," Egyptian Center for Economic Studies, Cairo, Working Paper 46, November.

Williamson, John. 2000. *Exchange Rate Regimes for Emerging Markets: Reviving the Intermediate Option.* Washington, D.C.: Institute for International Economics, September.

[2]

Expectations and Exchange Rate Dynamics

Rudiger Dornbusch

Massachusetts Institute of Technology

The paper develops a theory of exchange rate movements under perfect capital mobility, a slow adjustment of goods markets relative to asset markets, and consistent expectations. The perfect foresight path is derived and it is shown that along that path a monetary expansion causes the exchange rate to depreciate. An initial overshooting of exchange rates is shown to derive from the differential adjustment speed of markets. The magnitude and persistence of the overshooting is developed in terms of the structural parameters of the model. To the extent that output responds to a monetary expansion in the short run, this acts as a dampening effect on exchange depreciation and may, in fact, lead to an increase in interest rates.

I. Introduction

The paper develops a simple macroeconomic framework for the study of exchange rate movements. The purpose is to develop a theory that is suggestive of the observed large fluctuations in exchange rates while at the same time establishing that such exchange rate movements are consistent with rational expectations formation. In developing a formal model we draw on the role of asset markets, capital mobility, and expectations that have been emphasized in recent literature.[1] We draw, too, on the fact

I am indebted to Stanley Black, Franco Modigliani, and Edward Tower who provided the stimulus for this paper. In revising various drafts I have had the benefit of many comments. I wish, in particular, to acknowledge the helpful suggestions I have received from Wilfred Ethier, Stanley Fischer, Jacob Frenkel, and the thoughtful remarks of two anonymous referees. Financial support was provided by a grant from the Ford Foundation.

[1] For recent work on flexible exchange rates that shares some of the present emphasis, see Black (1973, 1975), Henderson (1975), Niehans (1975), Dornbusch (1976*a*, 1976*b*), Frenkel (1976), Kouri (1976), and Mussa (1976). The classics remain Fleming (1962) and Mundell (1964, 1968).

[*Journal of Political Economy*, 1976, vol. 84, no. 6]

of differential adjustment speeds in goods and asset markets. In fact, the dynamic aspects of exchange rate determination in this model arise from the assumption that exchange rates and asset markets adjust fast relative to goods markets.

The adjustment process to a monetary expansion in this framework serves to identify several features that are suggestive of recent currency experience. In the short run, a monetary expansion is shown to induce an immediate depreciation in the exchange rate and accounts therefore for fluctuations in the exchange rate and the terms of trade. Second, during the adjustment process, rising prices may be accompanied by an appreciating exchange rate so that the trend behavior of exchange rates stands potentially in strong contrast with the cyclical behavior of exchange rates and prices. The third aspect of the adjustment process is a direct effect of the exchange rate on domestic inflation. In this context the exchange rate is identified as a critical channel for the transmission of monetary policy to aggregate demand for domestic output.

The effect of monetary policy on interest rates and exchange rates is significantly affected by the behavior of real output. If real output is fixed, a monetary expansion will, in the short run, lower interest rates and cause the exchange rate to overshoot its long-run depreciation. If output, on the contrary, responds to aggregrate demand, the exchange rate and interest rate changes will be dampened. While the exchange rate will still depreciate, it may no longer overshoot, and interest rates may actually rise.

In Part II we develop a formal model in terms of explicit functional forms. That development allows us to derive an analytical solution for the time path of variables and, in Part III, for the expectations that generate the perfect foresight path. In Part IV, the model is used to investigate the effects of a monetary disturbance. While the major part of the analysis is developed for the case of fixed output, an extension to variable output is introduced in Part V.

II. The Model

We will assume a country that is small in the world capital market so that it faces a given interest rate. Capital mobility will ensure the equalization of expected net yields so that the domestic interest rate, less the expected rate of depreciation, will equal the world rate. In the goods market we will assume that the world price of imports is given. Domestic output is an imperfect substitute for imports, and aggregate demand for domestic goods, therefore, will determine their absolute and relative price.

A. Capital Mobility and Expectations

Assets denominated in terms of domestic and foreign currency are assumed to be perfect substitutes given a proper premium to offset anticipated exchange rate changes. Accordingly, if the domestic currency is expected to depreciate, interest rates on assets denominated in terms of domestic currency will exceed those abroad by the expected rate of depreciation. That relationship is expressed in (1) where r is the domestic interest rate, r^* is the given world rate of interest, and x is the expected rate of depreciation of the domestic currency, or the expected rate of increase of the domestic currency price of foreign exchange:

$$r = r^* + x. \tag{1}$$

Equation (1) is a representation of perfect capital mobility, and it is assumed that incipient capital flows will ensure that (1) holds at all times.

Consider next expectations formation. Here we distinguish between the long-run exchange rate, to which the economy will ultimately converge, and the current exchange rate. Denoting the logarithms of the current and long-run rate by e and $\bar{e}$, respectively, we assume that

$$x = \theta(\bar{e} - e). \tag{2}$$

Equation (2) states that the expected rate of depreciation of the spot rate is proportional to the discrepancy between the long-run rate and the current spot rate. The coefficient of adjustment θ is for the present taken as a parameter. The long-run exchange rate is assumed known, and an expression for it will be developed below. We note further that, while expectations formation according to (2) may appear ad hoc, it will actually be consistent with perfect foresight, as shown in Part III.

B. *The Money Market*

The domestic interest rate is determined by the condition of equilibrium in the domestic money market. The demand for real money balances is assumed to depend on the domestic interest rate and real income and will, in equilibrium, equal the real money supply. Assuming a conventional demand for money, the log of which is linear in the log of real income and in interest rates, we have[2]

$$-\lambda r + \phi y = m - p, \tag{3}$$

where m, p, and y denote the logs of the nominal quantity of money, the price level, and real income. For the remainder of this part we will take the nominal quantity of money and the level of real income as given.

Combining (1), (2), and (3) will give us a relationship between the spot exchange rate, the price level, and the long-run exchange rate, *given* that the money market clears and net asset yields are equalized:

$$p - m = -\phi y + \lambda r^* + \lambda\theta(\bar{e} - e). \tag{4}$$

[2] Equation (3) is obtained by taking the logarithm of the money market equilibrium condition $M/P = Y^{\phi} \exp(-\lambda r)$.

Equation (4) can be simplified by noting that with a stationary money supply long-run equilibrium will imply equality between interest rates, because current and expected exchange rates are equal. This implies that the long-run equilibrium price level, $\bar{p}$, will equal

$$\bar{p} = m + (\lambda r^* - \phi y). \tag{5}$$

Substituting (5) in (4) gives us a relationship between the exchange rate and the price level:[3]

$$e = \bar{e} - (1/\lambda\theta)(p - \bar{p}). \tag{6}$$

Equation (6) is one of the key equations of the model. For given long-run values of exchange rates and prices, it serves to determine the current spot price of foreign exchange as a function of the current level of prices. Given the level of prices, we have a domestic interest rate and an interest differential. Given the long-run exchange rate, there is a unique level of the spot rate such that the expected appreciation, or depreciation, matches the interest differential. An increase in the price level, because it raises interest rates, gives rise to an incipient capital inflow that will appreciate the spot rate to the point where the anticipated depreciation exactly offsets the increase in domestic interest rates.

C. The Goods Market

The demand for domestic output depends on the relative price of domestic goods, $e - p$, interest rates, and real income. The demand function is assumed to have the form

$$\ln D = u + \delta(e - p) + \gamma y - \sigma r, \tag{7}$$

where D denotes the demand for domestic output and where u is a shift parameter.[4] From (7) we note that a decrease in the relative price of domestic goods raises demand, as does an increase in income or a reduction in interest rates. The rate of increase in the price of domestic goods, $\dot{p}$, is described in (8) as proportional to an excess demand measure:

$$\dot{p} = \pi \ln (D/Y) = \pi[u + \delta(e - p) + (\gamma - 1)y - \sigma r]. \tag{8}$$

[3] In (3) we assumed that the appropriate deflator for money balance is the price of domestic output. An alternative is provided by a deflator that is a weighted average of domestic and import prices. In such a formulation the "price level," q, could be written as $q = \alpha p + (1 - \alpha)e$, where α and $(1 - \alpha)$ are the expenditure shares of domestic goods and imports. With such a formulation (6) would be amended to the following equation: $e = \bar{e} - \beta(p - \bar{p})$, where $\beta \equiv \alpha/[\lambda\theta + (1 - \alpha)]$. None of the qualitative results described below would be affected by this extension.

[4] The complete relative price argument in (7) is $(e + p^* - p)$ where p^* is the logarithm of the foreign price level. Setting the foreign price level equal to unity implies that $p^* = 0$.

We note that the long-run equilibrium exchange rate implied by (8) is[5]

$$\bar{e} = \bar{p} + (1/\delta)[\sigma r^* + (1 - \gamma)y - u], \tag{9}$$

where $\bar{p}$ is defined in (5). From (9) it is apparent that the long-run exchange rate depends with the conventional homogeneity properties on monetary variables, but obviously on real variables, too.

The price equation in (8) can be simplified by using the definition of the long-run rate in (9) and the fact that interest differences equal expected depreciation, $r - r^* = \theta(\bar{e} - e)$, to become[6]

$$\dot{p} = -\pi[(\delta + \sigma\theta)/\theta\lambda + \delta](p - \bar{p}) = -v(p - \bar{p}), \tag{10}$$

where

$$v \equiv \pi[(\delta + \sigma\theta)/\theta\lambda + \delta]. \tag{11}$$

The price adjustment equation in (10) can be solved to yield

$$p(t) = \bar{p} + (p_0 - \bar{p}) \exp(-vt), \tag{12}$$

which shows that the price of domestic output will converge to its long-run level at a rate determined by (11). Substitution of (12) in (6) gives the time path of the exchange rate

$$\begin{aligned} e(t) &= \bar{e} - (1/\lambda\theta)(p_0 - \bar{p}) \exp(-vt) \\ &= \bar{e} + (e_0 - \bar{e}) \exp(-vt). \end{aligned} \tag{13}$$

From (13) the exchange rate will likewise converge to its long-run level. The rate will appreciate if prices are initially below their long-run level and, conversely, if prices initially exceed their long-run level.

D. *Equilibrium Exchange Rates*

The adjustment process of the economy can be described with the help of figure 1. At every point in time the money market clears and expected yields are arbitraged. This implies a relationship between prices and the spot exchange rate shown in (6) and reflected in the QQ schedule in figure 1. The positively sloped schedule $\dot{p} = 0$ shows combinations of price levels and exchange rates for which the goods market and money market are in equilibrium.[7] Points above and to the left of that schedule

[5] Equation (9) is obtained by setting $\dot{p} = 0$ and $r = r^*$ as is appropriate for the long run where markets clear and exchange rates are constant.

[6] In (8) aggregate demand depends on the nominal interest rate. An alternative formulation allows aggregate demand to depend on the real interest rate, $r - \dot{p}$. Such a formulation requires that we substitute $\rho \equiv \pi/(1 - \sigma\pi) > 0$ in place of π in (11) and the equations below. The restriction that $\rho > 0$ is required for stability.

[7] The $\dot{p} = 0$ schedule represents combined goods- and money-market equilibrium. Setting $\dot{p} = 0$ in (8) and substituting for the domestic interest rate from (3) yields the equation of the goods-market equilibrium schedule:

$$p = [\delta\lambda/(\delta\lambda + \sigma)]e + [\sigma/(\delta\lambda + \sigma)]m + [\lambda/(\delta\lambda + \sigma)][u + (1 - \gamma)y - \phi\sigma y/\lambda].$$

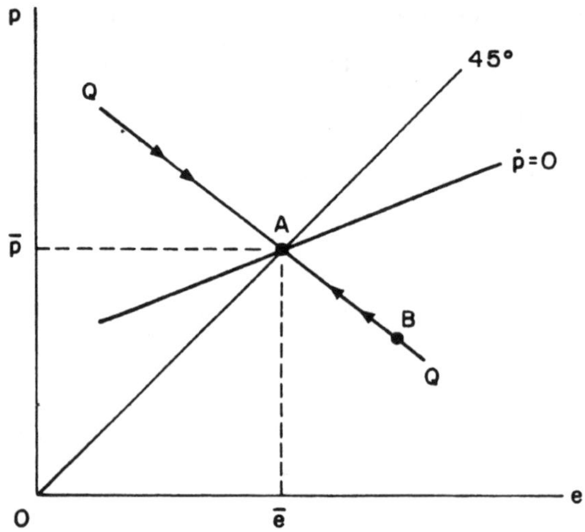

FIG. 1

correspond to an excess supply of goods and falling prices. Conversely, points to the right and below the schedule correspond to an excess demand. The $\dot{p} = 0$ schedule is positively sloped and flatter than a 45° line for the following reason.[8] An increase in the exchange rate creates an excess demand for domestic goods by lowering their relative price. To restore equilibrium, domestic prices will have to increase, though proportionately less, since an increase in domestic prices affects aggregate demand, both via the relative price effect and via higher interest rates.

For any given price level the exchange rate adjusts instantaneously to clear the asset market. Accordingly, we are continuously on the QQ schedule with money-market equilibrium and international arbitrage of net expected yields. Goods-market equilibrium, to the contrary, is only achieved in the long run. Conditions in the goods market, however, are critical in moving the economy to the long-run equilibrium by inducing rising or falling prices. Specifically, an initial position such as point B, with a price level below the long-run level and, correspondingly, an exchange rate in excess of the long-run equilibrium, implies an excess demand for goods because domestic output commands a low relative price and because the interest rate is low. Accordingly, prices will be rising, thereby inducing over time a reduction in excess demand. The path of rising prices is accompanied by an appreciation of the exchange rate. As interest rates rise, as a consequence of declining real balances, the spot

[8] The 45° line in fig. 1 is drawn through the origin on the assumption that, by appropriate choice of units, the prices of both goods are initially equal.

rate will approach the long-run rate. Once the long-run equilibrium at point A is attained, interest rates are equal internationally, the goods market clear, prices are constant, and expected exchange rate changes are zero.

III. Consistent Expectations

So far we have placed no restrictions on the formation of expectations other than the assumption that the expected rate of depreciation, as shown in (2) is proportional to the discrepancy between the long-run and the current exchange rate. From (12) and (13) we note that the rate at which prices and the exchange rate converge to equilibrium is given by v. From (11) it is apparent that the rate of convergence is a function of the expectations coefficient, θ.

Clearly, for the expectations formation process in (2) to correctly predict the actual path of exchange rates it must be true that $\theta = v$. Accordingly, the expectations coefficient, θ, that corresponds to perfect foresight, or, equivalently, that is consistent with the model is given by the solution to the equation

$$\theta = v \equiv \pi[(\delta + \sigma\theta)/\theta\lambda + \delta]. \tag{14}$$

The consistent expectations coefficient, $\tilde{\theta}$, obtained as the solution to (14), is a function of the structural parameters of the economy[9]

$$\tilde{\theta}(\lambda, \delta, \sigma, \pi) = \pi(\sigma/\lambda + \delta)/2 + [\pi^2(\sigma/\lambda + \delta)^2/4 + \pi\delta/\lambda]^{1/2}. \tag{15}$$

Equation (15) gives the rate at which the economy will converge to long-run equilibrium along the perfect foresight path. If expectations are formed according to (2) and (15), exchange rate predictions will actually be borne out.[10] The characteristics of the perfect foresight path are that the economy will converge faster the lower the interest response of money demand and the higher the interest response of goods demand and the price elasticity of demand for domestic output. The reason is simply that with a low interest response a given change in real balances will give rise to a large change in interest rates which, in combination with a high interest response of goods demand, will give rise to a large excess demand and therefore inflationary impact. Similarly, a large price elasticity serves to translate an exchange rate change into a large excess demand and, therefore, serves to speed up the adjustment process.

[9] In (16) we have taken the positive and therefore stable root of the quadratic equation implied by (14).

[10] Perhaps a remark about the perfect foresight path is in order here. Why should that path command our interest rather than being a mere *curiosum*? The reason is that it is the only expectational assumption that is not arbitrary (given the model) and that does not involve persistent prediction errors. The perfect foresight path is, obviously, the deterministic equivalent of rational expectations.

IV. The Effects of a Monetary Expansion

In this part we will study the adjustment process to a monetary expansion. The analysis serves to derive substantive results but also to highlight the manner in which expectations about the future path of the economy affect the current level of the exchange rate. This link is embodied in consistent expectations and makes the impact effect of a monetary disturbance depend on the entire structure of the economy.

In figure 2 we show the economy in initial full equilibrium at point A, with a long-run price level $\bar{p}$ and a corresponding long-run exchange rate $\bar{e}$ where the level of prices is determined, according to (5), by the nominal quantity of money, real income, and the interest rate. The long-run exchange rate by (9) will depend on the level of domestic prices and characteristics of the demand for domestic goods. The asset-market equilibrium schedule QQ that combines monetary equilibrium and arbitrage of net expected yields is drawn for the initial nominal quantity of money.

An increase in the nominal quantity of money that is expected to persist will cause a goods and asset market disequilibrium at the initial exchange rate and price. To maintain asset-market equilibrium, the increased quantity of money would have to be matched by higher prices and/or a depreciation in the exchange rate. The asset-market equilibrium schedule will shift out to $Q'Q'$, a shift that is (proportionately) equal to the increase in the nominal quantity of money.

It is immediately obvious that the new long-run equilibrium is at point C, where both goods and asset markets clear and exchange rate and price changes exactly reflect the increase in money.[11] This long-run homogeneity result is not surprising, since there is no source of money illusion or long-run price rigidity in the system.

Consider next the adjustment process. At the initial level of prices, the monetary expansion reduces interest rates and leads to the anticipation of a depreciation in the long run and, therefore, at the current exchange rate, to the expectation of a depreciating exchange rate. Both factors serve to reduce the attractiveness of domestic assets, lead to an incipient capital outflow, and thus cause the spot rate to depreciate. The extent of that depreciation has to be sufficient to give rise to the anticipation of appreciation at just sufficient a rate to offset the reduced domestic interest rate. The impact effect of a monetary expansion is, therefore, to induce an immediate depreciation in the spot rate and one that exceeds the long-run depreciation, since only under these circumstances will the public anticipate an appreciating exchange rate and thus be compensated for the reduced interest on domestic assets. This is shown in figure 2 by the move from point A to the short-run equilibrium at point B.

[11] We have not drawn in fig. 2, the $\dot{p} = 0$ schedule. It is apparent, however, from the homogeneity properties of the model that the $\dot{p} = 0$ schedule will pass through point C.

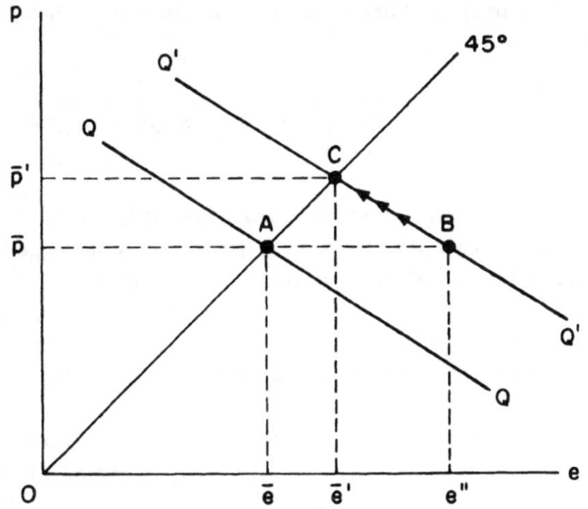

FIG. 2

From (4), noting that $d\bar{e} = dm = d\bar{p}$, we obtain a formal expression for the impact effect of a monetary expansion on the spot exchange rate:

$$de/dm = 1 + 1/\lambda\theta. \tag{16}$$

Equation (16) confirms that in the short run the exchange rate will overshoot. The extent of the overshooting will depend on the interest response of money demand and the expectations coefficient.

A high interest response of money demand will serve to dampen the overshooting because it implies that a given expansion in the (real) quantity of money will only induce a small reduction in the interest rate. A small reduction in the interest rate in turn requires only a small expectation of appreciation to offset it and therefore, given the coefficient of expectations and the long-run rate, only a small depreciation of the spot rate (in excess of the long-run rate) to generate that expectation. A similar interpretation applies to the coefficient of expectations in (16).

It is quite obvious from the preceding explanation that the short-term effects of a monetary expansion, in this model, are entirely dominated by asset markets and, more specifically, by capital mobility and expectations. This feature places in sharp relief the assumption that asset markets and exchange rates adjust fast relative to the goods market and the price of domestic output. It is under these circumstances that a change in the nominal quantity of money is, in fact, a change in the real quantity of money, and the spot rate adjustment serves to achieve equilibrium in the asset markets by creating the expectation of appreciation of just sufficient an extent to balance the reduced interest rate on domestic assets.

The interpretation of (16) has not so far used the restriction that expectations be rational. That restriction is introduced by substituting (15) in (16) to obtain

$$de/dm = 1 + 1/\lambda\tilde{\theta} = 1 + \frac{1}{\pi(\sigma + \delta\lambda)/2 + [\pi^2(\sigma + \delta\lambda)^2/4 + \pi\delta\lambda]^{1/2}}. \tag{17}$$

Equation (17) has two implications that cannot be derived from (16). The first is that with an interest response of money demand that approaches zero the initial depreciation remains finite and, in fact, approaches $de/dm = 1 + 1/\pi\sigma$. This result reflects the fact that, for the large interest rate changes that would result in these circumstances, the subsequent path of prices and the exchange rate is governed by the effect of interest rates on aggregate demand.

A second implication of (17) is the fact that the short-run overshooting of the exchange rate is inversely related to the speed of adjustment of the system, $\tilde{\theta}$. That fact is particularly obvious for the case where the speed of adjustment of prices, π, becomes infinite and where, accordingly, the economy jumps instantaneously to the new long-run equilibrium at point *C*.[12] More generally, those factors that serve to speed up the adjustment process, in particular high interest rate responsiveness of money demand, or aggregate spending, or high price elasticities, will therefore serve to dampen the impact effect of a monetary expansion on the exchange rate. This effect relies entirely on expectations about the subsequent path of the economy, rather than on *current* interaction between goods and asset markets.

Consider next the adjustment process from the short-run market equilibrium at point *B* to long-run equilibrium at point *C*. We note from figure 2 that at point *B* there is an excess demand for goods. That excess demand arises both from the decline in domestic interest rates and from the depreciation in the exchange rate that lowers the *relative* price of domestic goods. Each factor by itself is sufficient to account for this excess demand and, in fact, they constitute independent channels through which monetary changes affect demand for domestic output.

The exchange rate channel has been identified by Fleming and Mundell as an important avenue for monetary policy to act on aggregate demand.[13] In the present context the depreciation of the spot rate that is induced by the conditions of asset-market equilibrium serves to reduce the relative price of domestic goods and thereby to raise aggregate de-

[12] The slope of the *QQ* schedule is $dp/de = -\tilde{\theta}\lambda$, and the schedule becomes vertical as $\tilde{\theta}$ approaches infinity.

[13] In the Mundell–Fleming model with prices and interest rates fixed, the depreciation by worsening the terms of trade creates the necessary increase in aggregate demand to support the higher level of income required by monetary equilibrium (for a further discussion see Niehans [1975] and Dornbusch [1976]).

mand and give rise to inflationary pressure as opposed to an increase in output. The importance of this channel is larger, the higher the price elasticity of demand relative to the interest response of aggregate spending.

The lower interest rates and a lower relative price of domestic goods, that are characteristics of the impact effect, will cause domestic prices to rise and therefore be reflected in falling real money balances, rising interest rates, and an appreciating exchange rate. The adjustment process of rising prices over time restores the economy to the initial real equilibrium. An important feature of that adjustment process is the fact that rising prices are accompanied by an appreciating exchange rate. In terms of figure 2, this is described by the move along $Q'Q'$ from B to C. This result is due to the fact that rising prices cause the real money supply to be falling and interest rates to be rising. The rising interest rate, in turn, gives rise to an incipient capital inflow that appreciates the exchange rate at the same rate as interest rates are rising and thus maintains expected net yields in line. The model therefore confirms the link between interest rates and exchange rates that is emphasized in popular interpretations of foreign exchange events. The observation is correct, in the present circumstances, because rising interest rates are accompanied by the expectation of an appreciating exchange rate.

In summarizing this part we note that the ultimate effect of a monetary expansion is an equiproportionate increase in prices and the exchange rate. In the short run, however, the monetary expansion does exert real effects on interest rates, the terms of trade, and aggregate demand. The details of the adjustment process will depend on the economic structure. In particular, terms of trade changes will be both larger and more persistent the lower the speed of adjustment, $\tilde{\theta}$.

A key role in this analysis is played by the sluggish adjustment of prices as compared with asset markets. There is no very persuasive theoretical support for the slow adjustment of goods markets, but the facts clearly point in this direction. While the differential adjustment speed lacks theoretical backing, it implies, nevertheless, a behavior of exchange rates that is suggestive of recent experience.[14]

V. Short-Run Adjustment in Output

So far we have assumed that output is fixed at the full-employment level, $\bar{y}$. In the present part, the analysis is extended to allow for short-run adjustments in output in response to changes in aggregate demand.

[14] An extension of this paper would draw in an explicit manner on stochastic elements to provide a rationale for the short-run stickiness of prices. At the same time, such an extension would have interesting implications for the manner in which expectations are formed. Exchange rate determination in a stochastic setting has been studied by Black (1973), Kouri (1975), and Mussa (1976). Fischer (1976) has used a stochastic framework to evaluate fixed versus flexible exchange rate systems.

Therefore, we replace equation (8) by an equilibrium condition in the domestic goods market,

$$y = \ln D \equiv u + \delta(e - p) + \gamma y - \sigma r, \tag{18}$$

where y is the log of the actual level of output that in the short run is demand determined. In addition to (18), we require a price adjustment equation which is shown in (19):

$$\dot{p} = \pi(y - \bar{y}). \tag{19}$$

According to (19) the rate of inflation is proportional to the discrepancy between actual and full employment, or "potential" output, $\bar{y}$. This price adjustment equation is a combination of a relationship between wage and price inflation, a relation between wage inflation and unemployment as in a Phillips curve, and a relation between unemployment and the departure from potential output, $y - \bar{y}$, as described by Okun's law.

It is shown in the Appendix below that the extension that incorporates (18) and (19) in place of (8) leaves most of the analysis of adjustments to a monetary increase unchanged. In particular, the price adjustment will continue to be exponential although the speed of adjustment will depend now also on the income elasticities of demand for domestic goods and real balances, γ and ϕ.

In the present framework it continues to be true that in the short run an increase in the nominal quantity of money is an increase in the real quantity of money. Accordingly, a monetary expansion has the conventional effect of increasing in the short run the level of output and inducing inflation. Since the inflation that is induced by the expansion in real output serves to raise over time the price level, real balances will decline back to their initial level until in the long run the expansion in money is fully matched by increased prices and output has returned to the full-employment level.

The impact effect of a monetary expansion on exchange rates and interest rates may, however, differ significantly from the analysis in Part IV. The new possibility that arises from the expansion in output in the short run is that the exchange rate depreciation will fall short of the monetary expansion rather than exceed it as in (16). That possibility arises because, in the short run, the income expansion raises money demand and may do so sufficiently to actually increase interest rates. If the output expansion were sufficiently strong to raise interest rates, equalization of net yields internationally would require the expectation of a depreciation and therefore a spot rate that falls short of the long-run equilibrium rate. Since the long-run equilibrium rate increases in the same proportion as the nominal quantity of money, it follows that the spot rate would increase less than the quantity of money. The condition that gives rise to this case is

$$1 - \phi\delta/(1 - \gamma) < 0. \tag{20}$$

The term $\delta/(1 - \gamma)$ is the elasticity of equilibrium output with respect to the exchange rate. That term multiplied by the income elasticity of demand gives the increase in money demand due to a depreciation in the spot rate. Accordingly, (20) tells us whether at constant interest rates, and allowing the exchange rate to depreciate in the same proportion as the increase in money, we have an excess demand or supply of money and, accordingly, an increase or decrease in interest rates. The possibility of an excess demand and therefore an increase in interest rates is associated with a high income elasticity of money demand, high price elasticity, and a high income elasticity of demand for domestic goods.

The time path of exchange rates and the interest rate therefore depends on income and price elasticities, and the short-run overshooting of exchange rates is no longer a necessary feature of the adjustment process. In fact, if in the short run the interest rate rises and the exchange rate therefore depreciates less than proportionately to the increase in money, the adjustment process will be one of rising prices and a depreciating exchange rate. In this event, therefore, terms of trade fluctuations will be dampened as compared with the case described earlier where the exchange rate overshooting introduces large terms of trade variations in the adjustment process.

The analysis of a monetary expansion in this part confirms once more the Mundell-Fleming result that under conditions of capital mobility and flexible rates a small country can conduct, in the short run, an effective monetary policy. More important, the exchange rate proves a critical channel for the transmission of monetary changes to an increase in aggregate demand and output. That channel may, in fact, prove to be the only channel since, as was shown above, the interest rate may actually rise in the transition. Unlike in the Mundell-Fleming world, extension of the analysis to the long run shows that the effects of a monetary expansion are only transitory, since the inflation that is induced by the output expansion serves to reduce real balances and thereby return interest rates, relative prices, and real income to their initial level.

The possibility of short-run output adjustment has been shown to dampen exchange rate movements and possibly reverse the interest rate effects of a monetary expansion. It is appropriate, therefore, to ask which of the assumption, fixed or variable output, is a more relevant characteristic of the adjustment process. The answer no doubt is that the fixed output adjustment is a suitable characterization of the very short run. In the very short run we would not expect output to adjust instantaneously to meet an increase in aggregate demand and, accordingly, the adjustment will be primarily confined to the asset markets and will be characterized by a decline in interest rates and overshooting of exchange rates. In the intermediate run, on the contrary, the present analysis gains relevance, since here we would expect an adjustment of both output and prices in response to increased aggregate demand. On balance, therefore, the fixed output case retains relevance, and particularly so if output adjusts sluggishly to changes in aggregate demand.

Appendix

This Appendix extends the model to include short-run supply responses. For that purpose we replace the price adjustment equation in (8) by a goods-market equilibrium condition (A1) and a price equation (A2):

$$y = \mu[u + \delta(e - p) - \sigma r]; \; \mu \equiv 1/(1 - \gamma) > 0, \tag{A1}$$

$$\dot{p} = \pi(y - \bar{y}), \tag{A2}$$

where $\bar{y}$ denotes the full-employment level of output and where the price adjustment equation can be thought of as arising from a Phillips-curve relation between wage inflation and unemployment combined with an Okun's-law relation between the deviation from potential output, $y - \bar{y}$, and unemployment.[15]

The specification of the money market and exchange rate expectations remains unchanged, and equation (4) that represents these relations is repeated here for convenience:

$$p - m + \phi y = \lambda r^* + \theta\lambda(\bar{e} - e). \tag{A3}$$

Noting that in long-run equilibrium we have $y = \bar{y}$ and $r = r^*$, we obtain from (A1) the long-run goods-market relationship

$$\bar{y} = \mu[u + \delta(\bar{e} - \bar{p}) - \sigma r^*], \tag{A4}$$

and subtracting (A4) from (A1) we obtain the goods-market equilibrium condition expressed in terms of deviations from long-run equilibrium,

$$y - \bar{y} = \mu(\delta + \sigma\theta)(e - \bar{e}) + \mu\delta(\bar{p} - p), \tag{A5}$$

where we have used the fact that $r^* - r = \theta(e - \bar{e})$.

Next we proceed in a similar manner for the money market and rewrite the equilibrium condition as

$$\phi(y - \bar{y}) + (p - \bar{p}) = \lambda\theta(\bar{e} - e). \tag{A6}$$

Equations (A5) and (A6) can be simultaneously solved to yield the spot exchange rate and the level of output as a function of the existing price level. These solutions are, respectively,

$$y - \bar{y} = -w(p - \bar{p}). \tag{A7}$$

where

$$w \equiv [\mu(\delta + \theta\sigma) + \mu\delta\theta\lambda]/\Delta; \qquad \Delta \equiv \phi\mu(\delta + \theta\sigma) + \theta\lambda,$$

and

$$e - \bar{e} = -[(1 - \phi\mu\delta)/\Delta](p - \bar{p}). \tag{A8}$$

[15] To deal with steady-state inflation we would have to add in (A2) the long-run rate of inflation which is given by the rate of monetary growth, which in the present treatment is assumed equal to zero.

Substitution of (A7) in (A2) yields the equilibrium rate of inflation as a function of the price level:

$$\dot{p} = -\pi w(p - \bar{p}). \quad \text{(A9)}$$

Following the procedure in Part III, rational expectations require that the expectations coefficient, θ, equal the rate at which exchange rates actually adjust, πw:

$$\theta = \pi w, \quad \text{(A10)}$$

which can be solved for the rational expectations coefficient of adjustment, $\tilde{\theta}$.

Consider next the impact effect of a monetary expansion. Remembering that in the long run an increase in money causes an equiproportionate increase in prices and the exchange rate, we have $d\bar{e} = d\bar{p} = dm$. Therefore, from (A8) we obtain the impact effect of a monetary expansion on the exchange rate as

$$de/dm = 1 + (1 - \phi\mu\delta)/\Delta > 0. \quad \text{(A11)}$$

Whether the exchange rate increases more or less proportionately than the nominal quantity of money depends on the condition

$$1 - \phi\mu\delta \gtrless 0, \quad \text{(A12)}$$

which determines, too, whether the interest rate declines or increases.

By (A7) the impact effect on real output is unambiguously positive and equal to $dy/dm = w$. The increase in the rate of inflation is given by $d\dot{p}/dm = \pi w$.

Since from (A9) the inflation rate converges monotonically to the long-run level, we know that output declines monotonically back toward the level of full employment. The exchange rate, following the impact effect, will appreciate, or depreciate, depending on (A12).

References

Black, S. *International Money Markets and Flexible Exchange Rates.* Princeton Studies in International Finance, no. 32. Princeton, N.J.: Princeton Univ. Press, 1973.

———. "Exchange Rate Policies for Less Developed Countries in a World of Floating Rates." Mimeographed. Vanderbilt Univ., 1975.

Dornbusch, R. "Exchange Rate Expectations and Monetary Policy." *J. Internat. Econ.* (1976), forthcoming. (*a*)

———. "The Theory of Flexible Exchange Rate Regimes and Macroeconomic Policy." *Scandinavian J. Econ.* 2 (May 1976): 255–75. (*b*)

Fischer, S. "Stability and Exchange Rate Systems in a Monetarist Model of the Balance of Payments." In *The Political Economy of Monetary Reform*, edited by R. Aliber. London: Macmillan, 1976.

Fleming, M. "Domestic Financial Policies under Fixed and Floating Exchange Rates." *I.M.F. Staff Papers* 9 (November 1962): 369–79.

Frenkel, J. A. "A Monetary Approach to the Exchange Rate." *Scandinavian J. Econ.* 2 (May 1976): 200–221.

Henderson, D. "Monetary, Fiscal and Exchange Rate Policy in a Two-Country, Short-Run Macroeconomic Model." Mimeographed. Board of Governors, Federal Res., 1975.

Kouri, P. *Essays on the Theory of Flexible Exchange Rates.* Ph.D. dissertation, Massachusetts Inst. Tech., 1975.

———. "The Exchange Rate and the Balance of Payments in the Short Run and in the Long Run." *Scandinavian J. Econ.* 2 (May 1976): 280–304.

Mundell, R. A. "Exchange Rate Margins and Economic Policy." In *Money in the International Order*, edited by C. Murphy. Dallas: Southern Methodist Univ. Press, 1964.

———. *International Economics*. New York: Macmillan, 1968.

Mussa, M. "The Exchange Rate, the Balance of Payments and Monetary and Fiscal Policy under a Regime of Controlled Floating." *Scandinavian J. Econ.* 2 (May 1976): 229–48.

Niehans, J. "Some Doubts about the Efficacy of Monetary Policy under Flexible Exchange Rates." *J. Internat. Econ.* 5 (August 1975): 275–81.

[3]

Journal of International Economics 14 (1983) 3–24. North-Holland Publishing Company

EMPIRICAL EXCHANGE RATE MODELS OF THE SEVENTIES

Do they fit out of sample?

Richard A. MEESE*

University of California at Berkeley, Berkeley, CA 94720, USA

Kenneth ROGOFF

Board of Governors of the Federal Reserve System, Washington, DC 20551, USA

Received July 1981, revised version received April 1982

This study compares the out-of-sample forecasting accuracy of various structural and time series exchange rate models. We find that a random walk model performs as well as any estimated model at one to twelve month horizons for the dollar/pound, dollar/mark, dollar/yen and trade-weighted dollar exchange rates. The candidate structural models include the flexible-price (Frenkel–Bilson) and sticky-price (Dornbusch–Frankel) monetary models, and a sticky-price model which incorporates the current account (Hooper–Morton). The structural models perform poorly despite the fact that we base their forecasts on actual realized values of future explanatory variables.

1. Introduction

This study compares time series and structural models of exchange rates on the basis of their out-of-sample forecasting accuracy. We find that a random walk model would have predicted major-country exchange rates during the recent floating-rate period as well as any of our candidate models.[1] Significantly, the structural models fail to improve on the random walk model in spite of the fact that we base their forecasts on actual realized values of future explanatory variables.

*Both authors were at the Federal Reserve Board when this paper was written. This paper is a revised version of a paper presented at the International Monetary Fund and at the December 1981 Meetings of the Econometric Society. Robert Flood, Jeffrey Frankel, Robert Hodrick, Peter Hooper, and Julio Rotemberg gave us helpful comments on an earlier draft. We are indebted to Julie Withers and Catherine Crosby for research assistance. This paper represents the views of the authors and should not be interpreted as reflecting the views of the Board of Governors of the Federal Reserve System.

[1]Cornell (1977), Mussa (1979) and Frenkel (1981b) have noted that exchange rate changes are largely unpredictable. Mussa (p. 10) states that: 'The natural logarithm of the spot exchange rate follows approximately a random walk.' The present study systematically confirms this 'stylized fact'. Another point Mussa makes and the results of this study support, is that any serial correlation found in the exchange rates by in-sample tests is likely to be unstable over time.

0022–1996/83/0000–0000/$03.00 © 1983 North-Holland

In our experiment, each competing model is used to generate forecasts at one to twelve month horizons for the dollar/pound, dollar/mark, dollar/yen and trade-weighted dollar exchange rates.[2,3] The parameters of each model are estimated on the basis of the most up-to-date information available at the time of a given forecast. This is accomplished by using rolling regressions to re-estimate the parameters of each model every forecast period.

As representative structural models we choose the flexible-price monetary (Frenkel–Bilson) model, the sticky-price monetary (Dornbusch–Frankel) model, and the Hooper–Morton model. The latter empirical model extends the Dornbusch–Frankel model to incorporate the effects of the current account. We estimate these models using ordinary least squares, generalized least squares, and Fair's (1970) instrumental variables technique. We also try specifications which incorporate lagged adjustment.

A variety of univariate time series techniques are applied to the data as well. None of these techniques, including estimation of a random walk with drift model, generally yields any forecasting improvement in root mean square error or mean absolute error over the random walk model. Nor does an unconstrained vector autoregression composed of the exchange rate and all the explanatory variables from the structural models.

The forward rate does not predict any better than the random walk model either. But the interpretation of its relative performance is somewhat tangential to the main issue here, which is: How well do existing empirical exchange rate models fit out-of-sample?

A description of the competing models and the techniques used to estimate them is presented in section 2 of the paper. Section 3 discusses our methodology for comparing models out of sample, and section 4 contains the main results. In section 5 we list some possible explanations of these results.

2. A description of the models

Here we discuss the specification and statistical estimation of the various competing models.

2.1. The structural models

From the 'asset' models that have come to dominate the recent literature on exchange rate determination we select three which, perhaps due to the relative tractability of their data requirements, have been subjected to

[2]Haache and Townend (1981), using different methods than ours, conclude that none of the structural models can explain the behavior of the effective pound sterling exchange rate over the seventies.

[3]The trade-weighted dollar is a weighted-average of U.S. dollar exchange rates with the Group of Ten Countries plus Switzerland; see the data appendix.

extensive (in-sample) empirical testing. These are the flexible-price monetary (Frenkel–Bilson) model, the sticky-price monetary (Dornbusch–Frankel) model, and the sticky-price asset (Hooper–Morton) model.[4] The quasi-reduced form specifications of all three models are subsumed in the general specification (1):

$$\begin{aligned} s = {} & a_0 + a_1(m-\overset{*}{m}) + a_2(y-\overset{*}{y}) + a_3(r_s-\overset{*}{r}_s) \\ & + a_4(\pi^e-\overset{*}{\pi}^e) + a_5\overline{TB} + a_6\overline{\overset{*}{TB}} + u, \end{aligned} \tag{1}$$

where s is the logarithm of the dollar price of foreign currency, $m-\overset{*}{m}$ the logarithm of the ratio of the U.S. money supply to the foreign money supply, $y-\overset{*}{y}$ is the logarithm of the ratio of U.S. to foreign real income, $r_s-\overset{*}{r}_s$ is the short-term interest rate differential and $\pi^e-\overset{*}{\pi}^e$ is the expected long-run inflation differential.[5] $\overline{TB}$ and $\overline{\overset{*}{TB}}$ represent the cumulated U.S. and foreign trade balances, and u is a disturbance term. The disturbance term may be a serially correlated; we shall also consider allowing for lagged adjustment in eq. (1).

All of the models posit that, ceteris paribus, the exchange rate exhibits first-degree homogeneity in the relative money supplies, or $a_1=1$. The Frenkel–Bilson model, which assumes purchasing power parity, constraints $a_4=a_5=a_6=0$. The Dornbusch–Frankel model, which allows for slow domestic price adjustment and consequent deviations from purchasing power parity, sets $a_5=a_6=0$. None of the coefficients in eq. (1) is constrained to be zero in the Hooper–Morton model. This model extends the Dornbusch–Frankel model to allow for changes in the long-run real exchange rate. These long-run real exchange rate changes are assumed to be correlated with unanticipated shocks to the trade balance.[6] Imposing the constraint that domestic and foreign variables (except for trade balances) enter eq. (1) in differential form implicitly assumes that the parameters of the domestic and

[4]See Bilson (1978, 1979), Frenkel (1976), Dornbusch (1976), Frankel (1979, 1981), and Hooper and Morton (1982). Our nomenclature, which identifies particular models with authors who contributed significantly to their development is a conventional one. But it is not comprehensive in that some of these authors have worked with more than one of the three models, and there are other researchers who have studied these models or closely-related ones.

[5]Proxies for the unobservable $\pi^e-\overset{*}{\pi}^e$ are typically constructed from variables such as long-term interest rate differentials, the preceding twelve-month period CPI or WPI inflation rates, or with an inflation rate autoregression; see Frankel (1981) and Hooper and Morton (1982).

[6]Since current account data is available only on a quarterly basis, the monthly version of Hooper and Morton's empirical model uses the trade balance as a proxy. Cumulative deviations from trend balances (current accounts) enter Hooper and Morton's equation since they assume that deviations from trend balances are unanticipated. Frankel (1982b) employs a model with a very similar quasi-reduced form, in which the cumulated current accounts of both countries enter because of wealth terms in the money demand equations. Branson, Halttunen and Masson (1979) also include the cumulated current accounts in empirical exchange rate equations. Their justification derives from the joint assumptions of imperfect asset substitutability and differential asset preferences across countries.

foreign money demand and price adjustment equations are equal. While this parsimonious assumption is conventional in empirical applications, it is a potential source of misspecification; see Haynes and Stone (1981). As reported below, however, no gain in out-of-sample fit results from estimating separate coefficients for domestic and foreign money supplies and real incomes.

A conventional approach to comparing the models subsumed in eq. (1) involves estimating a model of the general form, and then testing the constraints implied by the competing models. When overall performance is measured by in-sample fit, regressions based on eq. (1) do reasonably well. [See, for example, Frankel (1979) or Hooper and Morton (1982).] One drawback to this approach is that it is difficult to deal with the statistical problems encountered in obtaining consistent estimates of the coefficients in eq. (1). Variables such as relative money supplies and relative incomes are typically treated as exogenous variables in the underlying theoretical models, but may be more realistically thought of as endogenous variables. Other variables, such as the short-term interest differential, are generally endogenous in these same theoretical models. Yet they are still treated as legitimate regressors in ordinary or generalized least squares regressions of eq. (1).

The possibility that the explanatory variables in eq. (1) are endogenous is supported by the vector autoregression results presented in Meese and Rogoff (1983), and by the block exogeneity specification tests presented in Glaessner (1982). Of course, endogeneity of the explanatory variables does not preclude consistent estimation of the structural parameters in eq. (1). If, for example, the error term follows an autoregressive process of known maximum order, then instrumental variables techniques such as Fair's (1970) method are available. Frankel (1979) takes this approach, assuming a first-order autoregressive process and treating long-term expected inflation differentials as endogenous; Frankel (1981) allows short-term interest rates to be endogenous as well. To also account for the possible endogeneity of the money supplies, he tries constraining the coefficient on relative money supplies to its theoretical value of one. Following Frankel, we estimate the models using ordinary least squares, generalized least squares (correcting for serial correlation),[7] and Fair's method. In the last case money supplies, short-term interest rates, and expected long-term inflation rates are treated as endogenous variables. Note that if one of the models summarized by eq. (1) is true, and if its structural and serial correlation parameters can be consistently estimated with instrumental variables techniques, then such techniques will outperform inconsistent techniques in large enough samples.

[7]Generalized least squares with a correction for a fifth-order autoregressive error term performs worse than GLS with a correction for a first-order autoregressive term (Cochrane–Orcutt). Cochrane–Orcutt also outperforms a stock-adjustment model.

However, generalized least squares parameter estimates did not yield inferior forecasts in our experiments.

While the forecasts generated in this study are based on models with freely-estimated coefficients, elsewhere [Meese and Rogoff (1983)] we try forecasting with the structural models using a grid of coefficient constraints drawn from the theoretical and empirical literature on money demand and purchasing power parity. Those results, which are discussed further below, do not lead to different conclusions than our experiements here with freely-estimated coefficients.

2.2. *Univariate and multivariate time series models*

Several univariate time series models involving a variety of prefiltering techniques and lag length selection criteria are employed in our experiments. All are estimated for the logarithm of the exchange rate.[8]

The prefiltering techniques involve differencing, deseasonalizing, and removing time trends. All six univariate time series techniques we consider are applied to both the actual and the prefiltered data. The first technique, the 'long AR', is an unconstrained autoregression (AR) where the longest lag considered (M) is a function of sample size (N), $M=N/\log N$. A deterministic rule like this has long been employed in spectral estimation [see Hannan (1970)] and has been applied to distributed lag models by Sims (1974b). If the true order of the autoregression is unknown but finite, this procedure is asymptotically inefficient relative to the Schwartz (1978) order selection criterion. We employ this procedure and the Akaike (1974) procedure in our study; the Schwartz criterion provides a consistent estimate of lag length, while the Akaike lag length criterion asymptotically produces minimum mean square prediction errors of the dependent variable. Our fourth procedure is like the long AR, except that in estimating the parameters more weight is given to recent observations. We arbitrarily choose to weight the observations by powers of 0.95. The fifth univariate technique involves direct application of the Wiener–Kolmogorov prediction formula in the frequency domain; see Sargent (1979).

A possible problem with all the techniques listed thus far is that they minimize criteria based on squared deviations. These type of criteria are inappropriate if, for example, exchange rates follow non-normal stable-Paretian distributions with infinite variance, as suggested by Westerfield (1977). Therefore, our final time series technique is based on minimizing absolute deviations. This 'MAD' estimator is more robust to fat-tailed distributions, and less sensitive to outlier observations.

[8]A Box–Cox transformation test indicates that the logarithmic transformation is slightly preferable to levels for all the exchange rates we consider. Theoretical reasons for preferring the logarithm of the exchange rate are given in section 3.

While the relative performance of the six univariate forecasting techniques is of interest in itself, we shall only report detailed results for the long AR model without trend, seasonal adjustment, or differencing. This model's performance characterizes those of the best univariate models; we will discuss the results of the other univariate models only to a lesser degree.

The random walk model, which uses the current spot rate as a predictor of all future spot rate is, of course, a univariate time series model. While the basic random walk model obviously requires no estimation, we also estimate a random walk model with drift parameter. The drift parameter is estimated as the mean monthly (logarithmic) exchange rate change.

An unconstrained vector autoregression (VAR), composed of the variables in eq. (1), serves as our representative multivariate time series model. A convenient normalization for estimation of the VAR is one in which the contemporaneous value of each variable is regressed against lagged values of itself and all the other variables, e.g. the exchange rate equation is

$$s_t = a_{i1}s_{t-1} + a_{i2}s_{t-2} + \cdots a_{in}s_{t-n} + B'_{i1}X_{t-1}$$
$$+ B'_{i2}X_{t-2} + \cdots B'_{in}X_{t-n} + u_{it}, \tag{2}$$

where X_{t-j} is a vector of the explanatory variables in eq. (1), lagged j periods. The error term u_{it} is serially uncorrelated, but may be contemporaneously correlated with the error terms in the other equations; thus the normalization used in (2) does not preclude contemporaneous interactions between variables. This normalization facilitates estimation since ordinary least squares equation by equation is an efficient strategy. The uniform lag length n across all (seven) equations is estimated using Parzen's (1975) lag length selection criterion.[9] To reduce the parameterization of the VAR, we also try constraining the domestic and foreign cumulated trade balances to enter in differenced form rather than separately. As is not unusual in a small sample, the more parsimoniously parameterized six-variable VAR yields better forecasts, so this is the model we report below. The VAR is important to include in our forecasting experiments since it does not restrict any variables to be exogenous a priori, and is therefore robust to some of the estimation problems that plague the structural models discussed in the previous section. We did not, however, experiment with algorithms designed to reduce the number of estimated coefficients in the profligately parameterized VAR; see Litterman (1979). Such algorithms can sometimes markedly reduce the mean square prediction errors produced by these models.

[9]Parzen's (1975) criterion asymptotically selects a lag order greater than or equal to the true order, assuming the true order is finite. The lag lengths chosen for the dollar/mark, dollar/pound, dollar/yen, and trade-weighted dollar VARs are 2, 2, 4, and 2.

2.3. Selecting the data

The data, which are described in an appendix, are chosen to conform to the theoretical assumptions underlying the specification of the structural models.

All of the raw data used in this study are seasonally unadjusted, which makes it possible to estimate seasonal and structural parameters on a consistent basis. The use of seasonally adjusted data is especially likely to distort structural parameter estimates when the variables are not all adjusted by the same method. [See Sims (1974a, 1974b) for a further discussion.] We experimented with two different seasonal adjustment procedures. One method uses seasonal dummy variables. The other is Sims' (1974a) method which explicitly allows the seasonal parameterization to expand with sample size. As the results of our experiment are robust to the choice between these two techniques, we only report the results for the more conventional dummy variables procedure. Another reason for using seasonally unadjusted data is to avoid the use of certain information not available at the time of a given forecast. Forecasts based on seasonally adjusted data, adjusted over the extended sample period or with a two-sided filter such as Census X-11, implicitly make use of information which would not have been available.

The dollar/mark, dollar/pound, and dollar/yen spot exchange rate data are monthly point-sample data. We use an average of daily rates for the trade-weighted dollar, partly because that data is more readily available and partly to be consistent with other work on the trade-weighted dollar. [See Hooper and Morton (1982).] For the purposes of this study, point sample data have a decided advantage over monthly average data. Suppose the exchange rate follows a random walk on a mid-day to mid-day basis. Then as Working (1960) observed, a series consisting of monthly averages of mid-day rates will exhibit positive serial correlation.

Bilateral forward rates of one, three, six, and twelve month maturities are drawn from the same day of the month as the spot rates; point-sample short-term and (where possible) long-term interest rate data also match the spot rate data. We use treasury bill rates and interbank rates for short-term interest rates. Using these interest rates makes sense when estimating models based on standard money demand specifications. However, Euromarket rates would be more likely to conform to another assumption underlying most of the structural models: perfect asset substitutibility. Some limited experimentation with Euromarket rates suggests that their use would have little effect on our results. As discussed below, the choice of monetary aggregates is potentially quite important. We try three different aggregates in our experiments: M1-B, M2, and the reserve-adjusted base. (Since the United Kingdom does not publish a series for M2, U.S. M3 and sterling M3 are employed in place of M2's for the dollar/pound rate experiments. Only M1-B type measures are used in the trade-weighted dollar experiments; we were unable to find or construct a reserve-adjusted base series for Japan.)

3. The methodology for comparing models out-of-sample

All the competing models are estimated over a monthly data series which starts in March 1973, the beginning of the floating rate period, and extends through June 1981. Each model is initially estimated for each exchange rate using data up through the first forecasting period, November 1976. Forecasts are generated at horizons of one, three, six, and twelve months; these forecast horizons correspond to the available forward rate data. Then the data for December 1976 are added to the sample, and the parameters of each model, including the seasonal adjustment parameters, are re-estimated using rolling regressions. New forecasts are generated at one, three, six, and twelve month horizons, etc.

The purpose of considering multiple forecast horizons in this type of experiment is to see whether the structural models do better than time series models in the long run, when adjustment due to lags and/or a serially correlated error term has taken place. Of course, when lags and serial correlation are fully incorporated into the structural models, a consistently-estimated true structural model will outpredict a time series model at *all* horizons in a large sample.

The choice of where to begin forecasting is predicted on our desire to have sufficient degrees of freedom available for initial parameter estimates of all the models, especially the profligately-parameterized vector autoregression. We also look at the subperiod beginning in November 1978, in part because that date marks a major change in U.S. intervention strategy, and in part to see whether the relative performances of the competing models are different over the recent subperiod than over the entire forecasting period. Finally, we try truncating the sample in November 1980 which, like November 1976, marks a U.S. presidential election.

The structural models require forecasts of their explanatory variables in order to generate forecasts of the exchange rate. To give these models the benefit of the doubt, we use actual realized values of their respective explanatory variables. This procedure directly addresses one possible defense of these models: structural exchange rate models have explanatory power, but predict badly because their explanatory variables are themselves difficult to predict.[10]

The methodology used here for comparing models out-of-sample is drawn from the macro literature; see, for example, Nelson (1972), Christ (1975),

[10]When the explanatory variables are endogenous they will in general be correlated with the error term in eq. (1). If available, information about this correlation could be used to construct better structural model forecasts.

Litterman (1979), or Fair (1979). Although out-of-sample comparisons have considerable intuitive appeal, formal tests of whether these differences are statistically significant generally require restrictive assumptions.[11] But this limitation of the experimental design does not turn out to be crucial for the interpretation of our major result. We shall postpone this discussion until the next section.

Out-of-sample accuracy is measured by three statistics: mean error (ME), mean absolute error (MAE) and root mean square error (RMSE). These are defined as follows:

$$\text{mean error} = \sum_{s=0}^{N_k-1} [F(t+s+k) - A(t+s+k)]/N_k, \tag{3a}$$

$$\text{mean absolute error} = \sum_{s=0}^{N_k-1} |F(t+s+k) - A(t+s+k)|/N_k, \tag{3b}$$

$$\text{root mean square error} = \left\{ \sum_{s=0}^{N_k-1} [F(t+s+k) - A(t+s+k)]^2/N_k \right\}^{1/2}, \tag{3c}$$

where $k=1$, 3, 6, 12 denotes the forecast step, N_k the total number of forecasts in the projection period for which the actual value $A(t)$ is known, and $F(t)$ the forecast value. Forecasting begins in period t. Because we are looking at the logarithm of the exchange rate, these statistics are unit-free (they are approximately in percentage terms) and comparable across currencies. By comparing predictors on the basis of their ability to predict the logarithm of the exchange rate, we also avoid any problems arising from Jensen's inequality. Because of Jensen's inequality, the best predictor of the level of the dollar/mark rate might not be the best predictor of the mark/dollar rate.[12]

Root mean square error is our principal criterion for comparing forecasters. But because RMSE is an inappropriate criterion if, as mentioned

[11]Granger and Newbold (1977, p. 281) propose a formal test of two forecasting techniques; the test is applicable only when both forecast errors are independent and normally distributed with zero means and constant variances. Thus, the test can only be applied at forecast intervals greater than one month if overlapping multi-horizon forecasts are omitted.

[12]Siegel (1972) notes that because $1/x$ is a convex function of the random variable x, $E(1/x)$ is not in general equal to $1/E(x)$. McCulloch (1975) suggests that this problem is not important empirically, given the historical variance of the exchange rate. Both analyses are based on an erroneous Taylor expansion which yields $E(1/x) - 1/E(x) \approx \operatorname{var}(x)/E(x)^3$. This approximation may be misleading because the Taylor expansion used to derive it is local, whereas the expectations integral is global. While the above approximation is precisely correct when x follows a lognormal distribution, it can be way off when the distribution of x is skewed. Consider the discrete probability density function: $P(x=1)=0.99$, $P(x=0.01)=0.01$. Then $E(1/x) - 1/E(x) = 1.99 - 1.01 = 0.98$. However, $\operatorname{var}(x)/E(x)^3 \cong 0.01$. The order of magnitude of the Jensen's inequality term is more likely to be large in data sets where an outside chance of a major intervention is incorporated into expectations.

in subsection 2.2, exchange rates are governed by a non-normal stable Paretian process with infinite variance, it is important to include mean absolute error. MAE is also a useful criterion when the exchange rate distribution has fat tails, even if the variance is finite. The last criterion, mean error, provides another measure of robustness. By comparing MAE and ME we can ascertain whether a model systematically over- or underpredicts.

4. The results

Table 1 lists the root mean square error statistics at one and twelve month horizons over the full November 1976 through June 1981 forecasting period for exchange rate for representative versions of each model. The structural models in table 1 are estimated using Fair's method as described in subsection 1.1. The measure of money is M1-B and, in the two sticky-price models, the long-term interest differential serves as the proxy for the long-run expected inflation differential. In addition, table 1 gives RMSE for the spot rate, the forward rate, the vector autoregression, and a long univariate autoregression (with order a function of sample size).

Ignoring for the present the fact that the spot rate does no worse than the forward rate, the striking feature of table 1 is that none of the models achieves lower, much less significantly lower, RMSE than the random walk model at any horizon. Although RMSE at three month horizons are not listed in table 1, they give the same result.

The structural models in particular fail to improve on the random walk model in spite of the fact their forecasts are based on realized values of the explanatory variables. They predict much worse, especially at one month horizons, if serial correlation is not accounted for. We obtain very similar results to those presented in table 1 using Granger and Newbold's (1977) method of combining the forecasts of structural models (without serial correlation) and time series models.[13] Estimating the models in first difference form does not help, nor does using either a stock-adjustment formulation or generalized least squares with a correction for a fifth-order autoregressive process. Generalized least squares with a correction for first-order serial correlation (Cochrane–Orcutt) does frequently yield marginally better results than Fair's method. But this is not particularly encouraging

[13]Granger and Newbold's technique for optimally combining forecasts involves regressing the realized exchange rate against the forecasts of different models, with the weights constrained to sum to one, but not constrained to be positive. Even a bad predictor can sometimes be profitably combined with a good predictor; the forecasting gain depends on their covariation. An estimated combination of all seven forecasts never improves upon the random walk model alone, but estimated linear combinations of the different forecasts taken two at a time do sometimes outperform the random walk model. However, the same combination never works for more than one exchange rate. (These results are based on a November 1976–November 1980 forecasting period; linear combination forecasts were only generated at one month horizons.)

Table 1

Root mean square forecast errors.[a]

Exchange rate	Model: / Horizon	Random walk	Forward rate	Univariate autoregression	Vector autoregression	Frenkel–Bilson[b]	Dornbusch–Frankel[b]	Hooper–Morton[b]
$/mark	1 month	3.72	3.20	3.51	5.40	3.17	3.65	3.50
	6 months	8.71	9.03	12.40	11.83	9.64	12.03	9.95
	12 months	12.98	12.60	22.53	15.06	16.12	18.87	15.69
$/yen	1 month	3.68	3.72	4.46	7.76	4.11	4.40	4.20
	6 months	11.58	11.93	22.04	18.90	13.38	13.94	11.94
	12 months	18.31	18.95	52.18	22.98	18.55	20.41	19.20
$/pound	1 month	2.56	2.67	2.79	5.56	2.82	2.90	3.03
	6 months	6.45	7.23	7.27	12.97	8.90	8.88	9.08
	12 months	9.96	11.62	13.35	21.28	14.62	13.66	14.57
Trade-weighted dollar	1 month	1.99	N.A.	2.72	4.10	2.40	2.50	2.74
	6 months	6.09	N.A.	6.82	8.91	7.07	6.49	7.11
	12 months	8.65	14.24	11.14	10.96	11.40	9.80	10.35

[a]Approximately in percentage terms.

[b]The three structural models are estimated using Fair's instrumental variable technique to correct for first-order serial correlation.

since Cochrane–Orcutt estimates are less often of the theoretically correct sign. Constraining the coefficients to be of the correct sign does not, however, improve the structural model forecasts. Meese and Rogoff (1983) report extensive constrained-coefficient experiments in which the structural models still fail to beat the random walk model at horizons of one to twelve months; see section 5 below.

Allowing for separate coefficients on domestic and foreign real incomes and money supplies yields no gain in out-of-sample forecasting accuracy. Nor does including domestic and foreign price levels as additional explanatory variables. Replacing M1-B with either M2 or the reserve-adjusted base almost always yields worse results, and never an improvement on the random walk model. Replacing long-term interest rates by other inflationary expectations proxies, such as current period inflation differentials, a moving average of past inflation differentials, or future inflation differentials, yields comparable results in both constrained- and freely-estimated coefficient experiments. The past twelve-month-period inflation differential works somewhat better (over the present sample). With that proxy, at one month horizons for the dollar/mark rate the Dornbusch–Frankel and Hooper–Morton models predict better than the random walk model in RMSE by 0.02 and 0.05 percent, respectively. They do worse at longer forecast horizons, though. The Hooper–Morton model (with the past year inflation rate proxy) also exhibits marginal improvement over the random walk model for the dollar/yen rate at six months (but not at one month or twelve months), and for the trade-weighted dollar at six months. At twelve months, the Hooper–Morton model improves by a more substantial 2 percent over the random walk model for the trade-weighted dollar.

The failure of the univariate time series models to beat the random walk model is similarly quite robust. None of the various univariate techniques improve on the random walk model at any horizon for the dollar/mark rate. The random walk with drift model improves by about 0.5 percent at six and twelve month horizons for the dollar/pound rate, but is 0.1 percent worse at one month and does much worse at predicting the dollar/yen and trade-weighted dollar. Given that we use monthly average data for the trade-weighted dollar, one would expect that in a large enough sample, the estimated univariate models would predict it better than the random walk model, even if the latter model is true for point-sample data (see subsection 2.3). But here only the long AR model (detrended) ever predicts the trade-weighted dollar better; it is only 0.5 percent better at twelve months. Only the Schwarz criterion together with detrending yields an improvement over the random walk model for the dollar/yen rate. The improvement is 1.5 percent at six months and 4.8 percent at twelve months.

It is worth emphasizing that even though exchange rates probably do not follow a random walk exactly, an estimated univariate model may not forecast better due to sampling error. It is well known that imposing a coefficient restriction which is approximately correct tends to improve forecast accuracy. [See Sims (1980) or Litterman (1979) for further discussion.] This reason may similarly explain why the multivariate vector autoregression fails to outpredict the random walk model. It is thus possible that a non-structural method of reducing the number of estimated VAR parameters, such as the one Litterman (1979) proposes, would lead to an improvement on the random walk model.

At the risk of detracting from central issues such as how well existing empirical exchange rate models fit out-of-sample, we briefly turn to a comparison of spot and forward exchange rates. In table 1 the forward rate only improves on the random walk model in RMSE for the case of the dollar/mark rate at twelve month horizons. Given the joint assumptions of market efficiency and rational expectations, the relative performance of the forward rate may be interpreted as evidence on the existence of a risk premium.[14] For example, the forward rate could predict worse than the random walk model when there is a time-varying risk premium, even if the risk premium is zero on average.

The dominance of the random walk model over the other models in RMSE remains when forecasting begins in November 1978, or alternatively if it ends in November 1980. The mean absolute error statistics, which are generally 20–25 percent smaller than RMSE, are not listed here since they yield virtually the same rankings as RMSE. Even the univariate technique designed to minimize mean absolute deviations fails to improve on the random walk model in out-of-sample MAE.

The mean forecast errors of the various models are listed in table 2. These errors are generally much smaller than the corresponding mean absolute errors, indicating that the models do not systematically over- or underpredict. (The structural models do tend to go systematically offtrack if no serial correlation is allowed for.) Note that the random walk model is somewhat less dominant in ME than in RMSE and MAE in our experiments, particularly for the dollar/mark rate. Estimating the structural models in first difference form generally produces lower ME but higher RMSE than does estimating the models in levels with a correction for serial correlation.

The results presented above do not answer the question of whether the random walk is *significantly* better than the other models in root mean square error, our primary criterion. However, given our finding that the

[14]A number of recent authors, including Bilson (1981), Cumby and Obstfeld (1981), Geweke and Feige (1979), Hakkio (1981), Hansen and Hodrick (1980, 1983), Meese and Singleton (1980), and Tryon (1979), have found evidence of the divergence of forward rates from expected future spot rates over the recent floating-rate period. Bilson (1981), however, is the only author who uses an out-of-sample testing methodology. Although his model is not discussed, it too failed to outperform the random walk model at one month forecast horizons.

Table 2

Mean forecast errors[a]

Exchange rate	Model / Horizon	Random walk	Forward rate	Univariate autoregression	Vector autoregression	Frenkel–Bilson[b]	Dornbusch–Frankel[b]	Hooper–Morton[b]
$/mark	1 month	0.04	0.35	0.26	−1.12	0.37	−0.17	0.07
	6 months	−0.92	1.31	1.99	−3.31	1.23	−0.59	−0.17
	12 months	−3.93	0.29	5.20	−5.22	0.55	−3.06	−1.52
$/yen	1 month	−0.46	−0.06	−0.15	−2.64	−1.36	−1.46	−0.18
	6 months	−3.32	−1.26	−3.17	−7.51	−8.00	−8.53	−1.81
	12 months	−6.48	−2.62	−8.91	−10.45	−14.05	−14.82	−2.38
$/pound	1 month	−0.31	−0.38	−0.12	−3.72	−0.48	−0.37	−0.52
	6 months	−3.09	−4.05	−1.32	−9.45	−5.55	−4.53	−5.30
	12 months	−7.75	−9.55	−4.17	−18.54	−13.21	−12.07	−11.69
Trade-weighted dollar	1 month	−0.03	N.A.	0.06	0.89	0.63	0.54	0.68
	6 months	0.77	N.A.	1.61	3.91	3.86	2.79	3.52
	12 months	3.18	7.66	6.44	7.11	7.69	5.30	5.78

[a]Approximately in percentage terms.

[b]The three structural models are estimated using Fair's instrumental variable technique to correct for first-order serial correlation.

random walk model almost invariably has the lowest root mean square error over all horizons and across all exchange rates, we *can* unambiguously assert that the other models do not perform significantly better than the random walk model. And while the random walk model may be as good a predictor as any of major-country exchange rates, it does not predict well. Even the RMSE in table 1 for the trade-weighted dollar — which as one might expect is more predictable than the bilateral rates — is 1.99 percent at one month and 8.65 percent at twelve months. The highest RMSE are for the dollar/yen rate: 3.70 percent at one month and 18.3 percent at twelve months.

One might hope to ultimately estimate a structural model which could perform substantially better than this, especially when forecasts are based on realized explanatory variable values. In the next section we address some possible explanations of our dissatisfying results. While the problem may lie in sampling error, it is also possible that these empirical models do not adequately capture expectations or other forces which influence exchange rates.

5. Possible reasons for the poor out-of-sample fit of the structural models

Since the structural model forecasts have been purged of explanatory variable uncertainty, their disappointing performance is most likely to be attributable to simultaneous equation bias, sampling error, stochastic movements in the true underlying parameters, or misspecification. Also, we make no attempt to account for possible non-linearities in the underlying models.

We have attempted to account for simultaneous equations bias by employing instrumental variables techniques, by estimating a vector autoregression, and by imposing theoretical coefficient constraints. The latter method is applied extensively in Meese and Rogoff (1983). There we develop and search a grid of coefficient constraints. The priors embodied in the grid are based on the fact that all the coefficients in the quasi-reduced form specification (1), except those on the cumulated trade balances, are functions of money demand parameters and the rate at which the real exchange rate returns to its long-run purchasing power parity level. [See Frankel (1979) or Hooper and Morton (1982).] Thus, we are able to base the coefficient on relative money supplies on the homogeneity postulate; the ranges for the income elasticity and interest rate semi-elasticity on the theoretical and empirical literature on money demand; and the range for the rate at which shocks to purchasing power parity are damped on empirical work on PPP.[15] Despite allowance for a serially correlated error term we find that no element of the grid yields a constrained-coefficient forecaster which improves on the

[15]The money demand and PPP literature is discussed and cited in Meese and Rogoff (1983).

random walk model for horizons under twelve months. While there is sometimes sporadic improvement at longer horizons, the overall results are similar to those presented here. (We examine longer forecasting periods in our other study, since the constrained coefficient models require estimation of only the intercept term.) These further results appear to demonstrate that simultaneous equations bias and/or sampling error cannot be regarded as the primary rationalization of the evidence presented here.

Another candidate explanation for the poor performance of the structural models is that their underlying parameters shifted over the course of the seventies due to the effects of the two oil shocks, changes in global trade patterns, or changes in policy regimes. But unless the structural model parameters themselves follow a random walk, it does not necessarily follow that parameter instability can explain why the random walk model outperforms the structural models. Nevertheless, it may be fruitful to account for parameter instability by utilizing a method such as Kalman filtering, which weights recent observations more heavily in forming parameter estimates; see Sargent (1979). We did employ one univariate technique along these lines, weighted least squares, but as we reported above this isolated effort failed. It should be noted that there is a sense in which parameter instability is equivalent to having omitted (perhaps binary) variables.

A useful approach to investigating the problem of omitted variables, or misspecification in general, is to examine the (not strictly independent) building blocks of the structural exchange rate models subsumed in eq. (1): uncovered interest parity,[16] the proxies for inflationary expectations, the goods market specifications, and the common money demand specification. Any or all of the above may be a source of misspecification; the discussion below is speculative.

Recent work on exchange rate risk premia has strongly challenged the assumption of uncovered interest parity. However, although the risk premia may be statistically significant, the evidence also suggests that the magnitudes are not large. (See the literature cited in footnote 14.) Therefore, it is not evident that deviations from uncovered interest parity can explain the poor forecasting performance of the structural models. [We note that empirical efforts to explain the risk premia in terms of portfolio-balance model variables have not been particularly successful; see, for example, Frankel (1982a).]

Measuring inflationary expectations presents many problems. The two sticky-price models, the Dornbusch–Frankel and Hooper–Morton models, are potentially quite sensitive to the proxy used for the long-run expected inflation differential. Proxies such as long-term interest rates and past inflation rates may be grossly inadequate. It is possible that the approach of

[16]Hooper and Morton allow for a risk premium as a function of central bank intervention in a more general version of their model.

estimating rational expectations versions of the models by imposing all the cross-equation restrictions, as in Driskell and Sheffrin (1981) or Glaessner (1982), will yield better expectations proxies. In that work, expectations of the exogenous forcing variables are formed using univariate or multivariate autoregressions. But it is not clear why autoregressions should necessarily yield good expectations proxies for the exogenous variables during a period when autoregressions yield poor proxies for the endogenous variables.

The goods market specifications of the models may also be suspect, though to differing degrees. There is little question that purchasing power parity did not hold in the short run during the seventies; see Isard (1977) or Frenkel (1981a). The Dornbusch–Frankel model assumes only long-run PPP; the evidence here is less clearcut [see Frenkel (1981b)]. The Hooper–Morton model attempts to empirically capture movements in the long-run real exchange rate, but it does not fit out-of-sample notably better than the other two models. Nevertheless, temporary or permanent movements in the PPP level of the exchange rate to real shocks may be a major cause of exchange rate volatility.

The final possible source of misspecification we shall discuss is the standard money demand function that underpins the models:

$$m-p=b_0-b_1r_s+b_2y. \tag{4}$$

In (4), p is the logarithm of the price of the domestic good (using a different deflator for money balances would not alter the discussion below), and other variables are defined as in eq. (1). The breakdown of empirical money demand relationships is widespread, and the phenomenon is particularly acute for U.S. money demand equations; see Simpson and Porter (1980). In an attempt to control for unexplained shifts in velocity, we tried using eq. (4) and its foreign equivalent to substitute price levels for monetary variables in eq. (1). For the Frenkel–Bilson model the theoretical values of the coefficients in eq. (1) are the same as the corresponding coefficients in eq. (4), so price levels alone remain as regressors after the substitution. The transformed model is thus a purchasing power parity equation. In the two sticky-price models, the coefficient on short-term interest rates differs from the coefficient b_1 in (4). For those models, the coefficient on short-term interest rates in the quasi-reduced form exchange rate eq. (1) is the negative of the inverse of the goods market speed of adjustment parameter; see Frankel (1979). Therefore the price substitution only eliminates money supplies and real incomes in their quasi-reduced forms. In table 3 the models are estimated in the same fashion as in table 1, using Fair's method. The models still fail after the price levels substitution to improve on the random walk model in root mean square error. Implementing other estimation techniques and trying other expected inflation rate proxies yields qualitatively similar

Table 3

Root mean square forecast errors with price levels substituted in for monetary variables.[a,b]

Exchange rate	Model: / Horizon	Random walk	Modified Frenkel–Bilson (relative PPP)	Modified Dornbusch–Frankel	Modified Hooper–Morton
$/mark	1 month	3.17	3.31	3.78	3.68
	6 months	8.71	9.78	11.28	10.51
	12 months	12.98	15.25	16.89	17.52
$/yen	1 month	3.70	3.70	4.42	4.18
	6 months	11.58	12.55	13.86	12.69
	12 months	18.31	21.80	20.55	20.65
$/pound	1 month	2.56	2.57	2.78	2.94
	6 months	6.45	7.83	8.64	8.92
	12 months	9.96	12.51	12.28	14.77
Trade-weighted dollar	1 month	1.99	2.18	2.29	2.48
	6 months	6.09	6.63	6.33	6.80
	12 months	8.65	10.48	9.52	9.45

[a]Approximately in percentage terms.

[b]The three structural models are estimated using Fair's instrumental variable technique to correct for first-order serial correlation.

results to those reported in section 3, where the models are estimated without the price level substitution.

As a final effort to investigate the money demand problem, we estimated the Dornbusch–Frankel model for the three cross-exchange rates, thereby abstracting from the particularly unstable demand for money in the U.S. The Dornbusch–Frankel model does not outperform the random walk model for the pound/yen or pound/mark rates, but does do 0.6 percent better at six months (12.0 vs. 12.6 percent for the random walk) and 3.4 percent better at twelve months (16.0 vs. 19.4 percent) for the yen/mark cross-rate. But even this improvement is not so great as to provide a basis for asserting that money demand instability or misspecification is the main problem with the models.

6. Conclusions

The random walk model performs no worse than estimated univariate time series models, an unconstrained vector autoregression, or our candidate structural models in forecasting three major bilateral rates (the dollar/mark, dollar/pound, and dollar/yen) and the trade-weighted dollar. The results of our paper contrast with those of previous studies based on in-sample fit. Thus, from a methodological standpoint, our paper supports the view that out-of-sample fit is an important criterion to consider when evaluating empirical exchange rate models.

The out-of-sample failure of the estimated univariate times series models and the vector autoregression suggests that major-country exchange rates are well-approximated by a random walk model (without drift). Of course, as long as the exchange rate does not exactly follow a random walk, we would expect one of the estimated time series models to prevail in a large enough sample.

Less certain is whether the failure of the stuctural models to outforecast the random walk model — even when uncertainty about the future values of the explanatory variables is removed — can similarly be attributed to sampling error. The constrained-coefficient experiments reported elsewhere in Meese and Rogoff (1983) suggest that neither sampling error nor simultaneous equations bias can fully explain the results presented here. We have listed other possible explanations without arriving at any definite conclusions. Structural instability due to the oil price shocks and changes in macroeconomic policy regimes, as well as the failure of the models to adequately incorporate other real disturbances, may be important. Misspecification of the money demand functions which underpin the structural models is another likely problem, although it is true that the structural models do not predict better when price levels are substituted in for monetary variables, or when M2 or the reserve-adjusted base are used in place of M1-B. Difficulties in modeling expectations of the explanatory variables are yet another obvious source of trouble. But determining the relative importance of the possible problems listed above, or any of the others listed in section 5, is at this point speculative.

Data appendix

The raw data consist entirely of seasonally unadjusted monthly observations over the period March 1973 to June 1981. In the bilateral data set for the United Kingdom, the spot and forward exchange rates, short-term interest rate, and long-term bond rate are all drawn from the same dates. Because daily long-term bond rate series are not readily available for Japan and Germany, only the exchange- and short-term interest rate dates correspond in those data sets. All other bilateral series as well as all of the series used in the trade-weighted data set are monthly data. All data are taken from publicly available sources. Data sources are listed below; a more detailed description of the data set can be found in Meese and Rogoff (1983).

United States data series

Long-term government bond yields, three-month Treasury bill rates, CPI, industrial production, M1-B, M2 and the reserve-adjusted base: Federal Reserve Board data base.

Trade Balance: U.S. Department of Commerce, Highlights of U.S. Export and Import Trade.

Foreign data series for the bilateral data sets

Forward rates: Data Resources Inc. data base.

Spot rates: Federal Reserve Board data base.

Trade balances, monetary aggregates, and industrial productions: O.E.C.D. Main Economic Indicators.

Long-term bond yields and consumer prices: *Monthly Report of the Deutsche Bundesbank, Financial Times and Employment Gazette* (U.K.), *Economics Statistics Monthly* (Japan).

Interest rates (three-month): Frankfurter Allegemeine Zeitung (three-month German interbank rate), *Financial Times* (three-month British local authorities deposits), FRB data base ('Over two-month ends' bill discount rate, Tokyo stock exchange).

The trade-weighted data set

The weights utilized to determine the trade-weighted statistics are: German mark, 0.208; Japanese yen, 0.136; French franc, 0.131; United Kingdom pound, 0.119; Canadian dollar, 0.091; Italian lira, 0.090; Netherlands guilder, 0.083; Belgian franc, 0.064; Swedish Krona, 0.042; and Swiss franc, 0.036. These weights represent each country's share of the total trade (measured by the sum of imports plus exports) of all ten countries in the period 1972 through 1976. See Hooper and Morton (1978).

All the trade-weighted (foreign) data is drawn from O.E.C.D. Main Economics Indicators and the Federal Reserve data base.

References

Akaike, H., 1974, A new look at the statistical model identification, IEEE Transaction on Automatic Control AC-19, 716–723.

Amemiya, T., 1980, Selection of regressors, International Economic Review 21, 331–354.

Bilson, John F.O., 1978, Rational expectations and the exchange rate, in: J. Frenkel and H. Johnson, eds., The economics of exchange rates (Addison-Wesley Press, Reading).

Bilson, John F.O., 1979, The deutsche mark/dollar rate — A monetary analysis, in: Karl Brunner and Allan H. Meltzer, eds., Policies for employment, prices and exchange rates, Carnegie-Rochester Conference 11 (North-Holland Publishing Company, Amsterdam).

Bilson, John F.O., 1981, The 'speculative efficiency' hypothesis, Journal of Business 54, 435–451.

Branson, William H., Hannu Halttunen and Paul Masson, 1979, Exchange rates in the short run: Some further results, European Economic Review 12, 395–402.

Christ, Carl F., 1975, Judging the performance of econometric models of the U.S. economy, International Economic Review 16, 54–74.

Cornell, Bradford, 1977, Spot rates, forward rates and exchange market efficiency, Journal of Financial Economics 5, 55–65.

Cumby, Robert and Maurice Obstfeld, 1981, A note on exchange-rate expectations and nominal interest differentials, The Journal of Finance 36, 697–703.

Dornbusch, Rudiger, 1976, Expectations and exchange rate dynamics, Journal of Political Economy 84, 1161–1176.

Driskell, Robert A. and Steven M. Sheffrin, 1981, On the mark: Comment, American Economic Review 71, 1068–1074.

Fair, Ray C., 1970, The estimation of simultaneous equations models with lagged endogenous variables and first order serially correlated errors, Econometrica 38, 507–516.

Fair, Ray C., 1979, An analysis of the accuracy of four macroeconometric models, Journal of Political Economy 87, 701–718.

Frankel, Jeffrey A., 1979, On the mark: A theory of floating exchange rates based on real interest differentials, American Economic Review 69, 610–622.

Frankel, Jeffrey A., 1981, On the mark: Reply, American Economic Review 71, 1075–1082.

Frankel, Jeffrey A., 1982a, In search of the exchange rate risk premium: A six-currency test assuming mean variance optimization, University of California at Berkeley, mimeo.

Frankel, Jeffrey A., 1982b, The mystery of the multiplying marks: A modification of the monetary model, Review of Economics and Statistics 64, 515–519.

Frenkel, Jacob A., 1976, A monetary approach to the exchange rate: Doctrinal aspects and empirical evidence, Scandinavian Journal of Economics 78, 200–224.

Frenkel, Jacob A., 1981a, The collapse of purchasing power parities during the 1970's, European Economic Review 16, 145–165.

Frenkel, Jacob A., 1981b, Flexible exchange rates, prices, and the role of news: Lessons from the 1970's, Journal of Political Economy 89, 665–705.

Geweke, John and Edward Feige, 1979, Some joint tests of the efficiency of markets for forward foreign exchange, Review of Economics and Statistics 61, 334–341.

Glaessner, Thomas, 1982, Theoretical and empirical essays on spot and forward exchange rate determination, Ph.D. Dissertation, University of Virginia.

Granger, Clive and Paul Newbold, 1977, Forecasting economic time series (Academic Press, New York).

Hacche, Graham and John Townend, 1981, Exchange rates and monetary policy: Modeling sterling's effective exchange rate, 1972–1980, in: W. Eltis and P. Sinclair, eds., The money supply and the exchange rate (Oxford University Press, Oxford).

Hakkio, Craig S., 1981, Expectations and the forward exchange rate, International Economic Review 22, 663–678.

Hannan, E.J., 1970, Multiple time series (John Wiley & Sons, New York).

Hansen, Lars P. and Robert J. Hodrick, 1980, Forward exchange rates as optimal predictors of future spot rates: An econometric analysis, Journal of Political Economy 88, 829–853.

Hansen, Lars P. and Robert J. Hodrick, 1983, Risk averse speculation in forward exchange markets: An econometric analysis, forthcoming in: Jacob A. Frenkel, ed., Exchange rates and international macroeconomics (University of Chicago Press, Chicago).

Haynes, Stephen E. and Joe A. Stone, 1981, On the mark: Comment, American Economic Review 71, 1060–1067.

Hodrick, Robert J., 1979, On the monetary analysis of exchange rates: A comment, in: Kark Brunner and Allan H. Meltzer, eds., Policies for employment, prices, and exchange rates, Carnegie-Rochester Conference 11 (North-Holland, Amsterdam).

Hooper, Peter and John E. Morton, 1978, Summary measures of the dollar's foreign exchange value, Federal Reserve Bulletin 64, 783–789.

Hooper, Peter and John E. Morton, 1982, Fluctuations in the dollar: A model of nominal and real exchange rate determination, Journal of International Money and Finance 1, 39–56.

Isard, Peter, 1977, How far can we push the law of one price?, American Economic Review 67, 942–948.

Litterman, Robert B., 1979, Techniques of forecasting using vector autoregressions, Working paper no. 115, Federal Reserve Bank of Minneapolis.

Maddala, G.S., 1977, Econometrics (McGraw-Hill, New York).

McCulloch, J. Huston, 1975, Operational aspects of the Siegel paradox, Quarterly Journal of Economics 86, 303–309.

Meese, Richard A. and Kenneth J. Singleton, 1980, Rational expectations, risk premia, and the market for spot and forward exchange, International Finance Discussion Papers no. 165, Board of Governors of the Federal Reserve System.

Meese, Richard A. and Kenneth S. Rogoff, 1983, The out-of-sample failure of empirical exchange rate models: Sampling error or misspecification?, forthcoming in: Jacob A. Frenkel, ed., Exchange rates and international macroeconomics (University of Chicago Press, Chicago).

Mussa, Michael, 1979, Empirical regularities in the behavior of exchange rates and theories of the foreign exchange market, in: Karl Brunner and Allan H. Meltzer, eds., Policies for employment, prices and exchange rates, Carnegie-Rochester Conference 11 (North-Holland, Amsterdam).

Nelson, Charles, 1972, The prediction performance of the F.R.B.–M.I.T.–Penn. model of the U.S. economy, American Economic Review 62, 902–917.

Parzen, Emanuel, 1975, Multiple time series: Determining the order of approximating autoregressive schemes, Technical Report no. 23, State University of New York at Buffalo.

Sargent, Thomas J., 1979, Macroeconomic theory (Acadmic Press, New York).

Schwarz, Gideon, 1978, Estimating the dimension of a model, Annals of Statistics 6, 461–464.

Siegel, Jeremy J., 1972, Risk, interest rates, and the forward exchange, Quarterly Journal of Economics 86, 303–309.

Simpson, Thomas D. and Richard D. Porter, 1980, Some issues involving the definition and interpretation of the monetary aggregates, in: Controlling monetary aggregates, vol. III, Federal Reserve Bank of Boston conference series no. 23.

Sims, Christopher A., 1974a, Seasonality in regression, Journal of the American Statistical Association 69, 618–626.

Sims, Christopher A., 1974b, Distributed lags, in: Michael D. Intrilligator and David A. Kendrick, eds., Frontiers of quantitative economics (North-Holland, New York).

Sims Christopher A., 1980, Macroeconomics and reality, Econometrica 48, 1–48.

Tryon, Ralph, 1979, Testing for rational expectations in foreign exchange markets, International Finance Discussion Papers no. 139, Board of Governors of the Federal Reserve System.

Westerfield, Janice M., 1977, An examination of foreign exchange risk under fixed and floating rate regimes, Journal of International Economics 7, 181–200.

Working, Holbrook, 1960, Note on the correlation of first differences in a random chain, Econometrica 28, 916–918.

[4]

Journal of International Economics 53 (2001) 29–52

Journal of INTERNATIONAL ECONOMICS

www.elsevier.nl/locate/econbase

Nominal exchange rates and monetary fundamentals Evidence from a small post-Bretton woods panel

Nelson C. Mark*, Donggyu Sul

Department of Economics, The Ohio State University, 410 Arps Hall, Columbus, OH 43210, USA

Received 16 December 1998; received in revised form 3 February 2000; accepted 11 February 2000

Abstract

We study the long-run relationship between nominal exchange rates and monetary fundamentals in a quarterly panel of 19 countries extending from 1973.1 to 1997.1. Our analysis is centered on two issues. First, we test whether exchange rates are cointegrated with long-run determinants predicted by economic theory. These results generally support the hypothesis of cointegration. The second issue is to re-examine the ability for monetary fundamentals to forecast future exchange rate returns. Panel regression estimates and panel-based forecasts confirm that this forecasting power is significant.

Keywords: Exchange rates; Panel cointegration; Prediction

JEL classification: F31; F47

1. Introduction

This paper re-examines the nominal exchange rate–monetary fundamentals link within a panel data framework. Our paper is motivated by Kilian (1997), Berkowitz and Giorgianni (1997), Groen (1997), and Berben and van Dijk (1998) who question the statistical robustness of the results from studies finding that monetary fundamentals forecast nominal exchange rate returns (percent changes in the exchange rate) (see MacDonald and Taylor, 1993; Mark, 1995; Chinn and

*Corresponding author. Tel.: +1-614-292-0413; fax: +1-614-292-3906.
E-mail address: mark.1@osu.edu (N.C. Mark).

0022-1996/01/$ – see front matter
PII: S0022-1996(00)00052-0

Meese, 1995; Chen and Mark, 1996; MacDonald and Marsh, 1997). Much of the favorable evidence for the prediction hypothesis centers around i) significant slope coefficient estimates in regressions of future exchange rate returns on the deviation of the log exchange rate from monetary fundamentals and ii) the dominance of prediction accuracy from these regressions over the random walk model in out out-of-sample forecasting. As in studies of stock returns (e.g. Fama and French, 1988; Campbell and Shiller, 1988; Hodrick, 1992), there is a tendency for exchange return regression slope coefficients and R^2s to increase in magnitude as the return horizon is lengthened. Similarly, out-of-sample forecast accuracy of monetary fundamentals relative to the random walk tend to improve with prediction horizon.

The relatively short time-series used in these studies combined with the high degree of dependence across overlapping observations of long-horizon exchange rate returns make statistical inference a thorny issue. As a result, the robustness of the link between monetary fundamentals and the nominal exchange rate has been called into question. Along these lines, Kilian (1997) finds the evidence for exchange rate predictability to be less favorable when he updates Mark's (1995) data set and employs a less restrictive data generating process in building parametric bootstrap distributions upon which to draw inference. Similarly, Berkowitz and Giorgianni (1997) and Berben and van Dijk (1998) argue that noncointegration between exchange rates and their monetary fundamentals render the independent variable in these regressions nonstationary so that standard hypothesis testing procedures produce misleading inferences and need to be modified.[1] Moreover, all these papers argue that long-horizon regressions offer no statistical power gains over short-horizon regressions.

This paper, which motivated by these recent critiques, aims to improve on the imprecise univariate estimates and forecasts by exploiting available cross-sectional information in a panel data set and imposing modest homogeneity restrictions in estimation. We focus our analysis on two main issues. The first of these is whether nominal exchange rates are cointegrated with monetary fundamentals. The second issue concerns the forecasting power of monetary fundamentals in a panel version of the long-horizon regression of currency returns on the deviation of the log exchange rate from the monetary fundamentals. We attack both of these issues within the framework of the panel regression of the one-period ahead nominal exchange rate return on the current deviation of the exchange rate from its

[1]The fragility of the results is not due entirely to the choice of statistical design. By extending Mark's quarterly sample, which ends in 1992, through 1994 Groen (1996) finds considerable deterioration in the accuracy of out-of-sample monetary fundamentals forecasts of US dollar prices of the yen, deutschemark, and Swiss franc. We speculate that reasons for the collapse of yen and deutschemark forecast accuracy in the 1990s include the ongoing banking crisis in Japan and residual fiscal consequences from German re-unification introduce important transient nonmonetary factors into the pricing of exchange rates.

fundamental value. The analysis is conducted on quarterly observations that begin on 1973.1 and extend through 1997.1 for 19 countries.

We study the issue of cointegration by employing a new panel based test of cointegration that combines ideas presented in Berben and van Dijk (1998) and Mark and Sul (1999). In the single-equation case, Berben and van Dijk build on Hansen (1995) to show that the predictive regression is well-specified when the regressor is nonstationary, in the sense that the estimator and its *t*-ratio have well-defined but non-Gaussian asymptotic distributions. In the framework, the test that the slope coefficient is zero is a test of the null hypothesis of no cointegration between the exchange rate and the fundamentals. Our test for cointegration exploits this argument and extends it to panel data.

Under the null hypothesis of no cointegration, the regressor in the panel predictive regression is nonstationary and the true value of the slope coefficient is zero. The standard least-squares dummy variable (LSDV) estimator is consistent, but suffers from second-order asymptotic bias that causes test statistics – such as its *t*-ratio – to diverge asymptotically. In order to draw inference, we use the panel dynamic OLS estimator whose *t*-ratio is asymptotically standard normal. To guard against potential small sample size distortion of the asymptotic tests, we supplement our asymptotic tests with tests based on both parametric and nonparametric bootstraps. We find that the null hypothesis of no cointegration can be rejected at standard significance levels and that these results are invariant as to whether inference is drawn from the asymptotic distribution or from the bootstrap.

We then proceed under the assumption that the exchange rate and the fundamentals cointegrate and examine the predictive content of deviations of the exchange rate from its fundamental value for future exchange rate returns. There are two aspects to this investigation. First, we study the slope coefficient in the panel short-horizon regression which we estimate by LSDV. We confine this analysis to a one-period forecast horizon to avoid the complications arising from serially correlated error terms that would be included by overlapping multiperiod forecast horizons and to reflect the growing consensus that long-horizon regressions offer no statistical power advantages over short-horizon regressions. The second aspect of the prediction issue is studied by conducting an out-of-sample forecast experiment using the panel regression over the period extending from 1983.1 through 1997.1. In this analysis we report results at two forecast horizons, 1 and 16 quarters. We note that it is not the objective of the paper to build the best exchange-rate forecasting model. In that regard, a fixed coefficient linear regression model is quite naive. Instead, our intent is to examine the extent to which monetary fundamentals matter at all for nominal exchange rate dynamics.

As in the cointegration tests, we augment the asymptotic analysis of the predictive regression under the assumption of cointegration and the forecasting exercise with parametric and nonparametric bootstraps to control for potential small sample size distortion. The bootstrap also allows us to model cross-sectional dependence in the data which surely is present in the data but which typically violates the regularity conditions under which the available asymptotic theory is derived.

As a basis for comparison, we also examine the predictive power contained in purchasing power parity (PPP) based fundamentals. A growing body of empirical research using panel data methods on post 1973 data concludes that PPP holds over the float.[2] With the re-emergence of PPP as a viable long-run equilibrium condition for nominal exchange rate determination, and its central role in motivating the use of monetary fundamentals it is a logical and useful exercise to compare its predictive performance to those of the monetary fundamentals. Since the monetary model is build upon PPP but imposes additional restrictions, the presumption must be that the monetary model will have better asymptotic prediction performance if the additional restrictions are true, and will have worse prediction performance if they are false. Our evidence suggests that the linkage between the exchange rate and monetary fundamentals is tighter than that between the exchange rate and purchasing power parities.

The remainder of the paper is organized as follows. The next section describes the form of the monetary fundamentals predicted by theory that we use in our empirical analysis. Section 3 describes our data set. Section 4 describes the econometric framework that we use. The panel cointegration tests are developed in Section 5, the panel prediction analysis is covered in Section 6, and Section 7 concludes.

2. Monetary fundamentals and the exchange rate

Let s_{it} be the time-t log nominal exchange rate between country $i = 1, 2, \ldots, N$ and the 'numeraire' country, which we label as country '0.' The exchange rate is country i's currency price of a unit of currency 0 so an increase in s_{it} means an appreciation in value of 0's money. Let the time-t log nominal money stock and log real income of country i be denoted by m_{it} and y_{it} respectively. Much of our analysis centers on the deviation x_{it}, of the exchange rate from it fundamental value,

$$x_{it} = f_{it} - s_{it}, \tag{1}$$

where $f_{it} = m_{it} - m_{0t} - \lambda(y_{it} - y_{0t})$ is the long-run equilibrium or the 'monetary fundamental value,' of the exchange rate. Notice that the long-run neutrality of money is imposed and λ is a scalar common across countries.

We think of f_{it} as a generic representation of the long-run equilibrium exchange rate implied by modern theories of exchange rate determination. The common feature shared by the various theories is that the long-run equilibrium exchange

[2] See, for example, Frankel and Rose (1996), Lothian (1997), MacDonald (1996), Papell (1997) and Wu (1996).

rate is governed by determinants of money market equilibrium at home and abroad. In the monetary models of Frenkel (1976) and Mussa (1976), for example, λ can be interpreted as the income elasticity of money demand and is predicted to be positive. In Lucas's (1982) equilibrium model, λ, which can depend on preference parameters, can possibly be negative but its value is bounded from above by 1.[3] The Obstfeld and Rogoff (1995) model on the other hand, predicts that per capita consumption enter in place of real income. The particular details – whether to include income, as in Lucas, or consumption levels as in Obstfeld and Rogoff – differ, but the general theoretical prediction is the same. Namely that the exchange rate is determined by monetary fundamentals. This is not a controversial proposition but establishing this principle with a satisfactory degree of statistical accuracy has been difficult.

Our analysis centers on two empirical questions. First, we examine whether the monetary fundamentals f_{it}, serve as an attractor for the nominal exchange rate. We address this problem in Section 5 by testing whether $\{f_{it}\}$ and $\{s_{it}\}$ are cointegrated using procedures developed for the analysis of panel data. Second, we examine the ability for deviations of the exchange rate from its monetary fundamentals value, to forecast future exchange rate returns in a panel regression.

3. The data

Our data consists of quarterly time series observations from 1973.1 through 1997.1 for the following 19 countries: Austria, Australia, Belgium, Canada, Denmark, Finland, France, Germany, Great Britain, Greece, Italy, Japan, Korea, the Netherlands, Norway, Spain, Sweden, Switzerland, and the United States. The composition of the sample was determined by data availability and by a requirement that the country's post Bretton Woods exchange rate experience was dominated by floating against the US dollar. While some of the countries in the sample did experience episodes of nominal exchange rate pegging, those periods were deemed to have been reasonably brief.

Nominal exchange rates are end-of-quarter observations from the IFS CD-ROM (line code AE). Quarterly GDP is unavailable for several countries in the sample so we used quarterly industrial production indices for all countries as a proxy for national income. The industrial production series are from the IMF's International Financial Statistics (IFS line code 66). Our measure of money is from the IFS and

[3] In the Lucas model, the log equilibrium nominal exchange rate is given by $m - m_0 + (y + \ln U_y) - (y_0 + \ln U_{y_0})$, where U_y and U_{y_0} is the representative agent's marginal utility of consumption. It is easy to see that a shock that raises y can lower the marginal utility of consuming y sufficiently to imply a negative value of λ. For example, let the period utility function $U = (Y_0^{1-\gamma_0})/(1 - \gamma_0) + (Y^{1-\gamma})/(1 - \gamma)$. Then $\lambda = 1 - \gamma$ and $\lambda = 1 - \gamma_0$. When the utility function displays curvature in excess of the log function, this model predicts negative λ coefficients.

is the sum of money (line code 34) plus quasi-money (line code 35) for all countries with the following exceptions for Great Britain, Norway, and Sweden due to availability. Money is M0 from the IFS for Great Britain, M2 from the OECD's Main Economic Indicators for Norway, and M3 also from the OECD for Sweden. Price levels, which we need for the comparison to PPP, are measured using the CPI from the IFS (line code 64). Neither money nor the CPIs are seasonally adjusted. To control for seasonality, we filter the money and price series by applying a one-sided moving average of the current observation and 3-lagged values.

4. The econometric specification

Our econometric analysis centers on panel estimation of the short-horizon predictive regression,

$$\Delta s_{it+1} = \beta x_{it} + e_{it+1} \tag{2}$$

$$e_{it+1} = \gamma_i + \theta_{t+1} + u_{it+1}, \tag{3}$$

where i indexes the country and t is the time period. We give the regression error e_{it+1} an unobserved components interpretation where γ_i is an individual-specific effect, θ_t is a time-specific effect that allow us to account for a limited amount of cross-sectional dependence, and u_{it+1} is the residual idiosyncratic error.

Eq. (2) is the panel version of the short-horizon predictive regression studied by Mark (1995), Berkowitz and Giorgianni (1997), Groen (1997), Kilian (1997), and Berben and van Dijk (1998) in connection with exchange rates and by Fama and French (1988), Campbell and Shiller (1988), and Hodrick (1992) in the study of stock returns. In the single equation context, the predictive regression is the linear least squares projection of the exchange rate return on the deviation of the exchange rate from its fundamental value so that e_t is uncorrelated with x_t by construction. The slope coefficient is an estimate of $\mathrm{Cov}(x_t, \Delta s_{t+1})/\mathrm{Var}(x_t)$ which does not disentangle contributions from short-run and long-run dynamics.

We follow the exchange rate studies cited above and condition our analysis by fixing $\lambda = 1$. An alternative strategy would be to estimate λ. Pedroni (1997) shows that when λ is estimated by panel regression, it can be treated as fixed in the asymptotic analysis of residual based tests of cointegration. However, we are also interested in modeling the exact distribution of our test statistics via the bootstrap and it is unclear whether treating the estimated value of λ as fixed is appropriate in this context. To avoid these complications, we proceed with $\lambda = 1$. We note that making such precise assumptions enables us to sharpen our testable predictions.

5. A panel cointegration test

For a single equation, Berben and van Dijk (1998) show that the predictive regression can be sensibly estimated whether x_t is I(0) or I(1). Building on Hansen (1995), they show under the null hypothesis that x_t is I(1) a test that $\beta = 0$ is a test of the hypothesis that s_t and f_t are not cointegrated. We extend this line of argument to panel data and take as the null hypothesis that x_{it} is *nonstationary* for all $i = 1, \ldots, N$.[4] Because Δs_{it+1} is stationary and x_{it} is not, they are asymptotically independent and the true value of β is zero under the null.[5]

Let $\Delta \underline{s}_i = (\Delta s_{1i}, \Delta s_{2i}, \ldots, \Delta s_{Ti})'$, and $\Delta \underline{s} = (\Delta \underline{s}_1, \Delta \underline{s}_2, \ldots, \Delta \underline{s}_N)'$ be the vectorization of the observations on exchange rate returns, $\underline{x}_i = (x_{1i}, x_{2i}, \ldots x_{T-1i})'$ be the $T-1 \times 1$ vector of observations on x_{it} for country i, $\underline{0}$ be a $T-1 \times 1$ vector of zeros, $\underline{\iota}$ be a $T-1 \times 1$ vector of ones, and $\mathbf{I}$ a $T-1$ dimensional identity matrix, and

$$\mathbf{X} = \begin{bmatrix} \underline{x}_1 & \mathbf{I} & \underline{0} & \underline{0} & \cdots & \underline{0} \\ \underline{x}_2 & \mathbf{I} & \underline{\iota} & \underline{0} & \cdots & \underline{0} \\ \underline{x}_3 & \mathbf{I} & \underline{0} & \underline{\iota} & \cdots & \underline{0} \\ \vdots & & & & & \vdots \\ \underline{x}_N & \mathbf{I} & \underline{0} & \underline{0} & \cdots & \underline{\iota} \end{bmatrix}$$

The least-squares dummy variable estimator of β is obtained by running OLS on the pooled observations, $\beta_{lsdv} = (\mathbf{X}'\mathbf{X})^{-1}\mathbf{X}'(\Delta \underline{s})$. Under the null hypothesis that x_{it} is I(1), $\beta_{lsdv} \xrightarrow{p} 0$ so that the LSDV estimator is a consistent estimator of the true value of $\beta = 0$. However, the panel regression is contaminated by second order asymptotic bias which causes $\sqrt{NT}\beta_{lsdv}$ to diverge. Since β_{lsdv} does not have a well defined asymptotic distribution neither does its t-ratio which prevents construction of appropriate t-tests for testing hypotheses about the slope coefficient.

To control for this asymptotic bias, we employ the panel dynamic OLS estimator discussed in Mark and Sul (1999). In panel dynamic OLS, the current value and p_i leads and lags of Δx_{it-1} are included in the equation for country i, and we estimate the system of equations,[6]

$$\Delta s_{it} = \gamma_i + \theta_t + \beta x_{i,t-1} + \sum_{j=-p_i}^{p_i} \delta_{ij} \Delta x_{i,t-j-1} + u_{it}, \tag{4}$$

[4] Evans (1997) has applied this methodology to test whether economic growth evolves according to endogenous or exogenous growth theories.

[5] The arguments sketched in this section are developed in more detail in the appendix.

[6] To relate the test to Hansen (1995), let X_t' be the vector of leads and lags of Δx_{it}, and subtract Δf_{it} from both sides of Eq. (4), we get,

$$\Delta s_{it} - \Delta f_{it} = \gamma_i + \theta_t + \beta x_{it-1} + X_t' b + \Delta f_{it} + u_{it}$$

which is in the form of Hansen's unit root test (on $x_{it} = f_{it} - s_{it}$) with covariates. Hansen showed that his test had better power than augmented Dickey–Fuller tests.

$i=1,\ldots,N$, $t=p_i+2,\ldots,T-p_i+1$. Let $\bar{p}$ be the largest p_i and let $\underline{z}_{it}=(\Delta x_{it+p_i-1},\ldots,\Delta x_{it-p_i-1})$, $\mathbf{Z}_i=(\underline{z}_{1i},\ldots \underline{z}_{Ti})'$, and

$$\tilde{\mathbf{X}}=\begin{bmatrix} \underline{x}_1 & \mathbf{Z}_1 & \mathbf{0}\cdot & \mathbf{0} & \cdots & \mathbf{0} & \mathbf{I} & \underline{0} & \underline{0} & \cdots & \underline{0} & \underline{0} \\ \underline{x}_2 & \mathbf{0} & \mathbf{Z}_2 & \mathbf{0} & \cdots & \mathbf{0} & \mathbf{I} & \underline{\iota} & \underline{0} & \cdots & \underline{0} & \underline{0} \\ \underline{x}_3 & \mathbf{0} & \mathbf{0} & \mathbf{Z}_3 & \cdots & \mathbf{0} & \mathbf{I} & \underline{0} & \underline{\iota} & \cdots & \underline{0} & \underline{0} \\ \vdots & & & & & \vdots & \vdots & & & & & \vdots \\ \underline{x}_N & \mathbf{0} & \cdots & \mathbf{0} & \cdots & \mathbf{Z}_N & \mathbf{I} & \underline{0} & \underline{0} & \cdots & \underline{0} & \underline{\iota} \end{bmatrix}$$

Then the panel dynamic OLS estimator of β is the first element of the vector $(\tilde{\mathbf{X}}'\tilde{\mathbf{X}})^{-1}\tilde{\mathbf{X}}'(\Delta \underline{s})$. Mark and Sul (1999) show that,

$$\sqrt{NT}(\beta_{pdols}-\beta)N(\underline{0},2\tilde{\mathbf{V}}) \tag{5}$$

as $T\to\infty$, $N\to\infty$ where $\tilde{\mathbf{V}}$ is consistently estimated by $\tilde{\mathbf{V}}_{NT}=\tilde{\mathbf{B}}_{NT}^{-1}\tilde{\mathbf{A}}_{NT}\tilde{\mathbf{B}}_{NT}^{-1}$, where $\tilde{\mathbf{B}}_{NT}=(1/NT^2)\sum_{i=1}^{N}\sum_{t=1}^{T}\tilde{x}_{it-1}\tilde{x}'_{it-1}$, $\tilde{\mathbf{A}}_{NT}=(1/NT^2)\sum_{i=1}^{N}\hat{\Omega}_i^2\sum_{t=1}^{T}\tilde{x}_{it-1}\tilde{x}'_{it-1}$ and $\hat{\Omega}_i^2$ is an estimate of the long run variance of u_{it}.[7]

The bootstrap: Mark and Sul report that the asymptotic distribution of $\hat{\beta}_{pdols}$ is reasonably accurate for their Monte Carlo experiments. But because there is no guarantee that this is true for all regions of the parameter space, we supplement the asymptotic analysis by drawing inference from the bootstrap. The data generating process (DGP) underlying the bootstrap is the restricted vector autoregression,

$$\begin{aligned} \Delta s_{it} &= \mu_s^i+\varepsilon_{st}^i \\ \Delta x_{it} &= \mu_x^i+\sum_{j=1}^{k_i} a_{21,j}^i\,\Delta s_{it-j}+\sum_{j=1}^{k_i} a_{22,j}^i\,\Delta x_{it-j}+\varepsilon_{xt}^i \end{aligned} \tag{6}$$

which imposes the null hypothesis that the exchange rate return is unpredictable and that x_{it} is nonstationary. The lag length in the Δx_{it} equations are determined by the Campbell–Perron rule on lagged Δx_{it} variables from an initial OLS regression.[8]

[7] To estimate $\Omega_i^2=\lim_{T\to\infty}\operatorname{Var} 1/\sqrt{T}\sum_{t=1}^{T}u_{it}$, we use the parametric autoregressive approximation described in Hamilton (1994) (p. 610). Let $\hat{u}_{it}$ be the panel dynamic OLS residuals. For each i, we fit the AR(g_i) $\hat{u}_{it}=\sum_{j=1}^{g_i}\phi_{ij}\hat{u}_{it-j}+\eta_{it}$. Let $\tilde{T}_i=T-1-2p_i-g_i$ and $\hat{\sigma}_{1i}^2=(1/\tilde{T}_i)\sum\hat{\eta}_{it}^2$. The long run estimate is $\hat{\Omega}_i=\hat{\sigma}_{1i}/(1-\sum_{j=1}^{g_i}\hat{\phi}_{ij})$. The lag length g_i is determined by Campbell and Perron's (1991) top-down t-test approach. That is start with some maximal lag order ℓ and estimate the autoregression on $\hat{\epsilon}_{it}$. If the absolute value of the t-ratio for $\hat{\phi}_{i\ell}$ is less than some appropriate critical value, c^*, reset g_i to $\ell-1$ and reestimate. Repeat the process until the t-ratio of the estimated coefficient with the longest lag exceeds the critical value c^*.

[8] That is, we estimate by OLS beginning with $k_i=8$. If the t-statistic on $a_{22,8}^i$ is significant, we stay with $k_i=8$. If not, reset $k_i=7$ and try again until we find a significant coefficient.

After determining the lag length, we fit the equations for Δx_{it} by iterated seemingly unrelated regression (SUR).

Let $\underline{\varepsilon}_t = (\varepsilon^1_{st}, \ldots, \varepsilon^N_{st}, \varepsilon^1_{xt}, \ldots, \varepsilon^N_{xt})'$ be the $(2N \times 1)$ error vector. We construct a *nonparametric* bootstrap by resampling the residual vectors $\{\hat{\varepsilon}_1, \hat{\varepsilon}_2, \ldots, \hat{\varepsilon}_T\}$ with replacement and build up the bootstrap observations of s_{it} and x_{it} recursively according to the estimated version of (6). Note that this resampling scheme preserves the cross-sectional dependence exhibited in the estimated residuals. We obtain start-up values for Δs_{it} and Δx_{it} by direct block resampling of the data.[9] Then we apply the estimation procedure outlined above for β_{pdols} and its asymptotic t-ratio to the bootstrapped data. We do this 2000 times and the resulting 2000 t-ratios form the bootstrap distribution.

We also build a *parametric* bootstrap conditioned on a normality assumption for the error vector. To do this, we estimate the joint error covariance matrix $\Sigma = E(\varepsilon_t \varepsilon_t')$ using the SUR $\hat{\epsilon}^i_{xt}$ residuals and the Δs_{it} residuals.[10] Now instead of resampling the residuals, the error terms in the DGP are drawn from $N(0, \hat{\Sigma})$. Vector sequences of the innovations of length $T + 100$ are initially drawn and pseudo values of s_{it} and x_{it} are built up recursively using the estimated versions of (6). The first 100 observations are then discarded and β_{pdols} and its t-ratio are calculated with the pseudo-data. Again, the process is repeated 2000 times with the resulting collection of t-ratios forming the parametric bootstrap distribution. Analogous procedures are followed to bootstrap all other statistics that we study in the paper.

We note that we model the cross-sectional dependence of the sample only through the covariance of the innovations. Ideally, we would like a DGP to jointly model the evolution of all of the variables across all 18 bilateral country pairs. This would imply an unrestricted VAR for 36 variables and would provide a proper accounting for the cross-sectional dependence across countries but estimating such a large system turns out not to be feasible. A quick calculation modestly assuming say 3 lags of each variable means that for each equation we have 108 regression coefficients (plus a constant) for each equation, but we have only 97 time series observations.[11]

---

[9] Let $r_{it} = (s_{it}, x_{it})'$. The data are arrayed as, $(r_{i1}, r_{i2}, \ldots, r_{iT})$. Four adjacent observations, $r_{it}, \ldots, r_{i,t-4}$, are required to start up the recursion. In a collection of T such vectors, there are $T - 3$ possible blocks of 4 adjacent observations. For each replication in the bootstrap, we draw a 4-block at random to start up the recursion in (6).

[10] We do not combine the Δs_{it} equations in the SUR estimation because they contain only a constant term.

[11] We did some checks for robustness. First, we looked (sequentially across $j \neq i$) to see if variables of country j belonged in the equation for x_{it} according to t-ratio size. They didn't. Secondly, we considered choosing lag length by BIC instead of the Campbell–Perron rule. Since we are letting lag length differ across individuals, we calculated BIC and determined lag length individually, then estimated the equations jointly by SUR. The main results are unaffected.

5.1. Panel cointegration test results

We consider three alternative numeraire countries: the US, Japan, and Switzerland. We run the panel dynamic OLS regressions with 2 leads and lags of first differences of the x_{it-1}, and 3 lags in the autoregression to estimate the long-run variance, Ω_i^2. We report bootstrap results only for the asymptotic t-ratio because the evidence suggests that bootstrapping the t-ratio gives more reliable inference than bootstrapping the slope coefficient.[12] The results of the panel test for cointegration are reported in Table 1.

The asymptotic test easily rejects the null hypothesis of no cointegration between the exchange rate and the monetary fundamentals but it evidently exhibits some small sample size distortion as evidenced by comparing the bootstrap P-values to the asymptotic t-ratios. However, both the parametric and nonparametric bootstrap P-values allow the hypothesis of no cointegration to be rejected at the 5% level and the results are robust to the three numeraire currencies considered.

We are also able to reject the hypothesis of no cointegration between the exchange rate and PPP fundamentals at standard levels of significance with asymptotic as well as with bootstrap tests. These results are consistent with Frankel and Rose (1996), Wu (1996), Lothian (1997), and Papell (1997), and others who reject nonstationarity of real exchange rates with panel unit root tests. Curiously, our panel dynamic OLS estimates of the slope coefficient are negative. The reason is that the regression is misspecified under the alternative hypothesis that x_{it} is stationary. We can use panel dynamic OLS to test for cointegration but cannot interpret its slope estimate of β if the null hypothesis of no cointegration is rejected. Under the alternative hypothesis, the future Δx_{it} do not belong in the regression. When the future Δx_{it} are dropped from the PPP regression (not reported), the estimated slope coefficients are positive.

Table 1
Panel dynamic OLS based cointegration tests

Fundamentals	Numeraire	β_{pdols}	t-ratio	P-value[a]	P-value[b]
Monetary	US	0.010	**4.930**	**0.000**	**0.002**
	Switzerland	0.006	**2.219**	**0.050**	**0.067**
	Japan	0.007	**3.877**	**0.002**	**0.001**
PPP	US	−0.016	**−4.626**	**0.998**	**0.999**
	Switzerland	−0.019	**−7.417**	**0.992**	**0.989**
	Japan	−0.022	**−4.077**	**1.000**	**1.000**

[a] Parametric bootstrap P-value.

[b] Nonparametric bootstrap P-value. P-value is the proportion of the bootstrap distribution that lies to the *right* of the asymptotic t-ratio calculated from the data. A two-tailed test rejects the null hypothesis at the 5% level if the P-value is above 0.975 or below 0.025.

[12] See Maddala and Kim (1998).

To summarize the empirical results of this section, we reject the hypothesis of no cointegration between the nominal exchange rate and the monetary fundamentals at small levels of significance. We also reject the hypothesis of no cointegration between the exchange rate and relative national price levels. The strength of the evidence for the monetary fundamentals and PPP fundamentals is roughly equivalent.

6. Panel short-horizon prediction regression

We now proceed under the assumption that x_{it} is stationary. Even under stationarity, however, the question remains whether the deviation of the exchange rate from the monetary fundamentals helps to predict future exchange rate returns. As discussed above, under the hypothesis of cointegration, the predictive regression is a regression of the stationary exchange rate return on stationary exchange rate deviations from the monetary fundamental x_{it}, and the study of monetary fundamentals forecasts of exchange rate returns can proceed along the standard analysis of a panel regression with stationary variables.

6.1. LSDV estimation results

We focus on short-horizon estimates ($k=1$) first to avoid complications of residual serial dependence induced by forecasting over horizons exceeding the sampling interval of the data and second, to reflect the growing consensus that long horizons yield no power advantages over short horizons. Our first task here is to estimate β and test the hypothesis that it is 0.

Because the regressor is only predetermined but not exogenous, in the single-equation context the OLS estimator of the slope coefficient in the predictive regression has been shown to exhibit small sample bias (Stambaugh, 1986; Mankiw and Shapiro, 1986). In Appendix A, we argue that this bias is attenuated, but not eliminated by panel estimation. We consider two alternative strategies to control for this small sample bias. Our first scheme is to correct for the bias using the bootstrap and then to do the asymptotic t-test using the bias corrected estimate. Our second strategy for accounting for small sample bias simply bootstraps the t-ratio of β_{lsdv}.

In the bootstrap, we assume that the exchange rate evolves according to a martingale but is cointegrated with the fundamentals. This null distribution is built from the DGP,

$$\begin{aligned} \Delta s_{it} &= \mu_s^i + \epsilon_{st}^i, \\ \Delta x_{it} &= \mu_x^i + \gamma_i x_{it-1} + \sum_{j=1}^{k_i} a_{21,j}^i \, \Delta s_{it-j} + \sum_{j=1}^{k_i} a_{22,j}^i \, \Delta x_{it-j} + \epsilon_{xt}^i. \end{aligned} \tag{7}$$

Table 2
Bias-adjusted LSDV estimates of panel predictive regression

Fundamentals	Numeraire	β_{bc} [a]	t-ratio[a]	β_{bc} [b]	t-ratio[b]
Monetary	US	0.033	**6.076**	0.023	**4.149**
	Switzerland	0.019	**3.663**	0.016	**3.006**
	Japan	0.037	**6.399**	0.026	**4.594**
PPP	US	0.031	**3.608**	0.026	**3.016**
	Switzerland	0.034	**2.749**	0.019	**2.291**
	Japan	0.033	**3.608**	0.029	**3.094**

[a] Bias correction by parametric bootstrap.
[b] Bias correction by nonparametric bootstrap.

Cointegration between s_{it} and f_{it} requires that $-2<\gamma_i<0$ so that Eq. (7) is equivalent to a restricted VAR in $(\Delta s_{it}, x_{it})$ and which in turn has an equivalent to a vector error-correction representation for $(\Delta s_{it}, \Delta f_{it})$ with cointegration vector (1, −1). The estimation of the DGP and the buildup of the parametric bootstrap distribution follows as before.

To correct for bias, let β^* be the median value of the bootstrap distribution for β_{lsdv} generated under the null hypothesis that $\beta=0$. Then the bias-corrected estimate is $\beta_{bc}=\beta_{lsdv}-\beta^*$. Next, we divide β_{bc} by the asymptotic LSDV standard error and conduct the standard t-test of the hypothesis that $\beta=0$.

The results of the panel tests of the null hypothesis that the deviation of the exchange rate from the fundamentals do not contain predictive content for the future exchange rate return are reported in Tables 2 and 3. First, all of the tests that we consider resoundingly reject the no-prediction hypothesis for both monetary and PPP fundamentals. Second, the PPP regressions exhibit larger bias but the bias corrected estimates for the monetary fundamentals and PPP fundamentals are similar.

In Table 4, we report the estimation results of the panel regression with both PPP and monetary fundamentals included in the regression,

Table 3
LSDV estimates and bootstrapped t-ratios for panel predictive regression

Fundamentals	Numeraire	β_{lsdv}	t-ratio	P-value[a]	P-value[b]
Monetary	US	0.036	**6.544**	**0.000**	**0.000**
	Switzerland	0.032	**5.932**	**0.001**	**0.004**
	Japan	0.038	**6.632**	**0.000**	**0.000**
PPP	US	0.054	**6.187**	**0.006**	**0.013**
	Switzerland	0.047	**5.541**	**0.023**	**0.031**
	Japan	0.057	**6.220**	**0.008**	**0.016**

[a] Parametric bootstrap P-value.
[b] Nonparametric bootstrap P-value. P-value is the proportion of the bootstrap distribution that lies to the *right* of the asymptotic t-ratio calculated from the data.

Table 4
LSDV estimation with both monetary and PPP fundamentals $\Delta s_{it+1} = \beta_m x^{m}_{i,t} + \beta_p x^{p}_{it} + e_{it+1}$; $e_{it+1} = \gamma_i + \theta_{t+1} + u_{it+1}$; $x^{m}_{it} = f_{it} - s_{it}$; and $x^{p}_{it} = p_{it} - p_{0t} - s_{it}$

	US	Japan	Switzerland
β_m	0.024	0.027	0.026
t-ratio	3.443	3.866	3.756
P-value[a]	**0.004**	**0.001**	**0.012**
P-value[b]	**0.000**	**0.001**	**0.000**
β_p	0.030	0.024	0.033
t-ratio	2.718	2.080	2.984
P-value[a]	0.356	0.501	0.121
P-value[b]	**0.084**	0.190	**0.070**

[a] Parametric bootstrap P-value.
[b] Nonparametric bootstrap P-value. P-value is the proportion of the bootstrap distribution that lies to the *right* of the asymptotic t-ratio calculated from the data.

$$\Delta s_{it+1} = \beta_m x^{m}_{i,t} + \beta_p x^{p}_{it} + e_{it+1},$$

where $e_{it+1} = \gamma_i + \theta_{t+1} + u_{it+1}$, $x^{m}_{it} = f_{it} - s_{it}$, and $x^{p}_{it} = p_{it} - p_{0t} - s_{it}$. Here it can be seen that the coefficient on the monetary fundamentals maintain their statistical significance whereas the coefficient on the PPP fundamentals generally become statistically insignificant.

6.2. Out-of-sample prediction

We generate out-of-sample forecasts both at a short-horizon ($k=1$) and at a long-horizon ($k=16$). We begin by estimating Eq. (2) by LSDV on observations available through 1983.1. The $k=1$ regression is then used to forecast the 1-quarter ahead exchange rate return in 1983.2 and the $k=16$ regression to forecast the 16 quarter ahead exchange rate return through 1987.1. We then update the sample by one period by adding the observation for 1983.2 and repeat the procedure. This recursive updating scheme gives us 57 $k=1$ forecasts and 41 overlapping $k=16$ forecasts. We compare the panel regression forecasts against those implied by the random walk model.[13] We do this for both for the monetary and PPP fundamentals.

We measure relative forecast accuracy with Theil's U-statistic – the ratio of the root-mean-square prediction error (RMSPE) from two competing models. We avoided using other statistics of prediction evaluation, such as Diebold and Mariano (1995) because, as documented in Berben and van Dijk, the difficulty in accurately estimating long-run variances often results in misleading inference. The

[13] We follow Kilian (1997) who argues that it is appropriate to employ the random walk with drift.

null hypothesis is that the monetary fundamentals (or PPP) and the random walk provide equally accurate forecasts ($U=1$). The alternative hypothesis is that the monetary fundamentals (or PPP) is more accurate than the random walk ($U<1$). We also perform joint tests of the hypothesis of equal forecast accuracy by using joint test statistics formed alternatively by taking the mean value and the median value of the U-statistics. P-values are the proportion of the bootstrap distribution that lie below (to the left) of the U-statistic calculated from the data. P-values are constructed under the hypothesis of cointegration.

US as numeraire. The prediction results for the US are displayed in Table 5. At the 1-quarter horizon, monetary fundamentals point predictions dominate the random walk in RMSPE for 13 of 18 exchange rates (Australia, Denmark, Finland, Greece, and Japan are the exceptions). The improvement in forecast accuracy over the random walk is generally statistically significant at the 10% level for these 13 exchange rates. Both of the joint tests reject the hypothesis at the 10% level of equal prediction accuracy under the parametric bootstrap whereas the mean value is significant under the nonparametric bootstrap.

The statistical evidence is less favorable towards PPP forecasts. Qualitatively, PPP point predictions exhibit a similar degree of accuracy in that they dominate the random walk for 12 of 18 exchange rates, but the U-statistic are not generally statistically significant. Looking at the last column, it can be seen that monetary fundamentals forecasts dominate PPP forecasts in root-mean-square error for 13 of the 18 exchange rates.

Upon inspection of the table, one gets the impression that the U-statistic is tightly distributed around 1.0. This impression is accurate. To provide a coarse description of the properties of the parametric bootstrap distribution of the 1-quarter horizon U-statistic, we note that the distributions for the monetary fundamentals are generally symmetric about a modal value of 1.0 to four significant digits. The mean values range only from 1.001 for Canada to 0.999 for Korea and Sweden. The standard deviations range from 0.018 to 0.004 and have an average value of 0.003 over the 18 distributions. Under PPP, the grand mean of the U-statistic distributions is 1.003, indicating a small upward bias. The PPP distributions are also more spread out. The average standard deviation is 0.010, which exceeds those under the monetary model by an order of magnitude.

At the 16-quarter horizon, monetary fundamentals forecasts again dominate the random walk in RMSPE for 17 of 18 exchange rates (Greece is the lone exception). The hypothesis that the monetary fundamentals and the random walk provide equal forecast accuracy can be rejected for 15 exchange rates at the 10% level. Moreover, both joint test statistics are significant at the 5% level.

PPP performance at 16 quarters is inferior to that of the monetary fundamentals. Monetary fundamentals forecasts dominate PPP forecasts in RMSPE for 10 of 18 exchange rates. While PPP point predictions have lower RMSPE than the random walk for 17 of 18 exchange rates, the improvement in prediction accuracy is significant at the 10% level for 13 of the exchange rates.

Table 5
Out-of-sample forecasts of US dollar returns. Bootstrapped P-values generated assuming cointegration

Country	U^a	P-value[d]	P-value[e]	U^b	P-value[d]	P-value[e]	U^c
A. One-quarter ahead forecasts							
Australia	1.024	0.991	0.904	**0.988**	**0.083**	0.102	1.036
Austria	**0.984**	**0.001**	**0.013**	**0.994**	0.231	0.259	**0.990**
Belgium	**0.999**	0.269	0.424	1.000	0.441	0.442	**0.998**
Canada	**0.985**	**0.020**	**0.074**	1.003	0.534	0.496	**0.982**
Denmark	1.014	0.989	0.912	**0.998**	0.361	0.365	1.016
Finland	1.001	0.708	0.527	**0.992**	0.137	0.152	1.009
France	**0.994**	**0.024**	0.155	1.000	0.440	0.426	**0.994**
Germany	**0.986**	**0.006**	**0.056**	**0.992**	0.188	0.222	**0.994**
Great Britain	**0.983**	**0.028**	**0.077**	**0.988**	0.102	0.131	**0.996**
Greece	1.016	0.995	0.909	1.012	0.883	0.891	**0.984**
Italy	**0.997**	0.174	0.269	1.004	0.598	0.537	**0.994**
Japan	1.003	0.831	0.579	**0.998**	0.343	0.332	1.005
Korea	**0.912**	**0.001**	**0.002**	**0.974**	**0.020**	**0.034**	**0.936**
Netherlands	**0.986**	**0.004**	**0.041**	**0.992**	0.193	0.226	**0.994**
Norway	**0.998**	0.202	0.380	**0.992**	0.164	0.193	1.006
Spain	**0.996**	0.115	0.341	1.024	0.736	0.691	**0.993**
Sweden	**0.975**	**0.008**	**0.034**	**0.987**	**0.079**	0.101	**0.988**
Switzerland	**0.982**	**0.002**	**0.008**	**0.988**	**0.073**	**0.092**	**0.995**
Mean	**0.991**	**0.002**	**0.010**	**0.996**	0.135	0.145	**0.995**
Median	**0.995**	**0.025**	0.163	**0.993**	0.131	0.173	**0.994**
B. Sixteen-quarter ahead forecasts							
Australia	**0.864**	0.127	0.222	**0.728**	**0.045**	**0.053**	1.186
Austria	**0.837**	**0.070**	0.131	**0.549**	**0.006**	**0.008**	1.525
Belgium	**0.405**	**0.001**	**0.001**	**0.577**	**0.009**	**0.015**	**0.703**
Canada	**0.552**	**0.005**	**0.009**	**0.601**	**0.015**	**0.023**	**0.919**
Denmark	**0.858**	**0.092**	0.174	**0.732**	**0.069**	**0.071**	1.172
Finland	**0.859**	**0.099**	0.164	**0.631**	**0.006**	**0.012**	1.360
France	**0.583**	**0.002**	**0.004**	**0.683**	**0.033**	**0.048**	**0.854**
Germany	**0.518**	**0.001**	**0.003**	**0.440**	**0.001**	**0.001**	1.178
Great Britain	**0.570**	**0.004**	**0.012**	**0.601**	**0.015**	**0.018**	**0.948**
Greece	1.046	0.657	0.594	**0.854**	0.738	0.817	**0.787**
Italy	**0.745**	**0.003**	**0.016**	**0.878**	0.195	0.207	**0.849**
Japan	**0.996**	0.476	0.433	**0.895**	0.222	0.219	1.113
Korea	**0.486**	**0.001**	**0.012**	**0.682**	**0.048**	**0.067**	**0.714**
Netherlands	**0.703**	**0.006**	**0.032**	**0.399**	**0.001**	**0.001**	1.762
Norway	**0.537**	**0.001**	**0.002**	**0.829**	0.126	0.133	**0.648**
Spain	**0.672**	**0.006**	**0.028**	1.219	0.178	0.182	**0.859**
Sweden	**0.372**	**0.001**	**0.001**	**0.541**	**0.004**	**0.004**	**0.687**
Switzerland	**0.751**	**0.019**	**0.049**	**0.575**	**0.007**	**0.007**	1.307
Mean	**0.686**	**0.001**	**0.001**	**0.690**	**0.001**	**0.001**	1.032
Median	**0.688**	**0.001**	**0.001**	**0.656**	**0.001**	**0.003**	**0.933**

[a] Monetary fundamentals versus random walk with drift.
[b] PPP fundamentals versus random walk with drift.
[c] Monetary versus PPP fundamentals.
[d] P-values from parametric bootstrap.
[e] P-values from nonparametric bootstrap.

Switzerland as Numeraire Country. The out-of-sample forecast results are shown in Table 6. At the 1-quarter horizon, monetary fundamental forecasts outperform the random walk for 17 exchange rates. The improvement in accuracy is significant at the 10%.level in each of these cases under the null of cointegration and for 16 of these countries under both the parametric and nonparametric bootstraps. PPP forecasts dominate the random walk for these same 17 currencies. The monetary fundamentals dominate PPP forecasts in RMPSE in 13 instances.

At the 16 quarter horizon, monetary fundamentals forecasts outperform the random walk in terms of RMPSE for 15 exchange rates. The U-statistics are significant at the 10% level in 12 cases under the parametric and nonparametric bootstrap. PPP forecasts are qualitatively similar, but are dominated in terms of point prediction accuracy by the monetary fundamentals in 10 cases. Joint tests soundly reject the hypothesis that the monetary fundamentals contain no predictive content.

Japan as Numeraire Country. The out-of-sample prediction results for the yen, displayed in Table 7 are less successful. At the 1-quarter horizon, monetary fundamentals forecasts dominate the random walk in terms of RMPSE for 8 exchange rates whereas PPP forecasts outperform the random walk for 10 exchange rates.

At the 16 quarter horizon, monetary fundamentals forecasts outperform the random walk in terms of RMPSE for 10 exchange rates but only 4 of the U-statistics are significant at the 10% level under the parametric bootstrap and 3 are significant under the nonparametric bootstrap. PPP forecasts outperform the random walk in terms of RMPSE for 9 exchange rates but only 5 of the individual U-statistics are significantly less than 1 at the 10% level under the bootstraps. The monetary fundamentals forecasts do dominate PPP forecasts in terms of RMPSE in 10 of the 18 yen exchange rates.

To summarize, full sample LSDV estimates of the panel predictive regression yield statistically significant slope coefficients on the monetary and PPP fundamentals. When both sets of fundamentals are included in the regression, only the coefficient on the monetary fundamentals maintain statistical significance. Dominance of monetary fundamentals over the random walk in out-of-sample forecasts for US dollar exchange rates and Swiss Franc exchange rates provide confirmatory evidence consistent with the full sample evidence. Out-of-sample forecasts from monetary fundamentals dominate forecasts from PPP fundamentals but the difference in accuracy is not overwhelming.

7. Conclusions

Univariate analyses of the relation between exchange rate returns and monetary fundamentals are imprecise. We sharpen our inference about this connection by

Table 6
Out-of-sample forecasts of SF returns. Bootstrapped *P*-values generated assuming cointegration

Country	U[a]	*P*-value[d]	*P*-value[e]	U[b]	*P*-value[d]	*P*-value[e]	U[c]
A. One-quarter ahead forecasts							
Australia	**0.988**	**0.031**	**0.060**	**0.979**	**0.018**	**0.018**	1.009
Austria	**0.982**	**0.016**	**0.020**	**0.982**	**0.031**	**0.040**	**0.999**
Belgium	**0.952**	**0.002**	**0.002**	**0.948**	**0.001**	**0.001**	1.005
Canada	**0.995**	0.223	0.257	**0.987**	0.116	0.135	1.008
Denmark	**0.960**	**0.002**	**0.004**	**0.972**	**0.008**	**0.006**	**0.988**
Finland	**0.962**	**0.001**	**0.002**	**0.978**	**0.017**	**0.014**	**0.984**
France	**0.915**	**0.001**	**0.001**	**0.957**	**0.001**	**0.002**	**0.956**
Germany	**0.979**	**0.015**	**0.029**	**0.962**	**0.001**	**0.001**	1.018
Great Britain	**0.966**	**0.003**	**0.008**	**0.981**	**0.027**	**0.036**	**0.984**
Greece	**0.985**	**0.023**	**0.046**	**0.995**	**0.068**	**0.094**	**0.963**
Italy	**0.965**	**0.006**	**0.012**	**0.995**	0.270	0.276	**0.970**
Japan	1.003	0.551	0.657	1.005	0.621	0.605	**0.999**
Korea	**0.976**	**0.003**	**0.003**	**0.988**	**0.077**	**0.083**	**0.988**
Netherlands	**0.950**	**0.001**	**0.001**	**0.972**	**0.008**	**0.006**	**0.977**
Norway	**0.960**	**0.001**	**0.001**	**0.959**	**0.005**	**0.008**	1.002
Spain	**0.958**	**0.001**	**0.001**	**0.989**	0.252	0.264	**0.996**
Sweden	**0.948**	**0.002**	**0.005**	**0.960**	**0.001**	**0.001**	**0.987**
USA	**0.984**	**0.055**	**0.086**	**0.988**	0.120	0.137	**0.995**
Mean	**0.968**	**0.001**	**0.001**	**0.978**	**0.001**	**0.001**	**0.990**
Median	**0.966**	**0.001**	**0.001**	**0.980**	**0.005**	**0.006**	**0.992**
B. Sixteen-quarter ahead forecasts							
Australia	**0.795**	**0.062**	**0.082**	**0.385**	**0.001**	**0.001**	2.063
Austria	**0.652**	**0.008**	**0.012**	**0.775**	**0.076**	**0.078**	**0.842**
Belgium	**0.653**	**0.027**	**0.042**	**0.477**	**0.003**	**0.003**	1.370
Canada	**0.587**	**0.002**	**0.006**	**0.681**	**0.046**	**0.056**	**0.862**
Denmark	**0.695**	**0.032**	**0.045**	**0.865**	0.156	0.183	**0.804**
Finland	**0.701**	**0.024**	**0.034**	**0.915**	0.246	0.258	**0.766**
France	**0.315**	**0.001**	**0.001**	**0.726**	**0.062**	**0.082**	**0.434**
Germany	**0.486**	**0.002**	**0.002**	**0.402**	**0.001**	**0.001**	1.208
Great Britain	1.474	0.949	0.884	**0.850**	0.151	0.150	1.735
Greece	**0.845**	0.116	0.134	**0.982**	**0.080**	**0.096**	**0.491**
Italy	**0.575**	**0.003**	**0.006**	1.119	0.653	0.628	**0.514**
Japan	1.006	0.468	0.565	1.503	0.922	0.932	**0.670**
Korea	**0.382**	**0.001**	**0.001**	**0.849**	0.127	0.147	**0.450**
Netherlands	1.382	**0.001**	**0.001**	**0.720**	**0.001**	**0.004**	1.920
Norway	**0.382**	0.874	0.812	**0.417**	**0.042**	**0.049**	**0.916**
Spain	**0.482**	**0.001**	**0.001**	**0.808**	0.361	0.369	1.046
Sweden	**0.954**	0.425	0.340	**0.519**	**0.002**	**0.002**	1.837
USA	**0.783**	0.130	0.152	**0.619**	**0.016**	**0.019**	1.265
Mean	**0.731**	**0.002**	**0.002**	**0.756**	**0.002**	**0.003**	1.066
Median	**0.674**	**0.001**	**0.003**	**0.750**	**0.005**	**0.007**	**0.889**

[a] Monetary fundamentals versus random walk with drift.

[b] PPP fundamentals versus random walk with drift.

[c] Monetary versus PPP fundamentals.

[d] *P*-values from parametric bootstrap.

[e] *P*-values from nonparametric bootstrap.

Table 7
Out-of-sample forecasts of Yen returns. Bootstrapped *P*-values generated assuming cointegration

Country	U[a]	*P*-value[d]	*P*-value[e]	U[b]	*P*-value[d]	*P*-value[e]	U[c]
A. One-quarter ahead forecasts							
Australia	**0.996**	**0.050**	0.211	**0.987**	**0.082**	**0.099**	1.008
Austria	**0.997**	**0.088**	0.342	1.007	0.670	0.626	**0.990**
Belgium	1.039	0.999	0.972	1.010	0.706	0.658	1.029
Canada	1.015	0.988	0.875	1.000	0.425	0.390	1.016
Denmark	**0.996**	**0.066**	0.292	**0.987**	**0.077**	**0.092**	1.009
Finland	**0.978**	**0.001**	**0.007**	**0.987**	**0.079**	**0.088**	**0.991**
France	1.007	0.933	0.696	**0.984**	**0.046**	**0.067**	1.023
Germany	1.006	0.951	0.792	1.017	0.819	0.763	**0.990**
Great Britain	1.051	1.000	0.954	**0.979**	**0.022**	**0.032**	1.074
Greece	**0.993**	**0.018**	0.155	**0.981**	0.759	0.648	**0.995**
Italy	**0.979**	**0.037**	**0.048**	**0.976**	**0.009**	**0.014**	1.003
Korea	**0.988**	**0.005**	**0.072**	**0.981**	**0.035**	**0.043**	1.007
Netherlands	1.001	0.713	0.582	1.016	0.805	0.741	**0.985**
Norway	1.044	1.000	0.957	**0.997**	0.318	0.345	1.047
Spain	**0.976**	**0.001**	**0.006**	1.008	**0.028**	0.034	**0.986**
Sweden	1.024	0.994	0.900	**0.993**	0.179	0.199	1.031
Switzerland	1.005	0.944	0.733	1.009	0.745	0.694	**0.997**
USA	1.009	0.970	0.761	1.000	0.419	0.397	1.010
Mean	1.006	0.956	0.724	**0.996**	0.152	0.162	1.010
Median	1.003	0.934	0.674	**0.995**	0.179	0.204	1.007
B. Sixteen-quarter ahead forecasts							
Australia	**0.959**	0.342	0.317	1.087	0.555	0.533	**0.881**
Austria	**0.945**	0.305	0.363	1.487	0.953	0.948	**0.636**
Belgium	1.551	0.999	0.964	1.724	0.970	0.953	**0.900**
Canada	**0.913**	0.192	0.247	**0.897**	0.243	0.265	1.017
Denmark	**0.832**	**0.056**	0.140	**0.915**	0.222	0.238	**0.910**
Finland	**0.657**	**0.002**	**0.014**	**0.792**	**0.071**	**0.095**	**0.830**
France	**0.973**	0.382	0.359	**0.941**	0.285	0.287	1.034
Germany	1.342	0.988	0.954	2.012	0.995	0.995	**0.667**
Great Britain	2.089	1.000	0.988	**0.782**	**0.080**	**0.096**	2.670
Greece	**0.910**	0.188	0.250	**0.621**	0.946	0.884	**0.904**
Italy	**0.771**	**0.002**	**0.032**	**0.649**	**0.011**	**0.013**	1.187
Korea	**0.909**	0.195	0.263	**0.533**	**0.002**	**0.005**	1.706
Netherlands	1.000	0.513	0.505	1.841	0.988	0.980	0.543
Norway	1.768	0.999	0.965	1.210	0.769	0.726	1.462
Spain	**0.562**	**0.001**	**0.004**	1.389	**0.008**	**0.010**	**0.656**
Sweden	1.020	0.999	0.940	1.594	0.863	0.820	**0.640**
Switzerland	1.567	0.555	0.505	1.323	0.983	0.979	1.185
USA	1.079	0.734	0.585	**0.961**	0.344	0.357	1.123
Mean	1.103	0.860	0.697	1.153	0.744	0.688	1.053
Median	**0.966**	0.304	0.322	1.024	0.432	0.418	**0.907**

[a] Monetary fundamentals versus random walk with drift.
[b] PPP fundamentals versus random walk with drift.
[c] Monetary versus PPP fundamentals.
[d] *P*-values from parametric bootstrap.
[e] *P*-values from nonparametric bootstrap.

exploiting cross-sectional information available in a small panel. The weight of the evidence – both from a panel cointegration test and the examination of panel short-horizon regression slope coefficients – suggests that the nominal exchange rate is cointegrated with monetary fundamentals and that the monetary fundamentals contain significant predictive power for future exchange rate movements. Moreover, the evidence does not appear to be solely a US dollar phenomenon.

Our results raise an economic question that is not solved by our analysis. The puzzle is why monetary fundamentals evidently dominate PPP in terms of predictive content despite the fact that PPP is one of the building blocks upon which the link between the exchange rate and monetary fundamentals are formed. When both PPP and monetary fundamentals are included in the panel predictive regression, significance is maintained only on the slope coefficient on the monetary fundamentals. Additionally, monetary fundamentals point predictions most clearly dominated those of PPP for US dollar exchange rates. Root-mean-square prediction errors for the alternative measures of the fundamentals were more evenly matched for the Swiss franc and yen exchange rates but the U-statistics of PPP forecasts displayed lower levels of statistical significance.

Engel and Kim (1999) and Canzoneri et al. (1999) report evidence that real exchange rates themselves contain relatively small, slow moving permanent components. One point of speculation for the poor PPP forecast performance may be the failure to account for embedded random walk dynamics. A second possibility may be that the monetary fundamentals provide a better estimate of the long-run equilibrium price level than does the currently observed price level. A third explanation may be that the long-run nominal exchange rate is determined directly by monetary fundamentals and not by relative price levels.

Acknowledgements

Some of Mark's work on this paper was supported by a 1998 Erskine Fellowship at the University of Canterbury, New Zealand. We thank seminar participants at the University of North Carolina Janice Breuer, Menzie Chinn, Kyung So Im, Lutz Kilian, Ronald MacDonald and Peter Pedroni. The comments of two anonymous referees and Charles Engel (the co-editor) led to substantial improvements in the paper. None of these individuals are responsible for any remaining errors or mistakes.

Appendix A

A.1. Panel regression when $x_{it} \sim I(1)$

We assume the following regularity conditions. First, the data generating process is given by,

$$\begin{bmatrix}\Delta s_{it}\\ \Delta x_{it}\end{bmatrix}=\begin{bmatrix}u_{it}\\ v_{it}\end{bmatrix}=\underline{w}_{it}=\mathbf{\Psi}_i(L)\underline{\epsilon}_{it} \tag{A.1}$$

where $\underline{w}_{it}$ is a covariance stationary vector process and is independent across $i=1,\ldots,N$, $\underline{w}_{i0}=\underline{0}$, $\underline{\epsilon}_{it}\overset{iid}{\sim}N(0,\mathbf{I})$, $\mathbf{\Psi}_i(L)=\Sigma_{j=0}^{\infty}\mathbf{\Psi}_{ij}L^j$ is a $(k+1)\times(k+1)$ dimensional matrix lag polynomial in the lag operator L, where $\Sigma_{r=0}^{\infty} r|\psi_{ir}^{mn}|<\infty$, and ψ_{ir}^{mn} is the m,nth element of the matrix $\mathbf{\Psi}_{ir}$. (A.1) is the vector Wold moving average representation.

(A.1) could equivalently be represented in terms of $(\Delta s_{it}, \Delta f_{it})$, but the algebra is messier. (A.1) implies that

$$\frac{1}{\sqrt{T}}\sum_{t=1}^{[Tr]}\underline{w}_{it}\mathbf{\Psi}_i(1)\underline{W}_i(r)=\underline{B}_i(r,\mathbf{\Omega}_i), \tag{A.2}$$

$$\mathbf{\Omega}_i=\sum_{j=-\infty}^{\infty}\mathbf{\Gamma}_j'=\sum_{j=-\infty}^{\infty}\mathrm{E}(\underline{w}_{it}\underline{w}_{it}')=\mathbf{\Gamma}_0+\sum_{j=1}^{\infty}(\mathbf{\Gamma}_j+\mathbf{\Gamma}_j'), \tag{A.3}$$

$$\mathbf{\Gamma}_j=\mathrm{E}(\underline{w}_{it}\underline{w}_{it-j}') \tag{A.4}$$

where $\overset{D}{\rightarrow}$ denotes convergence in distribution, $\underline{W}(r)$ is a vector standard Brownian motion for $0\le r\le 1$, $[Tr]$ denotes the largest integer value of Tr for $0\le r\le 1$, $\underline{B}_i(r,\mathbf{\Omega}_i)$ is a randomly scaled mixed Brownian motion with conditional (on individual i) covariance matrix, $\mathbf{\Omega}_i$. For each i, $\mathrm{E}_i(\int \underline{B}_i\underline{B}_i')=\frac{1}{2}\mathbf{\Omega}_i$, $\mathbf{\Omega}_i$ is independent and identically distributed across individuals i and satisfies the law of large numbers, $1/N\ \Sigma_{i=1}^{N}\mathbf{\Omega}_i\overset{D}{\rightarrow}\mathrm{E}(\mathbf{\Omega}_i)=\mathbf{\Omega}$.

Let $\xi_{it}=(s_{it},x_{it})'$. Then from Hamilton's (1994) proposition 18.1, we have,

$$\frac{1}{T^2}\sum_{t=1}^{T}\begin{bmatrix}s_{i,t-1}^2 & s_{i,t-1}x_{i,t-1}\\ x_{i,t-1}s_{i,t-1} & x_{i,t-1}^2\end{bmatrix}\overset{D}{\rightarrow}\begin{bmatrix}\int B_{1i}^2 & \int B_{1i}B_{2i}\\ \int B_{2i}B_{1i} & \int B_{2i}^2\end{bmatrix} \tag{A.5}$$

$$\frac{1}{T}\sum_{t=1}^{T}\begin{bmatrix}s_{i,t-1}u_{it} & s_{i,t-1}v_{it}\\ x_{i,t-1}u_{it} & x_{i,t-1}v_{it}\end{bmatrix}\overset{D}{\rightarrow}\int \underline{B}_i d\underline{B}_i'+\sum_{j=0}^{\infty}\mathbf{\Gamma}_j' \tag{A.6}$$

A.2. Properties of panel OLS

Our main points can be made efficiently by assuming there are no individual-specific or time-specific effects so LSDV simplifies to OLS run on pooled observations. Extensions to incorporate these factors is straightforward but tedious. The panel OLS estimator of β in (3) is,

$$\beta_{\text{pols}} = \frac{\sum_i \sum_t x_{it} \Delta s_{i,t+1}}{\sum_i \sum_t x_{it}^2} = \frac{\frac{1}{TN} \sum_i \frac{1}{T} \sum_t (x_{it} \Delta s_{i,t+1})}{\frac{1}{N} \sum_i \frac{1}{T^2} \sum_t x_{it}^2} \tag{A.7}$$

The key features of panel OLS are, first, $\beta_{\text{pols}} \xrightarrow{p} 0$, and second, $\sqrt{N}T\beta_{\text{pols}}$ diverges. We sketch out heuristically why this is true.

We begin with the denominator of (A.7). It follows from (A.5) that for each i, $1/T^2 \,\Sigma_t\, x_{it}^2 \xrightarrow{D} \int B_{2i}^2$. Now $\text{E}_i B_{2i}^2 = \frac{1}{2}\Omega_{22,i}$ and $1/N\, \Sigma_i\, \mathbf{\Omega}_i \xrightarrow{p} \text{E}(\mathbf{\Omega}_i) = \mathbf{\Omega}$, so $1/N\, \Sigma_i\, 1/T^2\, x_{it}^2 \xrightarrow{p} \frac{1}{2}\Omega_{22}$, which is a constant. Now turning to the numerator of (A.7), for each i, $1/T\, \Sigma_t\, x_{it} \Delta s_{i,t+1} = 1/T\, \Sigma_t\, x_{it} u_{i,t+1} \xrightarrow{D} \int B_{2i}\, \text{d}B_{1i} + \Lambda_{21,i}$ where $\Lambda_{21,i} = \Sigma_{j=0}^{\infty}\, \text{E}u_{it} v_{i,t-j}$ is the 2,1th element of $\Sigma_{j=0}^{\infty}\, \mathbf{\Gamma}_{j,i} = \mathbf{\Lambda}_i$. We get this term because we do not have a-priori restrictions to rule out possible correlation between $\Delta s_{1,t+1}$ and Δx_{it}. This is exactly the correlation that creates the second-order asymptotic bias that necessitates corrections in panel dynamic OLS so that we can do inference when estimating the cointegration vector. By the law of large numbers, $1/N\, \Sigma_{i=1}^{N}\, \Lambda_{21,i} \xrightarrow{p} \text{E}(\Lambda_{21,i}) = \Lambda_{21}$, thus for fixed N, $1/N\, \Sigma_{i=1}^{N}\, 1/T^2\, \Sigma_{t=1}^{T}\, x_{it-1} u_{it} \xrightarrow{p} 0$ as $T \to \infty$, so it follows that $\beta_{\text{pols}} \xrightarrow{p} 0$.

Panel OLS is a *consistent* estimator of the true value, which is zero. The problem with panel OLS, is that it is second-order asymptotically biased in which $\sqrt{N}T\beta_{\text{pols}}$ diverges. That means that test statistics constructed for β_{pols} will converge and are useless for conducting inference. Divergence can be seen by examination of

$$\sqrt{N}T\beta_{\text{pols}} = \frac{\frac{1}{\sqrt{N}} \sum_i \frac{1}{T} \sum_t x_{it} \Delta s_{i,t+1}}{\frac{1}{N} \sum_i \frac{1}{T^2} \sum_t x_{it}^2} \tag{A.8}$$

The denominator in (A.8) is the same as that in (A.7). The numerator in (A.8) is $\sqrt{N}$ times the numerator in (A.7). Since the numerator in (A.7) converges to a constant in probability, when we multiply by $\sqrt{N}$, it will diverge as N gets large. This is the issue that comes up in panel dynamic OLS.

A.3. Panel dynamic OLS

In this section, we sketch the intuition behind panel dynamic OLS. These results are developed more carefully in Mark and Sul (1999).

The offending term in panel OLS is $\Lambda_{21,i} = \Sigma_{j=0}^{\infty} \mathrm{E}(\Delta x_{it-j} u_{it})$. Assume that u_{it} is correlated with at most p_i leads and lags of $v_{it} = \Delta x_{it}$. Let $z_{it-1} = (\Delta x_{it+p_i-1}, \ldots, \Delta x_{it-p_i-1})$, and project Δs_{it} onto $z_{i,t-1}$. Using (2), the projection error can be written as, $e_{it} = \beta h_{it-1} + \tilde{u}_{it}$ where $e_{it} = \Delta s_{it} - \mathrm{P}(\Delta s_{it} | z_{it-1})$, $h_{it-1} = x_{it-1} - \mathrm{P}(x_{it-1} | z_{it-1})$, and $\tilde{u}_{it} = u_{it} - \mathrm{P}(u_{it} | z_{it-1})$. The projection error, $\tilde{u}_{it}$ is by construction orthogonal to $\Delta x_{i,t-j}$ for all j. Regressing e_{it} on h_{it-1} gives us the panel dynamic OLS estimator of β. The asymptotic distribution of the estimator is derived in Mark and Sul (1999).

A.4. LSDV bias when $x_{it} \sim I(0)$

In the single equation context, Stambaugh (1986) and Mankiw and Shapiro (1986) show that the OLS estimator in the predictive regression is biased in small samples. To see why the bias arises, let the predictive regression be $\Delta s_{it} = \beta x_{it-1} + u_{it}$ and suppose that x_{it} evolves according to an AR(1) process, $x_{it} = \rho x_{it-1} + v_{it}$, where $(u_{it}, v_{it})' \overset{iid}{\sim} N(0, \Sigma_i)$.

In the single equation context, for any i, $(\hat{\beta} - \beta) = \Sigma\ x_{it-1} u_{it} / \Sigma\ x_{it-1}^2$. Following Stambaugh, since u_{it} and v_{it} are contemporaneously correlated, we can project u_{it} onto v_{it} and represent it as $u_{it} = (\sigma_{12,i}/\sigma_{22,i}) v_{it} + \epsilon_{it}$ where ϵ_{it} is the projection error, which is orthogonal to x_{it-1}. Substitute the projection representation into the above expression and taking expectations yields, $\mathrm{E}(\hat{\beta} - \beta) = (\sigma_{12,i}/\sigma_{22,i}) \mathrm{E}(\hat{\rho} - \rho) = \mathrm{Bias}(\hat{\beta})$, where $\hat{\rho}$ is the OLS estimator of ρ. The bias in $\hat{\rho}$ has long been understood, and shown by Kendall (1954) to be $\mathrm{E}(\hat{\rho} - \rho) = -(1 + 3\rho)/T$. Thus, for any individual, the OLS bias is $\mathrm{E}(\hat{\beta} - \beta) = -(\sigma_{12,i}/\sigma_{22,i})(1 + 3\rho)/T$.

If we mimic the calculations above, we have in the panel context, $\hat{\beta} - \beta = \Sigma_i \Sigma_t x_{it-1} u_{it} / \Sigma_i \Sigma_t x_{it-1}^2 = \Sigma_i \Sigma_t x_{it-1} [(\sigma_{12,i}/\sigma_{22,i}) v_{it} + \epsilon_{it}] / \Sigma_i \Sigma_t x_{it-1}^2$. Now taking expectations, we have $\mathrm{E}(\hat{\beta} - \beta) = \Sigma_i (\sigma_{12,i}/\sigma_{22,i}) \mathrm{E}(\Sigma_t x_{it-1} v_{it} / \Sigma_i \Sigma_t x_{it-1}^2)$. We can simplify further if we assume $\Sigma_i = \Sigma$, in which case, $\mathrm{E}(\hat{\beta} - \beta) = (\sigma_{12}/\sigma_{22}) \mathrm{E}(\hat{\rho} - \rho)$. The bias in the estimator of ρ is attenuated, but not eliminated in the panel. Formulae for the bias $\mathrm{E}(\hat{\rho} - \rho)$ are given in Hsiao (1986).

References

Berben, R.B., van Dijk, D.J., 1998. Does the absence of cointegration explain the typical findings in long horizon regressions? Econometrics Institute. Erasmus University Rotterdam, Report 9814.

Berkowitz, J., Giorgianni, L., 1997. Long-horizon exchange rate predictability? International Monetary Fund working paper No. 97/6.

Campbell, J.Y., Perron, P., 1991. Pitfalls and opportunities: what macroeconomists should know about unit roots. In: Blanchard, O.J., Fisher, S. (Eds.). NBER Macroeconomics Annual, Vol. 6. MIT Press, Cambridge, MA.

Campbell, J.Y., Shiller, R.J., 1988. Stock prices, earnings, and expected dividends. Journal of Finance 43, 661–676.

Canzoneri, M.B., Cumby, R.E., Diba, B., 1999. Relative labor productivity and the real exchange rate in the long run: evidence for a panel of OECD countries. Journal of International Economics 47, 245–266.

Chen, J., Mark, N.C., 1996. Alternative long-horizon exchange rate predictors. International Journal of Finance and Economics 1, 229–250.

Chinn, M.D., Meese, R.A., 1995. Banking on currency forecasts: how predictable is change in money? Journal of International Economics 38, 161–178.

Diebold, F.X., Mariano, R.S., 1995. Comparing predictive accuracy. Journal of Business and Economic Statistics 13, 253–263.

Engel, C., Kim, C., 1999. The long-run US/UK real exchange rate. Journal of Money, Credit, and Banking 31, 335–356.

Evans, P., 1997. Government consumption and growth. Economic Inquiry 35, 209–217.

Fama, E.F., French, K.R., 1988. Dividend yields and expected stock returns. Journal of Financial Economics 22, 3–25.

Frenkel, J.A., 1976. A monetary approach to the exchange rate: doctrinal aspects and empirical evidence. Scandinavian Journal of Economics 78, 200–224.

Frankel, J.A., Rose, A.K., 1996. A panel project on purchasing power parity: mean reversion within and between countries. Journal of International Economics 40, 209–224.

Groen, J.J., 1997. Long horizon predictability of exchange rates. Tinbergen Institute Discussion Paper TI 97-095/2.

Hansen, B.E., 1995. Rethinking the univariate approach to unit root testing: using covariates to increase power. Econometric Theory 11, 1148–1171.

Hamilton, J.D., 1994. Time Series Analysis. Princeton University Press, Princeton, NJ.

Hodrick, R.J., 1992. Dividend yields and expected stock returns: alternative procedures for inference and measurement. Review of Financial Studies 5, 357–386.

Hsiao, C., 1986. Analysis of Panel Data. Cambridge University Press, New York.

Kilian, L., 1997. Exchange rates and monetary fundamentals: what do we learn from long-horizon regressions? Journal of Applied Econometrics, forthcoming.

Kendall, M.G., 1954. Note on bias in the estimation of autocorrelation. Biometrika 41, 403–404.

Lothian, J.R., 1997. Multi-Country evidence on the behavior of purchasing power parity under the current float. Journal of International Money and Finance 16, 19–35.

Lucas, Jr. R.E., 1982. Interest rates and currency prices in a two-country world. Journal of Monetary Economics 10, 335–359.

MacDonald, R., 1996. Panel unit root tests and real exchange rates. Economics Letters 50, 7–11.

MacDonald, R., Marsh, I., 1997. On fundamentals and exchange rates: a Casselian perspective. Review of Economics and Statistics 79, 655–664.

MacDonald, R., Taylor, M.P., 1993. The monetary approach to the exchange rate: rational expectations, long-run equilibrium and forecasting. IMF Staff Papers, 40 (1).

Maddala, G.S., Kim, I., 1998. Unit roots, cointegration, and structural change. Cambridge University Press, New York.

Mankiw, N.G., Shapiro, M., 1986. Do we reject too often? Small sample bias in tests of rational expectations models. Economics Letters 20, 139–145.

Mark, N.C., 1995. Exchange rates and fundamentals: evidence on long-horizon prediction. American Economic Review 85, 201–218.

Mark, N.C., Sul, D., 1999. A computationally simple cointegration vector estimator for panel data. Mimeo, Ohio State University.

Mussa, M., 1976. The exchange rate, the balance of payments, and monetary and fiscal policy under a regime of controlled floating. Scandinavian Journal of Economics 78, 229–248.

Obstfeld, M., Rogoff, K., 1995. Exchange rate dynamics redux. Journal of Political Economy 103, 624–660.

Papell, D.H., 1997. Searching for stationarity: purchasing power parity under the current float. Journal of International Economics 43, 313–332.

Pedroni, P., 1997. Panel cointegration: asymptotic and finite sample properties of pooled time series tests with an application to the PPP hypothesis. Mimeo, Indiana University.

Stambaugh, R.F., 1986. Bias in regression with lagged stochastic regressors. Mimeo, University of Chicago.

Wu, Y., 1996. Are real exchange rates non-stationary? Evidence from a panel-data test. Journal of Money, Credit, and Banking 28, 54–63.

Part II
Statistical Models of the Foreign Exchange Market

[5]

ELSEVIER

Journal of Empirical Finance 4 (1997) 115–158

Journal of EMPIRICAL FINANCE

Intraday periodicity and volatility persistence in financial markets

Torben G. Andersen [a], Tim Bollerslev [b,c,*]

[a] *Department of Finance, J.L. Kellogg Graduate School of Management, Northwestern University, Evanston, IL 60208, USA*

[b] *Department of Economics, Rouss Hall, University of Virginia, Charlottesville, VA 22901, USA*

[c] *NBER, Cambridge, MA 02138, USA*

Abstract

The pervasive intraday periodicity in the return volatility in foreign exchange and equity markets is shown to have a strong impact on the dynamic properties of high frequency returns. Only by taking account of this strong intraday periodicity is it possible to uncover the complex intraday volatility dynamics that exists both within and across different financial markets. The explicit periodic modeling procedure developed here provides such a framework and thus sets the stage for a formal integration of standard volatility models with market microstructure variables to allow for a more comprehensive empirical investigation of the fundamental determinants behind the volatility clustering phenomenon. © 1997 Elsevier Science B.V.

JEL classification: C14; C22; G14; G15
Keywords: Volatility; Intraday periodicity; Temporal aggregation; ARCH

1. Introduction

It is widely documented that return volatility varies systematically over the trading day and that this pattern is highly correlated with the intraday variation of trading volume and bid–ask spreads. Indeed, these strikingly regular patterns of market activity measures have provided the impetus for much theoretical work. On

* Corresponding author.

PII S0927-5398(97)00004-2

the other hand, the dynamics of the intraday return volatility process is mostly ignored in the empirical market microstructure literature. This is quite surprising given the notion that news arrivals and the resolution of their informational impact are intimately related to the dynamics of the return volatility process [1]. We conjecture that the intraday return dynamics is neglected primarily because standard time series models of volatility have proven inadequate when applied to high frequency returns data. In fact, previous results reported in the literature are often contradictory and generally defy theoretical predictions. Consequently, there is no well established paradigm for intraday volatility modeling, and at present its inclusion in market microstructure research is tenuous.

In this paper we demonstrate that the difficulties encountered by standard volatility models arise largely from the aforementioned systematic patterns in average volatility across the trading day. We further show how practical estimation and extraction of the intraday periodic component of return volatility is both feasible and indispensable for meaningful intraday dynamic analysis. Particular attention is paid to the differing impact of the periodic pattern on the dynamic return features at the various intraday frequencies. To illustrate the range of applicability of the developed procedures, the analysis is conducted in parallel for two different asset classes traded under widely different market structures, namely the over-the-counter foreign exchange interbank market and an organized exchange for futures equity index contracts. Moreover, to bring out the distinct character of the intraday returns process, the findings are contrasted to the corresponding features of interdaily returns series for the identical assets.

The empirical evidence on the properties of average intraday stock returns dates back to, at least, Wood et al. (1985) and Harris (1986a) who document the existence of a distinct U-shaped pattern in return volatility over the trading day i.e. volatility is high at the open and close of trading and low in the middle of the day. The existence of equally pronounced intraday patterns in foreign exchange markets has been demonstrated by Müller et al. (1990) and Baillie and Bollerslev (1991) [2].

Meanwhile, a separate time series oriented literature has modeled the dynamics of the intraday return volatility directly, building on the ARCH methodology of

[1] For example, theoretical work stress issues such as the process of price discovery, the optimal timing of trades designed to limit price impact, the differing price response to public versus private information, the clustering of discretionary liquidity trading and the associated increase in market depth when private information is short-lived and the particular market dynamics associated with periodic market openings and closures.

[2] Empirical work continues to refine and classify the regularities of high frequency returns in this dimension. Recent studies include Barclay et al. (1990) and Harvey and Huang (1991) on return variances over trading versus non-trading periods, Lockwood and Linn (1990) on overnight and intraday return volatility and Ederington and Lee (1993) on the impact of macroeconomic announcements on inter- and intraday return volatility.

Engle (1982). Most of these studies fall into one of three categories. Firstly, some authors investigate the interrelation between returns in geographically separated financial markets that trade sequentially, with a focus on the transmission of information as measured by the degree of spill-over in the mean returns and/or volatility from one market to the next [3]. A second strand of this literature is concerned with the lead–lag relations between two or more markets that trade simultaneously [4]. Finally, a third group of papers explores the role of information flow and other microstructure variables as determinants of intraday return volatility [5].

Direct comparison of these intraday volatility studies is complicated by the different sampling frequencies employed. Nonetheless, as noted by Ghose and Kroner (1994) and Guillaume (1994), the results regarding the implied degree of volatility persistence appear puzzling and in stark conflict with the aggregation results for ARCH models developed by Nelson (1990, 1992), Drost and Nijman (1993) and Drost and Werker (1996). One potential explanation is that these theoretical predictions about the relationship between parameter estimates at different sampling frequencies do not generally apply in the face of strong intraday periodicity, a fact that has gone largely unnoticed. The most comprehensive prior attempt at direct modeling of this intraday heteroskedastic pattern in returns is provided by a series of papers by the research group at Olsen and Associates on the foreign exchange market e.g. Müller et al. (1990, 1993) and Dacorogna et al. (1993). They apply time invariant polynomial approximations to the activity in the distinct geographical regions of the market over the 24-hour trading cycle [6]. Although this might be a reasonable assumption for the foreign exchange market, we propose an alternative and more general methodology that allows the shape of the periodic pattern to also depend on the current overall level of return volatility. This feature makes the procedure readily applicable to the analysis of high frequency financial data in general and turns out to be essential for our investigation of the stock market. While our approach accounts for the pronounced intraday patterns, we explicitly do not make any attempts to correct for the lower frequency interdaily patterns that also exist e.g. day-of-the-week and holiday effects which

[3] Examples of early contributions are Engle et al. (1990) for foreign exchange markets and Hamao et al. (1990) for various national equity index returns.

[4] See for example Baillie and Bollerslev (1991) and Chan et al. (1991).

[5] This literature is exemplified by Bollerslev and Domowitz (1993), Locke and Sayers (1993), Laux and Ng (1993), Foster and Viswanathan (1995) and Goodhart et al. (1993). This research is partially motivated by an attempt to identify the economic origins of the volatility clustering phenomenon as motivated by the mixture of distributions hypothesis; see for example Clark (1973), Tauchen and Pitts (1983), Harris (1986b, 1987), Gallant et al. (1991), Ross (1989) and Andersen (1994, 1996).

[6] One may note that the de-volatilization procedure proposed by Zhou (1992) implicitly adjusts for the intraday periodicity in the adaptive calculation of the volatility increments from tick-by-tick observations. Along similar lines, the notion of time deformation in modeling time varying volatility in financial markets has recently been advocated by Ghysels and Jasiak (1994).

are most certainly present in both of the data sets analyzed here. These inter-daily features are clearly less significant and not critical for the high frequency analysis pursued here. Yet, in analyses of longer run phenomena, accounting for these effects may be equally important and could in principle be incorporated along the same lines.

The remainder of the paper is organized as follows. Section 2 describes our data and summarizes the intraday average return patterns. Section 3 contains an analysis of the correlation structure of both raw and absolute 5-minute returns, as well as a comparison to the corresponding properties of the two daily time series. The impact of periodic heteroskedasticity on the 5-minute correlations is strong, while the evidence of standard conditional heteroskedasticity, although evident at the daily level, appears weak at many intraday frequencies. This motivates our simple model of intraday returns that renders formal assessments of the relation between the intra- and interdaily correlation patterns feasible. Section 4 investigates the properties of temporally aggregated intraday returns. Estimates of the degree of volatility persistence at the various sampling frequencies are contrasted to the theoretical aggregation results. Our estimation strategy for characterizing the intraday periodicity is presented in Section 5. A relatively simple model that allows for a direct interaction between the level of the daily volatility and the shape of the intradaily pattern provides a close fit to the average intradaily volatility patterns for both return series, with the interaction effect being less significant for the foreign exchange market. The corresponding time series properties of the filtered returns obtained by extracting the estimated volatility patterns from the raw series is also explored. Estimation results for these returns are much more in line with the theoretical predictions. Moreover, this analysis strongly suggests that several distinct component processes affect the volatility dynamics. This finding may help shed new light on the long-memory feature in low frequency return volatility documented by a number of recent studies. Section 6 contains concluding remarks. Details regarding the construction of the 5-minute foreign exchange and equity returns employed throughout and the flexible non-parametric procedure used in the estimation of the intraday periodicity are contained in the appendices.

2. Intraday return periodicity

Our primary data set consists of 5-minute returns for the Deutschemark–U.S.$ (DM–$) exchange rate from October 1, 1992 through September 30, 1993, comprising 74,880 observations, and the Standard and Poor's 500 (S&P 500) composite stock index futures contract from January 2, 1986, through December 31, 1989, consisting of a total of 79,280 observations. A more detailed description of the data sources and the calculation of the 5-minute returns is provided in Appendix A. In addition, we use two daily time series of 3,649 spot DM–$

exchange rates from March 14, 1979 through September 29, 1993 and 9,558 observations on the S&P 500 cash index from January 2, 1953 through December 31, 1990 [7]. All the empirical work is done in parallel, with tables and figures for the foreign exchange and equity data labelled 'a' and 'b', respectively.

2.1. The Deutschemark–U.S. dollar foreign exchange data

The sample mean of the 5-minute Deutschemark appreciation of 0.000175% is indistinguishable from zero at standard significance levels given the sample standard deviation of 0.047% [8]. However, the returns are clearly not normally distributed. For example, the sample skewness of 0.367 and the sample kurtosis of 21.5 are both highly statistically significant [9]. At the same time, the maximum and minimum 5-minute returns of 1.24% and −0.637% do not suggest the presence of sharp discontinuities in the series. A small negative first order autocorrelation coefficient of −0.04 provides some support for the hypothesis that foreign exchange dealers position their quotes asymmetrically relative to the perceived 'true market price' as a way to manage their inventory positions, thus causing the midpoint of the quoted prices to move around in a fashion similar to the bid-ask bounce often observed on organized exchanges [10]. A more detailed set of summary statistics are available in Andersen and Bollerslev (1994).

In order to evaluate the intraday periodicity of the returns, Fig. 1a plots the average sample mean for each 5-minute interval. The average returns are centered around zero but numerous violations of the constant 5% confidence band for the null of an i.i.d. series occur between 09.00 GMT and 18.00 GMT (interval range 108 to 216). Allowing for different return sample variances across the day produces a more realistic time-varying confidence band that is violated at seemingly random points in time and at a frequency consistent with the 5% band (13 violations over 288 intervals). Thus, there appears to be little evidence for any systematic DM–$ appreciation or depreciation through the regular trading day cycle [11].

[7] The initial observation on March 14, 1979 for the exchange rates corresponds to the beginning of the EMS. The Standard 90 was replaced by the broader S and P 500 composite index on January 2, 1953. Also, for reasons discussed below, the estimates for the S and P 500 data exclude the October 1987 crash period.

[8] Assuming the returns to be uncorrelated, the standard deviation for the mean equals $0.047/(74{,}880)^{1/2} = 0.000172\%$.

[9] The standard errors of these statistics in their corresponding asymptotic normal distributions are $(6/T)^{1/2}$ and $(24/T)^{1/2}$, or 0.009 and 0.018, respectively (see e.g. Jarque and Bera, 1987).

[10] The coefficient is small in an economic sense but given the large sample size it is highly statistically significant. Bollerslev and Domowitz (1993) also report a negative first order autocorrelation in 5-minute DM–$ returns over 3 months in 1989, but find the correlation for artificially constructed 5-minute pseudo transactions price returns to be positive.

[11] This is counter to Ito and Roley (1987) who found evidence for systematic dollar appreciation during the U.S. segment of the market but dollar depreciation during the European trading hours.

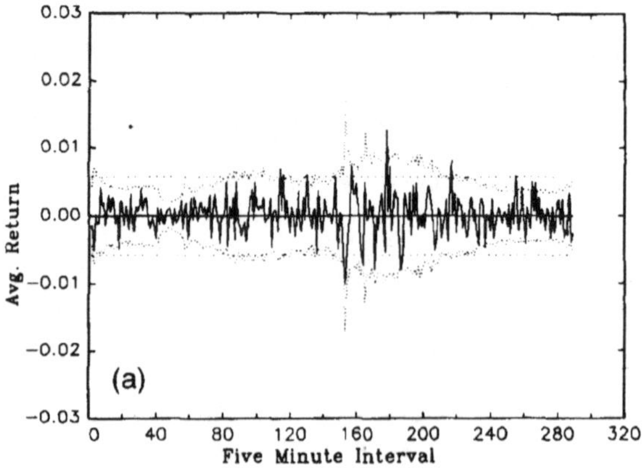

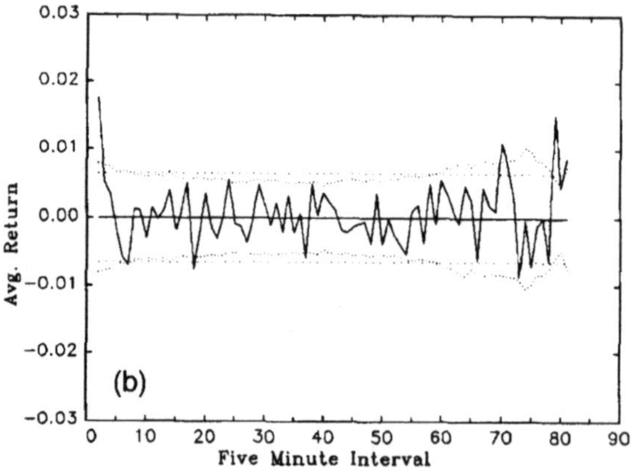

Fig. 1. Intraday average returns, (a) DM–$, (b) S&P 500.

In contrast, the exchange rate volatility fluctuates dramatically over the daily cycle. The average absolute returns over the 5-minute intervals are depicted in Fig. 2a. It reveals a pronounced difference in the volatility over the day, ranging from a low of around 0.01% at 04.00 GMT (interval 48) to a high of around 0.05% at 15.00 GMT (interval 180) [12]. This pattern is closely linked to the cycle of market activity in the various financial centers around the globe. The volatility starts out at a relatively high level followed by a slow decay up to around 03.00 GMT (interval 36). The strong drop between intervals 40 and 60 corresponds to the

[12] Since the average standard error for the absolute returns is 0.0022%, these differences are highly statistically significant.

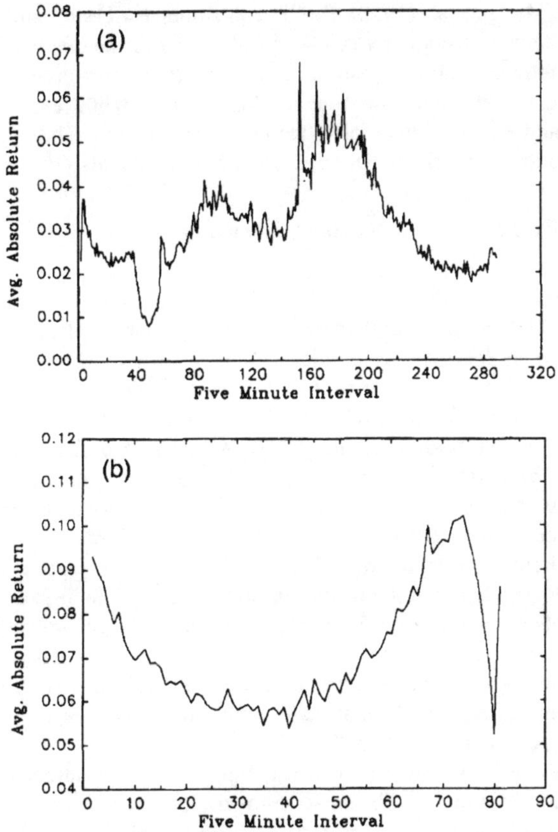

Fig. 2. Intraday average absolute returns, (a) DM–$, (b) S&P 500.

lunch hour in the Tokyo and Hong Kong markets. Activity then picks up during the afternoon session in the Far Eastern markets and is further fueled by the opening of the European markets around 07.00 GMT (interval 84). The market volatility then declines slowly until the European lunch hour at 11.30 GMT (interval 138), before it increases sharply during the overlap of afternoon trading in Europe and the opening of the U.S. markets around 13.00 GMT, or 7.00 a.m. New York (interval 156). After the European markets close volatility declines monotonically until trading associated with the Far Eastern markets starts to pick up again around 21.00 GMT (interval 252). The robustness of this intraday volatility pattern is confirmed by the sub-sample analysis and the sorting of days according to volatility levels reported in the more detailed analysis in Andersen and Bollerslev (1994), which is also consistent with earlier findings in Wasserfallen (1989), Müller et al. (1990), Baillie and Bollerslev (1991) and Dacorogna et al. (1993) [13]. Standard summary statistics further verify the overwhelming significance of this intraday volatility pattern. In particular, the first order autocorrelation coefficient for the absolute 5-minute returns of $\rho_1^A = 0.309$ exceeds the $1/\sqrt{T}$ asymptotic standard error by almost a factor of one hundred, while the Ljung–Box statistic for up to tenth order serial correlation in $|R_{t,n}|$ equals $Q^A(10) = 36{,}680$ [14].

2.2. The standard and poor's 500 stock index futures data

The basic features of the 5-minute S&P 500 are qualitatively similar to those of the 5-minute DM–$ returns. Perhaps, the most notable difference is that the standard deviation for the stock index futures return of 0.104% is more than double the value for the foreign exchange market. However, since the overnight returns for the S&P 500 are excluded, the average 5-minute standard deviation corresponds to active trading on the CME only, whereas the foreign exchange returns cover the entire 24-hour trading cycle and therefore include periods of relatively slow activity. Even so, when judged by auxiliary statistics such as the sample minimum and maximum of 2.22% and −2.76%, the equity market exhibits the more volatile returns. Another distinguishing feature is the virtual absence of autocorrelation in the futures returns. Although the first ten autocorrelation coefficients are highly significant, the coefficients are economically small and have unpredictable signs [15]. This lack of correlation contrasts sharply with results reported by most studies on the intraday S&P 500 cash market, where non-synchronous trading effects imply that stale prices may enter the calculation of the index (see e.g. Chan et al., 1991) [16].

The intraday periodic patterns over the eighty 5-minute intraday intervals are depicted in Fig. 1b and Fig. 2b. Apart from the positive returns over the initial 5-minute interval from 8.35 to 8.40 a.m. and towards the end of the trading day,

[13] We follow Dacorogna et al. (1993) in using GMT time scale throughout our analysis. Daylight savings time is observed in Europe and North America, but not in East Asia. From the sub-sample analysis in Andersen and Bollerslev (1994) this gives rise to a one hour difference in the peaks associated with the regular release of U.S. macroeconomic announcements at 08.30 a.m. corresponding to interval 162 for winter time and interval 150 for summer time. Ederington and Lee (1993) and Harvey and Huang (1991) also suggest that macroeconomic announcement effects have a distinct impact on the average volatility in early Friday morning trading in the U.S. segment of the market. We do not pursue this or any other day-of-the-week effects any further here, however.

[14] The first ten autocorrelations for $|R_{t,n}|$ are 0.309, 0.256, 0.238, 0.214, 0.212, 0.199, 0.204, 0.182, 0.185 and 0.182.

[15] The first ten autocorrelations of the returns are 0.009, −0.003, −0.009, 0.010, −0.004, 0.018, 0.009, 0.015, 0.013 and 0.008, respectively. The corresponding Ljung–Box statistic equals $Q(10) = 87.6$.

[16] The impact of non-synchronous trading has been explored extensively in the literature (see e.g. Scholes and Williams, 1977; Lo and MacKinlay, 1990).

the violations of the 5% confidence bands for the average returns are dispersed unpredictably over the trading day [17]. Nonetheless, as was the case for the foreign exchange market, the systematic return effects are dwarfed by the systematic movements in the return volatility, here documented in Fig. 2b. The average absolute returns attain the commonly observed intraday U-shape, starting out at 0.095% in the morning, followed by a smooth decline to a level of 0.055% around noon and a steady rise to 0.105% towards the end of trading in the cash market. The subsequent drop and rise over the last fifteen minutes corresponds to the post cash market trading on the CME [18]. The robustness of this intraday periodicity in the S&P 500 returns is again underscored by the more detailed analysis in Andersen and Bollerslev (1994) in which the full four year sample is divided into calendar years as well as four daily volatility categories. The only discernible difference across these sub-sample patterns is a tendency for the right part of the 'U' to occasionally rise above the left part, creating more of a 'J' shape. Interestingly, this tendency appears to be concentrated on high volatility days. The model proposed in Section 5 below explicitly accounts for this phenomenon.

Several recent studies have attempted to rationalize the pronounced U-shape pattern in intraday stock market volatility by strategic interaction of traders around market openings and closures (see e.g. Admati and Pfleiderer, 1988, 1989; Foster and Viswanathan, 1990; Son, 1991; Brock and Kleidon, 1992). Even though the foreign exchange market operates on a continuous basis, the volatility pattern for the DM–$ depicted in Fig. 2a may be viewed, tentatively, as a sum of two overlapping U-shapes corresponding to the Far East and European trading hours, along with an inverted U-shape for the U.S. segment of the market. Hence, in spite of obvious differences in market microstructures, the foreign exchange returns are calculated from quotes in a 24-hour over-the-counter market while the equity returns are obtained from transaction prices on an organized futures market with well defined daily closings, the pattern of intraday periodicity in the two markets share important common characteristics.

3. Characterization and modeling of the correlation structure in intraday returns

3.1. Intraday return correlations

While the intraday volatility patterns documented in the preceding section may be irrelevant for standard studies of the return dynamics based on price observa-

[17] This is related to the findings in Harris (1986a) who reports that the average positive returns in the equity markets tend to occur over the first 45 min of the trading day and the very last trade of the day. Notice also, that there is no indication of any abnormal positive returns after the cash market is closed.

[18] This U-shaped pattern in the volatility of S&P 500 futures prices following the closure of the cash market has also recently been documented by Chang et al. (1995).

tions at daily frequencies, conclusions drawn from the recent surge of empirical papers on return volatility and market microstructure variables at the intraday frequencies are likely subject to severe distortions due to the strong periodicity in returns. We therefore supplement the prior investigation of the unconditional volatility patterns with an explicit look at the dynamic features of our two return series.

Fig. 3a and b display the sample autocorrelations of the 5-minute returns for up to five days i.e. 1440 observations for the foreign exchange and 400 for the equity returns. All values are small and beyond the first few lags the series resemble realizations of white noise. Thus, we again detect little of interest in the mean

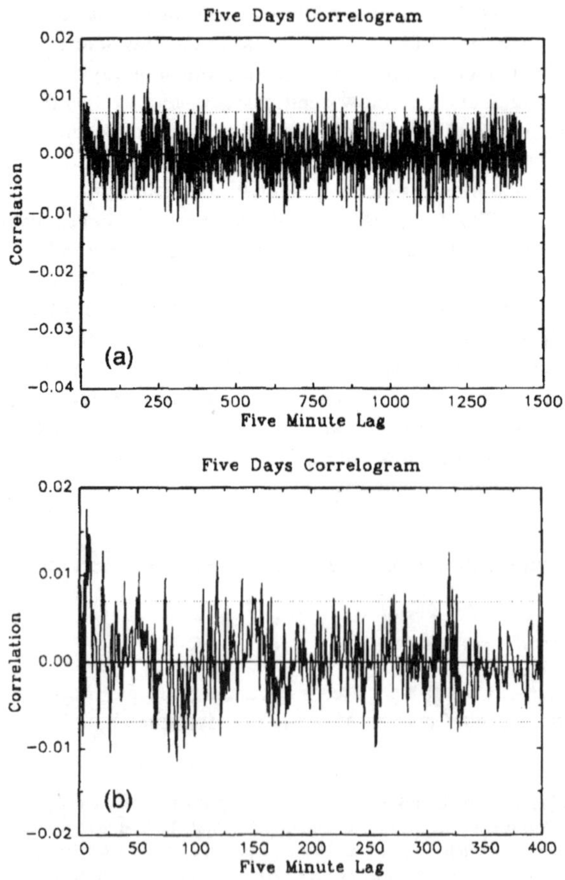

Fig. 3. Five days correlogram of intraday returns, (a) DM–$, (b) S&P 500.

returns. In contrast, the autocorrelation patterns for the absolute returns are strikingly regular. Consider the series for the DM–$ exchange rate in Fig. 4a. The strong intraday pattern induces a distorted U-shape in the sample correlogram [19]. Notice also how the size of the autocorrelations at the daily frequencies decay slowly over the first four days, only to increase slightly at the fifth, or weekly, frequency. This signals the presence of a minor day-of-the-week effect, which we ignore in the remainder. Fig. 4b for the S&P 500 futures returns is equally telling. The slowly declining U-shape occupies exactly 80 intervals, corresponding to the daily frequency.

3.2. Interpretation in terms of a suggestive intraday return model

The pronounced systematic fluctuations in the return correlogram provide an initial indication that direct ARCH modeling of the intraday return volatility would be hazardous. Standard ARCH models imply a geometric decay in the return autocorrelation structure and simply cannot accommodate strong regular cyclical patterns of the sort displayed in Fig. 4. Instead, it seems intuitively clear that the combination of recurring cycles at the daily frequency and a slow decay in the average autocorrelations may be explained by the joint presence of the pronounced intraday periodicity documented above coupled with the strong daily conditional heteroskedasticity [20]. The following stylized model provides a simple specification of the interaction between these two components,

$$R_t \equiv \sum_{n=1}^{N} R_{t,n} = \sigma_t \frac{1}{N^{1/2}} \sum_{n=1}^{N} s_n Z_{t,n}. \tag{1}$$

Here, R_t denotes the daily continuously compounded return calculated from the N uncorrelated intraday return components, $R_{t,n}$. The conditional volatility factor for day t is denoted by σ_t, while s_n refers to a deterministic intraday periodic component and $Z_{t,n}$ is an i.i.d. mean zero, unit variance error term assumed to be independent of the daily volatility process, $\{\sigma_t\}$. Both volatility components must be non-negative i.e. $\sigma_t > 0$ a.s. for all t and $s_n > 0$ for all n. The following terminology for the normalized, deterministic sample means and covariances for the periodic structure will prove convenient:

$$\frac{1}{N}\sum_{n=1}^{N} \equiv M(s) = 1, \qquad \frac{1}{N}\sum_{n=1}^{N} s_n s_{n-i} \equiv M(ss_i), \qquad \frac{1}{N}\sum_{n=1}^{N} S_n^2 \equiv M(s^2),$$

where $s_{n+jN} \equiv s_n$ for any integer j and $0 < n \leq N$.

[19] A corresponding figure is presented by Dacorogna et al. (1993). However, in their analysis the correlations at the daily frequencies are sharply diminished due to a strong weekend effect. By excluding weekend returns we have effectively eliminated this distortion.

[20] The temporal variation in daily financial market volatility have been successfully modeled by ARCH type processes (see Bollerslev et al. (1992) for a survey of this extensive literature).

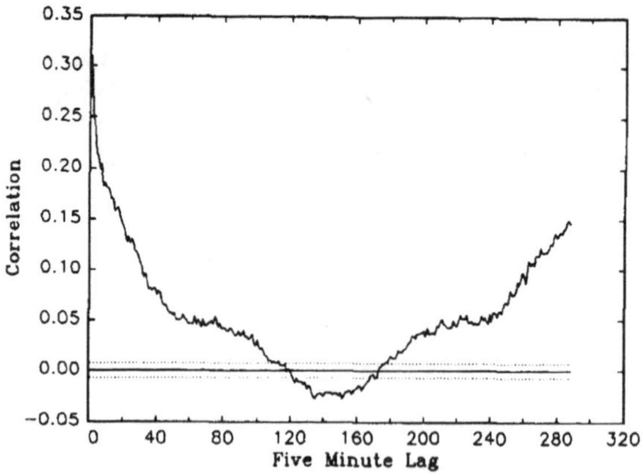

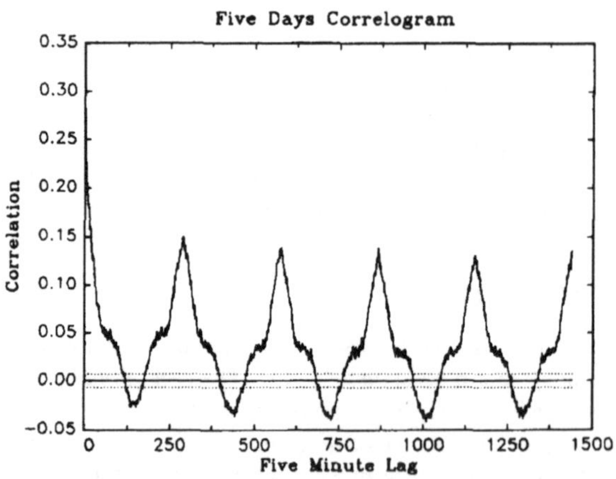

(a)

Fig. 4. Intraday absolute returns, (a) DM–$, (b) S&P 500.

In the absence of intraday periodicity ($s_n = 1$ for all n) the daily returns may be represented in the form $R_t = \sigma_t N^{-1/2} \Sigma_{n=1,N} Z_{t,n}$, where the return component $N^{-1/2} \Sigma_{n=1,N} Z_{t,n}$ is i.i.d. with mean zero and unit variance. Thus, Eq. (1) extends the standard volatility model for daily returns to an intraday setting with independent return innovations and deterministic volatility patterns. Of course, this type of periodicity is annihilated when the returns are measured at the daily frequency. In particular, letting Z_t denote an i.i.d. random variable with $E(Z_t) = 0$ and $\text{Var}(Z_t) = 1$, we have

$$R_t = M^{1/2}(s^2) \sigma_t Z_t, \qquad (2)$$

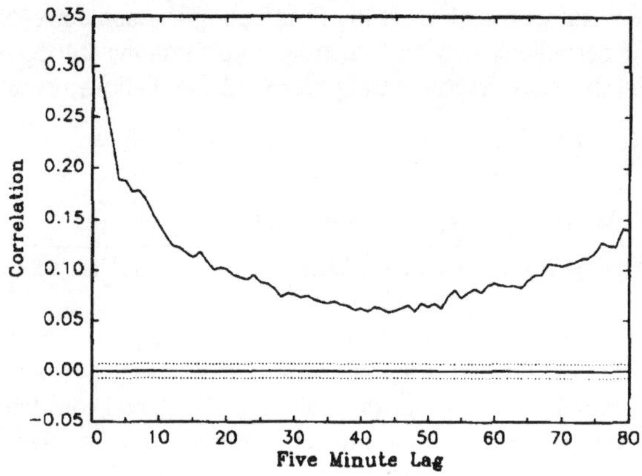

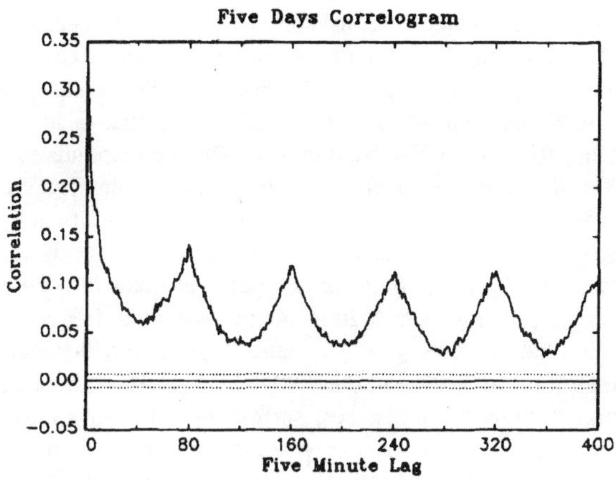

(b)

Fig. 4 (continued).

so that the expected absolute return equals $M^{1/2}(s^2)\sigma_t E|Z_t|$. Since $M^{1/2}(s^2) \geq 1$, the expected daily absolute return is an increasing function of the fluctuations in the intraday periodic pattern. However, this effect is limited to a scale factor. Letting $c \equiv (E|Z_t|)^{-2} - 1 > 0$, it follows that for $t \neq \tau$,

$$\mathrm{Corr}(|R_t|, |R_\tau|) = \frac{\mathrm{Cov}(\sigma_t, \sigma_\tau)}{\mathrm{Var}(\sigma_t) + cE(\sigma_t^2)}. \tag{3}$$

Hence, the presence of periodic components reduces the overall level of the interdaily return autocorrelations, without affecting the autocorrelation pattern [21]. In contrast, the periodicity may have a strong impact on the autocorrelation pattern for the absolute intraday returns. Straightforward calculations reveal

$$\mathrm{Corr}(|R_{t,n}|, |R_{\tau,m}|)$$

$$= \frac{M(ss_{n-m})\mathrm{Cov}(\sigma_t, \sigma_\tau) + \mathrm{Cov}(s_n, s_m)E^2(\sigma_t)}{M(s^2)\mathrm{Var}(\sigma_t) + c_N E(\sigma_t^2)M(s^2) + E^2(\sigma_t)\mathrm{Var}(s)}, \tag{4}$$

where $\mathrm{Var}(s) \equiv M(s^2) - M^2(s)$, $\mathrm{Cov}(s_n, s_m) \equiv M(ss_{n-m}) - M^2(s)$ and $c_N \equiv E^{-2}|Z_{t,n}| - 1$. Eq. (4) illustrates the interaction between the periodicity in absolute returns at the intradaily level and the conditional heteroskedasticity at the daily level. For adjacent trading days the impact of the positive correlation in the daily return volatility, captured by $\mathrm{Cov}(\sigma_t, \sigma_\tau)$, is strong and induces positive dependence in the absolute returns, but as the distance between t and τ grows this effect becomes less important which is consistent with the slow decay in the correlograms in the bottom panels of Fig. 4. At the same time, the correlograms are affected by the strong intraday periodicity. For example, consider the display for the absolute S&P 500 returns in Fig. 4b. The correlations attain their lowest values around lag forty, or half a trading day. This corresponds to the bottom of the U-shape for the average absolute returns depicted in Fig. 2b. Clearly, the population covariance, $\mathrm{Cov}(s_n, s_m)$, is minimized and significantly negative, at this frequency. Eq. (4) verifies that the negative correlation between the 5-minute absolute returns, realized about half-a-day apart, translates into a negative contribution to the corresponding correlogram at the 3–4 hour frequencies. Likewise, Fig. 2a indicates that there is strong negative correlation between the absolute foreign exchange returns in the intervals 80–225 (covering about half-a-day) and all the remaining 5-minute returns. Not surprisingly, the lower panel of Fig. 4a verifies that this again results in highly significant troughs in the correlogram around the 12 hour frequency (and its harmonics). Indeed, the impact is now sufficiently strong that the absolute return autocorrelations turn negative. This is truly remarkable given the very large positive autocorrelations found at the daily frequency and it is testimony to the profound impact of the periodic structure on the intraday return dynamics. In terms of the specification in Eq. (4), the size of the second, negative, term of the numerator exceeds the first, positive, term around the 12 hour frequency.

[21] Consistent with the findings of Granger and Ding (1996), informal investigations reveal that the dynamic dependencies are significantly more pronounced for the absolute as opposed to the squared sample returns. Consequently, our intraday modeling focuses on the patterns in $|R_t|$ and $|R_{t,n}|$, rather than R_t^2 and $R_{t,n}^2$.

3.3. Long-run implications and comparison to daily returns

To further assess the descriptive accuracy of the formulation in Eq. (1), we now investigate the long-run implications for the correlogram. It is convenient to focus on the daily frequency i.e. $n = m$,

$$\mathrm{Corr}(|R_{t,n}|, |R_{\tau,n}|) = \frac{\mathrm{Cov}(\sigma_t, \sigma_\tau) + (\mathrm{Var}(s)/M(s^2))E^2(\sigma_t)}{\mathrm{Var}(\sigma_t) + c_N E(\sigma_t^2) + (\mathrm{Var}(s)/M(s^2))E^2(\sigma_t)}. \tag{5}$$

Fig. 5a and b display the first forty autocorrelations for the absolute returns of the two daily time series on the DM–\$ spot exchange rate and the S&P 500 cash

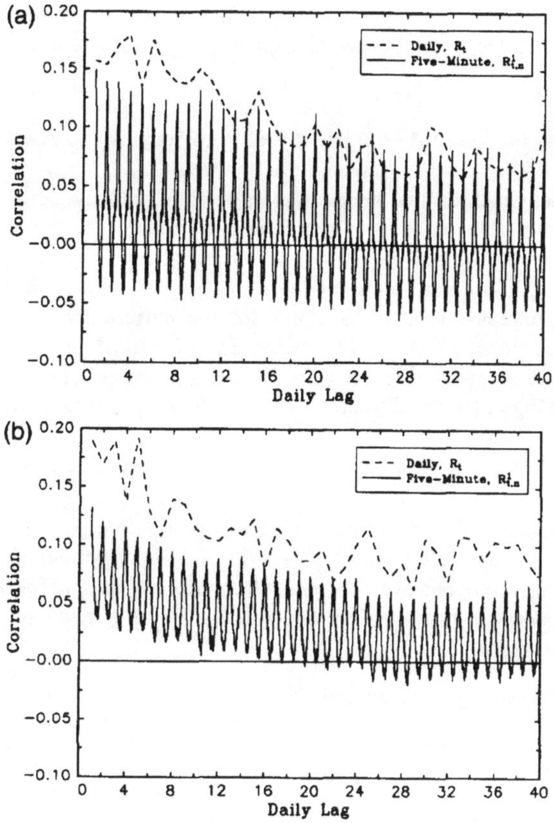

Fig. 5. Forty days correlogram of absolute returns, (a) DM–\$, (b) S&P 500.

index, along with the corresponding 5-minute intraday autocorrelations out to lag 11,520 and 3,200, respectively [22]. Direct comparison between the empirically estimated $\mathrm{Corr}(|R_t|, |R_\tau|)$ in Eq. (3) and the expression for $\mathrm{Corr}(|R_{t,n}|, |R_{\tau,n}|)$ above are complicated by the different sample periods required for reliable inference. Nonetheless, it is clear that the decay rate in the local maxima of the intradaily absolute correlogram and the daily return autocorrelations should be qualitatively comparable, as the $\mathrm{Cov}(\sigma_t, \sigma_\tau)$ term governs both. Comparing the peaks in the intraday correlograms to the daily autocorrelations in Fig. 5a and b confirms this implication of our stylized model; the dominant rate of decay is strikingly similar for both markets [23].

The findings in this section demonstrate a strong correspondence between the qualitative implications of the model outlined in Eq. (1) and the stylized empirical facts. It suggests that our model, stressing the conditional heteroskedasticity at the daily level along with the strong deterministic periodicity at the intradaily level, may serve as a good starting point for high frequency volatility modeling and as such it constitutes the basis for the subsequent analysis in Section 5.

4. Implications for volatility modeling and high frequency return aggregation

Section 3 demonstrates that the distinct intraday periodicity has a strong impact on the autocorrelation patterns of the 5-minute returns. The question therefore arises whether more formal time series modeling of return volatility is similarly affected by the presence of periodic features, and if so, whether some observation intervals are preferable relative to others for the purpose of drawing inference concerning the dynamic features of interest. In order to address these issues this section presents an extensive analysis of the properties of the return series obtained at a range of different intradaily and interdaily frequencies.

4.1. Characterization of the intraday returns at the various frequencies

Summary statistics for the foreign exchange market are provided in Table 1a for all seventeen possible intraday returns with a 24-hour periodicity. The returns are continuously compounded i.e. the nth return on day t for the series at $(k \cdot 5)$-minute intervals is defined by $R^k_{t,n} \equiv \Sigma_{i=(n-1)k+1,nk} R_{t,i}$, $t = 1, 2, \ldots, 260$,

[22] The sample autocorrelations are generally negatively biased and become less precise as the lag length grows; see Percival (1993) who point out that the sum of all the sample autocorrelations by construction equals zero. We therefore limit our analysis to lag-lengths which may appear large, but nonetheless constitute a modest fraction of the total intraday sample.

[23] The slow rate of decay in the autocorrelation functions is also in accordance with the apparent long-memory feature of asset return volatility documented by a number of recent studies (see e.g. Baillie et al., 1996; Ding et al., 1993).

$n = 1, 2, \ldots, K$ where $K \equiv 288/k$ refers to the number of returns per day. Note that while the 5-minute return series consists of 74,880 observations, the hourly series contains only 6,240 observations and the 1/2-day return series has a mere 520 observations. These differences should be kept in mind when interpreting the evidence.

The standard deviations in Table 1a grow at a rate almost proportional to the square root of the sampling frequency. This is consistent with the 5-minute returns being approximately uncorrelated, although there is a small, but highly significant, negative first order autocorrelation coefficients at the higher frequencies. As mentioned, the weak negative correlation may be the result of spread positioning by dealers causing mean reversion in the quote midpoints; an effect similar to a bid–ask bounce in transactions data [24]. In line with this explanation, the ρ_1 coefficients generally turn insignificant at the 40-minute and lower frequencies. Further corroborating evidence along these lines is provided by the variance ratio statistics,

$$\mathrm{VR} = \frac{K \cdot \mathrm{Var}_T\left(R^k_{t,n}\right)}{\mathrm{Var}_T\left(\Sigma^K_{n=1} R^k_{t,n}\right)}, \tag{6}$$

where $\mathrm{Var}_T(R^k_{t,n})$ and $\mathrm{Var}_T(\Sigma_{n=1,k} R^k_{t,n})$ denote the sample variances for the intraday and daily returns, respectively. Expanding the daily variance estimate in the denominator demonstrates that a value of the VR-statistic below unity will result from positive autocorrelation between adjacent return components, while a statistic above one is indicative of predominantly negatively correlated intraday returns [25]. Finally, it is worth noting from Table 1a, that the kurtosis of the DM–$ returns increases almost monotonically with the sampling frequency.

The first order autocorrelations of the absolute returns, ρ_1^A are, not surprisingly, all highly significant for the shorter intervals. However, beyond the 2-hour sampling frequency the autocorrelations drop off very sharply and in fact turn negative at the 8 and 12 hourly frequencies ($k = 96$, 144). This is, of course, consistent with the negative region of the 5-minute absolute return correlogram in Fig. 4a. The VR^A-statistic reported in the final column of Table 1a is calculated by replacing $R^k_{t,n}$ with $|R^k_{t,n}|$ in the definition of VR in Eq. (6) [26]. The statistic starts out at 0.05 for the 5-minute returns and rises almost monotonically to 0.69 for the

[24] Note that the standard deviation of the 5-minute returns is less than the average quoted bid–ask spread. According to Bollerslev and Melvin (1994), more than half of the DM–$ quotes are posted with a spread of 0.10%, while the second most common and lowest regularly posted spread of 0.05% accounts for about a quarter of the quotations.

[25] Formal tests for serial correlation based on the VR-statistic may be calculated as outlined in Lo and MacKinlay (1989).

[26] Note that the denominator in this VR^A-statistic involves the variance of the sum of the absolute returns rather than the absolute value of the sum of the returns. The expected value of the VR-statistic would not equal unity under the latter definition.

Table 1

k	T/k	Mean	St. Dev.	Skew.	Kurtosis	ρ_1	$Q(10)$	VR	ρ_1^A	$Q^A(10)$	VR^A
(a) Summary statistics for intraday DM–$ exchange rate											
1	74,880	0.018	0.047	0.368	21.5	−0.040	281	1.194	0.309	36,680	0.054
2	37,440	0.035	0.066	0.363	16.6	−0.070	263	1.162	0.313	17,563	0.071
3	24,960	0.053	0.079	0.200	13.6	−0.089	220	1.118	0.307	10,710	0.086
4	18,720	0.070	0.089	0.276	14.0	−0.082	154	1.084	0.287	6,296	0.099
6	12,480	0.105	0.107	0.534	12.6	−0.043	36.5	1.023	0.268	2,757	0.127
8	9,360	0.140	0.121	0.135	9.11	−0.023	22.0	0.994	0.272	1,736	0.149
9	8,320	0.158	0.126	0.345	10.1	0.002	18.9	0.948	0.251	1,212	0.161
12	6,240	0.210	0.148	0.326	11.0	−0.001	12.7	0.978	0.229	609	0.193
16	4,680	0.280	0.170	0.318	8.77	0.032	13.1	0.968	0.246	425	0.235
18	4,160	0.315	0.178	0.489	10.6	0.058	21.9	0.947	0.193	219	0.260
24	3,120	0.420	0.212	0.166	8.94	0.011	16.7	1.012	0.164	159	0.311
32	2,340	0.560	0.246	0.326	9.15	0.018	43.3	1.018	0.171	238	0.373
36	2,080	0.630	0.253	0.329	7.89	0.047	37.7	0.954	0.097	109	0.416
48	1,560	0.840	0.300	0.400	5.92	0.002	30.5	1.007	0.075	66.6	0.487
72	1,040	1.261	0.373	0.319	6.59	−0.019	20.6	1.042	0.007	67.6	0.679
96	780	1.681	0.423	0.389	5.19	−0.022	18.2	1.004	−0.025	53.2	0.653
144	520	2.521	0.520	0.192	4.31	−0.021	12.2	1.012	−0.033	28.2	0.692
(b) Summary statistics for intraday S&P 500 returns											
1	79,280	0.064	0.104	−0.597	29.3	0.009	87.6	0.774	0.292	32,425	0.099
2	39,640	0.128	0.150	−1.212	30.9	−0.009	81.5	0.801	0.285	12,641	0.128
4	19,820	0.255	0.212	−1.609	33.2	0.014	53.4	0.795	0.232	3,374	0.179
5	15,856	0.319	0.234	−1.755	33.3	0.032	60.6	0.780	0.243	2,323	0.205
8	9,910	0.511	0.299	−1.478	22.2	0.047	44.6	0.793	0.207	1,295	0.261
10	7,928	0.638	0.339	−1.417	21.2	0.039	41.7	0.819	0.211	973	0.300
16	4,955	1.021	0.437	−1.803	26.6	0.040	35.2	0.849	0.135	437	0.405
20	3,964	1.277	0.499	−1.869	27.4	0.016	24.4	0.884	0.114	268	0.463
40	1,982	2.553	0.728	−1.541	16.2	0.026	22.6	0.942	0.148	175	0.673

12 hourly returns. The results for the multiple day returns reported in Andersen and Bollerslev (1994) continue this near monotone ascent, reaching 1.94 for the biweekly sampling interval. The smooth increase suggests that a common component accounts for a substantial part of the positive higher order dependence in all of the return series. The corresponding ρ statistics of 0.123 and 0.118 for the weekly and biweekly sampling frequencies also testify to the importance of the interday heteroskedasticity [27].

[27] Hence, the VR^A-statistics convey a coherent message about the degree of conditional heteroskedasticity in the series. As a set of simple diagnostics, these statistics may therefore be more informative about the nature of the volatility process than the standard Ljung–Box statistics for tenth order serial correlation in the absolute returns, $Q^A(10)$, which appear both erratic and highly dependent on the sample size.

The summary statistics for the S&P 500 index futures returns in Table 1b largely parallel those for the DM–$ returns. However, in contrast to the results for the exchange rates, the first order autocorrelations and the VR-statistics in Table 1b all indicate a slight positive intraday dependence. Moreover, the equity returns are negatively skewed and display very significant excess kurtosis [28]. Finally, the intraday return periodicity, here depicted in Fig. 2b, again have a strong effect on the correlations for the absolute intraday returns, although the decay in the ρ_1^A coefficients for the lower frequencies is less pronounced than for the exchange rates.

4.2. Specification of the volatility model and the associated persistence measures

Numerous recent studies have relied on more formal time series techniques in the analysis of high frequency return dynamics both within and across different markets. The most commonly employed formulation is the GARCH(1, 1) model proposed independently by Bollerslev (1986) and Taylor (1986). Thus, in order to evaluate the potential impact of the strong intraday periodicity in this context we

Notes to Table 1:

(a) The percentage returns are based on interpolated 5-minute logarithmic average bid-ask quotes for the Deutschemark–U.S. dollar spot exchange rate from October 1, 1992 through September 29, 1993. Quotes from Friday 21.00 Greenwich mean time (GMT) through Sunday 21.00 GMT have been excluded, resulting in a total of 74,880 return observations. The length of the different intraday return sampling intervals equals $5 \cdot k$ minutes. Each time series has a total of T/k non-overlapping return observations. The sample means have been multiplied by one hundred. The columns indicated by ρ_1 and ρ_1^A give the first order autocorrelations for the returns and the absolute returns. The Ljung and Box (1978) portmanteau test for up to tenth order serial correlation in the returns and the absolute returns are denoted by $Q(10)$ and $Q^A(10)$, respectively. The variance ratio's for the different sampling frequencies versus the daily return variance are denoted by VR. The corresponding variance ratio statistics for the absolute returns are given in the VR^A column.

(b) The returns are based on 79,280 interpolated 5-minute futures transactions prices for the Standard and Poor's 500 composite index. The sample period ranges from January 2, 1986 through December 31, 1989, excluding the period from October 15, 1987 through November 13, 1987. Overnight five minute returns have also been deleted, resulting in a total of 80 intraday return observations from 08.35 through 15.15 for each of the 991 days in the sample. The length of the different intraday return sampling intervals equals $5 \cdot k$ minutes. Each time series has a total of T/k non-overlapping return observations. The sample means have been multiplied by one hundred. The columns indicated by ρ_1 and ρ_1^A give the first order autocorrelations for the returns and the absolute returns. The Ljung and Box (1978) portmanteau test for up to tenth order serial correlation in the returns and the absolute returns are denoted by $Q(10)$ and $Q^A(10)$, respectively. The variance ratio's for the different sampling frequencies versus the daily return variance are denoted by VR. The corresponding variance ratio statistics for the absolute returns are given in the VR^A column.

[28] The negative skewness may be interpreted as evidence of the so-called 'leverage' and/or 'volatility feed-back' effects discussed by Black (1976), Christie (1982) and Nelson (1991), and Campbell and Hentschel (1992), respectively.

present MA(1)–GARCH(1, 1) estimation results for each of the intradaily sampling frequencies in Table 2a and b. Formally, the model is defined by

$$R^k_{t,n} = \mu_{(k)} + \theta_{(k)}\epsilon^k_{t,n-1} + \epsilon^k_{t,n},$$

and

$$\left(\sigma^k_{t,n}\right)^2 = \omega_{(k)} + \alpha_{(k)}\left(\epsilon^k_{t,n-1}\right)^2 + \beta_{(k)}\left(\sigma^k_{t,n-1}\right)^2,$$

where $E_{t,n-1}(\epsilon^k_{t,n}) = 0$ and $E_{t,n-1}[(\epsilon^k_{t,n})^2] = (\sigma^k_{t,n})^2$ denotes the conditional return variance over the subsequent intraday period, with the subscript $(t, 0)$ defined to equal $(t-1, K)$. The reported parameter estimates for $\alpha_{(k)}$ and $\beta_{(k)}$ are obtained

Table 2

k	T/k	$\alpha_{(k)}$	$\beta_{(k)}$	$\alpha_{(k)}+\beta_{(k)}$	Half life	Mean lag	Median lag
(a) Persistence of MA(1)–GARCH(1, 1) models for intraday DM–$ exchange rate $R^k_{t,n} \equiv 100 \cdot \Sigma_{i=(n-1)k+1,nk} R_{t,i} = \mu_{(k)} + \theta_{(k)}\epsilon^k_{t,n-1} + \epsilon^k_{t,n}$ $(\sigma^k_{t,n})^2 = \omega_{(k)} + \alpha_{(k)}(\epsilon^k_{t,n-1})^2 + \beta_{(k)}(\sigma^k_{t,n-1})^2$, $t = 1, 2, \cdots, 260$, $n = 1, 2, \cdots, 288/k$							
1	74,880	0.193 (0.011)	0.822 (0.009)	1.015	∞	∞	∞
2	37,440	0.229 (0.012)	0.774 (0.008)	1.003	∞	∞	∞
3	24,960	0.273 (0.018)	0.708 (0.014)	0.981	533	725	488
4	18,720	0.287 (0.019)	0.677 (0.016)	0.964	375	488	320
6	12,480	0.322 (0.035)	0.579 (0.033)	0.901	200	233	138
8	9,360	0.286 (0.028)	0.581 (0.037)	0.868	195	207	108
9	8,320	0.306 (0.035)	0.521 (0.042)	0.828	165	167	81
12	6,240	0.311 (0.047)	0.395 (0.069)	0.706	119	105	35
16	4,680	0.261 (0.039)	0.456 (0.074)	0.718	167	136	< 40
18	4,160	0.270 (0.061)	0.246 (0.124)	0.516	94	67	< 45
24	3,120	0.018 (0.015)	0.969 (0.026)	0.988	6,771	5,919	1,878
32	2,340	0.016 (0.008)	0.975 (0.013)	0.991	12,159	11,219	4,318
36	2,080	0.011 (0.004)	0.978 (0.005)	0.989	11,311	8,293	266
48	1,560	0.011 (0.004)	0.979 (0.005)	0.990	17,084	13,229	1,748
72	1,040	0.007 (0.005)	0.987 (0.004)	0.987	19,585	10,153	< 180
96	780	0.014 (0.008)	0.969 (0.007)	0.983	19,637	13,202	< 240
144	520	0.010 (0.010)	0.960 (0.007)	0.970	16,329	5,988	< 360
(b) Persistence of MA(1)–GARCH(1, 1) models for intraday S&P 500 returns $R^k_{t,n} \equiv 100 \cdot \Sigma_{i=(n-1)k+1,nk} R_{t,i} = \mu_{(k)} + \theta_{(k)}\epsilon^k_{t,n-1} + \epsilon^k_{t,n}$ $(\sigma^k_{t,n})^2 = \omega_{(k)} + \alpha_{(k)}(\epsilon^k_{t,n-1})^2 + \beta_{(k)}(\sigma^k_{t,n-1})^2$, $t = 1, 2, \ldots, 991$, $n = 1, 2, \ldots, 80/k$							
1	79,280	0.137 (0.004)	0.838 (0.005)	0.975	137	168	105
2	39,640	0.180 (0.010)	0.765 (0.011)	0.945	121	138	79
4	19,820	0.223 (0.024)	0.664 (0.036)	0.887	116	118	57
5	15,856	0.230 (0.067)	0.630 (0.123)	0.861	116	112	49
8	9,910	0.053 (0.027)	0.935 (0.036)	0.988	2,213	2,602	1,559
10	7,928	0.048 (0.018)	0.940 (0.023)	0.988	2,947	3,437	2,043
16	4,955	0.148 (0.333)	0.764 (0.694)	0.912	606	575	240
20	3,964	0.060 (0.049)	0.890 (0.092)	0.951	1,376	1,124	246
40	1,982	0.108 (0.158)	0.798 (0.315)	0.906	1,397	1,128	228

by quasi-maximum likelihood methods assuming the innovations to be conditionally normally distributed. The corresponding robust standard errors for the estimates are provided in parentheses (see Bollerslev and Wooldridge, 1992). We note that, although it usually represents a reasonable approximation, the GARCH(1, 1) model is not necessarily the preferred specification for the return generating process in all, or even most, instances. However, estimating the same model across both asset classes and all return frequencies facilitates meaningful comparisons of the findings. Moreover, it corresponds to the class of models for which theoretical aggregation results are available. The MA(1) term is included to account for the economically minor, but occasionally highly statistically significant, first order autocorrelation in the returns.

Unfortunately, an unambiguous characterization of the estimated volatility dynamics and the associated persistence properties is not possible in this non-linear setting (see Bollerslev and Engle (1993), Bollerslev et al. (1994) and Gallant et al. (1993) for further discussion of these issues). Hence, we supplement the parameter estimates for $\alpha_{(k)}$ and $\beta_{(k)}$ in Table 2a and b with three additional summary measures for the implied degree of volatility persistence. In particular, if $\alpha_{(k)} + \beta_{(k)} < 1$, the j-step ahead prediction for the conditional variance may be written as

$$E_{t,n}\left[\left(\sigma^k_{t,n+j}\right)^2\right] = \sigma^2 + \left(\alpha_{(k)} + \beta_{(k)}\right)^j \left[\left(\sigma^k_{t,n}\right)^2 - \sigma^2\right]$$

where $\sigma^2 \equiv \omega_{(k)}(1 - \alpha_{(k)} - \beta_{(k)})^{-1}$ equals the unconditional variance of the

Notes to Table 2:

(a) The returns are based on 288 interpolated five minute logarithmic average bid–ask quotes for the Deutschemark–U.S. dollar spot exchange rate from October 1, 1992 through September 29, 1993. Quotes from Friday 21.00 Greenwich mean time (GMT) through Sunday 21.00 GMT have been excluded, resulting in a total of 74,880 return observations. The length of the different intraday return sampling intervals equal $5 \cdot k$ minutes. The model estimates are based on T/k non-overlapping return observations. The $\alpha_{(k)}$ and $\beta_{(k)}$ columns give the Gaussian quasi-maximum likelihood estimates for the GARCH(1, 1) parameters. Robust standard errors are reported in parentheses. The half life of a shock to the conditional variance at frequency k is calculated as $-\log(2)/\log(\alpha_{(k)} + \beta_{(k)})$ and converted into minutes. The mean lag of a shock to the conditional variance is given by $\alpha_{(k)} + \beta_{(k)} > 1$. The median lag of a shock to the conditional variance is calculated by $\frac{1}{2} + [\log(1 - \beta_{(k)}) - \log)\alpha_{(k)}) - \log(2)]/\log(\alpha_{(k)} + \beta_{(k)})$ and reported in number of minutes. For $2\alpha_{(k)} < 1 - \beta_{(k)}$ the median lag is less than $\frac{1}{2}$. The median lag is also not defined for $\alpha_{(k)} + \beta_{(k)} > 1$.

(b) The returns are based on 79,280 interpolated five minute futures transactions prices for the Standard and Poor's 500 composite index. The sample period ranges from January 2, 1986 through December 31, 1989, excluding the period from October 15, 1987 through November 13, 1987. Overnight five minute returns have also been deleted, resulting in a total of 80 intraday return observations from 08.35 through 15.15 for each of the 991 days in the sample. The length of the different intraday return sampling intervals equal $5 \cdot k$ minutes. The model estimates are based on T/k non-overlapping return observations. The $\alpha_{(k)}$ and $\beta_{(k)}$ columns give the Gaussian quasi-maximum likelihood estimates for the GARCH(1, 1) parameters. See (a) for the definition of the half life, mean lag and median lag statistics.

return innovations. The 'half-life' of the volatility process is then defined as the number of time periods it takes for half of the expected reversion back towards σ^2 to occur i.e. $-\log(2)\cdot\log(\alpha_{(k)}+\beta_{(k)})^{-1}$. Alternatively, by defining the conditional heteroskedastic squared return innovations, $\nu_{t,n}^k \equiv (\epsilon_{t,n}^k)^2 - (\sigma_{t,n}^k)^2$, the GARCH(1, 1) model may be expressed as an infinite MA model for $(\epsilon_{t,n}^k)^2$ with positive coefficients, θ_i^k,

$$\epsilon_{t,n}^k = \sigma^2 + \alpha(k)\sum_{i=1}^{\infty}\left(\alpha_{(k)}+\beta_{(k)}\right)^{i-1}\nu_{t,n-i}^k + \nu_{t,n}^k \equiv \sigma^2 + \sum_{i=0}^{\infty}\theta_i^k\nu_{t,n-i}^k.$$

This specification suggests the corresponding 'mean lag', $\alpha_{(k)}(1-\alpha_{(k)}-2\beta_{(k)}+\alpha_{(k)}\beta_{(k)}+\beta_{(k)})^{-1}$ and 'median lag', $\frac{1}{2}+[\log(1-\beta_{(k)})-\log(\alpha_{(k)})-\log(2)]\cdot\log(\alpha_{(k)}+\beta_{(k)})^{-1}$, as additional measures for characterizing the degree of volatility persistence and the duration of the dynamic adjustment process in squared returns across the different sampling frequencies [29]. Neither the mean nor the median lag is defined for $\alpha_{(k)}+\beta_{(k)}>1$. Also, the median lag is less than $1/2$ for $2\alpha_{(k)}+\beta_{(k)}<1$.

4.3. Interpretation of the GARCH results for different return frequencies

This section summarizes the evidence from fitting standard GARCH models to the return series at different frequencies. Particular emphasis is placed on the type of distortions that may be induced by the strong periodic intraday patterns which are ignored in these models. There are a couple of indirect ways to gauge the effect. First, there are theoretical predictions about the relation between the parameters at various frequencies. If these are most obviously violated at the particular frequencies where the intraday periodicity are expected to assert the maximal impact, this is therefore consistent with the periodic pattern being a dominant source of misspecification for these models. Second, to the extent that the periodic pattern is a strictly deterministic intraday phenomenon as suggested in Section 3, the distortions should be absent from models estimated at daily or multiple-day frequencies. Consequently, if the theoretical aggregation results work satisfactorily at the multiple-day frequencies but break down intradaily then this is further evidence of a significant impact of the periodic pattern on the dynamic properties of the intraday volatility process. We also relate our findings to the prior estimates reported from intraday volatility modeling. The comparison shows that our results are fully consistent with the diverse set of estimates reported in the literature once we control for the different return frequencies employed in the studies. Finally, the explicit incorporation of the cyclical pattern in Section 5 verifies that most of the distortions attributable to the intraday volatility cycle may

[29] The mean lag is given by $\Sigma_{i=0,\infty} i\theta_i^k$, whereas the median lag, m, is implicitly defined by $\Sigma_{i=0,m}\theta_i^k = 1/2\cdot\Sigma_{i=0,\infty}\theta_i^k$ (see Harvey, 1981).

be eliminated. Hence, our findings apply readily to the majority of the prior high frequency studies in the literature, and, in particular, provide an indication of the magnitude of their potential biases due to the neglect of the intraday periodicity in the volatility process.

The MA(1)–GARCH(1, 1) results for the intraday foreign exchange rates are given in Table 2a. The implied persistence measures reveal an alarming degree of irregularity across the different sampling frequencies. For the longer intraday intervals the estimates, converted into minutes, point to half lives around 18,000, or about $12\frac{1}{2}$ trading days and mean lags of around 8–9 days. However, the corresponding measures collapse at the intermediate $\frac{1}{2}$–$1\frac{1}{2}$ hour frequencies ($k = 6$–18), becoming less than 4 *hours*, only to resurrect again at the lowest, 5–10 minute, intervals ($k = 1, 2$) where violations of the $\alpha_{(k)} + \beta_{(k)} < 1$ inequality cause the estimated processes to be covariance nonstationary.

These intraday results contrast sharply with the findings for the interdaily DM–\$ returns reported in Table 3a i.e. $R \equiv \Sigma_{\tau=(t-1)k+1,tk} R_{\tau}$, $t = 1, 2, \ldots, [3{,}649/k]$, $k = 1, 2, \ldots, 10$ where $[\cdot]$ denotes the integer value. Here, the persistence measures appear quite consistent over the different return intervals, with the half lives and mean lags fluctuating around 20 and 15 days, respectively [30]. As for the intraday returns, the median lag is always substantially lower than the mean lag and measured with some imprecision resulting in numerous violations of the inequality governing the lower bound of the statistic, particularly for the smaller sample sizes.

A formal framework for assessment of the parameter estimates obtained at the various sampling frequencies is available from the results on temporal aggregation in ARCH models provided by Nelson (1990, 1992), Drost and Nijman (1993) and Drost and Werker (1996). Specifically, assuming that the GARCH(1, 1) model serves as a reasonable approximation to the returns process at the daily frequency, it follows from Drost and Nijman (1993) that the estimates for the corresponding weak GARCH(1, 1) models at the lower interdaily frequencies should be related to the daily parameters via the simple formula $\alpha_{(k)} + \beta_{(k)} = (\alpha_{(1)} + \beta_{(1)})^k$. This implies that the estimated half lives, when converted to a common unit of measurement as in our tables, should be stable across the frequencies [31]. Our evidence in Table 3a is in line with this prediction and it is also consistent with

[30] The intraday measures in Table 2a are converted to minutes whereas the interdaily results in Table 3a are given in days. Furthermore, recall that the weekend returns have been excluded from the intraday series. This may induce a distortion in the return dynamics but, again, our informal analysis found this effect to be inconsequential.

[31] Note that any serial dependence in the mean will generally increase the order of the implied low frequency weak GARCH model beyond that of the high frequency GARCH(1, 1) model (see Drost and Nijman (1993) for further details). However, the estimate for the MA(1) term for the daily DM–\$ GARCH(1, 1) model is only −0.034 with an asymptotic standard error of 0.018.

Table 3

k	$[T/k]$	$\alpha_{(k)}$	$\beta_{(k)}$	$\alpha_{(k)}+\beta_{(k)}$	Half life	Mean lag	Median lag
(a) Persistence of MA(1)–GARCH(1, 1) models for daily DM–$ exchange rates $R_t^k \equiv 100 \cdot \Sigma_{\tau=(t-1)k+1,tk} R_\tau = \mu_{(k)} + \theta_{(k)}\epsilon_{t-1}^k + \epsilon_t^k\ (\sigma_t^k)^2 = \omega_{(k)} + \alpha_{(k)}(\epsilon_{t-1}^k)^2 + \beta_{(k)}(\sigma_{t-1}^k)^2,\ t=1, 2, \ldots, [T/k]$							
1	3,649	0.105 (0.015)	0.873 (0.015)	0.978	31.2	37.7	23.2
2	1,824	0.150 (0.024)	0.784 (0.026)	0.934	20.6	21.4	10.9
3	1,216	0.106 (0.021)	0.813 (0.037)	0.919	24.8	21.2	6.1
4	912	0.167 (0.036)	0.713 (0.042)	0.879	21.6	19.2	6.5
5	729	0.182 (0.049)	0.611 (0.081)	0.794	15.0	11.4	< 2.5
6	608	0.191 (0.049)	0.646 (0.060)	0.838	23.5	20.9	5.6
7	521	0.129 (0.049)	0.674 (0.071)	0.803	22.2	14.2	< 3.5
8	456	0.170 (0.051)	0.563 (0.176)	0.733	17.8	11.7	< 4.0
9	405	0.133 (0.067)	0.641 (0.230)	0.774	24.3	14.7	< 4.5
10	364	0.174 (0.079)	0.434 (0.186)	0.607	13.9	7.8	< 5.0
(b) Persistence of MA(1)–GARCH(1, 1) models for daily S&P 500 returns							
1	9,558	0.089 (0.019)	0.906 (0.018)	0.995	147	202	137
2	4,779	0.087 (0.015)	0.902 (0.015)	0.990	135	175	114
3	3,186	0.108 (0.016)	0.870 (0.018)	0.979	98	119	74
4	2,389	0.093 (0.016)	0.889 (0.019)	0.983	158	194	121
5	1,911	0.101 (0.015)	0.900 (0.025)	1.000	∞	∞	∞
6	1,593	0.127 (0.037)	0.838 (0.044)	0.965	117	135	79
7	1,365	0.177 (0.085)	0.776 (0.076)	0.953	100	117	69
8	1,194	0.137 (0.050)	0.821 (0.044)	0.958	129	145	83
9	1,062	0.123 (0.035)	0.805 (0.052)	0.924	84	79	33
10	955	0.173 (0.066)	0.768 (0.030)	0.941	114	127	71

(a) The returns are based on 3,649 daily quotes for the Deutschemark–U.S. dollar spot exchange rate from March 14, 1979 through September 29, 1993. Weekend and holiday quotes have been excluded. The length of the return intervals equals k days, for a total of $[T/k]$ observations, where $[\cdot]$ denotes the integer value. See Table 2a for the definition of the half life, mean lag, and median lag. These measures are converted to trading days.

(b) The returns are based on 9,558 daily observations for the Standard and poor's 500 composite index from January 2, 1953 through December 31, 1990. The length of the return intervals equals k days, for a total of $[T/k]$ observations, where $[\cdot]$ denotes the integer value. See Table 2a for the definition of the half life, mean lag, and median lag. These measures are converted to trading days.

earlier evidence for other interdaily exchange rates reported in Baillie and Bollerslev (1989).

The observations above suggest that the results for the intraday exchange rates in Table 2a are indicative of serious model misspecification. For further analysis, we again use the estimates for the daily GARCH(1, 1) model ($\hat{\alpha}_{(288)} = 0.105$ and $\hat{\beta}_{(288)} = 0.873$) as a natural benchmark since these are unaffected by the intraday periodicity. The results of Drost and Nijman (1993) and Drost and Werker (1996) now imply that the intraday returns should follow weak GARCH(1, 1) processes with $\alpha_{(k)} + \beta_{(k)}$ converging to unity and $\alpha_{(k)}$ converging towards zero as the length of the sampling interval, k, decreases. In fact, Nelson (1990, 1992) establishes general conditions under which GARCH(1, 1) models, even if misspecified at all frequencies, will satisfy the above convergence results and produce consistent estimates for the true volatility process at the highest sampling frequencies. Unfortunately, these predictions do not allow for deterministic effects in the volatility process. Yet, given the estimated standard errors, the 12 hourly through 2 hourly returns ($k = 24–144$) are roughly in line with the qualitative predictions. Beyond this point the theoretical results are strongly contradicted, however. The most blatant violations are provided by the much lower volatility persistence, as measured by $\hat{\alpha}_{(k)} + \hat{\beta}_{(k)}$, for the models based on $\frac{1}{2}–1\frac{1}{2}$ hourly returns ($k = 6–18$). For the 5–15 minute returns ($k \leq 3$) the sum of the estimates for $\hat{\alpha}_{(k)}$ and $\hat{\beta}_{(k)}$ is again near unity, but the relative size of the coefficients does not conform to the theoretical predictions, as $\hat{\alpha}_{(k)}$ is too large.

Our intraday results in Table 2a are not unusual. They mirror the range of estimates previously obtained in the literature over corresponding return frequencies. In particular, Engle et al. (1990) and Hamao et al. (1990) who primarily rely on returns over six hours or longer find evidence of volatility persistence that is consistent with estimates from daily data. In contrast, Baillie and Bollerslev (1991) and Foster and Viswanathan (1995), on using hourly and half-hourly returns, find much lower volatility persistence [32]. However, the volatility persistence measures appear to rebound at the higher frequencies e.g. Bollerslev and Domowitz (1993) report 5-minute GARCH(1, 1) estimates for $\alpha_{(k)} + \beta_{(k)}$ close to one but, as in Table 2a, $\hat{\alpha}_{(k)}$ seems too large. For the very highest frequencies, Locke and Sayers (1993) find that 1-minute returns generally display little volatility persistence. Conversely, Goodhart et al. (1993) detect very strong persistence in quote-by-quote data, but also find a marked decline in the persistence once information events are taken explicitly into account, illustrating how specific news arrivals may overwhelm the underlying conditional heteroskedasticity at the extremely high frequencies.

Our findings provide strong, albeit indirect, evidence in support of the conjecture that a contributing factor to the systematic variation in volatility estimates across return frequencies is the interaction between the previously well documented interdaily conditional heteroskedasticity and the intraday periodicity. For the highest frequencies the change in the intraday pattern will generally appear smooth between adjacent returns, and thus have little impact on the overall estimated degree of volatility persistence. However, as argued more formally below, the existence of short-lived intraday volatility components (in addition to the intraday periodicity) will tend to increase the dependence of $(\sigma_{t,n}^{k})^2$ on the

[32] Interestingly, Laux and Ng (1993) deviate from these studies by finding high persistence in half-hourly data for the CME currency futures. However, the futures market only operates during the most active trading in the U.S. segment of the foreign exchange interbank market and this represents a period of relative stability for the intraday volatility pattern.

lagged squared innovation, $(\epsilon_{t,n-1}^{k})^2$, relative to the overall volatility level, $(\sigma_{t,n-1}^{k})^2$, hence explaining the relatively large estimates for $\alpha_{(k)}$ at the shortest return intervals. For the intermediate $\frac{1}{2}$–$1\frac{1}{2}$ hour return models the change in the average volatility between sampling intervals will typically appear much more abrupt, resulting in significantly lower persistence measures. Beyond the 2-hour intervals the periodic pattern is averaged over a substantial part of the 24-hour trading day, and the intraday exchange rate estimates are generally closer to the implications obtained from daily models.

The results for the S&P 500 equity returns tell a similar story. The interdaily estimates in Table 3b are again broadly consistent with the a priori predictions based on the daily GARCH(1, 1) model [33]. Although the volatility persistence is higher than for the foreign exchange returns, $\hat{\alpha}_{(k)} + \hat{\beta}_{(k)}$ again displays a general smooth decline and the explicit persistence measures are fairly stable across the different return horizons. The discrepancy between the half lives, mean lags and median lags implied by the intradaily and interdaily returns are even stronger than for the foreign exchange rate data, however [34]. Moreover, the pattern in the intraday estimates for $\alpha_{(k)} + \beta_{(k)}$ reported in Table 2b is again erratic, reaching lows at the $\frac{1}{2}$-day ($k = 40$) and 20–25 minute ($k = 4, 5$) return horizons, and highs at the 40–50 minute ($k = 8, 10$) and 5-minute ($k = 1$) horizons. We conclude that the daily GARCH models conform closely to the theoretical predictions, but the strong intraday periodic patterns in volatility render the intradaily estimates highly variable and generally hard to interpret.

5. The dynamics of filtered and standardized intraday returns

This section proposes a general framework for modeling of high frequency return volatility that explicitly incorporates the effect of the intraday periodicity. The preceding section suggests that this is a prerequisite for meaningful time series analysis. Our approach is motivated by the stylized model in Section 3. While the model almost certainly is overly simplistic, the previous analysis suggests that the representation does capture the dominant features of our foreign exchange and equity return series and thus may serve as a reasonable first approximation.

[33] In this case the estimate for the daily MA(1) term equals 0.186, which is highly significant when judged by the corresponding asymptotic standard error of 0.012. Consequently the GARCH(1, 1) models for the other frequencies are, at best, approximate representations of the data generating process (see Drost and Nijman (1993) for a formal analysis).

[34] The previous footnote about the deletion of weekend exchange rate returns are even more pertinent here as both weekend and overnight equity returns are excluded. However, our informal analysis again found this to be inconsequential (see Andersen and Bollerslev, 1994).

Specifically, consider the following decomposition for the intraday returns,

$$R_{t,n} = E(R_{t,n}) + \frac{\sigma_t s_{t,n} Z_{t,n}}{N^{1/2}}, \tag{7}$$

where $E(R_{t,n})$ denotes the unconditional mean, and N refers to the number of return intervals per day. Notice that this represents a generalization of the model in Section 3, in that the periodic component for the nth intraday interval, $s_{t,n}$, is allowed to depend on the characteristics of trading day, t [35]. Given the absence of any economic theory for stipulating a particular parametric form for the intraday periodic structure, a flexible nonparametric procedure seems natural. Although no one procedure is clearly superior, the smooth cyclical patterns documented in Fig. 2a and b naturally lend themselves to estimation by the Fourier flexible functional form introduced by Gallant, 1981, 1982 [36]. In a related context, Dacorogna et al. (1993) have proposed estimating the periodicity in the activity in the foreign exchange market as the sum of three polynomials corresponding to the distinct geographical locations of the market. Returns measured on their resulting theta-time scale correspond closely to our filtered returns defined and analyzed below. However, one advantage of the approach advocated here is that it allows the shape of the periodic pattern in the market to also depend on the overall level of the volatility; a feature which turns out to be important for the equity market. Also, the combination of trigonometric functions and polynomial terms are likely to result in better approximation properties when estimating regularly recurring patterns. Furthermore, our approach for estimating $s_{t,n}$ utilizes the full time series dimension of the returns data, as opposed to simply estimating the average pattern across the trading day. Full details of the approach are provided in Appendix B. Meanwhile, it is clear from the estimated average intraday periodic patterns depicted in Fig. 6a and b, that the fitted values, $\hat{s}_{t,n}$, provide a close approximation to the overall volatility patterns in both markets. Of course, the usefulness of the procedure will ultimately depend upon the degree to which it is successful in identifying the periodic components in a temporal dimension as well. If so, the approach may serve as the basis for a nonlinear filtering procedure that could eliminate the periodic components prior to the analysis of any intraday return volatility dynamics [37].

[35] This feature is particularly important for the equity returns for which the general U-shaped volatility pattern is transformed into more of a J-shape on the highest volatility days (see Andersen and Bollerslev, 1994).

[36] This technique has previously been applied to financial return series in a different context by Pagan and Schwert (1990).

[37] This same methodology may also be used directly for prediction of future volatility over different intraday time intervals. Such intraday volatility prediction may be particularly important in the pricing and/or continuous re-balancing of hedged intraday options positions. We shall not pursue this issue any further here, however.

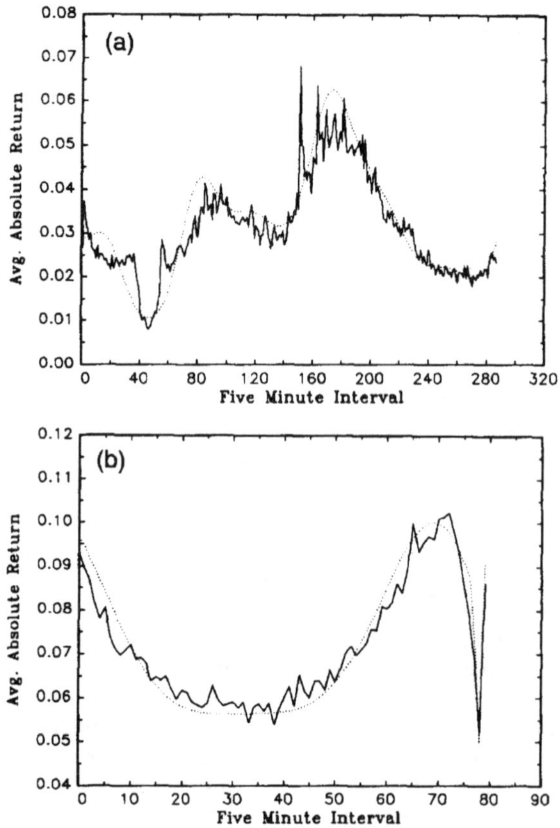

Fig. 6. Flexible Fourier functional form of intraday average absolute returns, (a) DM–$, (b) S&P 500.

5.1. Filtered foreign exchange returns

To further investigate these issues, define the filtered 5-minute return series; $\tilde{R}_{t,n} \equiv R_{t,n}/\hat{s}_{t,n}$ [38]. If the characterization of the 5-minute return series in Eq. (7) is perfect and the associated estimation error is negligible, then ignoring the impact of the weak first order return correlation, the filtered returns should conform more closely to the theoretical aggregation results for the GARCH(1, 1) model. We explicitly consider how well this hypothesis holds up, but we also keep in mind

[38] Alternatively, $\tilde{R}_{t,n}$ might also be mean adjusted. Since the mean return is practically zero, this is immaterial.

that the elimination of the main distorting effects of the intraday periodicity may bring out new features of the volatility process that were difficult to untangle prior to filtration.

First, we briefly summarize the main characteristics of the filtered series. While the mean and the standard deviation of these returns are virtually unchanged from Table 1a, both skewness and kurtosis are generally reduced by filtering the returns. For instance, the 5-minute skewness and kurtosis for $\tilde{R}_{t,n}$ equal 0.175 and 15.8, respectively. Interestingly, the evidence for negative return autocorrelations at the very highest frequencies becomes even more pronounced following the filtration, as measured by $\rho_1 = -0.090$ for the 5-minute returns. At the same time the first order absolute 5-minute return autocorrelations decline slightly to $\rho_1^A = 0.292$ [39]. The correlation structure for the absolute 5-minute filtered returns is further illustrated in Fig. 7a. The upper curves represent the correlogram for the raw returns, while the middle curves are for the filtered returns. The dramatic reduction in the periodic pattern is particularly striking for the longest lags. However, from the daily peaks in the 5 day correlogram it is clear that some periodicity remains, suggesting the presence of a stochastic periodic, or market specific, component in the intraday volatility [40]. Note also that the correlations for $|\tilde{R}_{t,n}|$ at the daily frequencies are always below the correlations for the raw absolute returns, $|R_{t,n}|$. This is consistent with the predictions from Eq. (5).

More direct evidence is provided by the estimated MA(1)–GARCH(1, 1) models reported in Table 4a. Compared to the results in Table 2a, the volatility parameters now display a much more coherent pattern across the return frequencies [41]. In accord with the theoretical aggregation results the estimates for $\alpha_{(k)} + \beta_{(k)}$ increase almost monotonically from the $\frac{1}{2}$ day to the 2 hour frequency. For the higher frequencies the theoretical predictions again begin to falter, however, although less starkly than before. The sum $\hat{\alpha}_{(k)} + \hat{\beta}_{(k)}$ remains high, but no longer increases monotonically and more importantly, $\hat{\alpha}_{(k)}$ starts to increase while $\hat{\beta}_{(k)}$ generally declines. These findings again should be interpreted in light of the absolute return autocorrelograms in Fig. 7a. The most striking feature is the initial rapid decay in the autocorrelations, followed by an extremely slow rate of decay thereafter. This pattern is not consistent with the exponential decay associated with a GARCH(1, 1) model for the 5-minute returns. Instead, these findings point to a slow hyperbolic rate of decay in the autocorrelation structure for the absolute returns, which is consistent with the presence of long-memory features in the

[39] See Andersen and Bollerslev for extensive documentation of the summary statistics for both filtered and standardized returns.

[40] The distinction between heat wave, or market specific, volatility as opposed to meteor shower, or global, volatility clustering was first discussed in Engle et al. (1990). This finding also points to the potential gains of more general dynamic periodic volatility type modeling (see e.g. Bollerslev and Ghysels, 1996).

[41] To conserve space, we do not report the half life or the mean and median lags.

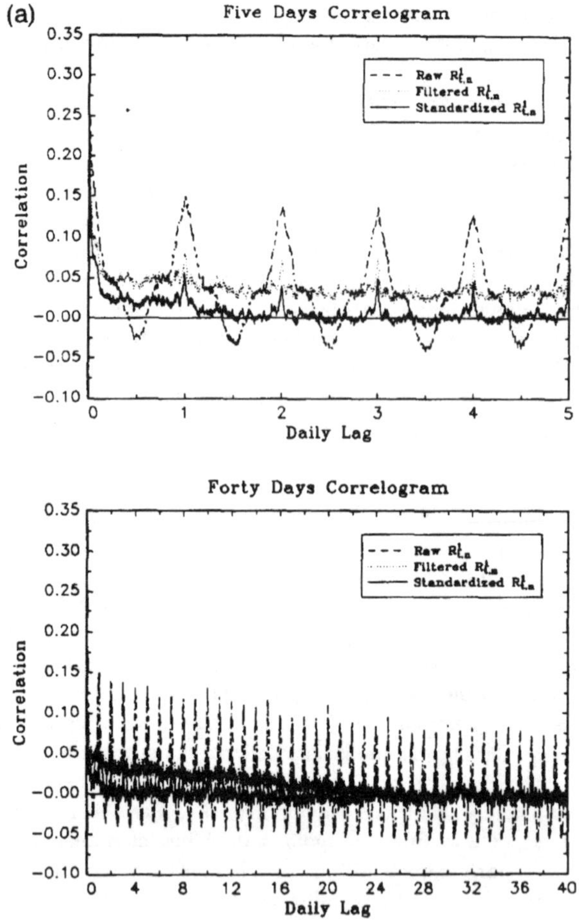

Fig. 7. Absolute returns, (a) DM–$, (b) S&P 500.

volatility process (see e.g. Baillie et al., 1996; Dacorogna et al., 1993; Ding et al., 1993). Note again the slightly higher peaks associated with the weekly frequencies.

Although the GARCH(1, 1) estimates for the high frequency filtered returns defy the theoretical predictions, the results are encouraging in terms of our ability to recover meaningful intraday volatility dynamics. In particular, by eliminating the deterministic periodicity we were able to uncover an interesting pattern in the absolute return correlogram which was largely invisible prior to the periodic filtering. A detailed investigation of the source of this phenomenon is well beyond

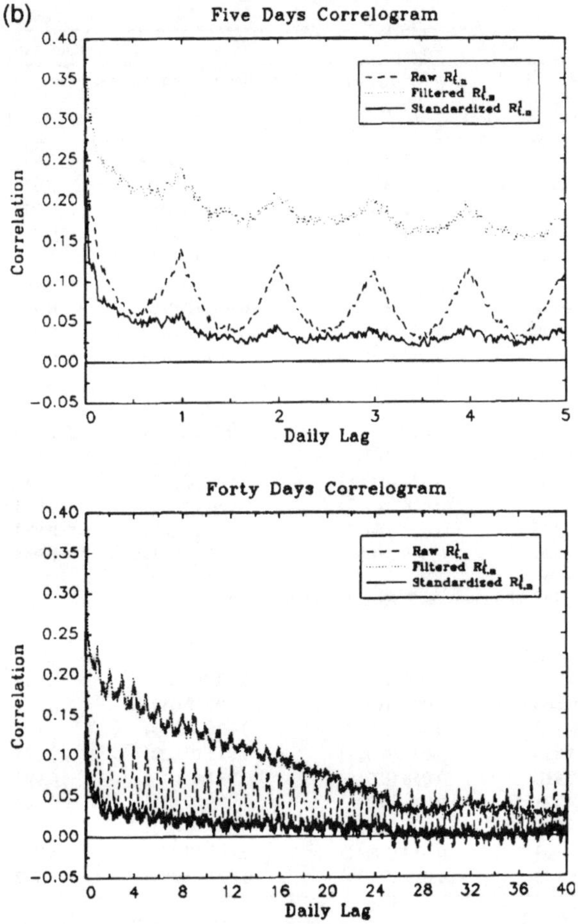

Fig. 7 (continued).

the scope of the present paper. However, we conjecture that the following factors have some impact on the observed correlation patterns. First, there may well be some positively cyclical correlated components left in the $|\tilde{R}_{t,n}|$ series, thus inducing spurious short-run dynamics in the return volatility. Second, and more importantly, the results also point to the potential importance of several distinct intraday volatility processes governed by e.g. economic announcements, the release of economic statistics, etc. each of which inherently may be of a less persistent nature than the volatility caused by changing trends in fundamental

Table 4

k	T/k	$\alpha_{(k)}$	$\beta_{(k)}$	$\alpha_{(k)}+\beta_{(k)}$
(a) MA(1)–GARCH(1, 1) models for filtered DM–$ exchange rate returns				
$\tilde{R}^k_{t,n} \equiv 100\cdot\Sigma_{i=(n-1)k+1,nk}\tilde{R}_{t,i} = \mu_{(k)} + \theta_{(k)}\epsilon^k_{t,n-1} + \epsilon^k_{t,n}\ (\sigma^k_{t,n})^2 = \omega_{(k)} + \alpha_{(k)}(\epsilon^k_{t,n-1})^2 + \beta_{(k)}(\sigma^k_{t,n-1})^2,\ t=1,2,\ldots,260,\ n=1,2,\ldots,288/k$				
1	74,880	0.176 (0.013)	0.795 (0.016)	0.971
2	37,440	0.167 (0.012)	0.787 (0.015)	0.954
3	24,960	0.172 (0.018)	0.756 (0.025)	0.928
4	18,720	0.171 (0.019)	0.746 (0.029)	0.917
6	12,480	0.135 (0.052)	0.788 (0.096)	0.923
8	9,360	0.064 (0.051)	0.904 (0.082)	0.968
9	8,320	0.043 (0.011)	0.938 (0.016)	0.981
12	6,240	0.032 (0.011)	0.953 (0.016)	0.985
16	4,680	0.033 (0.010)	0.951 (0.015)	0.984
18	4,160	0.030 (0.009)	0.951 (0.013)	0.981
24	3,120	0.020 (0.007)	0.969 (0.009)	0.989
32	2,340	0.023 (0.006)	0.967 (0.007)	0.990
36	2,080	0.022 (0.007)	0.964 (0.007)	0.986
48	1,560	0.022 (0.008)	0.966 (0.007)	0.987
72	1,040	0.028 (0.013)	0.950 (0.009)	0.978
96	780	0.029 (0.014)	0.951 (0.009)	0.980
144	520	0.040 (0.032)	0.915 (0.016)	0.955
(b) MA(1)-GARCH(1,1) models for filtered S&P 500 returns				
$\tilde{R}^k_{t,n} \equiv 100\cdot\Sigma_{i=(n-1)k+1,nk}\tilde{R}_{t,i} = \mu_{(k)} + \theta_{(k)}\epsilon^k_{t,n-1} + \epsilon^k_{t,n}\ (\sigma^k_{t,n})^2 = \omega_{(k)} + \alpha_{(k)}(\epsilon^k_{t,n-1})^2 + \beta_{(k)}(\sigma^k_{t,n-1})^2,\ t=1,2,\ldots,991,\ n=1,2,\ldots,80/k$				
1	79,280	0.096 (0.009)	0.892 (0.011)	0.988
2	39,640	0.086 (0.012)	0.905 (0.014)	0.991
4	19,820	0.088 (0.017)	0.904 (0.019)	0.992
5	15,856	0.071 (0.021)	0.923 (0.022)	0.994
8	9,910	0.058 (0.015)	0.937 (0.016)	0.994
10	7,928	0.058 (0.016)	0.936 (0.017)	0.994
16	4,955	0.109 (0.060)	0.869 (0.074)	0.978
20	3,964	0.084 (0.042)	0.893 (0.054)	0.977
40	1,982	0.099 (0.039)	0.873 (0.053)	0.972

(a) See Table 2a for construction of the raw return series. The method for obtaining the filtered returns, $\tilde{R}_{t,i}$, is described in the main text.
(b) See Table 2b for the construction of the raw return series. The method for obtaining the filtered returns, $\tilde{R}_{t,i}$, is described in the main text.

economic factors such as technology and productivity [42]. These distinct sources of volatility persistence could simultaneously influence the return series, resulting in a mixture distribution with different implications for the character of the short- and

[42] The distinct short-run volatility patterns induced by regularly scheduled macroeconomic announcements have been analyzed by Ederington and Lee (1993).

long-run dynamics. A promising first attempt at modeling this interaction between the volatility processes at different time resolutions within a unified framework have been suggested by Müller et al. (1995). In their so-called heterogeneous ARCH, or HARCH, model the volatility at the highest frequency is determined by the sum of numerous ARCH type processes defined over courser time intervals, where each of these components in turn may be linked to the actions of different types of traders with varying time horizons [43].

5.2. Standardized foreign exchange returns

The conjectures underlying a components type formulation of the volatility process are further reinforced by our analysis of the standardized 5-minute returns; $\hat{R}_{t,n} \equiv R_{t,n}/(\hat{\sigma}_t \hat{s}_{t,n})$. If our model provides a good approximation to the data generating process, then this series should display little ARCH effects at daily and lower frequencies, and the intraday ARCH effects should diminish. Consistent with this prediction, the absolute return autocorrelations at the lowest intraday frequencies have been reduced markedly. This is also manifest in the lower curves in Fig. 7a, which depict the correlograms for $|\hat{R}_{t,n}|$. Apart from small spikes associated with remaining stochastic periodicity at the daily frequency, the correlations for the absolute returns are generally close to zero beyond the two day lag. Thus, the daily GARCH(1, 1) volatility estimates appear to provide quite satisfactory estimates for the interday volatility dynamics [44]. At the same time, Fig. 7a is also indicative of important short-run dynamics that necessarily are unaccounted for by the daily GARCH(1, 1) volatility estimates. This again lends support to our conjecture of distinct short-run, or intraday, components in the fundamental return volatility generating process. The MA(1)–GARCH(1, 1) estimates for the standardized returns in Table 5a reinforce this interpretation by exhibiting a sharp decline in $\hat{\alpha}_{(k)} + \hat{\beta}_{(k)}$ as the return horizon increases from five minutes to one hour. In fact, beyond the one hour sampling frequency, the volatility clustering is sufficiently weak that the GARCH(1, 1) specification breaks down, and only ARCH(1) or homoskedastic MA(1) models are estimated.

5.3. Filtered equity returns

We now turn to the corresponding findings for the S&P 500 returns. In interpreting the results, it is important to recognize that the estimated intraday periodicity now involves interaction terms between the daily volatility level and

[43] Stationary conditions for this new class of time series models are developed in Darorogna et al. (1995).

[44] Of course, this apparent lack of any significant long-run correlations in the standardized returns may be due to the relatively short sample of only one year. With a longer span of data the GARCH(1, 1) model will most likely fail to capture all the low frequency dynamics (see e.g. Baillie et al., 1996).

Table 5

k	T/k	$\alpha_{(k)}$	$\beta_{(k)}$	$\alpha_{(k)}+\beta_{(k)}$
(a) MA(1)–GARCH(1, 1) models for standardized DM–$ exchange rate				
$\hat{R}^k_{t,n} \equiv 100 \cdot \Sigma_{i=(n-1)k+1,nk} \tilde{R}_{t,i} = \mu_{(k)} + \theta_{(k)}\epsilon^k_{t,n-1} + \epsilon^k_{t,n}\ (\sigma^k_{t,n})^2 = \omega_{(k)} + \alpha_{(k)}(\epsilon^k_{t,n-1})^2 + \beta_{(k)}(\sigma^k_{t,n-1})^2,\ t=1,2,\ldots,260,\ n=1,2,\ldots,288/k$				
1	74,880	0.182 (0.014)	0.766 (0.021)	0.948
2	37,440	0.167 (0.015)	0.760 (0.029)	0.927
3	24,960	0.172 (0.019)	0.706 (0.037)	0.877
4	18,720	0.177 (0.016)	0.666 (0.034)	0.843
6	12,480	0.173 (0.023)	0.603 (0.047)	0.776
8	9,360	0.177 (0.028)	0.484 (0.105)	0.661
9	8,320	0.123 (0.030)	0.607 (0.143)	0.729
12	6,240	0.158 (0.028)	0.376 (0.071)	0.534
16	4,680	0.184 (0.034)	—	0.184
18	4,160	0.089 (0.026)	—	0.089
24	3,120	0.088 (0.034)	—	0.088
32	2,340	0.072 (0.031)	—	0.072
36	2,080	0.083 (0.049)	—	0.083
48	1,560	—	—	—
72	1,040	—	—	—
96	780	—	—	—
144	520	—	—	—
(b) MA(1)–GARCH(1, 1) models for standardized S&P 500 returns				
$\hat{R}^k_{t,n} \equiv 100 \cdot \Sigma_{i=(n-1)k+1,nk} \tilde{R}_{t,i} = \mu_{(k)} + \theta_{(k)}\epsilon^k_{t,n-1} + \epsilon^k_{t,n}\ (\sigma^k_{t,n})^2 = \omega_{(k)} + \alpha_{(k)}(\epsilon^k_{t,n-1})^2 + \beta_{(k)}(\sigma^k_{t,n-1})^2,\ t=1,2,\ldots,991,\ n=1,2,\ldots,80/k$				
1	79,280	0.095 (0.007)	0.877 (0.012)	0.973
2	39,640	0.107 (0.012)	0.841 (0.022)	0.949
4	19,820	0.127 (0.021)	0.764 (0.053)	0.890
5	15,856	0.124 (0.024)	0.765 (0.047)	0.889
8	9,910	0.117 (0.027)	0.727 (0.070)	0.843
10	7,928	0.126 (0.023)	0.681 (0.047)	0.807
16	4,955	0.215 (0.074)	0.512 (0.051)	0.727
20	3,964	0.159 (0.096)	0.551 (0.037)	0.710
40	1,982	0.250 (0.160)	—	0.250

(a) See Table 2a for construction of the raw return series. The method for standardizing the returns, $\tilde{R}_{t,i}$, is described in the main text.
(b) See Table 2b for construction of the raw return series. The standardized returns, $\tilde{R}_{t,i}$, are generated as described in the main text.

the Fourier functional form, so that not only the level but also the shape of the volatility pattern varies with σ_t. Thus, our stylized deterministic periodic model discussed in Section 3 is not strictly valid in this context i.e. generally $s_{t,n} \neq s_{\tau,n}$ for $t \neq \tau$. Counter to the results for the DM–$ returns, this time-varying volatility component may weaken the autocorrelations for the raw absolute returns as, effectively, additional noise is injected into the returns process. Fig. 7b seem to indicate that this is indeed the case, as the correlogram for the filtered absolute returns, $|\tilde{R}_{t,n}|$, lies substantially above that for the raw series, $|R_{t,n}|$. Interestingly, this does not just occur at the 5-minute sampling frequency; the absolute return autocorrelation across the nine different intraday frequencies, as measured by ρ_1^A, $Q^A(10)$ and VR^A, are all markedly higher than the corresponding statistics for the raw returns in Table 1b [45]. This is also in line with the MA(1)–GARCH(1, 1) estimation results reported in Table 5b. The parameter estimates obtained as we move from the $\frac{1}{2}$ day to the 40-minute return horizon are again consistent with the theory. Thereafter, the sum $\hat{\alpha}_{(k)}$ and $\hat{\beta}_{(k)}$ decay slightly, but more importantly $\hat{\alpha}_{(k)}$ starts to increase. However, all the intraday estimates now consistently point towards a very high degree of volatility persistence and in all instances $\hat{\alpha}_{(k)} + \hat{\beta}_{(k)}$ are higher than the estimates for the raw return series in Table 2b. Note also, that in line with the findings for the DM–$ returns, the 5 day correlogram in Fig. 7b for the 5-minute filtered S&P 500 returns still retains a distinct periodic pattern, indicating the presence of even more complicated stochastic volatility components. Nonetheless, the simple filtering procedure again succeeds in eliminating a large proportion of the systematic intraday variation in the absolute returns and in so doing has unveiled a cleaner and starkly different picture of the volatility dynamics.

5.4. Standardized equity returns

In contrast to the results for the DM–$, the first order autocorrelations for the standardized absolute returns for the S&P 500, $|\hat{R}^k_{t,n}|$, remain highly significant for the lower intraday frequencies. Even at the $\frac{1}{2}$ day return frequency, $\rho_1^A = 0.094$ exceed the corresponding asymptotic standard error by more than a factor four. This is also confirmed by the much higher $\alpha_{(k)} + \beta_{(k)}$ estimates for the intraday GARCH(1, 1) models for $\hat{R}^k_{t,n}$ given in Table 5b. Similarly, the correlograms in Fig. 7b for the standardized returns indicate a much higher degree of volatility persistence in the 5-minute S&P 500 returns than was the case for DM–$ returns. In fact, the standardized absolute return correlogram stays mostly positive for the first 22 trading days, or about a month. This indication of more persistent volatility dynamics is likely attributable to the longer time span for the equity data. For example, Dacorogna et al. (1993) find that the absolute standardized return autocorrelations remain positive for one month when using 20-minute DM–$ data over a four year sample. Additionally, from Guillaume (1994) it is evident that our ability to detect significant long-horizon absolute return correlations is intimately linked to the length of the sampling period. Hence, although the interdaily GARCH(1, 1) model may capture a large portion of the day-to-day volatility clustering, the model's deficiency in dealing with long-memory behavior necessarily becomes more transparent when the time span of the data increases.

[45] For instance, ρ_1^A for the aggregated filtered returns, $|\tilde{R}^k_{t,n}|$, equal 0.371, 0.379, 0.341, 0.335, 0.305, 0.303, 0.292, 0.290 and 0.292 for $k = 1, 2, 4, 5, 8, 10, 16, 20$ and 40, respectively.

We conclude, that in spite of important institutional differences in the markets and the associated intradaily volatility patterns, there is strong indications that the volatility processes for the foreign exchange and the U.S. equity market share several important qualitative dynamic features. Moreover, these characteristics were largely invisible prior to our filtration of the intraday periodic structures in the high frequency return series. At the same time interesting differences between the average volatility level and volatility persistence in the two markets also emerge. These conclusions would be next to impossible to reach from the, at first sight, rather perplexing estimates obtained directly from the raw high frequency returns.

6. Concluding remarks

Our analysis of the intraday volatility patterns in the DM–$ foreign exchange and S&P 500 equity markets documents how traditional time series methods applied to raw high frequency returns may give rise to erroneous inference about the return volatility dynamics. Explicit allowance for the influence of the strong periodicity, as exemplified by our flexible Fourier form, is a necessary requirement for discovery of the salient intraday volatility features. Moreover, adjusting for the pronounced periodic structure appears critical in uncovering the complex link between the short- and long-run return components, which may help to explain the apparent conflict between the long-memory volatility characteristics observed in interday data and the rapid short-run decay associated with news arrivals in intraday data. More directly, however, our findings have immediate and important implications for a large range of issues in the rapidly growing literature using very high frequency financial data. Examples include investigations into the lead–lag relationship among returns and volatility both within and across different markets, the effect of cross listings of securities, the fundamental determinants behind the volatility clustering phenomenon, the development of real time trading and investment strategies and the evaluation of continuous option valuation and hedging decisions. Only future research will reveal the extent of the biases induced into these studies by the neglect of intraday periodic components.

Acknowledgements

We would like to thank Richard T. Bailie, the editor, an anonymous referee, Dominique Guillaume, Robert J. Hodrick, Charles Jones, Stephen J. Taylor, Kenneth F. Wallis, along with seminar participants at the Olsen and Associates Research Institute for Applied Economics, the workshop on 'Market Micro Structure' at the Aarhus School of Business, the Fall 1994 NBER Asset Pricing Meeting at the Wharton School, the HFDF-I Conference in Zürich, the 7th World

Congress of the Econometric Society in Tokyo, Duke University and the University of California at Santa Barbara for helpful comments.

Appendix A. Data description

A.1. The Deutschemark–U.S. dollar exchange rate data

The DM–\$ exchange rate data consist of all the quotes that appeared on the interbank Reuters network during the October 1, 1992 through September 29, 1993 sample period. The data were collected and provided by Olsen and Associates. Each quote contains a bid and an ask price along with the time to the nearest even second. Approximately 0.36% of the 1,472,241 raw quotes were filtered out using the algorithm described in Dacorogna et al. (1993). During the most active trading hours, an average of five or more valid quotes arrive per minute; see Bollerslev and Domowitz (1993). The exchange rate figure for each 5-minute interval is determined as the interpolated average between the preceding and immediately following quotes weighted linearly by their inverse relative distance to the desired point in time. For instance, suppose that the bid–ask pair at 14.14.56 was 1.6055–1.6065, while the next quote at 14.15.02 was 1.6050–1.6055. The interpolated price at 14.15.00 would then be $\exp\{1/3 \cdot [\ln(1.6055) + \ln(1.6065)]/2 + 2/3 \cdot [\ln(1.6050) + \ln(1.6055)]/2\} = 1.6055$. The nth 5-minute return for day t, $R_{t,n}$, is then simply defined as the difference between the midpoint of the logarithmic bid and ask at these appropriately spaced time intervals. This definition of the returns has the advantage, that it is symmetric with respect to the denomination of the exchange rate. However, as noted by Müller et al. (1990), the numerical difference from the logarithm of the middle price is negligible. All 288 intervals during the 24-hour daily trading cycle are used. However, in order to avoid confounding the evidence in the correlation analysis conducted below by the decidedly slower trading patterns over weekends, all the returns from Friday 21.00 Greenwich mean time (GMT) through Sunday 21.00 GMT were excluded (see Bollerslev and Domowitz (1993) for a detailed analysis of the quote activity in the DM–\$ interbank market and a justification for this 'weekend' definition). Similarly, to preserve the number of returns associated with one week we make no corrections for any worldwide or country specific holidays that occurred during the sample period. All in all, this leaves us with a sample of 260 days, for a total of 74,880 5-minute intraday return observations i.e. $R_{t,n}$, $n = 1, 2, \ldots, 288$, $t = 1, 2, \ldots, 260$.

A.2. The standard and poor's 500 stock index futures data

The intraday S&P 500 futures data are based on 'quote capture' information provided by the Chicago Mercantile Exchange (CME) from January 2, 1986 through December 31, 1989. The data specify the time, to the nearest 10 seconds and the exact price of the S&P 500 futures transaction whenever the price differs from the previously recorded price [46]. The calculation of the returns is based on the last recorded logarithmic prices for the nearby futures contract over consecutive five minute intervals. The price record covers the full trading day in the futures market from 8.30 a.m. (central standard time) to 3.15 p.m. Although, the New York Stock Exchange closes at 3.00 p.m., we retain the last three 5-minute returns from the futures market in the analysis reported on below. The first return for the trading day, i.e. from 8:30 to 8:35 a.m., constitutes another unusual time interval. This period incorporates adjustments to the information accumulated overnight, and consequently displays a much higher average return variability than any other 5-minute interval. In effect, this is not a 5-minute return, and we therefore delete it in the subsequent analysis. Alternatively, it would be possible to account for this special return interval using dummy variables. However, any such procedure is invariably ad hoc in nature. Furthermore, informal investigations reveal little sensitivity to the exact treatment of the overnight returns. We thus elect to work exclusively with the 5-minute returns. Following Chan et al. (1991), we also exclude the October 15 through November 13, 1987 time period around the stock market crash due to the frequent trading suspensions. Outside these four weeks trading suspensions were rare, but did occur. In these instances the missing prices were determined by linear interpolation, leading to identical returns over each of the intermediate intervals. This obviously smoothes the series over the missing data points which will mitigate the effect of sharp price changes subsequent to a trading suspension. Experimentation with exclusion of trading days with missing observations indicate that the findings pertaining to the degree of volatility persistence reported on here are virtually unaffected by this interpolation. All in all, these corrections result in a sample of 991 days, each consisting of 80 intraday 5-minute returns, for a total of 79,280 observations i.e. $R_{t,n}$, $n = 1, 2, \ldots, 80$, $t = 1, 2, \ldots, 991$.

Appendix B. Flexible Fourier form modeling of intraday periodic volatility components

From Eq. (7), define,

$$x_{t,n} \equiv 2\log[|R_{t,n} - E(R_{t,n})|] - \log \sigma_t^2 + \log N = \log s_{t,n}^2 + \log Z_{t,n}^2. \tag{A.1}$$

[46] We are grateful to G. Andrew Karolyi for providing us with this 5-minute price series. The same set of data has also been analyzed from a different perspective in Chan et al. (1991).

Our modeling approach is then based on a non-linear regression in the intraday time interval, n, and the daily volatility factor, σ_t,

$$x_{t,n} = f(\theta; \sigma_t, n) + u_{t,n}, \tag{A.2}$$

where the error, $u_{t,n} \equiv \log Z_{t,n}^2 - E(\log Z_{t,n}^2)$, is i.i.d. mean zero. In the actual implementation the non-linear regression function is approximated by the following parametric expression,

$$f(\theta; \sigma_t, n) = \sum_{j=0}^{J} \sigma_t^j \left[\mu_{0j} + \mu_{1j}\frac{n}{N_1} + \mu_{2j}\frac{n^2}{N_2} + \sum_{i=1}^{D} \lambda_{ij} I_{n=d_i} + \sum_{i=1}^{P}\left(\gamma_{pj}\cos\frac{pn2\pi}{N} + \delta_{pj}\sin\frac{pn2\pi}{N}\right)\right], \tag{A.3}$$

where $N_1 \equiv N^{-1}\Sigma_{i=1,N} i = (N+1)/2$ and $N_2 \equiv N^{-1}\Sigma_{i=1,N} i^2 = (N+1)(N+2)/6$ are normalizing constants. For $J=0$ and $D=0$, Eq. (A.3) reduces to the standard flexible Fourier functional form proposed by Gallant (1981, 1982). Allowing for $J \geq 1$ and thus a possible interaction effect between σ_t^j and the shape of the periodic pattern might be important in some markets, however. Each of the corresponding J flexible Fourier forms are parameterized by a quadratic component (terms with μ-coefficients) and a number of sinusoids (the γ- and δ-coefficients). Moreover, it may be advantageous to also include time specific dummies for applications in which some intraday intervals do not fit well within the overall regular periodic pattern (the λ-coefficients).

Practical estimation is most easily accomplished using a two-step procedure. Firstly, a generated $x_{t,n}$ series, $\hat{x}_{t,n}$, is obtained by replacing $E(R_{t,n})$ with the sample mean of the returns, $\bar{R}_{t,n}$ and σ_t with the estimates from a daily volatility model, say $\hat{\sigma}_t$. Substituting $\hat{\sigma}_t$ for σ_t and treating $\hat{x}_{t,n}$ as the dependent variable in the regression defined by Eqs. (A.2) and (A.3) allow the parameters to be estimated by ordinary least squares (OLS). Note that from Eq. (3), δ_t^2 represents an estimate of $M(s^2)\sigma_t^2$, so that after substitution for σ_t in Eq. (A.2), the term $-\log M(s^2)$ is implicitly included in the constant term in Eq. (A.3), μ_{00}. Let $\hat{f}_{t,n} \equiv f(\hat{\theta}; \hat{\sigma}_t, n)$ denote the resulting estimate for the right hand side of Eq. (A.3) [47]. The normalization $T^{-1}\Sigma_{n=1,N}\Sigma_{t=1,[T/N]} s_{t,n} \equiv 1$, where $[T/N]$ denotes the number of trading days in the sample, then suggests the following estimator of the intraday periodic component for interval n on day t,

$$\hat{s}_{t,n} = \frac{T \cdot \exp\left(\hat{f}_{t,n}/2\right)}{\Sigma_{t=1}^{[T/N]}\Sigma_{n=1}^{N}\exp\left(\hat{f}_{t,n}/2\right)}. \tag{A.4}$$

Note that although the periodic modeling procedure is designed for fitting the

[47] Given consistent estimates for $\hat{\sigma}_t$, the resulting parameter estimates will generally be consistent. However, the use of generated regressors may result in a downward bias in the conventional OLS standard errors for the parameter estimates (see Pagan, 1984).

average volatility pattern across the N intraday intervals, the second-stage estimation of Eq. (A.3) is based on a time series regression that include all T intraday returns. Utilizing this additional information in the data rather than simply fitting the average intraday pattern, enhances the efficiency of the estimation.

The first step of our procedure involves the determination of the daily volatility factor estimates i.e. $\hat{\sigma}_t$. Given the relative success of the daily MA(1)–GARCH(1, 1) models in explaining the aggregation results for the interdaily frequencies in both markets, this appears to be a natural choice. Next, the number of interaction terms, J and the truncation lag for the Fourier expansion, P, must be determined. This is done primarily on the basis of parsimony i.e. for each of the return series we choose the model that best matches the basic shape of the periodic pattern with the fewest number of parameters. The resulting estimates for the DM–\$ returns with $J=0$ and $P=6$ are,

$$\hat{f}_{t,n} = \begin{bmatrix} \underset{(1.06)}{0.72} & -\underset{(-4.14)}{8.39}\dfrac{n}{N_1} & +\underset{(4.14)}{5.59}\dfrac{n^2}{N_2} & \\ -\underset{(-6.15)}{2.51}\cos\dfrac{2\pi n}{N} & -\underset{(-10.44)}{0.40}\sin\dfrac{2\pi n}{N} & -\underset{(-3.71)}{0.38}\cos\dfrac{2\pi 2n}{N} & +\underset{(2.70)}{0.06}\sin\dfrac{2\pi 2n}{N} \\ +\underset{(8.79)}{0.42}\cos\dfrac{2\pi 3n}{N} & -\underset{(-4.89)}{0.09}\sin\dfrac{2\pi 3n}{N} & -\underset{(-0.53)}{0.02}\cos\dfrac{2\pi 4n}{N} & +\underset{(20.48)}{0.35}\sin\dfrac{2\pi 4n}{N} \\ -\underset{(-5.38)}{0.12}\cos\dfrac{2\pi 5n}{N} & +\dfrac{0.22}{(13.35)}\sin\dfrac{2\pi 5n}{N} & -\underset{(-12.67)}{0.23}\cos\dfrac{2\pi 6n}{N} & +\underset{(0.45)}{0.01}\sin\dfrac{2\pi 6n}{N} \end{bmatrix}$$

where the numbers in parentheses indicate heteroskedastic robust t-statistics. It is evident from the corresponding fit in Fig. 6a, that this representation provides an excellent overall characterization of the average intradaily periodicity in the DM–\$ market. Consistent with Fig. 2a, the basic shape of the periodic pattern appears invariant to the daily volatility level i.e. $J=0$.

In contrast, our preferred model, the S&P 500, returns sets $J=1$ and $P=2$,

$$\hat{f}_{t,n} = \begin{bmatrix} -\underset{(-3.03)}{1.85} & -\underset{(1.62)}{3.07}\dfrac{n}{N_1} & -\underset{(-2.05)}{2.68}\dfrac{n^2}{N_2} & \\ -\underset{(-0.53)}{0.16}\, I_{n=d_1} & -\underset{(-1.83)}{0.62}\, I_{n=d_2} & +\underset{(2.99)}{1.11}\, I_{n=d_3} & \\ +\underset{(3.11)}{1.18}\cos\dfrac{2\pi n}{N} & -\underset{(-6.14)}{0.59}\sin\dfrac{2\pi n}{N} & +\underset{(2.94)}{0.28}\cos\dfrac{2\pi 2n}{N} & -\underset{(-2.31)}{0.14}\sin\dfrac{2\pi 2n}{N} \end{bmatrix}$$
$$+\hat{\sigma}_t \begin{bmatrix} -\underset{(0.95)}{0.54} & -\underset{(-0.98)}{1.73}\dfrac{n}{N_1} & +\underset{(1.29)}{1.57}\dfrac{n^2}{N_2} & \\ -\underset{(-0.39)}{0.11}\, I_{n=d_1} & -\underset{(-0.97)}{0.30}\, I_{n=d_2} & -\underset{(-2.02)}{0.69}\, I_{n=d_3} & \\ -\underset{(-1.06)}{0.37}\cos\dfrac{2\pi n}{N} & +\underset{(1.30)}{0.12}\sin\dfrac{2\pi n}{N} & -\underset{(-1.97)}{0.17}\cos\dfrac{2\pi 2n}{N} & -\underset{(-0.50)}{0.03}\sin\dfrac{2\pi 2n}{N} \end{bmatrix}$$

Although few of the coefficients in the expansion corresponding to $J=1$ are individually significant, leaving out the interaction effect results in a seemingly inferior overall fit. As seen in Fig. 2b, the volatility profile for the last fifteen minutes of trading (intervals 78, 79 and 80) shows an abrupt change from the overall smooth intraday pattern. Three dummy variables are included to minimize the distortions that may otherwise arise from this distinct period i.e. $d_1 = 78$, $d_2 = 79$ and $d_3 = 80$. The resulting fit depicted in Fig. 6b again testifies to the success of this relatively simple procedure for modeling the periodicity in intraday financial market volatility.

References

Admati, A.R., Pfleiderer, P., 1988. A theory of intraday patterns: Volume and price variability. Review of Financial Studies 1, 3–40.

Admati, A.R., Pfleiderer, P., 1989. Divide and conquer: A theory of intraday and day-of-the-week mean effects. Review of Financial Studies 2, 189–224.

Andersen, T.G., 1994. Stochastic autoregressive volatility: A framework for volatility modeling. Mathematical Finance 4, 75–102.

Andersen, T.G., 1996. Return volatility and trading volume: An information flow interpretation of stochastic volatility. Journal of Finance 51, 169–204.

Andersen, T.G., Bollerslev, T., 1994. Intraday seasonality and volatility persistence in foreign exchange and equity markets. Working Paper #186. Department of Finance, J.L. Kellogg Graduate School of Management, Northwestern University.

Baillie, R.T., Bollerslev, T., 1989. The message in daily exchange rates: A conditional variance tale. Journal of Business and Economic Statistics 7, 297–305.

Baillie, R.T., Bollerslev, T., 1991. Intra-day and inter-market volatility in foreign exchange rates. Review of Economic Studies 58, 565–585.

Baillie, R.T., Bollerslev, T., Mikkelsen, H.O.Æ., 1996. Fractionally integrated generalized autoregressive conditional heteroskedasticity. Journal of Econometrics, forthcoming.

Barclay, M.J., Litzenberger, R.H., Warner, J.R., 1990. Private information, trading volume and stock-return variances. Review of Financial Studies 3, 233–253.

Black, F., 1976. Studies of stock market volatility changes. Proceedings of the American Statistical Association. Business and Economic Statistics Section, pp. 177–181.

Bollerslev, T., 1986. Generalized autoregressive conditional heteroskedasticity. Journal of Econometrics 31, 307–327.

Bollerslev, T., Chou, R.Y., Kroner, K.F., 1992. ARCH modeling in finance. Journal of Econometrics 52, 5–59.

Bollerslev, T., Domowitz, I., 1993. Trading patterns and prices in the interbank foreign exchange market. Journal of Finance 48, 1421–1443.

Bollerslev, T. and Engle, R.F., 1993. Common persistence in in conditional variances. Econometrica 61, 167–186.

Bollerslev, T., Engle, R.F., Nelson, D.B., 1994. ARCH models. In: Engle, R.F., McFadden, D. (Eds.), Handbook of Econometrics, vol.4. Elsevier Science B.V., Amsterdam.

Bollerslev, T., Ghysels, E., 1996. Periodic autoregressive conditional heteroskedasticity. Journal of Business and Economic Statistics 14, 139–151.

Bollerslev, T., Melvin, M., 1994. Bid–ask spreads and volatility in the foreign exchange market: An empirical analysis. Journal of International Economics 36, 355–372.

Bollerslev, T., Wooldridge, J.M., 1992. Quasi-maximum likelihood estimation of dynamic models with time varying covariances. Econometric Reviews 11, 143–172.

Brock, W.A., Kleidon, A.W., 1992. Periodic market closure and trading volume. Journal of Economic Dynamics and Control 16, 451–489.

Campbell, J.Y., Hentschel, L., 1992. No news is good news: An asymmetric model of changing volatility in stock returns. Journal of Financial Economics 31, 281–318.

Chan, K., Chan, K.C., Karolyi, G.A., 1991. Intraday volatility in the stock index and stock index futures market. Review of Financial Studies 4, 657–684.

Chang, E.C., Jain, P.C., Locke, P.R., 1995. S&P 500 index futures volatility and price around the NYSE close. Journal of Business 68, 61–84.

Christie, A.A., 1982. The stochastic behavior of common stock variances: Value, leverage and interest rate effects. Journal of Financial Economics 10, 407–432.

Clark, P.K., 1973. A subordinated stochastic process model with finite variance for speculative prices. Econometrica 41, 135–155.

Darorogna, M.M., Müller, U.A., Embrechts, P., Samorodnitsky, G., 1995. Moment conditions for HARCH(k) models. Working Paper. Olsen and Associates, Research Institute for Applied Economics, Zürich, Switzerland.

Dacorogna, M.M., Müller, U.A., Nagler, R.J., Olsen, R.B., Pictet, O.V., 1993. A geographical model for the daily and weekly seasonal volatility in the foreign exchange market. Journal of International Money and Finance 12, 413–438.

Ding, Z., Granger, C.W.J., Engle, R.F., 1993. A long memory property of stock market returns and a new model. Journal of Empirical Finance 1, 83–106.

Drost, F.C., Nijman, T.E., 1993. Temporal aggregation of GARCH processes. Econometrica 61, 909–927.

Drost, F.C., Werker, B.J.M., 1996. Closing the GARCH gap: Continuous time GARCH modeling. Journal of Econometrics 74, 31–57.

Ederington, L.H., Lee, J.H., 1993. How markets process information: News releases and volatility. Journal of Finance 48, 1161–1191.

Engle, R.F., 1982. Autoregressive conditional heteroskedasticity with estimates of the variance of United Kingdom inflation. Econometrica 50, 987–1007.

Engle, R.F., Ito, T., Lin, W.-L., 1990. Meteor showers or heat waves? Heteroskedastic intra-daily volatility in the foreign exchange market. Econometrica 58, 525–542.

Foster, F.D., Viswanathan, S., 1990. A theory of the interday variations in volume, variance and trading costs in security markets. Review of Financial Studies 3, 593–624.

Foster, F.D., Viswanathan, S., 1995. Can speculative trading explain the volume–volatility relation?. Journal of Business and Economic Statistics 13, 379–396.

Gallant, A.R., 1981. On the bias in flexible functional forms and an essentially unbiased form: The Fourier flexible form. Journal of Econometrics 15, 211–245.

Gallant, A.R., 1982. Unbiased determination of production technologies. Journal of Econometrics 20, 285–323.

Gallant, A.R., Hsieh, D.A., Tauchen, G.E., 1991. On fitting a recalcitrant series: The pound/dollar exchange rate, 1974–83. In: Barnett, W.A., Powell, J., Tauchen, G.E. (Eds.), Nonparametric and Semiparametric Methods in Econometrics and Statistics. Proceedings of the Fifth International Symposium in Economic Theory and Econometrics. Cambridge University Press, pp. 199–240.

Gallant, A.R., Rossi, P.E., Tauchen, G.E., 1993. Nonlinear dynamic structures. Econometrica 61, 871–908.

Ghose, D., Kroner, K.F., 1994. Temporal aggregation of high frequency data. Unpublished manuscript. Department of Economics, University of Arizona.

Ghysels, E., Jasiak, J., 1994. Stochastic volatility and time deformation: An application to trading volume and leverage effects. Unpublished manuscript. C.R.D.E., Université de Montreal.

Goodhart, C.A.E., Hall, S.G., Henry, S.G.B., Pesaran, B., 1993. News effects in a high-Frequency model of the sterling–dollar exchange rate. Journal of Applied Econometrics 8, 1–13.

Granger, C.W.J., Ding, Z., 1996. Some properties of absolute returns: An alternative measure of risk. Annales d'Economie et de Statistique 40, 67–92.

Guillaume, D.M., 1994. Forecasting foreign exchange rate price changes conditional on volatility: A heterogeneous time horizon approach. Unpublished manuscript. Department of Economics, Catholic University of Leuven.

Hamao, Y., Masulis, R.W., Ng, V., 1990. Correlations in price changes and volatility across international stock markets. Review of Financial Studies 3, 281–307.

Harris, L., 1986a. A transaction data study of weekly and intradaily patterns in stock returns. Journal of Financial Economics 16, 99–117.

Harris, L., 1986b. Cross-security tests of the mixture of distributions hypothesis. Journal of Financial and Quantitative Analysis 21, 39–46.

Harris, L., 1987. Transaction data tests of the mixture of distributions hypothesis. Journal of Financial and Quantitative Analysis 22, 127–141.

Harvey, A.C., 1981. The Econometric Analysis of Time Series. Philip Allan, Oxford.

Harvey, C.R., Huang, R.D., 1991. Volatility in the foreign currency futures market. Review of Financial Studies 4, 543–569.

Ito, T., Roley, V.V., 1987. News from the U.S. and Japan: Which moves the yen/dollar exchange rate?. Journal of Monetary Economics 19, 255–277.

Jarque, C.M., Bera, A.K., 1987. Test for normality of observations and regression residuals. International and Statistical Review 55, 163–172.

Laux, P., Ng, L.K., 1993. The sources of GARCH: Empirical evidence from an intraday returns model incorporating systematic and unique risks. Journal of International Money and Finance 12, 543–560.

Ljung, G.M. and Box, G.E.P., 1978. On a measure of lack of fit in time-series models. Biometrika 65, 297–303.

Lo, A.W., MacKinlay, A.C., 1989. The size and power of the variance ratio test in finite samples: A Monte Carlo investigation. Journal of Econometrics 40, 203–238.

Lo, A.W., MacKinlay, A.C., 1990. An econometric analysis of nonsynchroneous trading. Journal of Econometrics 45, 181–212.

Locke, P.R., Sayers, C.L., 1993. Intra-day futures price volatility: Information effects and variance persistence. Journal of Applied Econometrics 8, 15–30.

Lockwood, L.J., Linn, S.C., 1990. An examination of stock market return volatility during overnight and intraday periods, 1964–1989. Journal of Finance 45, 591–601.

Müller, U.A., Dacorogna, M.M., Davé, R.D., Olsen, R.B., Pictet, O.V., Weizsäcker, J.E., 1995. Volatilities of different time resolutions: Analyzing the dynamics of market components. Working Paper. Olsen and Associates, Research Institute for Applied Economics, Zürich, Switzerland.

Müller, U.A., Darorogna, M.M., Davé, R.D., Pictet, O.V., Olsen, R.B., Ward, J.R., 1993. Fractals and intrinsic time: A challenge to econometricians. Working Paper. Olsen and Associates, Research Institute for Applied Economics, Zürich, Switzerland.

Müller, U.A., Dacorogna, M.M., Olsen, R.B., Pictet, O.V., Schwarz, M., Morgenegg, C., 1990. Statistical study of foreign exchange rates, empirical evidence of a price change scaling law and intraday analysis. Journal of Banking of Finance 14, 1189–1208.

Nelson, D.B., 1990. ARCH models as diffusion approximations. Journal of Econometrics 45, 7–38.

Nelson, D.B., 1991. Conditional heteroskedasticity in asset returns: A new approach. Econometrica 59, 347–370.

Nelson, D.B., 1992. Filtering and forecasting with misspecified ARCH models I: Getting the right variance with the wrong model. Journal of Econometrics 52, 61–90.

Pagan, A.R., 1984. Econometric issues in the analysis of regressions with generated regressors. International Economic Review 25, 221–247.

Pagan, A.R., Schwert, G.W., 1990. Alternative models for conditional stock volatility. Journal of Econometrics 45, 267–290.

Percival, D.B., 1993. Three curious properties of the sample variance and autocovariance for stationary processes with unknown mean. American Statistician 47, 274–276.

Ross, S.A., 1989. Information and volatility: The no-arbitrage Martingale approach to timing and resolution irrelevancy. Journal of Finance 44, 1–18.

Scholes, M., Williams, J., 1977. Estimating betas from nonsynchronous data. Journal of Financial Economics 5, 309–327.

Son, G.S., 1991. Dealer inventory position and intraday patterns of price volatility, bid/ask spreads and trading volume. Working Paper. Department of Finance, University of Washington.

Tauchen, G.E., Pitts, M., 1983. The price variability–volume relationship on speculative markets. Econometrica 51, 485–505.

Taylor, S.J., 1986. Modeling Financial Time Series. John Wiley and Sons, Chichester.

Wasserfallen, W., 1989. Flexible exchange rates: A closer look. Journal of Monetary Economics 23, 511–521.

Wood, R.A., McInish, T.H., Ord, J.K., 1985. An investigation of transaction data for NYSE stocks. Journal of Finance 25, 723–739.

Zhou, B., 1992. Forecasting foreign exchange rates subject to de-volatilization. Working paper #3510. Sloan School of Management, MIT.

[6]

THE JOURNAL OF FINANCE • VOL LIII, NO. 1 • FEBRUARY 1998

Deutsche Mark–Dollar Volatility: Intraday Activity Patterns, Macroeconomic Announcements, and Longer Run Dependencies

TORBEN G. ANDERSEN and TIM BOLLERSLEV*

ABSTRACT

This paper provides a detailed characterization of the volatility in the deutsche mark–dollar foreign exchange market using an annual sample of five-minute returns. The approach captures the intraday activity patterns, the macroeconomic announcements, and the volatility persistence (ARCH) known from daily returns. The different features are separately quantified and shown to account for a substantial fraction of return variability, both at the intraday and daily level. The implications of the results for the interpretation of the fundamental "driving forces" behind the volatility process is also discussed.

THE EFFICIENT MARKET HYPOTHESIS contends that financial asset prices provide rational assessments of fundamental values and future payoffs. By implication, price changes should reflect the arrival and processing of all relevant new information. However, the proportion of return variability that can be ascribed to public news announcements is low. For example, Cutler, Poterba, and Summers (1989) find that even the largest daily price changes in the stock market generally cannot be associated with any significant economic news.[1] Moreover, proxies for the flow of public information, e.g., the number of news items released by Reuter's News Service (Berry and Howe (1994)) or Dow Jones & Company (Mitchell and Mulherin (1994)) explain little of the overall variation. Thus, if private information is ruled out, proponents of rational price formation have to assert the existence of important news items

*Andersen is at the J.L. Kellogg Graduate School of Management, Northwestern University. Bollerslev is with the Department of Economics, University of Virginia. We are grateful for financial support from the Institute for Quantitative Research in Finance (the Q-Group). Special thanks are also due to Olsen and Associates for making the foreign exchange quotes available. Furthermore, we have received valuable comments from seminar participants at Northwestern University, University of Chicago, University of Houston, University of Windsor, Pennsylvania State University, the NBER Universities Research Conference on the Determination of Exchange Rates, and the Econometric Society Summer Meetings in Iowa City. We are in particular indebted to comments from Mike Fishman, John Heaton, Bob Hodrick, Takatoshi Ito, Ken Kavajecz, Richard Lyons, Bruce Mizrach, an anonymous referee, and the editor, René Stulz. Needless to say, we remain fully responsible for the content.

[1] The evidence is not much more encouraging for commodities whose aggregate supply is relatively transparent (Roll (1984)), or, perhaps less surprisingly, at the individual firm level, where private information may be more prevalent (Roll (1988)).

that may be discerned by market agents, but not by economists. This is possible, but hardly convincing, and French and Roll (1986) provide strong evidence to the contrary. They document that return volatility is higher during trading than nontrading periods, independent of the flow of public news. They ascribe this to private information that is incorporated into prices through trading. One may, however, reiterate the question: What type of private information can individuals obtain that is relevant to the pricing of broad assets, while not being readily available to other investors and, even ex post, not being discernible to outside observers?

Furthermore, as stressed by Goodhart and O'Hara (1996), any satisfactory explanation for the behavior of volatility based on the private information hypothesis must be able to accommodate the striking empirical regularities in return volatility, not only over regular trading versus nontrading periods, but also within the trading day, within the trading week and over holiday periods. Moreover, a full account of the process governing price variability must also confront the pronounced volatility clustering, or ARCH effects, that are evident at the interday level. The one common observation across these dimensions is that "market activity" is strongly correlated with price variability. Trading volume, return volatility, and bid–ask spreads are highest around the open and close of trading; return variability per unit of time is higher over trading than nontrading periods; trading volume and spreads are particularly high on days with large return innovations; and public information releases—which theoretically may induce price jumps without any trading—are typically associated with extremely heavy volume.

Unfortunately, most empirical work has studied each of the above phenomena—the intraday and intraweekly patterns (calendar effects), the announcements (public information effects), and the interday volatility persistence (ARCH effects)—in isolation. This is ultimately not satisfactory. First, the similarity of the basic attributes across these dimensions suggests that there is a common component to the behavior which should be explicitly accounted for in any rationalization of the volatility process. Second, real-time decision-making requires that the agents recognize the various factors that exert a significant impact on current price movements. Since the factors display widely different stochastic properties, a decomposition of the contemporaneous effects is necessary in order to forecast volatility, even for the near future. Third, to judge the economic significance of the findings, it is important to gauge the influence of the features at different horizons. For example, the allocational role of the market, arguably, hinges on the information conveyed by prices at daily or lower frequencies, while studies of the market mechanism or institutions must pay close attention to the higher frequency patterns.

This paper takes a step in the direction called for above by providing a comprehensive characterization of the volatility process in the deutsche mark (DM)–dollar foreign exchange market based on a one-year sample of five-minute returns extracted from quotes on the Reuters interbank network. Although our emphasis is on the empirical identification of the various factors and their relative impact at different frequencies, we also stress the implications for theories of rational price fluctuations. The spot DM–dollar market constitutes a near ideal setting. It is the world's largest market measured by turnover, it is highly liquid, and it has low transaction costs. Moreover, it is linked globally through computerized information systems, so news is transmitted almost instantaneously to all participants. Further, it is a 24-hour market composed of sequential and partially overlapping trading in regional centers worldwide, so it has no definite closures, except those generated endogenously by the market. This allows for the study of the volatility process over periods that would be nontrading intervals under centralized market structures, thus including all public announcements, both in the United States and Germany, most of which fall outside the trading hours of the organized stock exchanges.

Our main findings are as follows: First, contrary to Cutler et al. (1989), but consistent with Ederington and Lee (1993), we show that the largest returns appear linked to the release of public information, and, in particular, certain macroeconomic announcements. Nonetheless, we conclude that these effects are secondary when explaining overall volatility. The major announcements dominate the picture immediately following the release, but their explanatory power is less than that of the intraday pattern at the high frequencies, and much less than that of standard volatility forecasts at the daily level. Thus, high-frequency data are critical for identification of news that impacts the market, but these rather spectacular episodes do not explain what generally "drives" markets. Second, the most significant U.S. announcements, namely the employment report, gross domestic product, trade balance figures, and durable goods orders, are all related to the real economy, while the important German announcements, the Bundesbank meetings and M3 supply figures, are monetary. This may reflect differences in the (perceived) central bank reaction functions, or that, over the sample period, monetary policy in the United States was stable, while in Germany it was highly controversial. Third, the clustering of public information releases on certain weekdays explains the day-of-week effect. Hence, if announcement effects are ignored, day-dummies provide biased predictions of excess volatility on specific weekdays. For days with important scheduled announcements, such dummies fail to capture the full elevation in volatility, but the volatility will be exaggerated when no announcements are pending. Fourth, the significant calendar effects include a distinct intraday volatility pattern, reflecting the daily activity cycle of the regional centers, as well as strong holiday, weekend, Daylight Saving Time, and Tokyo market opening effects. As a group, the calendar effects are the most important determinant of overall volatility at the highest frequencies. Fifth, standard ARCH effects permeate intraday returns. Not only are these effects identifiable, but the high-frequency data provide novel insights into this long-run component of volatility. For example, return variability over a given day is typically measured by the daily absolute (squared) return, but we find that procedures exploiting the entire sequence of intraday returns provide much improved measurements. In addition, the interday ARCH component displays dependencies of the so-called long-memory variety. This is an important result. Such features have been documented at daily and lower frequencies, but their origin has been much debated. For instance, it has been argued that infrequent exogenous shifts in the volatility process induces long-memory characteristics. Using daily data, these explanations are difficult to distinguish empirically. However, the presence of long-memory characteristics in high-frequency returns, covering a short time span, indicates that this feature is intrinsic to the system and not an artifact of exogenous shocks.

The empirical findings also have important implications for our understanding of the forces that determine the intensity of price movements. First, the pronounced activity pattern in intraday volatility suggests a significant role for the trading process itself. For trading to be informative, there must be an element of asymmetric information present in the market. Lyons (1995, 1997) develops a model of the interbank market in which dealers extract (private) signals from their customer (nondealer) order flow. This is rational if order flows speak to economic developments that only belatedly show up in statistics such as the trade balance and international capital flows. However, the aggregate net customer order flow is the variable of primary interest, and dealers only get to interpret the fraction of overall orders they receive individually. Because dealers also have a strong inventory control motive for trade, interdealer trade will not reveal, or perfectly aggregate, the information in order flows. In such settings, multiple trading rounds may be informative, even in the absence of additional news (see, e.g., Grundy and McNichols (1989), Brown and Jennings (1989), and Foster and Viswanathan (1996)). Moreover, most models stipulate that the precision of the information held by the different type of agents is common knowledge. If this assumption is relaxed, rational models again predict that the trading process provides a useful tool for inference about the structure and quality of the dispersed economy-wide information; see, e.g., Jacklin, Kleidon, and Pfleiderer (1992) and Romer (1993) for mostly theoretical arguments, and Peiers (1997) for an empirical investigation into Bundesbank interventions in the foreign exchange market.

Second, Hsieh and Kleidon (1996) document that return volatility and bid–ask spreads extracted from quotes pertaining to specific regional segments of the interbank market obey the usual u-shaped patterns that have been rationalized by clustering of informed trading (see, e.g., Admati and Pfleiderer (1988)). However, other regional segments, in the midst of their trading sessions, do not display any trace of a u-shape at the corresponding point in time. Hence, the regional u-shapes do not reflect particularly informative trading during the opening or closing hours, but may, instead, constitute a rational response to the abrupt changes in dealer exposure that occur as dealers periodically withdraw from the market place (see, e.g., Brock and Kleidon (1992) and Hong and Wang (1995)). In addition, the necessity of getting a "feel" for the market before engaging in active trading is cited as an explanation for the early parts of the regional u-shape by Hsieh and

Kleidon (1996). This is, of course, consistent with the importance of learning directly from the trading process.

Third, public information arrivals induce abrupt price changes, but the average price move is typically attained within minutes. Still, volatility and trading volume remain elevated for several hours (see, e.g., Kim and Verrecchia (1991)). If agents have identical information sets and interpret news similarly, the protracted response pattern is hard to explain, and as such provides yet another argument in favor of models with heterogeneously informed agents.

Finally, the long-memory characteristics of the volatility process speak to the potential importance of long-run persistence in the fundamental forces governing the price process. It is hard to imagine that one may rationalize such features without relying on strong dependence in the processes determining the rate of information flow and/or (private) order flow, and the associated degree of uncertainty regarding the state of the underlying economic system. On the other hand, it is clear that a study of high-frequency returns over a one-year sample can only address the issue indirectly. The origin of longer run volatility persistence remains an important topic for future research.

The paper is structured as follows. Section I reports on the data sources and the construction of the five-minute return series. Section II provides a preliminary data analysis. A robust regression procedure for estimation of the calendar and announcement effects is developed in Section III, and Section IV summarizes the empirical evidence with an emphasis on the instantaneous as well as the cumulative impact of each component. Section V assesses the explanatory power of the volatility factors for intraday and daily return variability. Section VI concludes. An appendix, available at the *Journal of Finance* web site, contains further discussion of the technical aspects of the estimation procedure.

I. Data Sources and Construction

Our primary data set consists of five-minute returns for the deutsche mark–dollar (DM–$) spot exchange rate from October 1, 1992, through September 30, 1993.[2] In addition, we utilize a longer daily time series of 3,649 spot DM–$ exchange rates from March 14, 1979, through September 29, 1993. The five-minute returns are constructed from the DM–$ exchange rate quotes that appear on the interbank Reuters network over the sample period. Each quote contains a bid and an ask price along with the time to the nearest even second. At the end of each five-minute interval, we use the immediately

[2] Going to a finer sampling interval results in the bid–ask bounce effect becoming dominant, as evidenced by the increasingly significant negative sample autocorrelations reported in Guillaume et al. (1995). These findings are also consistent with the standard deviation of our five-minute return series being slightly less than the average quoted spread (see Bollerslev and Melvin (1994)).

preceding and following quote to construct the relevant bid and ask prices. The quotes are weighted by their inverse relative distance to the endpoint, and the log-price, $\log(P_{t,n})$, is then defined as the midpoint of the logarithmic bid and ask. The nth return within day t, $R_{t,n}$, is the change in log-prices during the corresponding period. All $N = 288$ intervals during the 24-hour cycle are used. However, to avoid confounding the evidence by the decidedly slower trading patterns over the weekends, all returns from Friday 21:00 Greenwich Mean Time (GMT) through Sunday 21:00 GMT were excluded; see Bollerslev and Domowitz (1993) for an analysis of the interbank quote activity that justifies this "weekend" definition. To maintain a fixed number of returns over the span of one week, we do not remove any observations due to worldwide or country-specific holidays, although we control explicitly for their impact in the analysis below. This leaves us with a sample of $T = 260$ weekdays for a total of 74,880 five-minute return observations; i.e., $R_{t,n}$, $n = 1,2,\ldots,N$, $t = 1,2,\ldots,T$. The data set also includes all of the news headlines that appeared on the Reuters money news-alert screens. During the sample period from October 1, 1992 through September 30, 1993, a total of 105,065 such headlines appeared. These are time stamped to the second and constitute the basis for our analysis of announcement effects.

II. Preliminary Data Analysis

This section provides an initial investigation of our high-frequency foreign exchange return series that serves to motivate our formal model in Section III. It falls naturally in three parts, corresponding to each of the general factors that we identify as important determinants of the volatility process.

A. Daily ARCH Effects

Market microstructure theories concerning the relation between information flow, return volatility, and trading activity often ignore the lower frequency movements in volatility that are associated with the conditional heteroskedasticity of daily returns. This is probably related to the fact that, until recently, empirical studies have been unable to document that intraday return volatility displays characteristics that are consistent with those observed at the lower frequencies. At the face of it, this is utterly puzzling. How can the intraday return volatility process be void of ARCH features when the identical data, aggregated to the daily level, provide overwhelming evidence of conditional heteroskedasticity? An answer is provided by Andersen and Bollerslev (1997a) who demonstrate that the strong intraday volatility pattern interferes with, and garbles, the time series structure of interday volatility. Only by explicitly modeling the intraday pattern is it possible to recover meaningful volatility dynamics. Nonetheless, given the poor forecasting performance of ARCH models reported in a number of recent studies, the question remains as to whether ARCH effects are significant at the highest frequencies. This section documents, to the contrary, that the ARCH fea-

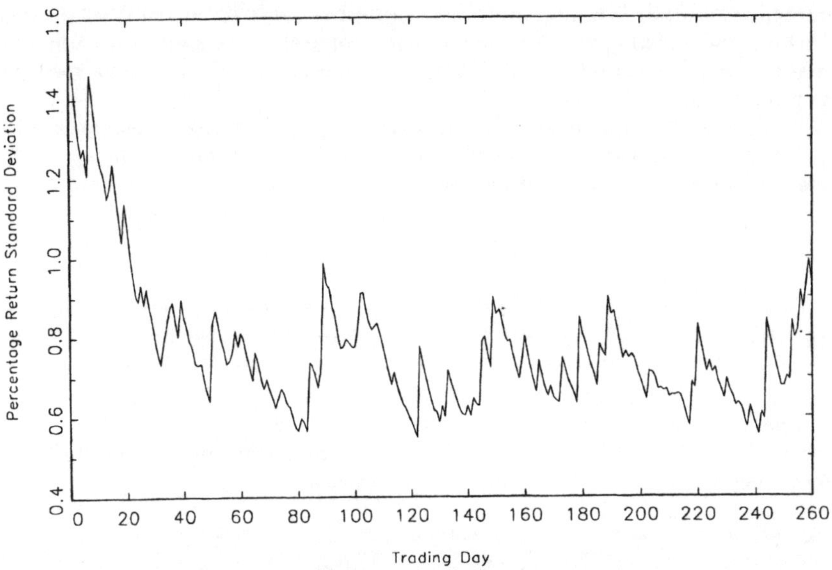

Figure 1. Daily GARCH(1,1) volatility forecasts. The figure plots the one-step-ahead conditional standard deviation forecasts from an MA(1)-GARCH(1,1) model for the daily deutsche mark–dollar spot exchange rate from October 1, 1992 through September 30, 1993, for a total of 260 nonweekend days. The model is estimated with data over the longer sample period from March 14, 1979 through September 29, 1993.

tures exert a pronounced and systematic impact on the high-frequency volatility process. In addition, we show that the forecasting performance of volatility models is much better than the recent evidence suggests. The key point is that these studies rely on daily returns to gauge the realized return variability. These measures are, however, extremely noisy, and when improved measurements are obtained from intraday data, the forecast performance improves dramatically.

For concreteness, we explore the relation between one-step-ahead volatility forecasts generated by an MA(1)-GARCH(1,1) model of daily returns and alternative measures of return variability based on intraday data.[3] The GARCH model is estimated from daily data over the longer sample period. The associated estimates of the conditional standard deviation for each day of our high-frequency sample are depicted in Figure 1. Volatility starts out at a high level, and consistently declines over the initial one and a half months, followed by a more stable level over the remainder of the sample. However, even the latter period is characterized by sudden bursts of volatility that die

[3] Although the GARCH(1,1) model is not necessarily the preferred model, it does represent a simple and popular model that provides a reasonable approximation to the second-order dependency in the series (see, e.g., Baillie and Bollerslev (1989)).

out only gradually. Finally, there is an apparent surge in volatility at the end of the sample. This overall development is broadly consistent with the dramatic events surrounding the European Monetary System (EMS) over the sample period.[4]

To discuss the properties of alternative (ex post) volatility measures, it is useful to contemplate an explicit model of intraday returns. Suppose that the exchange rate is determined by

$$d\log(P_\tau) = \mu_\tau \cdot d\tau + \sigma_\tau \cdot dW_\tau,$$

where $\tau \geq 0$, W_τ is a standard Brownian motion with unit variance per day, and the instantaneous mean, μ_τ, and volatility, σ_τ, may be governed by separate stochastic processes. Much of modern asset pricing theory is cast in terms of such continuous time diffusions. In the notation for the discretely sampled intraday returns defined above, $R_{t,n} \equiv \log(P_{t+n/N}) - \log(P_{t+(n-1)/N})$, where $t = 1,2,\ldots,T$, and $n = 1,2,\ldots,N$. In empirical applications to high-frequency data, it is often assumed that the mean return is constant,

$$E(R_{t,n}) = \mu_{t+n/N} = \mu,$$

while time variation in the corresponding volatility process is allowed,

$$E|R_{t,n} - \mu| = c \cdot \sigma_{t+n/N},$$

where $c = (\pi/2N)^{1/2}$, and μ is approximately zero. One common approach used for evaluation of daily (or lower) frequency volatility estimates, say $\hat{\sigma}_t$, relies on direct comparison with the corresponding realized absolute returns, $(t = 1,2,\ldots,T)$,

[4] In early September 1992, the Finnish markkaa gave up its peg to the main European currencies, and later that month the British pound and Italian lira left the EMS, which limited exchange rates, through the European Rate Mechanism (ERM), to fluctuate by only 2.25 percent versus each other. This created intense speculation that other currencies would leave the EMS, and the volatility in October 1992 reflects the repercussions of these events in the DM–dollar market. The more dramatic episodes include the abolition of the Swedish krona peg on 11/19, the 6 percent devaluation of the peseta and the escudo on 11/23, and the abolition of the Norwegian krone peg on 12/10. By Christmas, this round of turmoil had been weathered, but uncertainty arose again during a speculative attack on the Irish punt in late January. The punt was devalued by 10 percent on 01/30, and the market remained unsettled for most of February. Market sentiment focused on the willingness of the Bundesbank to support the weaker currencies by loosening its monetary policy. In fact, ERM tensions were reduced by a German interest rate cut on 02/04. Later, the peseta and escudo devalued again, on 05/13. This decision may have been associated with the upcoming vote, in Denmark, regarding the country's participation in the Maastricht treaty and the EMS, but the popular verdict, on 05/18, came out in favor of the treaty. The final bout of ERM-related volatility occurred during the latter three weeks of July, but came to a dramatic halt with the announcement, on 08/01, of a widening of the ERM band from 2.25 percent to 15 percent for all currencies except the Dutch guilder vis-à-vis the DM.

$$|R_t| = \left| \sum_{n=1}^{N} R_{t,n} \right| = |\log(P_t) - \log(P_{t-1})|. \tag{1}$$

Studies adopting this approach include Cumby, Figlewski, and Hasbrouck (1993), Figlewski (1995), Jorion (1995), and West and Cho (1995), among others. However, realized absolute or squared daily returns provide a very noisy measure of the underlying latent volatility. For example, the price may fluctuate rather wildly, but nonetheless end up close to the opening price, thus (falsely) signaling a low volatility state. A richer measure for volatility might instead be based on the sum of the intraday absolute returns, i.e.,

$$\sum_{n=1}^{N} |R_{t,n}|. \tag{2}$$

The measure in equation (2) is referred to as the *cumulative absolute returns* in the discussion below.[5]

Under simplifying assumptions it is readily shown that the return variability measure provided by equation (2) is much more efficient than the one in equation (1); see, e.g., Appendix A.[6] The practical implication of this result is illustrated in Figure 2, which displays the two alternative volatility measures along with the corresponding forecasts from Figure 1.[7] The weak relation between the GARCH forecasts and the absolute return measure in equation (1) is evident in Figure 2a. The daily absolute returns are scattered almost arbitrarily around the predicted values, reflecting the inherent noise in daily returns. Table I underscores the point. The sample correlation between the one-step-ahead GARCH volatility forecasts and two different ex post measures of the absolute and the squared daily returns are disturbingly low, attaining a maximum of 0.107.[8] Clearly, a regression of the ex post

[5] A similar measure is used by Hsieh (1991) in calculating daily stock return standard deviations from fifteen-minute returns. There also is a large literature attempting to extract additional information about volatility from sources other than the daily returns; for example, Garman and Klass (1980), Parkinson (1980), and Rogers and Satchell (1991) explored the information content in daily observations on high and low prices, while Latané and Rendleman (1976), Day and Lewis (1992), Canina and Figlewski (1993), Jorion (1995), and Xu and Taylor (1995) studied the implied volatility extracted from option prices, and Clark (1973), Epps and Epps (1976), Tauchen and Pitts (1983), Lamoureux and Lastrapes (1990a), Gallant, Rossi, and Tauchen (1992), Andersen (1994, 1996), and Jones, Kaul, and Lipson (1994) investigated trading volume.

[6] As mentioned earlier, the Appendix may be obtained from the *Journal of Finance* web site.

[7] Note that the GARCH volatility estimates rely solely on the *preceding* squared daily returns and the parameter estimates obtained over the longer sample. Because these parameter estimates are largely unaffected by the realization of returns over the final year of the sample, the volatility estimates are effectively one-step-ahead volatility forecasts based on prior daily returns only.

[8] The results are robust to the exclusion of holidays. Calculating the correlation between $|R_t|$ and the GARCH volatility estimate for nonholidays, rather than for the full sample, results in changes to the third decimal of the correlation number only.

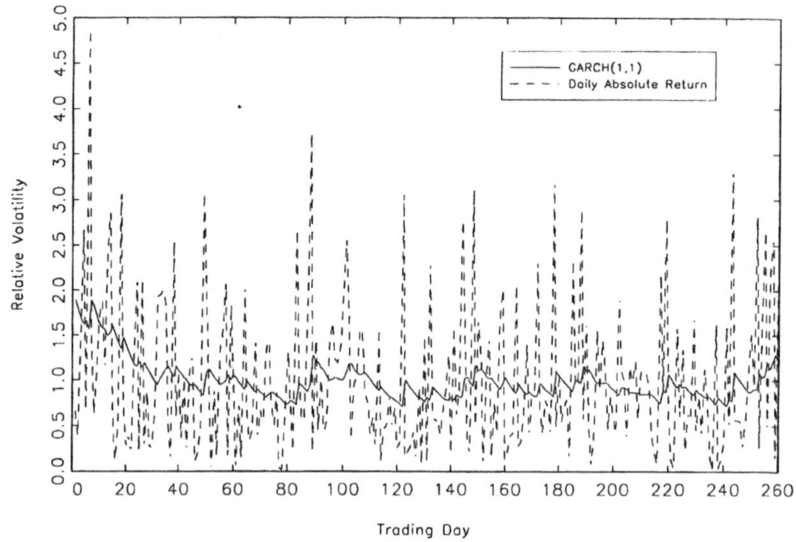

a

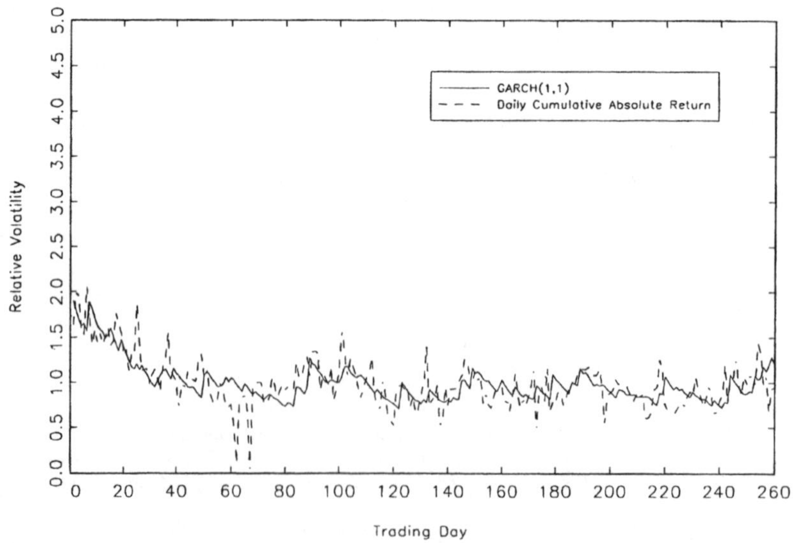

b

Figure 2. Daily GARCH(1,1) volatility forecasts versus ex post return variability measures. The figures plot the conditional return standard deviation forecasts from an MA(1)-GARCH(1,1) model for the daily deutsche mark–dollar returns from October 1, 1992 through September 29, 1993, along with the corresponding realized absolute daily returns (Figure 2a) and the corresponding cumulative absolute five-minute returns (Figure 2b). All series have been normalized to average unity over the one-year sample.

Table I

Ex Post Correlations between Forecasts of the Daily Deutsche Mark–Dollar Return Standard Deviation (Panel A) or the Daily Return Variance (Panel B) with Alternative Measures of the Ex Post Return Variability

The daily return standard deviation and variance for each weekday of the one-year sample, October 1, 1992 to September 29, 1993, is obtained from a MA(1)-GARCH(1,1) model estimated using daily data on the deutsche mark–dollar (DM–$) spot exchange rate over the longer sample period from March 14, 1979 through September 29, 1993. The measures of ex post return variability for the first two entries in Panel A, $\Sigma_{n=1}^{N}|R_{t,n}|$ and $(\Sigma_{n=1}^{N}R_{t,n}^2)^{1/2}$, and the first entry in Panel B, $\Sigma_{n=1}^{N}R_{t,n}^2$, are constructed from percentage returns based on interpolated five-minute logarithmic average bid–ask quotes for the DM–$ spot exchange rate. Quotes from Friday 21:00 GMT through Sunday 21:00 GMT are excluded, resulting in a total of 74,880 return observations. The last two entries in each of the panels, $|\Sigma_{n=1}^{N}R_{t,n}|$ and $|R_t|$, and $(\Sigma_{n=1}^{N}R_{t,n})^2$ and R_t^2, respectively, are based on ex post return variability measures constructed from daily continuously compounded DM–$ returns over the one-year sample. The returns denoted R_t are calculated from the spot exchange rate observed at 12:00 GMT, consistent with the definition used for the longer daily sample; the preceding entries use the exchange rates observed at 21:00 GMT, which is consistent with the definition of the trading day used for the five-minute return sample.

Panel A: Gaussian MA(1)-GARCH(1,1) estimates of σ_t

$\Sigma_{n=1}^{N}\lvert R_{t,n}\rvert$	$(\Sigma_{n=1}^{N}R_{t,n}^2)^{1/2}$	$\lvert\Sigma_{n=1}^{N}R_{t,n}\rvert$	$\lvert R_t\rvert$
0.672	0.618	0.046	0.086

Panel B: Gaussian MA(1)−GARCH(1,1) estimates of σ_t^2

$\Sigma_{n=1}^{N}R_{t,n}^2$	$(\Sigma_{n=1}^{N}R_{t,n})^2$	R_t^2
0.660	0.066	0.107

volatility measure on the GARCH forecasts has negligible explanatory power, with an explained variability of, at best, approximately $(0.107)^2 \approx 1.1$ percent. Given this evidence and the inadequacies of ARCH models when applied directly to intraday returns, it is perhaps understandable that many studies ignore such volatility estimates.

The fallacy of this approach, however, is evident from Figure 2b. The cumulative absolute returns from equation (2) are intimately related to the GARCH volatility predictions. The first two columns of Table I reinforce this conclusion. Over the annual sample, the correlation between the forecasts and the cumulative absolute returns is as high as 0.672. In other words, about $(0.672)^2 \approx 45.2$ percent of the variation in the sum of absolute intraday returns is predicted by the daily forecasts generated by a simple GARCH model.[9] Furthermore, this variation is at the daily level. It is impossible to explain this phenomenon by the intraday volatility pattern since this is an-

[9] This R^2 goes beyond 50 percent if simple adjustments are made for holidays with predictably low return volatility.

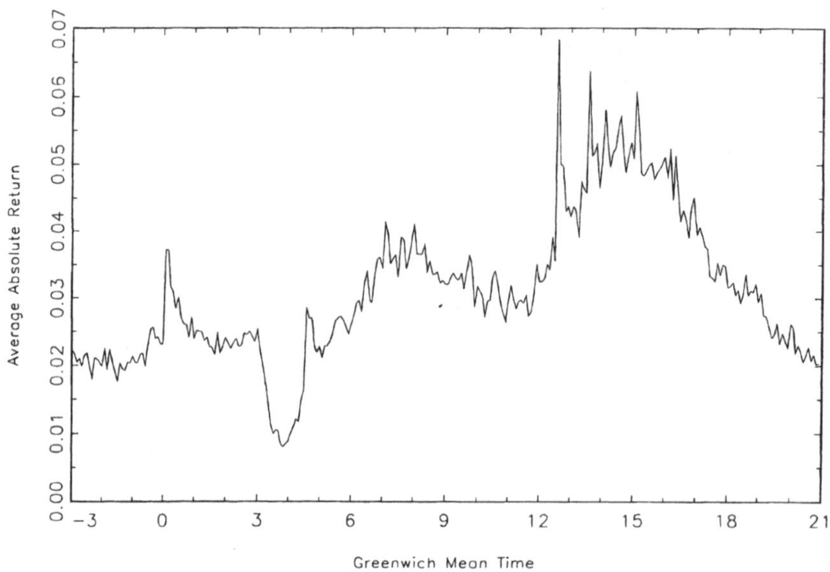

Figure 3. Intraday volatility pattern. The figure plots the average absolute five-minute deutsche mark–dollar (DM–$) return for each five-minute interval, starting with the interval 20:55–21:00 GMT and ending at 20:50–20:55 GMT. The returns are calculated from interpolated five-minute logarithmic average bid–ask quotes for the DM–$ spot exchange rate over the October 1, 1992 to September 29, 1993 sample period. Quotes from Friday 21:00 GMT through Sunday 21:00 GMT are excluded, resulting in a total of 74,880 return observations. All 260 weekdays are employed in calculating the averages.

nihilated when aggregated over the entire trading day. Thus, ignoring the ARCH volatility forecasts implies that a large component of *predictable* return variability is excluded from the high-frequency analysis. Clearly, a misleading picture may emerge if we fail to control for this source of common variation across the intraday returns.

B. Calendar Effects

Although there is very little evidence of predictability in the conditional mean of the five-minute DM–$ returns, the series displays pronounced intraday volatility and activity patterns.[10] Figure 3 depicts the average absolute return for each five-minute interval across all 260 weekdays in our sample. The initial observation corresponds to the interval ending at 21:00

[10] There is evidence of weak negative first-order autocorrelation, most likely induced by spread positioning of dealers attempting to correct inventory imbalances by posting quotes that attract customers on one side of the market only; see, e.g., Müller et al. (1990), Bollerslev and Domowitz (1993), and Zhou (1996). This explanation is confirmed by the analysis of actual transaction prices over seven hours in Goodhart, Ito, and Payne (1996).

GMT, and the last observation represents the interval 20:50–20:55 GMT. Thus, our week originates Monday morning in the Pacific segment where trading is dominated by banks located in Wellington and Sydney. Trading volume and return volatility is rather subdued at this hour. There is a significant jump in (average) volatility at 0:00 GMT, or 9 a.m. Tokyo time, corresponding to the simultaneous opening of trading in a number of financial markets, including the Tokyo foreign exchange interbank market and markets for U.S. debt securities. At this point, the market must interpret innovations to U.S. bond yields that have occurred since the close of U.S. trading and absorb any customer orders that have accumulated overnight at authorized currency-dealing banks in Japan.[11] Although yen–$ dealings comprise the largest portion of the Asian foreign exchange market, the yen–$ and DM–$ markets are intimately linked through a triangular arbitrage relationship. Thus, it is perhaps not surprising that the effects of the Tokyo market opening resemble those documented for equity markets by Wood, McInish, and Ord (1985) and Harris (1986). During lunch, 3:00–4:30 GMT, the Tokyo segment shuts down and the overall market typically approaches a standstill. This results in another market opening effect immediately thereafter. Ignoring this lunch effect, we may loosely identify a u-shaped pattern in volatility over the Asian segment, with the latter part leading into the European segment at 6:00 GMT. Volatility is notably higher during European trading, which remains active until about 15:00 GMT. This is to be expected, as it constitutes the most active trading period and more relevant economic news may hit the market during this part of the daily cycle. Although the rough outlines of a u-shape are again visible,[12] the latter part of the pattern may, as before, reflect an overlap in market activity: first the Asian market coexists with the European, and later, between 12:00 and 15:00 GMT, the two most active centers trade simultaneously as it is afternoon in London and morning in New York. Finally, after the close of the London market, volatility displays a monotonic decline until it reaches the plateau associated with the Pacific segment. There are thus no signs of elevated volatility when trading closes down in New York. Hence, although volatility increases when each of the main regional segments becomes active, there is no direct evidence of enhanced volatility associated with the termination of regional trading.[13] This overall pattern is consistent with the evidence reported in Baillie and Boller-

[11] Prior to December 1994, The Committee of Tokyo Foreign Exchange Market Customs prohibited all authorized foreign exchange trading in Japan prior to 9 a.m., between 12:00–1:30 p.m., and after 3:30 p.m. local time (see Ito, Lyons, and Melvin (1996)).

[12] We later demonstrate that the distinct peaks, at exactly 12:30 and 13:30 GMT, are caused by price movements associated with the release of U.S. macroeconomic news at 8:30 Eastern Standard Time (EST).

[13] Hsieh and Kleidon (1996) show that volatility computed from quotes specific to a given region may display a u-shape for reasons unrelated to informed trading. Because regional quoting intensity is low at the early and late stages of regional trading, market volatility is primarily determined by quotes emanating from the more active segments, rendering the regional u-shape irrelevant. However, if all other regions display thin quoting activity at this point in time, the regional pattern can impact the properties of returns computed from quotes on the overall market. This provides an alternative explanation of the Tokyo market opening effect.

slev (1991), Harvey and Huang (1991), and Dacorogna et al. (1993). We now turn to a discussion of the other systematic calendar features prevalent in the high-frequency returns.

Although there generally is a close coherence between the naive one-step-ahead volatility forecasts from the daily GARCH model and the cumulative absolute return volatility measure depicted in Figure 2b, there are a few dramatic deviations, most notably exemplified by the trading days 62 and 67. These are Christmas Day and New Year's Day, and both have close to zero quote activity, resulting in imputed intraday returns of near zero. Effectively, they are "weekends," as the low activity renders the intraday volatility computation meaningless. A similar, albeit weaker, manifestation of a low quoting intensity is at work on other U.S. holidays throughout the sample. The days 41, 98, 137–138, 173, 198, and 243, representing Thanksgiving, President's Day, Easter, Memorial Day, July 4, and Labor Day, are prominent examples. There are also instances of failures in the data transmission that cause gaps of several hours in our intraday time series. The most noticeable manifestation of this phenomenon is for day 258. The subsequent analysis explicitly controls for such spurious breaks in the volatility process.

A second type of calendar effect often recognized in high-frequency returns is day-of-the-week dependencies. The apparent need to allow for such effects is illustrated in Figure 4, where a set of two-hourly dummies is estimated along with dummies for each of the weekdays. Mondays appear the least volatile, while Thursdays and Fridays are the most volatile.

Third, the GMT time scale used in Figure 3 is dubious due to the observance of Daylight Saving Time in both North America and Europe. If the daily cycles of economic activity and trading in the different regions are underlying determinants of the intraday pattern, then it should differ across the Summer Time and Winter Time regimes. Figure 5 supports this conjecture. The volatility pattern appears translated leftward by exactly one hour between 6:00 and 21:00 GMT (the European and North American segments) during the U.S. Summer Time regime.[14]

Finally, motivated by the apparent importance of market openings and closures, we also consider the possibility that volatility behaves differently in periods leading into, or out of, such market closures. In particular, we find that Friday evenings and Monday mornings appear different from the identical periods on other weekdays, and the following analysis consequently controls for both of these effects.

C. Macroeconomic Announcement Effects

Figure 6 suggests that U.S. announcements released at 8:30 Eastern Standard Time (EST), or 12:30 GMT, are the source of the previously observed volatility spikes during the U.S. Summer Time regime. It displays the in-

[14] As detailed in the Appendix (on the *Journal of Finance* web site), we effectively delete the Tokyo lunch period by artificially assigning a low return to intervals between 3:00 and 4:45 GMT, thus causing the volatility pattern to appear rectangular over this period. These observations are further "dummied" out in the formal regression analysis conducted below.

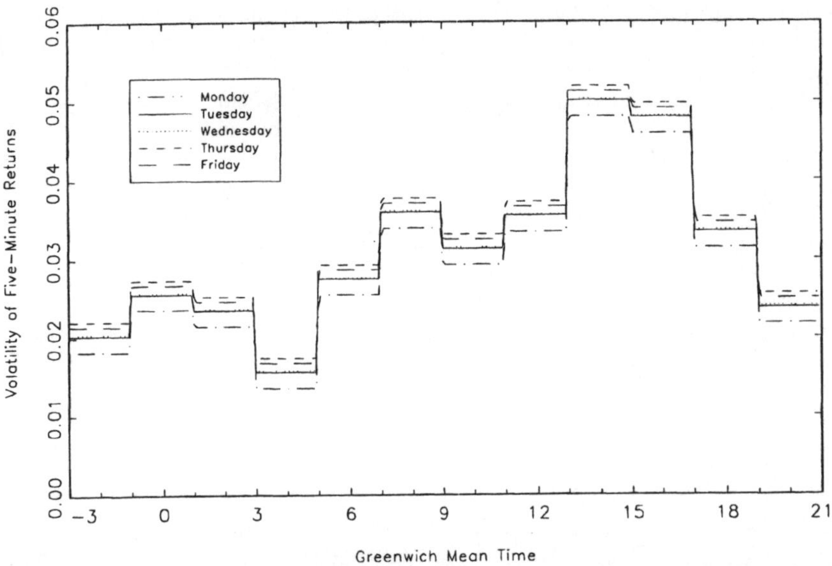

Figure 4. Daily and weekly volatility patterns. The figure displays the estimated average absolute five-minute deutsche mark–dollar (DM–$) returns obtained from a regression on two-hour and day-of-week dummies. The returns are calculated from interpolated five-minute logarithmic average bid–ask quotes for the DM–$ spot exchange rate over the October 1, 1992 through September 29, 1993 sample period. The two-hour intervals start out at 20:55–22:55 GMT and end at 18:55–20:55 GMT.

traday volatility pattern for Summer days that contain scheduled announcements on U.S. macroeconomic data, including the Employment Report, the Merchandise Trade Deficit, the Producer Price Index (PPI), Durable Goods, estimates and revisions to quarterly Gross Domestic Product (GDP), Retail Sales, Housing Starts, Leading Indicators, and Jobless Claims. It is apparent that the releases induce quite dramatic price adjustments. However, although there are signs of elevated volatility for several hours, the main impact seems to be gone within 10–20 minutes. Similar effects are evident for announcements at 13:30 GMT during the U.S. Winter Time regime (not displayed). These findings are consistent with the observation of heightened return volatility on days with macroeconomic announcements noted by, e.g., Harvey and Huang (1991) and Ederington and Lee (1993).

Table II displays the 25 largest absolute five-minute returns over the sample, and indicates whether any economic or political events may be identified as contributors to the abrupt price change. The latter exercise is, of course, subjective. Nonetheless, the evidence is striking, with the 7 largest, and 15 of the 25 largest, absolute returns directly associated with the release of economic news *in the same or the immediately preceding interval*. Among other events that seemingly induced "jumps" in the DM–$ exchange rate

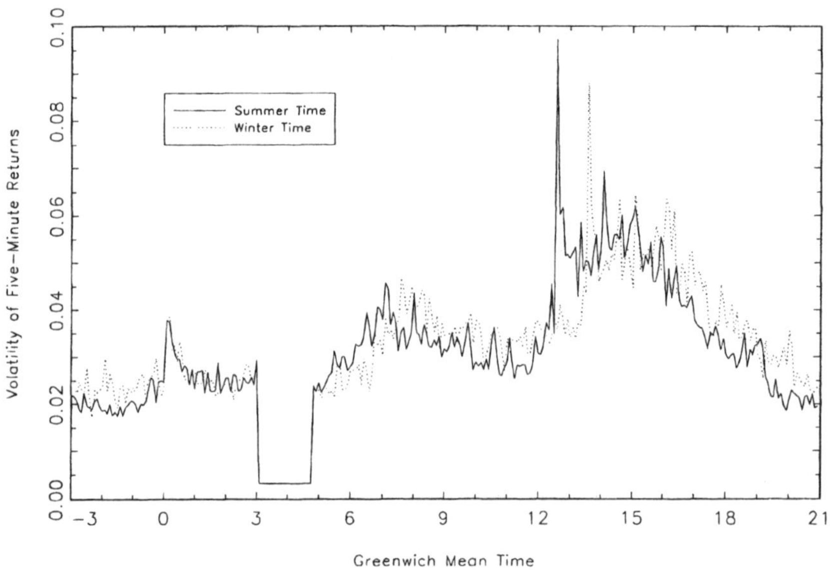

Figure 5. Intradaily U.S. Summer and Winter Time volatility patterns. The figure plots the average absolute five-minute deutsche mark–dollar (DM–$) return for each five-minute interval, starting with 20:55–21:00 GMT and ending at 20:50–20:55 GMT. The returns are calculated from interpolated five-minute logarithmic average bid–ask quotes for the DM–$ spot exchange rate over the October 1, 1992 through September 29, 1993 sample period. Quotes from Friday 21:00 GMT through Sunday 21:00 GMT are excluded, resulting in a total of 74,880 return observations. The Tokyo lunch period, 3:00–4:45 GMT, is assigned an artificially low return. All 145 weekdays during the U.S. Summer Time and the 115 weekdays during U.S. Winter Time are employed.

were the "Russia Crisis," involving a military confrontation between Yeltsin and hardliners in the Russian Parliament, the plunge of the U.S. stock market on October 5, the election of Bill Clinton as the next U.S. president, and various tumultuous episodes in the ERM, including the widening of the band to 15 percent, and the floating of the Swedish krona on 11/19 that culminated with a devaluation of the peseta and escudo the following weekend.

We conclude that scheduled releases occasionally induce large price changes, but the associated volatility shocks appear short-lived. The reason is probably their one-time character. Market participants may have different information sets, and thus differ in their interpretation of the news, but the market typically settles on a new equilibrium price after a brief period of hectic trading (see, e.g., Goodhart and Figliuoli (1992) and Goodhart et al. (1993)). This is contrary to the often more prolonged impact of unscheduled news. Examples include the Russia Crisis and the Stock Market Plunge which both are related to three separate, large innovations, and appear to exert longer-lasting effects. Announcements may thus constitute news arrivals with a well-defined content and clear-cut termination that endows them with a

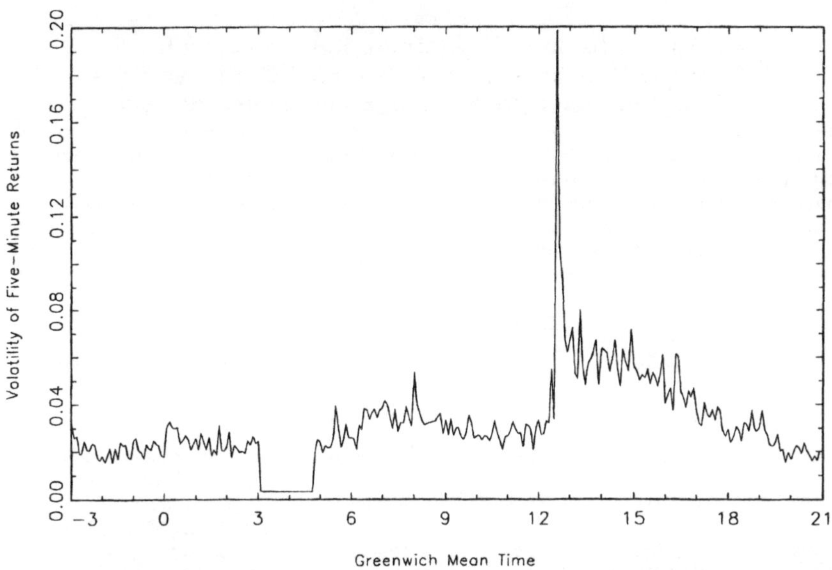

Figure 6. U.S. announcement day volatility. The figure plots the average absolute five-minute deutsche mark–dollar (DM–$) return for each five-minute interval, starting with 20:55–21:00 GMT and ending at 20:50–20:55 GMT for days with regularly scheduled U.S. macroeconomic announcements during the U.S. Summer Time regime. The returns are calculated from interpolated five-minute logarithmic average bid–ask quotes for the DM–$ spot exchange rate over the October 1, 1992 through September 29, 1993 sample period. Quotes from Friday 21:00 GMT through Sunday 21:00 GMT are excluded, resulting in a total of 74,880 return observations. The Tokyo lunch period, 3:00–4:45 GMT, is assigned an artificially low return. These days each contain at least one release, at 8:30 Eastern Standard Time, of one of the following U.S. macroeconomic announcements: the Employment Report, the Merchandise Trade Deficit, the Producer Price Index, the Advance Durable Goods Report, estimates or revisions to the Gross Domestic Product, Retail Sales, Housing Starts, Leading Indicators, and New Jobless Claims.

particularly short-lived impact, largely unrelated to the strong volatility persistence observed at the daily level. Nonetheless, they are sufficiently numerous that they induce an appreciable amount of predictable volatility in overall returns.

III. Modeling the Systematic Features of High-Frequency Volatility

The volatility dynamics of high-frequency foreign exchange returns are involved. There are pronounced intraday patterns, highly significant, albeit short-lived, announcement effects, and standard volatility clustering, or ARCH, effects at lower frequencies. Moreover, the latter cannot exist exclusively at the lower frequencies, as the aggregation of intraday returns would not be able to accommodate the persistent volatility processes present at the daily

Table II

Largest Absolute Five-Minute Returns Calculated from the Deutsche Mark–Dollar Spot Exchange Rate from October 1, 1992 through September 29, 1993

The absolute returns are obtained from interpolated five-minute logarithmic average bid–ask quotes. Quotes from Friday 21:00 GMT through Sunday 21:00 GMT are excluded, resulting in a total of 74,880 return observations. The 288 intraday returns per 24-hour trading day are numbered, starting at the interval 20:55–21:00 GMT, and ending with the interval 20:50–20:55 GMT. For each interval, we subjectively indicate whether any economic or political event appears to contribute to the large absolute five-minute return.

Absolute Return	Date	Interval	Weekday	Event
1.244	10/02	188	Friday	Employment Report
0.897	06/04	188	Friday	Employment Report
0.648	11/19	200	Thursday	Jobless Claims Housing Starts
0.637	03/04	189	Thursday	Bundesbank meeting
0.581	09/03	188	Friday	Employment Report
0.580	06/11	188	Friday	Retail Sales Producer Price Index
0.573	10/02	189	Friday	Employment Report
0.530	09/21	234	Tuesday	Russia crisis
0.529	11/20	37	Friday	ERM turmoil
0.527	01/29	200	Friday	Durable Goods
0.517	08/02	36	Monday	ERM band revision
0.510	10/05	243	Monday	U.S. stock market plunge
0.503	09/21	233	Tuesday	Russia crisis
0.501	03/05	200	Friday	Employment Report
0.498	09/16	197	Thursday	Industrial Output
0.494	08/31	188	Tuesday	Gross Domestic Product
0.480	07/02	188	Friday	Employment Report
0.478	10/05	240	Monday	U.S. stock market plunge
0.463	10/05	229	Monday	U.S. stock market plunge
0.458	11/04	39	Wednesday	U.S. Presidential Election
0.455	09/21	235	Tuesday	Russia crisis
0.449	08/19	188	Thursday	Jobless Claims Trade Balance
0.441	10/23	195	Friday	ERM turmoil
0.439	04/22	198	Thursday	Bundesbank meeting
0.434	10/27	200	Tuesday	Gross Domestic Product

level.[15] Thus, we stipulate that the volatility process is driven by the simultaneous interaction of numerous components, some associated with economic news releases, some with predominantly predictable calendar effects, and some with persistent, unobserved (latent) factors. We demonstrate how formal evaluation of the effects documented in Section II may be performed

[15] See the theoretical results regarding temporal aggregation for ARCH in Drost and Nijman (1993) and Drost and Werker (1996), and stochastic volatility in Andersen and Bollerslev (1996b) and Ghysels, Harvey, and Renault (1996).

using a simple two-step procedure, where the final step relies on standard regression techniques.

In full generality, our model takes the following form,

$$R_{t,n} - \bar{R}_{t,n} = \sigma_{t,n} \cdot s_{t,n} \cdot Z_{t,n} \tag{3}$$

where $\bar{R}_{t,n}$ is the expected five-minute return, $Z_{t,n}$ is an i.i.d. mean zero, unit variance, error term, $s_{t,n}$ represents the calendar features as well as the scheduled announcement effects, and $\sigma_{t,n}$ denotes the remaining, potentially highly persistent, volatility components, that traditionally are captured by ARCH or stochastic volatility models. All the return components are assumed to be independent, and the volatility components are nonnegative; i.e., $\sigma_{t,n}$, $s_{t,n} > 0$ for all t, n.[16]

Without additional restrictions, the components of equation (3) are not separately identifiable. By squaring and taking logs, we may isolate the calendar and announcement effects, $s_{t,n}$, as the sole explanatory variables,

$$2\log[|R_{t,n} - \bar{R}_{t,n}|] - \log \sigma_{t,n}^2 = c + 2\log s_{t,n} + u_{t,n} \tag{4}$$

where $c = E[\log Z_{t,n}^2]$, and $u_{t,n} = \log Z_{t,n}^2 - E[\log Z_{t,n}^2]$. It is evident that $\log s_{t,n}$, in general, will be stochastic. Each particular release of, say, the Employment Report is unique, with the figures providing a certain innovation relative to consensus forecasts. The price and volatility reaction will reflect this innovation (the news content), the dispersion of beliefs across traders, and probably a host of other market conditions at the time of the release. In order to capture these dynamic features directly, one must resort to explicit time series modeling based on a wider information set, including consensus forecasts, recent return innovations, etc.[17] Instead, our goal is more modest. We merely assume that the (log) volatility response, conditional on the type of announcement, the time of the release, and other relevant calendar information, has a well-defined expected value, $E[\log s_{t,n}]$. This average impact is then governed by purely deterministic regressors. Of course, the innovation, $\log s_{t,n} - E[\log s_{t,n}]$, will typically be highly correlated for the immediate period following a new release. This will induce serial correlation and heteroskedasticity in the error terms of the regression that we develop below, and we are careful to accommodate such features. Finally, we impose the analogous (weak) restriction that $\log \sigma_{t,n}$ is strictly stationary and has a finite unconditional mean, $E[\log \sigma_{t,n}]$.

[16] We clearly lose some information by focusing strictly on a model for the imputed five-minute returns. The recent work of Engle and Russell (1997) is motivated by the desire to utilize all of the "ultrahigh" frequency data.

[17] Payne (1996) shows that direct estimation of a system containing all three factors is feasible, but his stochastic volatility model accommodates only one persistent latent factor. In contrast, Andersen and Bollerslev (1997b) show that the long-run features of the five-minute DM–$ return series analyzed here are consistent with a heterogeneous information arrival interpretation of the volatility process, but only if the number of latent components, endowed with relatively strong volatility persistence, is large.

In order to obtain an operational regression equation, we impose some additional structure. First, we assume that $\bar{R}_{t,n}$ is constant and well approximated by the sample mean, $\bar{R}$. This is innocuous because the standard deviation dwarfs the mean return, implying that the inference is not sensitive to minor misspecification of the conditional mean. Second, we utilize an a priori estimate of the return standard deviation, $\hat{\sigma}_{t,n}$, to help control for this source of systematic volatility movements. Third, we impose a parametric representation on the regressor $E[\log s_{t,n}]$ of the form $f(\theta i, t, n)$. Since theory provides no specific guidelines regarding the shape of the intraday pattern, we allow for a flexible functional form that adapts well to the smooth cyclical pattern. Our choice is the following

$$f(\theta,t,n) = \mu_0 + \sum_{k=1}^{D} \lambda_k \cdot I_k(t,n) + \sum_{p=1}^{P} \left(\delta_{c,p} \cdot \cos \frac{p2\pi}{N} n + \delta_{s,p} \cdot \sin \frac{p2\pi}{N} n \right), \tag{5}$$

where $I_k(t,n)$ is an indicator for the event k during interval n on day t, θ denotes the full parameter vector to be estimated, and μ_0, λ_k, $\delta_{c,p}$, and $\delta_{s,p}$ are fixed coefficients. Apart from the dummy variables, equation (5) is a Fourier flexible form (FFF) and may be given a semi-nonparametric interpretation.[18]

Assembling all the pieces, we obtain the operational regression,

$$\hat{x}_{t,n} \equiv 2 \log[|R_{t,n} - \bar{R}|] - \log \hat{\sigma}^2_{t,n} = \hat{c} + f(\theta,t,n) + \hat{u}_{t,n} \tag{6}$$

where $\hat{c} = E[\log Z^2_{t,n}] + E[\log \sigma^2_{t,n} - \log \hat{\sigma}^2_{t,n}]$ and the error process $\{\hat{u}_{t,n}\}$ is stationary.

The two-step procedure is now apparent. The first step requires calculating $\bar{R}$, providing a reasonable estimator of $\hat{\sigma}_{t,n}$, and specifying the exact form of the announcement dummies and lag lengths to be included in the regressors of equation (5). Thus, the first step provides the observable regressand and regressors for equation (6). The resulting expression constitutes a nonlinear regression in the intraday time interval, n, and the event dummies, I_k. It is parameterized by a number of sinusoids (δ-coefficients), and dummies (λ-coefficients). It is estimated, in the second step, by ordinary least squares (OLS). We refer to equation (6) and the associated OLS procedure as the *FFF regression*. This two-step method is not fully efficient, but, as argued in Appendix B, given correct specification of the first-step FFF regressor, the parameter estimates are consistent. An important advantage of the

[18] The FFF is introduced by Gallant (1981). The trigonometric terms obey a strict periodicity of one day, as desired. One may add a quadratic function in the intraday interval, n, but these terms are not significant and thus simply omitted. Allowing for the intraday pattern to depend on the overall volatility level for the day, σ_t, appears important for some markets, but is not significant in this context. The more general specification is utilized in Andersen and Bollerslev (1997a).

regression specified in terms of $\hat{x}_{t,n}$, relative to, say, $R^2_{t,n}$, is that the log-transform effectively eliminates the extreme outliers in the five-minute return series, rendering the regression much more robust.

A final issue concerns the proper choice of the first-stage estimator, $\hat{\sigma}_{t,n}$. A simple candidate class may be derived from standard ARCH models, fit at the daily level. For example, the GARCH(1,1) estimates in Section II.A are directly applicable, if one stipulates that this volatility component is constant over the trading day. The associated intraday estimates are

$$\hat{\sigma}_{t,n}=\hat{\sigma}_t/N^{1/2}. \tag{7a}$$

Alternatively, the temporal variation in $\sigma_{t,n}$ could be ignored altogether, as in the estimator,

$$\hat{\sigma}_{t,n} = \bar{\sigma}/N^{1/2}, \tag{7b}$$

where $\bar{\sigma}$ denotes the sample mean of $\hat{\sigma}_t$. In either case, we do not capture the high-frequency movements in this component, but, as argued above, the consistency of the FFF regression is retained. The advantage of the (constant) estimator (7b) is that it eliminates any generated regressor problem. On the other hand, it does nothing to alleviate the heteroskedasticity. In contrast, the estimator, (7a), does provide a normalization with respect to the strong overall movements in volatility, which should improve the efficiency of the second step procedure, and allow for more accurate volatility forecasts, as documented further in Section V below.[19]

IV. Empirical Results

As in Section II, we report on the empirical findings in three separate sections. The first focuses on calendar, the second on announcement, and the third on ARCH effects. However, all coefficients are estimated simultaneously, so the full range of volatility features is controlled for throughout.

A. Calendar Effects

Decisions regarding the treatment of a number of distinct features in the five-minute return series are necessary prior to estimation of the intraday pattern. We briefly outline our approach, but refer to Appendix C for a more

[19] The robustness of the developed FFF regression is worth reiterating. The nature of conditional heteroskedasticity is left unspecified, and need not have anything to do with the preliminary estimator, $\hat{\sigma}_{t,n}$. Likewise, the distributional form for the conditional errors is unspecified, except for the existence of second-order moments. General stochastic dependencies are allowed in both the calendar and announcement effects. The only caveat is a "generated regressor" problem that may arise from the first step estimates of $\hat{\sigma}_{t,n}$, which may impart a bias in our standard errors (see Pagan (1984)). However, we document below that this problem is negligible in the current context, given our choice of first-step estimators.

extensive treatment. First, we observe that the extreme slowdown in market activity over some holidays as well as the Tokyo lunch period resembles weekends. Because we aim to characterize the overall, average volatility pattern, the systematic lack of reliable return observations over a given interval during the day is an overriding concern. Consequently, we treat these episodes as analogous to weekends and, effectively, eliminate them from the sample. Each Tokyo lunch period, from 12:00 to 1:45 p.m. local time, each major holiday, and each interval associated with a failure in data transmission, are assigned the identical low, positive return, and a dummy variable is introduced to account (perfectly) for the returns over these periods. This retains the strict periodicity in the data, while removing any impact from these episodes on the inference. Some regional holidays involve only subdued, rather than extremely thin, quoting activity, so we introduce a "Holiday" dummy to accommodate these predictable reductions in volatility. There is also some evidence of a slowdown in the periods surrounding the weekends, i.e., early Monday morning in the Pacific zone, and late Friday afternoon in the North American segment. We accommodate these by constrained second-order polynomials over the corresponding intervals, resulting in two regression coefficients for each period. The Tokyo market opening effect is captured by a single coefficient that allows for a linear decay in the associated volatility burst. U.S. Daylight Saving Time induces a one-hour parallel shift in the intraday pattern over parts of the day, which is readily accommodated. However, this increases volatility in the earlier part of the (Summer) day, and this is compensated by lower volatility during the now-longer hiatus between the North American and Pacific segments. This is captured by a restricted second-order polynomial (one free parameter) over the latter part of the day. We also incorporate day-of-the-week dummies for all weekdays except Monday. Finally, we need to select the sinusoids to be included in the seminonparametric component of equation (4). The removal of the Tokyo lunch period facilitates approximation of the intraday pattern by means of smooth functional, and we obtain an excellent fit using only four sets of sinusoids; see Andersen and Bollerslev (1997a), Payne (1996), and Kofman and Martens (1997) for earlier specifications of this form.

We control for four different types of macroeconomic announcements in this section. The most influential is the Employment Report—the "king of kings" among announcements (Carnes and Slifer (1991))—and it is allowed to abide by its own volatility decay rate. The other significant U.S. announcements are incorporated as "Category I" (more important) or "Category II" (less important) releases. The former includes GDP and trade balance figures, and Durable Goods Orders, while the latter contains the PPI, Retail Sales, Housing Starts, Leading Indicators, Initial Jobless Claims, Factory Orders, and German M3 figures. Finally, releases following the biweekly Bundesbank meeting have a major impact, so this effect is also treated separately. Each type of announcement effect is summarized by a single regression coefficient. Interpretation of these point estimates is discussed in the next section.

The estimation results for the full system, using the first-step estimator (7a), are recorded in the second column of Table III. All coefficients associated with the intraday pattern are highly significant, except for the last sine term.[20] As mentioned, the volatility slowdown over the latter part of the Summer days compensates for increased activity earlier in the day due to Daylight Saving Time. The strong market opening effect in Tokyo is noteworthy; the pronounced announcement and holiday effects were expected. In contrast, the Monday morning effect is insignificant, once all calendar effects are taken into account, and the Friday afternoon effect is at best borderline significant. Similarly, there is no indication of a day-of-the-week effect. Although the Friday coefficient is large when judged by conventional OLS standard errors, the effect is likely an artifact of specific events that happened to occur on Fridays. When evaluated against the robust standard error the effect is decidedly insignificant.

These results justify estimation without the day-of-the-week dummies, as given in Table III, column three. The only qualitative difference is that the Friday afternoon effect now is insignificant at the 5 percent level. As a last robustness check, we estimate the identical system, imposing the constant daily volatility factor, (7b). The results in Table III, column four, confirm that the parameter estimates are largely unchanged and the qualitative features of the inference unaffected. Thus, the inclusion of $\hat{\sigma}_t$ does not seem to give rise to a practical, generated regressors problem.

The Summer Time intraday volatility pattern, as dictated by the estimates in column three, Table III, is displayed in Figure 7. Both the Tokyo opening effect, and the increased volatility during the overlap in the Asian and European and, subsequently, the European and North American segments are apparent. The Monday morning and Friday afternoon effects also manifest themselves clearly, in spite of being marginally insignificant. The excellent overall fit is evident from Figure 8, which displays predicted and actual average absolute five-minute returns for the corresponding period in the FFF dimension underlying the estimation. The results for the Winter Time regime are similar.

Arguably, the corresponding fit in the absolute return dimension is a better gauge of the success of the model. To convert the FFF pattern into absolute returns, note that equations (3) through (7) imply

$$|R_{t,n} - \bar{R}| = N^{-1/2} \cdot \hat{\sigma}_t \cdot \exp(f(\theta, t, n)/2) \cdot \exp(\hat{u}_{t,n}/2). \tag{8}$$

One-day-ahead intraday forecasts, conditional on $\hat{\sigma}_t$, may therefore be generated by taking the conditional expectation in equation (8), and evaluating $f(\cdot; t, n)$ at the estimated θ. If we ignore potential correlation between $\hat{\sigma}_t$ and the transformed error term, we simply have to obtain the unconditional expectation, $E[\exp(\hat{u}_{t,n}/2)]$, which in turn may be estimated by averaging the corresponding expression, $\exp(\hat{u}_{t,n}/2)$, over the relevant residuals in the sam

[20] The large differences between the heteroskedasticity and autocorrelation consistent standard errors and the OLS standard errors signify the importance of accounting for the effects of the strong volatility clustering and outlying observations when conducting the inference.

Table III

Parameter Estimates for the Regression of Logarithmic Squared Demeaned Five-Minute Deutsche Mark–Dollar Returns on Deterministic Regressors Capturing Calendar and Announcement Effects

The returns are calculated from interpolated five-minute logarithmic average bid–ask quotes for the deutsche mark–dollar (DM–$) spot exchange rate from October 1, 1992 through September 29, 1993. Quotes from Friday 21:00 GMT through Sunday 21:00 GMT are excluded, resulting in a total of 74,880 return observations. The robust standard errors reflect a Newey and West (1987) type correction incorporating 289 lags. The regression equation takes the form

$$2\log\frac{|R_{t,n}-\bar{R}|}{\hat{\sigma}_{t,n}} = \hat{c} + \mu_0 + \sum_{k=1}^{D}\lambda_k\cdot I_k(t,n) + \sum_{p=1}^{4}\left(\delta_{c,p}\cdot\cos\frac{p2\pi}{N}n + \delta_{s,p}\cdot\sin\frac{p2\pi}{N}n\right) + \hat{u}_{t,n},$$

where $R_{t,n}$ denotes the five-minute returns for interval n on day t, $\bar{R}$ the sample mean of the five-minute returns, $\hat{\sigma}_{t,n}$ is an a priori estimate of the overall daily level of the five-minute return standard deviation, $\hat{u}_{t,n}$ is a mean zero error term, and the right-hand side variables represent the deterministic calendar and announcement regressors. The volatility estimates, $\hat{\sigma}_{t,n}$, for interval n on day t, are obtained from an MA(1)-GARCH(1,1) model fit to a longer daily sample of DM–$ spot exchange rates from March 14, 1979 through September 29, 1993. Denoting the daily return standard deviation estimate by $\hat{\sigma}_t$, the daily volatility factor is captured by $\hat{\sigma}_{t,n} \equiv N^{-1/2}\cdot\hat{\sigma}_t$. The "Daily Volatility Excluded" column indicates that $N^{-1/2}\cdot\bar{\sigma}$ is used in place of $\hat{\sigma}_{t,n}$, where $\bar{\sigma}$ denotes the sample mean of $\hat{\sigma}_t$. During the U.S. Summer Time, the sinusoid regressors are translated leftward by one hour and an additional restricted second-order polynomial allows for a volatility slowdown between 19:00 and 24:00 GMT. The $I_k(t,n)$ regressors indicate either regular dummy variables (in the case of holidays or weekdays) or a prespecified volatility response pattern associated with a calendar-related characteristic or an announcement. A separate linear volatility decay is allowed for the Tokyo open, 00:00–00:35 GMT. Similarly, a restricted second-order polynomial adapts to the volatility slowdown around the weekends, i.e., early Monday morning, 21:00–22:30 GMT, and late Friday, 17:00–21:00 GMT (U.S. Winter Time) or 16:00–21:00 GMT (U.S. Summer Time). Finally, the volatility decay pattern following announcements is restricted to last one hour (13 intervals), except for the Employment Report pattern which lasts two hours (25 intervals). All of the response patterns are approximated by a third-order polynomial restricted to reach zero at the end of the response horizon. The announcement coefficients measure the extent to which the absolute returns load onto this pattern following the announcement. Category I comprises U.S. announcements on GDP, the trade balance, and durable goods, and Category II covers U.S. releases of PPI, retail sales, housing starts, leading indicators, jobless claims, and factory orders, and the German M3 figures. Robust t-statistics are given in brackets and regular OLS t-statistics are in parentheses.

Parameter	Full System	Day-of-Week Effect Excluded	Day-of-Week, Daily Volatility Excluded
$\mu_0 + \hat{c}$	−1.77	−1.76	−1.85
	[−32.8]	[−69.2]	[−56.3]
	(−79.4)	(−155.6)	(−162.0)
$\delta_{c,1}$	−0.12	−0.13	−0.13
	[−4.41]	[−4.58]	[−4.78]
	(−8.27)	(−8.62)	(−8.77)
$\delta_{c,2}$	−0.13	−0.13	−0.13
	[−4.93]	[−5.09]	[−5.10]
	(−8.16)	(−8.30)	(−8.26)
$\delta_{c,3}$	−0.28	−0.28	−0.29
	[−11.8]	[−12.0]	[−11.4]
	(−18.4)	(−18.5)	(−18.5)

Table III—*Continued*

Parameter	Full System	Day-of-Week Effect Excluded	Day-of-Week, Daily Volatility Excluded
$\delta_{c,4}$	0.14 [8.10] (10.6)	0.14 [8.01] (10.6)	0.14 [8.10] (10.6)
$\delta_{s,1}$	−0.62 [−24.1] (−38.6)	−0.62 [−23.8] (−38.5)	−0.62 [−23.4] (−38.4)
$\delta_{s,2}$	−0.21 [−10.4] (−14.3)	−0.21 [−10.2] (−14.1)	−0.21 [−10.2] (−14.0)
$\delta_{s,3}$	0.17 [8.64] (11.9)	0.18 [8.76] (12.1)	0.17 [8.55] (11.8)
$\delta_{s,4}$	−0.01 [−0.68] (−0.91)	−0.01 [−0.46] (−0.62)	−0.01 [−0.68] (−0.94)
Summer slowdown	−1.14 [−5.91] (−10.6)	−1.15 [−5.95] (−10.7)	−1.08 [−5.06] (−9.93)
Tokyo opening	0.59 [8.96] (9.81)	0.58 [8.91] (9.76)	0.59 [9.06] (9.76)
Holiday	−0.698 [−5.76] (−13.86)	−0.712 [−6.28] (−15.25)	−0.703 [−6.87] (−14.93)
Employment Report	1.755 [10.38] (11.11)	1.746 [10.47] (11.09)	1.739 [8.82] (10.95)
Category I announcement	0.997 [7.23] (8.35)	0.991 [7.28] (8.33)	0.992 [7.48] (8.26)
Category II announcement	0.627 [6.71] (8.64)	0.620 [7.03] (8.65)	0.619 [6.89] (8.56)
Bundesbank meeting	1.465 [6.20] (10.01)	1.457 [6.20] (9.99)	1.492 [6.43] (10.13)
Monday early	−0.301 [−0.26] (−0.36)	−0.368 [−0.32] (−0.44)	−0.529 [−0.45] (−0.63)
	0.001 [0.001] (0.001)	0.069 [0.047] (0.065)	0.208 [0.14] (0.19)
Friday late	−0.609 [−2.04] (−3.36)	−0.412 [−1.43] (−2.37)	−0.437 [−1.39] (−2.49)
	0.068 [0.49] (0.88)	0.011 [0.08] (0.14)	0.017 [0.12] (0.22)

Table III—*Continued*

Parameter	Full System	Day-of-Week Effect Excluded	Day-of-Week, Daily Volatility Excluded
Tuesday	−0.065 [−0.95] (−2.17)	—	—
Wednesday	0.006 [0.08] (0.19)	—	—
Thursday	0.050 [0.74] (1.65)	—	—
Friday	0.096 [1.31] (2.99)	—	—

ple.[21] The unconditional volatility forecasts may be obtained in identical fashion, except that $\bar{\sigma}$ would be used in place of $\hat{\sigma}_t$. This resulting (unconditional) pattern for the Summer Time regime is displayed in Figure 9, and contrasted to the actual average absolute returns. While the more pronounced sensitivity to outliers renders the actual average pattern somewhat jagged, the overall fit is very good.

We end the section by assessing the economic significance of the estimated FFF coefficients. The point estimates associated with regular dummy variables in equation (5) are readily interpreted. For example, a coefficient of unity is tantamount to the addition, in equation (8), of a multiplicative factor of $\exp(1/2) \approx 1.65$. Thus, volatility for the corresponding interval increases by about 65 percent. Consequently, the holiday factor amounts to $\exp(-0.712/2) \approx 0.700$, or a reduction in volatility of about 30 percent. This effect applies uniformly to each interval covered by the Holiday dummy. Beyond less important U.S. "holidays," such as Veterans Day and weekdays between Christmas and New Year's Day, these also include regional holidays in Tokyo, Wellington, Sydney, and London.

Assessment of the remaining calendar and announcement effects is more complicated because the regressors are not simple indicators, but involve prespecified dynamic response patterns. In particular, assuming that event k impacts volatility over N_k intervals, the implied set of regressors are

$$\sum_{i=0}^{N} \lambda(k,i) \cdot I_k(t, n - i).$$

[21] Note that any correlation would enhance the predictive power of the daily volatility factor. Thus, the assessment of the explanatory power provided by $\hat{\sigma}_t$ in this context may be deemed a conservative estimate of its true predictive value.

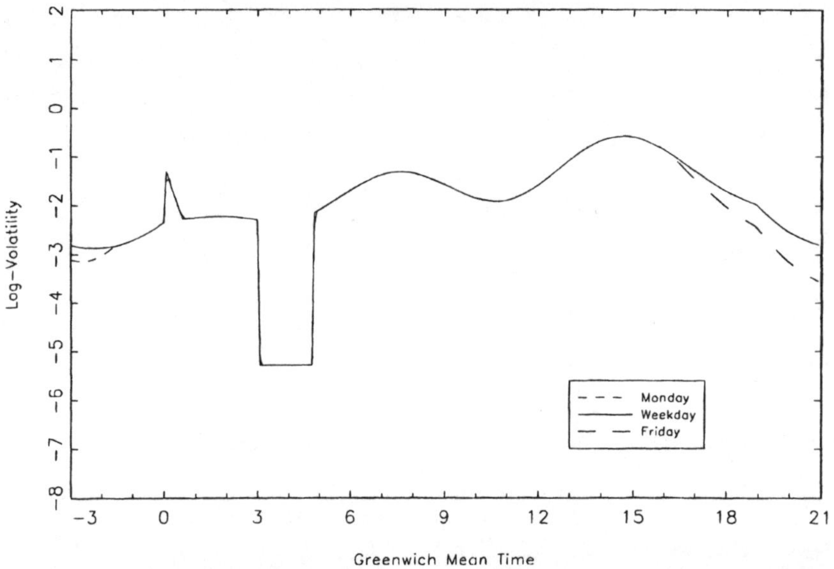

Figure 7. Flexible Fourier form fit. The figure graphs the fit to the average logarithmic-squared, normalized, and demeaned five-minute deutsche mark–dollar (DM–$) returns across the 24-hour weekday trading cycle during U.S. Summer Time. The returns are calculated from interpolated five-minute logarithmic average bid–ask quotes for the DM–$ spot exchange rate over the October 1, 1992 through September 29, 1993 sample period. Quotes from Friday 21:00 GMT through Sunday 21:00 GMT are excluded, resulting in a total of 74,880 return observations. The interval starts with 20:55–21:00 GMT and ends at 20:50–20:55 GMT. The Tokyo lunch period, 3:00–4:45 GMT, is artificially assigned low returns, so this part of the pattern is not estimated. The fit is based on four sets of sinusoids, dummies for the Tokyo open period, 00:00–00:35 GMT, and constrained second-order polynomials for early Monday and late Friday, as well as the latter part of the U.S. Summer Time trading day.

If the announcement affects volatility for an hour or two, there are 13 or 25 separate event-specific coefficients to estimate. Given the limited number of occurrences of each event and the inherent noise in the returns process, this is highly inefficient. Instead, we impose a reasonable decay-structure on the volatility response pattern, and simply estimate the degree to which the event "loads onto" this pattern, by imposing $\lambda(k,i) = \lambda_k \cdot \gamma(i)$, $i = 0,1,\ldots,N_k$, where $\gamma(i)$ dictates the prespecified pattern. Hence, $\exp(\lambda_k \cdot \gamma(0)/2)$ signifies the immediate response of the absolute returns, while the response at the ith lag equals $\exp(\lambda_k \cdot \gamma(i)/2)$. The corresponding cumulative response measure is naturally defined by

$$M(k) = \sum_{i=0}^{N_k} \left[\exp\left(\frac{\lambda_k \cdot \gamma(i)}{2} \right) - 1 \right]. \tag{9}$$

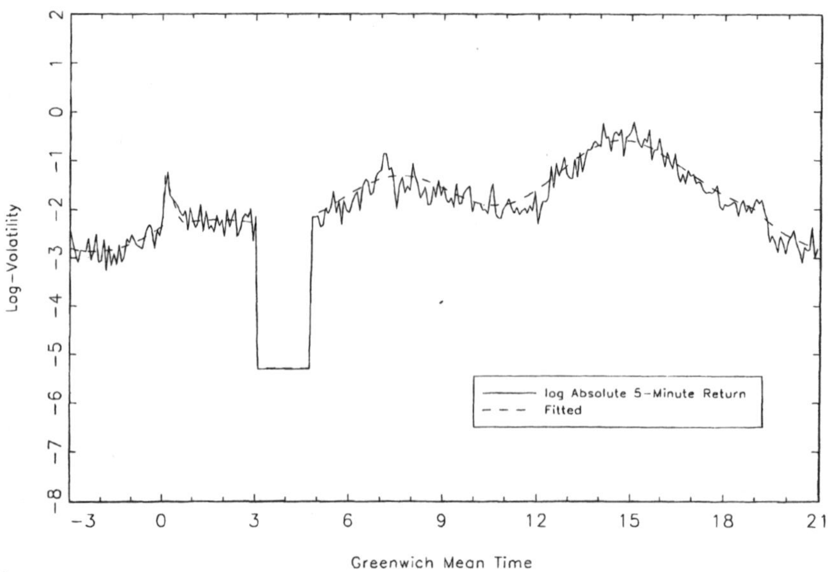

Figure 8. Average intradaily log-volatility fit. The figure graphs the fit to the average logarithmic-squared, normalized, and demeaned five-minute deutsche mark–dollar (DM–$) returns across the 24-hour weekday trading cycle plotted against the corresponding average sample values. The returns are calculated from interpolated five-minute logarithmic average bid–ask quotes for the DM–$ spot exchange rate over the October 1, 1992 through September 29, 1993 sample period. Quotes from Friday 21:00 GMT through Sunday 21:00 GMT are excluded, resulting in a total of 74,880 return observations. The GMT axis starts with the 20:55–21:00 GMT interval and ends at 20:50–20:55 GMT. The Tokyo lunch period, 3:00–4:45 GMT, is artificially assigned low returns, so this part is not fitted. The fit is based on four sets of sinusoids, dummies for the Tokyo open, 00:00–00:35 GMT, and constrained second-order polynomials for the latter part of the U.S. Summer Time trading day, as well as early Monday and late Friday. The latter "weekend effects" are not indicated on the figures. The Summer Time average is based on 145 weekdays.

This nonlinear function of the event-specific loading coefficient, λ_k, reflects the impact over the entire response horizon expressed as a multiplicative factor scaled in units of average volatility per interval over the period. The Tokyo market opening, for example, has an immediate response coefficient of 0.65 and a cumulative response measure of 2.12, implying that volatility jumps by 65 percent at 9 a.m. Tokyo time, while more than twice the usual volatility of a five-minute interval is added over the span of the half-hour response horizon. However, volatility is low at this point in the trading cycle, averaging about 0.025 percent per interval, so the full impact is only around 0.053 percent. Because the (median) cumulative absolute return is about 9 percent over our sample, this constitutes less than 0.6 percent of the return variability for a typical day. Although the effect is pronounced and robust, and market observers and traders clearly recognize it, it is thus arguably of limited overall economic importance. A similar calculation shows the eco-

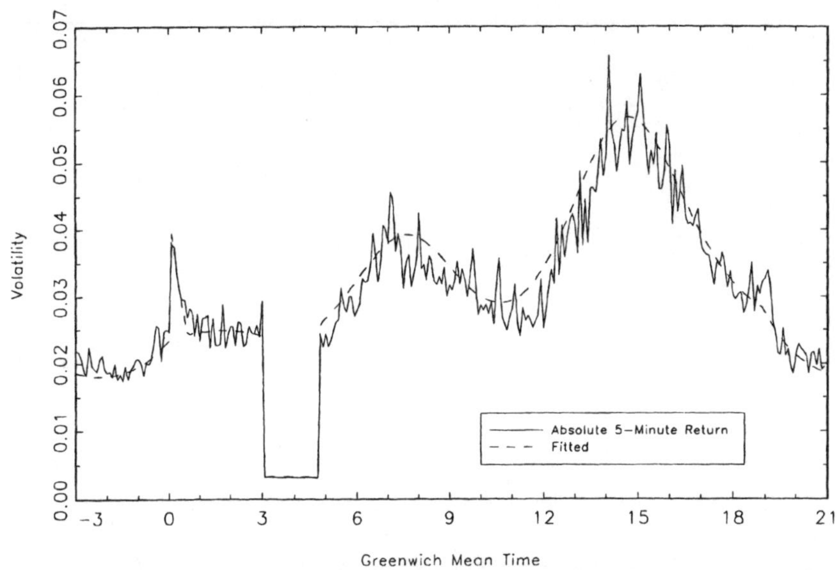

Figure 9. Average intraday absolute return fit. The figure graphs the fit to the average absolute five-minute deutsche mark–dollar (DM–$) returns across the 24-hour weekday trading cycle plotted against the corresponding average sample values. The returns are calculated from interpolated five-minute logarithmic average bid–ask quotes for the DM–$ spot exchange rate over the October 1, 1992 through September 29, 1993 sample period. Quotes from Friday 21:00 GMT through Sunday 21:00 GMT are excluded, resulting in a total of 74,880 return observations. The GMT axis starts with the 20:55–21:00 GMT interval and ends at 20:50–20:55 GMT. The Tokyo lunch period, 3:00–4:45 GMT, is artificially assigned low returns, so this part is not fitted. The fit is based on a Flexible Fourier Form regression of logarithmic-squared, normalized, and demeaned returns onto four sets of sinusoids, dummies for the Tokyo open, 00:00–00:35 GMT, and constrained second-order polynomials for the latter part of the U.S. Summer Time trading day, as well as early Monday and late Friday. The latter "weekend effects" are not indicated on the figures. The Summer Time average is based on 145 weekdays.

nomic significance of the early Monday effect to be negligible. The first few intervals have an estimated 14 percent reduction in volatility, but the total effect amounts to about 0.38 percent of the daily cumulative absolute returns. In contrast, the late Friday slowdown exerts a considerable effect. Due to Daylight Saving Time, separate estimates are obtained for Summer and Winter, but the reduction in volatility over the last interval of the day is 31 percent in both cases, with a cumulative impact of 3 to 4 percent at the daily level.

B. Announcement Effects

This section reports on our estimation of the volatility responses associated with regularly scheduled macroeconomic announcements in the United States, Germany, and Japan. Extensive experimentation reveals the qualitative fea-

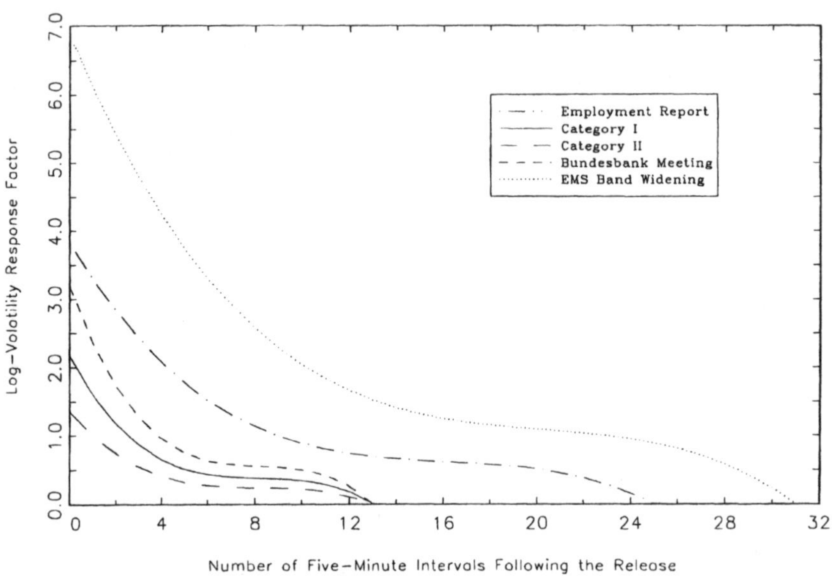

Figure 10. Dynamic announcement response patterns. The figure graphs the relative strength and duration of the estimated dynamic log-volatility response pattern of the five-minute deutsche mark–dollar (DM–$) returns following the release of macroeconomic announcements. The returns are calculated from interpolated five-minute logarithmic average bid–ask quotes for the DM–$ spot exchange rate over the October 1, 1992 through September 29, 1993 sample period. Quotes from Friday 21:00 GMT through Sunday 21:00 GMT are excluded, resulting in a total of 74,880 return observations. The response pattern estimates are obtained from a Flexible Fourier Form regression of the logarithmic-squared, normalized, and demeaned returns onto four sets of sinusoids, dummies for the Tokyo market opening, and constrained second-order polynomials for the latter part of the U.S. Summer Time trading day, as well as early Monday and late Friday.

tures of the average volatility impact to be remarkably similar across announcements, and well approximated by third-order polynomials constrained to reach zero at a one-hour horizon. In order to allow for simultaneous estimation of the multiple effects, we adopt this pattern as a universal format for the $\gamma(i)$ sequence. The announcements load onto the pattern in accordance with the logic underlying equation (9), except that a few releases, notably the Employment Report, follow elongated versions, so that their response horizons extend beyond one hour. Apart from this, the only source of variation across the estimated response patterns is the announcement-specific loading coefficients, λ_k.

A summary of the results may be based on the point estimates for the announcement coefficients in Table III, column three. The table includes all releases that are highly significant, with categories I and II consolidating those that have similar response patterns. The estimated average effects take the form displayed in Figure 10. For comparison, the figure also includes an estimated response pattern for the period following the widening of the ERM band. Because this decision arguably had the same one-shot character as regularly scheduled announcements, with no additional information to be released subsequently, the market response should share the qualitative features of the standard announcement responses. The remaining estimates are invariant to the inclusion of this event.

The relative size of the response patterns in Figure 10 is as expected. The revision of the EMS band is a major event, and the large and prolonged volatility response is no surprise. The ranking of the regular announcements reflects the fact that they are presorted according to apparent significance. More interesting is the size of the estimated effects. The coefficients displayed in Figure 10 represent $\lambda(k) \cdot \gamma(i)$ for $i = 0, 1, \ldots, 32$ where, e.g., $\gamma(0) = 2.18869$ and λ_k is given in Table III. For example, the contemporaneous response to an Employment Report is governed by $\lambda_k \cdot \gamma(0) = 1.746 \cdot 2.18869 = 3.822$. From equation (10), this is tantamount to a multiplicative impact on the absolute return of $\exp(3.822/2) = 6.76$, or an instantaneous jump in volatility of about 576 percent. The corresponding cumulative response from equation (9) amounts to 27.17. Since a conservative estimate of the expected absolute return during 8:30 to 10:30 EST, absent announcement effects, is approximately 0.05 percent per five-minute interval, the overall effect is an elevation of volatility by $27.27 \cdot 0.05 = 1.3585$ percent. Therefore, we find about a 15 (=1.3585/9.0) percent average increase in the cumulative absolute return for trading days that contain a scheduled Employment Report. Analogous calculations reveal that the instantaneous volatility nearly triples for Category I announcements, almost doubles for Category II announcements, and jumps by almost 400 percent following Bundesbank meetings, while the cumulative impact represents an increase in the daily cumulative absolute returns of about 3.6, 2.0, and 5.1 percent, respectively. Of course, the Bundesbank meetings are biweekly rather than monthly, so their overall impact, at least over this sample period, is estimated at close to two thirds of that of the U.S. Employment Report. Likewise, Categories I and II represent multiple monthly releases, so their combined impact is substantial. We again stress that these estimates represent average, or expected, responses. The most surprising releases are associated with a much larger impact. This point is exemplified by the ERM-band widening, which ranks eleventh on the list of large return innovations in Table II. The event is estimated to have raised the instantaneous absolute five-minute return by 3,000 percent, and to have increased the cumulative absolute return on August 2, 1993, by 36.6 percent. There are announcements within each of the four categories that are associated with even larger immediate responses than the ERM-band correction. Thus, some scheduled announcements induce truly spectacular bursts of volatility, although the responses, on average, are decidedly less pronounced.

The strict categorization in Table III is adequate for general characterization of the announcement effects, but clearly the categories cover quite diverse events. In order to convey more direct information regarding the importance of each individual type of release, Table IV reports loading coefficients for all U.S. and German announcements investigated in the study.

Table IV

Parameter Estimates of Specific Announcements Effects Obtained from Regressions of the Logarithmic Squared Demeaned Five-Minute Deutsche Mark–Dollar Returns on Deterministic Regressors Allowing for Calendar and Other Announcement Effects.

The returns are calculated from interpolated five-minute logarithmic average bid–ask quotes for the deutsche mark–dollar (DM–$) spot exchange rate from October 1, 1992 through September 29, 1993. Quotes from Friday 21:00 GMT through Sunday 21:00 GMT are excluded, resulting in a total of 74,880 return observations. The regression takes the form

$$2\log\frac{|R_{t,n}-\bar{R}|}{\hat{\sigma}_{t,n}} = \hat{c} + \mu_0 + \sum_{k=1}^{D}\lambda_k \cdot I_k(t,n) + \sum_{p=1}^{4}\left(\delta_{c,p}\cdot\cos\frac{p2\pi}{N}n + \delta_{s,p}\cdot\sin\frac{p2\pi}{N}n\right) + \hat{u}_{t,n},$$

where $R_{t,n}$ denotes the five-minute returns for interval n on day t, $\bar{R}$ the sample mean of the five-minute returns, $\hat{\sigma}^2_{t,n}$ is an a priori estimate of the overall daily level of the five-minute return standard deviation, $\hat{u}_{t,n}$ is a mean zero error term, and the right-hand side variables represent the deterministic calendar and announcement regressors. The volatility estimates, $\hat{\sigma}_{t,n}$, for interval n on day t, are obtained from an MA(1)-GARCH(1,1) model fit to a longer daily sample of DM–$ spot exchange rates from March 14, 1979 through September 29, 1993. Denoting the daily return standard deviation estimate by $\hat{\sigma}_t$, the daily volatility factor is captured by $\hat{\sigma}_{t,n} \equiv N^{-1/2}\cdot\hat{\sigma}_t$. During U.S. Summer Time, the sinusoid regressors are translated leftward by one hour and an additional restricted second-order polynomial allows for a volatility slowdown between 19:00 and 24:00 GMT. The $I_k(t,n)$ regressors indicate either regular dummy variables (for holidays or weekdays) or prespecified volatility response patterns associated with a calendar feature or an announcement. A separate linear volatility decay is allowed for the Tokyo open, 00:00–00:35 GMT. Similarly, a restricted second-order polynomial adapts to the volatility slowdown around weekends, early Monday morning, 21:00–22:30 GMT, and late Friday, 17:00–21:00 GMT (U.S. Winter Time) or 16:00–21:00 GMT (U.S. Summer Time). The volatility decay pattern following announcements is restricted to last one hour (13 intervals), except for the U.S. Employment Report pattern which lasts for two hours (25 intervals). All response patterns are approximated by a third-order polynomial restricted to reach zero at the end of the response horizon. The reported coefficients measure the extent to which the absolute returns load onto this pattern following the announcement. Beyond the specific announcement under investigation, all of the regressions allow for the independent influence of the U.S. Employment Report, the Bundesbank meeting, and category I and II announcements. Category I covers announcements on the U.S. GDP, trade balance, and durable goods. Category II includes U.S. releases of PPI, Retail Sales, Housing Starts, Leading Indicators, Jobless Claims, and Factory Orders, and German M3 figures. If the specific announcement under investigation belongs to one of these categories, it is dropped from the category. The instantaneous jump in volatility measures the estimated increase in the five-minute absolute return for the interval where the announcement is made; the estimated total cumulative absolute return induced by the announcement over the assumed response horizon is measured relative to the median cumulative absolute return over the sample of 9.0 percent per day.

Panel A: Important Announcement Effects

Announcement	Coefficient [robust t-stat]	Instantaneous Jump in Volatility (%)	Impact in Percent of Daily Cum. Abs. Return
Employment Report	1.75 [11.5]	576	15.1
Advance Report on Durable Goods	1.27 [5.75]	303	5.17

Table IV—*Continued*

Announcement	Coefficient [robust t-stat]	Instantaneous Jump in Volatility (%)	Impact in Percent of Daily Cum. Abs. Return
Bundesbank meeting	1.46 [9.74]	392	5.11
Merchandise Trade	0.889 [4.24]	164	3.12
Gross Domestic Product (GDP)	0.836 [3.43]	150	2.87
Producer Price Index (PPI)	0.703 [3.67]	116	2.31
Retail Sales	0.670 [2.86]	108	2.17
German M3	0.872 [4.77]	160	2.13
Leading Indicators	0.624 [3.55]	98	1.99
Housing Starts	0.515 [2.29]	76	1.59
Factory Orders	0.481 [2.05]	69	1.46
New Jobless Claims	0.334 [3.02]	44	0.968
Japanese Gross National Product	0.600 [2.40]	93	0.949
German Gross Domestic Product	0.506 [1.43]	74	0.931

Panel B: Less Important U.S. Announcements

Announcement	Coefficient	Robust t-stat
U.S. Treasury Report	0.338	1.62
Consumer Confidence (Conference Board)	0.273	1.20
Consumer Price Index (CPI)	0.236	1.02
Construction Spending	0.211	0.954
Car Sales	0.091	0.709
Business Inventories	0.124	0.704
Housing Completions	0.070	0.430
Import Prices	0.076	0.374
University of Michigan Survey	0.043	0.315
Current Account Deficit	0.084	0.314
Industrial Output/Capital Utilization	0.067	0.282
Non-Farm Productivity	0.035	0.154
M2 Figures	0.017	0.134
Personal Income	0.030	0.102
Real Earnings	0.005	0.021
Reserve Assets	−0.012	−0.062
House Sales	−0.041	−0.150
Minutes from FOMC Meeting	−0.177	−0.613
Capital Spending Survey	−0.261	−0.689

Table IV—*Continued*

Announcement	Coefficient	Robust *t*-stat
NAPM Survey	−0.205	−0.777
Consumer Installment Credit	−0.375	−1.02
Wholesale Sales	−0.181	−1.06

Panel C. Less Important German Announcements

Announcement	Coefficient	Robust *t*-stat
Wholesale Turnover	0.322	1.56
Retail Sales	0.124	0.668
Consumer Price Index (all states tallied)	0.072	0.668
East German Consumer Price Index	0.122	0.647
East German Industrial Orders	0.152	0.630
Industrial Orders	0.110	0.465
Producer Price Index	0.085	0.423
Wholesale Prices	0.054	0.295
Current Account	0.032	0.181
Consumer Price Index (First State)	0.010	0.051
Business Insolvencies	0.002	0.010
Employment Report	−0.004	−0.022
Import Prices	−0.011	−0.049
Consumer Price Index (Final)	−0.089	−0.427
East German Employment	−0.075	−0.438
East German Producer Price Index	−0.092	−0.503
Industrial Output	−0.176	−0.702
Capital Account	−0.238	−1.14
East German Industrial Output	−0.245	−1.18
Consumer Price Index (Preliminary)	−0.563	−1.84

These are obtained by treating each announcement in the manner afforded the Employment Report and Bundesbank meetings in Table III, i.e., we control for all remaining significant announcements while estimating the marginal impact of the release under investigation. All statistically significant releases are listed in Table IV, Panel A, and ranked according to their estimated impact on the cumulative absolute returns. The results largely confirm our earlier findings. Indeed, the first twelve announcements are the ones controlled for throughout in our estimation procedure. The set of significant U.S. releases also corresponds closely to those identified by Ederington and Lee (1993, 1995a, 1995b) and Payne (1996). Of course, we would expect the relative importance of the releases to differ across markets. For instance, Ederington and Lee (1993) and Jones, Lamont, and Lumsdaine (1995) find the PPI figures to be almost as important as the employment report for U.S. bond market volatility; see also Goodhart et al. (1993) and DeGennaro and Shrieve (1995) for analyses of high-frequency news effects in the U.S. dollar–British pound and U.S. dollar–Japanese yen foreign exchange markets, respectively.[22] The overwhelming significance of the two German monetary announcements is also interesting, especially in light of the fact that none of the corresponding U.S. monetary announcements have any explanatory power; for evidence pertaining to earlier periods and other rates see, e.g., Hardouvelis (1984), Goodhart and Smith (1985), Hakkio and Pearce (1985), Ito and Roley (1987), and Thornton (1989). However, it is worth recalling the intense scrutiny of German monetary policy over the sample period due to the frictions in the EMS.[23] Moreover, U.S. monetary policy was unusually uncontroversial over the period. For example, there were no changes in the Fed Funds rate over the sample. Only confirmation of our results over a longer sample period will allow us to gauge the robustness of these particular findings. Nonetheless, the results are consistent with the emphasis that the Bundesbank allegedly places on monetary targets as guidelines for its policy decisions.

Table IV, Panel A, also includes the only Japanese release of any significance, namely the Japanese GNP figures. Since there are only four annual releases of this statistic, the announcement is of limited overall importance, but the statistical significance is noteworthy. The directional response of the exchange rate is consistent with a strengthening of the dollar on positive innovations to the Japanese GNP. It suggests an interpretation that stresses the U.S.–Japanese trade imbalance. Strong growth in Japan would be conducive to imports from the United States, and a shrinkage of the overall U.S. deficit vis-à-vis Japan. However, the small sample precludes any firm conclusions. For comparison purposes the table also includes the German GDP figures. These are estimated to be of about the same economic importance as the Japanese GNP numbers, although the effect is not statistically significant at the 5 percent level.

The remaining 22 U.S. and 20 German news releases were all individually insignificant, but the mere fact that a majority of the coefficients are positive (15 versus 7 and 11 versus 9, respectively) suggests that on average these announcements contribute positively to the DM–$ volatility, although the economic impact in most instances is negligible. The complete listing is given in Table IV, Panels B and C.

The qualitative importance of the announcement effects is perhaps best illustrated by observing that they "explain" the significance of weekday dummies. A number of previous studies have noted the importance of allowing for day-of-the-week effects when modeling daily exchange rate move-

[22] Eddelbüttel and McCurdy (1996) and Chang and Taylor (1996) also find that a simple frequency count of the news headlines on the Reuters screen is positively related to the intradaily DM–$ volatility, but has low overall explanatory power.

[23] For a recent discussion of the Bundesbank monetary policy rules see Clarida and Gertler (1996). In a related context, Peiers (1997) provides an empirical analysis on the role of price leadership by Deutschebank in the DM–$ interbank market in the two hours surrounding Bundesbank foreign exchange interventions.

ments; see, e.g., McFarland, Pettit, and Sung (1982, 1987), So (1987), Hsieh (1988, 1989), and Baillie and Bollerslev (1989). Upon running the FFF regression, using the volatility estimates from equation (6), and including all calendar effects but *excluding the announcement effects*, we obtain the following coefficients on the weekday dummies for Tuesday through Friday: −0.038 [−0.54] (−1.26), 0.038 [0.53] (1.24), 0.118 [1.68] (3.85), and 0.165 [2.19] (5.09), where the square brackets provide robust t-statistics and the parentheses report standard OLS t-statistics. Thus, ignoring the announcement effects produces economically large day-of-the-week effects, with Friday having estimated excess absolute returns on the order of $\exp(\frac{1}{2}\cdot 0.165) - 1 \approx 8.6$ percent, and Thursday of $\exp(\frac{1}{2}\cdot 0.118) - 1 \approx 6.1$ percent. Moreover, the effect is highly significant based on the conventional heteroskedasticity adjusted OLS standard errors, and the Friday effect remains significant at the 5 percent level when judged against fully robust standard errors. Of course, Table III demonstrates that this result vanishes, if we account for the announcement effects. The large Thursday and Friday dummies reflect the clustering of scheduled news releases on these weekdays. Given the estimates in Table IV, a back-of-the-envelope calculation indicates the magnitude of the involved effects. For example, Fridays contain all 12 Employment Report releases, as well as 4 Trade Balance, 2 Housing Start, 5 CPI, 3 Retail Sales, 5 PPI, 5 Business Inventories, 3 Durable Goods, 3 GDP, 3 Factory Orders, 5 Industrial Output/ Capital Utilization, 1 Leading Indicator, 1 Jobless Claims, and 1 Bundesbank meeting releases over the year. In total, this increases the average cumulative absolute returns on Fridays by about 5.4 percent. The unexplained gap of about 3.1 percent is small, and certainly consistent with random variation. In fact, from Table II it is evident that the most influential releases of PPI, Retail Sales, and Durable Goods figures happen to occur on Fridays, and, in addition, there are two distinct episodes of "ERM turmoil" on this weekday. Hence, the enhanced volatility on Fridays is readily "explained," which is consistent with the message obtained from the robust inference. A similar analysis applies to Thursdays. The Bundesbank meetings typically take place on this weekday, resulting in 23 releases. This combined with 51 Jobless Claims, 6 Trade Balance, 6 Factory Orders, 5 Retail Sales, 4 PPI, 3 CPI, 3 GDP, and 2 Housing Start Releases plus numerous minor announcements explains an average elevation of volatility on the order of 5.0 percent. The residual 1.0 percent is comparable to the implied variation across the first three weekdays, and is clearly insignificant.

Consequently, there is no evidence of a day-of-the-week effect. The implication is that volatility forecasts based on such dummies are biased. For instance, if there are no scheduled announcements on a Friday, forecasts will tend to be inflated by about 7 to 8 percent, but volatility for a Friday containing just an Employment Report release, on average, will be underestimated by the same magnitude. If additional announcements are scheduled for the same Friday the downward bias in the forecast is further aggravated.

In summary, macroeconomic announcements have a large impact when they hit the market, with the largest five-minute returns over the entire sample readily being identified with such public releases. Clearly, for sensible inference around these periods, it is necessary to control for this effect. However, the induced bursts of volatility are short-lived. As such, the overall significance of these announcements for volatility at the daily level is tenuous. In fact, the majority of the releases induce average excess cumulative absolute returns of approximately, or less than, 5 percent of that for a typical trading day. Only the employment report is associated with a substantially higher impact. Section V further explores the significance of the documented effects for explaining overall volatility.

C. Longer-Run Volatility Components

A significant finding to emerge from our study is that the high-frequency returns contain valuable information for measurement of volatility at the daily level. Specifically, the cumulative absolute returns provide a much better ex post measure of the underlying daily latent volatility factor than either absolute or squared daily returns. These results encourage the development of new and improved techniques for the estimation and prediction of daily or lower frequency volatility that explicitly incorporate the information in high-frequency returns. In addition, as we show below, the intraday returns provide new insights that are of critical importance for the understanding of the lower frequency return dynamics.

Given our estimates of the systematic, or deterministic, calendar and announcement effects, we may filter the high-frequency returns to obtain an innovation process that retains only the purely stochastic components of the volatility process. If our modeling strategy is warranted, the properties of this (residual) return series should be largely void of calendar effects and display the type of volatility dependencies usually associated with ARCH-type processes. To investigate this hypothesis, Figure 11 displays the correlogram for the raw absolute five-minute returns, $|R_{t,n} - \bar{R}|$, as well as the corresponding filtered absolute returns, $\hat{s}_{t,n}^{-1} \cdot |R_{t,n} - \bar{R}|$. The former, depicted in Figure 11a, is dominated by the strong periodicity at the daily frequency and does not appear particularly informative.[24] Figure 11b, in contrast, features a strictly positive and slowly declining correlogram. Spikes are visible at the daily frequencies, but they are minor and do not distort the overall pattern. This may be interpreted as a testimony to the relative success of our model for $s_{t,n}$ in capturing the systematic calendar and announcement effects. The regularity of the correlogram in Figure 11b compares favorably to those of similarly filtered absolute returns presented in Andersen and Bollerslev (1997a) and Payne (1996). The excellent fit afforded by the hy-

[24] Both series are adjusted for missing observations, so that, e.g., the Tokyo lunch hour is removed. The daily periodicity is even more pronounced when the lunch time observations are retained.

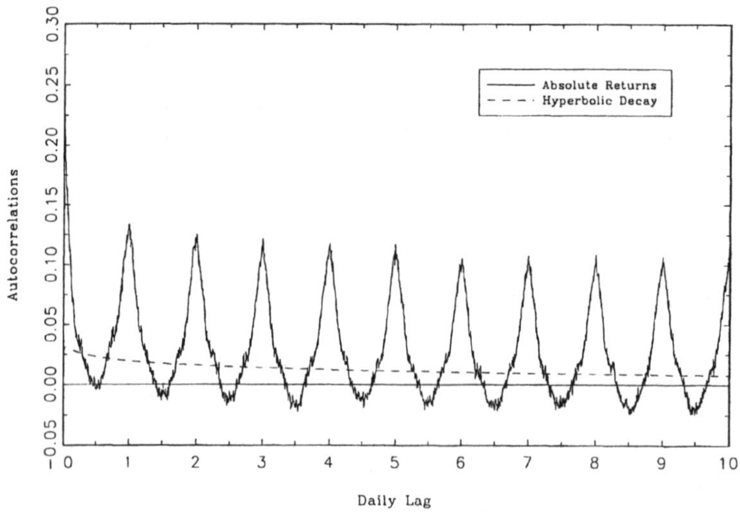

a

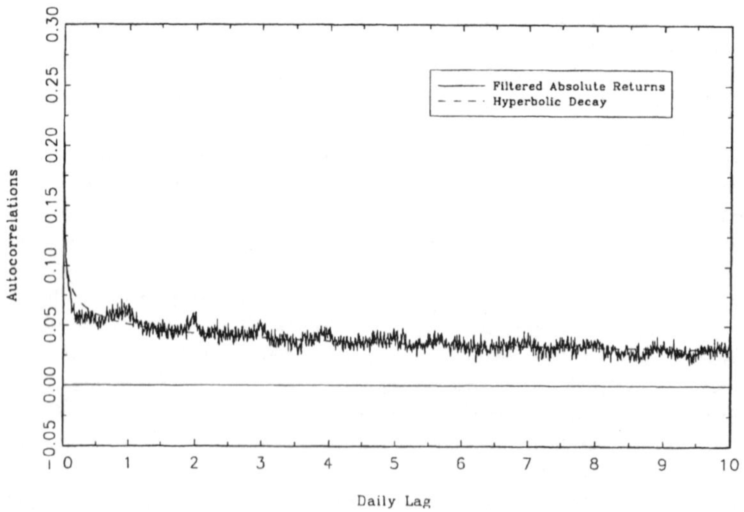

b

Figure 11. Absolute return correlograms. The figures display the autocorrelations for demeaned raw and filtered five-minute absolute returns. The returns are calculated from interpolated five-minute logarithmic average bid–ask quotes for the deutsche mark–dollar spot exchange rate over the October 1, 1992 through September 29, 1993 sample period. Quotes from Friday 21:00 GMT through Sunday 21:00 GMT, along with the Tokyo lunch period, 3:00–4:45 GMT, are not included, resulting in 267 weekday return observations, for a total of 69,420 five-minute returns. Additional minor corrections are also made for extremely low quoting activity during holidays and gaps in the data series. The filtered returns in Figure 11b are obtained by standardizing the raw demeaned absolute returns by the estimated volatility impact of calendar, holiday, and announcement effects.

perbolic decay superimposed in the figures is particularly noteworthy. This rate of decay is inconsistent with ordinary ARCH models, and instead points toward a fractionally integrated, or long-memory, volatility process, as proposed by Baillie, Bollerslev, and Mikkelsen (1996) in the ARCH framework, and Harvey (1994) and Breidt, Crato, and de Lima (1995) within the context of stochastic volatility models.[25] The estimate of the degree of fractional integration, or d, implied by the fitted hyperbolic decay in Figure 11 equals 0.387, which is in close accordance with the estimates obtained by semiparametric frequency domain methods in Andersen and Bollerslev (1997b) and Henry and Payne (1996).[26] Thus, the long-memory characteristics appear inherent to the return series, as they manifest themselves, even over shorter time spans. This suggests that the source of fractional integration in the volatility is related to the data generating process itself, rather than induced by infrequent structural shifts as suggested by Lamoureux and Lastrapes (1990b). Thus, once we account for announcement and calendar effects, the high-frequency data provide important evidence on the plausibility of two alternative hypotheses that appear almost observationally equivalent from the perspective of lower frequency returns.

V. The Relative Importance of Volatility Components at Different Frequencies

Different market participants are concerned with different features of the volatility process. Market makers, brokers, and money managers engaging in continuous trading or the implementation of dynamic portfolio and hedging strategies are exposed to short-run volatility, and consider information on this dimension vital. Conversely, more passive investors are mostly concerned with lower frequency movements. Likewise, research into the price mechanism or other market microstructure issues focuses on the extreme high-frequency movements, but standard asset pricing models typically are specified and tested at daily or lower frequencies. Although the higher and lower frequency characteristics cannot be entirely independent, the difference in perspective will lead to rather wide discrepancies in the assessment of the economic significance of the factors that we have explored above. This section formally evaluates the impact of each component at both the extreme high frequency and the daily level.

The FFF framework allows for a direct assessment of the joint and marginal predictive power of each of the three separate components; the daily volatility factor, the calendar effects, and the announcement effects. We let the indicator variable, I_σ, be unity if the daily (ARCH-based) volatility factor from equation (7a) is included in the construction of a given forecast, and

[25] The autocorrelations for a fractionally integrated process of order d eventually decay at the hyperbolic rate of j^{2d-l}.

[26] The reported estimate of 0.387 is obtained from the regression $\log(\hat{\rho}_j) = \beta_0 + \beta_1 \log(j) + u_j$, $j = 5, 6, \ldots, 2670$, where $\hat{\rho}_j$ denotes the sample autocorrelation for the absolute returns, and $\hat{d} = \frac{1}{2}(\hat{\beta}_1 + 1)$; see Andersen and Bollerslev (1997b) for details.

zero if the forecast is based on a constant daily volatility factor, as in equation (7b). Formally, this component takes the form,

$$\hat{\sigma}_{t,n} = \hat{\sigma}_t \cdot I_\sigma + \bar{\sigma} \cdot (1 - I_\sigma).$$

Likewise, the indicators I_c, I_a, and I_h signify whether calendar, announcement, and holiday effects are accounted for in the volatility forecast. The calendar coefficients, f_c, include the FFF sinusoids, the Tokyo open, the Daylight Saving Time, the early Monday, and the late Friday regressors, the announcement effects, f_a, signify the contribution of the four announcement regressors from Table III, and the holiday effects, f_h, refer to the predicted reduction in volatility associated with the holiday dummy and the control for missing observations. The latter effects were incorporated in all forecasts, so that this source of predictable return variability would not interfere with the interpretation of the results. Based on the FFF regressors in equation (5), it is now straightforward to construct a volatility forecast from equation (8), and identify the contribution from each of the three remaining sources of systematic variation. In particular, letting the vector of indicator variables, $I = (I_\sigma, I_c, I_a)$, identify a given model configuration, the set of one-day-ahead absolute return interval forecasts is calculated as

$$v(I;t,n) = c_0 \cdot \hat{\sigma}_{t,n} \cdot \exp\left(\frac{\hat{f}_c(t,n) \cdot I_c + \hat{f}_a(t,n) \cdot I_a + \hat{f}_h(t,n) \cdot I_h}{2}\right), \tag{10}$$

where $\hat{f}_c(t,n) = f_c(\hat{\theta},t,n)$ and so forth, and $\hat{\theta}$ is estimated conditional on the current variant of the model, as indicated by I. Thus, the parameters are allowed to vary across the designs in a manner that maximizes the explanatory power of the specific components for each configuration.

Table V provides the fraction of the total variation in absolute returns explained by each forecast. These are given as the R^2 from the following regressions of realized cumulative absolute returns, $(t = 1,\ldots,T)$,

$$\sum_{n=1}^{N} |R_{t,n} - \bar{R}| = b_0 + b_1 \cdot \sum_{n=1}^{N} v(I;t,n) + \epsilon_t, \tag{11}$$

and realized five-minute absolute returns, $(t = 1,\ldots,T;\ n = 1,\ldots,N)$,

$$|R_{t,n} - \bar{R}| = b_0 + b_1 \cdot v(I;t,n) + \epsilon_{t,n}, \tag{12}$$

on the corresponding volatility forecasts.

The results are telling. Consider the first data column in Table V, that refers to the degree of explained variation in daily cumulative absolute returns. The complete model accounts for an impressive 60.6 percent of the total variation. Moreover, this number drops only slightly if we remove the announcement or the calendar components from the forecast. In contrast, the explained variation drops precipitously when the daily volatility factor is omitted. In fact, the benchmark explanatory power, provided by the holiday effects alone (8 percent), is only marginally improved by incorporating calendar effects (8.3 percent) and only slightly improved when allowing for announcement effects (11.4 percent). In contrast, the daily GARCH volatility factor alone explains 57.8 percent. The message is clear. The daily volatility forecasts capture broader movements in volatility that generally are independent of calendar effects. This is perhaps not surprising given that the intraday pattern, which accounts for the majority of these features, is annihilated when aggregated to the daily level. More striking is the marginal impact of the announcements at the daily level. Although announcement effects explain a significant proportion of the return variability over shorter intervals, as also documented in Ederington and Lee (1993), this is not the case relative to the full 24-hour trading day, which is characterized by fairly large fluctuations in the overall level of volatility.[27] Finally, we note that the calendar effects pick up additional explanatory power if day-of-the-week effects are allowed, but remain less important than the announcement effects. This is fully consistent with the weekday dummies substituting (imperfectly) for the news releases.

Turning to the last column of Table V, we find that the explanatory power of the components is reversed when we consider the high-frequency return variability. The overall explained variation drops to 15.9 percent, but more revealing is the fraction explained by the calendar effects alone (8.1 percent) relative to the announcement effects (4.9 percent) and the daily volatility factor (3.4 percent). In other words, the intraday pattern accounts for the majority of the explained variation, but the announcements are sufficiently influential, in spite of the relatively few intervals they affect, that they also exert an appreciable impact, and, finally, the overall predictable movements in daily volatility have only a limited, although not negligible, impact at the five-minute return level.

VI. Concluding Remarks

The volatility process of the DM–$ spot exchange rate market is involved, with entirely new phenomena becoming visible as one proceeds from daily returns to high-frequency intraday returns. Nonetheless, it is possible to identify three general sets of characteristics that govern the systematic features of the process. At the high-frequency level, the pronounced intraday volatility pattern is dominant, accounting for an average variation in absolute returns of more than 250 percent across the 24-hour trading cycle (after exclusion of the Tokyo lunch period). At the intraday level, the magnitude of this effect overwhelms the predictable changes in volatility captured by, e.g.,

[27] Subsample analysis reveals that the explained variation drops when the overall level of volatility is more stable. However, the ranking of the effects remains the same across all investigated subsamples.

Table V

Explained Variation (R^2) from Regressions of Deutsche Mark–Dollar Daily Cumulative Absolute Returns or Five-Minute Absolute Returns on Alternative Absolute Return Forecasts

For the daily cumulative absolute returns, the regression takes the form

$$\sum_{n=1}^{N} |R_{t,n} - \bar{R}| = b_0 + b_1 \sum_{n=1}^{N} v(I;t,n) + \epsilon_t,$$

where $v(I;t,n)$ denotes the relevant absolute return forecast for interval n on day t, and ϵ_t is an error term. The regressions for the five-minute absolute returns are calculated as

$$|R_{t,n} - \bar{R}| = b_0 + b_1 \cdot v(I;t,n) + \epsilon_{t,n}.$$

The five-minute returns are based on interpolated logarithmic average bid–ask quotes for the deutsche mark–dollar (DM–\$) spot exchange rate from October 1, 1992 through September 29, 1993. Quotes from Friday 21:00 GMT through Sunday 21:00 GMT are excluded, resulting in a total of 74,880 five-minute observations. The daily cumulative absolute returns are aggregated from 21:00 GMT to 21:00 GMT the following day. The corresponding one-day-ahead five-minute absolute return forecasts are obtained as

$$v(I;t,n) = (N^{-1/2}[\hat{\sigma}_t \cdot I_\sigma + \bar{\sigma} \cdot (1 - I_\sigma)]) \cdot c_0 \cdot \exp\left(\frac{\hat{f}_c(t,n)I_c + \hat{f}_a(t,n)I_a + \hat{f}_h(t,n)}{2}\right),$$

where the first term on the right-hand side represents an estimate of the benchmark return volatility of the interval, while $\hat{f}_c(t,n)$, $\hat{f}_a(t,n)$, and $\hat{f}_h(t,n)$ denote the estimated calendar, announcement, and holiday effects from a regression of normalized, log-squared, demeaned five-minute DM–\$ returns on calendar, announcement, and holiday regressors. The functional form of the forecast equation translates the estimates into the absolute return dimension. The indicator variables I_σ, I_c, and I_a signify whether the features associated with a given effect are accounted for in the construction of a particular forecast. For example, the indicator vector $I \equiv (I_\sigma, I_c, I_a) = (0,1,1)$ corresponds to the model where the daily volatility is constant, and calendar (c) and announcement (a) effects are accounted for. Because the holiday effect, $\hat{f}_h(t,n)$, is included in all of the forecasts, the R^2's reported here exceed the simple correlations given in Table I. Estimates for the time-varying daily return standard deviations over the one-year sample, $\hat{\sigma}_t$, are obtained from an MA(1)-GARCH(1,1) model fit to a longer daily sample of DM–\$ returns covering the period from March 14, 1979, through September 29, 1993. The sample mean of $\hat{\sigma}_t$ is denoted by $\bar{\sigma}$. The "*" indicates the allowance for day-of-the-week dummies among the calendar effects, while they are excluded otherwise.

Design	Daily Cumulative Absolute Returns	Five-Minute Absolute Returns
Complete model $(I_\sigma,I_c,I_a) = (1,1,1)$	0.606	0.159
No announcements $(I_\sigma,I_c,I_a) = (1,1,0)$	0.579	0.113
No calendar effects $(I_\sigma,I_c,I_a) = (1,0,1)$	0.603	0.084
Only daily volatility $(I_\sigma,I_c,I_a) = (1,0,0)$	0.578	0.034
No daily volatility $(I_\sigma,I_c,I_a) = (0,1,1)$	0.119	0.124

Table V—*Continued*

Design	Daily Cumulative Absolute Returns	Five-Minute Absolute Returns
Only announcements $(I_\sigma, I_c, I_a) = (0,0,1)$	0.114	0.049
Only calendar effects $(I_\sigma, I_c, I_a) = (0,1,0)$	0.083	0.081
Calendar + Day-of-week $(I_\sigma, I_c, I_a) = (0,1,0)$*	0.107	0.083
Only holiday effects $(I_\sigma, I_c, I_a) = (0,0,0)$	0.080	0.002

ARCH models, which rarely move by more than 25 percent over any 24-hour period. Additionally, strong but short-lived announcement effects are prevalent at the highest frequencies.

Our results verify that the high-frequency calendar and announcement effects may be estimated efficiently, even without accounting for the broader movements in daily volatility. On the other hand, real-time decision-making and the analysis of one-time events require controlling not only for the intraday pattern and the release of economic or political news, but also for the overall level of volatility. Furthermore, when analyzing the economic implications of the identified factors, it is evident that the daily volatility factor dominates at the daily and lower frequencies. Thus, it might be argued that the intraday pattern and announcement effects are of lesser economic importance, and that high-frequency data are of interest only for the area of market microstructure.

Any such conclusion, dismissing the importance of intraday return series for broader economic issues, is misleading. First, the high-frequency returns contain extremely valuable information for the measurement of volatility at the daily level. Second, the intraday returns reveal that there are significant long-memory features in the return dynamics. These features are critical for portfolio management and derivatives pricing. Moreover, they are relevant for the analysis of information transmission and volatility spillover, both contemporaneously across markets and intertemporally between the geographical regions of the identical market (see, e.g., Engle, Ito, and Lin (1990), Hamao, Masulis, and Ng (1990), and Hogan and Melvin (1994)). In summary, the information provided by high-frequency returns is valuable to a broad range of issues in financial economics, both within and beyond the realm of market microstructure.

REFERENCES

Admati, Anat R., and Paul Pfleiderer, 1988, A theory of intraday patterns: Volume and price variability, *Review of Financial Studies* 1, 3–40.

Andersen, Torben G., 1994, Stochastic autoregressive volatility: A framework for volatility modeling, *Mathematical Finance* 4, 75–102.

Andersen, Torben G., 1996, Return volatility and trading volume: An information flow interpretation of stochastic volatility, *Journal of Finance* 51, 169–204.

Andersen, Torben G., and Tim Bollerslev, 1997a, Intraday periodicity and volatility persistence in financial markets, *Journal of Empirical Finance* 4, 115–158.

Andersen, Torben G., and Tim Bollerslev, 1997b, Heterogeneous information arrivals and return volatility dynamics: Uncovering the long run in high-frequency returns, *Journal of Finance* 52, 975–1005.

Baillie, Richard T., and Tim Bollerslev, 1989, The message in daily exchange rates: A conditional variance tale, *Journal of Business and Economic Statistics* 7, 297–305.

Baillie, Richard T., and Tim Bollerslev, 1991, Intra-day and inter-market volatility in foreign exchange rates, *Review of Economic Studies* 58, 565–585.

Baillie, Richard T., Tim Bollerslev, and Hans O. Mikkelsen, 1996, Fractionally integrated generalized autoregressive conditional heteroskedasticity, *Journal of Econometrics* 74, 3–30.

Berry, Thomas D., and Keith M. Howe, 1994, Public information arrival, *Journal of Finance* 49, 1331–1346.

Bollerslev, Tim, and Ian Domowitz, 1993, Trading patterns and prices in the interbank foreign exchange market, *Journal of Finance* 48, 1421–1443.

Bollerslev, Tim, and Michael Melvin, 1994, Bid-ask spreads and volatility in the foreign exchange market: An empirical analysis, *Journal of International Economics* 36, 355–372.

Breidt, F. Jay, Nuno Crato, and Pedro J. F. de Lima, 1995, On the detection and estimation of long memory in stochastic volatility, *Journal of Econometrics*, forthcoming.

Brock, William A., and Allan W. Kleidon, 1992, Periodic market closure and trading volume, *Journal of Economic Dynamics and Control* 16, 451–489.

Brown, David P., and Robert H. Jennings, 1989, On technical analysis, *Review of Financial Studies* 2, 527–552.

Canina, Linda, and Stephen Figlewski, 1993, The informational content of implied volatility, *Review of Financial Studies* 6, 659–681.

Carnes, W. Stansbury, and Stephen D. Slifer, 1991, *The Atlas of Economic Indicators: A Visual Guide to Market Forces and The Federal Reserve* (Harper Collins Publishers, Washington, D.C.).

Chang, Yuanchen, and Stephen J. Taylor, 1996, Information arrivals and intraday exchange rate volatility, Manuscript, Department of Accounting and Finance, Lancaster University, United Kingdom.

Clarida, Richard, and Mark Gertler, 1996, How the Bundesbank conducts monetary policy, Manuscript, Department of Finance, New York University, New York.

Clark, Peter K., 1973, A subordinated stochastic process model with finite variance for speculative prices, *Econometrica* 41, 135–155.

Cumby, Robert, Stephen Figlewski, and Joel Hasbrouck, 1993, Forecasting volatility and correlations with EGARCH models, *Journal of Derivatives* 1, 51–63.

Cutler, David M., Jim M. Poterba, and Lawrence H. Summers, 1989, What moves stock prices? *Journal of Portfolio Management* 15, 4–12.

Dacorogna, Michel M., Ulrich A. Müller, Robert J. Nagler, Richard B. Olsen, and Olivier V. Pictet, 1993, A geographical model for the daily and weekly seasonal volatility in the foreign exchange market, *Journal of International Money and Finance* 12, 413–438.

Day, Theodore E., and Craig M. Lewis, 1992, Stock market volatility and the information content of stock index options, *Journal of Econometrics* 52, 267–287.

DeGennaro, Ramon P., and Ronald E. Shrieves, 1995, Public information releases, private information arrival, and volatility in the foreign exchange market, Working paper, Department of Finance, University of Tennessee, Knoxville.

Drost, Feike C., and Theo E. Nijman, 1993, Temporal aggregation of GARCH processes, *Econometrica* 61, 909–927.

Drost, Feike C., and Bas J. M. Werker, 1996, Closing the GARCH gap: Continuous time GARCH modeling, *Journal of Econometrics* 74, 31–57.

Eddelbüttel, Dirk, and Thomas H. McCurdy, 1996, The impact of news on foreign exchange rates: Evidence from very high frequency data, Working paper, Department of Economics, Queen's University, Kingston, Ontario, Canada.

Ederington, Louis H., and Jae Ha Lee, 1993, How markets process information: News releases and volatility, *Journal of Finance* 48, 1161–1191.

Ederington, Louis H., and Jae Ha Lee, 1995a, The creation and resolution of market uncertainty: The impact of macroeconomic announcements on implied volatility, Manuscript, Department of Finance, University of Oklahoma, Norman.

Ederington, Louis H., and Jae Ha Lee, 1995b, Volatility prediction: ARCH, announcement, and seasonality effects, Manuscript, Department of Finance, University of Oklahoma, Norman.

Engle, Robert F., Takatoshi Ito, and Wen-Ling Lin, 1990, Meteor showers or heat waves? Heteroskedastic intra-daily volatility in the foreign exchange market, *Econometrica* 58, 525–542.

Engle, Robert F., and Jeffrey R. Russell, 1997, Forecasting the frequency of changes in quoted foreign exchange prices with the autoregressive conditional duration model, *Journal of Empirical Finance* 4, 187–212.

Epps, Thomas W., and Mary L. Epps, 1976, The stochastic dependence of security price changes and transaction volumes: Implications for the mixture-of-distributions hypothesis, *Econometrica* 44, 305–321.

Figlewski, Stephen, 1995, Forecasting volatility using historical data, Manuscript, Department of Finance, New York University, New York.

Foster, F., Doug, and S. Viswanathan, 1996, Strategic trading when agents forecast the forecast of others, *Journal of Finance* 51, 1437–1478.

French, Kenneth R., and Richard Roll, 1986, Stock returns variances: The arrival of information and the reaction of traders, *Journal of Financial Economics* 17, 5–26.

Gallant, A. Ronald, 1981, On the bias in flexible functional forms and an essentially unbiased form: The Fourier flexible form, *Journal of Econometrics* 15, 211–245.

Gallant, A. Ronald, Peter E. Rossi, and George E. Tauchen, 1992, Stock prices and volume, *Review of Financial Studies* 5, 199–242.

Garman, Mark B., and Michael J. Klass, 1980, On the estimation of security price volatilities from historical data, *Journal of Business* 53, 67–78.

Ghysels, Eric, Andrew Harvey, and Eric Renault, 1997, Stochastic volatility, forthcoming, in G. S. Maddala and C. R. Rao, eds.: *Handbook of Statistics*, vol. 14, *Statistical Methods in Finance* (North Holland, Amsterdam).

Goodhart, Charles A. E., and L. Figliuoli, 1992, The geographical location of the foreign exchange market: A test of the 'island' hypothesis, *Journal of International and Comparative Economics* 1, 13–28.

Goodhart, Charles A. E., S. Hall, S. Henry, and B. Pesaran, 1993, News effects in a high frequency model of the sterling-dollar exchange rate, *Journal of Applied Econometrics* 8, 1–13.

Goodhart, Charles A. E., Takatoshi Ito, and Richard Payne, 1996, One day in June 1993: A study of the working of Reuters' dealing 2000-2 electronic foreign exchange trading system, in Jeffrey A. Frankel, Giampaolo Galli, and Alberto Giovannini, eds.: *The Microstructure of Foreign Exchange Markets* (University of Chicago Press, Chicago).

Goodhart, Charles A. E., and Maureen O'Hara, 1997, High frequency data in financial markets: Issues and applications, *Journal of Empirical Finance* 4, 73–114.

Goodhart, Charles A. E., and Richard G. Smith, 1985, The impact of news on financial markets in the United Kingdom, *Journal of Money, Credit and Banking* 17, 507–511.

Grundy, Bruce D., and Maureen McNichols, 1989, Trade and revelation of information through prices and direct disclosure, *Review of Financial Studies* 2, 495–526.

Guillaume, Dominique M., Michel M. Dacorogna, R. R. Davé, Ulrich A. Müller, Richard B. Olsen, and Olivier V. Pictet, 1995, From the bird's eye to the microscope: A survey of new stylized facts of the intradaily foreign exchange markets, *Finance and Stochastics* 1, 95–129.

Hakkio, Craig, and Douglas Pearce, 1985, The reaction of exchange rates to economic news, *Economic Inquiry* 23, 621–635.

Hamao, Yasushi, Ronald W. Masulis, and Victor Ng, 1990, Correlations in price changes and volatility across international stock markets, *Review of Financial Studies* 3, 281–307.

Hardouvelis, Gilas, 1984, Market perceptions of Federal Reserve policy and the weekly monetary announcements, *Journal of Monetary Economics* 14, 225–240.

Harris, Lawrence, 1986, A transaction data study of weekly and intradaily patterns in stock returns, *Journal of Financial Economics* 16, 99–117.

Harvey, Andrew C., 1994, Long-memory in stochastic volatility, Manuscript, London School of Economics, U.K.

Harvey, Campbell R., and Roger D. Huang, 1991, Volatility in the foreign currency futures market, *Review of Financial Studies* 4, 543–569.

Henry, Marc, and Richard Payne, 1996, An investigation of long range dependence in intra-day foreign exchange rate volatility, Manuscript, Financial Markets Group, London School of Economics, U.K.

Hogan, Kedreth C., Jr., and Michael T. Melvin, 1994, Sources of heat waves and meteor showers in the foreign exchange markets, *Journal of International Economics* 37, 239–247.

Hong, Harrison, and Jiang Wang, 1995, Trading and returns under periodic market closures, Manuscript, Sloan School of Management, MIT, Cambridge, Massachusetts.

Hsieh, David A., 1988, The statistical properties of daily foreign exchange rates: 1974–1983, *Journal of International Economics* 24, 129–145.

Hsieh, David A., 1989, Modeling heteroskedasticity in daily foreign exchange rates, *Journal of Business and Economic Statistics* 7, 307–317.

Hsieh, David A., 1991, Chaos and nonlinear dynamics: Application to financial markets, *Journal of Finance* 46, 1839–1877.

Hsieh, David A., and Allen W. Kleidon, 1996, Bid-ask spreads in foreign exchange markets: Implications for models of asymmetric information, in Jeffrey A. Frankel, Giampaolo Galli, and Alberto Giovannini, eds.: *The Microstructure of Foreign Exchange Markets* (University of Chicago Press, Chicago).

Ito, Takatoshi, Richard K. Lyons, and Michael T. Melvin, 1996, Is there private information in the fx market? The Tokyo experiment, Manuscript, University of California at Berkeley.

Ito, Takatoshi, and V. Vance Roley, 1987, News from U.S. and Japan: Which moves the yen/dollar exchange rate?, *Journal of Monetary Economics* 19, 255–277.

Jacklin, Charles J., Allan W. Kleidon, and Paul Pfleiderer, 1992, Underestimation of portfolio insurance and the crash of October 1987, *Review of Financial Studies* 5, 35–63.

Jones, Charles, Gautam Kaul, and Marc L. Lipson, 1994, Transactions, volume and volatility, *Review of Financial Studies* 7, 631–651.

Jones, Charles, Owen Lamont, and Robin Lumsdaine, 1995, Public information and the persistence of bond market volatility, Manuscript, Department of Economics, Princeton University, New Jersey.

Jorion, Phillippe, 1995, Predicting volatility in the foreign exchange market, Journal of Finance 50, 507–528.

Kim, Oliver, and Robert E. Verrecchia, 1991, Market reaction to anticipated announcements, Journal of Financial Economics 30, 273–309.

Kofman, Paul, and Martin Martens, 1997, Interaction between the London and New York stock markets during common trading hours, *Journal of International Money and Finance* 16, 387–414.

Lamoureux, Christopher G., and William D. Lastrapes, 1990a, Heteroskedasticity in stock return data: Volume versus GARCH effects, *Journal of Finance* 45, 221–229.

Lamoureux, Christopher G., and William D. Lastrapes, 1990b, Persistence in variance, structural change and the GARCH model, *Journal of Business and Economic Statistics* 8, 225–234.

Latané, Henry A., and Richard J. Rendleman, Jr., 1976, Standard deviations of stock price ratios implied in option prices, *Journal of Finance* 31, 359–381.

Lyons, Richard, 1995, Tests of microstructural hypotheses in the foreign exchange market, *Journal of Financial Economics* 39, 321–351.

Lyons, Richard, 1997, A simultaneous trade model of the foreign exchange hot potato, *Journal of International Economics* 42, 275–298.

McFarland, James W., R. Richardson Pettit, and Sam K. Sung, 1982, The distribution of foreign exchange price changes: Trading day effects and risk measurement, *Journal of Finance* 37, 693–715.

McFarland, James W., R. Richardson Pettit, and Sam K. Sung, 1987, The distribution of foreign exchange price changes: Trading day effects and risk measurement—a reply, *Journal of Finance* 42, 189–194.

Mitchell, Mark L., and J. Harold Mulherin, 1994, The impact of public information on the stock market, *Journal of Finance* 49, 923–950.

Müller, Ulrich A., Michel M. Dacorogna, Richard B. Olsen, Olivier V. Pictet, Matthias Schwarz, and Claude Morgenegg, 1990, Statistical study of foreign exchange rates, empirical evidence of a price change scaling law, and intraday analysis, *Journal of Banking and Finance* 14, 1189–1208.

Newey, Whitney K., and Kenneth D. West, 1987, A simple, positive semi-definite, heteroskedasticity consistent covariance matrix, *Econometrica* 55, 703–708.

Pagan, Adrian R., 1984, Econometric issues in the analysis of regressions with generated regressors, *International Economic Review* 25, 221–247.

Parkinson, Michael, 1980, Extreme value method for estimating the variance of the rate of return, *Journal of Business* 53, 61–65.

Payne, Richard, 1996, Announcement effects and seasonality in the intraday foreign exchange market, Manuscript, Financial Markets Group, London School of Economics, United Kingdom.

Peiers, Bettina, 1997, Informed traders, intervention and price leadership: A deeper view of the microstructure of the foreign exchange market, *Journal of Finance* 52, 1589–1614.

Rogers, L. Chris G., and Stephen E. Satchell, 1991, Estimating variance from high, low and closing prices, *Annals of Applied Probability* 1, 504–512.

Roll, Richard, 1984, Orange juice and weather, *American Economic Review* 74, 861–880.

Roll, Richard, 1988, R^2, *Journal of Finance* 43, 541–566.

Romer, David, 1993, Rational asset-price movements without news, *American Economic Review* 83, 1112–1130.

So, Jacky C., 1987, The distribution of foreign exchange price changes: Trading day effects and risk measurement—A comment, *Journal of Finance* 42, 181–188.

Tauchen, George E., and Mark Pitts, 1983, The price variability–volume relationship on speculative markets, *Econometrica* 51, 485–505.

Thornton, Daniel, 1989, The effect of unanticipated money on the money and foreign exchange markets, *Journal of International Money and Finance* 8, 573–587.

West, Kenneth D., and Dongchul Cho, 1995, The predictive ability of several models of exchange rate volatility, *Journal of Econometrics* 69, 367–391.

Wood, Robert A., Thomas H. McInish, and J. Keith Ord, 1985, An investigation of transaction data for NYSE stocks, *Journal of Finance* 25, 723–739.

Xu, Xinzhong, and Stephen J. Taylor, 1995, Conditional volatility and the informational efficiency of the PHLX currency options market, *Journal of Banking and Finance* 19, 803–821.

Zhou, Bin, 1996, High frequency data and volatility in foreign exchange rates, *Journal of Business and Economic Statistics* 14, 45–52.

ELSEVIER

Journal of International Money and Finance
20 (2001) 327–347

Journal of International Money and Finance

www.elsevier.nl/locate/econbase

'Once-in-a-generation' yen volatility in 1998: fundamentals, intervention, and order flow

Jun Cai [a], Yan-Leung Cheung [a], Raymond S.K. Lee [a], Michael Melvin [b,*]

[a] *Department of Economics and Finance, City University of Hong Kong, Tat Chee Avenue, Kowloon, Hong Kong, PR China*
[b] *Department of Economics, Arizona State University, Tempe, AZ 85287-3806, USA*

Abstract

The dramatic yen/dollar volatility of 1998 has been popularly ascribed to order flow driven by changing tastes for risk and hedge-fund herding on unwinding yen 'carry trade' positions rather than fundamentals. High-frequency evidence of shifting fundamentals is provided by a comprehensive list of macroeconomic announcements. News is found to have significant effects on volatility, but order flow may play a more important role. Since portfolio shifts are revealed to the market through trading, the results are consistent with order flow playing a significant role in the revelation of private information and associated exchange rate shifts.

JEL classification: F31; G14; G15; C22

Keywords: Exchange rate volatility; Private information; Order flow; News announcements; Central bank intervention

1. Introduction

The yen/dollar exchange rate provided market participants with a year to remember in 1998. Not since the breakdown of the Bretton Woods system in the early 1970s has such volatility been witnessed. After many months of uneven yen depreciation, a surprise joint US–Japanese intervention on June 17 led to a yen appreciation of

* Corresponding author. Tel.: +1-480-965-6860; fax: +1-480-965-0748.
E-mail address: mmelvin@asu.edu (M. Melvin).

0261-5606/01/$ - see front matter
PII: S0261-5606(00)00056-5

more than 6 yen per dollar. This first-ever yen intervention by the Clinton Administration followed the yen hitting an 8-yr low against the dollar earlier that week. Then, after several months of continued yen depreciation, a sudden reversal was experienced where, on October 7, the yen price of a dollar fell from about 134 to 120 in one day. On the next day, the yen traded in a remarkably large range between 111 and 123. For the remainder of the year, sporadic volatility occurred and investor uncertainty was reflected in the implied volatility in yen options trading between 15 and 23%. Near year's end, the premium for one-month dollar puts reached an all-time high of 3.6%.[1]

A search of the news reveals three sources being most frequently mentioned as the cause of yen–dollar volatility: announcements related to macroeconomic fundamentals; intervention by the Bank of Japan, the US Treasury, and the Federal Reserve; and portfolio position switches by large institutions. Most analysts blamed the wide swings of late 1998 on hedge funds and panic trading. For instance, in a review of recent yen performance a *Financial Times* article reported that the fluctuations in the value of the yen in late 1998 were "driven by temporary market panic, rather than any economic fundamentals."[2] The rapid appreciation of the yen has been most commonly associated with investors unwinding positions in the 'yen-carry' trade where funds had borrowed yen at interest rates near zero and then invested in higher-yielding securities denominated in dollars and other currencies. During the period of yen depreciation in early 1998, such short-yen positions were quite profitable. The standard belief is that a reassessment of the risk environment was associated with a liquidity crunch and was brought about by a convergence of negative outcomes such as hedge fund losses in emerging markets and the near-collapse of Long Term Capital Management. This changed environment caused funds to unwind their short yen positions and resulted in yen appreciation. Once the appreciation began, herd behavior is said to have occurred where there was a stampede of investors to cover their short yen positions.[3]

The notable events of 1998 provide an interesting laboratory to assess the role of economic fundamentals and test if there was an independent role for order-flow induced exchange rate volatility where investor position switches were revealed through their trades. In a broad sense, the sample provides insights into the role of public information in the form of macroeconomic announcements versus private information revealed through order flow in determining exchange rates. Microstructure theories provide a framework for understanding the learning that occurs when a large fund reveals its position switching through trades with counterparty banks. The world learns about the yen carry-trade unwinding not via public announcements

[1] A good overview of the environment in late 1998 is provided in the March 1999 Federal Reserve Bulletin.

[2] See Tett (1999).

[3] A useful non-technical discussion of the yen carry-trade and its potential effects on exchange rate volatility is provided in Beranger et al. (1999).

but via trades of the firms holding the short-yen positions.[4] Beyond the particular interest in understanding the causes of yen volatility in 1998, it is also worthwhile to consider the broader issue of exchange rate determination. It has long been known that empirical models of exchange rates have not performed well. In the high-frequency data setting, researchers have examined the impact of macroeconomic news and found that intra-daily exchange rate volatility systematically responds to public information announcements (see Andersen and Bollerslev (1998) for a mark/dollar example). However, researchers have recently suggested that the act of trading, apart from any fundamentals—related news, may be an important source of exchange rate dynamics.[5]

The foreign exchange market is a market with a relative lack of transparency and asymmetrically-informed traders so that order flow should be expected to contain independent information. This is a view that is widely supported by practitioners and documented in several market surveys. For instance, Menkhoff (1998) found that the overwhelming majority of 205 German FX professionals he surveyed agreed with the following statement: "Big market participants can 'make' exchange rates for a while via own position taking and customer orders." This is consistent with the findings of a survey of 142 U.S. market participants by Cheung and Chinn (2000). They find that "large players are perceived to have a better customer and market network, which, in turn, give them better information on order flow and the activity of other trading banks" (p. 8). Cheung and Wong (1999) surveyed almost 400 traders in Hong Kong, Tokyo, and Singapore and find that roughly 25% of respondents identify their trading style to be determined by customer order flow rather than technical trading, fundamentals, or jobbing (continuously buying and selling small amounts to earn the spread). Cheung et al. (1999) found that 97% of the 110 UK FX professionals they surveyed disagreed with the statement: "Intraday exchange rate movements accurately reflect changes in the fundamental value." Based on their survey results and the role that order flow may play in revealing 'speculative forces' leads Cheung et al. to state that "A model capable of explaining exchange rate movements needs to consider another factor, over and above the usual suspects." We believe that this 'other factor' is order flow and hope to demonstrate the importance empirically in a setting incorporating major news releases so that the effect of order flow, independent of announcement effects, may be identified.

The response of the yen–dollar exchange rate to regularly scheduled news releases has been studied by others. Ederington and Lee (1994), DeGennaro and Shrieves (1997), Leng (1996) and Chatrath and Song (1998) are among those who investigate

[4] Evans and Lyons (1999) provide a theoretical model of the role of foreign exchange market order flow in determining exchange rates. Using data on signed order flow (whether a purchase or sale) from the Reuters Dealing 2000–1 system, they find evidence that order flow is a significant determinant of the mark–dollar and yen–dollar exchange rates over 89 days in 1996. Unfortunately, such data are not available for our sample period as the Bank of England only collected the data for four months in 1996. In addition, the EBS system is known to provide better coverage of the yen/dollar market than Reuters so one may wonder how representative the Reuters system would be for yen/dollar trades.

[5] See, for example, Ito et al. (1998) and Evans and Lyons (1999).

high-frequency news effects on the yen. All but DeGennaro and Shrieves focus on macroeconomic announcements during US trading hours and futures markets, with their limited trading hours constraint.[6] Earlier studies tend to emphasize one of the following three components-time-of-day patterns (intraday calendar effects), macroeconomic announcements (public information effects), and intra- and inter-day volatility persistence (ARCH effects). Recent findings suggest that all three factors should be accounted for simultaneously in high frequency studies of volatility processes, or else distorted estimates for the individual components may arise.

Building on the methodology in Andersen and Bollerslev (1997, 1998), this paper offers a comprehensive study of the intraday patterns in the volatility of the yen–dollar spot exchange rate that explicitly incorporates the different volatility components in a coherent framework. Our analysis is based on a one-year sample of five-minute returns in 1998. The impact of 32 US and 33 Japanese regularly released macroeconomic announcements is examined. The sample of macroeconomic news is more comprehensive than that used in any existing study on the yen–dollar exchange rate. From the US side, ten announcements are found to be significant. These include the employment report, the consumer price index (CPI), the Gross Domestic Product (GDP), the producer price index (PPI), the merchandise trade balance, consumer installment credit, real earnings, employment costs, reserve assets, and personal income. The six significant Japanese announcements include the Tankan report,[7] the unemployment rate, vehicle sales, the consumer sentiment index, electricity usage, and vehicle production. Dummy variables for central bank intervention are also found to have a significant effect on volatility. Order flow is proxied by yen positions held by major market participants such as commercial and investment banks. We find that yen volatility is positively associated with purchases of yen spot, forward, and futures contracts and negatively associated with sales. The results indicate that there is a significant role for order flow in understanding the yen volatility of 1998 apart from announcements regarding fundamentals or central-bank intervention.

Despite the extraordinary yen–dollar exchange rate volatility in 1998, we are able to capture a distinct intraday volatility pattern over different regional segments. The significant calendar effects include holiday, weekend, Tokyo opening, Tokyo and European lunch breaks, Monday morning, late Friday, and Daylight Saving Time. In contrast to previous studies, the day-of-the-week effects remain highly significant even after accounting for the clustering of regularly scheduled macroeconomic news releases on Thursdays and Fridays during the sample period.

The remainder of the paper is organized as follows. Section 2 describes the data, summarizes the intraday volatility patterns, and estimates various intraday calendar effects. Section 3 examines the implications of major macroeconomic announcements, intervention, and order flow. Section 4 assesses the overall importance of

[6] Hardouvelis (1984), Hakkio and Pearce (1985), Thornton (1989) and Ito and Roley (1987) examine announcement effects on the yen–dollar exchange rate using lower-frequency data. See Andersen and Bollerslev (1998) for a more detailed review of earlier studies on the impact of macroeconomic news on major currencies.

[7] The BOJ conducts a quarterly short-term economic survey (Tankan) of about 7500 companies.

different volatility components at the intraday and daily level. Finally, Section 5 provides a concluding discussion of results and implications.

2. Modeling the intraday patterns

2.1. Data

The Japanese yen–US dollar spot exchange rate quotes for 1998 are provided by Olsen and Associates Limited. Each quote contains a bid and ask price along with the time to the nearest second. At the end of each five-minute interval, we use the immediately preceding and following quotes to construct the relevant price. The log-price is first calculated as the midpoint of the logarithmic bid and ask. The log-prices are then weighted by their inverse relative distance to the endpoint. On weekdays, all 288 intervals during the 24-hour trading cycle are used. On weekends, however, all returns from 21:00 Greenwich Mean Time (GMT) Friday through 21:00 GMT Sunday are excluded. To maintain a fixed number of observations over the span of a week, returns during worldwide or country-specific holidays are not removed, although the holiday effects are explicitly accounted for by dummy variables. There are 260 trading days during the sample period so this leaves us with a total of 74,880 observations on returns, $R_{t,n}$, where n=1,2,...,288, and t=1,2,...,260.

To provide a sense of the range of fluctuations that occurred in 1998, daily data are plotted in Fig. 1.[8] The incredible range of prices is clearly illustrated in the figure

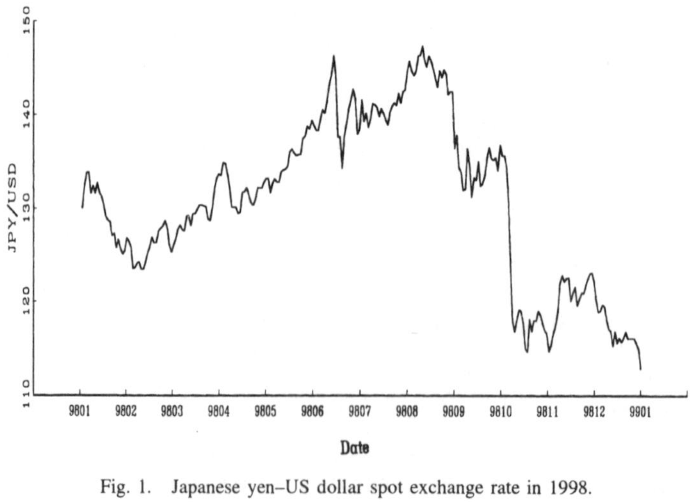

Fig. 1. Japanese yen–US dollar spot exchange rate in 1998.

[8] Daily observations on the yen–dollar spot rate are taken from Datastream. These are the midpoints of the bid and ask quotes in London from Barclays Bank International at 16:30 GMT.

and reflects the wild events of the year, which include spillovers from the Asian crisis, a Russian bond default, currency market interventions, and the near-collapse of a very large hedge fund, Long Term Capital Management.

2.2. Intradaily patterns

Although there is little evidence of a systematic pattern in the raw five-minute yen–dollar returns across the day, there is a pronounced pattern in intraday volatility. Fig. 2 depicts the average absolute return for each five-minute interval across 145

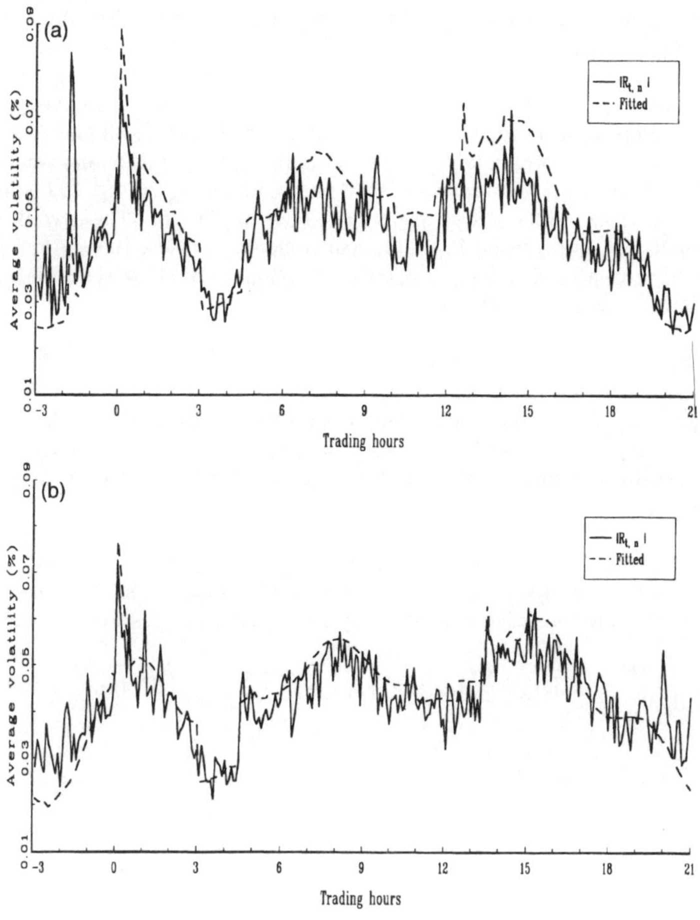

Fig. 2. (a) Japanese yen–US dollar summer time intraday five-minute average$|R_{t,n}|$; (b) Japanese yen–US dollar winter time intraday five-munite average $|R_{t,n}|$.

trading days during the US summer time and 115 trading days during the US winter time, respectively.[9] The initial observation corresponds to the interval beginning at 21:00 GMT, and the last observation represents the interval ending at 21:00 GMT. Thus, trading originates every morning in the Pacific segment where banks located in Wellington and Sydney dominate the market. Trading volume and return volatility are rather subdued at this hour. Fig. 2(a) shows a significant spike in volatility in the early Asian morning in summer. In both seasons, there is a significant jump in volatility at 00:00 GMT, or 9 a.m. Tokyo time, corresponding to the opening of the Tokyo foreign exchange interbank market, in which yen–dollar dealings comprise the largest portion of the trading volume.[10] The market slows down significantly during the Tokyo lunch time, 3:00–4:30 GMT. Volatility then picks up again at 6:00 GMT during summer time (7:00 GMT during Winter Time) when the European market begins to trade. The overlap of the European and North American market between 12:00 and 15:00 GMT constitutes another notable segment of high volatility. With the observance of daylight saving time in both Europe and North America, the volatility pattern appears to shift leftward between 6:00 and 21:00 GMT. In particular, the two peaks corresponding to the scheduled US macroeconomic announcements at 8:30 and 10:00 Eastern Standard Time (EST), or 13:30 and 15:00 GMT in Fig. 2(b) are shifted to the left by exactly one hour in Fig. 2(a). The overall pattern is consistent with those found in Baillie and Bollerslev (1991), Harvey and Huang (1991), Dacorogna et al. (1993), Andersen and Bollerslev (1998) and Melvin and Yin (2000) for major currencies.

2.3. *Flexible Fourier form estimates*

In order to explicitly model the periodic volatility component in the high-frequency returns, we apply the general framework developed by Andersen and Bollerslev (1997). Specifically, on decomposing the demeaned five-minute returns as,

$$R_{t,n}-E(R_{t,n})=s_{t,n}\cdot\sigma_{t,n}\cdot Z_{t,n} \tag{1}$$

where $\sigma_{t,n}$ denotes a daily volatility factor and $Z_{t,n}$ is an i.i.d. mean zero unit variance innovation term, the logarithmic seasonal component, $\ln(s^2_{t,n})$, may be conveniently estimated from the following flexible Fourier form (FFF) regression,

$$2\ln\frac{|R_{t,n}-\bar{R}|}{\hat{\sigma}_t/N^{1/2}}=c+\beta O_{t,n}+\sum_{k=1}^{D}\lambda_k\cdot I_k(t,n)+\delta_{0,1}\frac{n}{N_1}+\delta_{0,2}\frac{n^2}{N_2}+\sum_{p=1}^{P}\left(\delta_{c,p}\cdot\cos\frac{2\pi p}{N}n\right. \tag{2}$$

$$\left.+\delta_{s,p}\cdot\sin\frac{2\pi p}{N}n\right)+\varepsilon_{t,n},$$

where $\bar{R}$ denotes the sample mean of the five-minute returns, $\hat{\sigma}_t$ is an a priori estimate

[9] Summer time, or daylight saving time, is defined as the period from April 5 to October 25.

[10] According to the Japan Economic Almanac (Anon, 1999), yen–dollar dealings account for 72% of the total trading volume in Japan during the first 11 months of 1998.

of the daily volatility component.[11] N_1=(N+1)/2 and N_2=(N+1)(N+2)/6 are normalizing constants. N refers to the number of return intervals per day, and the tuning parameter P determines the order of the expansion. $O_{t,n}$ is the order flow of large market participants. The $I_k(t,n)$ indicator variable for event k during interval n on day t allows for the inclusion of specific calendar and news announcement effects that will be discussed in the following sections.[12]

2.4. Calendar effects and their estimates

We now briefly outline the treatment of a number of distinct calendar features in the absolute five-minute yen–dollar spot exchange rate returns. First, we observe a significant slow down in market activity over worldwide and regional holidays. The worldwide holidays include January 1, December 24–26, and December 31, during which a dummy variable is assigned to each of the 288 five-minute intervals. The regional holidays are from the following eight countries: New Zealand, Australia, Japan, Hong Kong, Singapore, Germany, France, Great Britain, and the United States. Regional holidays affect the corresponding trading segment only.[13] The volatility burst following the Tokyo opening is captured by a single coefficient that allows for a linear decay between 00:00 and 00:30 GMT. Volatility slows down significantly in the morning on Asian Monday (21:00–22:30 GMT) in winter, and late Friday afternoon (16:00–21:00 summer time and 17:00–21:00 winter time) in the North America segment. We model these periods by constrained second-order polynomials over the corresponding intervals, resulting in two regression coefficients for each period. During the US summer time, the sinusoid regressors are shifted leftward by one hour, resulting in lower volatility in the late afternoon between 19:00 and 21:00 GMT. This is adjusted by a restricted second-order polynomial with one free parameter. In order to compensate for the one-hour shift, we elongate the intraday pattern via sinusoid regressors between 20:00 and 22:00 GMT. We also add dummy variables to control for the lunch breaks in Tokyo (3:00–4:30 GMT) and Europe (10:00–11:30 GMT summer time and 11:00–12:30 GMT winter time). Finally, we incorporate day-of-the-week dummies for all weekdays except Monday.

After some experimentation we found that P=6 in Eq. (2) was sufficient to capture

[11] Following Andersen and Bollerslev (1998), the daily volatility component is calculated in two ways: a time varying $\hat{\sigma}_{t,n}=\hat{\sigma}_t/N^{1/2}$ where $\hat{\sigma}_t$ is the estimated daily volatility from a MA(1)-FIGARCH(1,d,1) model fitted over 3652 daily returns from January 2, 1985 to December 31, 1998, and a constant $\hat{\sigma}_{t,n}=\bar{\sigma}/N^{1/2}$, where $\bar{\sigma}$ is the sample mean of $\hat{\sigma}_t$.

[12] The actual estimation involves a two-step procedure, see Andersen and Bollerslev (1997) for more details.

[13] Holidays in the US include Martin Luther King Day (19/1), President's Day (16/2), Easter (12/4–13/4), Memorial Day (25/5), Independence Day (4/7), Labor Day (7/9), Columbus Day (12/10), Veteran's Day (11/11), and Thanksgiving Day (26/11). Holidays in Japan include Coming of Age Day (15/1), National Foundation (11/2), Vernal Equinox (21/3), Green Day (29/4), Constitution Memorial and National Holiday (3/5–4/5), Children's Day (5/5), Sea Day (20/7), Respect for the Aged Day (15/9), Autumn Equinox (23/9), Health and Sports Day (10/10), National Culture Day (3/11), Labor Thanksgiving Day (23/11), and Emperor's Birthday (23/12).

the basic shape. It is clear from the corresponding dashed lines plotted in Fig. 2(a,b) that the fitted values provide a close approximation to the general intradaily volatility pattern in the yen–dollar foreign exchange market.

3. Macroeconomic announcement, intervention, and order flow effects

3.1. Important announcements

In order to formally analyze the actual impact of the news announcements, we collected data on the dates and release times of 32 US macroeconomic news releases from Reuters and 33 Japanese macroeconomic news announcements from Bloomberg.[14] All US announcements are monthly except for quarterly announcements of GDP, employment costs and the current account deficit, weekly announcements of initial jobless claims and the money supply (M2), and irregular announcements of FOMC meeting minutes, productivity and costs, the Beige book, and auto sales. For Japan, except for the quarterly announcements of the Tankan report, consumer sentiment index, GDP, and Tokyo office vacancy rate, all macroeconomic announcements are released on a monthly basis. The US announcements are released widely and virtually instantaneously at a precise scheduled time. For the Japanese announcements, we cross-checked the scheduled release time with reports from Reuters. The release times are essentially the same. Our sample of macroeconomic news from the two countries is the most comprehensive set employed to study yen–dollar exchange rate volatility.

In addition to the regularly scheduled macroeconomic news, we also include dummy variables for two days when large-scale intervention in the yen–dollar market occurred. The Bank of Japan intervened in support of the yen on April 10. The *Financial Times* reported that Tokyo currency dealers estimated the magnitude of the intervention to be around $5 billion. On June 17, the Clinton Administration's first-ever intervention aimed at supporting a weak yen was carried out in tandem with the BOJ. The *Financial Times* estimated the magnitude of the intervention to be $2 billion. Despite rumors of intervention later in the year, there was no intervention in the fourth quarter.

3.2. Order flow

Data on foreign exchange market order flow are not made public. Historically, this was due to the bilateral nature of direct-dealing trades where only the two participants to the trade knew the quantity traded and price. More recently with the advent of electronic brokerages, it is feasible to provide data representing a large cross-

[14] US non-farm payrolls and employment reports are always released at the same time, as are industrial production and capacity utilization. Simultaneous releases of news in Japan include the unemployment report and job-to-applicant ratio, housing starts and construction orders, and CPI nationwide and in the Tokyo area.

section of the market, but the firms providing the major platforms (EBS and Reuters) do not make such data public in order to preserve the confidentiality of the trading parties. In the past, the only view of order flow has been through individual traders (Lyons, 1995; Yao, 1998). Recently, Evans (1997) obtained four months of data in 1996 from the Reuters direct-dealing 2000–1 system that contains transaction prices and whether a trade was a purchase or sale (Reuters would not provide the quantities traded).

Note that there exists no way to capture the order flow of the entire market at the high frequency level across the spectrum of telephone and electronic trading venues. Obtaining the trading records over a short sample period from one trading venue, like the Reuters 2000–1 system, is the best one can hope for. However, at a lower frequency level there exist time-series data on quantities in the form of positions held by major market participants. For our study of 1998 yen volatility, we employ these data. The data source is the US Treasury. Market participants with positions greater than $50 billion in foreign exchange contracts on the last business day of any quarter must file weekly reports on their purchases and sales. The Treasury does not reveal the participants identities and only provides aggregated data. However, the size threshold for required reporting suggests that these major market participants are essentially the largest commercial and investment banks. We use the weekly data on purchases and sales of spot, forward, and futures contracts on the yen as our proxy for order flow.[15] It is the order flow that reveals the private information regarding position changes as there are no public announcements when a large fund switches from long to short or vice versa. In the context of the yen in 1998, the financial press frequently reported that a liquidity crunch associated with losses in emerging markets like Southeast Asia and Russia and the tightening of credit following the losses of Long Term Capital Management led to unwinding the yen carry-trade positions. In fact, a search of Reuters news associated with the 25 largest 5-min absolute returns in our sample reveals that many of these intervals are associated with the yen carry trade. The increased dollar selling and yen buying associated with unwinding positions was reported to be the force behind the dramatic periods of yen appreciation.

When a hedge fund initiates a trade aimed at unwinding its short yen position, this trade is not known to anyone other than the counterparty to the trade. As the magnitude of such trading grew and the yen rose in value, rumors regarding the scale of the position switches were common. The important point is that it is the order flow related to the position switching that results in the exchange rate changing and this order flow may be orthogonal to public information associated with current fundamentals. In the context of the 'portfolio shifts' model presented in Evans and Lyons (1999), this result requires that (1) portfolio shifts are not common knowledge as they occur and (2) they are large enough that clearing the market requires adjust-

[15] Wei and Kim (1997) use these data to establish that the major market participants' positions Granger-cause exchange rate volatility for the UK pound, Swiss franc, yen, mark, and Canadian dollar over the 1994–1996 period.

ment of the spot exchange rate.[16] In the case under study, the first condition is correct at the time trades are initiated. Furthermore, in the case of the yen in 1998, the second condition is fulfilled to such a degree that news services quickly search for a causal factor. This results in news reports of major hedge fund yen purchases with a short lag (within the day) after the trades.

Some additional comments on order flow in the context of our model are needed. First, since the measure of order flow, O, is only available weekly, O will not enter into the determination of the intradaily volatility patterns. Instead, O may be thought of as shifting the intercept term to account for shifts in average weekly volatility. As will be seen below, there are significant shifts in average weekly volatility that would be missed in the absence of the O variable. Second, the time aggregation embodied in O creates a potential simultaneity problem. As a result, we utilize an instrumental variable estimation procedure where the instruments are two lags of order flow and two lags of the absolute weekly exchange rate returns (a volatility proxy). It should be kept in mind that our measure of O is the only market-wide proxy for order flow available and our study is the first to incorporate such a measure in an intradaily model of exchange rate dynamics.

3.3. Initial estimation results

We begin our analysis with the announcement effects. Given the limited number of occurrences of each type of news announcement and the inherent noise in the return process, it is not possible to simultaneously estimate separate coefficients for each event and time interval following the news releases. Instead, we impose a reasonable decay structure on the volatility response pattern and estimate the degree to which the event 'loads onto' this pattern. Following Andersen and Bollerslev (1998), we choose the dynamic response pattern to be of the form $\lambda(k,i)=\lambda_k \cdot \gamma(i), i=0,1,2,\ldots,12$, where the pre-specified $\gamma(i)$ coefficients are determined by a third-order polynomial, the general shape of which is given in Fig. 3.[17] This approach restricts the response horizon to be one hour.

Table 1 summarizes the estimates of the full system in Eq. (2) including the intradaily calendar effects, time-varying daily volatility factor, intervention effects, holiday and day-of-the-week dummies, order flow, and macroeconomic data announcements. For the latter, the table just includes those announcements that were found to have a statistically significant effect on volatility. Significant announcements were identified by estimating a version of Eq. (2) for each specific announcement, where

[16] Evans and Lyons develop a model of daily exchange rate returns depending upon macroeconomic news and order flow. They use daily interest differential changes as their proxy for macro news and the number of purchases minus sales per day as their measure of order flow. While their model is aimed at estimating returns, one can derive their model in absolute value terms to address volatility.

[17] We calibrate this pattern by fitting all three parameters for a set of announcements of about equal significance, without the λ_k coefficient. This uniquely identifies the three parameters. For the rest of the announcement effects, we fix the response pattern and estimate the λ_k coefficient that loads onto the pattern. Details are available upon request.

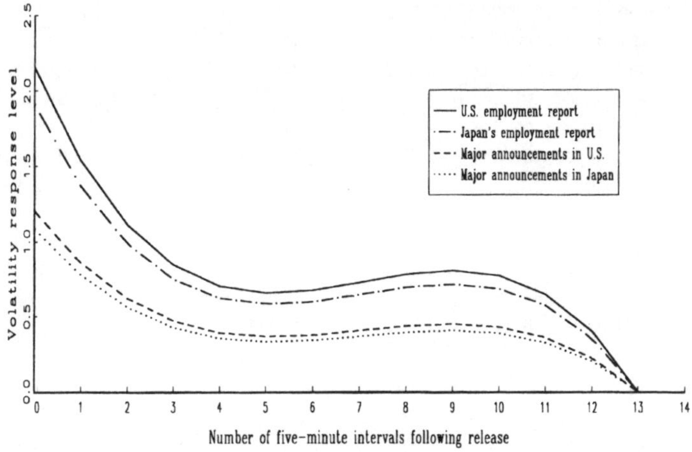

Fig. 3. Estimated announcement response patterns.

each announcement is, in turn, entered into the equation separately while other announcements are entered jointly with a separate 'all other announcements' coefficient. Appendix A provides details on the individual announcement effects. Of the 32 US and 33 Japanese announcements analyzed, the following announcements were employed in the estimates reported in Table 1: US employment report, CPI, GDP, PPI, merchandise trade balance, consumer installment credit, real earnings, employment costs, reserve assets, and personal income; Japanese employment report, Tankan report, unemployment rate, vehicle sales, consumer sentiment index, electricity usage, and vehicle production. Given the importance of the two employment reports, their coefficients are estimated separately. The remaining announcements are aggregated into the 'major announcement' variable.

Table 1a reports results using the time-varying daily volatility-scaling factor $\hat{\sigma}$. Table 1b contains the results based on the constant daily volatility-scaling factor $\bar{\sigma}$. Column 2 of Table 1a reports estimates of the complete model. The coefficients associated with the intraday patterns are significant except for the US afternoon summer slowdown and the second-order term on winter Monday morning. Andersen and Bollerslev (1998) found day-of-the-week effects to be insignificant for the dollar–mark exchange rate once the other calendar effects and announcements were included. However, the coefficients reported in column 2 indicate that the daily dummies are significant. Column 3 reports estimates for the yen–dollar with the day-of-the-week dummies excluded. A chi-square test of the exclusion restriction indicates that the day-of-the-week dummies are highly significant. Whether this difference between the results found by Andersen and Bollerslev and our results reflects a systematic difference between the mark and yen volatility dynamics or is due to the special nature of the year we study is open to further analysis.

Focusing on the separate sources of volatility, we see that both intervention

Table 1a
Using time-varying daily volatility factor

Parameter	Full system	Day-of-the-week dummies excluded	Intervention dummies excluded	Macro-announcements excluded	Order flow variables excluded
Constant intercept	−4.65 (−4.32)	−4.43 (−4.11)	−4.63 (−4.29)	−4.20 (−3.90)	−6.08 (−5.66)
Holiday	−0.91 (−18.48)	−0.93 (−18.98)	−0.91 (−18.53)	−0.91 (−18.38)	−0.89 (−18.05)
Tokyo open	1.52 (6.77)	1.52 (6.74)	1.52 (6.77)	1.47 (6.54)	1.53 (6.80)
US afternoon summer slowdown	−0.01 (−0.25)	−0.01 (−0.43)	−0.01 (−0.24)	−0.01 (−0.18)	−0.03 (−1.69)
Winter Asian Monday morning	−2.01 (−2.98)	−2.13 (−3.15)	−2.01 (−2.98)	−2.01 (−2.98)	−1.95 (−2.88)
	0.12 (0.49)	0.09 (0.35)	0.12 (0.49)	0.12 (0.49)	0.14 (0.57)
Friday late	−0.04 (−5.06)	−0.03 (−4.32)	−0.04 (−5.12)	−0.04 (−5.19)	−0.04 (−4.96)
	0.06×10^{-2} (3.57)	0.05×10^{-2} (3.04)	0.06×10^{-2} (3.60)	0.07×10^{-2} (3.66)	0.06×10^{-2} (3.47)
Tokyo lunch break	−0.81 (−11.15)	−0.81 (−11.13)	−0.81 (−11.15)	−0.81 (−11.21)	−0.79 (−10.88)
European lunch break	−0.21 (−3.18)	−0.21 (−3.17)	−0.21 (−3.20)	−0.19 (−2.86)	−0.21 (−3.24)
Summer high volatility at 2210–2225 GMT	1.47 (5.45)	1.51 (5.62)	1.47 (5.45)	1.46 (5.44)	1.36 (5.04)
Tuesday	0.12 (3.84)		0.12 (3.84)	0.13 (4.10)	0.12 (3.95)
Wednesday	0.17 (5.51)		0.17 (5.60)	0.17 (5.57)	0.17 (5.59)
Thursday	0.26 (8.49)		0.26 (8.49)	0.27 (8.80)	0.26 (8.58)
Friday	0.23 (7.10)		0.24 (7.29)	0.26 (7.99)	0.24 (7.13)
FED and BOJ intervention on June 17	2.65 (2.75)	2.67 (2.77)		2.58 (2.67)	2.68 (2.77)
BOJ intervention on April 10	1.09 (2.92)	1.16 (3.13)		1.05 (2.82)	1.23 (3.30)
US employment reports	2.00 (5.60)	2.16 (6.06)	1.98 (5.54)		2.01 (5.62)
Japan's employment reports	1.78 (5.06)	1.88 (5.36)	1.77 (5.02)		1.80 (5.08)
Major announcements in US	1.14 (8.13)	1.21 (8.58)	1.13 (8.06)		1.15 (8.12)
Major announcements in Japan	1.01 (5.54)	1.03 (5.65)	1.00 (5.50)		1.02 (5.60)
Spot, forward purchased	3.21×10^{-2} (8.18)	3.26×10^{-2} (8.29)	3.20×10^{-2} (8.14)	3.24×10^{-2} (8.25)	
Spot, forward sold	-3.82×10^{-2} (−9.62)	-3.86×10^{-2} (−9.73)	-3.81×10^{-2} (−9.60)	-3.85×10^{-2} (−9.69)	
Log-likelihood	−179,444.33	−179,488.04	−179,458.73	−179,496.30	−179,577.42

Table 1b
Using constant daily volatility factor

Parameter	Full system	Day-of-the-week dummies excluded	Intervention dummies excluded	Macro-announcements excluded	Order flow variables excluded
Constant intercept	−8.63 (−7.96)	−8.40 (−7.75)	−8.60 (−7.94)	−8.19 (−7.57)	−6.28 (−5.79)
Holiday	−0.91 (−18.33)	−0.93 (−18.80)	−0.92 (−18.39)	−0.91 (−18.24)	−0.90 (−17.97)
Tokyo open	1.51 (6.67)	1.50 (6.63)	1.51 (6.67)	1.47 (6.45)	1.52 (6.67)
US afternoon summer slowdown	0.01 (0.37)	0.01 (0.19)	0.01 (0.38)	0.01 (0.43)	−0.01 (−0.37)
Winter Asian Monday morning	−2.03 (−2.96)	−2.15 (−3.14)	−2.03 (−2.96)	−2.03 (−2.97)	−1.98 (−2.94)
	0.11 (0.44)	0.07 (0.30)	0.11 (0.44)	0.11 (0.44)	0.13 (0.52)
Friday late	−0.04 (−5.07)	−0.03 (−4.31)	−0.04 (−5.14)	−0.04 (−5.20)	−0.04 (−5.11)
	0.06×10^{-2} (3.62)	0.05×10^{-2} (3.08)	0.07×10^{-2} (3.66)	0.07×10^{-2} (3.71)	0.07×10^{-2} (3.67)
Tokyo lunch break	−0.82 (−11.17)	−0.82 (−11.14)	−0.82 (−11.16)	−0.82 (−11.23)	−0.81 (−10.95)
European lunch break	−0.21 (−3.11)	−0.21 (−3.10)	−0.21 (−3.13)	−0.18 (−2.80)	−0.21 (−3.13)
Summer high volatility at 2210–2225 GMT	1.50 (5.60)	1.55 (5.76)	1.50 (5.60)	1.50 (5.59)	1.46 (5.46)
Tuesday	0.10 (3.28)		0.10 (3.27)	0.11 (3.52)	0.10 (3.33)
Wednesday	0.16 (5.36)		0.17 (5.46)	0.17 (5.42)	0.17 (5.40)
Thursday	0.29 (9.32)		0.29 (9.32)	0.30 (9.62)	0.30 (9.46)
Friday	0.24 (7.16)		0.25 (7.40)	0.27 (8.04)	0.24 (7.20)
Fed and BOJ intervention on June 17	2.76 (2.86)	2.77 (2.88)		2.69 (2.79)	2.57 (2.67)
BOJ intervention on April 10	1.36 (3.66)	1.44 (3.88)		1.33 (3.56)	1.05 (2.82)
US employment reports	2.02 (5.68)	2.18 (6.16)	1.99 (5.61)		1.99 (5.61)
Japan's employment reports	1.65 (4.59)	1.73 (4.88)	1.63 (4.54)		1.63 (4.68)
Major announcements in US	1.12 (7.87)	1.19 (8.34)	1.11 (7.80)		1.16 (8.22)
Major announcements in Japan	1.00 (5.41)	1.03 (5.54)	0.99 (5.35)		0.98 (5.23)
Spot, forward purchased	5.28×10^{-2} (13.40)	5.33×10^{-2} (13.51)	5.26×10^{-2} (13.36)	5.31×10^{-2} (13.47)	
Spot, forward sold	-4.09×10^{-2} (−10.27)	-4.14×10^{-2} (−10.38)	-4.08×10^{-2} (−10.25)	-4.12×10^{-2} (−10.34)	
Log-likelihood	−179,909.25	−179,961.42	−179,927.55	−179,958.42	−180,414.24

dummy variables are positive and significant, indicating that volatility was higher on the intervention days. Column 4 of Table 1a reports estimates of the model with the intervention dummies omitted. A likelihood ratio test of the exclusion restriction indicates that the intervention dummies are jointly significant. Among macroeconomic announcements, the employment reports have the largest effect on yen–dollar volatility similar to the mark–dollar findings of Andersen and Bollerslev (1998). The other major announcements also have positive and significant effects on volatility. Column 5 of Table 1a reports estimates of the model with the macroeconomic announcements variables excluded. A likelihood ratio test of the exclusion restriction indicates they are jointly highly significant. Finally, order flow, as proxied by purchases and sales of spot, forward, and futures contracts by major market participants, is seen to have a significant effect on volatility. Purchases are associated with higher volatility and sales with lower volatility. The positive and significant effect of purchases is consistent with volatility being caused by the unwinding of yen carry-trade positions. Periods with large yen sales by major participants are associated with lower yen volatility. This suggests that the establishment of short yen positions was consistent with a tranquil market. Column 6 of Table 1a reports model estimates with the order flow variables excluded. A likelihood ratio test of the exclusion restriction indicates that the order flow variables are also jointly highly significant.

The estimates reported in Table 1b, using the constant daily volatility-scaling factor are generally quite similar to those reported in Table 1a. The variables that were found to be insignificant determinants of yen/dollar volatility in Table 1a are also the variables with insignificant coefficients in Table 1b. The qualitative results of Table 1a all carry over to Table 1b. The greatest difference between the two tables is with regard to the order-flow variables. There appears to be collinearity between the time-varying daily volatility factor used in Table 1a and order flow. When the constant daily volatility factor is used in Table 1b, we find order flow to have larger coefficients and a greater level of statistical significance. The likelihood-ratio statistic on the joint significance of the order flow variables implied by the results reported in the last column of each table increases from 266 in Table 1a to 1010 in Table 1b. It seems likely that the generated time-varying daily volatility-scaling variable $\hat{\sigma}$ is, at least partially, reflecting shifts in order flow over time.

The results of Tables 1a and 1b indicate that each of the major factors we examine has a statistically significant role in explaining volatility. Now we would like to have an idea of the relative contributions of each to understanding yen–dollar volatility in 1998. The next section will provide a measure of the marginal predictive power of each individual component.

4. The relative importance of different volatility components

In this section we provide a direct assessment of the joint and marginal predictive power of each of the four volatility components—intraday calendar effects, announcement effects, intervention effects, and order flow. The basic idea is to construct a series of five-minute volatility forecasts $v(\mathrm{I}{:}t,n)$ that in turn omits or includes only the contribution from each of the four components. The day-of-the-week and holiday effects are always included in the regressions. The joint and marginal contribution of the four volatility components at the daily and intraday frequencies are then measured by the coefficient of explained variation, R^2, from the regressions of the realized daily cumulative absolute returns, $\Sigma^N_{n=1}|R_{t,n}-\bar{R}|$, and the realized five-minute absolute returns, $|R_{t,n}-\bar{R}|$, on the corresponding volatility forecasts, $\Sigma^N_{n=1}v(I{:}t,n)$ and $v(I{:}t,n)$, respectively.

Table 2 summarizes the results for the different model configurations. Columns 2 and 3 contain results for models based upon the time-varying daily volatility-scaling factor while results reported in columns 4 and 5 are for models using the constant daily volatility-scaling factor. The numbers in the second and fourth columns refer to the degree of explained variation in the daily cumulative absolute returns. The complete model using the time-varying daily volatility-scaling factor $\hat{\sigma}$ accounts for 49.7% of the cumulative daily volatility.[18] The complete model with the constant daily volatility-scaling factor $\bar{\sigma}$ explains 23.7% of the total variation. The explanatory power is similar when the calendar effects are removed from the forecast. The R^2 drops slightly when the announcement variables are deleted. It drops

Table 2
Explained variation (R^2) from regressions of Japanese yen–US dollar daily cumulative absolute returns or five-minute absolute returns on absolute return forecasts[a]

Model	Time-varying daily volatility: Daily cumulative absolute return	Time-varying daily volatility: Five-minute absolute return	Constant daily volatility: Daily cumulative absolute return	Constant daily volatility: Five-minute absolute return
Complete model	0.497	0.072	0.237	0.046
No intraday calendar effects	0.497	0.053	0.237	0.028
No announcements	0.490	0.071	0.228	0.045
No intervention dummies	0.482	0.069	0.218	0.043
No order flow	0.477	0.073	0.031	0.027
Intraday calendar effects only	0.469	0.069	0.024	0.022
Announcements only	0.470	0.050	0.029	0.007
Intervention dummies only	0.478	0.052	0.034	0.007
Order flow only	0.489	0.049	0.228	0.024

[a] The table reports the explained variation (R^2) from regressing $\Sigma^N_{n=1}|R_{t,n}-\bar{R}|$ on $\Sigma^N_{n=1}v(I{:}t,n),t=1,2,\ldots T$ for daily cumulative absolute returns and from regressing $|R_{t,n}-\bar{R}|$ on $v(I{:}t,n),t=1,2,\ldots T,n=1,2,\ldots N$, for five-minute absolute returns. $v(I{:}t,n)$ is the five-minute volatility forecast that in turn leaves out or includes only the contribution from each of the following components, the intraday calendar effects, the announcement effects, the intervention dummies, and predicted order flow by big market participants. The first two columns report estimates for the complete model using the time-varying daily volatility factor $\hat{\sigma}$. The remaining columns report estimates using the constant daily volatility factor $\bar{\sigma}$. The day-of-the-week dummies and holiday effects are included in all regressions.

[18] Explanatory power may be increased for the cumulative absolute returns when some components are deleted since the forecasts at this horizon involve a nonlinear transformation of the components.

somewhat more without the intervention dummies. The biggest drop in explanatory power for the daily cumulative absolute returns occurs when order flow is omitted.

As one would expect, the models estimated for five-minute absolute returns reveal significant explanatory power for the intraday calendar effects. Five-minute absolute return models based on $\hat{\sigma}$ find that the deletion of announcements, intervention dummies, or order flow all have about the same minor effect on explanatory power. The five-minute absolute return models based on $\bar{\sigma}$ find the same results for announcements or intervention, but now we see the omission of order flow cutting explanatory power roughly in half. This different inference on order flow effects between models based on $\hat{\sigma}$ or $\bar{\sigma}$ is due to the collinearity that exists between order flow and $\hat{\sigma}$.

Examining the explanatory power when each source of volatility is used by itself to forecast, provides the R^2 results reported in the last four rows of Table 2. Standing alone, the R^2 estimates for daily cumulative absolute returns are listed in ascending order as calendar, announcement, intervention, and order flow effects; with time-varying (constant) daily volatility values ranging from 46.9 (2.4) to 48.9 (22.8)%. For the five-minute absolute returns, results using time-varying daily volatility indicate calendar effects have the highest R^2 of 6.9% while the other three components have approximately the same values of 5%. With constant daily volatility, the five-minute absolute returns range from a low of 0.7% for announcements and intervention to 2.4% for order flow. The evidence presented in Table 2 suggests that, compared to the effect of order flow, the announcement and intervention effects are of secondary importance in understanding yen–dollar volatility in 1998.

5. Discussion and conclusion

This paper provides a detailed characterization of the Japanese yen–US dollar spot exchange rate return volatility over 1998. The yen–dollar exchange rate was extraordinarily volatile during the year with periods of both rapid yen depreciation and rapid yen appreciation. A review of the news during the year suggests the following candidates as sources of the dramatic volatility: foreign exchange market intervention by the Bank of Japan, the US Treasury and the Federal Reserve; shifting fundamentals related to US and Japanese macroeconomic conditions; and spillover from the Asian and Russian financial crises and Long Term Capital Management losses resulting in a liquidity crunch that caused large investment funds to unwind short yen positions. Our analysis is focused on identifying the relative contributions of these various factors in understanding the yen–dollar volatility of 1998.

In order to obtain meaningful estimates of the effects of intervention, macroeconomic announcements, and big-trader order flow, a model capturing the typical intradaily volatility pattern over a 24-h trading day must be employed. The resulting model incorporates intradaily calendar effects to account for the regular daily pattern of activity in the yen–dollar market. Our analysis also details the impact of a comprehensive list of 32 US and 33 Japanese regularly released macroeconomic announcements. Most of the ten significant US announcements and six significant Japanese announcements are associated with the real side of the economies, with employment reports from both countries on top of the list. In contrast to previous studies, the day-of-the-week effects cannot be attributed to the clustering of scheduled macroeconomic news releases on Thursdays and Fridays during the morning session of US trading hours.

Comparing the alternative sources of volatility, we find that order flow is most important. The significance of order flow by itself could simply reflect the effect of some underlying true causal factor like macroeconomic announcements or intervention. However, even accounting for a lengthy list of announcements and the actual interventions that occurred during 1998, we find an independent role for order flow in explaining yen–dollar volatility. This finding lends support to the assertion that portfolio shifts were responsible for much of the volatility. The popular story is that early in the year there was a large-scale shift into short yen positions associated with the yen 'carry trade' of borrowing yen at extremely low interest rates and then investing in higher-yielding assets denominated in other currencies. Later in the year, following losses in Asian and Russian markets and credit constraints associated with new perceptions of risk following Long Term Capital Management's problems, there was a large-scale unwinding of the short-yen positions. The market learns about such portfolio shifts through order flow rather than public announcements. Our results lend support to the effect of order flow being an important determinant of yen–dollar volatility in 1998.

In a broader context than our particular yen–dollar application, are the implications for understanding the structure of the foreign exchange market. It has long been known that empirical exchange rate models based on fundamentals perform poorly. This has led to an ongoing search for better approaches to modeling exchange rate dynamics. Recently, some studies have provided suggestive evidence that the act of trading, apart from any news regarding fundamentals, may be an important source of exchange rate movements. As a market with a relative lack of transparency and asymmetrically informed traders, it should not be surprising to find that order flow contains independent information. Just as news regarding macro announcements can affect volatility by providing information to the market, so does large order flow convey new information. While we might expect order flow to reflect macro news, what else could drive position changes? In general, order flow that is orthogonal to current macro news may reflect expectations of future changes in fundamentals or revised expectations due to institutional changes. In the most dramatic period of yen volatility in 1998, it is likely that changing risk perceptions and associated credit constraints associated with the Russian bond default, losses in Asian markets, and the LTCM debacle contributed to the order flow associated with unwinding the yen carry trade. Such an effect will not be revealed by macroeconomic announcements. As discussed in the introduction, practitioners have long argued that order flow is a major source of price movements. However, only now is the evidence accumulating to support this view. It is in this sense that our findings have implications beyond the yen–dollar application studied. We provide new evidence in support of the role of order flow and its associated information as a determinant of exchange rate dynamics.

Acknowledgements

We would like to thank City University of Hong Kong for its support. In addition, financial support from RGC Competitive Earmarked Research Grants 1994–1996 and 1996–1998 (Cai) is gratefully acknowledged. Helpful comments on an earlier draft were provided by Charles Goodhart, Richard Lyons, Bettina Peiers, and the anonymous referees. Finally, we thank Tim Bollerslev for sharing his programs.

Appendix A. Individual macroeconomic news announcement effects

The dependent variables are based on raw five-minute returns on the Japanese yen–US dollar spot exchange rate. The sample period is from January 1998 to December 1998 for a total of 74,880 observations. The regression takes the form as in Table 1. The volatility response pattern following announcements is approximated by a third-order polynomial restricted to reach zero at the end of the response horizon of one hour, or the 13th five-minute interval. The reported coefficients measure the extent to which the absolute returns load onto this pattern following the announcement. The sample of macroeconomic news includes 32 announcements from the US and 33 announcements from Japan. The instantaneous jump in volatility measures the estimated increase in the five-minute absolute return for the interval when the announcement is made. The estimated total cumulative absolute return induced by the announcement over the assumed horizon is measured relative to the median cumulative absolute return over the sample period of 11.7% per day.

Table 3 only summarizes the results for the significant announcements from both the US and Japan. In descending order based on the estimated volatility jump, the insignificant US announcements include construction spending, FOMC meeting minutes, factory inventories, housing starts, new single-family home sales, housing completion, NAPM survey, industrial production, productivity and costs, initial jobless claims, existing home sales, beige book, federal budget, durable goods orders, import prices, leading indicators, money supply (M2), consumer confidence, retail sales, business inventories, current account deficit, and auto sales. The insignificant Japanese announcements in descending order include the current account, vehicle exports, foreign currency reserves, housing starts, GDP, merchandise trade balance, Tokyo new condo sales, vehicle imports, money supply (M2+CD), leading indicators, Tokyo department store sales, large scale retail sales, bank lending, bankruptcies, average lending rate, wholesale price index, nationwide department store sales, corporate service price, Tokyo office vacancy rate, steel production, machine tool orders, household spending, industrial production, machinery orders, international securities investment, crude oil imports, and consumer price index.

Table 3
Important annnouncement effects

Announcement	OBS	GMT	Coefficient	Robust t-statistic	Instantaneous jump in volatility (%)	Impact on daily cum absolute return (%)
US						
Employment report	12	1330	2.01	5.59	188	3.2
CPI	12	1330	1.63	4.03	136	2.4
GDP	4	1330	1.40	3.70	110	2.0
PPI	12	1330	1.26	2.84	94	1.8
Merchandise trade balance	12	1330	1.24	3.00	92	1.7
Consumer instalment credit	12	2000	1.17	2.54	85	1.0
Real earnings	12	1500	0.93	2.96	63	1.3
Employment costs	4	1330	0.91	1.73	61	1.2
Reserve assets	12	2000	0.84	1.80	56	0.7
Personal income	12	1330	0.71	2.10	46	0.9
Japan						
Tankan report	4	2350	2.71	5.66	317	5.0
Unemployment report	12	30	1.75	4.81	151	2.4
Vehicle sales	12	500	1.09	3.37	78	1.2
Consumer sentiment index	4	500	0.85	1.75	57	0.9
Electricity usage	12	200	0.82	2.75	54	0.8
Vehicle production	12	400	0.75	1.77	49	0.7

References

Anon, 1999. Japan Economic Almanac. Nihon Keizai Shimbun Inc.

Andersen, T., Bollerslev, T., 1997. Intraday periodicity and volatility persistence in financial markets. Journal of Empirical Finance 4, 115–158.

Andersen, T., Bollerslev, T., 1998. Deutsche mark–dollar volatility: intraday activity patterns, macroeconomic announcements, and longer-run dependencies. Journal of Finance 1, 219–265.

Baillie, R., Bollerslev, T., 1991. Intra-day and inter-market volatility in foreign exchange rates. Review of Economic Studies 58, 565–585.

Beranger, F., Galati, G., Tsatsaronis, K., von Kleist, K., 1999. The yen carry trade and recent foreign exchange market volatility. International Banking and Financial Market Developments, Bank for International Settlements, 33–38.

Chatrath, A., Song, F., 1998. Information and volatility in futures and spot markets: the case of the Japanese yen. Journal of Futures Markets 18, 201–223.

Cheung, Y., Wong, C., 1999. Foreign exchange traders in Hong Kong, Tokyo, and Singapore: a survey study. Advances in Pacific Basin Financial Markets 5, 111–134.

Cheung, Y., Chinn, M., 2000. Currency traders and exchange rate dynamics: a survey of the U.S. market. Journal of International Money and Finance, in press.

Cheung, Y., Chinn, M., Marsh, I., 1999. How do U.K.-based foreign exchange dealers think their market operates? CEPR Working Paper no. 2230.

Dacorogna, M., Müller, U., Nagler, R., Olsen, R., Pictet, O., 1993. A geographical model for the daily and weekly seasonal volatility in the FX market. Journal of International Money and Finance 12, 413–438.

DeGennaro, R., Shrieves, R., 1997. Public information releases, private information arrival, and volatility in the foreign exchange market. Journal of Empirical Finance 4, 295–315.

Ederington, L., Lee, J., 1994. The response of the dollar–yen exchange rate to economic announcements. Financial Engineering and the Japanese Markets 1, 111–128.

Evans, M., 1997. The microstructure of foreign exchange dynamics, Working Paper, Georgetown University.

Evans, M., Lyons, R., 1999. Order flow and exchange rate dynamics, Working Paper, University of California at Berkeley.

Hakkio, C., Pearce, D., 1985. The reaction of exchange rates to economic news. Economic Inquiry 23, 621–636.

Hardouvelis, G., 1984. Market perceptions of Federal Reserve policy and the weekly monetary announcements. Journal of Monetary Economics 14, 225–240.

Harvey, C., Huang, R., 1991. Volatility in the foreign currency futures market. Review of Financial Studies 4, 543–569.

Ito, T., Lyons, R., Melvin, M., 1998. Is there private information in the FX market? The Tokyo experiment. Journal of Finance 53, 1111–1130.

Ito, T., Roley, V., 1987. News from the U. S. and Japan: which moves the yen/dollar exchange rate? Journal of Monetary Economics 19, 255–277.

Leng, H., 1996. Announcement versus nonannouncement: a study of intraday transaction price paths of Deutsche mark and Japanese yen futures. Journal of Futures Markets 16, 829–857.

Lyons, R., 1995. Tests of microstructural hypotheses in the foreign exchange market. Journal of Financial Economics 39, 321–351.

Melvin, M., Yin, X., 2000. Public information arrival, exchange rate volatility, and quote frequency. The Economic Journal 110, 644–661.

Menkhoff, L., 1998. The noise trading approach—questionnaire evidence from foreign exchange. Journal of International Money and Finance 17, 547–564.

Tett, G., 1999. Bruised investors wait for rising yen bubble to burst, Financial Times, June 25, p. V.

Thornton, D., 1989. The effect of unanticipated money on the money and foreign exchange markets. Journal of International Money and Finance 8, 573–587.

Yao, J., 1998. Market making in the interbank foreign exchange market. New York University Salomon Center Working Paper no. 5-98-3.

Wei, S.-J., Kim, J. 1997. The big players in the foreign exchange market: do they trade on information or noise? NBER Working Paper 6256.

Part III
Technical Analysis of Foreign Exchange Markets

[8]

ELSEVIER Journal of International Economics 58 (2002) 211–232

Journal of INTERNATIONAL ECONOMICS

www.elsevier.com/locate/econbase

The temporal pattern of trading rule returns and exchange rate intervention: intervention does not generate technical trading profits

Christopher J. Neely*

Research Department, Federal Reserve Bank of St. Louis, 411 Locust Street, St. Louis, MO 63102, USA

Received 8 December 2000; received in revised form 5 March 2001; accepted 1 July 2001

Abstract

This paper characterizes the temporal pattern of trading rule returns and official intervention for Australian, German, Swiss and U.S. data to investigate whether intervention generates technical trading rule profits. The data reject the hypothesis that intervention generates inefficiencies from which technical rules profit. In particular, high frequency data show that abnormally high trading rule returns precede German, Swiss and U.S. intervention. Australian intervention precedes high trading rule returns, but trading/intervention patterns make it implausible that intervention actually generates those returns. Rather, intervention responds to exchange rate trends from which trading rules have recently profited. © 2002 Elsevier Science B.V. All rights reserved.

Keywords: Technical analysis; Trading rule; Intervention; Exchange rate; Central bank

JEL classification: G0; G14

1. Introduction

Evidence has accumulated in recent years that technical analysis – the use of past price behavior to determine trading decisions – can be useful in the foreign

*Tel.: +1-314-444-8568; fax: +1-314-444-8731.
E-mail address: neely@stls.frb.org (C.J. Neely).

0022-1996/02/$ – see front matter
PII: S0022-1996(01)00163-5

exchange market (Sweeney, 1986; Levich and Thomas, 1993; Neely et al., 1997; Osler and Chang, 1999). This finding has challenged the efficient markets hypothesis, which holds that exchange rates reflect information to the point where the potential excess returns do not exceed the transactions costs of acting (trading) on that information (Jensen, 1978).

Researchers have been less successful in explaining why excess returns accrue to technical rules than in documenting those returns. The literature has focused on three hypotheses: (1) the return to technical trading rule strategies compensates traders for bearing risk (Kho, 1996); (2) the apparent success of technical trading can be explained by data snooping (Ready, 1998; Sullivan et al., 1999); and (3) official intervention in foreign exchange markets generates inefficiencies from which technical rules profit.

Many authors have speculated that intervention by monetary authorities is the source of technical trading rule profitability (Friedman, 1953; Dooley and Shafer, 1983; Corrado and Taylor, 1986; Sweeney, 1986; Kritzman, 1989). More recently, a seminal paper by LeBaron (1999) found a remarkable correlation between daily U.S. official intervention and returns to a typical moving average rule.[1] Further research extended this result. Szakmary and Mathur (1997) found that monthly trading rule returns were correlated with changes in reserves – a proxy for official intervention. Saacke (1999) extended LeBaron's results using Bundesbank data and examined the profitability of intervention for both the U.S. and Germany. Sapp (1999) used U.S. and Bundesbank data and explored whether other macroeconomic and financial variables help explain technical trading rule profits. These findings further convinced many researchers that technical trading profits were generated by intervention (Martin, 2001).

No paper, however, has carefully considered whether the timing of intervention and returns supports the hypothesis that intervention generates trading rule profits. This study uses high-frequency trading rule returns and five intervention series from four central banks to investigate that issue. The timing of signals/returns around intervention and the direction of trading are inconsistent with the idea that intervention generates technical trading rule profits. In particular, high trading rule returns *precede* U.S., German and Swiss intervention and trading rules consistently trade contrary to the direction of intervention. While high trading rule returns in the AUD/USD do appear to lag Australian intervention, the direction and timing of intervention and trading rule signals makes it implausible that intervention generates trading rule returns even in this case. Rather, intervention is correlated with trading rule returns because monetary authorities intervene in response to short-term trends from which trading rules have recently profited.[2]

[1] Davutyan and Pippenger (1989) explored similar issues with Canadian data from the 1950s.

[2] This does not, of course, mean that monetary authorities seek to minimize technical trading profits. Instead, authorities seem to dislike the trends themselves.

2. The data

This analysis uses five intervention series from four monetary authorities – Australia, Germany, Switzerland and the United States. The interventions of Australia, Germany and Switzerland were conducted in the respective national currencies (AUD, DEM, CHF) against the U.S. dollar (USD), while the U.S. data involve in-market transactions in the DEM/USD and Japanese yen/U.S. dollar (JPY/USD) markets.[3] Full summary statistics are available in the working paper but are omitted here for brevity.

To correspond with the U.S., German and Swiss intervention series, this paper uses noon New York (1700 Greenwich Mean Time (GMT)) buying rates for the USD against the DEM, JPY, and CHF from the H.10 Federal Reserve Statistical Release. The daily exchange rate corresponding to the Australian intervention data was the AUD/USD rate collected by the Reserve Bank of Australia at 4:00 p.m. Eastern Australian Time, 0600 GMT.

The Bank for International Settlements (BIS) provided daily interest rate data, collected at 0900 GMT. Australian interest rate data were unavailable over an extended sample, so returns for this exchange rate were calculated exclusive of interest differentials. These exchange rate and interest rate series have been described in Neely et al. (1997) and Neely and Weller (2001); summary statistics are omitted for brevity.

The use of daily exchange rates almost inevitably leaves some ambiguity about the timing of returns and intervention. To address the timing question, four sets of intraday exchange rates have been assembled from daily exchange rates series observed at different times during the day. In choosing daily series for inclusion in the intraday data set, a tradeoff was made between maximizing the number of observations per day and retaining the possible greatest sample length for the intraday data. This strategy permitted six observations per day for the DEM/USD and CHF/USD, at 0600, 1000, 1400, 1600, 1700 and 2200 GMT.[4] The JPY/USD had one more observation per day, at 0800 GMT. The Australian data were limited to three observations per day, at 2300, 0600, and 1600 GMT. For each intervention series, the maximum sample in which the intervention series, the daily exchange rate and the intraday exchange rates all exist was selected. The data were filtered to remove outliers. Sample lengths ranged from 10 years for the Swiss intervention in CHF/USD to 15 years, 6 months for the U.S. and German cases. Experiments and summary measures – omitted for brevity – show that the irregular nature of

[3]Intervention is defined narrowly to include only transactions, not other types of policies that affect exchange rates.

[4]Describing the time of collection of the intraday exchange rate data in GMT is an approximation. The data were collected during specified local times, which were then translated into GMT without allowance for daylight savings time changes. Thus, actual times of collection in GMT could vary by an hour from those described. For purposes of this paper, the approximation is not important.

the data does not introduce any seasonality that would be significant for this paper's results.

3. Daily returns and intervention

3.1. Daily return results

For continuity with the previous literature, this paper follows LeBaron (1999) and examines the profitability of signals from a moving average (MA) 150 trading rule. The rule prescribes:

$$\text{Buy USD if } S_t \geq \frac{1}{150}\sum_{i=0}^{149} S_{t-i}, \text{ and sell USD if } S_t < \frac{1}{150}\sum_{i=0}^{149} S_{t-i}, \tag{1}$$

where S_t is the spot foreign exchange price of USD at time t.

Excess returns to the rule are calculated under the assumption that a trader holds an amount of money in a margin account that collects the U.S. interest rate. The trader borrows against that margin to either invest in the foreign currency (short the USD) or to invest in USD assets (short the foreign currency). The continuously compounded excess return to switching back and forth between fully margined long and short positions in USD is approximated by $z_t r_t$. The variable z_t takes the values of $+1$ (-1) for a long (short) position in USD and r_t is defined as

$$r_t = \ln S_{t+1} - \ln S_t - \ln(1 + i_t^*) + \ln(1 + i_t) \tag{2}$$

where i_t^* and i_t denote daily interest rates on foreign and U.S. investments, respectively. The total excess return, r, for a trading rule from time zero to time T is the sum of the signed daily returns:

$$r = \sum_{t=0}^{T-1} z_t r_t.^5 \tag{3}$$

Panel A of Table 1 shows the mean annual return, standard deviation, t-statistic, trades-per-year and risk-adjusted returns from applying an MA 150 trading rule to each of the five samples. The rule makes positive returns in all five samples, ranging from 8.72% per annum for the JPY/USD from July 1983 to December 1998 to 2.44% for the AUD/USD from March 1985 through June 1999. The row

[5] This definition of r_t introduces a very small approximation error in the case of a short position. Note that these calculations include no adjustment for transactions costs. A reasonable adjustment for the transactions costs of a large trader (five basis points per round trip) would lower annual returns by 25 to 40 basis points, leaving them still well above zero.

Table 1
Daily trading rule returns conditional on removing periods of intervention

Monetary Authority exchange rate	United States DEM/USD	Germany DEM/USD	United States JPY/USD	Switzerland CHF/USD	Australia AUD/USD
Panel A: All observations					
obs	3892	3892	3891	2512	3629
mean	6.03	6.03	8.72	5.10	2.44
std	0.69	0.69	0.68	0.79	0.62
t-stat	2.17	2.17	3.17	1.28	0.93
ntrades	7.55	7.55	5.23	6.41	8.17
P-value	0.01	0.00	0.00	0.05	0.14
Sharpe	0.55	0.55	0.80	0.41	0.25
α	6.09	6.09	8.59	5.07	2.75
Panel B: Remove $p(t)/p(t-1)$ when $I(t) \neq 0$					
obs	3661	3302	3692	2410	2080
mean	2.61	1.28	4.50	4.44	−2.27
std	0.67	0.67	0.66	0.78	0.55
t-stat	0.99	0.51	1.74	1.16	−1.30
ntrades	7.42	7.29	5.23	6.21	5.52
P-value	0.13	0.40	0.02	0.11	0.86
Markov-*P*	0.00	0.00	0.00	0.29	0.00
Sharpe	0.25	0.13	0.44	0.37	−0.34
date 1	7/1/83	7/1/83	7/1/83	1/3/86	3/4/85
date 2	12/31/98	12/31/98	12/30/98	12/29/95	6/30/99

Notes: The table shows the results of an MA 150 rule on daily foreign exchange rate data (Eq. (3)). Panel A shows the results for all observations. Panel B excludes return observations from $t-1$ to t for which there was non-zero intervention at t. *obs* is the number of observations in each sample. *mean* is the mean annualized percentage return to the rule. *std* is the standard deviation of the daily percentage returns. *ntrades* is the number of trades per year. *t-stat* is the *t*-statistic for the null hypothesis that the mean annual return is zero. *P-value* is the bootstrapped *P*-value for the test that the mean return is zero. Low *P*-values reject the null hypothesis. *Sharpe* is the annualized Sharpe ratio. α is the estimate of the risk-adjusted annual return from a four-factor pricing model. See Eq. (4). *Markov-P* shows the simulated *P*-value for the test of the null that the change in the mean annual return from Panel A to Panel B would have been as great by randomly removing returns. *Date 1* and *date 2* are the beginning and ends of the samples in m/d/y format.

labeled *P*-value shows the probability – computed via bootstrap – that such returns would be produced under the null hypothesis of a zero mean return. The only case in which the *P*-value is greater than 0.05 is that of AUD/USD, for which it is 0.14.

The final rows of Panel A display two risk-adjusted-return measures, the Sharpe ratio and the constant from a linear factor model (α). The Sharpe ratio – the expected excess return per unit of risk for a zero-investment strategy – is the annual excess return to the trading rule over that excess return's annual standard deviation. A linear multifactor model 'explains' the return to the rule as compensation for exposure to risk factors. One may write the linear factor model for the return to the rule as:

$$z_t r_t = \alpha + \sum_{k=1}^{N} \beta_k X_{k,t} + \varepsilon_t \tag{4}$$

where $X_{k,t}$ is the kth risk factor at time t. The choice of risk factors is always arbitrary, but CAPM theory suggests that returns that are correlated with the market portfolio may impose undiversifiable risk and therefore have positive excess return. Thus the first three risk factors were the excess returns over riskless rates to the German Commerzbank index, the Japanese Nikkei index and the U.S. S&P 500 index. The fourth risk factor was the mean squared daily return over the previous five business days, a proxy for time-varying univariate risk. The linear factor models were estimated at the daily and monthly frequency by ordinary least squares to produce risk-adjusted returns (α).

Consistent with most of the previous literature on risk adjustment of foreign exchange trading rule returns, neither the Sharpe ratios nor any of the four linear factor models provide any evidence that the returns compensate the trading rules for bearing risk. The Sharpe ratios range from 0.25 to 0.8, comparing favorably with those from equity markets. The risk-adjusted returns (α) are close to the unadjusted returns. Analogous results at the monthly frequency – omitted for brevity – lead to similar conclusions. Risk adjustment does not reduce the technical returns significantly; unadjusted returns will be used in the rest of the paper.

3.2. Removing periods of official intervention

Panel B of Table 1 shows the results from LeBaron's (1999) procedure that removes returns from $t-1$ to t when there is intervention at t.[6] LeBaron's (1999) sample comprised in-market U.S. intervention in the DEM/USD and JPY/USD markets from 1979 through 1992. LeBaron showed that removing periods of U.S. intervention from the trading rule return series reduced the returns to insignificance. This has been interpreted as evidence that intervention caused those trading rule returns. Panel B confirms LeBaron's results for other series and different samples to a remarkable degree, with only minor discrepancies. For example, even after removing U.S. intervention in the JPY/USD market from July 1983 through 1998, the mean return is still a healthy and statistically significant 4.5%.

The row labeled Markov P-value shows the bootstrapped probability that

[6] The timing of the daily data (1700 GMT for the DEM/USD, JPY/USD and CHF/USD, 0600 for the AUD/USD) includes all Australian, German and Swiss business hours in the return from $t-1$ to t, but only half of the U.S. business day.

randomly removing returns – assuming that intervention follows a Markov process – would lower the return as much as removing actual intervention observations. The only case in which the Markov *P*-value indicates an insignificant relation between returns and intervention is that of the Swiss intervention in the CHF/USD market: the MA 150 rule has a 4.4% annual return after removing intervention and a Markov *P*-value of 0.29. The sign of the relation is consistent with other results, however, and the failure to obtain a statistically significant fall in return might simply reflect the poor power of the test statistic in the presence of relatively sparse Swiss intervention and a shorter sample. Therefore, the Markov *P*-values reject the hypothesis that randomly removing returns would lower the return as much as removing actual interventions.

Some of the strongest results are in the AUD/USD market, which has not been previously studied in this context. Removing Australian intervention periods from March 1985 through June 1999 reduces the annual return from 2.44 to −2.27%. Strong results also are generated by removing Bundesbank intervention in the DEM/USD market from July 1983 through December 1998. Removing Bundesbank intervention periods reduces the annual return from 6.03 percent to only 1.28%.

Fig. 1 illustrates the predicted daily trading rule returns, with a one-standard error band, around days of intervention. Predicted returns were constructed by regressing daily trading rule returns on leads and lags of an indicator variable for non-zero intervention:

$$z_{t-1}r_{t-1} = a_0 + \sum_{j=-2}^{2} b_j I_{t+j} + \varepsilon_{t-1} \qquad (5)$$

where I_{t+j} is an indicator variable taking the value one if there is any intervention on day $t+j$. The regression coefficients $(\{a_0 + b_j\} | j = -2, -1, 0, 1, 2)$ are the predicted returns in the 2 days prior to, on the day of and in the 2 days after intervention. The horizontal axis of Fig. 1 is labeled in hours from the beginning of the intervention day in GMT; the dating convention has made the returns backward looking in the figure. For example, because the USD, DEM and JPY daily data were collected at 1700 GMT, the predicted return from $t-1$ to t coincides with the label 17 for those cases. Similarly, the predicted return from t to $t+1$ coincides with the label 41, etc.[7] The vertical lines in each panel denote business hours for the intervening country.

On the whole, Table 1 and Fig. 1 confirm LeBaron's (1999) finding that high technical trading rule returns tend to be correlated with periods of intervention. The results – using a broader sample of intervention series and different time periods – are similar to those found by LeBaron (1999) in U.S. data, Szakmary

[7]Twenty four hours after 1700 would be 41 in the notation of the figure.

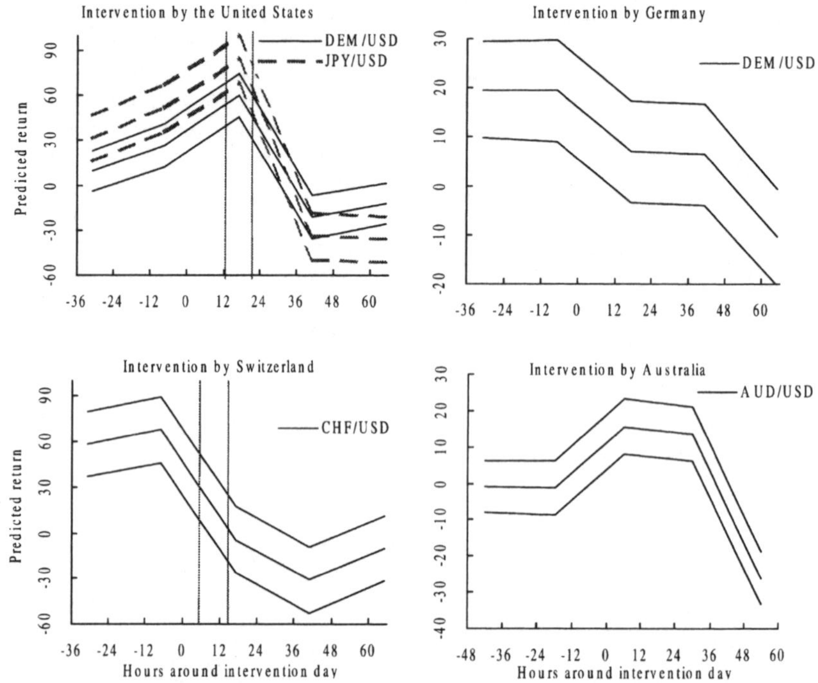

Fig. 1. Daily trading rule returns around periods of intervention. *Notes*: The figure depicts predicted daily backward-looking returns and a one-standard error confidence interval to an MA 150 rule around periods of intervention. The figures were obtained by regressing trading rule returns on leads and lags of intervention. The vertical lines depict business day hours in the intervening country. Australian business hours are 0200 to 0600 GMT; German and Swiss business hours are 0600 to 1400 GMT; U.S. business hours are 1300 to 2100 hours GMT. The horizontal axis shows hours before (negative) and after (positive) midnight on the day of intervention in GMT.

and Mathur (1997) in multinational monthly data or by Saacke (1999) and Sapp (1999) in U.S. and German data.

4. Why might intervention be correlated with technical trading rule profits?

This section lays out two alternate explanations for the correlation between intervention and trading rule returns and develops testable hypotheses to discriminate between those explanations.

Explanation 1. *Intervention generates or amplifies patterns that trading rules detect and from which they profit.*

Explanation 2. *Intervention leans against the wind. That is, intervention reacts to recent trends in exchange rates from which trading rules profit.*

Although the mechanism by which intervention might generate profits to trend-following trading rules is not fully developed in the literature, one can reason out three possibilities. First, intervention to buy dollars might generate a sustained appreciation in the value of the dollar. This would require intervention to precede the sustained appreciation and for the trading rule to trade with the central bank – when the central bank buys dollars, the trading rule also buys dollars. This story implies the following testable hypothesis:

TH (1.1). *Intervention precedes trading rule profits and trades in the same direction as the trading rule.*

The second story is that intervention might temporarily delay a change in the exchange rate, permitting trading rules time to switch positions and profit by trading against the central bank. That is, a central bank might sell dollars as the dollar is appreciating, temporarily depressing the price and allowing traders to buy dollars cheaply and profit on the resumption of the trend. Of course, if the trading rule does not switch positions during intervention, it can't take advantage of a delayed movement. That is, the data must show:

TH (1.2). *Intervention precedes trading rule profits, and the trading rule switches positions during or shortly after the intervention to trade against the intervention.*

The third story is that expectations of future intervention (e.g. USD purchases) cause a sustained appreciation of the USD from which the trend-following trader profits.[8] This implies testable hypothesis (1.3):

TH (1.3). *Intervention follows trading rule profits and trades with the trading rule.*

On the other hand, if Explanation (2) is correct – intervention is correlated with technical trading profits because it reacts to the same strong trends in exchange rates from which trend following rules profit – then one might expect the following:

[8] Although intervention is predictable to a certain extent, the author's prior is that expectations of intervention are unlikely to induce such substantial changes in exchange rates.

TH (2.1). *Intervention follows or is coincident with trading rule returns. Exchange rate changes predict intervention. Intervention trades against the trend-following rule.*

To summarize, if intervention generates or amplifies trading rule returns, then either TH (1.1), TH (1.2) or TH (1.3) must be true. If, instead, intervention reacts to trends from which trading rules profit, then TH (2.1) will be true.

A natural procedure to determine the relationship between trading rule returns and central bank intervention would be to write down reduced form equations for trading rule returns and intervention, to make identifying assumptions, to estimate the model and to derive the implied structural relationship between intervention and trading rule returns. While this procedure is natural and attractive, it is not necessary to investigate the issues of this paper and it entails making heroic assumptions about the timing of intervention and identification. For example, the first choice in such a procedure would be to match up intervention observations with contemporaneous observations of trading rule returns. Because the exact timing of intervention is uncertain, however, one cannot match intervention one-for-one to high-frequency return data. On the other hand, the use of daily data would ignore information on the high-frequency timing of returns and intervention. Further, the possibility of high frequency feedback between trading rule returns and intervention precludes any obvious way to identify the contemporaneous relationship.

To determine whether intervention generates trading rule returns, the next section characterizes the timing of high frequency returns, signals and intervention, and examines with which testable hypotheses such patterns are consistent.

5. Intraday results

5.1. Results with intraday data

Intraday returns are calculated as the log change from one intraday price to the next, exclusive of overnight interest differentials. That is, the ith return on day t is calculated as:

$$r_{i,t} = \ln S_{i+1,t} - \ln S_{i,t} \tag{6}$$

where $S_{i,t}$ is the ith observation on day t of the foreign exchange price of USD. Intraday returns whose initial observation occurred at or after the time of daily exchange rate collection day t but before the collection time on day $t+1$ are signed with the day *t* signal from the MA 150 rule.[9] The return during a period is the sum of signed intraday returns. It should be emphasized that these are intraday returns – several hours long – not simply daily returns recorded at different times of the day.

Table 2 displays the trading rule statistics from signed daily returns, constructed from intraday exchange rates. Comparing Table 2 with Table 1 shows that including or excluding interest differentials makes little difference to the results. All of the annualized intraday returns, excluding interest rate differentials, are within 75 basis points of the interest-adjusted daily results in Table 1. The bootstrapped *P*-values for the null of zero return are only slightly higher than those in Table 1. The largest such statistics are 0.07 and 0.17 for the Swiss and Australian cases, respectively. The similarity between Tables 1 and 2 is consistent

Table 2
Daily trading rule returns with intraday data

Monetary Authority exchange rate	United States DEM/USD	Germany DEM/USD	United States JPY/USD	Switzerland CHF/USD	Australia AUD/USD
Panel A: All observations					
obs	3892	3892	3891	2512	3629
mean	5.98	5.98	8.29	5.84	2.44
std	0.69	0.69	0.68	0.79	0.62
t-stat	2.15	2.15	3.01	1.47	0.93
ntrades	7.55	7.55	5.23	6.41	8.17
P-value	0.02	0.02	0.00	0.07	0.17
Sharpe	0.55	0.55	0.76	0.47	0.25
Panel B: Remove $p(t)/p(t-1)$ when $I(t)/=0$					
obs	3661	3302	3692	2410	2080
mean	2.59	1.47	4.20	5.21	−2.27
std	0.67	0.67	0.66	0.78	0.55
t-stat	0.99	0.59	1.62	1.37	−1.30
ntrades	7.42	7.29	5.23	6.21	5.52
P-value	0.19	0.32	0.05	0.12	0.91
Markov-*P*	0.00	0.00	0.00	0.32	0.00
Sharpe	0.25	0.15	0.41	0.43	−0.34
date 1	7/1/83	7/1/83	7/1/83	1/3/86	3/4/85
date 2	12/31/98	12/31/98	12/30/98	12/29/95	6/30/99

Notes: See the notes to Table 1.

[9] Recall that the daily DEM/USD, JPY/USD and CHF/USD exchange rates were collected at 1700 GMT while the daily AUD/USD exchange rate was collected at 0600 GMT. One could permit trade at hours other than noon; given the low frequency of trading for the MA 150 rule, however, this would not make much difference in the performance of the rule.

with LeBaron's (1999) finding that the correlation between trading rule returns and intervention is robust to the treatment of interest differentials.

As in Table 1, removing daily returns from $t-1$ to t when there is intervention at t reduces the mean annual return in every case, though again, the size of the reduction varies. Removing Swiss intervention from the CHF/USD return series leaves a still substantial 5.21% annual return, whereas removing days of Australian intervention from the AUD/USD series reduces the annualized return to −2.27%. The only Markov P-value greater than 0.05 was 0.32, for the Swiss case. In other words – except for the Swiss case – we can reject the null hypothesis that randomly removing returns would lower the mean as much as removing actual intervention.

5.2. The temporal pattern of intraday returns and intervention

To characterize the high-frequency temporal pattern of trading rule returns and intervention, a procedure similar to that used to create Fig. 1 is followed. Intraday trading rule returns – where periods are hours long rather than one day – are regressed on leads and lags of intervention signals. That is, returns around intervention are predicted by fitted values from the following regression:

$$z_{i,t}r_{i,t} = a_{i,0} + \sum_{j=-2}^{2} b_{i,j}I_{t+j} + \varepsilon_{i,t} \tag{7}$$

where $z_{i,t}$ is the $\{-1,1\}$ signal from the MA 150 rule associated with the ith period on day t, $r_{i,t}$ is the intraday return from period i to $i+1$ on day t and I_{t-j} is the jth lag of the indicator variable for non-zero intervention at t.

Panel A of Fig. 2 displays the backward-looking predicted intraday returns in the five business days around intervention ($\{a_{i,0} + b_{i,j}\}|j = -2, -1, 0, 1, 2$), as well as one-standard-error bands. The estimated $a_{i,0}$ coefficients were very small. To facilitate the discernment of patterns in the noisy data, Panel B shows a backward-looking, 24-h moving average of the predicted returns. The horizontal axes of the figures are labeled in hours from the beginning of the intervention day in GMT. For example, in panel B, an observation labeled −5 would denote the moving average of the returns from 1900 GMT 2 days prior to intervention to 1900 GMT on the day prior to intervention. The vertical lines in each panel again denote the business hours of the day for each of the intervening monetary authorities.

Business hours are significant because one might reasonably assume that most intervention transactions take place during those hours. Although the U.S. authorities do not publicly release the times of intervention, Goodhart and Hesse (1993) and Humpage (1998) report that it generally occurs before the close of the London markets, at 1600 GMT. There is more information about the timing of Swiss intervention, which is publicly announced. Generally, the Swiss National

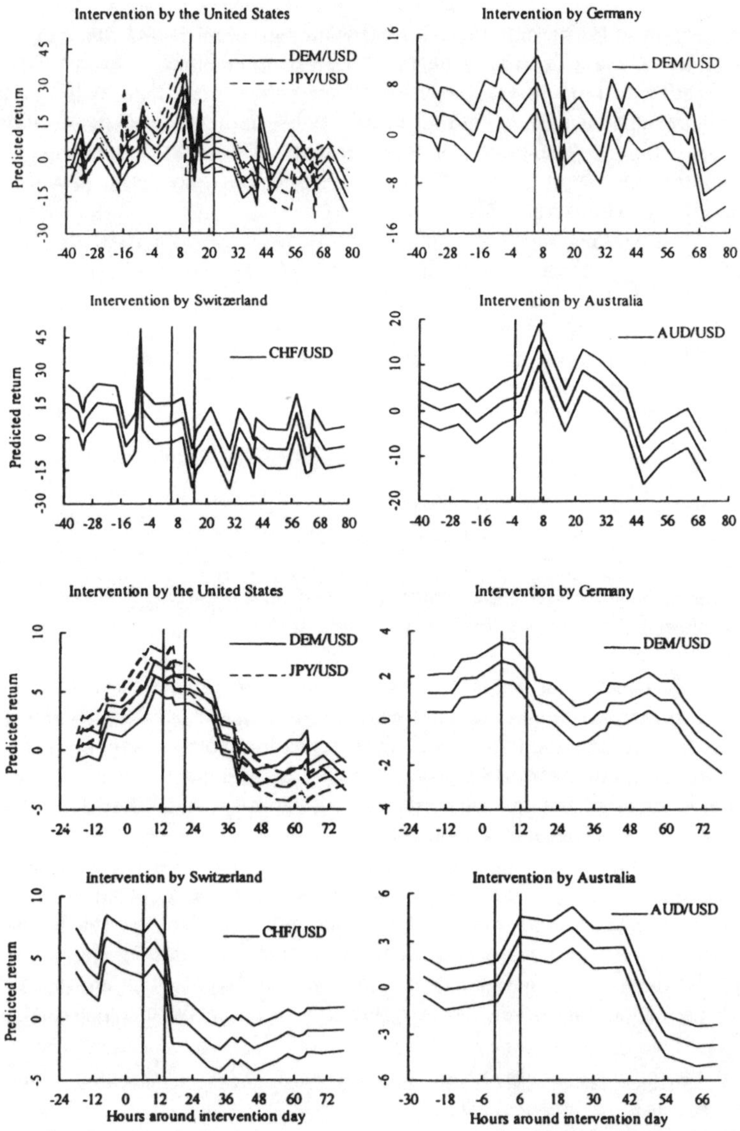

Fig. 2. Intraday trading rule returns around periods of intervention. Notes: The top panel depicts backward-looking predicted intraday returns to an MA 150 trading rule around periods of intervention with a one-standard error band. The bottom panel shows a backward-looking, 24-h moving average of those predicted returns with its error band. Vertical lines depict business day hours in the intervening country. The horizontal axis shows hours before (negative) and after (positive) midnight on the day of intervention in GMT.

Bank intervened for the first time at 1400 GMT during joint intervention with the Federal Reserve. As these joint interventions often also involve the Bundesbank, one might surmise that most Bundesbank intervention in the DEM/USD markets occurs contemporaneously with SNB intervention – during the European afternoon or U.S. morning.[10] The timing of Reserve Bank of Australia operations is less certain; the RBA specifically states that intervention may occur during non-business hours (Rankin, 1998).

Fig. 2 is consistent with Fig. 1 and Tables 1 and 2 in that the backward-looking trading rule returns are usually high from −700 to 1700 GMT on the day of interventions for the U.S., Swiss, and German cases. Fig. 2 also reveals patterns that were not apparent from the tables, however. Most importantly, it is clear that the highest U.S., Swiss, and German excess returns precede the business hours during which most intervention would be carried out.[11] The highest returns are finished by 0800 GMT for the U.S. and German cases and by 1000 GMT for the Swiss case.

5.3. Morning-to-morning and business day results

One can quantify how much of the abnormal returns in Fig. 2 likely preceded intervention by computing the daily returns from intraday returns from early morning to early morning – prior to the business day – instead of noon-to-noon as in Table 2. Panel A of Table 3 shows that the unconditional results for early-morning to early-morning returns for each of the five cases are very similar – not surprisingly – to the noon-to-noon cases presented in Table 2. Panel B shows that removing observations in the 24 hours prior to the beginning of the business day of intervention reduces the mean returns substantially. But, these high returns almost surely precede intervention and therefore could not plausibly have been caused by intervention.[12] In contrast, Panel C removes returns in the 24 hours after the beginning of the intervention day. Intervention might have preceded – and therefore plausibly caused – these returns. But, removing these returns that follow intervention still leaves significant technical trading rule mean returns. The U.S. and Swiss cases still have high mean returns (4.23 and 6.04%) that are statistically significant at the 10% level. These results are consistent with hypothesis (2.1);

[10]The correlations between signed indicators of U.S., Swiss, and German intervention range from 0.55 to 0.62 during the 1986–1995 sample.

[11]As a check on the robustness of the methodology, the same figure was created for isolated interventions – those for which there was no other intervention within 2 days of another intervention. With 70 to 95% fewer observations, results for the U.S. and Swiss cases were consistent with Fig. 2; those for Germany showed no clear pattern and those for Australia were inconsistent with results shown in Fig. 2.

[12]This statement assumes that expectations of intervention are unlikely to systematically create significant changes in exchange rates.

Table 3
Morning to morning returns with and without days and business days of intervention

Monetary exchange	Authority rate	United States DEM/USD	Germany DEM/USD	United States JPY/USD	Switzerland CHF/USD	Australia AUD/USD
Panel A: All observations						
	mean	5.87	5.89	8.28	5.91	2.40
	P-value	0.02	0.01	0.01	0.05	0.20
Panel B: Remove $p(t)/p(t-1)$ when $I(t) \neq 0$						
	mean	2.28	0.05	3.69	2.95	−0.65
	P-value	0.18	0.49	0.07	0.19	0.61
	Markov-*P*	0.00	0.00	0.00	0.00	0.05
Panel C: Remove $p(t+1)/p(t)$ when $I(t)/=0$						
	mean	4.23	2.18	6.02	6.04	−2.65
	P-value	0.07	0.22	0.00	0.09	0.86
	Markov-*P*	0.00	0.00	0.00	0.67	0.01
Panel D: Remove business hour returns prior to the day of intervention						
	mean	3.32	1.95	5.75	3.56	1.32
	P-value	0.11	0.28	0.03	0.24	0.29
	Markov-*P*	0.00	0.00	0.00	0.00	0.35
Panel E: Remove business hour returns on the day of intervention						
	mean	3.90	3.31	6.99	5.91	−0.30
	P-value	0.10	0.11	0.02	0.05	0.57
	Markov-*P*	0.00	0.02	0.04	0.52	0.11
	date 1	7/1/83	7/1/83	7/1/83	1/3/86	3/4/85
	date 2	12/31/98	12/31/98	12/30/98	12/29/95	6/30/99

Notes: The table provides statistics on returns calculated from morning-to-morning or morning-to-evening, around periods of intervention. Morning-to-evening (business day) hours are calculated as 1000–2200, 0600–1700, 1000–2200, 0600–1700, and 1600 (day $t-1$) to 0600 GMT for each of the five cases, respectively. Local times would be −5, +1, −5, +1 and +10 h from the GMT figures, respectively. The notes to Table 1 define *mean, P-value,* and *Markov-P.* Panel A shows the results for all observations. Panel B removes the returns in the 24 h prior to the beginning of the morning observation when there is intervention. Panel C removes the returns in the 24 h after the morning observation when there is intervention. Panel D removes the returns during the business day prior to the day of intervention. Panel E removes the returns during the business day of intervention.

intervention responds to short-term trends in the market but does not generate trading rule returns.

The German intraday results from Panel C of Table 3 show that removing returns during the 24 hours after the start of the day of intervention does reduce the return on the DEM/USD trading rule to 2.18%. However, Fig. 2 suggests that part of this reduction is caused by high returns *after* the business day of intervention. One can argue that such post-business returns should be excluded from the calculations because they are less likely to have been caused by intervention. Neely (2000) provides some evidence from a survey of central bankers themselves to support this proposition: 61% of respondents believe that the full effect of intervention is felt in a few hours or less. Panels D and E show the results of excluding returns on the business day prior to and the business day of intervention. Excluding returns on the business day of intervention (Panel E) generally leaves the return to the trading rule at significant (or nearly significant) levels for the U.S., Swiss, and German cases. The JPY/USD trading rule returns a hefty 6.99%, for example, after excluding business days of U.S. intervention.

Fig. 2 and Table 3 show that for the U.S., Swiss, and German cases, most abnormally high returns precede business hours and thus precede intervention. This timing is consistent with either testable hypothesis (1.3) or (2.1). In other words, the correlation between intervention and trading rule returns probably results from fulfilled expectations of future intervention or monetary authorities 'leaning against the wind' of exchange rate trends. For the Australian case, however, the timing evidence is consistent with hypotheses (1.1), (1.2) and (2.1) as intervention precedes or is contemporaneous with high returns. The next section examines the timing and direction of trading and intervention to determine with which hypotheses they are consistent.

5.4. The timing and direction of intervention and trading rule signals

Hypotheses (1.1), (1.2) and (1.3) all require the trading rule either to trade with intervention – i.e. to buy USD when the central bank buys USD – or to switch positions to trade against the central bank. In contrast, hypothesis (2.1) implies that intervention trades contrary to technical trading signals. To investigate the facts on the timing and direction of intervention and trading rule signals, Table 4 shows that the MA 150 rule consistently (typically more than 80% of the time) trades against the position taken by central banks in periods around intervention. Thus, the timing and direction of trading signals around intervention rejects hypotheses (1.1), (1.2) and (1.3) for each case; intervention does not generate or amplify trading rule profits. Instead, this evidence is consistent with hypothesis

Table 4
Do the technical traders trade with or against central banks?

Authority rate	United States DEM/USD	Germany DEM/USD	United States JPY/USD	Switzerland CHF/USD	Australia AUD/USD
−2	0.05	0.06	0.06	0.05	0.19
−1	0.06	0.07	0.07	0.04	0.19
0	0.15	0.12	0.13	0.13	0.28
1	0.06	0.07	0.07	0.04	0.20
2	0.04	0.06	0.06	0.05	0.20

Notes: The table shows the proportion of the time that the MA 150 trader and the monetary authority were on the same side of the market from 2 days prior to intervention to 2 days after intervention. For example, the first row, second column shows that MA 150 traders were purchasing (selling) dollars only 5% of the time before U.S. authorities purchased (sold) dollars. The timing convention is that intervention at t is contemporaneous with the trading position from $t-1$ to t.

(2.1), that central bank intervention responds to strong trends in exchange rates. The next section formally investigates intervention reaction functions.

5.5. Under what conditions do these monetary authorities intervene?

The fact that the technical trading rules trade against intervention – that is, the rules are buying dollars when the central banks are selling dollars and vice versa – implies that central banks intervene to lean against the wind, to counter recent short-term trends in exchange rates. Such a finding would be consistent with empirical research on intervention (Almekinders and Eijffinger, 1996), results of a survey on intervention practices (Neely, 2000) and the public pronouncements of monetary authorities (Board of Governors, 1994, p. 64 or Rankin, 1998).

To test the proposition that intervention is a reaction to exchange rate changes, one would want to use the most recent exchange rate changes that are unlikely to be contemporaneous with intervention. For each of the five intervention series, the nearest 24 hours of intraday returns just prior to the business day of intervention are aggregated into the first lag of returns; the 24 hours of returns prior to that are aggregated into the second lag of returns and so on. For the U.S. intervention in DEM and JPY, the last returns used to predict day t intervention end at 1000 GMT; for German and Swiss intervention, the last such returns end at 0600; and for Australian intervention the last returns used end at 1600 GMT on day $t-1$. (The Australian business day on day t begins at 2200 GMT of day $t-1$).

Intervention might also be used to signal to the market that exchange rates are misaligned with their fundamental determinants. Neely (2000) finds that 66.7% of responding authorities stated that a desire to return exchange rates to fundamental values sometimes or always motivated intervention. A simple measure of a monthly purchasing-power-parity exchange rate is constructed with the following regression:

$$\ln(S_t) - \ln(P_t^*) + \ln(P_t) = \mu + \beta t + \varepsilon_t \tag{8}$$

where S_t is the foreign exchange price of dollars, P_t^* and P_t are the foreign and U.S. price levels, and t denotes a time trend. The fitted values for $\ln(S_t)$ are linearly interpolated to business day frequency. The deviations of the actual exchange rate from its fitted values measure the misalignment from what the monetary authorities might regard as long-run fundamentals.

To characterize the reaction of intervention to past returns and the measure of misalignment, an intervention reaction function is estimated in a friction-model framework.[13] A friction model permits the dependent variable – intervention – to be insensitive to changes in the independent variables over some range of values.

[13] Almekinders and Eijffinger (1996) and Kim and Sheen (1999) have studied intervention with friction models.

This is appropriate for a variable like intervention that takes the value zero for a large proportion of observations. The likelihood function is given by:

$$L(\gamma_1,\gamma_2,\beta,\sigma|I_t,x_t) = \prod_{t\in T_1} \frac{1}{\sigma}\phi\left(\frac{I_t+\gamma_1-\beta' x_t}{\sigma}\right) \times \prod_{t\in T_2}\left[\Phi\left(\frac{\gamma_2-\beta' x_t}{\sigma}\right)-\Phi\left(\frac{\gamma_1-\beta' x_t}{\sigma}\right)\right] \times \prod_{t\in T_3} \frac{1}{\sigma}\phi\left(\frac{I_t+\gamma_2-\beta' x_t}{\sigma}\right) \tag{9}$$

where I_t is intervention at time t, γ_1 (<0) is the lower bound on insensitivity for changes in the linear combination of explanatory variables $(\beta' x_t)$ to affect I_t, γ_2 (>0) is the corresponding upper bound, $\{\phi, \Phi\}$ denote the normal density and cumulative normal density, respectively, and T_1, T_2 and T_3 denote the sets of observations for which I_t is negative, zero and positive, respectively.

Up to five lags of intervention, up to five lags of 24-hours cumulated returns and the deviation of the exchange rate from fundamentals were permitted for each intervention series; the models were estimated by maximum likelihood, subject to the constraint that the estimated model be stationary.[14] The best model was selected by the Schwarz criterion (SC).

Table 5 displays the coefficients from the best models as well as the results of two likelihood ratio (LR) tests. Consistent with the autocorrelation found in the summary statistics, the coefficients on lagged intervention (I1–I3) are generally positive. Coefficients on lagged returns (R1–R4) are negative – indicating leaning-against-the-wind behavior. The coefficient on the exchange rate deviation (XRD) is also negative in each case, meaning that monetary authorities tend to buy (sell) dollars when the value of the dollar is below (above) its purchasing-power-parity fundamental measure. The restriction that the coefficient(s) on the lag(s) of the exchange rate return are jointly zero is overwhelmingly rejected by a likelihood ratio test in each case. Intervention leans against the wind.[15] The only case for which the LR test fails to reject that the coefficient on the exchange rate deviation is zero is that of the AUD/USD, for which the coefficient is correctly signed but insignificant.

The reaction function evidence indicates that intervention leans against the wind and is conducted against misalignment. The leaning-against-the wind behavior is inconsistent with hypotheses (1.1), (1.2) and (1.3) but consistent with Explanation (2)/hypothesis (2.1). Intervention reacts to counter recent trends in exchange rates from which trading rules profit.

[14]There was great difficulty fitting the models for U.S. intervention with more than three intervention lags, so those results were not considered.

[15]Although intervention leans against the wind and loses money in the short run, Neely (1998) shows that U.S. foreign exchange intervention has been profitable in the long run.

Table 5
Under what conditions do monetary authorities intervene?

	United States DEM/USD		Germany DEM/USD		United States JPY/USD		Switzerland CHF/USD		Australia AUD/USD	
I1 (s.e.)	0.95	(0.00)	0.60	(0.06)	0.95	(0.00)	0.95	(0.00)	0.74	NA
I2 (s.e.)			0.33	(0.05)					−0.09	NA
I3 (s.e.)									0.13	NA
R1 (s.e.)	−6.95	(1.26)	−4.40	(0.62)	−6.63	(1.28)	−3.40	(0.90)	−0.52	NA
R2 (s.e.)			−2.75	(0.61)			−2.85	(0.89)	−0.27	NA
R3 (s.e.)			−3.31	(0.62)			−3.11	(0.92)		
R4 (s.e.)							−2.58	(0.93)		
XRD (s.e.)	−0.41	(0.06)	−0.51	(0.03)	−0.63	(0.08)	−0.88	(0.12)	−0.16	NA
σ (s.e.)	0.31	(0.02)	0.17	(0.01)	0.29	(0.02)	0.16	(0.01)	0.08	NA
γ_1 (s.e.)	−0.59	(0.03)	−0.28	(0.01)	−0.59	(0.04)	−0.29	(0.03)	−0.11	NA
γ_2 (s.e.)	0.65	(0.04)	0.40	(0.02)	0.64	(0.04)	0.49	(0.04)	0.06	NA
LR test 1, *P*-value	52.50	(0.00)	433.61	(0.00)	83.00	(0.00)	88.15	(0.00)	153.52	(0.00)
LR test 2, *P*-value	33.33	(0.00)	101.03	(0.00)	28.77	(0.00)	47.10	(0.00)	3.45	(0.18)

Notes: The table shows the results from a friction model estimating monetary authority reaction functions (see Eq. (9)). The best models were selected from maximal lag lengths of five lags of intervention and five lags of returns by the Schwarz criterion. Coefficients on lags of intervention are labeled I1 to I5, those on the lagged return variable as R1 to R4 and the coefficient on the exchange rate deviation as XRD. σ denotes the estimated standard deviation and γ_1 and γ_2 denote the estimated inactivity boundaries. NA indicates that standard errors were unavailable as the Hessian matrix was nearly singular. The last two rows show the likelihood ratio test statistics and *P*-values for two hypotheses: (1) that the coefficients on lagged returns are zero – that the authority doesn't lean against the wind; (2) that the coefficient on the deviation from purchasing power parity is zero – that the authority does not intervene to correct misalignments.

A common problem in estimating time series relations, such as reaction functions, is structural instability. Wald tests for structural breaks in the middle of each sample failed to reject structural stability in every case, except that of the AUD/USD. Even in this case, the qualitative inference on the coefficients over each subsample was the same as that drawn from the whole sample: Intervention is negatively related to recent trends in exchange rates and to deviations from the purchasing-power-parity fundamental means. Thus, the determinants of central bank intervention appear structurally stable. Full results are omitted for brevity.

6. Conclusion

During the last 15 years, researchers have accumulated evidence that technical trading rules can produce excess returns in foreign exchange markets. These returns cannot be readily explained by reasonable transactions costs, conventional measures of risk or data mining. For a long time, some have speculated that these trading rule returns result from official intervention. Many have interpreted recently found correlations between intervention and trading rule returns as confirming this suspicion. The primary contribution of this paper is to show that the high frequency evidence disproves the hypothesis that intervention generates trading rule profits. Instead, intervention reacts to the same strong short-run trends from which the trading rules have recently profited.

In addition to showing that intervention does not generate trading rule profits, this paper characterizes the temporal patterns of high frequency trading rule returns and intervention for Australian, German, Swiss and U.S. intervention. Positive correlations found in German and U.S. data are also present – with minor variations – in longer samples, as well as in Australian and Swiss data. For the U.S., Swiss, and German cases, the highest returns probably precede intervention by less than 24 hours. For Australia, the highest returns appear to be coincident with or follow the likely hours of intervention. However, examination of the direction of trading signals and intervention make it implausible that intervention is actually generating those returns.

The explanation for the puzzle of technical trading profitability might lie in the way that information is transmitted through the microstructure of the foreign exchange market (Treynor and Ferguson, 1985; Brown and Jennings, 1989; Banerjee, 1992). Recently, Evans and Lyons (1999, 2000) have used an interdealer data set to examine several features of the data including the following: (1) imperfect substitutability of international assets; (2) signaling; (3) and a lower bound on the price impact of trades. In addition, they find a strong relation between order flow and exchange rate changes. In another line of attack, Naranjo and Nimalendran (2000) relate the adverse selection component of the bid-ask spread to the variance of unexpected intervention. Of course, this implies that unexpected intervention may reduce real-world trading profits by widening the spread.

Acknowledgements

The views expressed are those of the author and do not necessarily reflect official positions of the Federal Reserve Bank of St. Louis or the Federal Reserve System. The author thanks the Federal Reserve Bank of New York, the Board of Governors of the Federal Reserve, the Reserve Bank of Australia, the Bundesbank, the Swiss National Bank, the Bank of England and the Reserve Bank of New Zealand for assistance in obtaining data. The author also thanks Blake LeBaron, Suk-Joong Kim, Carol Osler, Paul Weller, Jeffrey Wrase, two anonymous referees and the editor, Andrew Rose, for helpful comments; Mrinalini Lhila and Charles Hokayem for research assistance; and Andreas Fischer of the Swiss National Bank for private communications regarding the timing of Swiss intervention.

References

Almekinders, G.J., Eijffinger, S.C.W., 1996. A friction model of daily Bundesbank and Federal Reserve intervention. Journal of Banking and Finance 20, 1365–1380.

Banerjee, A.V., 1992. A simple model of herd behavior. Quarterly Journal of Economics 107, 797–817.

Board of Governors of the Federal Reserve System, 1994. The Federal Reserve System: Purposes and Functions. Washington, DC.

Brown, D.P., Jennings, R.H., 1989. On technical analysis. The Review of Financial Studies 2, 527–551.

Corrado, C.J., Taylor, D., 1986. The cost of a central bank leaning against a random walk. Journal of International Money and Finance 5, 303–314.

Davutyan, N., Pippenger, J., 1989. Excess returns and official intervention: Canada 1952–1960. Economic Inquiry 27, 489–500.

Dooley, M.P., Shafer, J.R., 1983. Analysis of short-run exchange rate behavior: March 1973 to November 1981. In: Bigman, D., Taya, T. (Eds.), Exchange Rate and Trade Instability: Causes, Consequences, and Remedies. Harper & Row, Ballinger, Cambridge, pp. 43–69.

Evans, M.D.D., Lyons, R.K., 2000. The price impact of currency trades: Implications for intervention. Georgetown University, Manuscript.

Evans, M.D.D., Lyons, R.K., 1999. Order flow and exchange rate dynamics. Georgetown University, Manuscript.

Friedman, M., 1953. The case for flexible exchange rates. In: Essays in Positive Economics. University of Chicago Press, Chicago.

Goodhart, C.A.E., Hesse, T., 1993. Central bank forex intervention assessed in continuous time. Journal of International Money and Finance 12, 368–389.

Humpage, O.F., 1998. U.S. Intervention: Assessing the probability of success. Journal of Money, Credit, and Banking 31, 731–747.

Jensen, M.C., 1978. Some anomalous evidence regarding market efficiency. Journal of Financial Economics 6, 95–101.

Kho, B.-C., 1996. Time-varying risk premia, volatility, and technical trading rule profits: evidence from foreign currency futures markets. Journal of Financial Economics 41, 249–290.

Kim, S., Sheen, J., 1999. The determinants of foreign exchange intervention by central banks: evidence from Australia. The University of New South Wales, Manuscript.

Kritzman, M., 1989. Serial dependence in currency returns: Investment implications. Journal of Portfolio Management 16, 96–102.

LeBaron, B., 1999. Technical trading rule profitability and foreign exchange intervention. Journal of International Economics 49, 125–143.

Levich, R.M., Thomas, L.R., 1993. The significance of technical trading rule profits in the foreign exchange market: A bootstrap approach. Journal of International Money and Finance 12, 451–474.

Martin, A.D., 2001. Technical trading rules in the spot foreign exchange markets of developing countries. Journal of Multinational Finance 11, 59–68.

Naranjo, A., Nimalendran, M., 2000. Government intervention and adverse selection costs in foreign exchange markets. The Review of Financial Studies 13, 453–477.

Neely, C.J., 2000. The practice of central bank intervention: Looking under the hood. Central Banking 11, 24–37.

Neely, C.J., 1998. Technical analysis and the profitability of US foreign exchange intervention. Federal Reserve Bank of St. Louis Review 80, 3–17.

Neely, C.J., Weller, P.A., 2001. Technical analysis and central bank intervention. Federal Reserve Bank of St. Louis working paper 97-002C. Journal of International Money and Finance 20, 949–970.

Neely, C., Weller, P., Dittmar, R., 1997. Is technical analysis in the foreign exchange market profitable? A genetic programming approach. Journal of Financial and Quantitative Analysis 32, 405–426.

Osler, C.L., Chang, P.H.K., 1999. Methodical Madness: Technical Analysis and the Irrationality of Exchange-Rate Forecasts. Economic Journal 458, 636–661.
Rankin, B., 1998. The exchange rate and the reserve bank's role in the foreign exchange market. Reserve Bank of Australia, http://www.rba.gov.au/publ/pu_teach_98_2.html.
Ready, M.J., 1998. Profits from technical trading rules. University of Wisconsin, Manuscript.
Saacke, P., 1999. Technical analysis and the effectiveness of central bank intervention. University of Hamburg, Manuscript.
Sapp, S., 1999. The role of central bank intervention in the profitability of technical analysis in the foreign exchange market. University of Western Ontario, Manuscript.
Sullivan, R., Timmermann, A., White, H., 1999. Data-snooping, technical trading rule performance, and the bootstrap. Journal of Finance 54, 1647–1691.
Sweeney, R., 1986. Beating the foreign exchange market. Journal of Finance 41, 163–182.
Szakmary, A.C., Mathur, I., 1997. Central bank intervention and trading rule profits in foreign exchange markets. Journal of International Money and Finance 16, 513–535.
Treynor, J.L., Ferguson, R., 1985. In defense of technical analysis. Journal of Finance 40, 757–773.

Part IV
Central Bank Intervention in the Foreign Exchange Market

Pergamon

Journal of International Money and Finance, Vol. 16, No. 6, pp. 909–919, 1997

Printed in Great Britain
0261-5606/97 $17.00 + 0.00

PII: S0261-5606(97)00012-0

Why do central banks intervene?

RICHARD T BAILLIE*

Michigan State University, East Lansing, MI 48824, USA

AND

WILLIAM P OSTERBERG

Federal Reserve Bank of Cleveland, Cleveland, OH 44126, USA

Intervention by central banks, in terms of buying and selling foreign currency, has been a major activity in recent years. This paper investigates the motivations for such policy and the evidence for its effectiveness. We use high quality daily data on the dollar amounts of intervention by the central banks of the US and Germany. We also use information on agreed G7 target levels for the $/DM and $/Yen nominal exchange rates. Daily, nominal dollar exchange rate returns are well described as a Martingale–GARCH process, and we find little evidence that the different types of intervention have had much effect on the conditional mean of exchange rate returns. There is some evidence that intervention is associated with slight increases in the volatility of exchange rate returns. While little evidence is found for the effectiveness of intervention, the motivations are more clear. In particular, from the application of probit analysis we find that the probability of intervention is determined by the magnitude of the deviation of the nominal exchange rate from the agreed target level and, to a lesser extent, by the current volatility of exchange rates. (JEL C22 E41 E31).

The US dollar was generally perceived as being substantially overvalued against most other major currencies in the mid-1980s. As a result, the G5 and G7 meetings, known as the Plaza Agreement of September 22, 1985 and the Louvre Accord of February 21 and 22, 1987, ostensibly decided that coordinated multilateral policies were necessary to depreciate the US dollar and to

*This paper is dedicated to the memory of Patrick McMahon, a great friend and colleague and to his work in international finance. The views in this paper do not necessarily reflect the views of the Federal Reserve Bank of Cleveland or of the Board of Governors of the Federal Reserve System. The authors wish to acknowledge very helpful comments from Jim Lothian, Eric Girardin, Charles Goodhart, Owen Humpage and seminar participants at Johns Hopkins University, North Carolina State University and the Tinbergen Institute at Rotterdam.

restore equilibrium in current account balances. The Plaza Agreement included a plan to use central bank intervention in the sense of buying and selling foreign currency to depreciate the dollar, while the Louvre Accord advocated central bank intervention to reduce the volatility of the dollar. Such intervention was typically sterilized, so that relative money supplies were unchanged and the intervention was viewed as an additional policy tool beyond the usual mix of fiscal and monetary policy. The failure of structural models to explain how the G7 managed to achieve the depreciation of the US dollar that occurred from 1985 onwards suggests the possible importance of sterilized intervention. If economic policies, excluding intervention, were in terms of manipulating macroeconomic and structural variables, then the results of such policy actions should have been apparent in the estimation of structural models.

On denoting the logarithm of the nominal spot exchange rate in period t as s_t and the fundamentals as z_t; and assuming transversality, so that bubbles are excluded, the standard asset pricing model approach implies

$$\langle 1\rangle \qquad s_t = \Sigma_{j=0,\infty} \lambda^j E_t(z_{t+j}),$$

where λ is a discount parameter, $0 < \lambda < 1$ and E_t is the expectations operator conditioned on a set of relevant and available information at time t. However, little evidence has been obtained to overturn the results of Meese and Rogoff (1983) concerning the lack of success of structural exchange rate models in outperforming a simple random walk. Studies such as Baillie and McMahon (1989), Diebold and Nason (1990), Engel and Hamilton (1990), Baillie and Pecchenino (1991), Meese and Rose (1991) and Edison and Pauls (1993) have failed to detect much evidence for even long run relationships between exchange rates and fundamentals. Somewhat more positive results are reported by Mark (1995), who found a role for the fundamentals in explaining nominal exchange rates, but only over very long horizons.

The plan of the rest of this paper is as follows. Section I discusses the probable channels for intervention and briefly reviews some of the previous research in this area. Section II discusses the data and addresses the issue of the magnitude of central bank intervention in respect to the size of the overall market. Here we consider some of the arguments for and against intervention being large enough to matter. The historical period focused on in this study is 1985–1990, a period in which intervention was relatively intense, particularly in the $/DM market.

Section III then examines the evidence for intervention affecting the conditional mean and conditional variance of nominal exchange rate returns, within the estimation of a Martingale–GARCH model for nominal returns. The use of daily data allows us to more easily detect the effects of intervention. Section IV then considers the various factors that motivate central bank intervention. Our model links the probability of intervention to the level of volatility in nominal exchange rates and also to the deviation of the current exchange rate from the target rate as defined in the study by Funabashi (1989). The paper ends with a short concluding section.

I. The effects of intervention

The two theorized transmission mechanisms for intervention in the foreign exchange market are the portfolio balance approach and signalling to market participants of the central bank's future monetary policy. Interventions by the US, German and Japanese central banks generally are considered to be sterilized through open market operations; although Takagi (1991) has questioned whether the Bank of Japan has sterilized on a regular basis. Sterilized intervention occurs when the purchase or sale of foreign currency is offset by a corresponding sale or purchase of domestic government debt to eliminate the effects on domestic money supply. Clearly unsterilized intervention is equivalent to monetary policy and is more likely to directly affect exchange rates.

The portfolio balance mechanism is usually considered in terms of mean-variance optimization, where agents are concerned with their terminal wealth, which is composed of domestic and foreign currencies and bonds. Sterilized intervention will change the relative supplies of domestic and foreign bonds. Risk averse investors who view German denominated assets (bonds) as imperfect substitutes for US assets (bonds) therefore may be induced to trade currencies as a result of an intervention. For example, if an intervention increases the supply of DM to dollar assets, then investors must either accept the increased DM assets into their portfolios or alternatively force down the price of these DM denominated assets.

According to the signalling theory, a sterilized purchase of foreign currency will lead to a depreciation of the exchange rate if the foreign currency purchase is assumed to signal a more expansionary domestic monetary policy. Thus public information that a central bank is intending to intervene to support a currency may cause speculators to expect an appreciation of the currency. Dominguez (1990) has discussed the interpretation and possible credibility games involving signalling. For example, following a purchase of foreign currency, monetary authorities might not follow through with the expected change in the domestic monetary base and thus mislead the market. A signalling role may also imply that the impact of coordinated and unilateral intervention would differ since the former may lead to more concerted monetary actions.

The application of the signalling theory can vary depending on whether exchange rates are purely floating or varying within bands. Palm and Vlaar (1993) have shown that the behavior of ERM rates can be quite different from other purely floating rates. Froot and Obstfeld (1989) and Klein and Lewis (1991) suggest that intervention is a signal of exchange rate target bands.

An excellent survey of the previous literature on intervention is provided by Edison (1993). Most previous empirical studies have been inconclusive as to the validity of the two transmission mechanisms. Danker et al. (1987) estimated inverted asset demand equations as implied by portfolio balance models and found mixed evidence for the impact of sterilized intervention. Frankel (1982) incorporated mean-variance optimization in a portfolio balance model, but failed to find empirical support. Ghosh (1992) and Dominguez and Frankel (1993) both attempted to disentangle the portfolio balance and signalling effects; and while both found some impact for the portfolio balance channels, the effect was quite weak. The signalling hypothesis is usually interpreted in terms of conveying information concerning future monetary policy. Dominguez (1990) examined weekly data on money surprises and concluded that intervention anticipated monetary policy. Other articles have found less effect. For example, Klein and Rosengren (1991) found the impact of intervention to decline with time, while Kaminsky and Lewis (1992) on using a regime switching model, found inconclusive evidence as to whether intervention correctly signalled changes in monetary policy. Lewis (1995) examined the links between intervention, monetary policy and exchange rates; and found little evidence that monetary policy influenced exchange rates. An alternative line of research is provided by Baillie and Osterberg (1993) who considered an inter-temporal asset pricing model that allows intervention to directly affect the risk premium in forward markets. They found evidence that intervention affected excess returns from uncovered interest parity.

II. Data

This study uses data provided by the Board of Governors of the Federal Reserve System on intervention in the $/DM and $/Yen spot exchange rate markets by the US, Japanese and German central banks. Only the data on US intervention is routinely made available to the public, by the Board of Governors of the Federal Reserve System[1]. This study uses the amount of net dollar purchases (sales) from August 6, 1985 through March 1, 1990. The intervention variables are defined as the logarithm of the number of US dollars purchased or sold over a 24 h period at the close of the previous day. If no intervention occurs, which is the case for 86% of the observations, then the intervention variable is set to zero. The daily exchange rate data are bid rates at 10.00 h each day. We distinguish between purchases and sales of dollars. For the $/DM we include purchases and sales of dollars by the Federal Reserve Board and the Bundesbank separately. However, for the Yen/$ we are restricted to include only the Federal Reserve Board's operations. The Federal Reserve usually intervenes in integer multiples of either $10 m or $100 m, with the highest recorded amount in our sample period being $1.25 bn. Osterberg and Wetmore-Humes (1993) analyzed a slightly larger sample and found that the arithmetic mean of US dollar intervention exceeded US $100 m. The longest continuous stretch of Federal Reserve Bank intervention in the sample used in this study, is 11 business days.

Clearly the dollar amounts of intervention are extremely small when compared to the total activity in the foreign exchange market. Recent surveys of the market have concluded that the total value of transactions on a daily basis is at least $700 bn in the spot market alone, and close to $1000 bn including the derivative markets. Such a figure represents daily transactions of over 15% of

[1]We are grateful to the German Bundesbank for making daily data on their intervention operations available to us.

annual US GNP. Of this level of transactions, it is estimated that approximately 1.5% is motivated by merchandise trade, so that the majority is due to arbitrage, money managers taking positions and speculative activities. As noted by Obstfeld (1989) and Humpage (1988) the small size of intervention relative to the total amount of trading suggests that it is unlikely that the portfolio approach will have much impact following a sterilized intervention. Also, since studies of the portfolio approach require information concerning the stocks of assets, they are likely to be restricted to using monthly or quarterly data. Clearly this is not very satisfactory given that intervention decisions are made on a daily basis.

Intervention has been studied at the micro market level by Goodhart and Hesse (1993). They found some evidence that intervention was motivated by deviations from target levels, but also noted the possibility of small sample bias since they examined only a little over two months of Reuters screen activity. Lyons (1995) studied the activities of individual foreign exchange market traders and noted that many large currency transactions led to as many as eight subsequent trades as traders readjusted their positions, to prevent them taking excessively long or short positions in certain currencies. Hence the volume of 'market moving' transactions may well be considerably smaller than the $1000 bn stated earlier and hence allows a potentially greater role for central bank intervention.

III. The effect of intervention on the exchange rate

The model relating movements in the rates of return of the dollar exchange rates is built around the standard Martingale model with time dependent conditional heteroskedasticity. Following Bollerslev (1986) and Baillie and Bollerslev (1989), the conditional variance is modeled as a linear GARCH(1,1) process and the conditional density may be either Gaussian or Student t. Hence

$$\langle 2\rangle \qquad \Delta logS_t = \epsilon_t + b'x_t,$$

$$\langle 3\rangle \qquad \epsilon_t|\Omega_{t-1} \sim D(0,\sigma_t^2),$$

$$\langle 4\rangle \qquad \sigma_t^2 = \omega + \alpha\epsilon_{t-1}^2 + \beta\sigma_{t-1}^2 + \gamma'x_t,$$

where S_t is the level of the spot exchange rate in terms of number of foreign currency per one US$, so that $\Delta \log S_t$ is the approximate continuously compounded rate of return; and x_t denotes a vector of explanatory variables that includes the intervention variables, and possibly daily and holiday dummy variables. McFarland *et al.* (1982), Baillie and Bollerslev (1989) and Hsieh (1989a,b) have analyzed daily exchange rate returns, and found their volatility varies with the day of the week. The usual explanation for this phenomena is that volatility reflects the volume of trading and the flow of information to the market as hypothesized by French and Roll (1986). The intervention variables are lagged to ensure they are predetermined, and are the logarithms of net purchases or sales of intervention over the 24 h period ending at 17.00 h on day $t-2$, while the variable ΔS_t is the continuously compounded return on the exchange rate between 10.00 h on day $t-1$ and 10.00 h on day t.

The details of the estimated models are given in Table 1. The empirical results are consistent with Baillie and Bollerslev (1989) and Hsieh (1989a), providing support for the Martingale specification and confirming the presence of strong persistence in volatility with the α and β parameters summing close to unity. Day of the week effects were found to be significant but did not change our interpretation of the effects of intervention. For reasons of parsimony and to facilitate comparison of our results with other research on the impacts of intervention we only report the coefficient estimates for the specifications excluding various dummy variables.

The most important finding regarding the first equation is that intervention has been unable to influence the change in the exchange rate. While this is consistent with the results of studies such as Humpage (1988), it is sharply at odds with the findings of Dominguez and Frankel (1993). In addition, there is some tendency for the impact of intervention to imply that the purchase of dollars is associated with subsequent dollar depreciation. This effect is sometimes known as the 'leaning against the wind' phenomenon, and suggests the possibility of policy endogeneity, with central banks buying dollars because the dollar is depreciating. We avoid the possible simultaneous bias by having specified the intervention variable so as to be predetermined.

Table 1 also reports the effects of intervention on the conditional variance of exchange rate returns. Although the Louvre Accord advocated the use of intervention to reduce exchange rate volatility, there is some moderate evidence that intervention may have actually Granger caused an increase in volatility. This is contrary to much previous research and may reflect the fact that intervention by providing more information to market participants can induce increased volatility as agents adjust their positions.

IV. Modeling the probability of intervention

A separate issue concerns the motivation for central banks to intervene in the foreign exchange market. The stated goals for intervention following the Plaza and Louvre meetings were to depreciate the dollar and to create market stability, respectively. The perceived desire to adjust the level of the dollar can be proxied by its distance of the nominal exchange rate from its target level. Although there exists no analogous target for volatility, the goal of 'calming disorderly markets' is frequently referenced by the Working Group on Exchange Market Intervention (1983) and by Dudler (1988) who noted that disorderly markets were indicated by widening bid-ask spreads and by high volatility. Below we adopt a closely related measure; namely the amount the current conditional variance exceeds the average conditional variance, which is the unconditional variance.

On denoting US_t^b as the amount of dollar purchases vis a vis the DM by the Federal Reserve Bank in time period t, and G_t^b as the equivalent action by the Bundesbank; we then analyze the determinants of the combined intervention variable, $X_t^b = (US_t^b + G_t^b)$ from the following model:

$$X_t^b = \gamma_{i1} + \gamma_{i2}(s_t^* - s_t) + \gamma_{i3}(\sigma_t^2 - \sigma^2) + \epsilon_{1t}.$$

TABLE 1. Estimation of Martingale–GARCH(1,1) intervention model

$$\Delta \log S_t = b_0 + b_1 \mathrm{US}_t^b + b_2 \mathrm{US}_t^s + b_3 \mathrm{G}_t^b + b_4 \mathrm{G}_t^s + \epsilon_t,$$
$$\epsilon_t | \Omega_{t-1} \sim \mathrm{td}(0, \nu, \sigma_t^2),$$
$$\sigma_t^2 = \omega + \alpha \epsilon_{t-1}^2 + \beta \sigma_{t-1}^2 + \gamma_1 \mathrm{US}_t^b + \gamma_2 \mathrm{US}_t^s + \gamma_3 \mathrm{G}_t^b + \gamma_4 \mathrm{G}_t^s$$

	DM/\$	Yen/\$
b_0	−0.351(0.182)	−0.107(0.168)
b_1	−0.002(0.201)	−0.429(0.173)
b_2	0.283(0.177)	0.256(0.162)
b_3	−0.276(0.197)	
b_4	−0.011(0.167)	
ω	3.398(1.155)	2.555(0.805)
α	0.107(0.024)	0.122(0.026)
β	0.834(0.036)	0.829(0.031)
γ_1	−0.319(0.527)	0.282(0.650)
γ_2	0.207(0.721)	0.951(0.606)
γ_3	0.298(0.670)	
γ_4	−0.064(0.647)	
ν^{-1}	0.144(0.001)	0.275(0.001)
m_3	0.07	−0.59
m_4	4.42	8.30
$Q(10)$	9.73	12.94
$Q^2(10)$	2.36	14.23
T	1486	1485

The dependent variable is the daily nominal returns on the exchange rate in terms of either \$/DM or \$/Yen. The intervention variables representing the purchasing and selling \$ are given by US_t^b and US_t^s, respectively. The equivalent actions by the German Bundesbank are given in the first column, but similar actions for the Japanese central bank are omitted from the model on the grounds of confidentially. Asymptotic standard errors are in parentheses alongside corresponding parameter estimates. The statistics m_3 and m_4 are the sample skewness and kurtosis of the standardized residuals, respectively; $Q(10)$ and $Q^2(10)$ are the portmanteau statistics for autocorrelation and ARCH effects respectively, and T is the sample size.

Similarly, on defining US_t^s as the amount of dollar sales for DM purchases by the Federal Reserve Bank in time period t, and G_t^s as the equivalent action by the Bundesbank, we then analyze the combined intervention variable, $X_t^s = (\mathrm{US}_t^s + \mathrm{G}_t^s)$ from the model:

$$X_t^s = \gamma_{i4} + \gamma_{i5}(s_t^* - s_t) + \gamma_{i6}(\sigma_t^2 - \sigma^2) + \epsilon_{2t},$$

where s_t^* is the 'target' nominal exchange rate at time t, defined as the target rates documented by Funabashi (1989). The regressor σ^2 is the average conditional variance, i.e. the unconditional variance, so that $(\sigma_t^2 - \sigma^2)$ reflects the deviation of current volatility from average volatility. We define

$$I_t^b = 1, \text{ if } X_t^b > 0; \text{ and } I_t^b = 0, \text{ otherwise,}$$

$$I_t^s = 1, \text{ if } X_t^s > 0; \text{ and } I_t^s = 0, \text{ otherwise.}$$

Then the following two equations can be estimated by MLE to obtain

$$I_t^b = \gamma_{i1} + \gamma_{i2}(s_t^* - s_t) + \gamma_{i3}(\sigma_t^2 - \sigma^2) + \epsilon_{3t}$$

and

$$I_t^s = \gamma_{i4} + \gamma_{i5}(s_t^* - s_t) + \gamma_{i6}(\sigma_t^2 - \sigma^2) + \epsilon_{4t}.$$

The results of the above probit estimation are given in Table 2 and are designed to address the issue as to whether volatility of the exchange rate Granger causes intervention. The conditional variance σ_t^2 of the exchange rate was generated by estimating the model given by ⟨2⟩–⟨4⟩ with $b = \gamma = 0$. The generated conditional variance was then used as a regressor along with deviations of the nominal exchange rate from the agreed target rate in the probit, with intervention as the dependent variable. For the DM/\$ exchange rate the deviations from the target rate levels appears to have a significant effect, Granger causing intervention measured as either the buying or selling of US dollars. Conversely, there is no evidence that excess volatility increases the probability of intervention.

The findings for the Yen/\$ differ to those of the DM/\$. Volatility in the Yen/\$ market is strongly related to the buying of US dollars by the two central banks. There is less evidence that increased volatility induced a selling of dollars. Also in contrast to the findings for the DM/\$, deviations of the Yen/\$ from its target rate Granger caused the selling of US dollars, but did not affect the buying of US dollars.

It is not immediately clear why the determinants for intervention should differ between currencies, nor why there should be differences between buying and selling. It is possible that the results are specific to the particular time

TABLE 2. Estimation of probit intervention model for nominal exchange rate returns

	Germany		Japan	
Dependent Variable	$US^b + G^b$	$US^s + G^s$	$US^b + J^b$	$US^s + J^s$
Constant	−0.92(0.32)	−2.23(0.41)	−2.08(0.23)	−2.09(0.27)
$(s^* - s_{t-1})$	20.76(2.22)	10.95(1.90)	7.82(8.44)	3.58(1.12)
σ_{t-1}^2	−0.33(0.48)	0.49(0.62)	1.22(0.32)	0.63(0.35)
LR Test with 2 d.f.	94.01	44.05	14.79	13.49

The dependent variable is the total buying or total selling of dollars by either the Federal Reserve Bank (US^b and US^s) and the foreign central Bank, i.e. the German Bundesbank (G^b and G^s), or the Japanese central bank (J^b and J^s). Hence the first and third columns reflect total intervention purchases of \$ in the DM and Yen markets, respectively; while the second and fourth columns reflect total sales of \$ in the DM and Yen markets. The regressor s^* is the target rate as estimated by Funabashi (1989) in his study of central bankers estimated target nominal exchange rates. The regressor σ_{t-1}^2 is the conditional variance of spot returns and is generated from estimating the model in ⟨1⟩ with $b = \gamma = 0$. Asymptotic standard errors are in parentheses alongside corresponding parameter estimates.

period under investigation. For example, it is possible that having assessed market conditions authorities determined that buying dollars was the appropriate response to the increased volatility, perhaps to stabilize the market by exerting upward pressure on the dollar. Or it could be that actual exchange rates tended to be persistently on one side of the target rate so that either buying or selling but not both, was deemed the appropriate action.

V. Conclusion

A continued reliance on foreign exchange intervention by central banks is rationalized by claims that such activity is effective in either influencing the levels of exchange rates or in reducing their volatility. By the use of a Martingale–GARCH model, we investigated these claims in a time period which included stated efforts to achieve both objectives. Since intervention may occur as a response to the perceived need to meet these objectives, we also investigate the determinants of intervention by a probit model which measures the determinants of intervention as the deviations of exchange rates from their target levels, and as the difference between their conditional variance from their unconditional or average variance.

We find little support for the hypothesis that intervention can consistently influence the level of the exchange rate. When any significant effect is found it is usually of the 'leaning against the wind' variety, with dollar purchases depreciating the dollar. Additionally, we find evidence that intervention tends to increase volatility rather than 'calm disorderly markets'. While we find some support for the notion that intervention occurs because the exchange rate has substantially deviated from the target rate, or by increases in volatility above its average level, these effects differ between currencies and between the buying of US dollars as opposed to the selling of US dollars. These results cast considerable doubt on the efficacy of intervention and cautions against the conventional acceptance of intervention as an important policy instrument.

References

Baillie, R. T. and Bollerslev, T. (1989) The message in daily exchange rates: a conditional variance tale. *Journal of Business and Economic Statistics* 7, 297–305.

Baillie, R. T. and McMahon, P. C. (1989) *The Foreign Exchange Market: Theory and Econometric Evidence*. Cambridge University Press, New York.

Baillie, R. T. and Osterberg, W. P. (1993) Central Bank Intervention and Risk in the Forward Premium. Michigan State University Working Paper.

Baillie, R. T. and Pecchenino, R. A. (1991) The search for equilibrium relationships in international finance: the case of the monetary model. *Journal of International Money and Finance* **10**, 582–593.

Bollerslev, T. (1986) Generalized autoregressive conditional heteroskedasticity. *Journal of Econometrics* **31**, 307–327.

Danker, D. J., Haas, R. A., Henderson, D. W., Symansky, S. A. and Tryon, R. W. (1987) Small empirical models of exchange market intervention: applications to Germany, Japan and Canada. *Journal of Policy Modeling* **9**, 143–173.

Diebold, F. X. and Nason, J. N. (1990) Nonparametric exchange rate prediction? *Journal of International Economics* **28**, 315–332.

Dominguez, K. (1990) Market responses to coordinated central bank intervention. *Carnegie Rochester Conference Series on Public Policy* **32**, 121–164.

Dominguez, K. and Frankel, J. A. (1993) Does foreign exchange intervention matter? *American Economic Review* **83**, 1356–1369.

Dudler, H. J. (1988) Monetary Policy and Exchange market management in Germany. In *Exchange Market Intervention and Monetary Policy*, edited by The Bank for International Settlements, Basel, pp. 65–96.

Edison, H. J. (1993) The effectiveness of central-bank intervention: a survey of the literature after 1982. *Special Papers in International Economics*. Princeton University, New Jersey.

Edison, H. J. and Pauls, B. D. (1993) A re-assessment of the relationship between real exchange rates and real interest rates: 1974–1990. *Journal of Monetary Economics* **31**, 165–187.

Engel, C. M. and Hamilton, J. D. (1990) Long swings in the dollar: are they in the data and do the markets know it? *American Economic Review* **80**, 689–713.

Frankel, J. A. (1982) In search of the exchange risk premium: a six currency test assuming mean-variance optimization. *Journal of International Money and Finance* **1**, 255–274.

French, K. R. and Roll, R. (1986) Stock return variances: the arrival of information and the reaction of traders. *Journal of Finance* **17**, 5–26.

Froot, K. A. and Obstfeld, M. (1989) *Exchange rate dynamics under stochastic regime shifts: a unified approach*. Harvard Institute of Economic Research discussion paper 1451.

Funabashi, Y. (1989) *Managing the Dollar: From the Plaza to the Louvre*. Institute for International Economics, Washington, DC.

Ghosh, A. (1992) Is it signalling? exchange intervention and the dollar–deutschemark rate. *Journal of International Economics* **32**, 201–220.

Goodhart, C. A. E. and Hesse, T. (1993) Central bank forex intervention assessed in continuous time. *Journal of International Money and Finance* **12**, 368–389.

Hsieh, D. A. (1989a) The statistical properties of daily foreign exchange rates: 1974–1983. *Journal of International Economics* **24**, 129–145.

Hsieh, D. A. (1989b) Modeling heteroskedasticity in daily foreign exchange rates. *Journal of Business and Economic Statistics* **7**, 307–317.

Humpage, O. F. (1988) Intervention and the dollar's decline. *Federal Reserve Bank of Cleveland Economic Review* **2**, 2–16.

Kaminsky, G. L. and Lewis, K. K. (1992) *Does foreign exchange intervention signal future monetary policy?* Board of Governors of the Federal Reserve, Washington DC.

Klein, M. W. and Lewis, K. (1991) Learning About Intervention Target Zones. NBER working paper 3674.

Klein, M. W. and Rosengren, E. (1991) Foreign exchange intervention as a signal of monetary policy. *New England Economic Review* May/June, 39–50.

Lewis, K. K. (1995) Are foreign exchange intervention and monetary policy related and does it really matter? *Journal of Business* **68**, 185–214.

Lyons, R. K. (1995) Tests of microstructural hypotheses in the foreign exchange market. *Journal of Financial Economics* forthcoming.

Mark, N. C. (1995) Exchange rates and fundamentals: evidence on long-horizon predictability. *American Economic Review* **85**, 210–218.

McFarland, J. W., Pettit, R. R. and Sung, S. K. (1982) The distribution of foreign exchange price changes: trading day effects and risk measurement. *Journal of Finance* **37**, 693–715.

Meese, R. A. and Rogoff, K. (1983) Empirical exchange rate models of the seventies: do they fit out of sample? *Journal of International Economics* **14**, 3–24.

Meese, R. A. and Rose, A. K. (1991) An empirical assessment of non-linearities in models of exchange rate determination. *Review of Economic Studies* **58**, 603–619.

Obstfeld, M. (1989) The effectiveness of foreign exchange intervention. NBER working paper, 2796.

Osterberg, W. P. and Wetmore-Humes, R. (1993) The inaccuracy of newspaper reports of US foreign exchange intervention. *Federal Reserve Bank of Cleveland, Economic Review* 4, **29**, 25–33.

Palm, F. and Vlaar. (1993) The message in weekly exchange rates in the European Monetary System: mean reversion, conditional heteroskedasticity and jumps. *Journal of Business and Economic Statistics* **11**, 351–360.

Takagi, S. (1991) Foreign exchange market intervention and domestic monetary control in Japan 1973–1989. *Japan and the World Economy* **3**, 147–180.

Working Group on Exchange Market Intervention, 1983.

[10]

RASMUS FATUM
MICHAEL HUTCHISON

Is Intervention a Signal of Future Monetary Policy? Evidence from the Federal Funds Futures Market

Sterilized foreign exchange market intervention may affect the exchange rate if it signals future monetary policy actions. Signaling will be effective if the central bank backs up intervention with predictable changes in the stance of monetary policy and, in turn, affects current expectations. We investigate whether intervention operations in the United States are related to changes in expectations over the stance of future monetary policy, where expectations are proxied by federal funds futures rates. This relatively new futures market instrument has proved to be an efficient and unbiased predictor of the future spot federal funds rate. Estimates obtained from a GARCH time-series model over the 1989–93 period using daily data do not support the signaling hypothesis: dollar-support intervention is not related to a rise in expected future short-term interest rates (monetary tightening). However, intervention appears to significantly increase the conditional variance of federal funds futures rates, suggesting that it adds considerable noise to the market and possibly increasing the degree of uncertainty ovet the future course of monetary policy.

THE EFFECT OF FOREIGN EXCHANGE MARKET INTERVENTION on exchange rates is a subject of continuing controversy. Few doubt that unsterilized intervention may affect nominal exchange rates by changing interest rates and monetary aggregates. However, the effect of sterilized intervention on exchange rates is less clear. The "portfolio balance" channel, through which sterilized intervention changes the currency denomination of relative asset supplies and thereby the exchange risk premium if assets are imperfect substitutes, has received little empirical support (for example, Rogoff 1984; Humpage 1991; Edison 1993; Sweeney 1995, 1996).

The evidence in favor of a "signaling" channel, through which sterilized intervention may provide new information about policy intentions and hence future fundamentals, is somewhat more supportive. Watanabe (1994) finds that intervention tends to lead discount rate changes and help predict changes in the monetary aggregates in

The authors thank the Board of Governors of the Federal Reserve System and the Federal Reserve Bank of San Francisco for providing data, two anonymous referees, Yin-Wong Cheung and seminar participants at EPRU and the Department of International Economics and Management of the Copenhagen Business School for detailed comments, and Niels Alsing of the Danish Ministry of Economic Affairs for his assistance in the statistical work.

RASMUS FATUM *and* MICHAEL HUTCHISON *are in the Department of Economics at the University of California-Santa Cruz.* FATUM *is on leave from the Ministry of Economic Affairs, Copenhagen, and* HUTCHISON *is also a member of the Economic Policy Research Unit of the University of Copenhagen.*

Journal of Money, Credit, and Banking, Vol. 31, No. 1 (February 1999)

Japan. Using U.S. data, Lewis (1995) finds that intervention (on a daily, weekly, or biweekly basis) helps predict changes in the interbank interest rate and various monetary aggregates. Lewis finds, however, that intervention only helps predict monetary indicators within a two-week period, and attributes this not to signaling but rather to the particular nature of the Federal Reserve operating procedures (especially the required reserves accounting period) which induce a lag between intervention and sterilization.

Kaminsky and Lewis (1996) also find that U.S. intervention provides a signal to future changes in interbank rates and monetary aggregates, but sometimes in the opposite direction of that predicted by the conventional signaling hypothesis. Klein and Rosengren (1991), investigating the signaling hypothesis around two important intervention episodes, find no consistent relationship between U.S. intervention and subsequent monetary policy actions. More generally, Humpage's (1991) review of the literature on signaling finds mixed results.

In this paper we test for linkages between U.S. daily intervention operations and expected changes in future monetary policy, where a proxy for the latter are obtained from the new federal funds futures market. Our objective is to use information from the federal funds future market to test for the effect of intervention on expected monetary policy. We wish to determine whether intervention provides an effective signal that influences expectations over the future course of monetary policy, as opposed to simply introduces "noise" in the system and raising monetary uncertainty. The federal funds futures contract, introduced by the Chicago Board of Trade in 1988, has not been used in this context previously but should prove a useful proxy for market expectations. The predictive content of fed funds futures rates is very good, particularly over shorter horizons, and they appear to be rational forecasts of future rates (Carlson and McIntire 1995; Carlson, McIntire, and Thomson 1995; Krueger and Kuttner 1995). These future contract prices, written for any calendar month up to twenty-four months ahead, also change on a daily basis and may be matched with the daily observations of the Federal Reserve's intervention activities.

We test whether Federal Reserve intervention operations are systematically related to the change in the federal funds futures rate and its conditional variance—where the former provides evidence of a "signaling" channel and the latter may provide evidence of uncertainty over the course of future monetary policy.

The empirical work is based on estimation of a regression model with a time-varying variance term using a Generalized Autoregressive Conditional Heteroskedastic (GARCH) model. This model fits well with our financial markets data and allows us to address the questions of interest. In particular, we are able to simultaneously model and estimate the effect of intervention both on the change in the federal funds future rate and on its conditional variance. We consider several alternative model specifications to check the robustness of the results.

We focus on the March 1989–December 1993 period. The fed funds futures market for contracts maturing one and two months ahead became active at the beginning of this sample period. In addition, U.S. intervention policy was operating under one regime in terms of its intensity and intent during this sample period. Focussing attention on this period decreases the likelihood that a change has occurred in the use of intervention as a signal of future monetary policy actions.

The next section discusses our empirical approach and highlights some of the difficulties in testing the signaling hypothesis. Section 2 explains the data in some detail. Section 3 presents the empirical results. Section 4 concludes the paper.

1. SIGNALING AND MONETARY POLICY

The basic signaling hypothesis may be illustrated by a simple model of the exchange rate and fundamentals. Consider the familiar formulation of the nominal exchange rate (s_t) as a function of the discounted value (with discount factor θ) of current and expected future fundamentals ($E_t f_{t+j}$):

$$s_t = (1-\theta)\sum_{j=0}^{\infty} \theta^j E_t f_{t+j} . \qquad (1)$$

To be a useful signal of the future fundamental, intervention at time $t-k, n_{t-k}$ must help predict the future value of the fundamental. To illustrate this point, assume Lewis's (1995) formulation where the fundamental follows a simple autoregressive process with the intervention signal entering exogenously together with a random disturbance term (μ_t):

$$f_t = \rho_f f_{t-1} + \beta n_{t-k} + \mu_t . \qquad (2)$$

Intervention itself may also demonstrate various degrees of persistence which may be illustrated by an AR(1) process:

$$n_t = \rho_n n_{t-1} + \epsilon_t . \qquad (3)$$

With the specific processes followed by fundamentals and intervention given, expectations of future fundamental values may be determined, and an explicit solution for the exchange rate obtained (assuming $k = 1$ for simplicity):[1]

$$s_t = \Omega[f_t + (\theta\beta/(1-\theta\rho_n))n_t] \qquad (4)$$

where $\Omega = (1-\theta)/(1-\theta\rho_f)$.

One test of the signaling hypothesis is to estimate (4) directly, attempting to measure the effect of current intervention on the exchange rate over and above the contribution of the current fundamental. This approach is followed by Dominguez (1993), Dominguez and Frankel (1993a), and others. If intervention is a good signal (β is large in absolute value) and persistent (ρ_n is substantially greater than zero), then one

1. Assuming away bubble solutions.

would expect a large effect of intervention on the exchange rate. Dominguez (1993), for example, considers the effect of foreign exchange market intervention on both the conditional mean and conditional variance of daily (and weekly) exchange rate changes. She concludes that intervention (and, more generally, exchange rate policy variables) belong in daily GARCH models of the exchange rate. Changes in contemporaneous monetary policy and intervention policy were found in several cases to influence the conditional variance of exchange rates, and the causal link (using Granger causality tests) appears to run from the policy variables to exchange rate volatility and not vice versa.

Another approach, followed by Lewis (1995), Kaminsky and Lewis (1996), Klein and Rosengren (1991), Watanabe (1994), and others, is to estimate the fundamental process (2) and measure the ability of intervention to forecast movements in the fundamental. Lewis (1995), for example, uses VARs of interventions and monetary policy to investigate whether intervention "Granger causes" monetary policy (that is, monetary policy is the only fundamental considered). She then uses VARs of monetary policy and exchange rates to determine whether monetary policy Granger causes exchange rates. Kaminsky and Lewis (1996) investigate whether interventions that were consistent with expected future monetary policy movements affected the exchange differently than those that were inconsistent. They find some evidence for this proposition.

A third approach, pursued in this paper, is to directly estimate the effect of intervention on changes in expected monetary policy—the "fundamental" being considered—where one has an independent (not model-based) measure of changes in expectations:

$$E_{t+1}f_{t+j} - E_t f_{t+j} = \varphi_o + \varphi_1 n_t + \epsilon_t \tag{5}$$

where changes in expected future monetary policy is given by $E_{t+1}f_{t+j} - E_t f_{t+j}$. One innovation of this study is that we use changes in the federal funds futures rate (FF) as our independent proxy of changes in expected monetary policy, and the conditional variance of FF as a measure of monetary policy uncertainty. The error term, ϵ_t, is modeled as a GARCH process and is considered in some detail in section 3. This "direct" approach is similar to Dominguez and Frankel (1993b) in their investigation of the link between intervention and survey-based measures of exchange rate expectations.

The maintained hypothesis contained in the approach we follow is that intervention is systematically related to expected future policy. We need not assume a particular process driving monetary policy or attempt to capture structural shifts in these processes.[2] Limiting the focus to whether intervention acts as a reliable signal of future policy may be measured directly through surveys of expectations or through futures prices (that is, no assumptions about the processes driving monetary policy are necessary).[3] An important auxiliary assumption imposed, however, and a limitation

2. However, policy regime changes affecting the link between intervention and monetary policy, for example, changes in the degree of systematic sterilization, still need to be identified using the direct approach.

3. A full test of the model suggested by equation (4) also requires—for intervention to have an effect on

of the "direct" approach is that the expected future fed funds rate (the measure of monetary policy stance) is assumed equal to the fed funds futures price. That is, it is assumed that there is no risk premium between the fed funds rate expected to prevail at some future point and the current fed funds future rate of the same maturity. This is the "cost" of not estimating a monetary policy process. This assumption seems reasonable judging from several studies showing that, although the fed funds futures rates appear to exhibit a small forward premium, the market seems so efficiently incorporate all publicly available information on the likely direction of future funds rates movements (Krueger and Kuttner 1995; Carlson, McIntire, and Thomson 1995).

2. DATA

We detail below why the daily change in the federal funds futures rate is a good proxy for changes in expectations over the future stance of monetary policy. We focus on the March 1989–December 1993 period. The federal funds future market for contracts maturing one and two months ahead was established at the beginning of this sample period. In addition, the U.S. intervention policy regime was roughly unchanged in terms of its intensity and intent (post-Plaza Accord and post-Louvre Agreement) during this sample period.

The Fed Fund Futures Market

The Chicago Board of Trade (CBT) began trading an interest rate futures contract based on the month-long average of daily fed funds rates in 1988.[4] This contract may be written for any calendar month up to twenty-four months ahead and is known as the thirty-day fed funds futures. The CBT lists contracts for six consecutive delivery dates at any one time. The contracts call for delivery of interest paid on a principal amount of $5 million in overnight fed funds, but in practice is cash-settled daily (that is, whenever the price changes) through margin accounts held with brokers. Fed funds futures provide instruments to hedge or speculate against future changes in the fed funds rate. Though banks buying and selling fed funds may naturally find a use for the futures market, it is also open to others so long as margin requirements are satisfied.

The thirty-day interest rate futures contract differs from most other interest rate futures in that the final settlement price is based on an average of *past* interest rates. Final settlement is based on an arithmetic average of the effective overnight rate, as reported by the Federal Reserve Bank of New York, for the thirty-day period immediately preceding the contract maturity date. The average includes weekends and holidays, whose rates are carried over from the rate prevailing on the most recent trading day. As with all other money market futures, prices for the thirty-day fed funds rate fu-

the exchange rate—that (i) it adds information not otherwise available in predicting future policy, and (ii) that expected future policy is an important determinant of the exchange rate (see Watanabe 1994).

4. See Carlson, McIntire, and Thomson (1995) for a detailed description of the federal funds futures market. Cook and LaRoche (1993) give a thorough introduction to money market futures generally and also include a detailed description of the Fed funds futures contract.

tures are quoted as an index equal to one hundred minus the futures rate. The price of the current month's contract would reflect a weighted average of the average fed funds rate for the expired fraction of the current month, plus the term fed funds rate for the remaining fraction of the month.[5,6] For example, the June settlement price applied to a futures contract purchased on June 21 would be

$$100 - \textit{price index} = (20/30) \times (\textit{average effective overnight federal funds rate for the previous 20 days}) + (10/30) \times (\textit{term fed funds rate for the 10 days beginning June 21})\,.$$

The price of a deferred month contract—that is, a contract maturing after the current month's settlement date—reflects entirely the thirty-day average term fed funds rate for the month in question. On June 21 (to June 30), for example, the one-month futures contract would consist of the average term fed funds rate for the month of July. On July 1, the one-month future contract would consist of the average term fed funds rate for the month of August.

Current and one-month futures contracts (termed "first nearby" and "second nearby," respectively) are the most heavily traded, but trading is also active in two- and three-month futures contracts. However, trading activity diminishes markedly when the maturity extends beyond three months. Contracts beyond five months exist, but appear rather infrequently (Carlson, McIntire, and Thomson 1995).

We investigate the effects of intervention on the one- and two-month ("second nearby" and "third nearby") federal funds futures rates. These are the longest maturities in which contracts are actively traded and with enough depth to the market so that inferences may be confidently drawn about expectations over future developments in the federal funds market. Our data cover daily observations for the period March 27, 1989, when this segment of the fed funds futures market opened, to December 31, 1993. The level and first differences of the one-month contracts are shown in Figures 1 and 2, respectively. The data here are expressed as the implied future term interest rate rather than the index quoted on the CBT exchange. Our sample consists only of outstanding deferred contracts, that is, always reflecting thirty-day averages of the fed funds term rates for periods either one or two months ahead. No maturing contracts (or expiration dates) are included in the sample. Since past spot rates do not enter into the calculation of the price of the contract (unlike the case of the current or "nearby" contracts), maturity effects should not be present. That is, the changes in the fed interest rate futures contracts with one-month maturities shown in Figure 2 do not exhibit the type of trend associated with current-month futures contracts where the average of past spot rates must equal the settlement price on the date of expiration.

Recent studies by Carlson, MacIntire, and Thomson (1995) and Krueger and Kutt-

5. For contracts maturing after the current month's settlement date, the futures rate corresponds approximately to a forward interest rate on one-month term fed funds. See Cook and LaRoche (1993, p. 198).

6. For examples of fed fund futures price quotations, see Carlson, MacIntire, and Thomson (1995, p. 23), and Cook and LaRoche (1993, p. 198).

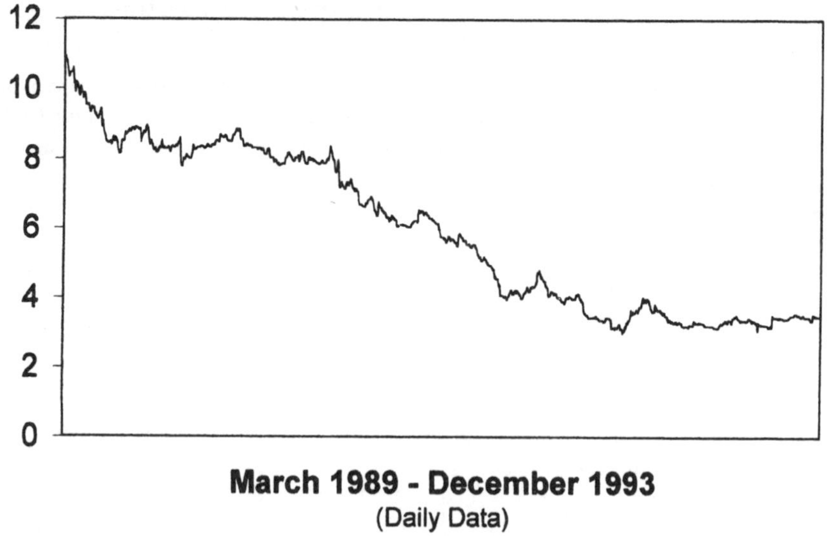

FIG. 1. Federal Funds Futures Rate, One-Month-Ahead Delivery

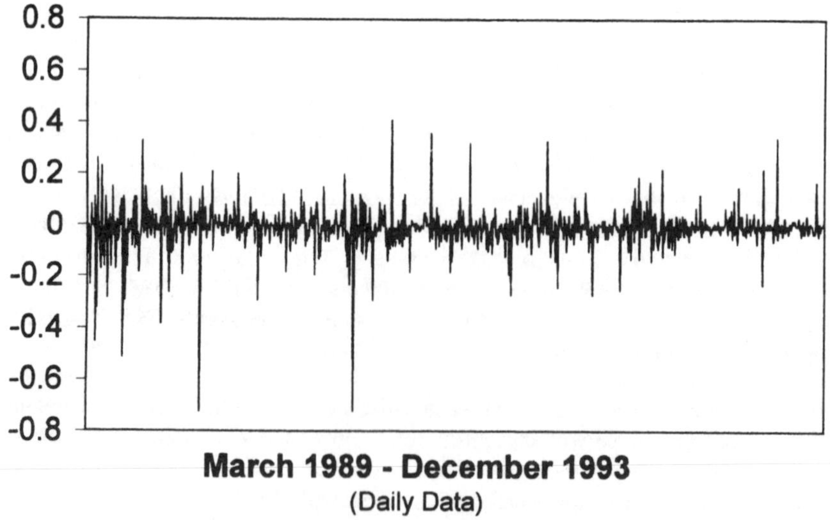

FIG. 2. Changes in Federal Funds Futures Rate, One-Month-Ahead Delivery

ner (1995) show that over the 1989-to-1994 period, fed funds futures rates provide very accurate forecasts of short-term changes in the fed funds rate. In fact, both studies find a small ex post forward premium, but that all systematic variation in the fed funds rate is anticipated by the market and incorporated into futures prices.[7] The small forward premium bias observed may be specific to the sample chosen, however, as the economy was generally weaker, and the fed funds rate as a consequence set lower by the FOMC, than had been anticipated by most analysts at the time (Carlson, McIntire, and Tompson 1995, p. 27). The general conclusion is that the market for fed fund futures "efficiently incorporates virtually all publicly available information on the likely direction of future funds rate movements."[8] The fed funds futures rate appears a good proxy for the rational expectation of the future spot rate in that the futures-based forecast errors are not generally correlated with other information publicly available at the time of the forecast.

Fed funds futures rates also provide good proxies for expected short-term monetary policy developments at different maturities. This is because the fed funds rate—upon which the futures rates are based—is the primary operating instrument of monetary policy. It is also the most widely cited indicator of policy stance. Rudebusch (1995), for example, finds that the fed funds rate adequately reflects monetary policy in the very short term, that is, within a month or two. Similarly, Bernanke and Blinder (1992) also find that the fed funds rate is a good indicator of monetary policy actions, arguing further that it contains information about future movements of real macroeconomic variables. These considerations, combined with its high predictive power, suggest that fed funds future rates are likely to provide good proxy measures of expected future short-term monetary policy developments.[9]

Foreign Exchange Market Intervention

The intervention variable is daily fed sales (negative values) and purchases (positive values) of USD (millions of U.S. dollars) against all other currencies in the foreign exchange market. This is official foreign exchange market intervention data, provided by the Board of Governors of the Federal Reserve System, from which we exclude so-called customer transactions. Customer transactions, which sometimes can be timed to constitute a type of "passive" intervention, consist of fed sales or purchases of foreign exchange directly with customers, usually central banks or governments, that would otherwise need to transact with market agents. Excluding these transactions is in line with previous research in this area.

Table 1 shows how often the fed has been active in the foreign exchange market and whether the daily intervention was mostly small or large scale. During our sample period, March 27, 1989, to December 31, 1993 (1,207 trading days), the fed sold USD in

7. Not surprisingly, both studies find that the predictive accuracy diminishes as the contract horizon is extended, and that errors tend to be relatively large when the fed funds rate changes direction or when it changes rapidly over a short period.

8. Krueger and Kuttner (1995, p. 14).

9. See also Krueger and Kuttner (1995, p. 1), and Carlson, MacIntire, and Thomson (1995, p. 29) for similar arguments.

TABLE 1

TOTAL U.S. INTERVENTION, MARCH 27, 1989, TO DECEMBER 31, 1993 (1207 TRADING DAYS)

Intervention sales (million USD)	Number of days	Cumulated amount (million USD)
>250[a]	37	15019
>150[b]	16	2887
>100[c]	33	3483
> 0[d]	15	817
Total sales	101	22207
Intervention purchases (million USD)	**Number of days**	**Cumulated amount (million USD)**
>250[a]	7	2352
>150[b]	7	1348
>100[c]	4	440
> 0[d]	16	897
Total purchases	34	5037

NOTES: (a) Daily intervention operations of USD 250 million or greater.
(b) Daily intervention operations of USD 150 million or greater, but less than USD 250 million.
(c) Daily intervention operations of USD 100 million or greater, but less than USD 150 million.
(d) Daily intervention operations of less than USD 100 million.

the foreign exchange market on 101 days and purchased USD on 34 days. The bulk of USD sales on active days was fairly large scale, with trades of more than 250 million USD. USD purchases on active days, by contrast, were usually much smaller in magnitude, that is, trades of less than one hundred million USD. Official USD sales for foreign exchange were particularly heavy during April–October 1989, February–March 1990, and March 1991. Official USD purchases against foreign exchange were largest in scale during May–July 1990, February 1991, late summer 1992, and May–June 1993.

This sample period, chosen in light of the availability of the fed funds futures data, omits the strong "leaning against the wind" policy of late 1987 and 1988.

3. EMPIRICAL METHODS AND RESULTS

If the signaling channel is an important channel through which foreign exchange intervention works, then intervention should change the current perception of the stance of future monetary policy, measured as changes in expectations over the level of future interest rates under the control of the Federal Reserve. In particular, the basic hypothesis is that positive intervention (a purchase of USD against foreign currencies) invokes the expectation of monetary tightening in the future and hence a rise in the fed funds future rate. The null hypothesis, of course, is that intervention is not interpreted as providing information about the stance of future monetary policy, and hence does not affect interest rate expectations in a systematic and predictable way.

Even if intervention does not provide a clear signal of the stance of future monetary policy, it may still cause varying reactions in the market depending on how a particular action is interpreted. In this case, intervention may simply be creating noise in the market as opposed to providing a clear signal. We also investigate this hypothesis by examining the effect of intervention on conditional volatility of the Federal funds future rate.

3.1 Testing the Signaling Hypothesis

Studies of the variance of financial market time series data often find the variance to be changing over time (heteroskedastic), (for example, Engle (1982); Bollerslev 1986; Bollerslev, Chou, and Kroner 1992). Large and small residuals frequently come in clusters, leading to a notion of the variance of an error being dependent on the size of the preceding error. This particular form of heteroskedasticity is denoted autoregressive conditional heteroskedasticity (ARCH) and is modeled by letting the variance of the current error be a linear function of the square of the preceding error. A natural generalization of the ARCH model is found in the Generalized ARCH (GARCH) model, in which the conditional variance is a function not only of preceding errors, but also of past conditional variances. Baillie and Bollershev (1989) use the GARCH approach to model the conditional mean and conditional variance of daily exchange rate changes.

Our basic approach follows Engle (1982) where a regression equation is estimated with the residuals modeled as a GARCH process. In addition, we follow Baillie and Bollershev (1989) and others by simultaneously modeling the focus independent variable (in our case, intervention), both in the mean and variance equations of the process governing the dependent variable (change in fed funds future rate). The basic regression model with GARCH(1, 1) errors that we estimate is equation (5) and

$$\epsilon_t \sim N(0,h_t)\ ; \tag{6}$$

$$h_t = \alpha_0 + \alpha_1 e_{t-1}^2 + \alpha_2 h_{t-1} + \alpha_3 |n_t| \tag{7}$$

where equation (6) states that the error term is normally distributed with zero mean and time dependent (conditional) variance, h_t, and equation (7) shows the conditional variance, where e_t^2 is the squared error of the previous period, h_{t-1} the conditional variance of the previous period, $|n_t|$ the absolute value of intervention (millions of U.S. dollars), and the αs are parameters.

We also test for day-of-the-week effects, in line with the studies of French (1980), Gibbons and Hess (1981), and others (focussed mainly on expected daily stock returns) to investigate whether there are significant differences in the change in fed funds future rate depending on the day of the week trading is conducted. A significant effect is found on the Friday dummy variable (*FRIDAY*), and this is included in the regressions, but not for any other day of the week. In addition, we test for the possibility that the conditional variance enters into the mean equation (5), that is, a garch-in-mean specification (GARCH-M). We find that strong evidence for the GARCH-M specification, and this is also included as part of basic specification of the model.

The unconditional variance is time invariant, and so the OLS estimation technique produces BLUE estimates of equation (5), but because of the heteroskedastic conditional variance it is possible to find a more efficient nonlinear estimator by the use of the maximum likelihood (ML) estimation technique. We follow this approach in estimating our model.

3.2 Model Statistics

The results are presented in Table 2 for the one-month-ahead futures rate and Table 3 for the two-month-ahead futures rate. The two sets show the model estimates with and without intervention entering the mean equation. The basic model specification is given at the top of the table, defining the parameters associated with the ML estimates (and *t*-statistics given in parentheses) shown in each row. The model is estimated with the federal funds future rate in first-difference form since unit root tests indicated that the fed funds futures rate is difference stationary. The augmented Dickey-Fuller test (DF) is utilized using the Bayesian information criteria to indicate lag length. (However, zero lag is indicated for both tests.) The DF statistic (critical value) on the level of the fed funds future rate is −2.361 (−2.864) and on first differences is −32.160 (−2.864).

A number of estimated model diagnostic statistics are presented at the foot of each column. Log *L* denotes the value of the log-likelihood function; *LR* denotes the log-likelihood ratio test comparing the log-likelihood function from the final interaction

TABLE 2

GARCH MODEL ESTIMATES: FEDERAL FUNDS FUTURES RATE, ONE MONTH AHEAD, MARCH 28, 1989–DECEMBER 31, 1993

$$\Delta FF_t = \beta_0 + \beta_1 \Delta FF_{t-1} + \beta_2 FRIDAY_t + \beta_3 \sqrt{h_t} + \beta_4 n_t + \varepsilon_t$$
$$\varepsilon_t \sim N(0, h_t)$$
$$h_t = \alpha_0 + \alpha_1 e_{t-1}^2 + \alpha_2 h_{t-1} + \alpha_3 |n_t|$$

Parameter Estimates and Statistics	(1)		(2)	
β_0	0.005	(1.51)	0.005	(1.61)
β_1	0.10**	(2.46)	0.101**	(2.47)
β_2	−0.011**	(−5.57)	−0.011**	(−5.59)
β_3	−0.158*	(−1.79)	−0.170*	(−1.93)
β_4	2.11e-05	(1.18)		
α_0	2.78e-04**	(16.09)	2.87e-04**	(17.43)
α_1	0.285**	(11.72)	0.287**	(11.62)
α_2	0.657**	(36.26)	0.651**	(36.82)
α_3	2.85e-06**	(4.51)	3.08e-06**	(4.98)
Log *L*	3157.22		3156.72	
LR	308.80		306.76	
$Q(15)$	7.46		7.35	
$Q^2(15)$	10.75		11.24	
m_3	−1.73		−1.74	
m_4	14.29		14.28	
ARCH	0.78		0.78	
OBS	1205		1205	
Iterations	138		138	

TABLE 3

GARCH MODEL ESTIMATES: FEDERAL FUNDS FUTURES RATE, TWO MONTHS AHEAD, MARCH 28, 1989–DECEMBER 31, 1993

$$\Delta FF_t = \beta_0 + \beta_1 \Delta FF_{t-1} + \beta_2 FRIDAY_t + \beta_3 \sqrt{h_t} + \beta_4 n_t + \varepsilon_t$$

$$\varepsilon_t \sim N(0, h_t)$$

$$h_t = \alpha_0 + \alpha_1 e_{t-1}^2 + \alpha_2 h_{t-1} + \alpha_3 |n_t|$$

Parameter Estimates and Statistics	(1)		(2)	
β_0	5.17e-04	(0.07)	1.25e-03	(0.17)
β_1	0.09**	(2.20)	0.09**	(2.20)
β_2	−0.011**	(−4.31)	−0.011**	(−4.32)
β_3	−0.071*	(−0.41)	−0.089	(−0.52)
β_4	9.46e-06	(0.55)		
α_0	4.05e-04**	(10.08)	4.11e-04**	(10.65)
α_1	0.112**	(8.48)	0.113**	(8.75)
α_2	0.69**	(26.15)	0.690**	(27.42)
α_3	2.56e-06**	(4.81)	2.59e-06**	(4.94)
Log *L*	3130.31		3130.10	
LR	124.68		124.46	
$Q(15)$	11.69		11.67	
$Q^2(15)$	6.84		6.90	
m_3	−2.21		−2.22	
m_4	14.49		14.48	
ARCH	0.76		0.77	
OBS	1205		1205	
Iterations	70		70	

with that calculated initially for just the constant term; $Q(15)$ and $Q^2(15)$ denote the Box-Pierce Q-statistic with fifteen lags on the standardized residuals and squared standardized residuals, respectively; m_3 and m_4 denote the standard measures of skewness and kurtosis, respectively; *ARCH* is the F-statistic value of the null hypothesis of no *ARCH* in the standardized residuals; *OBS* is the number of observations in the sample estimated, and "iterations" is the number of interations taken to converge to the final ML estimates.

The results reported in both Tables 2 and 3 provide strong support for the GARCH models. The estimated α_j coefficients ($j = 1$ to 2), estimating the autoregressive and moving average components in the heteroskedastic variance, are highly significant. The log-likelihood ratio test, providing a test of the overall explanatory power of the model, clearly rejects the null hypothesis that the unrestricted (final estimated model) and restricted model (with only the constant term included) have the same value of the likelihood function. No evidence of autocorrelation (Q statistic), heteroskedasticity (Q^2), or ARCH effects is indicated in the standardized residuals. The degree of skewness and kurtosis is much less in the standardized residuals compared with the unstandardized residuals, but some evidence of non-normality remains.

3.3 Conditional Mean and Variance

The estimates of the conditional mean equations in both tables indicate that the autoregressive term (β_1) is statistically significant, as is the "Friday effect" (the fed funds future rate tends to decrease on Fridays) and the conditional variance term (higher variance tends to decrease the fed funds futures rate). However, there is little evidence that a U.S. dollar purchase in the foreign exchange market tends to signal a future monetary tightening, and hence a rise in the fed funds future rate. The estimated coefficient on the n_t term (the sensitivity of the federal funds futures rate to dollar purchase in the foreign exchange market) is not significant at the 90 percent level of confidence or better.

However, the absolute value of intervention by the Federal Reserve, $|n_t|$, does appear to raise the conditional variance of the federal funds futures rate. In all four models estimated in Tables 2 and 3, intervention operations—either in buying or selling dollars for foreign exchange—is positively associated with increased volatility in the fed funds futures market. These estimates are significant at the 95 percent level of confidence or better. This is consistent with the Diebold and Nerlove (1989) hypothesis that ambiguous signals—in this case, the intent of the monetary authorities with respect to monetary policy and intervention operations—may increase market volatility.

3.4 Discussion

Our results may be compared to other studies in this area using different methodologies, sample periods, and data sets. Most relevant is the work of Kaminsky and Lewis (1996), who reject the hypothesis that interventions convey no signal over future monetary policy developments. However, they find that intervention "signaled" changes in monetary policy in the *opposite* direction of the conventional signaling story for much of the sample period (1985–90). Dominguez (1993) finds reported intervention reduced exchange rate volatility over the 1985–88 period, but increased it during 1989–91. Hung (1991) finds that U.S. intervention raises exchange rate volatility in some periods, but not in others, and suggests that the disparate results may depend on market conditions and the skill of those intervening.

This leads to at least two caveats in the interpretation of our own results. First, we concentrate attention on one episode when the fed funds future data is available. Although we find no evidence of signaling, it may have been important during other periods. It is noteworthy that our sample omits the strong "leaning against the wind" U.S. intervention policy of late 1987 and 1988. This may be why our study finds no relationship between intervention and monetary policy while some studies, considering other sample periods, have found an opposite and significant relationship, that is, dollar purchases positively correlated with dollar depreciation reflecting the policy reaction function of the authorities.

Second, signaling may be an effective channel only when combined with other policy actions such as an official announcement by the Federal Reserve over its policy intentions. This is examined in Kaminsky and Lewis (1996) with some success using several monetary policy variables. This is on our agenda for future research using the fed funds future rate data.

4. CONCLUDING COMMENTS

We exploit information from the new federal funds future market to test whether foreign exchange intervention is an effective and predictable signal of monetary policy actions in the United States. Interpreting changes in federal funds futures rates as reflecting revisions in expectations over future spot federal funds rates, and hence over monetary policy, seems appropriate given (i) the high predictive power of the futures rate in forecasting the fed funds rate, and (ii) that the fed funds rate is a good indicator of monetary policy stance. By investigating measures of expectations directly, we avoid having to specify a complete model of the process driving the monetary indicator of interest from which to derive a measure of expected (forecast) policy changes. Daily U.S. intervention and federal funds futures rates data over the 1989–93 period is considered, an episode which may be viewed as encompassing a single intervention and monetary policy "regime."

Estimating a model with a time-varying conditional variance (GARCH residuals), we do *not* find that purchases of U.S. dollars in the foreign exchange market by the fed (dollar support intervention) raises the federal funds futures rate. This result is robust to different estimation specifications and different maturities in the federal funds futures rate. However, the conditional variance of the federal funds future rate is positively and significantly related to the magnitude of intervention operations. Intervention may not convey a clear signal about future monetary policy actions—judging by the failure of interest rate expectations to respond—but apparently increases "noise" and market volatility. At a minimum, our results suggest that it is difficult to identify a clear and effective "signaling" channel, and that the sporadic intervention policy followed by the fed (and ultimately the U.S. Treasury) could lead to greater monetary uncertainty.

LITERATURE CITED

Baillie, Richard T., and Tim Bollershev. "The Message in Daily Exchange Rates: A Conditional Variance Tale." *Journal of Business and Economic Statistics* 7 (1989), 297–305.

Bernanke, Ben S., and Alan S. Blinder. "The Federal Funds Rate and the Channels of Monetary Transmission." *American Economic Review* 82:4 (1992), 901–21.

Bollerslev, Tim. "Generalized Autoregressive Conditional Heteroskedasticity." *Journal of Econometrics* 31 (1986), 307–27.

Bollerslev, Tim, Ray Y. Chou, and Kenneth F. Kroner. "ARCH Modeling in Finance: A Review of the Theory and Empirical Evidence." *Journal of Econometrics* 52 (1992), 5–59.

Carlson, John B., and Jean M. McIntire. "Monetary Policy and the Federal Funds Futures Market." Federal Reserve Bank of Cleveland *Economic Commentary* (July 1995).

Carlson, John B., Jean M. McIntire, and James B. Thomson. "Federal Funds Futures as an Indicator of Future Monetary Policy: A Primer." Federal Reserve Bank of Cleveland *Economic Commentary* 31 (May 1, 1995), 20–30.

Cook, T. Q., and R. K. LaRoche. "The Money Market." In *Instruments of the Money Market,* edited by T. Q. Cook and R. K. LaRoche. Federal Reserve Bank of Richmond, Virginia, 1993.

Diebold, Francis X., and Mark Nerlove. "The Dynamics of Exchange Rate Volatility: A Multivariate Latent Factor ARCH Model." *Journal of Applied Econometrics* 4 (1989), 1–21.

Dominguez, Kathryn M. "The Informational Role of Official Foreign Exchange Intervention Policy: The Signaling Hypothesis." In *Exchange Rate Efficiency and the Behavior of International Asset Markets,* pp. 41–80. New York: Garland Publishing, 1992.

______. "Does Central Bank Intervention Increase the Volatility of Foreign Exchange Rates?" National Bureau of Economic Research, Working Paper Series no. 4532, November 1993.

Dominguez, Kathryn M., and Jeffrey A. Frankel. "Does Foreign-Exchange Intervention Matter? The Portfolio Effect." *The American Economic Review* 83:5 (1993a).

______. "Foreign Exchange Intervention: An Empirical Assessment." Ch. 16 in *On Exchange Rates,* by J. A. Frankel, pp. 327–45. Cambridge, Mass.: MIT Press, 1993b.

______. *Does Foreign Exchange Intervention Work?* Washington, D.C.: Institute for International Economics, 1993c.

Edison, Hali J. *The Effectiveness of Central-Bank Intervention: A Survey of the Literature after 1982.* Princeton University International Finance Section, Special Papers in International Economics no. 18, 1993.

Engle, Robert F. "Autoregressive Conditional Heteroskedasticty with Estimates of the Variance of U.K. Inflation." *Econometrica* 50 (1982), 987–1008.

French, K. R. "Stock Returns and the Weekend Effect." *Journal of Financial Economics* (March 1980).

Gibbons, M. R., and P. Hess. "Day of the Week Effects and Asset Returns." *Journal of Business* (October 1981).

Humes, Rebecca Wetmore, and William P. Osterberg. "The Inaccuracy of Newspaper Reports of U.S. Foreign Exchange Intervention." Federal Reserve Bank of Cleveland *Economic Review* 29:4 (1993), 25–33.

Humpage, Owen, F. "Central Bank Intervention: Recent Literature, Continuing Controversy." Federal Reserve Bank of Cleveland *Economic Review* 27:2 (1991), 12–26.

______. "Institutional Aspects of U.S. Intervention." Federal Reserve Bank of Cleveland *Economic Review* 30:1 (1994), 2–19.

______. "Are Successful Interventions Random Events?" Federal Reserve Bank of Cleveland *Economic Commentary,* March 1, 1996.

Hung, Juann H. "Noise Trading and the Effectiveness of Sterilized Foreign Exchange Intervention." Federal Reserve Bank of New York, Research paper no. 9111, March 1991.

Kaminsky, Graciela L., and Karen K. Lewis. "Does Foreign Exchange Intervention Signal Future Monetary Policy?" *Journal of Monetary Economics* 37 (April 1996).

Klein, Michael W. "The Accuracy of Reports of Foreign Exchange Intervention." *Journal of International Money and Finance* 12 (1993), 644–53.

Klein, Michael W., and Eric Rosengren. "Foreign Exchange Intervention as a Signal of Monetary Policy." Federal Reserve Bank of Boston *New England Economic Review* (May/June 1991), 39–50.

Krueger, Joel T., and Kenneth N. Kuttner. "The Fed Funds Futures Rate as a Predictor of Federal Reserve Policy." Federal Reserve Bank of Chicago, Research Department, Working Paper Series, no. 4, 1995

Lewis, Karen K. "Are Foreign Exchange Intervention and Monetary Policy Related and Does It Really Matter?" *Journal of Business* 68 (April 1995).

Osterberg, William P. "Can Foreign Exchange Intervention Signal Monetary Policy Changes?" Federal Reserve Bank of Cleveland *Economic Commentary,* May 1, 1995.

Rogoff, Kenneth. "On the Effects of Sterilized Intervention: An Analysis of Weekly Data." *Journal of Monetary Economics* 14 (1984), 133–50.

Rudebusch, Glen. "Federal Reserve Policy and the Predictability of Interest Rates." Federal Reserve Bank of San Francisco *Weekly Letter* 95–23 (1995).

Sweeney, Richard. "Does the Fed Move the Foreign-Exchange Market?" Unpublished Georgetown School of Business, November 6, 1995.

______. "Does the Foreign Exchange Market Beat the Fed?" Unpublished, Georgetown School of Business, April 10, 1996.

Watanabe, T. "The Signaling Effect of Foreign Exchange Intervention: The Case of Japan." In *Exchange Rate Policy and Interdependence: Lessons from the Pacific Basin,* edited by Reuven Glick and Michael M. Hutchison. Cambridge University Press, 1994.

ELSEVIER Journal of Banking & Finance 24 (2000) 665–694

Journal of BANKING & FINANCE

www.elsevier.com/locate/econbase

Does the Fed beat the foreign-exchange market?

R.J. Sweeney *

McDonough School of Business, Georgetown University, Room 323 Old North, 37th and "O" Sts., NW, Washington, DC 20057, USA

Received 7 February 1999; accepted 8 March 1999

Abstract

This paper's estimates and tests of Fed intervention profits are the first that explicitly adjust for foreign-exchange risk premia; failure to adjust may grossly affect estimated profits. Profits appear economically and statistically significant, whether risk premia are modeled as time-constant or as appreciation's market beta depending on Fed intervention. The estimates are sensitive to the method of risk adjustment and to the periods used. Because a key variable, cumulative intervention, is $I(1)$, test statistics may have non-standard distributions, a problem affecting past tests; this paper's tests account for non-standard distributions. Possible explanations of these profits have mixed empirical support in the literature. © 2000 Elsevier Science B.V. All rights reserved.

JEL classification: F31; F33; G15; E58

Keywords: Foreign-exchange intervention; Fed intervention; Central bank profits; Risk-adjustment of intervention profits

1. Introduction

The profitability of central bank intervention is a contentious issue. (i) Some observers expect speculators to make money at the expense of central banks,

* Corresponding author. Tel.: +1-202-687-3742; fax: +1-202-687-7639.
E-mail address: sweeneyr@msb.georgetown.edu (R.J. Sweeney).

PII: S0378-4266(99)00047-3

partly because of beliefs of government inefficiency relative to private activities, partly because some central banks assert they sometimes lean against the wind in attempts to slow down exchange-rate movements (Sweeney, 1986; Corrado and Taylor, 1986). (ii) Others note that if the foreign-exchange market is strong-form efficient relative to intervention, a central bank makes zero expected profits on its intervention. (iii) Those who expect central bank intervention profits offer differing sources of profits. Some argue that central banks have information unavailable to the public, particularly regarding future monetary policy, and may make intervention profits from using this information. Others argue that central banks profit from intervention to reduce volatility in "disorderly markets". Related, some argue that central banks profit from intervening against destabilizing speculation or from supplementing insufficiently strong private stabilizing speculation (Leahy, 1995); still others argue the contrary, that central banks may profit from intervention that is destabilizing. [1]

Empirical results have not settled the debate because they are conflicting. Some authors present evidence of central bank losses (Taylor, 1982a,b; Schwartz, 1994), others of profits (Leahy, 1989, 1995; Fase and Huijser, 1989, among others). Sweeney (1997) provides a review of the literature.

Previous estimates of central bank intervention profits are unreliable for several reasons. Previous work incorrectly measures profits by not accounting for the foreign-exchange risk central banks bear from intervention and the premia they can expect to earn for bearing this risk, though some papers note that an unknown part of measured profits may be due to risk premia (Leahy, 1989, 1995). Further, previous work takes no account of the implications of the Efficient Markets Hypothesis in formulating measures and tests of intervention profits, though some paper discuss implications of estimated profits for efficiency (Leahy, 1989, 1995). Finally, previous work does not take account of the fact that profit measures depend on a variable integrated of order one, and thus the asymptotic distributions both of the profit measure and its test statistics can easily be non-normal. This paper presents estimates and tests of Fed intervention profits that account for all of these problems. [2]

Central banks have goals beyond profitability and may intervene to achieve desired outcomes even at the cost of intervention losses (Bank of England, 1983; Edison, 1993; Dominguez and Frankel, 1993a). Most central banks argue

[1] Despite (Friedman's, 1953) famous conjecture that stabilizing intervention generates central bank profits, there is no consensus that profits are either necessary or sufficient for intervention to be stabilizing. Some argue that destabilizing speculation may be profitable (for the debate, see Baumol, 1957; Kemp, 1963; Johnson, 1976; Hart and Kreps, 1986; Szpiro, 1994). Others note that profitable intervention may have no effect on exchange rates and thus fail to be stabilizing (Leahy, 1989, 1995; Edison, 1993; Dominguez and Frankel, 1993a).

[2] This paper builds on Sweeney (1996a). Sweeney (1997) discusses some results from the older paper.

that they make profits on average from their intervention. Obviously, acknowledged losses might present serious political problems. This paper does not attempt to identify and measure the benefits the Fed achieves by its intervention, but instead focuses on estimates and tests of the Fed's risk-adjusted intervention profits.

In some speculative crises central banks clearly make or lose money, for example, the European Monetary System (EMS) crises of September 1992 and July–August 1993. Dispute seems to turn on the profitability of ongoing intervention, not necessarily just crisis-period profits. This paper uses daily data on Fed intervention in Deutsche Marks (DEM) and Japanese Yen (JPY) from 1985 to 1991, the data available when this project began. There were patches of important exchange-market stress during this period, including the Plaza (September 1985) and Louvre (February 1987) Accords, but no events on the order of the 1992 and 1993 EMS crises.

Risk-adjusted profits are measured here under two assumptions: Foreign-exchange risk premia are time-constant (less stringently, risk-premium variations are uncorrelated with Fed intervention); or, time variations in risk premia arise in an augmented market model where beta risk varies with Fed intervention. Under the strong form of the efficient markets hypothesis (EMH), expected risk-adjusted profits are zero for the investor tracking Fed intervention. Alternatively, the expected return from bearing foreign-exchange risk may vary around the risk premium. If the Fed buys (sells) a currency whose expected appreciation exceeds (falls short of) the premium, the Fed earns positive expected risk-adjusted profits. This alternative might hold because Fed intervention creates divergences between expected appreciation and the risk premium, or because the Fed anticipates divergences but does not eliminate them or perhaps is unable to influence them.

Section 2 discusses the data used. Based on the implications of the EMH, Section 3 develops the test statistics used. Because cumulative intervention is integrated of order one, test-statistic distributions may be non-standard. How non-standard distributions arise, and how to handle them, is discussed. Section 4 discusses risk-adjustment models. Section 5 presents profit estimates for time-constant risk premia, Section 6 for time-varying risk premia arising in an augmented market model. In Sections 5 and 6, estimates of intervention profits over the 1985–1991 period range from 0.903 to 15.58 percent/year for the DEM and from 2.66 to 8.61 percent/year for the JPY, with some estimates significant, others not. Estimated profits tend to be larger under the assumption of time-constant rather than time-varying risk premia. Estimated profits, and their significance, can vary substantially depending on whether estimated for the period as a whole or one year at a time, or equivalently, whether estimates for multi-year periods allow for separate year effects. Failure to adjust for risk can grossly affect estimated profits.

Section 7 offers a summary and discusses possible explanations for estimated Fed intervention profits. Fed intervention profits may derive from superior Fed information about coming monetary policy, but studies find mixed results that are only weakly consistent with the view that Fed intervention contains information regarding coming monetary policy (Lewis, 1995; Kaminsky and Lewis, 1996; Fatum and Hutchison, 1999). Fed profits may arise from interaction with private speculators. LeBaron (1996) and Sweeney (1996b) report that technical analysis allows risk-adjusted profits for private speculators, but neither find evidence that the Fed profits from opposing destabilizing speculation or from re-enforcing stabilizing speculation. Dominguez (1997) and Baillie and Osterberg (1996) find conflicting evidence on whether the Fed intervenes to try to reduce the conditional volatility of appreciation and hence possibly profits by calming "disorderly markets". Clearly, Fed intervention profits require further research.

2. Data

Daily intervention, exchange-rate and interest-rate data are from the Board of Governors of the Federal Reserve System for 2 January 1985 to 31 December 1991, the period for which intervention data were available when this project began. This gives 1757 trading days (days the New York foreign-exchange market is open).

Intervention. Intervention data are the USD value of Fed interventions in DEM and JPY ("purchases or sales (-) of dollars"; a positive number means sales of foreign currency). Transactions are on the Fed's own account (open market or "market" intervention); either the Fed or the U.S. Treasury initiates the intervention. [3] Over the sample, Fed intervention is relatively small and infrequent, but somewhat clustered. In Table 1, the average absolute value of intervention in DEM is about USD 135 million (m), in JPY about USD 138 m; the maximum was USD 0.797 billion (b) for DEM, USD 0.720 b for JPY. The Fed intervened in DEM on 11.33% of the days, in JPY on 9.68%.

In Figs. 1 and 2, cumulative intervention is the sum of the USD value of the Fed's daily foreign-currency purchases (i.e., the negative of daily intervention); the right-hand scale is in millions of USD. Sporadic intervention gives prolonged periods of constant cumulative intervention, for example, no intervention in 1986. For each cumulative intervention series, conventional tests cannot reject the null of a unit root.

[3] The data also include trades with multinational lending agencies (customer intervention). Results here are for market intervention, but use of total intervention does not importantly affect results.

Table 1
Properties of the data[a]

Panel A: Absolute values of non-zero daily interventions (millions of USD)

Mean:	134.97 (DEM), 137.74 (JPY)	Maximum:	797.00 (DEM), 720.20 (JPY)

Panel B: Frequency and patterns of intervention, purchases and sale of USD

Days: Purchases	Sales	Any	Sales of both	Purchases of both
61 (DEM), 65 (JPY)	138 (DEM), 105 (JPY)	341	28	63

			Interventions	
Period dates	Sample	Trading days	DEM	JPY
2 January 1985, 31 December 1985:	1–250	250	22	21
2 January 1986, 31 December 1986:	251–501	251	0	0
2 January 1987, 31 December 1987:	502–753	252	32	43
4 January 1988, 31 December 1988:	754–1004	251	36	22
3 January 1989, 29 December 1989:	1005–1255	251	77	67
2 January 1990, 31 December 1990:	1256–1506	251	19	16
2 January 1991, 31 December 1991:	1507–1757	251	13	1
2 January 1985, 31 December 1991:	1–1757	1757	199	170

Panel C: Sample statistics for variables in conditional market models, 1985–1991[b]

	DEM		JPY	
Variable	Mean	S.D.	Mean	S.D.
Appr.	0.0003572	0.0073671	0.0003274	0.0066054
Market	0.0006373	0.0101128	0.0006373	0.0101128
Interact	−0.6382563	55.971523	−0.2058985	40.635282
Cum. Int.	6448.5155	5834.4705	452.27109	4211.7833
Appr. Lag	0.0003590	0.0073674	0.0003220	0.0066039

Correlations	DEM	JPY	Correlations	DEM	JPY
Appr., Market	−0.0350556	−0.0519708	Market, Cum. Int.	−0.0108216	−0.0047965
Appr., Interact	0.0890038	0.1340992	Market, Appr. Lag	−0.0039459	−0.0081450
Appr., Cum. Int	0.0106655	0.0438949	Interact, Cum. Int.	0.0563552	0.0707623
Appr., Appr. Lag	0.0565260	0.0599036	Interact, Appr. Lag	0.0437198	0.0221508

Table 1 (Continued)

Correlations	DEM	JPY	Correlations	DEM	JPY
Market, Interact	−0.2636177	−0.2863563	Cum. Int., Appr. Lag	0.0091332	0.0411650

[a] Wednesday, 2 January 1985 to Tuesday 31 December 1991: Number of trading-day observations, 1757.

[b] Definitions Appr.: The continuously compounded rate of appreciation of the foreign currency relative to the USD from day t to day t+1, plus the difference in the continuously compounded rates of return on foreign and USD overnight deposits, as of day t. Market: The CRSP value-weighted rate of return on the market, including dividends, from day t to day t+1. Interact: The product of cumulative intervention by the end of day t and the market rate of return from day t to day t+1. Appr. Lag: The lagged value of the dependent variable.

Exchange rates. The New York Fed obtains dollar (bid) prices at approximately noon New York time. Figs. 1 and 2 show appreciation rates in USD per unit of foreign currency, net of interest-rate differentials. Intervention's timing is unknown; observers say intervention tends to occur in the morning (New York time), that is, before exchange-rate data are collected. Each appreciation rate shows important, but small first-order correlation that varies across years, but is positive in five of the six years. [4]

Interest rates. The interest rates are daily overnight Euro rates for USD and DEM deposits, and JPY call money (Euro-yen data were unavailable). These rates are not collected simultaneously with the exchange rate data, and this timing discrepancy might cause difficulties; results below suggest interest-rate differentials have small influence. [5]

Transaction costs. The only cost is the bid–ask spread. Results below conservatively assume costs of 1/16th of one percent of transaction value per one-way trip; knowledgeable observers say this may overstate Fed transactions costs on average by a factor of 2–4. [6] Because transactions are infrequent, much larger transaction costs do not importantly affect results. The opportu-

[4] Standard tests cannot reject the null hypothesis that the log of the exchange rate has a unit root for either currency. Engel and Hamilton (1990), however present evidence that some exchange rates have mean rates of appreciation that shift in a two-state Markov process. At conventional significance levels the data cannot reject the null hypothesis that the log levels of the DEM and JPY exchange rates are not cointegrated in Engle–Granger tests. Baillie and Bollerslev (1994), however, find evidence for fractional co-integration of seven USD exchange rates, including the DEM and the JPY.

[5] For each currency, the appreciation rate dominates the series of appreciation net of the interest-rate differential. The hypotheses that the two differentials are not cointegrated and that each differential has a unit root cannot be rejected at conventional significance levels.

[6] Sweeney (1986) and Surajaras and Sweeney (1992) use one-way transaction costs of 1/16th for private speculators. The Fed may have more and larger transactions in uncertain times when bid–ask spreads are larger than usual. Checking suggests that this is unimportant.

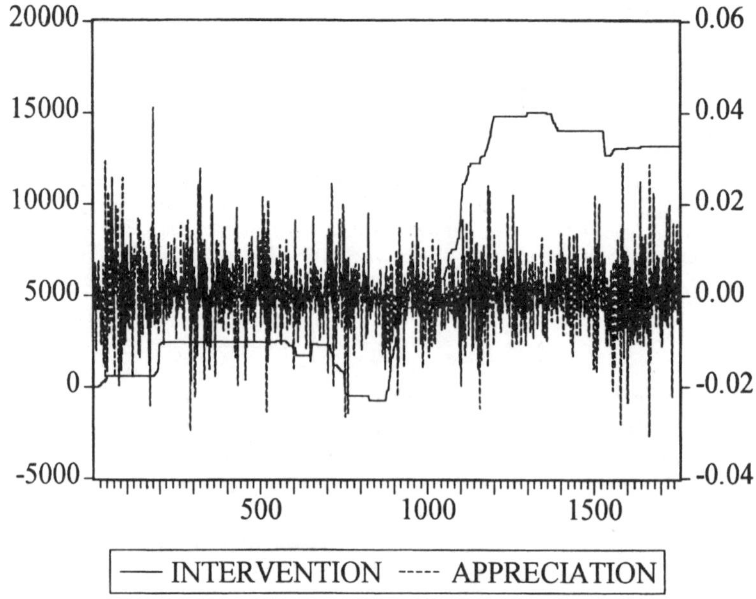

Fig. 1. DEM appreciation and cummulative intervention.

nity cost for DEM holdings is taken as the spread between USD and DEM Euro deposits (similarly for JPY). There are no transaction costs for deposits in this experiment.

Rates of return on the stock market. The augmented market model results below use the CRSP value-weighted rate of return on the market (including dividends); as discussed below, using CRSP equally weighted, S&P500 or Morgan–Stanley World Market Index rates of return makes no important difference.

3. Test statistics for risk-adjusted profits

In day 1, from $t=0$ to $t=1$, the USD value of net purchases of foreign currency (say, the DEM) is I_1. Each day, this position earns the continuously compounded net appreciation rate, $R_{t+1} = \Delta e_{t+1} + r_{\text{DEM},t} - r_{\text{USD},t}$, where e_t is the natural logarithm of the exchange rate in USD per DEM at day t, $r_{\text{DEM},t}$ and $r_{\text{USD},t}$ the continuously compounded overnight Euro rates, and Δ the backwards differencing operator ($\Delta e_{t+1} = e_{t+1} - e_t$). The economic profit from this position in period 2 is the product $I_1\ AR_2$, and over a window of T days is $I_1 \sum_{t=1}^{T} AR_{t+1}$, where AR_t is the abnormal return in period t, that is, the rate of

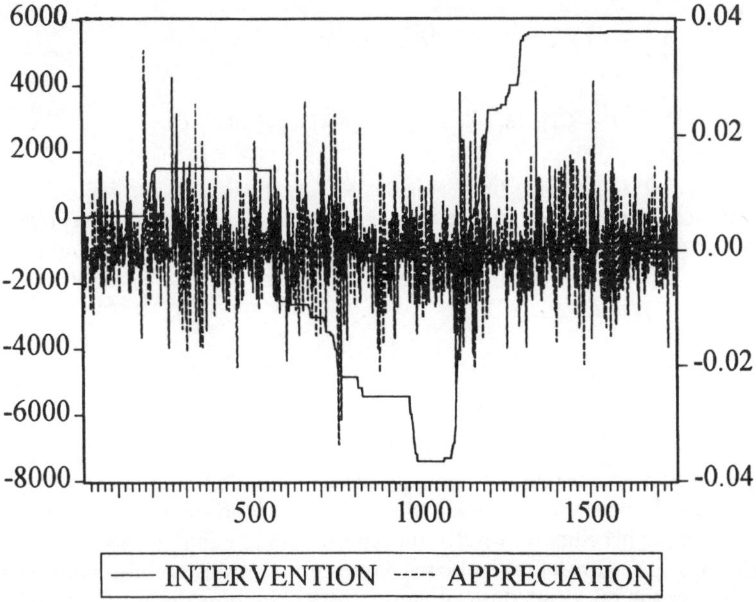

Fig. 2. JPY appreciation and cummulative interaction.

return less the risk premium pr_t, $AR = R_t - pr_t$. Summing over the I_t from $t = 1,T$ gives $\sum_{t=1}^{T} I_t \sum_{j=t}^{T} AR_{j+1}$. Define cumulative intervention through t as $CI_t = I_1 + I_2 + \cdots + I_t$ (taking initial cumulative intervention as zero); then $\sum_{t=1}^{T} I_t \sum_{j=t}^{T} AR_{j+1} = \sum_{t=1}^{T} CI_t AR_{t+1}$. Risk-adjusted profits are

$$S = \sum_{t=1}^{T} CI_t(R_{t+1} - pr_{t+1}) = \sum_{t=1}^{T} CI_t AR_{t+1}. \tag{1}$$

This experiment can be interpreted as an event study, where the events are exposure to foreign-exchange rate risk, and S is a weighted cumulative abnormal return. Below, S is divided by exposure to foreign-exchange risk to give profits per dollar of risk exposure or the risk-adjusted profit rate. Abnormal rates of return can also be discounted before calculating profit measures, as illustrated below.

The EMH requires $E_t(R_{t+h}|\Omega_t) = pr_{t+h}$ for $h > 0$, where E_t is the expectations operator at t, conditional on the information set Ω_t. Under strong-form efficiency, $\{I_j\}_{j=1}^{t}$ is in Ω_t. Alternatively, expected appreciation fluctuates around pr_t, or $E_t\, R_{t+h} \gtrless pr_{t+h}$, $h > 0$; the market is inefficient, allowing potential risk-adjusted profits.

The AR_t are estimated, conditional on some risk model. If the AR_t are fit over the sample being evaluated, the AR_t have sample mean zero. In this case,

$$S = \sum_{t=1}^{T} CI_t AR_{i,t+1} = \sum_{t=1}^{T} CI_t(AR_{t+1} - AR)$$
$$= \sum_{t=1}^{T}(CI_t - CI)(AR_{t+1} - AR) = (T-1)\text{cov}(AR_{t+1}, CI_t), \qquad (2)$$

where CI and AR are the sample means of CI_t and AR_{t+1} and cov is the sample covariance operator. Covariance measures like S are commonly interpreted as measuring profits from timing ability. Alternatively, AR_t may be found with risk models fit out of the sample being evaluated. In this case, generally $AR \neq 0$ and

$$S = \sum_{t=1}^{T} CI_t AR_{i,t+1} = \sum_{t=1}^{T}(CI_t - CI)(AR_{t+1} - AR) + \text{Adj}$$
$$= (T-1)\text{cov}(AR_{t+1}, CI_t) + \text{Adj}.$$

Adj is an adjustment that measures profits to a buy-and-hold strategy if some out-of-sample benchmark is used. Because there is no obvious choice for an out-of-sample benchmark, results are reported for the timing measure. [7]

Previous measures of central-bank intervention profits are not adjusted for risk. To see the problems this can cause, form C by substituting R_t for AR_t in Eq. (1),

$$C = \sum_{t=1}^{T}\left[I_t\left(\sum_{i=t}^{T} R_{i+1}\right)\right] = \sum_{t=1}^{T} CI_t R_{t+1}.$$

Then, $C - S = \sum_{i=t}^{T} CI_t pr_{t+1}$, and in the case of constant risk premia ($pr_t = pr$), $C - S = pr\ T\ CI$, where CI is the sample mean of CI_t. When risk-adjusted profits are zero ($S = 0$), $C \neq 0$ unless $CI = 0$ or $pr = 0$. Past studies of central bank intervention profit use measures similar to C; [8] reported profits are thus valid only in special cases. [9]

---

[7] $\text{Adj} = CIT(R_{\text{in}} - R_{\text{out}})$ for mean adjustment or $\text{Adj} = CIT(R_{\text{in}} - R_{\text{out}}) + CITb_{\text{out}}(R_{\text{M,in}} - R_{\text{M,out}})$ for market-model adjustment, with R_{in} and $R_{\text{M,in}}$ the evaluation period's mean rate of net appreciation and mean market rate of return, and similarly for R_{out} and $R_{\text{M,out}}$ where risk model is fit, and b_{out} the fitted market-model beta. If b_{out} is approximately zero, Adj is the same in both the mean and market-model adjustment cases. Sweeney (1999b) reports CI, R_{in} and $R_{\text{M,in}}$ for each year and the whole period; Adj may be calculated for any R_{out}, $R_{\text{M,out}}$, b_{out} considered.

[8] Sjöö and Sweeney (1996, 1998), discuss how Taylor's (1982a,b, 1989) and Leahy's (1989, 1995), and others' profit measures are analogous (though not identical) to the C-statistic.

[9] Spencer (1985, 1989), uses returns unadjusted for risk but suggests using $(CI_t - CI)$ rather than CI_t in the profits measure, though his economic rationale for this is unconvincing (Taylor, 1989). This gives $C_1 = \sum_{t=1}^{T}(CI_t CI)R_{t+1} = (T-1)\text{cov}(R_{t+1}, CI_t)$. In general $C_1 \neq S$ because $R_t \neq AR_{t+1}$. If however, AR_t is a linear transformation of R_t and $AR = 0$, then $C_1 = S$; this holds for in-sample mean adjustment, $AR_{t+1} = R_t - R$, but not for market-model adjustment.

Tests of significance. The standard error is

$$\hat{\sigma}_s = \left[\sum_{t=1}^{T}(CI_t - CI)^2\hat{\sigma}^2_{AR_{t+1}}\right]^{1/2},$$

where $\hat{\sigma}^2_{AR_t}$ is the estimated conditional variance of the abnormal return in period t. For $\hat{\sigma}^2_{AR_t}$ this paper either assumes homoscedasticity and uses the sample variance of AR_t, or uses GARCH estimates h_t. The null of a zero S-statistic is tested below with the S-test statistic, $S/\hat{\sigma}_S$. [10]

Distribution of the test statistic. Because CI_t appears to be integrated of order 1 in conventional unit-root tests, the usual assumption that $S/\hat{\sigma}_S$ is asymptotically distributed N(0,1) may be inappropriate. Sjöö and Sweeney (1999a) discusses conditions where $S/\hat{\sigma}_S$ is asymptotically N(0,1): AR_{t+1} and I_{t+h} must be weakly stationary and uncorrelated for *all h* for asymptotic normality. The EMH, however, implies only that AR_{t+1} and I_{t+h} are uncorrelated for $h \leqslant 0$: today's intervention can have no information about coming abnormal returns, but intervention may respond to past and current AR_t. With such correlation, the fact that CI_t is integrated implies $S/\hat{\sigma}_S$ has a non-normal asymptotic distribution. [11] Sjöö and Sweeney (1999a) report simulations that give the appropriate critical values for the S-test for a range of correlations. At one extreme, where intervention varies solely in reaction to abnormal returns, the test statistic is distributed as the (negative of the) Dickey–Fuller distribution for the test of a unit root when an intercept is estimated. At the other extreme, intervention does not respond to abnormal returns and the asymptotic distribution is normal. In the general case, the distribution is a weighted average of the two extremes.

In the Fed data used here, I_t is correlated with current and lagged AR_t. One may use the simulation results in Sjöö and Sweeney (1999a) to find critical values conditional on the correlation in the data used here. Alternatively, one may judge the evidence against normality small enough to be ignored. Results below are both for normal and non-normal distributions of the test statistic. For data used here, results are much the same whichever distribution is used.

Previous work has not taken account of the fact that an integrated variable is involved in tests of intervention profits. Taylor (1982a, p. 361) presents a test

[10] Mikkelson and Partch (1988), Karafiath and Spencer (1991), Salinger (1992) and Sweeney (1991) argue that standard errors in typical event studies must be adjusted to take account of the ratio of observations in the benchmark sample to those in the window; the S-test statistic is already appropriately adjusted.

[11] If CI_t is integrated of order 0 but shows substantial serial correlation, $S/\hat{\sigma}_S$ has a non-normal distribution in limited samples Mankiw and Shapiro (1986), but is asymptotically N(0, 1) (Bannerjee et al., 1993).

statistic that is widely used (with modifications), for example, Leahy (1989, 1995), Fase and Huijser (1989). Taylor argues the test statistic is distributed N(0, 1) under the assumption that "random purchases and sales of dollars, with the same standard deviation as actual intervention figures, are made at historically prevailing exchange rates". Randomness of I_t is not necessary – I_t and AR_{t+1} need only be weakly stationary. Finding the variance of profits conditional on the historical sequence of exchange rates is valid only if AR_{t+1} and I_{t+h} are uncorrelated for *all h* (Johansen, 1995). Because the EMH allows for correlation of AR_{t+1} and I_{t+h} for $h \geqslant 1$, the assumption of no correlation for all h is overly restrictive in testing for intervention profits. The null in Taylor's test is "no correlation", not the joint null of zero profits and the EMH.

Taylor (1989) criticizes Spencer's (1985) profit measure on the grounds that in simulations the test statistic is positive approximately 96% of the time if intervention arises only from leaning against the wind. This is the extreme Dickey–Fuller case mentioned above, and Taylor's simulation results are to be expected.

Regression approaches to testing. Testing for intervention profits can alternatively use regressions of the form

$$AR_{t+1} = g_0 + gCI_t + u_{t+1}.$$

Because the OLS estimate is $\hat{g} = \text{cov}(AR_{t+1}, CI_t)/\text{var}(CI_t)$, then $\hat{g}(T-1)\text{var}(CI_t) = S$. Asymptotically, the OLS t-value for g is the same as the S-test statistic (Sjöö and Sweeney, 1999a). [12]

The above regression is a two-pass approach: First, AR_{t+1} is found; second, it is regressed on CI_t. Single-pass approaches may have better properties. A single-pass approach for mean adjustment is

$$R_{t+1} = g_0 + gCI_t + u_{t+1}$$

because under mean adjustment $AR_t = R_t - R$. Section 6 discusses single-pass regression approaches for augmented-market-model adjustment.

The t_g-statistic has the same distribution as $S/\hat{\sigma}_S$; the simulation approach to finding critical values for $S/\hat{\sigma}_S$ applies directly to t_g. An alternative (Saikkonen, 1991) is to include an appropriate number of *leading* values of intervention in the regression to ensure that t_g is asymptotically distributed N(0, 1) even if CI_t is non-stationary. With $T \approx 1750$, a rule of thumb suggests six leads,

$$R_{t+1} = g_0 + \sum_{h=1}^{6} a_{I,h} I_{t+h} + gCI_t + u_{t+1}.$$

[12] Spencer (1985) suggests interpreting intervention-profit test statistics as regression t-values.

4. Adjustment for risk

Results are reported for mean adjustment and for market-model adjustment.[13] Under mean adjustment, $AR_t = R_t - R$, $t = 1,T$, where R is the sample mean of R_t. Mean adjustment accounts for risk by comparing R_t to a "buy-and-hold" strategy (Fama and Blume, 1966; Praetz, 1976; 1979; Sweeney, 1986). Mean adjustment is appropriate if risk premia are time-constant over the evaluation period or, more weakly, CI_t and pr_{t+1} are orthogonal.

Market-Model Adjustment. Available daily data include financial and commodities prices and rates of return (spot, and in some cases futures, forwards or options, and so forth). The researcher may use these data as proxies for risk-factor realizations; the rate of return on some market index is frequently used.[14] This paper uses the market rate of return as the single risk factor. This is in the spirit of an arbitrage pricing model, or a multi-factor capital asset pricing model, that omits non-market factors as well as predetermined variables such as dividend yields that are useful in predicting monthly stock-market returns and exchange-rate changes.

The usual market model is $R_t = a_0 + bR_{Mt} + \varepsilon_t$. R_{Mt} is the rate of return on the market; the slope b measures beta risk; and ε_t is an error term orthogonal to R_{Mt} and the estimated error is AR_{t+1}. Important mean-adjusted profits reported below may arise from association of intervention with time-varying beta risk. To allow for time-varying systematic risk, Sweeney (1996a, 1999a) makes beta a linear function of some Fed intervention[15] variable IV_t. A simple case is $b_t = b_0 + b_1 IV_{t-1}$. Including lagged appreciation, the augmented market model[16,17] is

[13] A common alternative to market adjustment. Under some conditions these three methods have similar size and power (Brown and Warner, 1980, 1985). Market adjustment is inappropriate here: The appreciation betas are small and often insignificant, and appreciation rates' standard deviations are substantially and significantly less than the markets.

[14] Alternatively, risk-factor realizations can be estimated by a factor-analytic approach; the market rate of return generally shows high correlation with extracted factors.

[15] IV_t might include other central bank's intervention; parameter estimates may be biased from omitting other central bank's intervention. It is difficult to get intervention data from other central banks; Weber (1993) and Dominguez and Frankel (1993a) report that Fed and Bundesbank intervention are not at cross purposes and in an important number of cases are in the same direction. IV_t may be non-linear function of intervention or a vector of Fed intervention variables (with b_1 a conformable coefficient vector).

[16] Serial correlation that does not allow trading profits is consistant with the EMH (Fama and Blume, 1966).

[17] Sweeney (1999b) discusses market models where beta also depends on contemporaneous cumulative intervention, $R_{t+1} = a_0 + b_0 R_{M+1} + b_1(R_{M+1} IV_t) + b_2(R_{M+1} IV_{t+1}) + cR_t + \varepsilon_{t+1}$. Because R_{t+1} and IV_{t+1} are contemporaneous allowing $b_2 \neq 0$ may result in simultaneous equations bias; the biggest part of intervention-appreciation correlation is contemporaneous rather than lead–lag (Loopesko, 1984).

$$R_{t+1} = a_0 + b_0 R_{Mt+1} + b_1 IV_t R_{Mt+1} + cR_t + \varepsilon_{t+1}. \quad (3)$$

Cumulative intervention [18] is used here as the intervention measure, as in the S-statistic. Explaining profits as due to time-varying risk requires that correlation of CI_t and R_{t+1} arise from correlation of CI_t with the time-varying risk measure $[b_0 R_{Mt+1} + b_1(R_{Mt+1} IV_t)]$.

5. Estimates of the profitability of Fed intervention: Mean-adjustment for risk

Results are for data for 1985–1991, the intervention data available when this project started. Analysis focuses on the whole period and on calendar years, chosen as sub-periods before work stated.

Calendar-year profits. Table 2:A shows mean-adjusted S-statistics in millions of USD. [19] There was no intervention in 1986. Test statistics show some instability across years, but estimated profits are mostly positive, mostly economically significant and sometimes statistically significant. Ten of 12 S-statistics are positive, and three of the six DEM S-statistics are significant at the 5% or better level.

In comparison, profits calculated over the whole period, as $S = 1756$ $\text{cov}(R_{t+1}, CI_t)$, are 785.67 m for the DEM and 2143.28 m for the JPY. In these estimates, DEM profits are significant at only the 0.6627 level, but JPY profits are significant at the 0.0658 level.

Transaction costs. In Table 2:A yearly profit rates before and after transaction costs are very close. Because Fed intervention is infrequent (Table 1) inthis sample, transaction costs have small effects and are henceforth neglected. [20]

Economic significance of risk-adjusted profits. Table 2:A emphasizes the economic importance of calendar-year profits by restating them as *percentage rates of profit* per dollar exposed to exchange-rate risk. The amount exposed to exchange-rate risk is the average across the year of the absolute value of each day's cumulative intervention [21].

[18] Dominguez and Frankel (1993a,b) and Sweeney (1999a) use intervention, cumulative intervention and (1, 0, −1) qualitative variables.

[19] These results assume that the Fed buys at today's reported noon rate, adding to cumulative intervention that earns the rate of appreciation from noon today to tomorrow. To assess the sensitivety of profits to transaction timing, Sweeney (1999b) reports experiments assume that the Fed buys at yesterday's or tomorrow's rate. The S-statistics and test-statistics are similar to, though smaller than, those in Table 2:A. Transaction timing is not an important issue.

[20] These costs can be calculated from data in Sweeney (1999b).

[21] Each day's risk depends on the absolute, not algebraic, value of exposure. Alternating between ± USD 1 *b* daily exposure gives mean daily risk exposure of USD 1b, not zero.

Table 2
S-statistics, millions of USD: Mean adjustment[a]

Year	Currency	*S*-statistic	Standard error	Test stastistic	Profit rate (%)	Profit rate (%) (Trans. cost)	Av^b $\lvert CI_t \rvert$, |net	Int. diff *S*-stat.[c]
Panel A: Calendar-year profits								
1985	DEM	99.21856	110.8731	0.894884	10.723	10.557	925.30	0.9785
	JPY	56.17096	50.39125	1.114697	16.066	15.780	349.63	1.0477
1987	DEM	3.780948	57.28459	0.066003	0.666	0.127	440.16	2.4535
	JPY	12.51137	201.3925	0.062124	0.371	0.287	3347.23	2.3812
1988	DEM	533.2567	214.9831	2.480458**	26.704	26.502	1987.60	1.0037
	JPY	−6.206608	41508	−0.083405	−0.735	−0.925	916.40	1.0762
1989	DEM	1119.661	393.9701	2.841996***	16.033	15.933	6955.75	1.0332
	JPY	685.1543	495.5930	1.382494	13.093	12.963	5212.06	1.0762
1990	DEM	−37.35826	41.78255	−0.894112	−8.317	−8.484	450.41	1.0328
	JPY	73.33963	63.62394	1.152705	4.451	4.379	1891.16	1.0335
1991	DEM	87.35964	41.23514	2.118573**	10.418	10.278	829.05	0.9931
	JPY	1.044932	1.163779	0.897878	4.332	4.254	24.00	1.0176
Σ	DEM	1805.9					11588.17	
	JPY	822.0					11639.76	

Panel B. Analysis of year effects[d]

1. *Year effects, separate slopes*: $R_{t+1} = \sum_{i=1}^{7} g_{0,i}D_{0,i} + \sum_{i=1}^{7} g_i D_i CI_t + u_{t+1}$

Estimated profits (annual percentage rate):	DEM	JPY
unconstrained $g_{0,i}$	1805.92 (15.584%)	822.00 (7.062%)
Wald test (prob.)	(0.0034)***	(0.5207)

2. *No year effects, common slope*: $R_{t+1} = g_0 + gCI_t + u_{t+1}$

Estimated profits (annual percentage rate):	DEM	JPY
$g_{0,i}$ constrained: 1985–91	785.67 (1.719%)	2143.28 (8.605%)
slope (prob.)	1.35×10^{-8} (0.6627)	6.89×10^{-8} (0.0658)*

3. *Unconstrained year effects, common slope*: $R_{t+1} = \sum_{i=1}^{7} g_{0,i}D_{0,i} + gCI_t + u_{t+1}$

Estimated profits (annual percentage rate):	DEM	JPY
$g_{0,i}$ unconstrained	1806.22 (15.586%)	824.09 (7.080%)
slope (prob.)	3.82×10^{-7} (0.0004)***	1.35×10^{-7} (0.1105)

continued overleaf

4. *Constrained year effects, common slope*: $R_{t+1} = \sum_{i=1}^{7} g_{0,i}D_{0,i} + gCI_t + u_{t+1}$		
Estimated profits (annual percentage rate):	DEM	JPY
$g_{0,i}$ constrained: 1985–88	–	866.82 (7.447%)
slope (prob.)	–	1.42×10^{-7}(0.0131)***
$g_{0,i}$ constrained: 1985–88; 1989–91	–	891.24 (7.657%)
slope (prob.)	–	1.46×10^{-7} (0.0008)***
$g_{0,i}$ constrained: 1985–87	1669.10 (14.403%)	–
slope (prob.)	3.53×10^{-7} (0.0007)***	–
$g_{0,i}$ constrained to zero: 1986–87	1740.03 (15.015%)	–
slope (prob.)	3.68×10^{-7} (0.0000)***	–
5. *Leading* I_{t+h}: *Year effects, common slope*: $R_{t+1} = \sum_{i=1}^{7} g_{0,i}D_{0,i} + \sum_{h=1}^{6} a_{1,h}I_{t+h}gCI_t + u_{t+1}$		
Estimated profits (annual percentage rate):	DEM	JPY
$g_{0,i}$ unconstrained	1446.22 (12.485%)	817.99 (7.028%)
slope (prob.)	3.06×10^{-7} (0.0046)***	1.34×10^{-7} (0.1105)
$g_{0,i}$ constrained: 1985–88; 1989–91	–	726.42 (6.241%)
slope (prob.)	–	1.19×10^{-7} (0.0065)***

[a] The *S*-statistic is $S = \sum_{t=1}^{T}(CI_t - CI)(R_{t+1} - R)$, where CI_t is cumulative intervention as of day *t*, *CI* its sample mean, R_{t+1} the net appreciation rate from day *t* to day *t*+1, and *R* its sample mean. The standard error of the *S*-statistic is $\hat{\sigma}_S = \sum_{t=1}^{T}(CI_t - CI)^2\hat{\sigma}_t^{2^1}/2$, where $\hat{\sigma}_t^2$ is the estimated conditional variance of R_t, with $\hat{\sigma}_t$ assumed time constant in this table (see Sweeney, 1999b) for time-varying conditional variances).

[b] Period averages of the daily absolute value of cumulative intervention, CI_t. The net concept sets the period's initial value of CI_t to zero, because the initial level of cumulative intervention cannot affect the period's profits/losses in this paper's measure of profits to timing ability. The gross concept intervention does not adjust CI_0. Intervention is in millions of USD.

[c] This column reports the ratio of the *S*-statistic calculated with and without the interest-rate differential. Definitions: $g_{0,i}$: year effect in *i*, g_i: slope for year *i*, $\hat{\sigma}^2_{i,CI}$: sample variance of CI_t for year *i*, R_{t+1}: currency's rate of appreciation from *t* to *t*+1, net of the interest-rate differential, $\hat{\sigma}^2_{av,CI}$: average across the seven years of yearly variance of CI_t: DEM, 2,692,672.88 m; JPY, 3,476,302.47 m, $\hat{\sigma}^2_{W,CI}$: the sample variance of CI_t over the whole seven-year period: for the DEM, 34,025,944; for the JPY, 17,719,030, g_0: common intercept with no year effects, *g*: common slope across years.

[d] Profits are calculated as follows. Case 1: $S = \sum_{i=1}^{7}(T_i - 1)\hat{g}_i\hat{\sigma}^2_{i,CI}$. Case 2: $S = \hat{g}(T-1)\hat{\sigma}^2_{W,CI}$. Cases 3, 4 and 5: $S = \hat{g}\sum_{i=1}^{7}(T_i - 1)\hat{\sigma}^2_{av,CI}$. T_i: the number of days in year *i* (=251 save for 1985 [250] and 1987 [252]), $D_{0,i}$: a dummy equal to unity in year *i*, zero elsewhere, D_i: a dummy equal to unity in year *i*, zero elsewhere; for 1986, zero always because intervention was zero in 1986.

* Significant at the 1% level.

** Significant at the 10% level.

*** Significant at the 5% level.

In the timing measure used here, yearly profits are independent of that year's initial cumulative intervention, CI_0: Ex post, CI_0 must earn zero *abnormal* returns over the year *i*, $\sum_{t=1}^{Ti} CI_0 AR_{t+1} = 0$, because the measure sets $\sum_{t=1}^{Ti} AR_{t+1} = 0$. But CI_0 affects the *percentage* rate of profits. Hence, in percentage profit rates here, the amount exposed to exchange-rate risk is found with $CI_0 = 0$. This is net exposure; the alternative, which uses the actual amounts including CI_0, is gross exposure. [22]

Alternative estimates of percentage profit rates. Consider three measures of overall percentage profit rates. First, the simple average of the yearly profit rates in Table 2:A for the DEM and JPY are 9.470 and 6.109 percent/year. Second, the sum of the calendar year profits in Table 2:A, divided by the sum of each year's net exposure, gives DEM and JPY profit rates of 15.584 and 7.062 percent/year. The DEM profit rate is substantially larger than in the first measure because 1988 and 1989 dominate profits and exposure, and have large profit rates, 26.704 and 16.033 percent/year.

A third way of estimating profit rates over the entire 7-year period is to calculate a whole-period *S*-statistic, $S = 1756 \operatorname{cov}(R_{t+1}, CI_t)$. Profits are 785.67 m for the DEM and 2143.28 m for the JPY. Over the 7 years, the average absolute value of each day's cumulative intervention is 6533.41 m for the DEM and 3559.39 m for the JPY. Thus, annual profit rates are 1.719% [$= 100 \times (785.67/6533.41)/7$] for the DEM and 8.605% for the JPY.

The large difference in DEM profit rates between the first and third measures arises from different treatments of year effects in the data.

Importance of year effects. Table 2:B reports profit estimates from alternative restrictions on the overall regression

$$R_{t+1} = \sum_{i=1}^{7} g_{0,i} D_{0,i,t} + \sum_{i=1}^{7} g_i D_{i,t} CI_t + u_{t+1}. \tag{4}$$

To allow for year effects in the intercept, $D_{0,i,t}$ is a dummy variable equal to unity each day in year *i*, zero otherwise. To allow for separate slopes, $D_{i,t}$ is the same save for 1986 where $D_{i,t} = 0$ for all *t* because there was no intervention (with both a year effect and a separate slope, the data matrix is singular). On the one hand, the $g_{0,i}$ represent calendar-year risk premia that may vary across years. Similarly, marginal profit rates from foreign-exchange exposure, g_i, may vary across years. On the other hand, including year effects or separate slopes that the data do not require reduces estimating efficiency and may substantially affect profit estimates and their significance.

[22] Table 2:A reports net exposure; Sweeney (1999b) reports gross exposure and compares profit rates for gross and net exposure. Gross equals net risk exposure for whole-period profit rates and 1985.

In Table 2:B.1, the overall regression (4) has year effects and separate slopes, is the same as running a separate regression for each year, and gives the same calendar-year results as Table 2:A. In this case, $S = \sum_{i=1}^{7} S_i = \sum_{i=1}^{7}(T_i - 1)\hat{g}_i\hat{\sigma}^2_{i,CI}$, where $\hat{\sigma}^2_{i,CI}$ is the sample variance of CI_t in year i and T_i is the number of trading days in year i (see Section 3, "Regression Approaches..."). Profits are 1805.92 m for DEM, and 822.00 m for JPY intervention. A Wald test of the null that all the slopes g_i, and hence the calendar-year S-statistics, are zero is rejected at the 0.0034 significance for the DEM but only the 0.5207 level for the JPY. (A Wald test requires all t-values have an asymptotically normal distribution.)

The experiment in 2:B.2 has no year effects and a single slope. This corresponds to finding profits over the whole period as in $S = 1756\ \mathrm{cov}(R_{t+1}, CI_t)$, with profits as reported above of 785.67 m and 2143.28 m for the DEM and JPY. Here, profits are calculated as $S = \hat{g}(T-1)\hat{\sigma}^2_{W,CI}$.

The experiment in 2:B.3 retains the seven year effects in 2:B.1 but imposes a time-constant slope. For both currencies, imposing a common slope does not degrade performance, as judged from Wald- and t-tests. As compared to 2:B.1, profits change only slightly, to 1806.22 m and 824.09 m for the DEM and JPY. Analogous to 2:B.1, these profits are calculated as $S = \sum_{i=1}^{7} S_i = \sum_{i=1}^{7}(T_i - 1)\hat{g}\hat{\sigma}^2_{i,CI} = \hat{g}\sum_{i=1}^{7}(T_i - 1)\hat{\sigma}^2_{i,CI} \approx \hat{g}(T-1)\hat{\sum}^2_{ac,CI}$.

With a time-constant slope, a t-test is appropriate. As discussed in Section 3, the t-value may, but need not, be asymptotically N(0, 1). For the data used here, but not of course in general, the critical value in a two-tailed test under the normal distribution, and the critical value found from simulation for a one-tail test under the non-normal distribution discussed above, are approximately the same for a specified significance level. In a t-test of the hypothesis $g = 0$, DEM profits are significant at the 0.0004 level. JPY profits are significant at only the 0.1105 level, but note that imposing a common slope increases significance from 0.5207.

Restrictions on year effects can importantly change results, as 2:B.4 shows. For the JPY, if the 1985–1988 year effects are set equal, the significance level is 0.0131; in both Wald- and t-tests, these restrictions do not degrade performance. With only two effects, for 1985–88 and 1989–91, the significance level is 0.0008; again, in both Wald- and t-tests, these restrictions do not degrade performance. These restrictions have little effect on the estimated common slope – 1.35, 1.46 and 1.18 (all times 10^{-7}) across the three specifications. But the restrictions can greatly affect the significance level.

Similarly, for the DEM, both Wald- and t-tests support restricting 1985–1987 year effects to be equal, or alternatively, setting both 1986 and 1987 year effects to zero; in the first case, the significance level is 0.0007, in the second 0.0000. These restrictions have little effect on the estimated common slope – 3.82, 3.53 and 3.68 (all times 10^{-7}) across the three specifications. As opposed to the JPY case, these restrictionss have little effect on the significance level.

Table 2:B.4 shows profits calculated in the same way as in 2:B.1 and 2:B.3. But the estimated g may be used to calculate risk-adjusted profits either as the sum of calendar-year profits, $S = \sum_{i=1}^{7} S_i = \sum_{i=1}^{7}(T_i - 1)\hat{g}\hat{\sigma}^2_{i,CI} = \hat{g}\sum_{i=1}^{7}(T_i - 1)\hat{\sigma}^2_{i,CI} \approx \hat{g}(T - 1)\hat{\sigma}^2_{av,CI}$, or as whole period profits, $S = \hat{g}(T - 1)\hat{\sigma}^2_{W,CI}$. (Sections 2:B.1 and 2:B.3 use the sum of calendar-year profits; Section 2:B.2 uses whole-period profits.) The ratio of these two profit measures is $\hat{\sigma}^2_{av,CI}/\hat{\sigma}^2_{W,CI}$:

	$\hat{\sigma}^2_{av,CI}$	$\hat{\sigma}^2_{W,CI}$	$\hat{\sigma}^2_{av,CI}/\hat{\sigma}^2_{W,CI}$
DEM	2,692,672	34,025,944	0.07914
JPY	3,476,302	17,719,030	0.19619

Strikingly, for any specification with a common slope, whole-period profits exceed the sum of calendar-year profits. This arises because CI_t is non-stationary: $\hat{\sigma}^2_{CI}$ calculated across the seven years is expected to be larger than the $\hat{\sigma}^2_{CI}$ for any one calendar year or the average of the $\hat{\sigma}^2_{CI}$ across calendar years.

Thus, tacitly, profits calculated with mean-adjustment over the whole period, as in 2:B.2, are calculated with $\hat{\sigma}^2_{W,CI}$; and yearly mean-adjusted profits, as in 2:B.3, are calculated with $\hat{\sigma}^2_{av,CI}$. If profits were calculated in both cases with the same variance measure, profits in 2:B.3 would be even larger for the DEM relative to those in 2:B.2. Restricting year effects to be constant reduces the estimated slope g greatly for the DEM (from 3.82×10^{-7} to 1.32×10^{-8}) and importantly for the JPY (from 1.35×10^{-7} to 6.89×10^{-8}) in comparing 2:B.2 to 2:B.3. Using the larger $\hat{\sigma}^2_{W,CI}$ to calculate profits in 2:B.2 does not offset the fall in the slope for the DEM, but more than offsets the fall in the slope for the JPY.

Using leading values of I_{t+h}. Table 2:B.5 reports results when leading I_{t+h} are included. Including the leading I_{t+h} ensures the t-value of g is asymptotically N(0, 1). In comparing Sections 2:B.3 and 2:B.5, in each case with 7 year effects and a common slope, DEM profits fall by 19.9%, to 1446.87 m, but JPY profits fall by less than 1% to 817.99 m. $\hat{g}$ is significant at the 0.0046 level for the DEM, at the 0.1105 level for the JPY. Thus, the approach with leading I_{t+h} and the simulation approach give similar results. Note that results with leading I_{t+h} are sensitive to restrictions on year effects: As an example, if the JPY is constrained to have only two effects, 1985–1988 and 1989–1991, $\hat{g}$ is significant at the 0.0065 level.

Quantitative importance of adjusting for risk. Previous estimates of intervention profits are not adjusted for risk. As an example of how important this omission can be, for the 1985–1991 period, comparing the S-statistic (in millions of USD, found with a common slope and without year effects) to the C-statistic in Section 3

Currency	C-statistic	S-statistic	$C-S$	$(C-S)/C$	$(C-S)/S$
DEM	4846.868	785.665	4061.202	0.8379	5.1619
JPY	2403.298	2143.281	260.017	0.1082	0.1213

Failure to adjust for risk grossly overstates DEM intervention profits and importantly overstates JPY profits. $C - S = \sum_{t=1}^{T} CI_t R = TRCI$ implies that $(C - S) >< 0$ as $(RCI) >< 0$. Even with negligible risk-adjusted profits ($S \approx 0$), large $|C|/T$ is expected whenever both $|R|$ and $|CI|$ are large.

Influence of Interest Rates on Estimated Profits. Many authors argue that inclusion of interest rates plays a key role in measuring intervention profits (for example, Bank of England, 1983; Fase and Huijser, 1989). Further, the interest rates may be measured with error if the investor cannot obtain the rates used or if the collection time differs for interest rates versus other data. The final column in Table 2:A gives evidence on the importance of interest-rate differentials. It shows the ratio of the S-statistics net of interest-rate differentials relative to those that omit these differentials. Results are much the same whether or not interest-rate differentials are included. In many cases, inclusion of the differential raises the S-statistics. In cases where omitting the differential has important effects on the ratio, the S-statistics are small. Interest-rate differentials do not drive Table 2's results; in cases where interest-rate data are not available to form net appreciation rates, gross appreciation rates may be adequate. [23]

Using discounted profits. If the abnormal returns are discounted to the start of the period, estimated profits S are expected to fall, but so are discounted standard errors and exposure. The results of many experiments are well represented by an example where the investor puts profits in his/her euro-USD account at an annual rate of 5% compounded daily. For the DEM and the JPY without separate year effects, whole period profits fall from 785.7 and 2143.3 m to 709.3 and 1777.6 m, but with smaller standard errors of 1543.02 m and 986.48 m, giving S-test values of 0.460 and 1.802, marginally higher for the DEM, lower for the JPY. Discounting profits reduces dollar values but has small effects on test results or profit rates.

[23] For mean-adjusted S-statistics, the difference from including interest rates and not is $\sum_{t=1}^{T}(CI_t - \overline{CI})[(i_{\mathrm{DEM},t} - i_{\mathrm{USD},t}) - (\bar{i}_{\mathrm{DEM}} - \bar{i}_{\mathrm{USD}})]$, where $\overline{CI}$, $\bar{i}_{\mathrm{DEM}}$ and $\bar{i}_{\mathrm{USD}}$ are sample means; interest-rate differentials have non-zero effects only if correlated with cumulative intervention. Further, Δe_t and CI_t show much larger fluctuation than the interest-rate differential. Thus the criticism of neglecting interest rates is perhaps misplaced; if profit measure is risk-adjusted, interest rates may be irrelevant. Similarly, results may be insensitive to which interst rates are used.

Summary for mean-adjusted profits estimates. Fed intervention makes positive risk-adjusted profits in many of the years from 1985 to 1991, with the profits economically significant and sometimes statistically significant at conventional levels.[24] Clearly, the Fed does not lose money, and arguably it makes statistically significant profits.

6. Estimates of the profitability of Fed intervention: Market-model adjustment for risk

Market models with *time-constant* betas, $R_t = a_0 + b_0 R_{M,t} + \varepsilon_t$, give risk-adjusted profits close to those for mean-adjustment. For comparison to mean-adjusted whole-period profits (Table 2:B.2), DEM and JPY S-statistics for the whole 1985–1991 period calculated from standard market models are 757.30 m and 2130.00 m versus 785.67 m and 2143.28 m; mean-adjusted profits are only 3.75% and 0.62% larger for the DEM and JPY.

Market models that *condition* beta on cumulative intervention often yield importantly smaller estimated profits than under mean-adjustment, but these declines in profits do not qualitatively affect conclusions. From Section 4, the general market model is $R_{t+1} = a_0 + b_0 R_{Mt+1} + b_1 (R_{Mt+1} CI_t) + cR_t + \varepsilon_{t+1}$: Model 1 excludes lagged appreciation ($c = 0$), Model 2 includes lagged appreciation (fits c).

Calendar-year results. Table 3:A shows calendar-year S-statistics for Models 1 and 2. Model 1's S-statistics are similar to mean-adjusted results in Table 2:A, though often smaller. As compared to the sum of the calendar-year S-statistics for Model 1, the mean-adjusted value is larger in Table 2:A by 3.54% for the DEM, by 24.32% for the JPY.

Importance of year effects. Table 3:B examines the same cases discussed around Table 2:B. Different profit estimates arise from different restrictions on

$$R_{t+1} = \sum_{i=1}^{7} D_{0,i,t} a_{0,i} + \sum_{i=1}^{7} b_{0,i} D_{0,i,t} R_{Mt+1} + \sum_{i=1}^{7} b_{1,i} D_{0,i,t} CI_t R_{Mt+1} + \sum_{i=1}^{7} d_i D_{i,t} CI_t + \sum_{i=1}^{7} c_i D_{0,i,t} R_t + \varepsilon_{t+1}. \qquad (5)$$

[24] These results assume, abnormal returns have conditionally constant varinces. Appreciation-rates appear to be leptokurtic (Surajaras and Sweeney, 1992), with GARCH effects in their variances (Baillie and Bollerslev, 1989; Dominguez, 1993). Sweeney (1999b) compares S-statistic standard errors from four GARCH models with those used in Table 2. Differences are quite small for both currencies. GARCH effects have little influence on S-test results.

Again, $D_{0,i,t}$ are dummy variables equal to unity for every day t in year i, zero otherwise, and $D_{i,t}$ the same except for $D_{1986,t} = 0$ for all t because there was no intervention in 1986.

Table 3:B.1 reports the sum of the calendar-year profits as 1,744.1 m for the DEM and 661.2 m for the JPY, as in Table 3:A. DEM profits are significant at the 0.0078 level in a Wald test that all slopes equal zero, but JPY profits are significant at only the 0.5227 level; this test requires that all t-values are asymptotically normal. The comparable mean-adjusted profits in Table 2:B.1 are 1805.9 m for the DEM, 822.0 m for the JPY, larger by 3.54% for the DEM, 24.32% for the JPY.

In Table 3:B.2, profits found with no year effects and a common slope on CI_t are 412.07 m for the DEM and 1691.38 m for the JPY. Comparable mean-adjusted profits are larger by 90.66% and 26.72% for the DEM and JPY. In t-tests, the DEM and JPY slopes are significant at only the 0.82 and 0.15 levels, compared to 0.66 and 0.07 for mean adjustment; significance levels are approximately the same even if t-values have non-standard distributions.

Table 3:B.3 reports profit estimates with separate year effects but a common slope as 1743.81 m for the DEM, 668.43 m for the JPY. t-tests for the slopes and hence the profits are significant at the 0.0005 and 0.1923 levels, under the assumption that the t-values are asymptotically normal; as in the preceding section, significance levels are approximately the same even if the non-standard distribution is assumed for the test statistic. Comparable mean-adjusted profits are larger by 3.58% and 24.28%, with t-values significant at the 0.0004 and 0.1105 levels.

Table 3:B.4 reports results for the same restrictions on year effects as in Table 2:B.4 in the case of a common slope. Imposing restrictions on year effects has little effect on estimated slopes. The restrictions substantially increase significance levels for the JPY, from 0.1916 in Section 3:B.3 to either 0.0116 or 0.0032.

Table 3:B.5 reports results when leading I_{t+h} are included to ensure the t-value's slope is asymptotically normal. Profits are 1390.09 m for the DEM, with a significance level of 0.0005. These profits are lower by 20.08% than in the comparable case in 3:B.3. Profits are 668.43 m for the JPY, with a significance level of 0.1923; profits and significance are slightly higher than in the comparable case in 3:B.3. Mean-adjustment profits in the similar case in Table 2:B.5 are higher by 4.08% and 23.34% for the DEM and JPY. For the JPY, restricting year effects to equal across 1985–1988, and 1989–1991, gives a significance level of 0.0194 in 3:B.5 as compared to 0.0032 in 3:B.4 and 0.0065 in 2:B.5.

Economic significance of risk-adjusted profits. Table 4 summarizes estimates of percentage profit rates for mean adjustment and market-model adjustment (Model 1 is used). First, risk-adjusted profits are economically significant in

Table 3
S-statistics, millions of USD: time-varying betas, market-model adjustment[a]

Panel A: S-statistics

Period	DEM			JPY		
	S-statistic	Std. Err.	Test-statistic	*S*-statistic	Std. Err.	Test-statistic
Model 1						
1985	101.2363	92.67599	1.092368	54.22020	57.70792	0.939562
1987	−8.100405	61.93517	−0.130788	5.366977	194.4426	0.027602
1988	521.2067	252.1780	2.066821*	−11.67622	74.84239	−0.156011
1989	1089.620	418.1521	2.605798***	542.3030	459.6625	1.179785
1990	−42.31908	52.29881	0.809179	69.71066	62.71270	1.111588
1991	82.47932	35.11797	2.348636**	1.307806	1.242263	1.052760
Model 2						
1985	98.36944	92.34550	1.065233	49.97051	57.59636	0.867598
1987	5.609141	61.88135	−0.090643	9.541198	194.2202	0.049126
1988	494.9018	251.9588	1.964217**	−11.10842	74.75677	−0.148594
1989	−1031.872	417.7888	2.469841**	504.1863	459.1367	1.098118
1990	−40.03501	52.25337	−0.766171	64.54240	62.64096	1.030355
1991	78.05002	35.08745	2.224443**	1.275045	1.240842	1.027564
$\sum$ (for mod. 1)	1744.1			661.2		

Panel B. Analysis of year effects[b]

1. *Year effects, separate slopes*: $R_{t+1} = \sum_{i=1}^{7} a_{0,i}D_{0,i} + \sum_{i=1}^{7} b_0 D_{0,i}R_{M,t+1} + \sum_{i=1}^{7} b_1 D_{0,i}R_{M,t+1}(CI_t - CI) + \sum_{i=1}^{7} d_i D_i CI_t + u_{t+1}$

	DEM	JPY
Estimated profits (annual percentage rate):	DEM	JPY
	1744.1 (15.309%)	661.2 (5.680%)
Wald test	(0.0078)***	(0.5227)

2. *No year effects, common slope*: $R_{t+1} = a_0 + b_0 R_{M,t+1} + b_1 R_{M,t+1}(CI_t - CI) + dCI_t + u_{t+1}$

Estimated profits (annual percentage rate):	DEM	JPY
$a_{0,i}$ constrained: 1985–91	412.07 (0.903%)	1691.38 (6.791%)
slope (prob.)	6.94×10^{-9} (0.8157)	5.46×10^{-8} (0.1420)

3. *Unconstrained year effects, common slope*: $R_{t+1} = \sum_{i=1}^{7} a_{0,i}D_{0,i} + b_0 R_{M,t+1} + b_1 R_{M,t+1}(CI_t - CI) + dCI_t + u_{t+1}$

Estimated profits (annual percentage rate):	DEM	JPY
$a_{0,i}$ unconstrained	1743.81 (15.049%)	663.11 (5.696%)
slope (prob.)	3.69×10^{-7} (0.0005)***	1.10×10^{-7} (0.1916)

continued overleaf

Table 3 (Continued)

4. *Constrained year effects, common slope*: $R_{t+1} = \sum_{i=1}^{7} a_{0,i}D_{0,1} + b_0 R_{M,t+1} + b_1 R_{M,t+1}(CI_t - CI) + dCI_t + u_{t+1}$		
Estimated profits (annual percentage rate):	DEM	JPY
$a_{0,i}$ constrained: 1985–88	–	587.85 (5.050%)
slope (prob.)	–	$9.63\ 10^{-8}$ (0.0116)**
$a_{0,i}$ constrained: 1985–88; 1989–91	–	775.26 (6.659%)
slope (prob.)	–	1.27×10^{-7} (0.0032)***
$a_{0,i}$ constrained: 1985–87	1602.91 (13.833%)	–
slope (prob.)	3.39×10^{-7} (0.0003)***	–
$a_{0,i}$ constrained to zero: 1986–87	1721.11 (14.853%)	–
slope (prob.)	$3.64\ 10^{-7}$ (0.0000)***	–
5. *Leading* I_{t+h}: *Year effects, common slope*: $R_{t+1} = \sum_{i=1}^{7} a_{0,i}D_{0,i} + \sum_{h=1}^{6} a_{I,h}I_{t+h} + b_0 R_{M,t+1} + b_1 R_{M,t+1}(CI_t - CI) + dCI_t + u_{t+1}$		
Estimated profits (annual percentage rate):	DEM	JPY
$a_{0,i}$ unconstrained	1390.09 (11.996%)	668.43 (5.742%)
slope (prob.)	2.94×10^{-7} (0.0062)***	1.09×10^{-7} (0.1923)
$a_{0,i}$ constrained: 1985–88; 1989–91	–	616.54 (5.296%)
slope (prob.)	–	1.01×10^{-7} (0.0194)**

[a] General model: $R_{t+1} = a + b_0 R_{M,t+1} + b_1 R_{Mt+1}(CI_t - CI) + cR_t + \epsilon_{t+1}$. Model 1, $c = 0$; Model 2, c is fit. Definitions $a_{0,i}$: year effect for i, d_i: slope for year i, $\hat{\sigma}^2_{i,CI}$: Sample variance of CI_t for year i, R_{t+1}: currency's rate of appreciation from t to t+1, net of the interest-rate differential $\hat{\sigma}^2_{av,CI}$: average across the seven years of the sample variance of CI_t. DEM: 2,692,672.88 m. JPY: 3,476,302.47 m, $\hat{\sigma}^2_{W,CI}$: The sample variance of CI_t over seven-year period. DEM: 34,025,944 m. JPY: 17,719,030 m. T_i: the number of days in year i (=251 save for 1985 [250] and 1987 [252]), a_0: common intercept with no year effects, d: common slope across years, $D_{0,i}$: a dummy equal to unity in year i, zero elsewhere, D_i: a dummy equal to unity in year i, zero elsewhere; but in 1986 equals zero always because intervention was zero in 1986.

[b] Profits are calculated as follows. Case 1: $S = \Sigma_{i=1}^{7}(T_i - 1)\hat{g}_i\hat{\sigma}^2_{i,CI}$. Case 2: $S = (T-1)^2_{W,CI}$. Cases 3, 4 and 5: $S = \sum_{i=1}^{7}(T_i - 1)^2_{av,CI}$.

*, **, *** Significant at the 10, 5 and 1 percent levels.

Table 4
Risk-adjusted profit rates (percent/year): mean and market-model adjustment

Measure	DEM		JPY	
	Mean Adj.	Mkt.-Mod. 1	Mean Adj.	Mkt.-Mod. 1
Yearly rates				
1985	10.723	10.941	16.066	15.508
1987	0.666	−1.840	0.371	0.1603
1988	26.704	26.223	−0.735	−1.2741
1989	16.033	15.665	13.093	10.4048
1990	−8.317	−9.396	4.451	3.861
1991	10.418	9.949	4.332	5.4492
Average of yearly rates [a, b, c]	9.470	8.590	6.109	5.656
No year effects, common slope [a, b, c]	1.7188	0.9031	8.605	6.791
Sum of yearly profits/sum of yearly exposure [a, b, c]	15.584	15.309	7.062	5.680

[a] The "Average of yearly rates" finds the yearly rates using estimates that allow for year effects and separate slopes – Tables 2:A and 3:A (or comparably, Tables 2:B.1 and 3:B.1). The "No year effects, common slope" is for the *S*-statistic calculated with a single slope and with no year effects – the final entry in Tables 2:B.2 and 3:B.2. The "Sum of yearly profits ÷ sum of yearly exposure" is the sum of each year's *S*-statistic divided by the sum across years of each year's average absolute value of daily cumulative intervention, times 100.
[b] Transaction costs – Table 2:A shows the minor effects of transaction costs. Because transaction costs have such minor effects, the profit rates reported here are gross of transaction costs.
[c] The profit *rates* are calculated as the *S*-statistic (profits) for a period relative to the period average of the absolute value of "net" cumulative intervention. In the "net" concept, cumulative intervention outstanding at the start of the period is set to zero. The text explains that the net concept is appropriate for the measures of profits from timing ability used here. In contrast, in the "gross" concept cumulative intervention at the start of the period is not adjusted.

many measures. Relative to amount of dollars exposed to exchange-rate risk, the estimated profits tend to give large profit rates. Second, across the alternative profit-rate estimates, use of market-model rather than mean adjustment reduces profit rates by between 28 and 82 basis points for the DEM, 45 to 181 basis points for the JPY. On the one hand, time-varying risk premia, in market models that condition beta on predetermined cumulative intervention, explain an economically important part of the mean-adjusted profits in Table 2. On the other hand, these adjustments for time-varying risk leave economically important profits. [25]

[25] Sjöö and Sweeney (1999b) show using whole-period or in-sample market model residuals does not affect estimated calender-year profits importantly or in a consistant direction. Further, different market indices give qualitatively similar results. When the conditional variance of appreciation is estimated simultaneously under M-GARCH, profits are similar to those in Tables 2 and 3.

Summary for market-model adjustment for risk. Using augmented market models to risk-adjusted profits results in lower profit rates than under mean adjustment, by from 22 to 86 basis points for the DEM, 45 to 181 for the JPY. Nevertheless, many of the profit rates are still economically important. Similarly, significance levels tend to fall, but many remain important.

7. Summary and conclusions

The profitability of central banks' foreign-exchange intervention is an important, contentious issue. Past estimates of Fed profits have failed to resolve conflicting opinions (see Sweeney (1997) for a review). In estimating Fed profits, this paper supersedes previous work in three ways. First, it takes account of premia that compensate investors for bearing foreign-exchange risk, as must be done to estimate economic profits. Failure to include risk premia can greatly change estimated profits. This paper's approach can be used with any estimatable risk model. Second, the paper bases its profit measures and tests on the Efficient Markets Hypothesis. Third, it recognizes that the profits involve a variable integrated of order 1 and hence the profit measures and test statistics may have non-normal distributions. It discusses how this may arise and how to handle the problem in testing.

Results are reported here for two ways of adjusting for risk. Mean adjustment subtracts the sample-mean rate of appreciation (net of the interest-rate differential) from daily net appreciation. This adjustment is most appropriate if risk premia in foreign-exchange markets are time-constant or, more weakly, intervention and risk premia are orthogonal. Market-model adjustment subtracts the market-model estimates of net appreciation from actual net appreciation. This approach allows for time-varying risk premia. In particular, the market beta of appreciation is conditioned on Fed intervention.

A central bank may have intervention goals beyond profits, and may arguably do a good job overall even if it makes intervention losses. But a central bank may well face political difficulties if it makes intervention losses; almost every central bank claims that it makes money on intervention, save in those speculative crises where it clearly makes losses. Because the outside observer cannot know which portion of intervention a central bank undertakes for goals beyond profits and perhaps in the expectation of losses, this paper's tests do not adjust for such activities.

This paper's estimates on daily data for the period, 1985–1991 suggest the Fed makes risk-adjusted profits. For the entire period, estimates of profit rates range from 0.90 to 15.58 percent/year for the DEM, and from 5.66 to 8.61 percent/year for the JPY. In some years, profits are significant, in others not. Mean adjustment tends to give larger profits than market-model adjustment. Using an adequate risk model is then crucial to evaluating risk-adjusted intervention profits. On balance, estimated profits appear economically and statistically significant.

Observers who think central banks lose money from their intervention have an important prima facie case against intervention. The burden is on the central bank to justify the losses in terms of other benefits from intervention. This paper's results, that conditional on the risk models used, the Fed appears to make risk-adjusted profit from its intervention, suggest that evaluating intervention requires more detailed, quantified cost–benefit analysis than has yet been attempted.

If these estimated profits are taken at face value, they raise an important theoretical, empirical and policy issue: *Why* does the Fed make profits on its intervention? Evidence that intervention profits arise from the Fed acting on its superior knowledge about coming monetary policy is mixed. Lewis (1995) finds that Fed intervention helps predict changes in interbank interest rates and various monetary aggregates, but only over a two-week period; she views this relationship as arising less from signaling than from Fed operating procedures with a lag between intervention and sterilization. Kaminsky and Lewis (1996) find that Fed intervention gives signals of changes in interbank rates and monetary aggregates, but in the contrary direction from what the signaling hypothesis usually predicts. Fatum and Hutchison (1999) investigate whether Fed intervention is associated with changes in the Fed Funds futures rate, with the Fed Funds rate taken as an indicator of monetary policy and the futures rate as a predictor of the coming Fed Funds rate. They report no systematic relationship.

Fed intervention may make profits from countering "disorderly markets". Some see "disorderly markets" as directly related to conditional volatility as found in GARCH models. In this view, periods of high volatility induce intervention aimed to reduce volatility. Evidence is mixed. Dominguez (1997) finds no evidence that volatility induces Fed intervention. Baillie and Osterberg (1996), allowing different reactions to up and down movements, find intervention reacts directly to volatility in the JPY but not the DEM.

Fed profits might arise from interaction with private speculators. Speculator and Fed positions may be opposite; the Fed profits reported here would be speculators' losses. Alternatively, the Fed and speculators take positions in the same direction, and the Fed profits reported here imply speculator profits. The interpretation in this case is that the Fed supplements stabilizing private speculation that is occasionally insufficient in volume to stabilize the market; profits arise from offsetting destabilizing shocks from the private sector or other governments. [26] Sweeney (1996b) reports that technical analysis offers

[26] Conceptually, the profits might arise from destabilizing-but-profitable currency purchases and sales by both the Fed and speculators. There has been no empirical work that bears on this view.

risk-adjusted profits for private speculators, but that the implied private trades are essentially uncorrelated with Fed intervention. Thus, it is not possible to explain Fed or speculator profits as arising at the expense of the other, nor can the actors' profits be explained as arising from stabilizing the same exchange-market shocks. LeBaron (1996) argues that technical analysis allows speculators to make profits and these profits are largely associated with days the Fed intervenes, with the speculator taking positions counter to the Fed's. This is a possible explanation for speculator profits but does not explain the Fed profits estimated here. Clearly, much remains to be done to explain Fed risk-adjusted intervention profits.

Acknowledgements

For helpful comments, thanks are due to the editor, Giorgio Szegö, and in particular to Boo Sjöö. Thanks are also due to Richard Baillie, Hali Edison, Mats-Ola Forsman, Lorenzo Giorgianni, Dale Henderson, Alex Humer, Michael Hutchison, Michael Leahy, Christine P. Ries, Clas Wihlborg, Thomas D. Willett and Othmar Winckler. The paper benefited from comments by participants in the Claremont Seminar in Money and Finance, the workshop series of the Board of Governors of the Federal Reserve System, the seminar series at the Gothenburg School of Economics, Lund University and the Institute of Finance at the Copenhagen Business School. Ma Jun and Feng Yuanshi were research assistants on this project. The Board of Governors of the Federal Reserve System kindly provided the intervention data. Georgetown University summer and sabbatical grants and McDonough School of Business summer grants supported part of this project; the Capital Markets Research Center at Georgetown University provided summer research assistance. Part of the work on this paper was done at the Gothenburg School of Economics, Sweden.

References

Baillie, R.T., Bollerslev, T., 1989. Common Stochastic Trends in a System of Exchange Rates. Journal of Finance 44, 167–194.

Baillie, R.T., Bollerslev, T., 1994. Cointegration, fractional cointegration and exchange rate dynamics. Journal of Finance 49, 737–745.

Baillie, R.T., Osterberg, W.P., forthcoming. Why Do Central Banks Intervene. Journal of International Money and Finance.

Bank of England, 1983. Intervention, stabilization and profits. Quarterly Bulletin 23, 384–391.

Bannerjee, A., Dolado, J., Galbraith, J.W., Hendry, D., 1993. Cointegration error-correction and the econometric analysis of non-stationary data. Oxford University Press, Oxford.

Baumol, W., 1957. Speculation profitability, and stability. Review of Economics and Statistics 39, 263–271.

Brown, S., Warner, J., 1980. Measuring security price performance. Journal of Financial Economics 8, 205–258.

Brown, S., Warner, J., 1985. Using daily stock returns: The case of event studies. Journal of Financial Economics 14, 3–31.

Corrado, C.J., Taylor, D., 1986. The cost of a central bank leaning against a random walk. Journal of International Money and Finance 5, 303–314.

Dominguez, K.M., 1993. Does central bank intervention influence the volatility of foreign exchange rates? Working paper, Harvard University, Cambridge, MA.

Dominguez, K.M., 1997. Central bank intervention and exchange rate volatility. Working paper, Harvard University, Cambridge, MA.

Dominguez, K.M., Frankel, J.A., 1993a. Does Foreign Exchange Intervention Work. Institute for International Economics, Washington, DC.

Dominguez, K.M., Frankel, J.A., 1993b. Does foreign-exchange intervention matter? The portfolio effect, American Economic Review 83, 1356–1369.

Edison, H.J., 1993. The effectiveness of central-bank intervention: A survey of the literature after 1982. Special Papers in International Economics International Finance Section. Department of Economics, Princeton University, Princeton, NJ.

Engel, C., Hamilton, J.D., 1990. Long swings in the dollar: Are they in the data and do markets know it? American Economic Review 80, 689–713.

Fama, E.F., Blume, M., 1966. Filter rules and stock-market trading. Journal of Business 39, 226–241.

Fatum, R., Hutchison, M., 1999. Is intervention a signal of future monetary policy? Evidence from the federal funds futures market. Journal of Money, Credit and Banking 31, 54–69.

Fase, M.M.G., Huijser, A.P., 1989. The profitability of official foreign exchange intervention: A case study for the Netherlands 1974–1989. Research Memorandum WO and E nr 8821, De Nederlandsche Bank, Amsterdam.

Friedman, M., 1953. The Case for Flexible Exchange Rates, Essays in Positive Economics, University of Chicago Press, Chicago.

Hart, O.D., Kreps, D.M., 1986. Price destabilizing speculation. Journal of Political Economy 94, 927–952.

Johansen, S., 1995. The role of ancillarity in inference for non-stationary variables. Economic Journal 105, 302–320.

Johnson, H.G., 1976. Destabilizing speculation: A general equilibrium approach. Journal of Political Economy 84, 101–108.

Kaminsky, G., Lewis, K.K., 1996. Does foreign exchange intervention signal future monetary policy? Journal of Monetary Economics 37, 285–312.

Karafiath, I., Spencer, D., 1991. Statistical inference in multiperiod event studies. Review of Quantitative Finance and Accounting, pp. 353–371.

Kemp, M.C., 1963. Speculation, profitability, and price stability. The Review of Economics and Statistics, 185–189.

Leahy, M., 1989. The profitability of US intervention. International Finance Discussion Paper No. 343, Board of Governors of the Federal Reserve System, Washington, DC.

Leahy, M., 1995. The profitability of US intervention in the foreign-exchange markets. Journal of International Money and Finance 14, 823–844.

Lewis, K., 1995. Are foreign exchange intervention and monetary policy related, and does it really matter. Journal of Business 68, 185–214.

LeBaron, B., 1996. Technical Trading Rule Profitability and Foreign Exchange Intervention. Working Paper, University of Wisconsin, Madison, WI.

Loopesko, B., 1984. Relationships among exchange rates, intervention, and interest rates: An empirical investigation. Journal of International Money and Finance 3, 257–277.

Mankiw, N.G., Shapiro, M., 1986. Do we reject too often? Small sample properties of tests of rational expectations models. Economics Letters 20, 139–145.

Mikkelson, W.H., Partch, M.M., 1988. Withdrawn securities offerings. Journal of Financial and Quantitative Analysis 23, 119–133.

Praetz, P., 1976. Rates of return on filter tests. Journal of Finance 31, 71–75.

Praetz, P., 1979. A general test of a filter effect. Journal of Financial and Quantitative Analysis 14, 385–394.

Saikkonen, P., 1991. Asymptotic efficient estimation of cointegrating regression. Economic Theory 7, 1–21.

Salinger, M., 1992. Standard errors in event studies. Journal of Financial and Quantitative Analysis 27, 39–53.

Sjöö, B., Sweeney, R.J., 1996. Foreign exchange intervention: New methods and results on the profitability of central bank intervention. Working paper, Gothenburg School of Economics, Gothenburg, Sweden.

Sjöö, B., Sweeney, R.J., 1998. The foreign-exchange costs of central bank intervention: Evidence from Sweden. Working paper, Gothenburg School of Economics, Gothenburg, Sweden.

Sjöö, B., Sweeney, R.J., 1999a.Testing the Efficient Markets Hypothesis with An Integrated Regressor. Working paper, Gothenburg School of Economics, Gothenburg, Sweden.

Sjöö, B., Sweeney, R.J., 1999b. Time-varying foreign-exchange risk and central bank intervention: Estimating profits from intervention and speculation. Working paper, Gothenburg School of Economics, Gothenburg, Sweden.

Spencer, P.D., 1985. Official intervention in the foreign exchange market. Journal of Political Economy 93, 1019–1024.

Spencer, P.D., 1989. How to make the central bank look good: A reply. Journal of Political Economy 97, 233–235.

Surajaras, P., Sweeney, R.J., 1992. Profit Making Speculation in Foreign Exchange Markets Westview Press, Boulder, CO.

Sweeney, R.J., 1986. Beating the foreign exchange market. Journal of Finance 41, 163–182.

Sweeney, R.J., 1991. Levels of significance in event studies. Review of Quantitative Finance and Accounting 1, 373–382.

Sweeney, R.J., 1996a. Does the foreign-exchange market beat the Fed? Working paper, Georgetown School of Business, Washington, DC.

Sweeney, R.J., 1996b. Do foreign exchange speculators beat the Fed? Working Paper, Georgetown School of Business, Washington, DC.

Sweeney, R.J., 1997. Do central banks lose on foreign-exchange intervention? A review article. Journal of Banking and Finance 21, 1667–1684.

Sweeney, R.J., 1999a. Does the Fed move the foreign-exchange market? Working paper, Georgetown School of Business, Georgetown University, Washington, DC.

Sweeney, R.J., 1999b. More results on Fed profits from foreign-exchange intervention. Working paper, Georgetown School of Business, Georgetown University, Washington, DC.

Szpiro, G.G., 1994. Exchange rate speculation and chaos-inducing intervention. Journal of Economic Behavior and Organization 24, 363–368.

Taylor, D., 1982a. Official intervention in the foreign exchange market, or bet against the central bank. Journal of Political Economy 90, 356–368.

Taylor, D., 1982b. The mismanaged float: Official intervention by the industrialized countries, In Connolly, M.B. (Ed.), The International Monetary System: Choices for the Future, Praeger, New York, pp. 49–84.

Taylor, D., 1989. How to make the central bank look good. Journal of Political Economy 97, 226–232.

Weber, A., 1993. International policy coordination and the future of EMU: A German perspective. Working paper, University of Siegen, Siegen, Germany.

[12]

The Economic Journal, **109** (*October*), 662–676. © Royal Economic Society 1999. Published by Blackwell Publishers, 108 Cowley Road, Oxford OX4 1JF, UK and 350 Main Street, Malden, MA 02148, USA.

EXCHANGE RATE EFFECTS OF CENTRAL BANK INTERVENTIONS: AN ANALYSIS OF TRANSACTION PRICES*

Andreas M. Fischer and Mathias Zurlinden

The impact of sterilised interventions by the Swiss National Bank on the Swiss franc/U.S. dollar exchange rate is examined for the 1986–94 period. The paper extends results from earlier studies by using the actual prices of interventions. Based on the fact that all Swiss National Bank interventions are announced, our test exploits the informational differences between interventions and customer transactions. A key finding is that only initial interventions matter; customer transactions and subsequent interventions have no influence.

When the Bretton Woods system of fixed exchange rates broke up in the early 1970s, central banks continued to intervene on the foreign exchange market. In the meantime, a substantial literature has emerged that focuses on the effectiveness of official interventions. This literature has been summarised by Edison (1993) and Almekinders (1995, chapter 3). Its central policy issue is whether sterilised interventions, defined as interventions that leave the monetary base unchanged, can have a significant influence on exchange rate behaviour.

Macroeconomic theory proposes various channels for interventions to operate through. But the empirical evidence accumulated over the years is less encouraging. It suggests that there is no permanent effect of (sterilised) interventions on the exchange rate. More surprisingly perhaps, even short-term effects are hard to pin down. The evidence is weak and sample dependent at best. In most cases, coefficients are either insignificant or have the wrong sign; see Almekinders (1995, chapter 6), Baillie and Humpage (1992), Dominguez (1998), Dominguez and Frankel (1993), Klein and Rosengren (1991), Lindberg (1994), and Osterberg and Wetmore Humes (1995).

During the last decade, the bulk of the empirical research has concentrated on the analysis of daily or weekly data. This line of research, which adopts the view that exchange rate markets are highly efficient, was stimulated by the decision of the Federal Reserve Board and the Deutsche Bundesbank to make their daily intervention data available to outside researchers. To rationalise the gap between the fragile empirical evidence and the manifest interest paid by the media and other observers to interventions, various explanations have been offered. In this paper, we stress two measurement problems.

First, there is the problem of properly defining the exchange rate change in the regression analysis. Since intervention exchange rates are not available, the

* The authors are indebted to Philippe Bacchetta and Charles Goodhart for helpful conversations and seminar participants at the Austrian National Bank, the University of Bern, the 1997 EEA meeting, and the 1998 Konstanz Seminar for useful criticism of a previous draft. Two anonymous referees provided helpful suggestions.

timing of the intervention usually falls inside the interval of the exchange rate change, leading to a simultaneity problem and questionable interpretations of the results. In particular, it is possible that the estimated intervention coefficient is downward biased due to an intervention policy of leaning against the wind. The second problem stems from the observation that numerous Bundesbank and Federal Reserve interventions were conducted secretly and therefore were unknown to the market. This is unsatisfactory for empirical research, if interventions are thought to work through an information channel. The remedy used in most studies is to comb the financial press to create a new series based on reported interventions. Osterberg and Wetmore Humes (1995) have pointed out, however, that media reports on interventions are often vague and that the constructed series may differ depending on the source and the selection criteria.

This paper circumvents both problems by using a new data set of foreign exchange transactions of the Swiss National Bank (SNB). The set includes all transactions the SNB carried out on the Swiss franc/U.S. dollar market between 1986 and 1994. It has several attractive features. First, and most important, the data go down to the micro level where every SNB transaction is observed with respect to its amount, price, and time of day. This allows us to create an improved measure of the exchange rate change associated with interventions. Second, all SNB interventions during the 1986–94 period were announced to the market to achieve maximum visibility. This eliminates the necessity to distinguish between actual and reported interventions. We can work instead with two clearly distinguishable groups of SNB operations on the foreign exchange market: interventions and other transactions (referred to as customer transactions).

A drawback of the SNB data is that transactions occur at irregular intervals forcing us to work with irregularly spaced time series. More importantly, we do not know the bid-ask spreads that correspond to the observed SNB transactions. This is irrelevant as long as the spread is constant over the sample period. It is well known, however, that the spread fluctuates widely between tranquil and turbulent periods (often associated with interventions). We therefore refrain from combining our data with the common daily exchange rate series available from various sources. Continuous-time data such as tick-by-tick market quotes assembled by Olsen and Associates would be helpful. However, such data are not available to us (due to cost reasons).

The data used in this paper allow us to look at intra-day effects of interventions. Moreover, since all SNB interventions were made public, we can exploit the informational differences between interventions and SNB customer transactions. The basic idea is that the two operations by differing in motive entail different information. We suspect that interventions reveal the central bank's discontent with exchange rate conditions and may signal news about future monetary policy, whereas customer transactions probably do not. If the market perceives them in this manner, then interventions unlike customer transactions should affect market expectations and thereby the exchange rate.

The paper is organised as follows. The next section discusses SNB intervention policy and presents descriptive statistics on interventions, customer transactions, exchange rates, and time intervals. The second section outlines the empirical model for irregularly spaced time series data. The estimation results of the model and of various extensions thereof are given in the third section. The final section contains some concluding remarks.

1. SNB Interventions and Customer Transactions

Institutional Issues

The interventions in this study are SNB spot transactions in the Swiss franc/U.S. dollar spot market during the period 1986–94. November 1986 marks the resumption of interventions by the SNB after a three-year break. All interventions considered are sterilised; i.e., the SNB did not allow the interventions to affect the monetary base. In addition, they are co-ordinated in the sense that the Bundesbank or the Federal Reserve intervened on the same day and in the same direction as the SNB. There were only three days when the SNB intervened alone in the market. These interventions are excluded from the sample, because the SNB did not sterilise the effect on liquidity entirely.[1] Also excluded are interventions involving the Japanese yen or the German mark, which were rare during the period.

The SNB intervened to affect the trend of the exchange rate or to counteract market disturbances. Solidarity with other central banks may also have been an important motive since virtually all interventions were co-ordinated. This does not imply that the SNB always followed the lead of key central banks. The Federal Reserve and the Bundesbank intervened more frequently than the SNB during the sample period.

The other group of SNB transactions in the Swiss franc/U.S. dollar spot market are purchases of U.S. dollars triggered by the Swiss government's request for foreign currency. If the government needs U.S. dollars, the SNB will supply the currency by reducing its dollar holdings. If the government requires other foreign currencies, the SNB usually buys these currencies with U.S. dollars in the market. The government's currency requests thus result in a steady dollar outflow. In turn, the SNB compensates this outflow by repurchasing U.S. dollars against Swiss francs either directly from commercial banks or through the BIS. The latter channel is sometimes used to avoid potential contradictions in the direction of dollar repurchases and interventions.[2] Throughout the remainder of the paper, we refer to the dollar repurchases by the SNB from commercial banks as customer transactions.[3]

[1] We do not have (matching) intra-daily observations of short-term interest rates to control for liquidity effects. The dates of the excluded Swiss franc/U.S. dollar interventions are December 27, 1989, March 6 and 11, 1992.

[2] All transactions with the BIS are excluded from our sample.

[3] Our usage of the term customer transactions is somewhat unconventional since the actual customer transaction is the purchase of (other) foreign currencies for dollars on behalf of the government. Only transactions in the Swiss franc/U.S. dollar market are considered in this paper, however, This allows us to define customer transactions as the subsequent repurchase of dollars for Swiss francs.

The interventions considered and customer transactions cover all spot transactions conducted by the SNB in the Swiss franc/U.S. dollar market (with the few exceptions mentioned above). All operations are based on market exchange rates since the SNB does not act as a market-maker. The SNB informs her counterparties that the transaction is an intervention straight after the deal is concluded. According to SNB officials, the intervention announcement spreads swiftly across the market and is picked up by news agencies. It is safe to assume that the market encounters no difficulties in distinguishing interventions from customer transactions.

Data and Their Properties

The data on interventions and customer transactions are compiled from transaction slips filled out by the SNB dealer. These slips provide information on the transacted amount, the price, and the time when the slip was filled out. We assume that this is done without delay and that the reported time coincides with the time of the executed transaction. The slips indicate that numerous transactions were conducted within the same minute. The interventions and customer transactions in question are aggregated separately and weighted average exchange rates are calculated.

Table 1 provides descriptive statistics on interventions, customer transactions, exchange rate changes, and time intervals. All amounts for interventions and customer transactions are given in millions of dollars. The respective variables are INT_{t_i} and CT_{t_i}, where i is the ith transaction on day t.

The figures reveal that the SNB intervened on 87 days during the period 1986–94. The total number of interventions, INT_{t_i}, is 362, implying that the SNB averaged more than four interventions per day.[4] Interventions went in both directions; i.e., the SNB traded U.S. dollars for Swiss francs and Swiss francs for U.S. dollars. Overall, there were more dollar sales. This is reflected in the negative mean (−4.0 million dollars) and the large number of dollar sales (208). Customer transactions, CT_{t_i}, were approximately as frequent as interventions (367 versus 362), though they were less concentrated on particular days. As a result, there are more days with customer transactions than with interventions (226 versus 87) and the average amount of customer transactions (21.5 million dollars) is larger.[5]

The exchange rate changes, ΔS_{t_i}, are defined as the natural log difference between exchange rates of two consecutive interventions or customer transactions of the same day (multiplied by 100). The statistics in Table 1 indicate that an intervention involving the purchase of dollars by the SNB was usually followed by a strengthening of the U.S. dollar. Similarly, the U.S. dollar weakened, when the SNB was selling dollars. Customer transactions do not need to be differentiated between sales and purchases, because all transactions

[4] The number of interventions before interventions of the same minute are aggregated is 432.

[5] There were 14 days when the SNB carried out interventions and customer transactions on the same day. In these cases, the interventions involved U.S. dollar purchases by the SNB.

are purchases. The evidence suggests that the dollar weakened after the SNB bought U.S. dollars to rebalance previous dollar outflows. It is tempting to associate the weakening of the dollar with the dollar outflow, i.e. the sale of dollars for foreign currencies that precedes the dollar repurchase captured by our definition of customer transactions. This conjecture is rather unconvincing, however, because the dollar outflow is not compensated immediately in most cases.[6]

The time interval between consecutive interventions or customer transactions is denoted by Δt_i. According to the figures in Table 1, the average time interval between interventions is 0.4 hours, while for customer transactions the rhythm is much slower (1.6 hours). The corresponding figures for the median time interval are 0.03 hours and 0.8 hours, implying that interventions are bunched together.

Information on the intra-daily pattern of interventions and customer transactions is provided by Fig. 1. The graph exhibits the number of transactions by the hour from 07:00 to 18:00 (Zurich local time). Interventions rise during the morning hours, dip around midday and peak in the afternoon. The peak in the afternoon may reflect the fact that Zurich is six hours ahead of New York so that co-ordinated interventions with the Federal Reserve usually start after 15:00.[7] Customer transactions have a similar pattern as interventions, but peak during the morning hours.

Table 1
Descriptive Statistics 1986–94

	mean	median	std	min	max	NOB
Interventions						
INT_{t_i}	−4.0	−5.0	15.2	−50.0	35.0	362
$INT_{t_i} > 0$	11.0	10.0	6.3	5.0	35.0	154
$INT_{t_i} < 0$	−15.1	−10.0	8.9	−5.0	−50.0	208
ΔS_{t_i}	−0.0046	0	0.0661	−0.4553	0.2055	266
ΔS_{t_i} if $INT_{t_i} > 0$	0.0083	0	0.0631	0.4105	0.2055	123
ΔS_{t_i} if $INT_{t_i} < 0$	−0.157	−0.0040	0.0669	−0.4553	0.1504	143
Δ_{t_i}	0.37	0.03	1.10	0.02	6.27	266
Customer Transactions						
CT_{t_i}	21.5	10.0	40.2	0.7	500.0	367
ΔS_{t_i}	−0.0105	−0.0034	0.767	−0.2989	−0.2728	138
Δt_i	1.62	0.80	1.89	0.02	7.12	138

Notes: Interventions, *INT*, and customer transactions, *CT*, are in millions of US dollars. $INT > 0$ means a dollar purchase by the SNB. Time duration, Δt, is in hours. *S* is defined as Swiss francs per U.S. dollar. The changes in the exchange rates, ΔS, are log-changes multiplied by 100. *NOB* denotes the number of observations.

[6] Daily data suggest that the SNB purchased foreign currencies (with U.S. dollars) on 68% of the working days between 1986 and 1994, but repurchased U.S. dollars (with Swiss francs) on 18% of the working days.

[7] The time difference between New York and Zurich is not constant due to different regimes of Daylight Savings Time (DST). In the United States, DST begins at 2 a.m. on the first Sunday in April and ends at 2 a.m. on the last Sunday in October. In Switzerland DST begins at 2 a.m. on the last Sunday in March; before 1996 it ended at 3 a.m. on the last Sunday in September. As a result, for some observations the time difference is 5 or 7 hours instead of 6 hours.

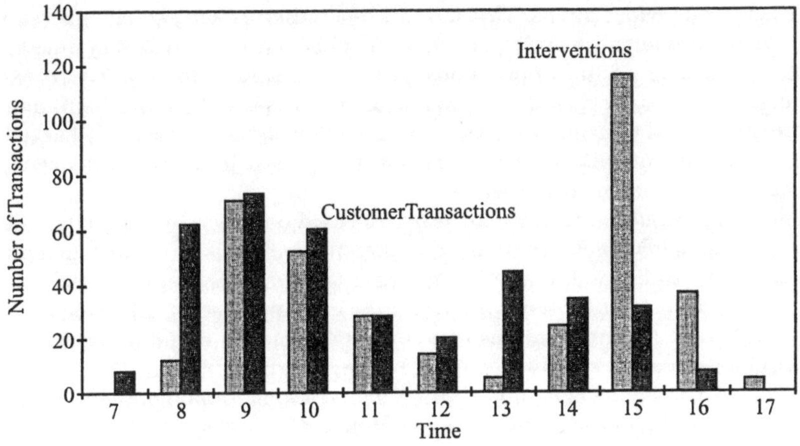

Fig. 1. *Number of Interventions and Customer Transactions 07:00 to 18:00 (1986–94)*

The dual humped patterns reveal a similar picture as the trading volumes in the foreign exchange market documented by Müller *et al.* (1990). This suggests that the SNB does not try to influence the market when trading is thin.[8] Taking into account that all interventions are announced, we may conclude that Swiss monetary authorities do not build on 'chartists' to affect exchange rates.[9]

2. The Empirical Model

Early studies of intervention effects were based on portfolio models. In these models domestic and foreign bonds are assumed to be imperfect substitutes so that sterilised interventions by changing the relative supply of the two assets may affect the expected returns and the exchange rate. Because the portfolio balance channel requires data of the relative asset supplies, these studies are usually based on monthly or quarterly data. The evidence as summarised by Edison (1993) does not lend much empirical support for the portfolio channel.

An alternative channel, which may operate even in the absence of imperfect substitutability between domestic and foreign assets, is the signalling channel. The prerequisite is that interventions cause market participants to alter their

[8] In contrast, Goodhart and Hesse (1993), based on Reuter's announcements of interventions during the period 4/4/1989–26/6/1989, find that central banks prefer to intervene in relatively thin markets.

[9] Huang (1997) develops a model where interventions affect exchange rates through a noise-trading channel. The basic idea is that interventions induce noise traders to buy or sell a currency in a way that the otherwise temporary effect of sterilised interventions is prolonged. Huang argues for secret interventions in relatively thin markets to achieve a maximum effect.

exchange rate expectations. This may arise because market participants reassess their views about future monetary or fiscal policy, or because they change their assessment of the implications these policies have for the future exchange rate. Empirical studies by Kaminsky and Lewis (1996) and Klein and Rosengren (1991) attempt to detect whether interventions are actually backed up by subsequent shifts in monetary policy, but find no direct evidence in favour of the signalling hypothesis.

Most papers published in recent years are based on a loose interpretation of the signalling channel. They assume that interventions influence market expectations and examine whether the data are consistent with this assumption. In particular, a time series model for the exchange rate is built using daily or weekly data for interventions and sometimes interest rate differentials to control for monetary conditions. An interesting feature of several studies is the distinction between actual and reported interventions. Dominguez and Frankel (1993), and Osterberg and Wetmore Humes (1995) regress the change in the exchange rate on reported interventions and unreported interventions. This allows them to test the hypothesis that only reported interventions matter under the signalling hypothesis.[10]

This paper takes a similar approach in that it attempts to exploit informational differences between various central bank operations. Since all SNB interventions are announced and none are secret, we do not have to differentiate between reported and unreported interventions. Instead, we can design a test that reflects the novel features of the SNB data set and regress the change in the transaction exchange rate on interventions and customer transactions.

A problem in working with transaction exchange rates are the irregular time intervals between observations. As revealed in Table 1, Δt_i ranges between 0.02 and 7.12 hours and notable differences in the first two moments arise between interventions and customer transactions. However, irregular time intervals need not create difficulties for regression analysis as long as the variables are scaled properly and/or the parameters are allowed to vary in response to differing time intervals. The analysis below works with exchange rate returns scaled by the corresponding time interval, $\Delta s_{t_i} = \Delta S_{t_i}/\Delta t_i = 100(lnS_{t_i} - lnS_{t_{i-1}})/(t_i - t_{i-1})$, where ΔS_{t_i} is the natural log change of the exchange rate at time t_i, and Δt_i is the time interval between two adjacent observations. The transformation of ΔS_{t_i} is motivated by the scaling law proposed by Müller *et al.* (1990), which relates the mean absolute value of the price change to the size of the time interval.[11]

The equation for the irregular time series model is written as

$$\Delta s_{t_i} = \Phi_0(\cdot) + \Phi_1(\cdot)\, INT\_D_{t_{i-1}} + \Phi_2(\cdot)\, CT\_D_{t_{i-1}} + \epsilon_{t_i}, \qquad (1)$$

[10] Further references on the difference between actual and reported interventions include Klein (1993) Klein and Rosenberg (1991) and Osterberg and Wetmore Humes (1993).

[11] This is more formally defined as $|\Delta \overline{S}| = c\Delta t_i$, where the term on the left hand side defines the absolute average over the whole sample period and Δt_i is the time interval. Müller *et al.* (1990) allow for a drift exponent, which we do not consider. Empirically, we find the correlation between $|\Delta S_{t_i}|$ and Δ_{t_i} to be positive and highly significant.

where the variables $INT\_D_{t_i}$ and $CT\_D_{t_i}$ are dummy variables for interventions and customer transactions defined as +1 when dollars are purchased and −1 when dollars are sold by the SNB. The use of dummy variables is motivated by the observation that the SNB usually splits her interventions among serveral commercial banks and does not provide information on the total intervention amount to the market.

The parameters of interest are the response functions $\Phi_1(\cdot)$ and $\Phi_2(\cdot)$ for interventions and customer transactions. Following the irregular-spaced model by Pai and Polasek (1995), two parameterisations are used: constant and reciprocal response functions. These can be written as

$$\Phi_j(\Delta t_i) = \alpha_{aj},$$

$$\Phi_j(\Delta t_i) = \alpha_{aj} + \alpha_{bj}/\Delta t_i,$$

$$\text{for } j = 0, 1, 2. \qquad (2)$$

The constant response function is the standard model for equally spaced time series. It assumes that the coefficient capturing the intervention response is time invariant. More flexibility is provided by the reciprocal function, which is composed of a constant component, α_{aj}, and a time dependent component, $\alpha_{bj}/\Delta t_i$.[12] Because the dependent variable, $\Delta s_{t_i} \equiv \Delta S_{t_i}/\Delta t_i$, is scaled, α_{aj} may be considered as measuring a growth effect and α_{bj} a level effect. The reciprocal function can generate different response patterns depending on the size of Δt_i and the sign on the coefficients α_{aj} and α_{bj}. When α_{aj} and α_{bj} are signed differently, the response function $\Phi_j(\Delta t_i)$ may change sign over time. Otherwise, when α_{aj} and α_{bj} have the same sign, $\Phi_j(\Delta t_i)$ is either a monotone increasing or decreasing function. Finally, when Δt_i is large, the time-varying component, $\alpha_{bj}/\Delta t_i$, is close to zero, and the reciprocal function behaves similarly to the constant response function.

Equation (1) represents our basic model to examine the effectiveness of interventions. If the interventions affect the exchange rate in accordance with the objectives stated in Section 1, we expect $\Phi_1(\cdot) > 0$ and $\Phi_2(\cdot) = 0$.[13] The estimation poses the problem that the simultaneous nature of exchange rate changes and interventions may bias the coefficients. This is a common problem in the literature, especially in studies that utilise high-frequency data. Nonetheless, it may be less severe here than in previous studies, because transaction prices allow us to avoid the overlap between the exchange rate change and the timing of the intervention. We also face the problem that intra-daily intervention data from other central banks are not available. This problem of omitted variables is mitigated somewhat by the fact that central banks always seem to have intervened in the same direction. In addition, the

[12] Pai and Polasek (1995) consider also an exponential response function, where $\alpha_{bj}/\Delta t_i$ is replaced by $\alpha_{bj}e^{-\Delta t_i}$ in (2).

[13] In the case of the reciprocal response function when α_{aj} and α_{bj} are of opposite sign, the restriction $\Phi_1(\cdot) > 0$ is fulfilled only for certain time intervals: $\Delta t_i < \alpha_{bj}/\alpha_{aj}$ if $\alpha_{aj} < \alpha_{bj}$, or $\Delta t_i > \alpha_{bj}/\alpha_{aj}$ if $\alpha_{aj} > \alpha_{bj}$.

Swiss National Bank presumably was the only central bank intervening in the Swiss franc/U.S. dollar market.

3. Empirical Results

The empirical investigation is based on the intra-daily data set discussed in Section I. The sample includes only those days when the SNB conducted interventions and/or customer transactions. The results presented are thus conditional on the observation that an intervention or a customer transaction occurred that day. The construction of our data set also implies that the exchange rate reaction of the last intervention or the last customer transaction of each day is not considered.[14]

The date November 1, 1988 is used as a breakpoint to test for sample dependency. We acknowledge some arbitrariness in the choice of this date. A more obvious candidate would be the Louvre meeting on 21–2 February 1987 when the G-7 countries agreed to stabilise dollar exchange rates. This breakpoint is dismissed on the grounds that the SNB had intervened only twice before this date. There is also no commonly accepted terminal date of the Louvre accord and proposals on this issue vary widely in the literature.[15] As a result, the breakpoint is set to divide the sample observations roughly in half.[16]

Preliminary tests showed that ARCH effects do not arise in our data set of exchange rate changes. The GARCH framework widely used in recent intervention studies based on daily or weekly data is thus not employed. The regressions are carried out with OLS. Robust standard errors are calculated with the Newey-West method allowing for serial correlation when necessary.

Table 2 reports the response of Δs_{t_i} to interventions and customer transactions. In the constant response function model, the intervention coefficient (α_1) is statistically significant at conventional levels for the full sample and the second sub-period. The positive sign of the coefficient suggests that the exchange rate change associated with interventions is consistent with the central bank's objectives. In the reciprocal response function model, we find that the positive time-varying coefficient for interventions is significant in the full sample. The coefficient for the customer transactions, on the other hand, is insignificant for all samples and both specifications.[17]

[14] The number of valid observations (418) is slightly higher than the total given for ΔS_{t_i} in Table 1 ($404 = 138 + 266$), because the dependent variables Δs_{t_i} in the empirical section is calculated as the exchange rate change between two adjoining transactions irrespective of whether it is an intervention or a customer transaction.

[15] Based on the frequency of interventions, Humpage (1997) suggests that the Louvre period ended in April 1990. Baillie and Humpage (1992), in turn, find evidence for a mark/dollar target zone before October 1988, but not thereafter.

[16] The exact midpoint falls on a lengthy intervention sequence

[17] We experimented with a number of alternative breakpoints. The results for the constant response function indicate that the (positive) intervention coefficient is statistically significant at the 5% level for the first sub-samples ending in March 1989 or later. For the second sub-sample, the intervention coefficient is significant whatever the starting date.

Table 2

Basic Exchange Rate Equation

Constant Response Function	$\Delta s_{t_i} = \alpha_0 + \alpha_1 INT\_D_{t_{i-1}} + \alpha_2 CT\_D_{t_{i-1}} + \varepsilon_{t_i}$		
	I	II	III
α_0	0.0599	0.0887	0.4380
	(0.902)	(1.107)	(1.558)
α_1	0.2276***	0.0773	0.6552**
	(3.438)	(0.965)	(2.341)
α_2	−0.0506	−0.1051	−0.4063
	(0.600)	(0.874)	(1.415)
$\overline{R}^2$	0.022	0.003	0.055
DW	2.30	2.12	2.48
NOBS	418	219	199
Reciprocal Response Function	$\Delta s_{t_i} = \alpha_0 + \alpha_1/\Delta t_{t_i} + (\alpha_2 + \alpha_3/\Delta t_{t_i}) INT\_D_{t_{i-1}} + (\alpha_4 + \alpha_5/\Delta_{t_i}) CT\_D_{t_{i-1}} + \varepsilon_{t_i}$		
α_0	−0.0749	−0.0860	−0.4210
	(0.931)	(0.602)	(0.810)
α_1	0.0048	0.0055	0.0303
	(1.159)	(1.560)	(1.051)
α_2	−0.0668	−0.0124	−0.4283
	(0.838)	(0.087)	(0.836)
α_3	0.0092**	0.0031	0.0364
	(2.210)	(0.905)	(1.271)
α_4	0.0656	0.1076	0.3710
	(0.798)	(0.614)	(0.701)
α_5	−0.0034	−0.0087	−0.0246
	(0.553)	(1.615)	(0.843)
H_0: $\alpha_2 = \alpha_3 = 0$	12.68***	1.39	6.07**
H_0: $\alpha_4 = \alpha_5 = 0$	0.64	1.82	1.07
$\overline{R}^2$	0.042	0.023	0.124
DW	2.27	2.08	2.31
NOBS	418	219	199

Notes: Absolute values of t-statistics in parentheses. Robust standard errors are calculated, allowing for heteroscedasticity and first-order serial correlation in samples I and III. Samples: I = full sample 1986:01–1994:12, II = first subsample 1986:01–1988:10, III = second subsample 1988:11–1994:12. Wald tests $\sim \chi^2(2)$ are used to test the restriction under H_0.

* p-value of hypothesis test < 0.10,

** p-value of hypothesis test < 0.05,

*** p-value of hypothesis test < 0.01.

Next, we consider the point estimates of the reciprocal response function which are of opposite sign. In the full sample, for example, they imply that an intervention has a positive effect on the exchange rate up to eight minutes and a negative effect thereafter. If the equation is evaluated at the median time interval between adjacent interventions (0.03 hours or 2 minutes according to Table 1), a positive effect in accordance with the results for the constant response function model is obtained. The coefficients of the reciprocal response function are not estimated with much precision, however. The standard error for the estimated break-even point of eight minutes after the intervention is 13 minutes.[18] This leads us to opt for a more parsimonious model and to present further results only for the constant response function model.

The first extension of our basic equation focuses on the effect of intervention concentration on the exchange rate. The SNB often executed several transactions simultaneously with various commercial banks. Thus, a natural question is whether the number of trading partners involved affects the results. One might expect that a widely dispersed intervention has a larger informational effect than an intervention carried out with a single bank. To examine this question, an index $DISP_{t_i}$ is constructed that gives the number of transactions executed within the same minute. The variables $DISP_{t_i} INT\_D_{t_i}$ and $DISP_{t_i} CT\_D_{t_i}$ are then included as additional variables in the regression.

Table 3 summarises the results for the effects of dispersion. The variables $DISP_{t_i} INT\_D_{t_i}$ and $DISP_{t_i} CT\_D_{t_i}$ are insignificant across all samples. The estimates for $INT\_D_{t_i}$ on the other hand remain significant in the full sample (10% level) and the second sub-sample (1% level) with point estimates close to those exhibited in Table 2. A Wald test cannot reject the null hypothesis that both intervention coefficients are zero. The results suggest that our measure of dispersion does not offer explanatory power beyond that already provided by

Table 3

Exchange Rate Equation with Dispersion Variable

$$\Delta s_{t_i} = \alpha_0 + \alpha_1 INT\_D_{t_{i-1}} + \alpha_2 DISP_{t_{i-1}} INT\_D_{t_{i-1}} + \alpha_3 CT\_D_{t_{i-1}} + \alpha_4 DISP_{t_{i-1}} CT\_D_{t_{i-1}} + \varepsilon_{t_i}$$

	I	II	III
α_0	0.0648	0.0768	0.4427
	(0.822)	(0.886)	(1.510)
α_1	0.2026*	0.1469	0.6337***
	(1.827)	(0.721)	(2.620)
α_2	0.0157	−0.0457	0.0138
	(0.201)	(0.371)	(0.153)
α_3	−0.0495	−0.1340	−0.3499
	(0.439)	(0.298)	(1.238)
α_4	−0.0054	0.0389	−0.0502
	(0.166)	(0.095)	(1.159)
H_0: $\alpha_1 = \alpha_2 = 0$	14.19***	0.68	6.93**
H_0: $\alpha_3 = \alpha_4 = 0$	0.50	0.36	2.31
$\bar{R}^2$	0.017	−0.006	0.045
DW	2.30	2.11	2.48
NOBS	418	219	199

Notes: See Table 2.

[18] The delta method was used for constructing the standard error for the non-linear function of the parameters.

the intervention dummies. This outcome is consistent with the view that the information content of an intervention is independent of the number of trading partners involved.[19] We have also examined the exchange rate effect of the intervention amount (aggregated by the minute), which is highly correlated with the number of trading partners. A regression with the intervention amount as an additional variable in the basic equation finds the intervention amount to be statistically insignificant (this result is not shown in Table 3).

To determine whether interventions are more successful during a certain hour of the day, a set of hourly dummy variables, $HOUR(j)_{t_i}$ for $j = (7, \ldots, 17)$, are created. These dummy variables represent the hours between 07:00 and 18:00 in which the interventions were executed. To test for hourly intervention and customer transaction effects, the hourly dummy variables are multiplied by the intervention and the customer transaction dummies, yielding $HOUR(j)_{t_i} INT\_D_{t_i}$ and $HOUR(j)_{t_i} CT\_D_{t_i}$.

Table 4 presents the regression results with hourly dummies. Because of the large number of dummy variables, the impact of interventions and customer transactions are estimated separately. The results show that the exchange rate response to interventions is significant for the second and third hour of the day, i.e., for the time between 09:00 and 11:00 and after 15:00. The positive signed coefficient implies that the Swiss franc depreciated as the SNB bought U.S. dollars. The largest intervention effect occurs between 15:00 and 16:00, i.e. the time when the Federal Reserve first enters the market.[20] The coefficient of 0.48 for α_{15} is more than two standard deviations above the average of all hourly intervention coefficients (0.08).[21] Point estimates for most of the other hours exhibit positively signed coefficients. A notable exception is the negative coefficient in the final hour; we do not know whether the dropping of the last transaction of each day influences this result. Finally, no statistically significant exchange rate response is detected for customer transactions (except for the weakly significant final-hour response in the second sub-sample).[22]

The significant exchange rate response to morning interventions is consistent with the notion that interventions influence the exchange rate through the impact of news. To test this more directly, we distinguish between initial and subsequent interventions. The dummy variable $FIRST_{t_i}$ takes the value +1 for those interventions or customer transactions that occur within three

[19] If the equation is evaluated at the mean dispersion, the overall intervention effects are close to those obtained for the basic equation in Table 2. The average number of banks involved in an intervention was 1.61 for the full sample, 1.38 for the first sub-sample, and 1.87 for the second sub-sample. The corresponding figures for customer transactions are 1.13, 10.5, and 1.22.

[20] The main results in Table 4 remain unchanged if the explanatory variables were adjusted for Daylight Savings Time keeping and time difference between New York and Zurich constant.

[21] More formally, we can regress the exchange rate changes on a constant, the variable $INT\_D_{t_i}$ and a full set of hourly intervention variables with the restriction that the coefficients of the hourly dummy variables add to zero (see Greene and Seaks, 1991).

[22] The results presented in Table 4 are somewhat sensitive to the scaling of the exchange rate by Δt_i. If the unscaled exchange rate change is regressed on the hourly interventions and the hourly customer transactions, the picture for interventions remains broadly the same, while some customer transaction dummies become statistically significant.

Table 4

Exchange Rate Equation with Hourly Dummies

$$\Delta s_{t_i} = \alpha_0 + \sum_{j=7}^{17} \alpha_j HOUR(j)_{t_{i-1}} X_{t_{i-1}} + \varepsilon_{t_i}$$

	$X_{t_i} = INT\_D_{t_i}$ Interventions				X_{t_i} $CT\_D_{t_i}$ Customer Transactions		
	I	II	III		I	II	III
α_0	0.0735	0.0503	0.2070	α_0	0.0437	0.1307*	−0.0522
	(1.391)	(0.789)	(1.557)		(0.634)	(1.908)	(0.413)
α_1				α_7	−0.0787	−0.1796	0.0730
					(1.019)	(0.437)	(0.577)
α_8	0.0040	0.0203	0.2070	α_8	−0.0199	−0.2335	0.1710
	(0.030)	(0.077)	(1.557)		(0.094)	(1.060)	(0.984)
α_9	0.0858	0.0941	0.1654	α_9	−0.0651	−0.1296	−0.0187
	(0.769)	(0.800)	(0.606)		(0.907)	(0.697)	(0.137)
α_{10}	0.1574**	−0.0533	0.4574***	α_{10}	−0.0441	−0.1807	0.1013
	(1.972)	(0.268)	(2.830)		(0.528)	(0.741)	(0.709)
α_{11}	0.1380*	0.2444	−0.1073	α_{11}	−0.0462	−0.1702	0.0744
	(1.656)	(1.121)	(0.616)		(0.624)	(0.504)	(0.555)
α_{12}	−0.0577	−0.0849	0.1778	α_{12}	−0.1145	−0.1138	−0.0713
	(0.666)	(0.275)	(0.686)		(1.076)	(0.241)	(0.391)
α_{13}	0.1526	0.1410		α_{13}	0.0315	−0.0250	0.0908
	(0.0)	(0.348)			(0.307)	(0.074)	(0.708)
α_{14}	0.0722	0.1217	0.0963	α_{14}	−0.0706	−0.0195	−0.2509
	(1.327)	(0.521)	(0.791)		(0.537)	(0.058)	(1.300)
α_{15}	0.4841***	0.2087	0.6773**	α_{15}	0.0975	−0.1497	0.3078*
	(2.727)	(1.153)	(2.558)		(0.695)	(0.4057)	(1.760)
α_{16}	0.4021*	0.1329	0.5258**				
	(1.799)	(0.325)	(2.149)				
α_{17}	−0.5599*		−0.4264				
	(1.756)		(1.248)				
$\bar{R}^2$	0.022	−0.024	0.027	$\bar{R}^2$	−0.021	−0.032	−0.044
DW	2.37	2.14	2.49	DW	2.24	2.10	2.30
NOBS	418	219	199	NOBS	418	219	199

Notes: See Table 2.

minutes after the first intervention or customer transaction of the day and 0 for the rest of the day.[23] Initial interventions and initial customer transactions represent 61% and 68% of their respective total.

Table 5 presents the results for initial versus subsequent transactions. The evidence suggests that only initial interventions matter and that the market digests this information within minutes. The estimated coefficients for initial interventions are positive and significant at the 10% level for the full sample

[23] The determination of the three minutes was initiated by a search process. The definition of initial interventions is the narrowest where a statistically significant exchange rate response to initial interventions can be found. This suggests that it may take a few minutes for the information to spread.

Table 5

Exchange Rate Equation with First Dummies

$$\Delta s_{t_i} = \alpha_0 + \alpha_1 FIRST_{t_{i-1}} INT\_D_{t_{i-1}} + \alpha_2 INT\_D_{t_{i-1}} + \alpha_3 FIRST_{t_{i-1}} CT\_D_{t_{i-1}} + \alpha_4 CT\_D_{t_{i-1}} + \varepsilon_{t_i}$$

	I	II	III
α_0	0.0947	0.0981	0.4589
	(1.228)	(1.188)	(1.614)
α_1	0.2850*	0.0706	0.4704**
	(1.929)	(0.509)	(1.978)
α_2	0.0568	0.0359	0.3365
	(0.746)	(0.314)	(1.405)
α_3	0.0275	0.0508	0.0531
	(0.356)	(0.232)	(0.622)
α_4	−0.1047	−0.1543	−0.4588
	(1.209)	(1.732)	(1.536)
H_0: $\alpha_1 = \alpha_2 = 0$	12.25***	0.76	6.39**
H_0: $\alpha_3 = \alpha_4 = 0$	1.49	0.60	2.43
$\bar{R}^2$	0.026	0.005	0.060
DW	2.32	2.13	2.50
NOBS	418	219	199

Notes: See Table 2.

and at the 5% level for the second sub-sample. Subsequent interventions and customer transactions are insignificant.

4. Concluding Remarks

This paper investigates the effectiveness of Swiss interventions under the assumption that interventions operate through a signalling or expectations channel. The data consist only of days when there was an intervention or a customer transaction. The results therefore reflect the effect of interventions on the exchange rate given that the SNB was in the market that day. The evidence for interventions suggests that initial SNB purchases (sales) of dollars are significantly associated with dollar appreciations (depreciations) against the Swiss franc. The paper finds no evidence that subsequent interventions or that customer transactions are related to exchange-rate movements. The analysis also offers evidence that the time of the day may have a significant bearing on the success of an intervention. The number of counterparties to a transaction, however, does not appear to matter.

The paper makes several contributions to the literature on foreign exchange intervention. The first is the recognition that intervention effects, while difficult to detect in weekly or even in daily data, can be observed with intra-daily data. On balance, the results are more encouraging than those of previous studies. Zurlinden (1996) found no significant intervention effects in daily and weekly Swiss data, and his point estimates of the intervention coefficient are negative. These results were typical for studies with daily or weekly data. The second contribution is to provide an alternative test for the effectiveness of central bank interventions, which exploits informational differences between interventions and customer transactions. Such a test is feasible for Swiss data, because the SNB does not intervene secretly. Both contributions go some way in solving measurement problems.

Swiss National Bank, University of Bern, and CEPR

Swiss National Bank

Data of receipt of first submission: September 1997
Data of receipt of final typescript: March 1999

References

Almekinders, Geert J. (1995). *Foreign Exchange Intervention: Theory and Evidence* Cheltenham: Edward Elgar.

Baillie, R. T. and Humpage, O. F. (1992). 'Post-Louvre intervention: did targets stabilize the dollar?' Federal Reserve Bank of Cleveland, Working Paper 9203.

Dominguez, K. M. (1998). 'Does central bank intervention increase the volatility of foreign exchange rates?' *Journal of International Money and Finance*, vol. 17, pp. 161–90.

Dominguez, K. M. and Frankel, J. A. (1993). 'Does foreign exchange intervention work?' Washington, D.C.: Institute for International Economics.

Edison, H. J. (1993). 'The effectiveness of central-bank intervention: a survey of the literature after 1982,' Special Papers in International Economics No. 18, Princeton University, New Jersey.

Goodhart, C. A. E. and Hesse, T. (1993). 'Central bank FOREX interventions assessed in continuous time,' *Journal of International Money and Finance*, vol. 12, pp. 368–89.

Greene, W. H. and Seaks, T. G. (1991). 'The restricted least squares estimator: a pedagogical note,' *Review of Economics and Statistics*, vol. 73, pp. 563–7.

Humpage, O. F. (1997). 'Recent U.S. interventions: is less more?' Federal Reserve Bank of Cleveland, *Economic Review*, vol. 33, pp. 2–10.

Huang, J. H. (1997). 'Intervention strategies and exchange rate volatility: a noise trading perspective,' *Journal of International Money and Finance*, vol. 16, pp. 779–93.

Kaminsky, G. and Lewis, K. K. (1996). 'Does foreign exchange intervention signal future monetary policy?' *Journal of Monetary Economics*, vol. 37, pp. 285–312.

Klein, M. W. (1993). 'The accuracy of reports of foreign intervention,' *Journal of International Money and Finance*, vol. 12, pp. 644–53.

Klein, M. W. and Rosengren, E. S. (1991). 'Foreign exchange intervention as a signal of monetary policy,' Federal Reserve Bank of Boston *New England Economic Review*, pp. 39–49.

Lindberg, H. (1994). 'The effects of sterilized interventions through the signalling channel: Sweden 1986–1990,' Sveriges Riksbank, Arbetsrapport No. 19.

Müller, U. A., Dacorogna, M. M., Olsen, R. B., Pictet, O. V., Schwarz, M. and Morgenegg, C. (1990). 'Statistical study of foreign exchange rates, empirical evidence of a price changing scaling law, and intraday analysis.' *Journal of Banking and Finance*, vol. 14, pp. 1189–208.

Osterberg, W. P. and Wetmore Humes, R. (1993). 'The incaccuracy of newspaper reports of U.S. foreign exchange intervention,' Federal Reserve Bank of Cleveland, *Economic Review*, vol. 29, pp. 25–33.

Osterberg, W. P. and Wetmore Humes, R. (1995). 'More on the differences between reported and actual U.S. central bank interventions,' Federal Reserve Bank of Cleveland, Working Paper 9501.

Pai, J. S. and W. Polasek, W. (1995). 'Irregularly spaced AR and ARCH (ISAR-ARCH) models,' paper presented at the First International Conference on High Frequency Data in Finance, Zurich, Switzerland, March 29–31, 1995.

Zurlinden, M. (1996). 'Devisenmarktinterventionen der Schweizerischen Nationalbank 1986–1994,' Schweizerische Nationalbank, *Geld, Währung und Konjunktur* vol. 14, pp. 163–87.

[13]

ELSEVIER

Journal of International Economics 59 (2003) 25–45

Journal of INTERNATIONAL ECONOMICS

www.elsevier.com/locate/econbase

The market microstructure of central bank intervention

Kathryn M.E. Dominguez*

University of Michigan, Gerald R. Ford School of Public Policy, Ann Arbor, MI 48109, USA

Received 2 September 1999; received in revised form 7 September 2001; accepted 31 August 2002

Abstract

How quickly do central bank intervention operations impact the foreign exchange market? And, do intra-daily market conditions influence the effectiveness of central bank interventions? This paper uses high-frequency intra-daily data to examine the relationship between the efficacy of intervention operations and the "state of the market" at the moment that the operation is made public. The results indicate that some traders typically know that the Fed is intervening at least 1 h prior to the public release of the information in newswire reports. Also, the evidence suggests that the timing of intervention operations matters—interventions that occur during heavy trading volume, that are closely timed to scheduled macro announcements, and that are coordinated with another central bank are the most likely to have large effects.

Keywords: Central bank intervention; Foreign exchange rates; Market micro structure

JEL classification: F31; G14; G15; E58

1. Introduction

How does information influence intra-daily exchange rate behavior? Standard models of exchange rate determination distinguish the types of information that should influence exchange rate movements, but there has been little focus on the way this information is assimilated by market participants. For example, in most

*Tel.: +1-734-764-9498; fax: +1-734-763-9181.

E-mail address: kathrynd@umich.edu (K.M.E. Dominguez).

0022-1996/02/$ – see front matter
PII: S0022-1996(02)00091-0

models of exchange rate determination an unanticipated (and exogenous) monetary contraction in the home country leads to an appreciation of the home currency relative to foreign currencies. Standard models have little to say about how market participants learn of the monetary contraction, or of how the state of the foreign exchange market might influence the immediate and longer-term reactions of individual foreign exchange traders to the news of such a contraction. One possible explanation for the inadequate empirical performance of standard exchange rate models is that they put so little emphasis on the market microstructure of the foreign exchange market.[1]

This paper focuses on one important source of information to the foreign exchange markets, the intervention operations of the G-3 central banks. Previous studies using daily and weekly foreign exchange rate data suggest that central bank intervention operations can influence both the level and variance of exchange rates,[2] but little is known about how exactly traders learn about these operations and whether intra-daily market conditions influence their effectiveness. This paper uses high-frequency intra-daily spot market data to examine the relationship between the efficacy of intervention operations and the "state of the market" at the moment that the operation is made public to traders. The results indicate that some traders know that the Fed is intervening at least 1 h prior to the public release of the information in newswire reports. Also, the evidence suggests that the timing of intervention operations matter—interventions that occur during heavy trading volume and that are closely timed to scheduled macro announcements are the most likely to have large effects. Finally, results indicate that interventions that are coordinated with another central bank have the largest price impact.

The data used in this study include all the days that the Fed intervened in the USD–DEM or USD–JPY markets over the period 1987 through 1995, allowing tests for systematic influences of interventions over a relatively long time series, though the nature of the data do not allow tests for the persistence of interventions' influence beyond the day.[3] Previous intra-daily studies of intervention have had to focus on much shorter time spans due to the relative unavailability of both intervention data and high-frequency exchange rate data.[4] This study is also able to control for the influence of other intra-daily news using time-stamped Reuters' newswire reports.

Section 2 of the paper presents stylized facts on the foreign exchange market,

---

[1] See, for example, Meese and Rogoff (1983) and Frankel and Rose (1995), and see Lyons (2001) for a thorough discussion of the role of market microstructure in international finance.

[2] See, for example, Dominguez (1992, 1998) and Dominguez and Frankel (1993a,b).

[3] Two additional Fed intervention operations have occurred since August 1995. On June 17, 1998 the Fed sold $833 million against the yen in cooperation with the BOJ and on September 22, 2000 the Fed purchased a total of 1.5 billion euros against the dollar in cooperation with the ECB, the BOJ, the Bank of Canada and the Bank of England.

[4] For example, Goodhart and Hesse (1993), Peiers (1997), Chang and Taylor (1998), Beattie and Fillion (1999), Fischer and Zurlinden (1999), Payne and Vitale (2000), and Neely (2002).

central bank interventions, and Reuters' news reports. Section 3 reviews the role of interventions in the market microstructure of foreign exchange markets. Section 4 examines empirically the influence of market microstructure on the efficacy of central bank intervention, and Section 5 is the conclusion.

2. Stylized facts

2.1. The foreign exchange market

The foreign exchange market is de-centralized and open 24 hours a day. Even though foreign exchange trading occurs at all hours, there appear to be three distinct geographical "markets" defined by daylight hours in Tokyo, London and New York. There is a small overlap between Asian and European trading, substantial overlap between European and American trading, and no overlap between American and Asian trading. It is during the overlap in European and American trading that volume is typically highest in the foreign exchange market.

The exchange rate data used in this paper are the Reuter's FXFX series tick-by-tick indicative quotes on Fed intervention days as well as a control sample of 25 days with no interventions.[5] The FXFX data identify a potential source of market heterogeneity by including in the data set the names and locations of quoting banks. A limitation of the FXFX data, however, is that because they are quotes and not transactions they do not provide volume information, so it is not possible to examine the joint dynamics of volume (or order flow) and price.[6] Another disadvantage of the data set is that, because it includes only intervention days, it is not possible to measure persistent effects of interventions.

2.2. Central bank intervention

In the United States, the New York Fed implements intervention operations, while the decision to intervene is made by the Treasury Department.[7] As with any other foreign exchange transaction, intervention trades are officially anonymous.

[5]The data are collected by Olsen and Associates (Research Institute for Applied Economics, Zurich Switzerland) using O&A proprietary real-time data collection software and are filtered as recommended by Dacorogna et al. (1993). The control dates were selected to provide a representative sample of non-intervention days over the period when the intervention operations take place. These data are used to test whether the volatility of exchange rates differs in periods when central banks are intervening as compared to periods of non-intervention.

[6]See Goodhart et al. (1996), Evans (1998, 1999) and Lyons (1995, 1996, 2001) for comparisons of the FXFX quote data and transaction data.

[7]Prior to 1992 the Fed conducted its foreign exchange transactions exclusively with commercial bank dealers, but in 1992 the Federal authorized relationships (for intervention purposes) with securities dealers (Federal Reserve Bank of New York, 1992).

However, most central banks have developed relationships with traders that allow them to inform the market of their presence within minutes of the original transaction, or to keep their intervention operations secret.[8]

The G-3 central banks intervened sporadically over the period 1987 through 1995. There are 273 days in the 9-year sample when the Fed intervened in the USD–DEM or the USD–JPY market. Moreover, the Bundesbank and the BOJ frequently intervened on the same days as the Fed, so that the sample of Fed intervention days also includes interventions by all three central banks.[9] In order to analyze the influence of intervention on the intra-daily data, ideally one would like to know the exact time that each central bank entered the market to buy or sell foreign exchange. Unfortunately, such data (rounded to the nearest minute) are only available for the Fed in the last two years of the sample.[10] However, on most days when central banks are in the market, Reuters reports the timing of their interventions and the time-stamped history of these reports are also available from Olsen and Associates.[11] To illustrate, Fig. 1 presents the DEM–USD tick-by-tick FXFX quotes for one of the last days in the sample, May 31, 1995, along with an indication of when the Reuters' time-stamped reports of the three Fed intervention operations appeared. On this particular day the DEM–USD price jumped from 1.38 to over 1.40 just before the first Reuters' report of Fed intervention and there are no signs of price mean reversion within the day.

It is possible that some traders in the market will learn that a central bank is in the market before the story appears in a Reuters' report. (It is indeed likely that the trading desks in the first bank (or banks) with which the central bank purchases or sells foreign exchange will know about the intervention before all the other banks.) Therefore, although we can assume that all traders know about the occurrence of intervention when the Reuters' report is released, it is possible that some (or even the bulk) of the influence of intervention will occur before the Reuters' time-

[8]Dominguez and Frankel (1993b) provide a detailed description of this process and the possible reasons that central banks might want to keep their intervention operations secret (the so-called stealth operations). Neely (2000) notes that central banks are moving increasingly toward electronic trading methods, which suggests that they are less interested in keeping operations secret.

[9]In 111 of the 273 days in the full sample the Fed was reported to have intervened unilaterally. On 80 of the remaining days (or 29%) two central banks (from among the Fed, Bundesbank and BOJ) were reported to have intervened. On 10 days (or 4%) all three G-3 central banks were reported to have intervened. And, on 29 days (11%) more than 3 central banks were reported to have intervened.

[10]The two other central banks that have kept records of the timing of their interventions (and provided the data to researchers) are the Swiss National Bank and the Bank of Canada.

[11]At a daily frequency, 25% (25 out of 101 days) of the Fed interventions that occurred over the period 1989–1995, were not reported by Reuters. 8 of the days occurred in August and September 1989 and the other 13 days occurred between May and July 1990. The average absolute daily value of non-reported Fed interventions was \$80m (median \$77m), whereas the value of reported Fed interventions averaged \$319m (median \$188m). It is not possible to check whether Reuters reported interventions that did not occur (false positives) because the Reuters data were only made available on the days on which the Fed (officially) intervened.

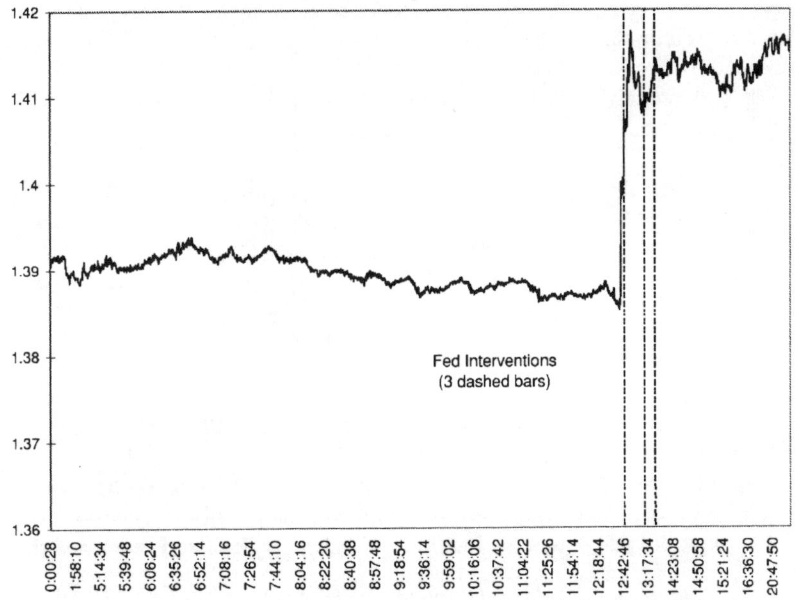

Fig. 1. DEM-USD exchange rate and Fed interventions on May 31, 1995.

stamp. (This is the likely explanation for why the DEM–USD rate in Fig. 1 jumped prior to the Reuters' report.)

Typically, central banks intervene during business hours in their own respective markets. For example, the Fed generally intervenes between 8 am and 5 pm Eastern Standard Time. According to the Reuters times-stamp, on average the Fed intervenes at 14:57:10 GMT (or 10 am EST), the Bundesbank intervenes at 11:31:16 GMT (or at 12:30 pm in Frankfurt) and the BOJ intervenes at 3:56:36 GMT (or around the Tokyo lunch hour). Fig. 2 presents the frequency distribution of Reuters reports of intervention times for the Fed. The graph clearly illustrates that there is a wide range of times at which the Fed enters the market.

Quite apart from the decision of when and how to intervene, central banks have varied goals for their intervention operations. The Fed describes four different reasons for its interventions in foreign exchange markets: to influence trend movements in exchange rates, to calm disorderly markets, to rebalance its foreign exchange reserve holdings, and to support fellow central banks in their exchange rate operations. Unfortunately, central banks rarely provide traders (or researchers) information regarding their specific goals for particular intervention operations. This lack of information, in turn, makes it difficult to access the "success" of individual intervention operations. Further, the magnitude and persistence of

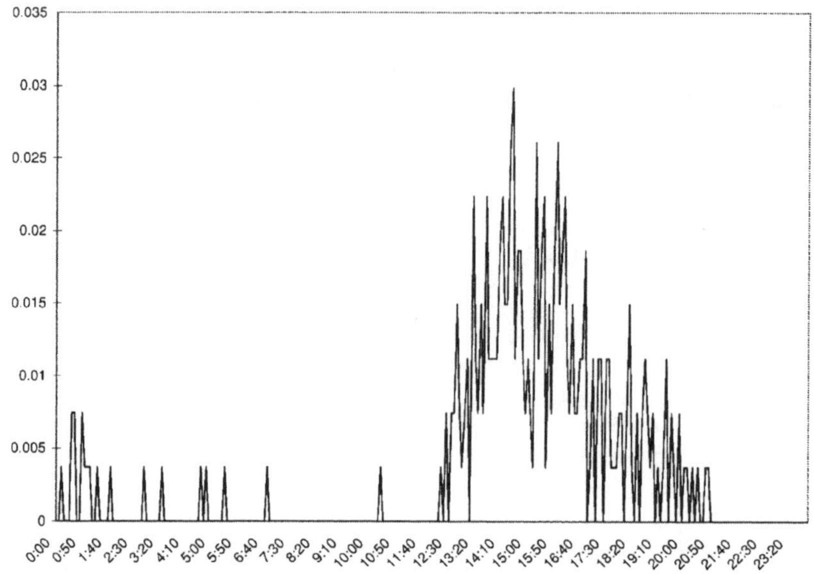

Fig. 2. Frequency distribution of the intradaily timing of Fed interventions, 1987–1995.

intervention's influence are likely to depend importantly on the interaction of the central bank's goals and the market's perception of those goals.

Theory provides at least two channels whereby central bank interventions may influence exchange rates, the portfolio balance and the signaling channel. A recent study by Evans and Lyons (2001) focuses on the portfolio balance channel by assuming that private transactions can serve as a proxy for secret interventions. The interventions studied here are explicitly non-secret, in that the timing information for the operations is taken from contemporaneous Reuters' newswire reports, so that both channels of influence may be operative.[12]

The empirical work that follows measures the impact of intervention operations on foreign exchange rate prices and volatility, and the extent to which this impact,

[12]See Mussa (1980) and Dominguez (1992) for further discussion of the intervention-signaling hypothesis. Montgomery and Popper (2001) suggest that central bank intervention may also serve to aggregate and disseminate traders' information and thereby serve an informational sharing role for a heterogeneously informed market. Naranjo and Nimalendran (2000) hypothesize that non-secret interventions create significant adverse selection problems for dealers. They find evidence in daily data that dealers increase exchange rate spreads around interventions and suggest that in doing so they protect themselves against the greater informational asymmetry around interventions.

and subsequent effects of intervention, depend on the "state of the market".[13] In particular, the tests will examine the relevance of the: (1) volume of trading, (2) proximity to other macro news, and the (3) presence of other central banks in the market, to the efficacy of intervention. The data also allow us to examine whether different central banks have different impacts on currencies, whether the market anticipates Reuters' reports of intervention operations, and whether exchange rates exhibit intra-daily mean reversion in reaction to intervention news.

2.3. Reuters news reports

The Reuters news reports are available from the Reuters AAMM Page News (Money Market Headline News) starting in 1989. Along with reports of central bank intervention, the Reuters data include announcements of various macroeconomic statistics, statements by central bank and government officials and reports of major economic events. In order to control for the impact of other news on exchange rate returns, a subsample of these Reuters news reports are also included in the empirical work. In particular, dummy variables indicate the timing of all major macroeconomic announcements and statements regarding exchange rate policy by officials of the G-3 central banks on the intervention sample days.[14]

3. The role of interventions in market microstructure models

The market microstructure literature analyzes ways in which specific trading mechanisms affect the price formation process.[15] The two branches of microstructure theory, the inventory approach and the informational approach, both provide implications for the effects of intervention operations on exchange rate movements.[16]

The inventory branch of the microstructure literature examines the question of what happens when orders to buy or sell are not always balanced in the selected time period. How does the price change to reflect order flow? In the context of inventory models, a central bank's order (intervention) can have both temporary and persistent effects. Interventions can influence bid-ask spreads, order flow and depending on the degree of risk aversion among market participants, the level of

---

[13]Of the four reasons that the Fed intervenes, only one (when the goal is to rebalance its portfolio) does not involve a desired change in the level or volatility of exchange rates. The tests in this paper are predicated on the assumption that relatively few interventions take place for the sole purpose of portfolio rebalancing.

[14]Table 2 in Dominguez (1999) lists the fifteen dummy variables created from the Reuters News Reports and the day-of-week and average time (GMT) when the announcements are made.

[15]See, for example, Admati (1991), O'Hara (1995) and Lyons (2001).

[16]See Pasquariello (2001) for a thorough theoretical treatment.

the exchange rate through the portfolio balance channel. Unfortunately the nature of the indicative quotes used in this study do not allow examination of either spreads or order flow,[17] but they will allow tests for whether interventions influence returns (and therefore prices).

The information branch of the microstructure literature focuses on the question of how prices may be affected by the fact that traders in the market may have different information. In these models periods of high variance correspond to periods of high concentration of informed trading (because during heavy volume informed traders can more easily hide their trades). If we assume that intervention operations constitute private information (at least initially), information theory suggests that volume and volatility are likely to rise during and immediately after an intervention operation. Currency prices and returns are also likely to change in reaction to intervention news, depending on how the news influences traders' forecasts of future currency movements. Once intervention news is fully revealed to the market (and all uncertainty is resolved), theory suggests that volatility (and volume) should revert back to initial levels.

4. Systematic influences of central bank interventions

A fundamental property of high frequency data in general, and the FXFX indicative quotes used in this study, is that observations occur at varying time intervals resulting in irregular spacing of data. Standard econometric techniques require regularly spaced data. As a consequence, a 5-min price (and returns) series was formed from the irregularly spaced data by averaging the two immediately adjacent bid and ask observations to the round 5-min mark with weights proportional to the distance from the end of the interval.[18]

Table 1 presents descriptive statistics (means, variance, skewness, kurtosis) of the 5-min FXFX returns data used in this study as well as corresponding statistics on the full sample of FXFX returns data from 1987 to 1993 (this data set contains 8,238,532 observations for the USD–DEM rate and 4,230,041 observations for the USD–JPY rate).[19] Mean returns and sample variances on the Fed intervention days are significantly larger than they are over the full sample period or the control sample.[20] Interestingly, mean returns are positive on the Fed intervention days, while they are negative over the full sample and of mixed signs in the control

[17]The FXFX indicative bid-ask spreads have not been found to be good proxies for actual transaction spreads. Likewise, the technical limitations of the FXFX transmission process are likely to bias measures of volume particularly during times of heavy trading.

[18]Results are essentially unchanged when data are sampled at 5-, 10- or 15-min intervals. Central banks often intervene on multiple occasions during 1 day, the 5-min intervals allow a maximal disaggregation of these individual operations.

[19]The full sample statistics in the upper panel of Table 1 are reproduced from Table 4 in Guillaume et al. (1997).

[20]This is also true at a daily frequency, see Chaboud and LeBaron (2001) and LeBaron (1999).

Table 1
Descriptive statistics of the FXFX return distribution

Rate	Time int.	Mean	Variance	Skewness	Kurtosis
Full sample of FXFX data 1987–1993 (based on 8,238,532 obs for DEM and 4,230,041 obs for JPY)					
USD/DEM	10 m	$-2.73\cdot10^{-7}$	$2.62\cdot10^{-7}$	0.17	35.10
	1 h	$-1.63\cdot10^{-6}$	$1.45\cdot10^{-6}$	0.26	23.55
	6 h	$-9.84\cdot10^{-6}$	$9.20\cdot10^{-6}$	0.24	9.44
	24 h	$-4.00\cdot10^{-5}$	$3.81\cdot10^{-5}$	0.08	3.33
USD/JPY	10 m	$-9.42\cdot10^{-7}$	$2.27\cdot10^{-7}$	−0.18	26.40
	1 h	$-5.67\cdot10^{-6}$	$1.27\cdot10^{-6}$	−0.09	25.16
	6 h	$-3.40\cdot10^{-5}$	$7.63\cdot10^{-6}$	−0.05	11.65
	24 h	$-1.37\cdot10^{-4}$	$3.07\cdot10^{-5}$	−0.15	4.81
Rate	Time int.	Mean	Variance	Skewness*	Kurtosis*
Fed intervention days 1987–1995 (based on 1,169,684 obs for DEM and 438,039 obs for JPY)					
USD/DEM	5 m	$4.94\cdot10^{-6}$	$6.85\cdot10^{-9}$	0.33	2.31
	10 m	$9.89\cdot10^{-6}$	$1.20\cdot10^{-8}$	−0.17	3.23
	1 h	$5.42\cdot10^{-5}$	$5.13\cdot10^{-8}$	1.22	3.98
	24 h	$1.05\cdot10^{-3}$	$5.95\cdot10^{-5}$	−0.32	1.93
USD/JPY	5 m	$9.90\cdot10^{-6}$	$5.02\cdot10^{-9}$	0.58	0.66
	10 m	$1.98\cdot10^{-5}$	$9.23\cdot10^{-9}$	0.41	−2.63
	1 h	$1.14\cdot10^{-4}$	$6.56\cdot10^{-8}$	0.57	−0.32
	24 h	$2.99\cdot10^{-3}$	$2.95\cdot10^{-5}$	0.01	−3.14
Rate	Time int.	Mean	Variance	Skewness*	Kurtosis*
Control sample: 25 days 1987–1993 (based on 108,973 obs for DEM and 49,132 obs for JPY)					
USD/DEM	5 m	$-6.84\cdot10^{-7}$	$1.52\cdot10^{-9}$	0.95	5.75
	10 m	$-1.37\cdot10^{-6}$	$3.15\cdot10^{-9}$	1.21	1.79
	1 h	$1.13\cdot10^{-6}$	$2.61\cdot10^{-8}$	0.46	2.80
	24 h	$1.10\cdot10^{-3}$	$2.16\cdot10^{-5}$	2.29	8.53
USD/JPY	5 m	$-3.26\cdot10^{-7}$	$1.07\cdot10^{-9}$	0.27	1.66
	10 m	$-6.53\cdot10^{-7}$	$1.96\cdot10^{-9}$	0.50	−2.54
	1 h	$1.42\cdot10^{-5}$	$2.73\cdot10^{-9}$	−0.53	0.59
	24 h	$2.25\cdot10^{-4}$	$1.37\cdot10^{-5}$	0.61	0.42

The top panel of data are reproduced from Table 4 in Guillaume et al. (1997).
** The skewness and kurtosis formulas are from Kendall and Stuart (1958).

sample depending on the particular sampling frequency used to create the data series. In the full sample, the degree of kurtosis of the returns rises with increasing sample frequency, while for both the Fed intervention days and the control sample the degree of kurtosis is relatively stable over sampling frequencies and is less pronounced.

4.1. The influence of intervention on returns

The empirical work uses an "event study" approach to test for the influence of intervention (and other announcements) on exchange rates. If R denotes the 5-min return series and D^k denotes the (time-stamped to the nearest 5-min) signed intervention[21] and other announcement dummy variables, then a general "event study" regression specification is:

$$R_{t_i} - \overline{R_{t_i}} = \alpha_0 + \sum_k \sum_n \alpha_{1,n}^k D_{t_{i+n}}^k + \varepsilon_{t_i} \quad (1)$$

where $\bar{R}$ is set to zero and the intra-daily returns data include only the days on which the Fed intervened in the market over the sample. Using this general regression specification it is possible to test for the impact and intra-day effects of signed intervention (and other macro news) by examining whether the D^ks are statistically significant.[22] Further, the specification can be adjusted to test whether market participants react to the intervention operations of different central banks similarly by including these operations separately in the regression. The possibility that certain market participants know about the interventions before others can be tested by looking for evidence of price effects prior to the time-stamped Reuters release of D^k news. The influence of the "state of the market" can be measured by examining information releases during specific times-of-day. It is also possible to measure whether the effects of interventions that are closely timed with other macroeconomic news announcements differ from those that occur in low news times. Finally, in order to investigate the intra-day persistence of intervention's influence, a test for mean reversion can be constructed by checking whether the n time lags on the D^ks sum to zero.

Results of the various event-study regressions using USD–DEM and USD–JPY data, respectively, are presented in Tables 2 and 3.[23] In the case of USD–DEM returns, signed interventions by all three G-3 central banks are statistically

[21] Interventions by all three central banks take the value 1 if they involve a purchase of dollars, the value −1 if they involve a sale of dollars and 0 otherwise. Interventions are included as (1, 0, −1) dummy variables both because the dollar magnitudes are generally only available at a daily (not intra-daily) frequency, and because there is some evidence that the size of interventions depend on market reaction to initial trades suggesting that including magnitudes might engender simultaneity bias.

[22] If the Fed bases its decision to intervene on intra-daily exchange rate movements or volatility then estimation of Eq. (1) will be subject to simultaneity bias. Neely's (2000) survey of central banks suggests that they are more likely to base intervention decisions on longer term objectives (though he suggests that central banks may determine the size of interventions based on market reaction to initial trades).

[23] Various regression specifications were attempted, including imposing a polynomial distributed lag (pdl) structure on the leads and lags of the intervention variables. Tests of the pdl restrictions suggested that the data do not conform to this specification. Experimentation with various lead and lag combinations indicated that a [−1 h, +2 h] window for the intervention variables and a [0, 1 h] window for the macroeconomic announcements was appropriate. In specifications that only included one-time influences (impact effects) of each announcement and intervention variable the right-hand-side variables were generally not found to be significant explainers of returns behavior. Subsample robustness checks for the event-study regressions are available from the author upon request and suggest that the influence of Fed interventions was strongest in the latter part of the sample.

Table 2
Influence of interventions on USD–DEM returns

$$R_{t_i} = \alpha_0 + \sum_k \sum_n \alpha^k_{1,n} D^k_{t_{i+n}} + \varepsilon_{t_i}$$

where R is the 5-min USD–DEM return; the D^ks include signed intervention, official central bank announcements and macro announcements; $n = -1$ to $+2$ h for the G-3 intervention variables and official announcements and $n=0$ to $+1$ h for the macro announcements; t_i is the sequence of the regular-spaced (every 5 min) intra-daily data for all the days on which the Fed intervened against the mark from 1989 to 1995 (69 days and a total of 151 reports of Fed operations). The reported coefficients are multiplied by 1000

	Do All G-3 interventions matter?	Does trade volume matter?[a]	Does proximity to macro news matter?[b]	Does coordination matter?[c]
Independent variable	Max signf. coefficient[d]	Max signf. coefficient	Max signf. coefficient	Max signf. coefficient
Fed intervention	0.685**			
Buba intervention	2.404**	2.331**	2.413**	na
BOJ intervention	0.627*	0.509†	0.554†	na
Official announcements	Yes	yes	Yes	yes
Macro controls	Yes	yes	Yes	yes
Fed interventions during high trade volume		0.881*		
Fed interventions during low trade volume		0.322		
Fed interventions close to macro news			0.734*	
Isolated Fed. interventions			0.521†	
Coordinated G-3 interventions				1.091**
Unilateral Fed. interventions				0.553†
R2	0.017	0.16	0.16	0.14
D.W.	1.88	1.88	1.88	1.87

Number of observations = 19,833. [a]High trade volume is defined as the overlap in US and European trading hours. [b]Interventions that occur within 2 h of a macro news announcement are defined as "close". [c]Coordinated interventions are defined as Fed interventions that occur on the same day as at least one other of the G-3 central banks. [d]The maximum significant coefficient is the largest of the 36 lead and lag coefficients on each of the intervention variables. **, *, † denote statistical significance at the 1, 5 and 10% levels, respectively, using robust standard errors.

significant, have the intended direction of influence on returns,[24] and in the cases of the Fed and the Bundesbank there is evidence of 1-h Reuters' announcement lags, suggesting that traders were aware of the interventions before the Reuters'

[24]A positive coefficient on the intervention variables indicates that a purchase (sale) of dollars results in a rise (fall) in the value of the dollar.

Table 3
Influence of interventions on USD–JPY returns

$$R_{t_i} = \alpha_0 + \sum_k \sum_n \alpha^k_{1,n} D^k_{t_{i+n}} + \varepsilon_{t_i}$$

where R is the 5-min USD–JPY return; D^ks include signed intervention, official central bank announcements and macro announcements; $n = -1$ to $+2$ h for the G-3 intervention variables and official announcements and $n = 0$ to $+1$ h for the macro announcements; t_i is the sequence of the regular-spaced (every 5 min) intra-daily data for all the days on which the Fed intervened against the yen from 1989 to 1995 (66 days and a total of 192 reports of Fed operations). The reported coefficients are multiplied by 1000

	Do All G-3 interventions matter?	Does trade volume matter?[a]	Does proximity to macro news matter?[b]	Does coordination matter?[c]
Independent variable	Max signf. coefficient[d]	Max signf. coefficient	Max signf. coefficient	Max signf. coefficient
Fed intervention	0.921**			
Buba intervention	1.877**	1.826**	1.901**	na
BOJ intervention	0.753†	0.762†	0.764†	na
Official announcements[5]	yes	yes	yes	yes
Macro controls	yes	yes	yes	yes
Fed interventions during high trade volume		1.023**		
Fed interventions during low trade volume		0.759*		
Fed interventions close to macro news			1.117**	
Isolated Fed. interventions			0.617	
Coordinated G-3 interventions				0.887**
Unilateral Fed. interventions				1.535
R2	0.011	0.010	0.010	0.010
D.W.	1.902	1.901	1.902	1.898

Number of observations = 18,969. [a]High trade volume is defined as the overlap in US and European trading hours. [b]Interventions that occur within 2 h of a macro news announcement are defined as "close". [c]Coordinated interventions are defined as Fed interventions that occur on the same day as at least one other of the G-3 central banks. [d]The maximum significant coefficient is the largest of the 36 lead and lag coefficients on each of the intervention variables. [5]Excluding BOJ official announcements. **, *, † denote statistical significance at the 1, 5 and 10% levels, respectively, using robust standard errors.

reports were released. For all three central banks lagged values of the intervention coefficients continued to be significant for at least 1 h after the release of the Reuters' report. Four of the twelve macro announcements were found to be significant; and lag effects were found up to 30 min after the Reuters' time-stamp.[25] The impact of the U.S. GNP announcement on USD–DEM returns was the largest by a wide margin, with U.S. consumer credit and Bundesbank intervention ranked second and third. If we measure the cumulative effect of an average-sized dollar purchase by the Fed (starting 1 h before the Reuters' report and cumulating the lead and lag coefficients on the signed Fed intervention variable) we find that the maximal effect (of about 7 basis points) comes 30 min after the Reuters report, and reverts toward zero after 2 h.[26] This suggests that a billion dollar intervention by the Fed would lead to a 29 basis point maximal price impact.[27]

Fed and Bundesbank interventions are also found to significantly influence USD–JPY returns, although Reuters' announcement lags are only found for the Fed. Interestingly, BOJ intervention was not found to significantly influence USD–JPY returns when the dummy variable denoting official BOJ exchange rate comments is also included in the regression specification. If the BOJ comments are omitted (as reported in the table), BOJ interventions are found to significantly influence the USD–JPY returns with a 30 min Reuters' announcement lag. For all three central banks lagged values of the intervention coefficients continued to be significant in the 2-h period after the release of the Reuters' report. Once again, four of the twelve macro announcement variables were found to be significant, and U.S. GNP had the largest impact on USD–JPY returns by a wide margin. There is little evidence of mean reversion in the coefficient values for Fed intervention in the USD–JPY returns regression, the maximal effect of an average-sized Fed intervention (about 10 basis points) comes 55 min after the Reuters' report, and declines to about 7 basis points after 2 h.

Tables 2 and 3 also report the results of three alternative specifications of the event study regression. The first of these alternative specifications provides a test of whether signed interventions that occur during high volume periods (as proxied by the overlap in the European and NY market)[28] have different effects from those

[25]Coefficient values for the macro variables are not reported in the tables because they serve only as controls in the regression. If there is an expected component to some of the macro announcements, leading to mis-measurement of the news component, this could potentially lead to a bias in all the coefficient values. As a robustness check, the regressions were also run without the macro controls (allowing the error term to capture all the effects of the macro news). The results of this specification of Eq. (1) are qualitatively similar to those reported in the paper and are available from the author upon request.

[26]The estimates suggest that there is mean reversion in exchange rate returns after an intervention event, though this does not preclude the possibility that intervention has lasting effects on the level of exchange rates. For example, in continuous time, if intervention causes the level of the exchange rate to quickly (although not instantaneously) converge to a new equilibrium, the first derivative (returns) will undergo mean reversion. I thank Jay Levin for pointing this out to me.

[27]This is based on the assumption that the average daily Fed intervention operation over this period was \$319m and the average intra-daily operation was \$240 million.

[28]It is also possible to interpret this specification as a test of whether Fed interventions that occur in the NY morning differ from those that occur at other times.

that occur in low volume times. Market microstructure models suggest that it is during high volume periods that information flow tends to be highest. The reported coefficient estimates in the second column of Tables 2 and 3 support this, in that they indicate that the influence of signed Fed interventions on returns is higher during high volume trading hours (defined as 8:30–12 EST or 13:30–17:00 GMT with adjustments for daylight savings time) relative to low volume periods in both currency markets[29], though the difference in the point estimates on the maximal coefficient values is smaller in the USD–JPY market.[30] Given that the majority of Fed interventions in the sample period in both markets occurred during high volume trading hours, the Fed seems to have already (perhaps inadvertently) exploited this phenomenon.

Previous studies using high frequency data have found evidence that volume and volatility tend to rise in foreign exchange markets in reaction to macro announcements. Along with controlling for the possible influence of these announcements in the event studies, it might also be the case that there exists an interaction effect between these announcements (and the high volume that ensues) and the influence of intervention operations. For example, it may be that traders are more sensitive to news (including intervention news) at times when other major announcements are released. In order to test this hypothesis, Fed interventions that are timed within a 2-h window of a macro announcement are distinguished from the other interventions in the event study regressions. In the case of Fed interventions in the USD–DEM market, 28% fell into this category, whereas for Fed interventions in the USD–JPY market, 63% of interventions were timed close to macro announcements. The results reported in column 3 of Tables 2 and 3 suggest that there does indeed seem to be evidence that signed interventions that closely follow macro announcements have a larger impact on returns than do other interventions. Interestingly, this effect is found to be largest for the Fed interventions in the USD–JPY market where a larger percentage of interventions were closely timed to macro announcements.[31]

In the sample period under study, 81% of Fed interventions in the USD–DEM market and 88% of the Fed interventions in the USD–JPY market occur on days when either the Bundesbank or the BOJ (or both) are also intervening. The final alternative specification, tests whether Fed interventions that are coordinated with

[29]The USD–DEM coefficient estimates suggest that when volume is high, the price impact of intervention is 28% higher. Linear restrictions imposing equality of the full set of leads and lags on Fed intervention interacted with the high trading volume dummy variable and the coefficient values for the remaining Fed intervention operations are rejected at the 5% level for both currencies.

[30]One potential explanation for why the results might differ across the two currency markets is that the US and Europe market overlap may not be the appropriate proxy for high trading volume for the Fed interventions in the USD–JPY market. In order to check whether this might be the case, similar regressions distinguishing interventions that occurred during alternative times were examined. The results did not suggest that any alternative timing would provide a better proxy for high trading volume in the USD–JPY market.

[31]Evans and Lyons (2001) also find that secret interventions are the most effective when the flow of macro news is strong.

one or both of the other G-3 central banks are more influential than unilateral interventions. The results, reported in the final column of Tables 2 and 3, suggest that coordinated G-3 interventions are indeed more effective than unilateral ones for all three central banks.[32] Similar results have also been found at a daily and weekly frequency, suggesting that the signaling (or information) value of an intervention operation is significantly strengthened by the presence of other central banks in the market (intervening in the same direction).

4.2. The influence of intervention on volatility

Along with influencing prices and returns, microstructure theory predicts that interventions may affect volume and volatility through both the inventory and information channels. Further, theory predicts that once intervention information is fully public and all uncertainty is resolved, volatility should revert to its original level. One way to examine the influence of intervention on volatility involves arranging squared returns around interventions according to the intervention event rather than clock time. In this approach, the first observation before an intervention report is the return recorded 5 min before the intervention report. A 2-h (before and after) window is selected to surround each Fed intervention operation in the two currency markets, USD–DEM and USD–JPY. Subsequent intervention reports that are clustered within the 2-h window are excluded from the sample.[33] The squared 5-min returns from this "intervention sample" are then compared against a control sample of matched (by time-of-day and day-of-week) 5-min volatility observations when no intervention was reported. (This sample comes from the control group of 25 days for each currency when no intervention occurred.) So, for example, if the Fed intervened in the USD–JPY market on a Monday at 3:55 GMT, then the 5-min returns 2 h before and after this event are included in the Fed intervention sample. The matched control sample likewise includes an average of returns on all Mondays in the 2-h window around 3:55 GMT.

The differences between exchange rate volatility surrounding the 2-h Fed intervention and non-intervention periods can be seen in Figs. 3 and 4 for the USD–DEM and USD–JPY markets, respectively. There are a total of 47 (5-min) volatility observations for each intervention: 23 before the report, one for the time that the report appears on the Reuters screen, and 23 volatility observations after the report. The figures indicate that volatility surrounding intervention periods is substantially higher than during non-intervention periods in the full 4-h window and especially in the [−30, +30] min interval.[34] The peak difference in volatility

[32]It is possible that the larger coordination effect is coming from the fact that the aggregate size of intervention tends to be higher when intervention is coordinated. Because intradaily intervention magnitudes are unavailable, it is not possible to distinguish whether coordination per se is at work here.

[33]This criteria disqualified 151 out of 268 Fed interventions.

[34]There are four 5-min returns in the USD–JPY control sample that are at least three standard deviations away from the mean return, these three observations (out of a total of 6888 observations) were dropped from the control sample.

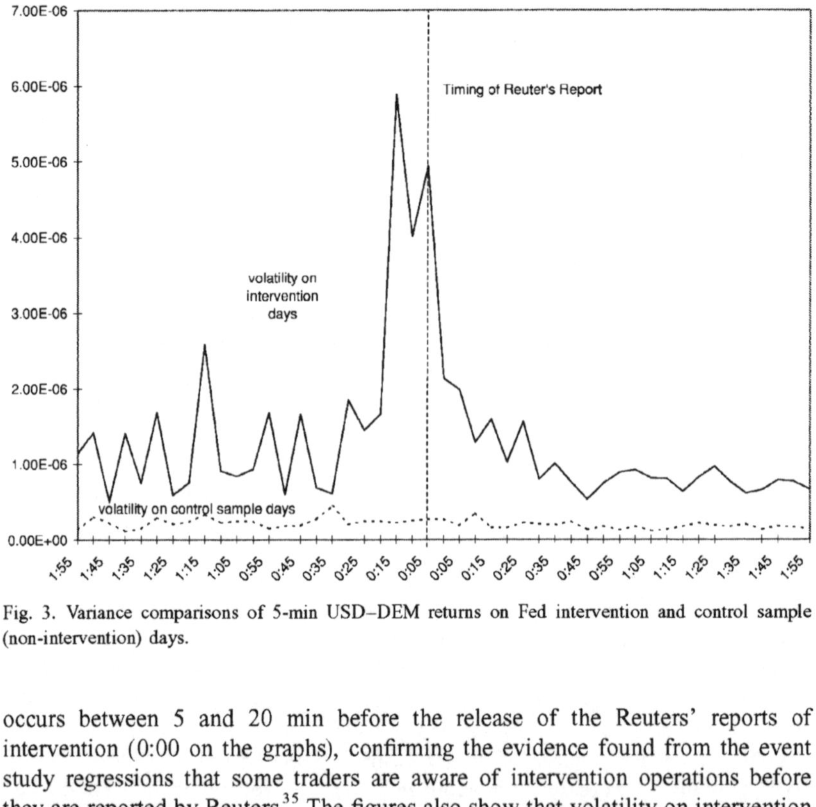

Fig. 3. Variance comparisons of 5-min USD–DEM returns on Fed intervention and control sample (non-intervention) days.

occurs between 5 and 20 min before the release of the Reuters' reports of intervention (0:00 on the graphs), confirming the evidence found from the event study regressions that some traders are aware of intervention operations before they are reported by Reuters.[35] The figures also show that volatility on intervention days, while always higher than in the control sample, tends to revert back to its initial level approximately 1 h after the initial signs of volatility increase.[36]

In order to test the equality of return variances through time in the period surrounding the intervention event versus the matched non-intervention sample a

[35]It is also interesting to note in Fig. 4 that there is a second spike in USD–JPY volatility 50 min after the Reuter's news release, suggesting that trader reactions to the intervention news are neither immediate nor monotonically decreasing. It may also be that other news events are influencing the volatility measure in the second 2-h period, although there is no evidence of specific outliers in the sample data.

[36]One of the objectives for intervention policy often cited by the Fed (as well as other central banks) is to "calm disorderly markets" and therefore presumably to lower market volatility. Figs. 3 and 4, however, suggest that volatility is higher during intervention days than it is in the control sample of non-intervention days. The figures also show that volatility rises just prior to the Reuters' announcement of a Fed intervention and falls back to its original level about 1 h later. This suggests that the Fed tends to intervene on days with higher than usual volatility, that operations temporarily increase volatility, but this increase is offset within the hour. The figures provide no evidence that interventions lower volatility at least within the day.

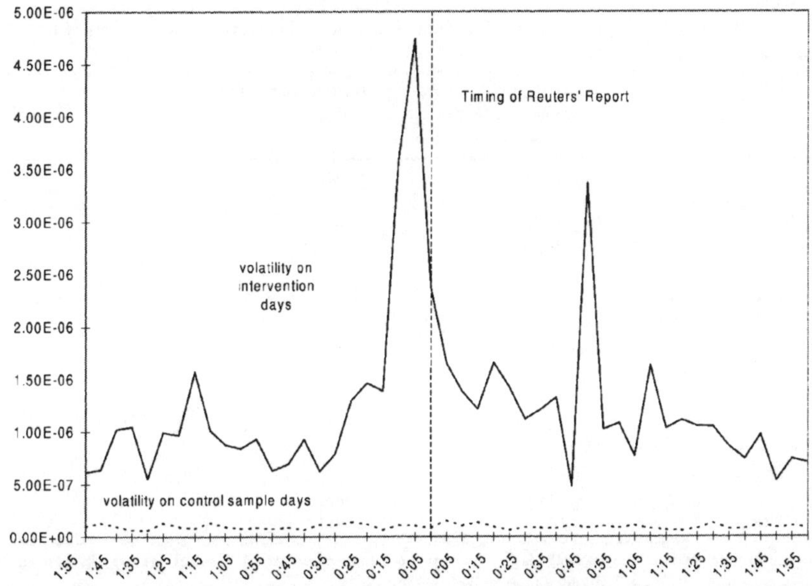

Fig. 4. Variance comparisons of 5-min USD–DEM returns on Fed intervention and control sample (non-intervention) days.

Brown–Forsythe (1974) modified Levene test is used.[37] The null hypothesis is that the variances at 5-min intervals surrounding the two samples are homoskedastic. Results of these tests are presented in Table 4. The return variance of both the USD–DEM and USD–JPY rates are found to vary significantly around Fed interventions, while in the two control samples, we cannot reject the hypothesis of equal variances

In addition to analyzing whether average volatility in the period surrounding interventions is significantly higher than volatility during matched non-intervention periods, the FXFX data permit a test of whether the variance of quotes from specific banks is responsible for any significant differences. In other words, the test consists of examining quotes from the major banks that deal in the USD–DEM and USD–JPY markets to see if they are more variable around intervention events than is typical at the same times of day on non-intervention days. If certain banks systematically receive information regarding intervention before other banks, then these banks are likely to drive up volatility around intervention events. Table 4

[37]The Brown and Forsythe (1974) test is robust to departures of the underlying data from normality. Chang and Taylor (1998) also use this test to examine the intra-day effects of BOJ intervention on USD–JPY volatility.

Table 4
Tests of the equality of return variances 2 h before and after fed interventions and in matched control samples

	Equality of return variance in Fed. intervention sample	Equality of return variance in control sample
	F-stats	*F*-stats
Full sample quotes		
USD–DEM	3.4509**	0.9034
USD–JPY	1.7147**	0.8851
Individual bank quotes		
USD–DEM		
Chemical Bank	0.7657	0.9034
Morgan Guaranty	0.7000	0.9034
Citibank	1.3546	0.9034
USD–JPY		
Chemical Bank	1.4175*	0.8851
Morgan Guaranty	0.9438	0.8851
Citibank	1.108	0.8851

The control sample includes 25 days when no interventions occurred. Control sample observations are matched by time-of-day and day-of-week to the intervention sample. The equality of variances is tested using the Brown–Forsythe (1974) modified Levene test. The null hypothesis is that the sample variances at 5-min intervals are homoskedastic over the [−120, +120] interval. Critical values are distributed as $F(38,2691)=1.4094$ (5%) denoted with * and 1.6202 (1%) denoted with **. The Fed intervention sample includes 70 Reuters reports. The three banks are listed by Euromoney magazine as the most popular among corporate customers in the New York market.

also presents *F*-statistics for equality of variance in the 2 h surrounding Fed interventions using quotes from individual banks. The banks selected were those listed by Euromoney magazine as the most popular among corporate customers in the New York market.[38] With the exception of Chemical Bank in the USD–JPY market, the statistics generally do not support the hypothesis that it is individual banks that systematically influence return variance surrounding intervention events. It is said that the Fed generally attempts to use a wide and variable selection of banks for their intervention transactions in order not to give any one bank unfair advantage. The results suggest that these attempts have been quite successful.[39]

[38]Euromoney magazine publishes its survey on the foreign exchange market annually. The banks selected appeared regularly (from 1989 to 1995) in the list of the five most popular banks in the NY market.

[39]Alternatively it may be that the indicative quote data are too noisy to pick up individual bank effects. During heavy information periods such as the period surrounding an intervention event it may be that banks are less conscientious about updating quotes.

5. Conclusions

The tests in this paper explore whether aspects of market microstructure influence the effectiveness of central bank intervention. In particular, this study examines the importance of the "state of the foreign exchange market" at the moment that central bank intervention operations (and macro announcements) are made public to traders. The empirical evidence indicates that Fed intervention operations significantly influenced both USD–DEM and USD–JPY intra-day returns and volatility. The evidence also suggests that some traders know at least 1 h prior to the Reuters' report that a central bank is intervening, and the effects of interventions generally persist, at least to the end of the day. There is evidence of mean reversion in returns subsequent to Fed interventions particularly in the USD–DEM market, suggesting some initial over-reaction by the market. Fed interventions that occurred when the US and European markets are open (a proxy for relatively heavy trading volume periods), and in the aftermath of macro announcements had relatively larger effects than those that occurred at other times in the day. Coordinated interventions were also found to have large effects on exchange rates. There is little evidence in the FXFX data that specific large banks in the USD–DEM and USD–JPY markets systematically act as price leaders in reaction to news of Fed intervention.

Overall, the tests in the paper support the hypothesis that central bank interventions influence intra-daily foreign exchange returns and volatility. The results also support the hypothesis that the efficacy of central bank intervention depends on the characteristics of the foreign exchange market at the time the operations become known to traders. The evidence suggests that policy makers that hope to have the largest intra-daily influence on exchange rate returns using intervention operations should time interventions to take place when trading volume is high (when both London and New York are trading) in the aftermath of the release of other macroeconomic news, and when other central banks are also in the market (intervening in the same direction).

Acknowledgements

I thank Andy Rose (the editor), the referees, seminar participants at the NBER, University of Michigan, and Georgetown University and, in particular, Jay Levin, Richard Lyons, Chris Neely, Matthew Shapiro, Larry Summers, Carol Osler and Shang-Jin Wei for useful comments and suggestions. Tatiana Nenova provided outstanding research assistance. I am grateful to Olsen and Associates for providing the intradaily exchange rates and Reuter's news tape analyzed in the paper.

References

Admati, A., 1991. The informational role of prices: A review essay. Journal of Monetary Economics 28, 347–361.

Beattie, N., Fillion, J., 1999. An Intraday Analysis of the Effectiveness of Foreign Exchange Intervention. Bank of Canada Working Paper 99-94.

Brown, M.B., Forsythe, A.B., 1974. Robust tests for the equality of variance. Journal of the American Statistical Association 69, 364–367.

Chaboud, A., LeBaron, B., 2001. Foreign exchange market trading volume and federal reserve intervention. Journal of Futures Markets 21, 851–860.

Chang, Y., Taylor, S., 1998. Intraday effects of foreign exchange intervention by the Bank of Japan. Journal of International Money and Finance 18, 191–210.

Dacorogna, M.M., Muller, U.A., Nagler, R.J., Olsen, R.B., Pictet, O.V., 1993. A geographical model for the daily and weekly seasonal volatility in the FX market. Journal of International Money and Finance 12, 413–438.

Dominguez, K., 1992. The informational role of official foreign exchange intervention operations: the signalling hypothesis. In: Dominguez, K. (Ed.), Exchange Rate Efficiency and the Behavior of International Asset Markets. Garland Publishing Company, NY, pp. 41–80, Chapter 2.

Dominguez, K., 1998. Central Bank intervention and exchange rate volatility. Journal of International Money and Finance 18, 161–190.

Dominguez, K., 1999. The Market Microstructure of Central Bank Intervention. NBER working paper 7337.

Dominguez, K., Frankel, F., 1993a. Does foreign exchange intervention matter? The Portfolio effect. American Economic Review 83, 1356–1369.

Dominguez, K., Frankel, F., 1993b. Does Foreign Exchange Intervention Work? Institute for International Economics, Washington, D.C.

Evans, M., 1998. The Microstructure of Foreign Exchange Dynamics. Georgetown University.

Evans, M., 1999. What are the Origins of Foreign Exchange Movements. Georgetown University.

Evans, M., Lyons, R., 2001. Portfolio Balance, Price Impact and Secret Intervention. National Bureau of Economic Research Working Paper 8356.

Federal Reserve Bank of New York, 1992. Administration of Relationships with Foreign Exchange Trading Counter-parties, February 28.

Fischer, A.M., Zurlinden, M., 1999. Exchange rate effects of central bank interventions: An analysis of transaction prices. Economic Journal 109, 662–676.

Frankel, J., Rose, A., 1995. Empirical research on nominal exchange rates. In: Grossman, G., Rogoff, K. (Eds.). Handbook of International Economics, Vol. 3. Elsevier Science, Amsterdam, pp. 1689–1729.

Goodhart, C., Hesse, T., 1993. Central Bank forex intervention assessed in continuous time. Journal of International Money and Finance 12, 368–389.

Goodhart, C., Ito, T., Payne, R., 1996. One day in June 1993: A study of the working of the Reuters 2000–2 Electronic foreign exchange trading system. In: Frankel, J., Galli, G., Giovannini, A. (Eds.), The Microstructure of Foreign Exchange Markets. The University of Chicago Press for NBER, pp. 107–179.

Guillaume, D., Dacorogna, M., Dave, R., Muller, U., Olsen, R., Pictet, O., 1997. From the bird's eye to the microscope: A survey of new stylized facts on the intra-daily foreign exchange markets. Finance and Stochastics 1 (2), 95–129.

Kendall, M.G., Stuart, A., 1958. Advanced Theory of Statistics. Griffin and Company, London.

LeBaron, B., 1999. Technical trading rule profitability and foreign exchange intervention. Journal of International Economics 49 (1), 125–143.

Lyons, R., 1995. Tests of microstructural hypotheses in the foreign exchange market. Journal of Financial Economics 39, 321–351.

Lyons, R., 1996. Foreign exchange volume: Sound and fury signifying nothing. In: Frankel, J., Galli, G., Giovannini, A. (Eds.), The Microstructure of Foreign Exchange Markets. The University of Chicago Press for NBER, pp. 183–201.

Lyons, R., 2001. The Microstructure Approach to Exchange Rates. MIT Press.

Meese, R., Rogoff, K., 1983. Empirical exchange rate models of the seventies: Do they fit out of sample? Journal of International Economics 14 (1–2), 3–24.

Montgomery, J., Popper, H., 2001. Information sharing and Central Bank intervention in the foreign exchange market. Journal of International Economics 55 (2), 295–316.

Mussa, M., 1980. The Role of Official Intervention. Group of Thirty, New York, NY.

Naranjo, A., Nimalendran, M., 2000. Government intervention and adverse selection costs in foreign exchange markets. Review of Financial Studies 13, 453–477.

Neely, C., 2000. The practice of Central Bank intervention: Looking under the hood. Central Banking XI (2), 24–37.

Neely, C., 2002. The temporal pattern of trading rule returns and Central Bank intervention: Intervention does not generate technical trading rule profits. Journal of International Economics 58, 211–232.

O'Hara, M., 1995. Market Microstructure Theory. Blackwell Business.

Pasquariello, P., 2001. Central Bank Intervention and the Intraday Process of Price Formation in the Currency Markets, Stern School of Business, NYU.

Payne, R., Vitale, P., 2000. A Transaction Level Study of the Effects of Central Bank Intervention on Exchange Rates. London School of Economics.

Peiers, B., 1997. Informed traders, intervention and price leadership: A deeper view of the microstructure of the foreign exchange market. Journal of Finance 52 (4), 1589–1614.

Part V
Micro Structure of the Foreign Exchange Market

[14]

ELSEVIER Journal of Financial Economics 39 (1995) 321–351

JOURNAL OF Financial ECONOMICS

Tests of microstructural hypotheses in the foreign exchange market

Richard K. Lyons

Haas School of Business, University of California at Berkeley, Berkeley, CA 94720, USA
National Bureau of Economic Research, Cambridge, MA 02138, USA

(Received August 1993; final version received March 1995)

Abstract

Data in this paper support both the inventory-control and asymmetric-information approaches to microstructure theory. Strong evidence of an inventory-control effect on price is new. The transactions dataset chronicles a trading week of a spot foreign exchange dealer whose daily volume averages over $1 billion. In addition to controlling inventory with his own price, the dealer also lays off inventory at other dealers' prices and through brokers. These results highlight the importance of inventory-control theory in understanding trading in this market.

Key words: Foreign exchange; Microstructure; Inventory; Information
JEL classification: G15; F31

1. Introduction

Empirical work on microstructures focuses primarily on the NYSE and its specialist structure. At least two reasons account for this focus on the specialist: Theory is better developed in this area, and the concentration of the market provides more readily available data. Current interest, however, is shifting towards various nonspecialist markets. This paper exemplifies that shift. It examines the spot deutschemark/dollar (DM/$) market, which has a decentralized

I thank the following for helpful comments: two anonymous referees, Charles Engel, Richard Levich, James McCarthy, Eric Noyes, Carol Osler, Linda Tesar, Sabine Toulson, Jianxin Wang, and seminar participants at Columbia, Harvard, Rochester, Berkeley, Santa Cruz, the NBER Summer Institute, and the ASSA Meetings. I also thank Euysung Kim and Eric Noyes for valuable research assistance and Merrill Lynch and Lasser Marshall for access to dealers and brokers while trading. Financial assistance from the National Science Foundation and the Berkeley Program in Finance is gratefully acknowledged. Any errors are my own.

SSDI 0304405X9500832 Y

dealership structure. The objective is to test models of price determination using a dataset appropriate for this market.

Microstructure theory emphasizes two channels through which order flow affects price. First, an inventory-control channel emerges when dealers adjust price to control inventory fluctuation due to order flow (e.g., Amihud and Mendelson, 1980; Ho and Stoll, 1983; O'Hara and Oldfield, 1986; among others). Second, an information channel emerges when dealers adjust price in response to order flow that may reflect private information (e.g., Kyle, 1985; Glosten and Milgrom, 1985; Admati and Pfleiderer, 1988; among others). Note that both channels imply that buyer-initiated trades push price up, while seller-initiated trades push it down. In empirical work, disentangling them is the central objective.

I find that both channels are significant in the foreign exchange (FX) market, providing support for both modeling approaches. Specifically, information asymmetry induces dealers to decrease price about one pip – or DM 0.0001/$ – for every incoming sell order of $10 million (conversely for buy orders); inventory control induces dealers to decrease price about three-quarters of a pip per $10 million of undesired inventory. Though information effects on price have been found elsewhere (e.g., Madhavan and Smidt, 1991; Hasbrouck, 1988, 1991; among others), strong evidence of an inventory effect on price is new (see Madhavan and Smidt, 1991; Manaster and Mann, 1992; Laux, 1993; among others). The previous evidence supporting inventory control is indirect, relying wholly on the time-series properties of inventory (e.g., Hasbrouck and Sofianos, 1993; Madhavan and Smidt, 1993).

Why is the direct effect on price so strong in FX when it leaves little trace in equity and futures markets? The following facts provide some prima facie evidence. Most FX dealers – including the one I track – begin and end each trading day with a zero net position. This, coupled with per-dealer volumes over $1 billion per day, implies substantial inventory control. Still, it is not clear why this should show up so clearly in price. (For example, FX dealers have other methods for controlling inventory, such as laying it off on another dealer's price or through a broker.) I offer two additional thoughts. First, dealers in FX quote bilaterally, so shading the quote provides a signal of inventory to one person only, not to the whole market. Second, the dataset available is remarkably powerful. It distinguishes between incoming orders (counterparty initiated), outgoing orders, and brokered orders. Specialist datasets, in contrast, provide no such taxonomy. These different categories provide extra power for disentangling inventory effects from information effects.[1]

[1]Another reason inventory effects may be relatively sharp here involves hedging. Dealers in the major currencies trade only one currency. Specialists, in contrast, typically trade several stocks and hedge their overall risk, rather than focusing on any one stock, which may mute the price effects of inventory. Similarly, futures traders sometimes cross-hedge in neighboring pits.

My dataset has significant advantages over FX data used previously. In particular, it chronicles the trading activity of a spot DM/$ dealer over a five-day trading week. The time-stamps on the quotes and trades are assigned by computer, without lags. Previous work on intraday spot trading has relied on a series of indicative quotes called FXFX, which is provided by Reuters (see Goodhart and Figliuoli, 1991; Goodhart et al., 1994). There are two key shortcomings of the FXFX data: These 'quotes' are not firm prices at which dealers can transact; and there is no measure of order flow or transaction prices. Clearly, the FXFX data are not sufficient for addressing the issues considered here.

The paper is organized as follows: Section 2 develops the model; Section 3 describes the dataset and provides some relevant institutional detail; Section 4 presents the model's results; and Section 5 concludes.

2. A Bayesian model of pricing behavior

This model extends the Madhavan and Smidt (1991) model in two ways. First, on the information side, it introduces a role for marketwide order flow. This is an important dimension of dealing in a decentralized multiple-dealer setting (see Lyons, 1994). Second, on the inventory-control side, it incorporates the fact that FX dealers use tools not available to a specialist (e.g., laying off inventory at another dealer's price).

Consider a pure exchange economy with two assets, one riskless (the numeraire) and one with a stochastic liquidation value, representing FX. The FX market is organized as a decentralized dealership market with n dealers. Here, I focus on the pricing decision of a representative dealer, denoted dealer i; accordingly, a period is defined by an incoming order at dealer i's quote, where incoming means initiated by dealer i's counterparty, denoted dealer j. Periods run from $t = 1, 2, \ldots, T$.

To accommodate the model's information asymmetry, I assume that transactions are *ex post* regret-free for the quoting dealer, in the sense of Glosten and Milgrom (1985). This means, for example, that when dealer i quotes an offer for quantity ten, built into the quote is an answer to the question: How would my expectation of value change if dealer j bought ten, given that he may have private information? Similarly, the bid side rationally incorporates any updating a sale of ten would engender. To accommodate all possible order sizes, the dealer quotes a schedule assigning a price to each quantity, buy or sell. This schedule therefore internalizes the proper inference for any potential order, and ensures the quoting dealer will not regret the quote *ex post*.

The rest of the model's specification is presented in three blocks: First the information environment, then the formation of expectations conditional on the information environment, and finally the determination of bid/offer quotes as a function of expectations and current inventory.

2.1. *The information environment*

The full information price of FX at time T is denoted by $\tilde{V}$, which is composed of a series of increments – e.g., interest differentials – so that $\tilde{V} = \sum_{i=0}^{T} \tilde{r}_i$, where r_0 is a known constant. The increments are i.i.d. mean zero. Each increment r_t is realized immediately after trading in period t. Realizations of the increments represent the flow of public information over time. The value of FX at t is thus defined as $V_t = \sum_{i=0}^{t} r_i$. At the time of quoting and trading in period t, i.e., before $\tilde{r}_t$ is realized, V_t is a random variable. Given this structure, without transaction costs or further information, the quoted price of FX at time t would equal V_{t-1}, which is the expected value of the asset conditional on public information at t.

The following three signals define each period's information environment prior to dealer i's quote to dealer j. The first two are received simultaneously, prior to the third:

$$\tilde{S}_t = V_t + \tilde{\eta}_t, \tag{1}$$

$$\tilde{C}_{jt} = V_t + \tilde{\omega}_{jt}, \tag{2}$$

$$\tilde{Q}_t = V_t + \tilde{\xi}_t. \tag{3}$$

The noise terms η_t, ω_{jt}, and ξ_t are normally distributed about zero, are independent of one another and across periods, and have variances σ_η^2, σ_ω^2, and σ_ξ^2, respectively. At the outset of each period t, all dealers receive a public signal S_t of the full-information value V_t. Also at the outset of each period t, dealer j receives a private signal C_{jt} of V_t. One potential source of private signals at the FX dealer level is order flow from nondealer customers. Each dealer has sole knowledge of his own-customer order flow; to the extent this flow conveys information it is private information, and can be exploited in interdealer trading (Lyons, 1994).

The third signal, Q_t, is an additional public signal introduced here to reflect the institutions of the FX market. It is distinct from S_t in that it is measurable by the econometrician. In particular, Q_t represents a signal of marketwide order flow. As indicated above, there is one source of information on marketwide order flow that provides transparency in an otherwise opaque FX trading process. This signal is provided verbally by interdealer brokers via intercoms at the dealers' desks. Specifically, when a brokered trade clears either the bid or offer at that broker, this is communicated to dealers marketwide. Though the precise quantity is not announced, dealers can infer a quantity on the basis of their knowledge of typical sizes; since the direction of the aggressor is established by whether the bid or offer was cleared, the quantity can be signed. To put this statistic in perspective, note that (i) about half of interdealer trading is arranged through brokers, (ii) typically 50% or more of brokered transactions clear the best bid or offer, and (iii) this is the only source of marketwide order flow available to dealers. The next section provides some additional institutional background regarding brokers and the precise information they convey. The important point for this model is that in the FX market, dealers do receive information regarding other dealers' orders, and proxies for this information are available to the econometrician.

The last conditioning variable dealer i uses to determine his quote schedule is the quantity dealer j might trade in period t, denoted Q_{jt}. That is, consistent with the regret-free property discussed above, dealer i quotes a schedule of prices that protects him from adverse selection. Of course, the realized quantity Q_{jt} still provides a signal of the $\tilde{C}_{jt}$ received by dealer j. Under the usual assumptions (exponential utility defined over end-of-period wealth), the quantity dealer j chooses to trade is linearly related to the deviation between dealer j's expectation and the transaction price, plus a quantity representing liquidity demand X_{jt} that is uncorrelated with V_t (e.g., inventory-adjustment trading):

$$Q_{jt} = \theta(\mu_{jt} - P_{it}) + X_{jt}, \tag{4}$$

where μ_{jt} is the expectation of V_t conditional on information available to dealer j at t, and the value of X_{jt} is known only to dealer j. Note that Q_{jt} can take either sign.

Fig. 1 summarizes the timing of the model in each period.

2.2. *The formation of expectations*

Dealer i's quote schedule is a function of the expectation of V_t at the time of quoting, which is denoted μ_{it}. This expectation, in turn, is conditioned on the

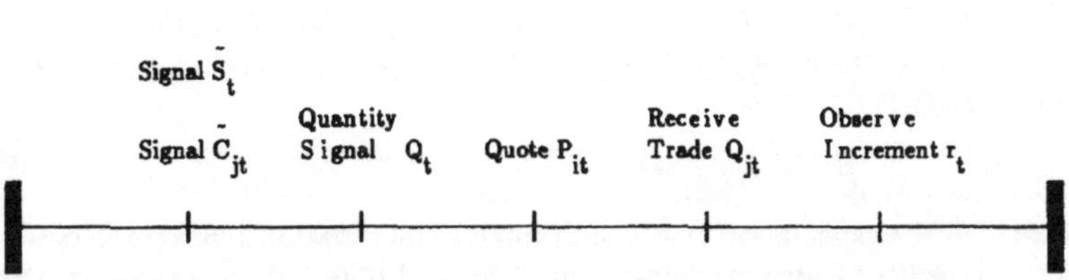

Fig. 1. Timing within each period, where a period is defined over each incoming order at dealer i's quote.

Definitions: $\tilde{S}_t$ is a public signal of the full information value V_t; $\tilde{C}_{jt}$ is dealer j's private signal of V_t, where j denotes the dealer requesting the quote from dealer i; Q_t is a public signal of interdealer trading not involving dealer i; P_{it} is dealer i's bilateral quote to dealer j, a schedule matching each transaction quantity with a particular price; Q_{jt} is the signed incoming order, positive for dealer j purchases, negative for sales; and r_t is the period t increment to V_t.

signals described above: S_t, Q_t, and Q_{jt} (the fourth variable described above, $\tilde{C}_{jt}$, is the signal embedded in Q_{jt}).

Dealer i's prior belief regarding V_t is summarized by the first public signal S_t. After observing the second public signal Q_t, dealer i's posterior belief, denoted μ_t, can be expressed as a weighted average of S_t and Q_t:

$$\mu_t \equiv \rho S_t + (1 - \rho) Q_t , \tag{5}$$

where $\rho \equiv \sigma_\xi^2/(\sigma_\xi^2 + \sigma_\eta^2)$. These posterior beliefs μ_t are normally distributed with mean V_t and variance $\sigma_\mu^2 \equiv \rho^2\sigma_\eta^2 + (1-\rho)^2\sigma_\xi^2$.

After observing Q_t, dealer i then conditions on various possible Q_{jt}'s (and the schedule he quotes internalizes this inference). In particular, dealer i can form the statistic Z_{jt} (see Appendix):

$$Z_{jt} \equiv \frac{Q_{jt}/\theta + P_{it} - \lambda\mu_t}{1-\lambda} = V_t + \tilde{\omega}_{jt} + [1/\theta(1-\lambda)]\tilde{X}_{jt} , \tag{6}$$

where $\lambda \equiv \sigma_\omega^2/(\sigma_\mu^2 + \sigma_\omega^2)$. This statistic is also normally distributed, with mean V_t and variance equal to the variance of the last two terms, both of which are orthogonal to V_t. Let σ_{Zj}^2 denote this variance. Note that Z_{jt} is statistically independent of μ_t, since Z_{jt} is orthogonal to both S_t and Q_t. Thus, dealer i's posterior μ_{it}, expressed as a function of any Q_{jt}, takes the form of a weighted average of μ_t and Z_{jt}:

$$\mu_{it} = \kappa\mu_t + (1-\kappa) Z_{jt} , \tag{7}$$

where $\kappa \equiv \sigma_{Zj}^2/(\sigma_{Zj}^2 + \sigma_\mu^2)$. This expectation plays a central role in determining dealer i's quote, to which I now turn.

2.3. *The determination of bid/offer quotes*

Consider the following prototypical inventory model: Here, price P_{it} is linearly related to the dealer's current inventory, which is optimal in a number of inventory-control models:

$$P_{it} = \mu_{it} - \alpha(I_{it} - I_i^*) + \gamma D_t , \tag{8}$$

where μ_{it} is the expectation of V_t conditional on information available to dealer i at t, I_{it} is dealer i's current inventory position, and I_i^* is i's desired position. The inventory-control effect, governed by α, will in general be a function of relative interest rates, firm capital, and carrying costs.

The term γD_t picks up bid–offer bounce in the model. D_t is a direction-indicator variable that equals one when the transaction price P_{it} is the offer and minus one when P_{it} is the bid. For a given expectation μ_{it}, γD_t thus picks up half of the spread. (Of course, to protect against adverse selection, the quoted spread widens with quantity due to effects on μ_{it}; γD_t should therefore be viewed as half the spread for quantities close to zero.) This term can be interpreted as compensation resulting from execution costs, price discreteness, or rents.

Consistent with the regret-free property of quotes, I substitute dealer i's expectation μ_{it} in Eq. (7) into Eq. (8), yielding

$$P_{it} = \kappa\mu_t + (1 - \kappa)Z_{jt} - \alpha(I_{it} - I_i^*) + \gamma D_t \,, \qquad (9)$$

which is equivalent to (see Appendix)

$$P_{it} = (1 - \rho)Q_t + \rho S_t + \left[\frac{1 - \phi}{\phi\theta}\right]Q_{jt} - \left[\frac{\alpha}{\phi}\right](I_{it} - I_i^*) + \left[\frac{\gamma}{\phi}\right]D_t \,, \qquad (10)$$

where the parameter $\phi \equiv (\kappa - \lambda)/(1 - \lambda)$ and $0 < \phi < 1$ since $0 < \kappa < 1$, $0 < \lambda < 1$, and $\kappa < \lambda$.

2.4. *An estimable equation*

Eq. (10) is not directly estimable for two reasons: First, the signal of market-wide order flow Q_t must be proxied in estimation (and I have to take into account that the proxy does not have the simple stochastic properties of the signal Q_t). Second, S_t is not observable to the econometrician.

I address first the impact of the proxy for Q_t. In estimation, I use data on marketwide order flow at a particular broker as a proxy for Q_t. This brokered order flow does not involve dealer i, but provides a signal observed by dealer i. I specify the signal of brokered order flow, B_t, in the following way:

$$B_t = \sum_{k=1}^{m} Q_{kt} + \psi_t \,. \qquad (11)$$

The sum represents the net order flow of m brokered trades not involving dealer i. The noise ψ_t is independently distributed normal, with mean zero and variance σ_ψ^2. I assume that the information content of these m trades has the same structure as the trade of dealer j; that is, using the definition of Q_{jt} in Eq. (4), I have

$$\sum_{k=1}^{m} Q_{kt} = \sum_{k=1}^{m} [\theta(\mu_{kt} - \mu_t) + \tilde{X}_{kt}] \,, \qquad (12)$$

where μ_{kt} is the expectation of V_t conditional on information available to dealer k at t, and X_{kt} is a liquidity component of each trade, the value of which is known only to the aggressor. The individual expectations μ_{kt} are a function of private signals C_{kt}, where

$$\tilde{C}_{kt} = V_t + \tilde{\omega}_{kt} \,, \qquad (13)$$

which parallels Eq. (2) describing the private signal available to dealer j, the dealer trading on i's prices. The ω_{kt}'s are distributed i.i.d. normal with mean zero and variance σ_ω^2. With this specification, the relationship between the observable B_t and a canonical signal Q_t is (see Appendix)

$$Q_t = \left[\frac{1}{m\theta(1-\lambda)\rho}\right]B_t + S_t\,. \tag{14}$$

Substituting this relationship into Eq. (10) yields

$$P_{it} = S_t + \left[\frac{1-\phi}{\phi\theta}\right]Q_{jt} - \left[\frac{\alpha}{\phi}\right](I_{it} - I_i^*) + \left[\frac{\gamma}{\phi}\right]D_t + \left[\frac{1-\rho}{m\theta(1-\lambda)\rho}\right]B_t\,. \tag{15}$$

I turn now to the unobservability of S_t. The assumptions about the signals available and the evolution of V_t allow me to express the period t prior as equal to the period $t-1$ posterior from Eq. (8) lagged one period, plus an expectational error term ε_{it}:

$$S_t = \mu_{it-1} + \varepsilon_{it} = P_{it-1} + \alpha(I_{it-1} - I_i^*) - \gamma D_{t-1} + \varepsilon_{it}\,. \tag{16}$$

Substituting this expression for S_t into Eq. (15) yields

$$P_{it} = [P_{it-1} + \alpha(I_{it-1} - I_i^*) - \gamma D_{t-1} + \varepsilon_{it}] + \left[\frac{1-\phi}{\phi\theta}\right]Q_{jt}$$

$$- \left[\frac{\alpha}{\phi}\right](I_{it} - I_i^*) + \left[\frac{\gamma}{\phi}\right]D_t + \left[\frac{1-\rho}{m\theta(1-\lambda)\rho}\right]B_t\,.$$

Therefore,

$$\Delta P_{it} = \left[\frac{\alpha}{\phi} - \alpha\right]I_i^* + \left[\frac{1-\phi}{\phi\theta}\right]Q_{jt} - \left[\frac{\alpha}{\phi}\right]I_{it} + \alpha I_{it-1} + \left[\frac{\gamma}{\phi}\right]D_t - \gamma D_{t-1}$$

$$+ \left[\frac{1-\rho}{m\theta(1-\lambda)\rho}\right]B_t + \varepsilon_{it}\,. \tag{17}$$

This corresponds to a reduced-form estimating equation of

$$\Delta P_{it} = \beta_0 + \beta_1 Q_{jt} + \beta_2 I_{it} + \beta_3 I_{it-1} + \beta_4 D_t + \beta_5 D_{t-1} + \beta_6 B_t + \varepsilon_{it}\,. \tag{18}$$

The model thus predicts that $\{\beta_1, \beta_3, \beta_4, \beta_6\} > 0$, $\{\beta_2, \beta_5\} < 0$, $|\beta_2| > \beta_3$, and $\beta_4 > |\beta_5|$, where the latter inequalities derive from the fact that $0 < \phi < 1$.

2.5. The error structure

As in Madhavan and Smidt (1991), this model implies a particular structure for the error term ε_{it} in Eq. (18). To see this, note that Eq. (16) allows me to write: $\varepsilon_{it} = S_t - \mu_{it-1}$. The two components on the right-hand side reduce to

$$S_t = V_t + \eta_t, \tag{16a}$$

$$\mu_{it-1} = \kappa\mu_{t-1} + (1-\kappa)Z_{jt-1}, \tag{16b}$$

using Eqs. (1) and (7), respectively. The latter expression for μ_{it-1}, after substitutions from Eqs. (5), (6), and (A.1), can be expressed as

$$\mu_{it-1} = V_{t-1} + \kappa\rho\eta_{t-1} + \kappa(1-\rho)\Bigg[m^{-1}\sum_{k \neq j}^{m}\tilde{\omega}_{kt-1} + [m\theta(1-\lambda)]^{-1}\sum_{k \neq j}^{m}\tilde{X}_{kt-1}$$
$$+ [m\theta(1-\lambda)]^{-1}\tilde{\psi}_{t-1}\Bigg] + (1-\kappa)[\tilde{\omega}_{jt-1} + [1/\theta(1-\lambda)]\tilde{X}_{jt-1}]. \tag{16c}$$

Now, to determine $E[\varepsilon_{it}\varepsilon_{it-1}]$, recall that $\tilde{\psi}$ and the increments to V are independent across time, and that ω, $\tilde{X}$, and $\tilde{\psi}$ are independent across dealers and time. Accordingly, $E[\varepsilon_{it}\varepsilon_{it-1}] = E[-\kappa\rho\eta_{t-1}\eta_{t-1}] = -\kappa\rho\sigma_\eta^2$, where the first η_{t-1} comes from the μ_{it-1} component of ε_{it} and the second comes from the S_{t-1} component of ε_{it-1}. Thus, the model predicts the error term ε_{it} should conform to an MA(1):

$$\varepsilon_{it} = \beta_7 v_{it-1} + v_{it}, \tag{19}$$

with $\beta_7 < 0$. Henceforth, I include this substitution in Eq. (18).

2.6. Additional tools for controlling inventory

I can extend the model further by incorporating the fact that FX dealers control inventory in ways not available to a specialist. Specifically, a dealer can sell inventory at another dealer's price (i.e., an outgoing trade), or a dealer can sell inventory through a broker. To capture this, I decompose dealer i's inventory at time t:

$$I_{it} = I_{it-1} + Q^{\mathrm{o}}_{i\Delta t} + Q^{\mathrm{b}}_{i\Delta t} - Q_{jt}, \tag{20}$$

or equivalently,

$$\Delta I_{it} = Q^{\mathrm{o}}_{i\Delta t} + Q^{\mathrm{b}}_{i\Delta t} - Q_{jt}. \tag{21}$$

Here, $Q^{o}_{i\Delta t}$ denotes dealer i's outgoing trades (net) occurring between $t-1$ and t (recall that periods are defined by incoming trades), $Q^{b}_{i\Delta t}$ denotes dealer i's brokered trades (net) occurring between $t-1$ and t, and ΔI_{it} denotes dealer i's inventory change from $t-1$ to t, which includes the incoming order Q_{jt}.[2]

To provide perspective on this decomposition, note that disentangling information effects from inventory-control effects requires breaking the perfect collinearity in a pure specialist market between incoming trades Q_{jt} and inventory changes ΔI_{it}. In this model, perfect collinearity is broken in two ways: (i) In addition to incoming trades Q_{jt}, ΔI_{it} includes outgoing trades and brokered trades; and (ii) brokered trades not involving dealer i provide signed volume information, but have no effect on I_{it} (proxied here by B_t). The first of these is made explicit by the decomposition.

Bringing this back to the reduced form in Eq. (18), I can write

$$\Delta P_{it} = \beta_0 + \beta_1 Q_{jt} + \beta_2 \Delta I_{it} + (\beta_2 + \beta_3) I_{it-1} + \beta_4 D_t + \beta_5 D_{t-1} + \beta_6 B_t + \beta_7 v_{it-1} + v_{it}. \quad (22)$$

Clearly, collinearity prevents estimation of separate coefficients for each of the three components of ΔI_{it} in Eq. (21). The data do, however, provide enough discriminating power to estimate an equation of the form:

$$\Delta P_{it} = \beta_0 + \beta_1 Q_{jt} + \beta_2 Q^{o}_{i\Delta t} + \beta_2'(Q^{b}_{i\Delta t-1} - Q_{jt}) + (\beta_2 + \beta_3) I_{it-1} + \beta_4 D_t + \beta_5 D_{t-1} + \beta_6 B_t + \beta_7 v_{it-1} + v_{it}. \quad (23)$$

Here, $Q^{o}_{i\Delta t}$ is included as a separate inventory-control variable. The model then predicts that the inventory-control effects β_2 and β_2' should be equal. Note, too, that $\beta_2 + \beta_3 = \alpha(1 - \phi^{-1})$, which approaches zero from below as the structural parameter $\phi \in (0, 1)$ approaches one (a larger ϕ implies that private information is imprecise relative to public information). Finally, I can test whether the presence of outgoing trades or brokered trades affects the other estimated coefficients in the model.

2.7. Two final comments on the model

The empirical implementation of the model warrants two further comments. First, note that with a slight reinterpretation, the model can accommodate variability in desired inventories, that is, an I_i^* that varies through time. Consider the following model: $I_{it}^* = \bar{I}_i + \delta(\mu_{it} - \mu_t)$, which is consistent with the

[2]In addition to incoming and outgoing orders and brokered trades (all of which are interdealer), FX dealers also trade with nondealer customers. Over this sample, the dealer did virtually no customer trading. For the FX market as a whole, interdealer trading accounts for about 90% of volume, and customer–dealer trading accounts for about 10%.

linear demands arising from negative exponential utility, where μ_t represents the market price away from dealer i. Since Q_{jt} is the only information available to dealer i that is not reflected in μ_t, it can be shown under the assumptions of this model that $(\mu_{it} - \mu_t)$ is proportional to Q_{jt}. Accordingly, I write $(\mu_{it} - \mu_t) = \pi Q_{jt}$, and can therefore express the desired inventory as follows: $I^*_{it} = \bar{I}_i + \delta\pi Q_{jt}$. In estimation, $\bar{I}_i$ will be absorbed in the constant. The estimate of β_1 now represents $[(1 - \phi)/\phi\theta] + [(\alpha/\phi) - \alpha]\delta\pi$, whose significance still evinces an information effect, though I have to be more careful in interpreting its magnitude.

A second issue relevant to empirical implementation is simultaneity. To see that simultaneity is not a problem here, recall that though quoting precedes trading, a quote is a schedule from which dealer j, by selecting Q_{jt}, determines the transaction price P_{it}. By design, there is no intrinsic-value information available to dealer i that is not available to dealer j. Hence, under the null there is no feedback here from P_{it} to the information content of Q_{jt}, which is what the coefficient β_1 measures. To think of it a different way, suppose a public announcement occurs during this period that raises the expectation of V_t conditional on public information. Though P_{it} will be higher, this does not help predict dealer j's trade this period since j's trade reflects only the orthogonal component of his beliefs relative to P_{it}, i.e., his C_{jt}.[3]

3. Data

The dataset introduced in this paper is qualitatively different from any yet employed in the exchange rate literature. The main difference is that it contains transaction prices and quantities. The existing alternative is constructed from what are called 'indicative' quotes, which are input to Reuters by trading banks (see Goodhart and Figliuoli, 1991; Bollerslev and Domowitz, 1993; Bessembinder, 1994). Some of the shortcomings of the indicative quotes include the following: First, they are not transactable prices. Second, while it is true that the indicated spreads usually bracket actual quoted spreads in the interbank market, they are typically two to three times as wide (documented below). Third, the indications are less likely to bracket true spreads when volatility is highest since there are limits to how frequently the indications can change. And finally, my experience, sitting next to dealers at major banks, indicates that they pay no attention whatsoever to the current indication; rather, dealers garner most of their high-frequency market information from signals

[3]The argument that the correlation between S_t and ε_{it} from Eq. (16) implies that Q_{jt} and ε_{it} are correlated is flawed: Both S_t and ε_{it} are known by dealer i at the time of quoting; correlation between Q_{jt} and ε_{it} is thus inconsistent with regret-free quoting.

transmitted via intercoms connected to interdealer brokers (see Lyons, 1994). In reality, the main purpose of the indicative quotes is to provide nondealer participants with a gauge of where the interdealer market is trading.

The dataset employed here consists of three interlinked components, covering the five trading days of the week August 3–7, 1992 from the informal start of trading at 8:30 a.m. Eastern Standard Time to roughly 1:30 p.m. Eastern Standard Time. The first component includes the time-stamped quotes, prices, and quantities for all the direct interdealer transactions of a single DM/$ dealer at a major New York bank. The second component comprises the same dealer's position cards, which include all indirect (brokered) trades. The third component includes the time-stamped prices and quantities for transactions mediated by one of the major New York brokers in the same market. These trades do not involve 'our' dealer.

3.1. Dealer data: Direct quotes and trades

The first component of the dataset includes the dealer's quotes, prices, and quantities for all direct transactions. The availability of this component is due to a recent change in technology in this market, the Reuters Dealing 2000-1 system. This system – very different from the system that produces the Reuters indications – allows dealers to communicate bilateral quotes and trades via computer rather than verbally over the telephone. Dealers can request multiple quotes simultaneously, and the computerized documentation reduces paperwork. The use of this technology differs by dealer and is growing rapidly. For example, our dealer uses Dealing 2000-1 for nearly all of his direct interdealer trades: Less than 0.4% of all transactions were done over the phone during the sample week, as indicated on the position cards.

Each record for the data covering the dealer's direct trades includes the following seven variables:

(1) the time the communication is initiated (to the minute, with no lag),
(2) whether the quote request is incoming or outgoing,
(3) the quote quantity,
(4) the bid quote,
(5) the offer quote,
(6) the transaction quantity (providing Q_{jt} if trade is incoming),
(7) the transaction price (providing P_{it} if trade is incoming).

This part of the dataset includes 952 transactions amounting to $4.1 billion. Fig. 2 provides an example of a dealer communication as recorded by the Dealing 2000-1 printout (see Reuters, 1990, for more details). Note especially

```
From CODE   FULL NAME HERE  * 1250GMT 030892 */1080
Our Terminal : CODE   Our user  : DMK
   SP DMK 10
# 8891
   BUY

#  10 MIO AGREED
#  VAL 6AUG92
#  MY DMK TO FULL NAME HERE
#  TO CONFIRM AT 1.5891 I SELL 10 MIO USD
#
    TO CONFIRM AT 1.5891 I SELL 10 MIO USD
    VAL 6AUG92
    MY USD TO FULL NAME HERE  AC 0-00-00000
    THKS N BIFN
#
#  #END LOCAL#
#
   ## WRAP UP BY DMK DMK 1250GMT 3AUG92

   #END#

( 265 CHARS)
```

Fig. 2. Example of a Reuters Dealing 2000-1 communication.

'From' establishes this as an incoming call; the caller's four-digit code and institution name follow; 'GMT' denotes Greenwich Mean Time; the date follows, with the day listed first; 'SP DMK 10' identifies this as request for a spot DM/$ quote for $10 million; '8891' denotes a bid of 88 and an offer of 91 (only the last two digits are quoted); the confirmation provides the complete transaction price of DM 1.5891/$, and verifies the transaction quantity.

that all Dealing 2000-1 transactions in the dataset takes place at the quoted bid or the quoted offer; the interdealer FX market is not one in which transaction prices are negotiated within the spread.

3.2. Dealer data: Position cards

The second component of the dataset is composed of the dealer's position cards over the same five days covered by the direct-transaction data, August 3–7, 1992. To track their inventories, dealers in the spot market record all their transactions on handwritten position cards as they go along. An average day consists of approximately twenty cards, each with about fifteen transaction entries.

There are two key benefits to this part of the dataset. First, it provides a clean measure of the dealer's inventory I_t at any time since it includes both direct trades and any brokered trades. Second, it provides a means of error-checking the first part of the dataset.

Each card includes the following information for every trade:

(1) the quantity traded (which determines I_t),
(2) the transaction price,
(3) the counterparty, including whether brokered.

Note that the bid/offer quotes at the time of the transaction are not included, so this component of the dataset is not sufficient for estimating the model. Note also that each entry is not time-stamped; at the top of every card, and often within the card too, the dealer records the time to the minute. Hence, the exact timing of some of the brokered transactions is not pinned down, since these trades are not confirmed via a Dealing 2000-1 record. Nevertheless, this is not a drawback for the purposes of this paper: The observations for the empirical model are the direct transactions initiated at our dealer's quoted prices; since the timing of these is pinned down by the Dealing 2000-1 records, and since these transactions appear sequentially in both components, any intervening changes in inventory due to brokered trades can be determined exactly.

3.3. *Broker data*

The data covering the New York broker's activities include time-stamped transaction prices and quantities over the same week covered by the other two components of the dataset. These data are transcribed from transaction tickets, which are filled out by the brokers themselves in their dealing room. The tickets are collected in small batches by an attendant and time-stamped. This component of the dataset includes 1172 transactions amounting to roughly $6.7 billion.

The data on the broker's transactions do not include the bid and offer at the time of each transaction, so I infer the trade direction from the transaction prices. I use the method recommended by Lee and Ready (1991), which codes price upticks as buyer-initiated, price downticks as seller-initiated, and no change in price as initiated by the same side as the previous transaction.

The resulting series provides a measure of B_t for the model. To insure that information in B_t is prior to the transaction Q_{jt}, I construct B_t by summing the signed trades from the two minutes prior to the minute in which Q_{jt} is effected, where two minutes corresponds to the median intertransaction time.

To put these data in perspective, remember that dealers in the major currencies trade while listening to so-called 'broker boxes', the intercoms over which interdealer brokers provide information on dealer prices and, when transactions occur, signed quantities. For each of the major currencies, there are typically four or five brokers who account for nearly all of the brokered trading. Hence, by listening to these brokers, dealers receive a common signal of signed volume and transaction prices. This statistic is the core of the dealer's high-frequency information set.

In spot FX, there is no source other than broker intercoms for marketwide order-flow information. While it is true that dealers have other motivations for using brokers, the fact that brokered trading defines the degree of transparency is undeniable. To determine the overall degree of order-flow transparency, consider first the share of spot trading that is brokered: 39% on average in 1989 across the seven countries with the highest turnover whose statistics are comparable, with a high of 44% and a low of 35% (Bank for International Settlements, 1990). (The remaining shares of total volume not brokered are about 50% from direct interdealer trades and about 10% customer–dealer trades.) Of the $\approx$ 40% of total trading that is brokered, only a portion of these trades generates a signal of signed volume. This is because a sale or purchase is announced only when it clears the bid or offer at the given broker. Though the likelihood of this depends on the currency, two dealers that trade different currencies for different firms estimated for me that this occurs for 50% to 75% of brokered trades. For example, if a broker is advertising underlying dealer prices of DM1.6045–DM1.6050 per dollar, and a buyer of dollars clears the offer, the broker will announce '50 paid', which indicates that the aggressor was a buyer. Though the exact size is not known, the median brokered quantity is about $5 million.

In light of this institutional background, three concerns regarding the broker data deserve attention. First, the data cover the trading activity of only one of the four for five main DM/$ brokers. Hence, just as dealer data reflect but a piece of the whole market, the broker data reflect only a piece of the brokered trading activity. Second, there is no way to determine on the basis of broker data available whether the bid or offer was cleared by any given transaction. Hence, some of the trades in this component of the dataset did not provide a signal to our dealer. Third, while the Dealing 2000-1 records include a precise, to-the-minute time stamp, the time stamps on the brokered transactions have a slight lag that corresponds to the time it takes the attendant to collect the tickets and stamp them. Due to these data shortcomings, I present estimates both with and without the signed brokered order flow B_t.

3.4. Descriptive statistics

Tables 1–3 present descriptive statistics. Because the dataset is new, the statistics are more detailed than usual. To convey a sense of the typical day's activity, Table 1 presents the data in the form of daily averages. This masks some daily variation in the sample: The heaviest day (8/7/92) is nearly twice as active as the lightest day (8/5/92). Note that this dealer averages well over $1 billion of interdealer trading daily (brokered trades are necessarily interdealer). With respect to quoting, because our dealer is among the larger players in this market, he has $10 million 'relationships' with many other dealers; that is, quote requests from other high-volume dealers that do not specify a quantity are

Table 1
Overview statistics, August 3–7, 1992

Data for the dealer's direct (not brokered) interdealer transactions are from the Reuters Dealing 2000-1 communications; these statistics include all direct transactions executed using Dealing 2000-1, regardless of which party is the aggressor. Incoming refers to communications initiated by another dealer; outgoing refers to communications initiated by our dealer. Data for the dealer's brokered transactions are from the dealer's position sheets; it is not possible to identify the aggressor from these data. Data from the broker are transcribed from transaction tickets; it is not possible to identify the aggressor from these data. The trades in the two dealer columns reflect more than 95% of this dealer's trading; the trades that make up the remainder are executed either (i) over the phone, (ii) with a nondealer customer, or (iii) in the futures market (IMM). The dealer's average trading day begins at 8:30 a.m. and ends around 1:30 p.m. EST.

	Dealer		
	Direct	Brokered	Broker
(1) Ave. # transactions daily	190	77	234
(A) incoming	170		
(B) outgoing	20		
(2) Ave. value transactions daily	$0.8 B	$0.4 B	$1.3 B
(A) incoming	$0.65 B		
(B) outgoing	$0.15 B		
(3) Median transaction size	$3 M	$4 M	$5 M
(A) incoming	$3 M		
(B) outgoing	$5 M		
(4) Median spread	DM 0.0003		
(A) incoming	DM 0.0003		
(B) outgoing	DM 0.0003		

understood to be good for $10 million. Note the tightness of the median spread. For comparison, the median spread in the Reuters indications dataset constructed by Goodhart is DM 0.001, more than three times as large. A bid/offer spread of three pips corresponds to less than 0.02% of the spot price.

Tables 2 and 3 present sample moments and a sample correlation matrix for the relevant variables used in estimation plus the intertransaction times. The first column of Table 3 bodes well for the model; these regressors all have the predicted correlation with the dependent variable ΔP_{it}. Note also that the intertransaction times are uncorrelated with the model variables (all are insignificant).

Figs. 3 and 4 present two plots. The first is the transaction price over the full sample, Monday, August 3 to Friday, August 7, 1992. The second plot provides the position (inventory) variability over the week; the maximum long dollar position was $56.8 million, the maximum short dollar position $42.7 million.

Table 2
Descriptive statistics: Sample moments

SD denotes standard deviation. 25% and 75% denote the 25th and 75th percentile values, respectively. ΔP_{it} is the change in the incoming transaction price (DM/$) from $t-1$ to t, expressed in pips, or DM 0.0001. All quantity variables are in $ millions. Q_{jt} is the quantity transacted directly at dealer i's quoted prices, positive for purchases (i.e., effected at the offer) and negative for sales (at the bid). I_t is i's position at the end of period t. B_t is the net quantity of third-party brokered trading over the previous two minutes, positive for buyer-initiated trades and negative for seller-initiated trades. Δt denotes the intertransaction time, in minutes. Sample: August 3–7, 1992, 839 observations.

	Mean	SD	25%	75%
ΔP_{it}	−0.2	4.7	−3.0	2.0
$\lvert\Delta P_{it}\rvert$	3.2	3.4	1.0	4.0
Q_{jt}	−0.4	5.2	−3.0	2.0
$\lvert Q_{jt}\rvert$	3.8	3.6	1.0	5.0
I_{it}	2.2	15.4	−6.7	9.3
$\lvert I_{it}\rvert$	11.3	10.7	3.4	16.0
B_t	−0.1	4.5	0.0	0.0
$\lvert B_t\rvert$	1.3	4.3	0.0	0.0
Δt	1.8	2.7	0.0	2.0

Table 3
Descriptive statistics: Sample correlation matrix

ΔP_{it} is the change in the incoming transaction price (DM/$) from $t-1$ to t, expressed in pips, or DM 0.0001. All quantity variables are in $ millions. Q_{jt} is the quantity transacted directly at dealer i's quoted prices, positive for purchases (i.e., effected at the offer) and negative for sales (at the bid). I_t is i's position at the end of period t. ΔI_t is $I_t - I_{t-1}$. D_t is an indicator variable with value 1 if the incoming order is a purchase and value −1 if a sale. B_t is the net quantity of third-party brokered trading over the previous two minutes, positive for buyer-initiated trades and negative for seller-initiated trades. Δt denotes the intertransaction time, in minutes. Sample: August 3–7, 1992, 839 observations.

	ΔP_{it}	Q_{jt}	I_{it}	ΔI_{it}	D_t	B_t	Δt
ΔP_{it}	1.00						
Q_{jt}	0.38	1.00					
I_{it}	−0.14	−0.28	1.00				
ΔI_{it}	−0.32	−0.58	0.22	1.00			
D_t	0.38	0.73	−0.12	−0.44	1.00		
B_t	0.08	−0.02	0.00	0.02	0.03	1.00	
Δt	0.00	−0.01	−0.02	−0.01	−0.01	0.02	1.00

A natural concern is whether our dealer is representative of the interbank spot market. While I cannot answer this definitively, I can offer a few relevant facts. First, he has been trading in this market for many years and is well known among the other major dealers. Second, in terms of trading volume, he is

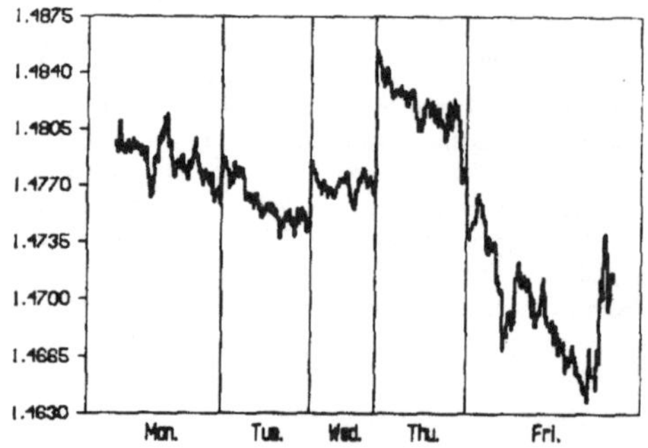

Fig. 3. Plot of the transaction price (DM/$) for all incoming orders in the sample, Monday, August 3 to Friday, August 7, 1992.

These 843 price observations are recorded by Reuters Dealing 2000-1. Their first differences correspond to the dependent variable in the model, ΔP_{it}. The vertical lines designate the four overnight periods through which the dealer did not trade. The discrete jumps at the vertical lines reflect price movements during these inactive periods.

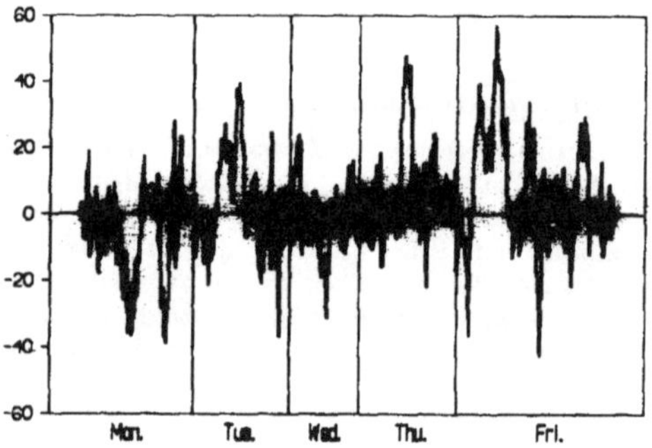

Fig. 4. Plot of dealer's dollar inventory I_{it} (in millions) at the time of each incoming order in the sample, Monday, August 3 to Friday, August 7, 1992.

These 843 inventory observations are constructed from the dealer's position sheets. Short dollar positions correspond to long DM positions, and vice versa. The vertical lines designate the four overnight periods through which the dealer did not trade.

without doubt one of the key players, trading well over $1 billion per day and maintaining $10 million quote relationships with a number of other dealers. Though this would probably not put him in the top five in terms of volume, he is not far back, possibly in the sixth to fifteenth range. He is certainly representative, at least with respect to the issues addressed here. There is no doubt, however, that different trading styles exist.

3.5. Relevant institutional background

Here, I highlight two institutional factors relevant to this analysis, trading limits imposed on dealers, and trading on the IMM futures market.

There is an important distinction between intraday trading limits and overnight limits. At our dealer's bank, which is typical of major banks, there is no explicit intraday limit on senior dealers, though dealers are expected to communicate particularly large trades to their immediate supervisor (about $50 million and above for many banks in the current DM/$ market). In contrast, most banks impose overnight limits on their dealers. Currently, a common overnight limit on a single dealer's open position is about $75 million, considerably larger than the largest open position in the sample. Most dealers, however, close their day with a zero net position; carrying an open position means monitoring it through the evening, an unattractive prospect after a full day of trading. Our dealer ends his day with a zero net position each of the five days in the sample. Finally, though broader risk-management programs are in place at the bank for which our dealer trades, it is rare in FX that a dealer's position is hedged because it aggregates unfavorably with others. When this does occur, it is typically without the participation of the individual dealer.

Trading on the IMM futures market while dealing spot differs by dealer. Our dealer's position cards show that he trades less than $1 million daily over the sample period, which is negligible relative to his daily spot volume. Like other spot dealers, he listens to an intercom that communicates futures prices. [Unlike equity markets, the spot FX market is many times larger than the futures market: In 1992, the average daily volume in New York in spot DM/$ was roughly $50 billion (New York Federal Reserve Bank, 1992). In the same year, the average daily volume on all IMM DM/$ contracts was less than $5 billion.]

4. Model estimation

4.1. The baseline model

Table 4 presents estimation results over the full five-day period. The sample size is determined by the number of incoming direct transactions, for a total of 839 observations. I have excluded the four overnight price changes, since the model is intended to explain intraday quoting dynamics, not price changes over periods through which the dealer is not active. The first row presents estimates of the full reduced form, i.e., including the information effects of third-party brokered order flow. The second row excludes the brokered-order-flow variable. It is therefore more directly comparable to results from work on the stock market, for example, Glosten and Harris (1988), Foster and Viswanathan (1990), and

340 R.K. Lyons/Journal of Financial Economics 39 (1995) 321–351

Table 4
Baseline model estimates

$$\Delta P_{it} = \beta_0 + \beta_1 Q_{jt} + \beta_2 I_{it} + \beta_3 I_{it-1} + \beta_4 D_t + \beta_5 D_{t-1} + \beta_6 B_t + \beta_7 v_{it-1} + v_{it}$$

T-statistics in parentheses. The last row indicates the signs predicted by the model. ΔP_{it} is the change in the incoming transaction price (DM/\$) from $t-1$ to t. Q_{jt} is the incoming order transacted at dealer i's quoted prices, positive for purchases (i.e., effected at the offer) and negative for sales (at the bid). I_t is dealer i's inventory at the end of period t. D_t is an indicator variable with value 1 if the incoming order is a purchase and value -1 if a sale. B_t is the net quantity of third-party brokered trading over the previous two minutes, positive for buyer-initiated trades and negative for seller-initiated trades. All quantity variables are in \$ millions. All coefficients are multiplied by 10^5. Sample: August 3–7, 1992, 839 observations. I use the Hildreth–Lu procedure to estimate β_7.

β_0	β_1	β_2	β_3	β_4	β_5	β_6	β_7	R^2
− 1.30	1.44	− 0.98	0.79	10.15	− 8.93	0.69	− 0.09	0.23
(− 0.96)	(3.10)	(− 3.59)	(3.00)	(4.73)	(− 6.12)	(2.21)	(− 2.55)	
− 1.34	1.40	− 0.97	0.78	10.43	− 9.16		− 0.09	0.22
(− 0.99)	(3.03)	(− 3.56)	(2.95)	(4.86)	(− 6.28)		(− 2.61)	
	> 0	< 0	> 0	> 0	< 0	> 0	< 0	

Madhavan and Smidt (1991). Row three indicates the predicted signs of the coefficients under the null that both information and inventory-control effects are present.

The main results from Table 4 are the very significant and properly signed coefficients on the information (order-flow) variables Q_{jt} and B_t and the inventory variables I_{it} and I_{it-1}. The size of β_1 implies that our dealer widens his spread about 2.8 pips per \$10 million (1.4 doubled) to protect against adverse selection. The size of the inventory-control coefficient β_3 [which equals α in Eq. (8)] implies that our dealer motivates inventory decumulation by shading his DM price of dollars by 0.8 pips for every \$10 million of net open position.

The coefficients on the indicator variables D_t and D_{t-1}, which measure the effective spread for Q_{jt} close to zero, are very significant, and have the predicted relative size as well, $\beta_4 > |\beta_5|$. (Recall that there is a one-to-one correspondence between D_t and the sign of Q_{jt}, so D_t controls perfectly for whether Q_{jt} is at the bid or the offer.) The coefficient β_4 suggests that once I control for the information and inventory effects, the baseline spread for this dealer is about two pips (2 times β_4 divided by 10^5). Note too that the moving average coefficient β_7 is significant and properly signed, providing further support for the model. Finally, the levels of the R^2's reflect the fact that Q_{jt} and B_t together are a small fraction of the trading activity in the wider market.

One possible way to control for the wider market would be to include ΔP from the broker data in the regression. Given the broker data available, however, there are three problems: First, the ΔP_{it}'s that make up the dependent variable come from the dealer data, which are strictly ordered and time stamped to the minute (no lag). With a mean intertransaction time less than two minutes, in many cases P_{it-1} and P_{it} have the same time stamp. Even if the broker data were time stamped immediately, there would be no way to determine whether a brokered transaction carrying the same time stamp as two dealer transactions actually occurred between the two transactions. Second, a short lag is present in the time stamping of the brokered transactions, as described in the data section. Finally, ΔP's from the broker data would incorporate bid–ask bounce that could not be netted as the dealer data can. These arguments notwithstanding, I experimented by including brokered price changes in the regression with various lags, and even leads up to five minutes to account for the time stamp lags; these proxies proved too crude to generate any significance.

4.2. Other methods of inventory control

Section 2.6 outlines two methods of inventory control available to the dealer that are not reflected in the baseline model: Trading directly on another dealer's price (outgoing trades) and trading indirectly via a broker. First, I determine whether our dealer uses these methods. Then, I determine whether use of these additional methods biases the baseline estimates of inventory control via own price. Finally, I present estimates that show exactly how these other methods of inventory control enter the baseline model.

To determine if the dealer manages inventory by trading directly on other dealers' prices or trading through brokers, I perform the following simple test: My null hypothesis is that outgoing direct trades and brokered trades are unrelated to inventory control, and are therefore equally likely to result in inventory accumulation as decumulation. Under the alternative that these trades are used for inventory control, I expect that significantly more than half of these trades result in decumulation. Table 5 presents the results.

The results are unambiguous: The incidence of decumulating trades in these two categories is far too high to explain under the null of equal likelihood. Note, too, that the test is conservative, in the sense that nonzero desired inventories can result in trades that accumulate inventory in an absolute sense, even though they are decumulating undesired inventory.

In light of the strong results in Table 5, I examine whether these two additional methods of inventory control affect the baseline estimates of inventory control via own price. That is, these three methods may be substitutes, and their relative appeal may vary over time with the value of immediacy, anonymity, and other factors. I test this in the following way: At any given time, a dealer reveals his preference for these two other methods of inventory control by using

Table 5
Null hypothesis: Outgoing direct trades and brokered trades are as likely to be inventory decumulating as accumulating

The test statistic corresponds to a test of the null that trades of the specified type - outgoing direct or brokered - are inventory decumulating with probability 1/2 (normal approximation of binomial). Sample: August 3-7, 1992.

	Outgoing direct trades	Brokered trades
Total observations	96	383
Decumulating trades	76	297
Accumulating trades	20	86
Test statistic: Standard deviations	5.7	10.8

them. Accordingly, I construct a dummy variable that equals one if either of these two methods is used between the realization of transaction prices P_{it} and P_{it-1} (which determine the dependent variable ΔP_{it} in the model), and equals zero otherwise. Of 839 observations of ΔP_{it} there are 270 for which there is at least one intervening outgoing or brokered trade. I then re-estimate the baseline model with two additional variables, the dummy multiplied by I_{it} and this product's lagged value. Under the null hypothesis, the coefficients on the inventory-control variables should not vary with my proxy for the attractiveness of the other methods; that is, the coefficients on the additional regressors should not be significantly different from zero. The alternative hypothesis is that inventory control via own prices is affected by the attractiveness of these other methods. The result: I could not reject the null that both of these additional variables have zero coefficients (p-value = 59%). In summary, though there is strong evidence that all three inventory-control methods are used, I found no evidence that this biases the baseline model estimates.

Below are estimates that show how these other methods of inventory control enter the baseline model. The way they enter follows from the decomposition of ΔI_{it} in Eq. (21) and the reformulation of the baseline model that isolates ΔI_{it} in Eq. (22). Indeed, it is precisely the systematic effect that changes in inventory have on changes in price that allows me to disentangle inventory control in the data. Substituting Eq. (21) into Eq. (22) yields

$$\Delta P_{it} = \beta_0 + \beta_1 Q_{jt} + \beta_2(Q^{o}_{i\Delta t} + Q^{b}_{i\Delta t} - Q_{jt}) + (\beta_2 + \beta_3) I_{it-1} + \beta_4 D_t + \beta_5 D_{t-1} + \beta_6 B_t + \beta_7 v_{it-1} + v_{it}, \tag{24}$$

where $Q^{o}_{i\Delta t}$ denotes dealer i's outgoing trades (net) occurring between $t-1$ and t, $Q^{b}_{i\Delta t}$ denote dealer i's brokered trades (net) occurring between $t-1$ and t, and $Q^{o}_{i\Delta t} + Q^{b}_{i\Delta t} - Q_{jt} = \Delta I_{it}$. Table 6 presents estimates of Eq. (24).

Table 6
Inventory change specification

$$\Delta P_{it} = \beta_0 + \beta_1 Q_{jt} + \beta_2(Q^{o}_{i\Delta t} + Q^{b}_{i\Delta t} - Q_{jt}) + (\beta_2 + \beta_3)I_{it-1} + \beta_4 D_t + \beta_5 D_{t-1} + \beta_6 B_t + \beta_7 v_{it-1} + v_{it}$$

T-statistics in parentheses. The last row indicates predicted signs. ΔP_{it} is the change in the incoming transaction price (DM/\$) from $t-1$ to t. Q_{jt} is the incoming order transacted at dealer i's quoted prices, positive for purchases (i.e., effected at the offer) and negative for sales (at the bid). $Q^{o}_{i\Delta t}$ is the net quantity of dealer i's outgoing trades in the interval $t-1$ to t. $Q^{b}_{i\Delta t}$ is the net quantity of dealer i's brokered trades in the interval $t-1$ to t. I_t is dealer i's inventory at the end of period t. D_t is an indicator variable with value 1 if the incoming order is a purchase and value -1 if a sale. B_t is the net quantity of third-party brokered trading over the previous two minutes, positive for buyer-initiated trades and negative for seller-initiated trades. All quantity variables are in \$ millions. All coefficients are multiplied by 10^5. Sample: August 3–7, 1992, 839 observations. I use the Hildreth–Lu procedure to estimate β_7.

β_0	β_1	β_2	$\beta_2+\beta_3$	β_4	β_5	β_6	β_7	R^2
-1.30	1.44	-0.98	-0.19	10.15	-8.93	0.69	-0.09	0.23
(-0.96)	(3.10)	(-3.59)	(-2.09)	(4.73)	(-6.12)	(2.21)	(-2.55)	
	>0	<0	<0	>0	<0	>0	<0	

This formulation of the model shows more clearly the role of $Q^{o}_{i\Delta t} + Q^{b}_{i\Delta t}$ in disentangling information effects from inventory control. The coefficient β_2 here picks up the strong control effect. (Recall that $\beta_2 + \beta_3$ approaches zero from below as the relative precision of private to public information goes to zero.) Finally, though collinearity prevents estimation of separate coefficients for each of the three components of ΔI_{it}, I can test the Eq. (23) prediction that separate coefficients for $Q^{o}_{i\Delta t}$ and $(Q^{b}_{i\Delta t} - Q_{jt})$ should be equal [coefficients β_2 and β_2' in Eq. (23)]. This null hypothesis is not rejected (p-value = 27%).

4.3. Nonlinearities and time-of-day effects

This subsection addresses two additional questions. First, are there (simple) nonlinearities in the information and inventory-control effects of trading activity? And second, are there important time-of-day effects in the data, such as increased inventory control near the end of the trading day?

First, I test for nonlinearities in the information effect of received trades by introducing a piecewise linear specification. I create a dummy variable L_t that equals one when the absolute value of Q_{jt} is above its median absolute value (\$2.5 million), and zero otherwise. I then re-estimate the baseline model in Table 4 with the additional explanatory variable $L_t Q_{jt}$, and test whether its coefficient is significant. The p-value of the test is 49%. Defining L_t with the 10th, 25th, 75th, and 90th percentiles produced similar results. Hence, I find no evidence for a piecewise linear specification of the impact of Q_{jt}. Note the significance of this in light of the incentive to break up larger trades that is implicit in the estimated coefficient on Q_{jt}. Comments from dealers on this point typically emphasize the offsetting cost of the additional time required to execute multiple orders in such a rapidly traded market.

Next I consider nonlinearities in the inventory-control effect. In a market like FX, inventory-control effects must exhibit a nonlinearity at some level: Arbitrage is possible if the quoting dealer's offer falls below another's bid, or if the bid rises above another's offer. Recall that the inventory-control effect corresponds to the size of α in Eq. (17), and is estimated as the coefficient on I_{t-1}: $\beta_3 \approx 0.79$ pips per $10 million net open position. Thus, a $40 million open position translates into prices that are adjusted about three pips to induce decumulation. To examine more formally the incremental inventory-control effects at high inventory levels, I perform the following test: I distinguish between inventory up to some threshold level, and increments beyond that threshold. Specifically, in lieu of the series I_t in the baseline model, I use I_t^{T} and I_t^{+}, where (i) I_t^{T} is defined equal to I_t if $|I_t|$ is less than the threshold $\bar{I}$, and $\bar{I}R$ otherwise, with R an indicator variable equal to one when $I_t > 0$ and minus one when $I_t < 0$, and (ii) I_t^{+} is defined equal to zero if $|I_t| < \bar{I}$, and equal to the increment $I_t - \bar{I}R$ otherwise. Accordingly, I test whether the coefficient on $I_{t-1}^{+} = 0$, i.e., that the α for these incremental positions is zero, and find that incremental effects are significant up to the $40 million level. Beyond that level, however, the coefficient is no longer significant. This is consistent with avoidance of arbitrage. From the dealer's position sheets it is clear that at higher inventory levels, it is preferable to reduce inventory via outgoing or brokered trades. Fig. 4 provides prima facie evidence that open positions above $40 million are reduced rapidly.

Concerning time-of-day effects, it is well known that FX dealers typically zero out their positions by the end of the trading day, and this is the case for each of the five days in this sample (see Fig. 4). This temporal structure may influence the inventory-control parameters, among others. Accordingly, I perform chow tests to determine whether coefficients are stable through the day. For each day, I cut the sample into an early and late period, three different ways: (i) at the median transaction time, (ii) at the time when 25% of the transactions remain, and (iii) at the time when 10% of the transactions remain. I find no evidence at conventional significance levels for instabilities in any of the coefficients at any of the breaks except the inventory-control coefficients. Table 7 presents the results in that case.

In the case of the final 10%, the coefficients β_2 and β_3 are muted at the end of the day, rather than amplified. When I asked the dealer about this result, he responded: 'Of course. Remember, all of us listen to broker prices, so when I shade my price it gives the caller a sense of my position. At the end of my trading day it is important to keep my position to myself, since other dealers are also getting rid of positions in order to go home flat'. This dealer clearly prefers the other methods of inventory control late in the day.

Table 7
Null hypothesis: Inventory-control coefficients β_2 and β_3 are constant through the day

$$\Delta P_{it} = \beta_0 + \beta_1 Q_{jt} + \beta_2 I_{it} + \beta_3 I_{it-1} + \beta_4 D_t + \beta_5 D_{t-1} + \beta_6 B_t + \psi_{it} + \beta_7 \psi_{it-1}$$

P-values correspond to the marginal significance level of the Chow test that both β_2 and β_3 in the baseline model are the same value late in the day as early, where 'late in the day' is defined as either the final 50%, 25%, or 10% of the trades each day. ΔP_{it} is the change in the incoming transaction price (DM/\$) from $t-1$ to t. Q_{jt} is the incoming order transacted at dealer i's quoted prices, positive for purchases (i.e., effected at the offer) and negative for sales (at the bid). I_t is dealer i's inventory at the end of period t. D_t is an indicator variable with value 1 if the incoming order is a purchase and value -1 if a sale. B_t is the net quantity of third-party brokered trading over the previous two minutes, positive for buyer-initiated trades and negative for seller-initiated trades. Sample: August 3–7, 1992, 839 observations.

	Final 50%	Final 25%	Final 10%
P-value	79.7%	10.8%	3.8%

4.4. Transaction time versus real time

The last dimension of my analysis addresses the use of transaction time as the empirical basis. Though intertransaction times are tightly distributed and uncorrelated with the model's variables (Tables 2 and 3), the coefficient β_1 on Q_{jt} will be affected if the flow of information from the various sources is not proportional to real time. To see this, note that the structural interpretation of β_1 is $(1-\phi)/\phi\theta$ [see Eq. (17)]. The key here is ϕ, defined equal to $(\kappa - \lambda)/(1-\lambda)$. κ and λ, in turn, are signal extraction coefficients that are time-invariant if the relative precision of the various signals in the model does not change. The question, then, is whether intertransaction time is related to relative precision, in which case the information content of order flow is related to intertransaction time. In the context of this model, it is not clear a priori why intertransaction time should be related to relative signal precision.

Other modeling approaches do imply a relation between intertransaction time (or 'trading intensity') and the information content of order flow. For example, in the Admati and Pfleiderer (1988) model, order flow is less informative when trading intensity is high, due to bunching of discretionary liquidity traders. In contrast, order flow in the Easley and O'Hara (1992) model is more informative when trading intensity is high, because intense trading signals that uncertain information events have occurred. Of course, the trading mechanisms of these models differ substantially from the FX market, so caution should be used in applying their insights here.

To determine in the context of FX whether intertransaction time is related to the informativeness of order flow, I perform the following test: I introduce two dummy variables, s_t and l_t. The dummy variable s_t equals one if the time since

Table 8
Is order-flow less informative when intertransaction time is short?

$\Delta P_{it} = \beta_0 + \beta_1 s_t Q_{jt} + \beta_1' l_t Q_{jt} + \beta_2 I_{it} + \beta_3 I_{it-1} + \beta_4 D_t + \beta_5 D_{t-1} + \beta_6 B_t + \beta_7 v_{it-1} + v_{it}$

T-statistics in parentheses. The coefficient β_1 measures the information effect of incoming orders for which the time since the previous incoming order is short ($s_t = 1$ and $l_t = 0$ in the equation in the heading), where short is defined as having the same time stamp (stamps are precise to the minute); 262 of 839 observations conform to this definition of a short intertransaction time. The coefficient β_1' measures the information effect of incoming orders for which the time since the previous incoming order is long ($s_t = 0$, $l_t = 1$), where long is defined as 'not short'. ΔP_{it} is the change in the incoming transaction price (DM/\$) from $t-1$ to t. Q_{jt} is the incoming order transacted at dealer i's quoted prices, positive for purchases (i.e., effected at the offer) and negative for sales (at the bid). I_t is dealer i's inventory at the end of period t. D_t is an indicator variable with value 1 if the incoming order is a purchase and value -1 if a sale. B_t is the net quantity of third-party brokered trading over the previous two minutes, positive for buyer-initiated trades and negative for seller-initiated trades. All quantity variables are in \$ millions. All coefficients are multiplied by 10^5. Sample: August 3–7, 1992, 839 observations. I use the Hildreth–Lu procedure to estimate β_7.

β_0	β_1	β_1'	β_2	β_3	β_4	β_5	β_6	β_7
−0.97	0.07	2.33	−0.88	0.67	9.82	−8.94	0.69	−0.09
(−0.72)	(0.12)	(4.55)	(−3.25)	(2.57)	(4.62)	(−6.18)	(2.24)	(−2.71)

β_1: short, β_1': long.

the previous incoming order is short, and zero if long, where short is defined as having the same time stamp (262/839 observations). The dummy variable l_t equals one if intertransaction time is long, zero if short. These dummies allow me to partition the information content of the incoming-order-flow variable Q_{jt} by including $s_t Q_{jt}$ and $l_t Q_{jt}$ in the baseline specification in lieu of Q_{jt}. Table 8 presents the results.

The coefficients on $s_t Q_{jt}$ and $l_t Q_{jt}$ imply that incoming trades occurring when trading is less intense are more informative. A test of the restriction that these two coefficients are equal is rejected at the 1% level.

I view this result as an early step in the empirics of the endogeneity of time in trading models. Earlier work (e.g., Hausman, Lo, and MacKinlay, 1992) rejects the assumption of exogenous intertransaction times, but makes little progress in establishing empirical regularities. Whether these effects are specific to the FX market remains to be determined.

5. Conclusion

I find that order flow affects prices through both an information channel and an inventory-control channel, providing support for both branches of microstructure theory. Of the two channels, the evidence for inventory control is the more novel. I estimate that inventory control induces price shading of about three-quarters of a pip for every $10 million of net open position. The strong inventory-control effect on price contrasts with previous work on the NYSE and futures markets. Further, this applies even though FX dealers have tools for controlling inventory that a specialist does not. In fact, there is strong evidence that our dealer uses these other tools: He systematically lays off inventory at other dealers' prices, trading both directly and through brokers. These results highlight the importance of inventory-control theory for understanding trading in this market.

For the information channel, the coefficient on incoming order flow implies a price response of about one pip for every $10 million. Since inside information in the usual sense is less relevant in FX, this finding calls for a broader view of what constitutes private information at the dealer level. One possibility, for example, is that the information in incoming order flow also pertains to inventories, though in an aggregate sense. Aggregate inventories may be price-relevant due to transitory liquidity effects or – at the other extreme – they may be communicating more fundamental information, because they are themselves caused by informative trades. Either way, the traditional distinction between information and inventory effects is less clear. Put differently, under this view the key distinction is aggregate versus idiosyncratic inventories. This role for aggregate dealer inventories is given further credence by the fact that price discovery relies on signals at the interdealer level; customer–dealer trades in spot FX are not publicly observed. Unfortunately, the multiple-dealer data required to test this interpretation of the information effect are not currently available.

This points to an important difficulty in focusing on a dealership market like FX. Empirical work on the specialist structure has the luxury of describing the behavior of a lone dealer. It is much more difficult to argue that by documenting the behavior of a single dealer in the FX market, I have similarly captured the FX market. Nevertheless, the dealer tracked here is without a doubt one of the key players in this market, trading well over $1 billion per day and maintaining $10 million quote relationships with a number of other dealers. Is he representative of dealers in the core of the wholesale spot market? Probably yes, at least with respect to the issues addressed here.

Appendix

A.1. Derivation of the statistic Z_{jt} in Eq. (6)

Beginning with

$$Q_{jt} = \theta(\mu_{jt} - P_{it}) + X_{jt}, \tag{4}$$

$$\Rightarrow$$

$$Q_{jt}/\theta + P_{it} = \mu_{jt} + X_{jt}/\theta,$$

and since $\mu_{jt} = \lambda\mu_t + (1-\lambda)C_{jt}$, where $\lambda \equiv \sigma_\omega^2/(\sigma_\mu^2 + \sigma_\omega^2)$, I have

$$Q_{jt}/\theta + P_{it} - \lambda\mu_t = (1-\lambda)(V_t + \tilde{\omega}_{jt}) + \tilde{X}_{jt}/\theta \quad \text{since} \quad C_{jt} = V_t + \tilde{\omega}_{jt}\,,$$

$$\Rightarrow$$

$$Z_{jt} \equiv \frac{Q_{jt}/\theta + P_{it} - \lambda\mu_t}{1-\lambda} = V_t + \tilde{\omega}_{jt} + [1/\theta(1-\lambda)]\tilde{X}_{jt}\,. \tag{6}$$

A.2. Derivation of the price representation in Eq. (10)

Beginning with

$$P_{it} = \mu_{it} - \alpha(I_{it} - I_i^*) + \gamma D_t\,, \tag{8}$$

I can write:

$$\mu_{it} = \kappa\mu_t + (1-\kappa)Z_{jt} \quad \text{where} \quad \kappa \equiv \sigma_{Zj}^2/(\sigma_{Zj}^2 + \sigma_\mu^2)$$

$$= \kappa\mu_t + \left[\frac{1-\kappa}{1-\lambda}\right][Q_{jt}/\theta + P_{it} - \lambda\mu_t]$$

$$= \kappa\mu_t - \left[\frac{\lambda(1-\kappa)}{1-\lambda}\right]\mu_t + \left[\frac{1-\kappa}{1-\lambda}\right][Q_{jt}/\theta + P_{it}]$$

$$= \left[\kappa - \frac{\lambda(1-\kappa)}{1-\lambda}\right]\mu_t + \left[\frac{1-\kappa}{1-\lambda}\right][Q_{jt}/\theta + P_{it}]$$

$$\equiv \phi\mu_t + (1-\phi)[Q_{jt}/\theta + P_{it}] \quad \text{since} \quad \left[\kappa - \frac{\lambda(1-\kappa)}{1-\lambda}\right] + \left[\frac{1-\kappa}{1-\lambda}\right] = 1\,.$$

Note also that $0 < \phi < 1$ since $0 < \kappa < 1$, $0 < \lambda < 1$, and $\kappa > \lambda$ – each of which follows from the definitions of κ and λ, above, and the fact that $\sigma_{Zj}^2 = \sigma_\omega^2 + [\theta(1-\lambda)]^{-2}\sigma_X^2$.

Substituting this expression for μ_{it} into Eq. (8) yields

$$P_{it} = \phi\mu_t + (1-\phi)[Q_{jt}/\theta + P_{it}] - \alpha(I_{it} - I_i^*) + \gamma D_t\,,$$

$$\Rightarrow$$

$$P_{it} = \mu_t + \left[\frac{1-\phi}{\phi\theta}\right]Q_{jt} - \left[\frac{\alpha}{\phi}\right](I_{it} - I_i^*) + \left[\frac{\gamma}{\phi}\right]D_t\,,$$

but from Eq. (5) μ_t can be written as

$$\mu_t = \rho S_t + (1-\rho)Q_t \quad \text{where} \quad \rho \equiv \sigma_\xi^2/(\sigma_\xi^2 + \sigma_\eta^2)\,.$$

Hence, I can write:

$$P_{it} = (1-\rho)Q_t + \rho S_t + \left[\frac{1-\phi}{\phi\theta}\right]Q_{jt} - \left[\frac{\alpha}{\phi}\right](I_{it} - I_i^*) + \left[\frac{\gamma}{\phi}\right]D_t\,.$$

A.3. Derivation of the relation between B_t and Q_t in Eq. (14)

The approach is as follows: I begin with the definition of the observable order-flow signal, B_t. I then determine a Q_t from B_t with the properties set out in Section 1, i.e., such that $Q_t = V_t + \tilde{\xi}_t$, where ξ_t is distributed normally and independently of the noise in S_t and C_{jt}. The resulting relation between Q_t and B_t establishes the structural interpretation of the coefficient β_6 in Eq. (18).

Beginning with Eq. (11):

$$B_t = \sum_{k=1}^{m} Q_{kt} + \tilde{\psi}_t = \sum_{k=1}^{m} [\theta(\mu_{kt} - \mu_t) + \tilde{X}_{kt}] + \tilde{\psi}_t\,. \tag{11}$$

But:

$$\mu_{kt} = (1-\lambda)C_{kt} + \lambda\mu_t = (1-\lambda)C_{kt} + \lambda[\rho S_t + (1-\rho)Q_t]\,.$$

Substituting this value for μ_{kt} into Eq. (11) yields

$$B_t = \theta(1-\lambda)\sum_{k=1}^{m} C_{kt} + m\theta(\lambda - 1)[\rho S_t + (1-\rho)Q_t] + \sum_{k=1}^{m} \tilde{X}_{kt} + \tilde{\psi}_t\,,$$

$$\Rightarrow$$

$$B_t + m\theta(1-\lambda)[\rho S_t + (1-\rho)Q_t] = \theta(1-\lambda)\sum_{k=1}^{m} [V_t + \tilde{\omega}_{kt}] + \sum_{k=1}^{m} \tilde{X}_{kt} + \tilde{\psi}_t\,,$$

$$\Rightarrow$$

$$[B_t + m\theta(1-\lambda)[\rho S_t + (1-\rho)Q_t]][m\theta(1-\lambda)]^{-1}$$

$$= V_t + m^{-1}\sum_{k=1}^{m} \tilde{\omega}_{kt} + [m\theta(1-\lambda)]^{-1}\sum_{k=1}^{m} \tilde{X}_{kt} + [m\theta(1-\lambda)]^{-1}\tilde{\psi}_t$$

$$\equiv V_t + \xi_t\,,$$

where ξ_t is composed of the independent sources of noise $\tilde{\omega}_{kt}$, $\tilde{X}_{kt}$, and $\tilde{\psi}_t$. I now define implicitly a statistic Q_t, such that:

$$Q_t \equiv [B_t + m\theta(1-\lambda)[\rho S_t + (1-\rho)Q_t]][m\theta(1-\lambda)]^{-1} = V_t + \xi_t\,, \quad \text{(A.1)}$$

$$\Rightarrow$$

$$Q_t = [B_t + m\theta(1-\lambda)\rho S_t][m\theta(1-\lambda)]^{-1} + [m\theta(1-\lambda)(1-\rho)][m\theta(1-\lambda)]^{-1}Q_t\,,$$

$$\Rightarrow$$

$$Q_t[1-(1-\rho)] = [B_t + m\theta(1-\lambda)\rho S_t][m\theta(1-\lambda)]^{-1}\,,$$

$$\Rightarrow$$

$$Q_t = \left[\frac{1}{m\theta(1-\lambda)\rho}\right]B_t + S_t\,. \quad (14)$$

References

Admati, A. and P. Pfleiderer, 1988, A theory of intraday patterns: Volume and price variability, Review of Financial Studies 1, 3–40.

Amihud, Y. and H. Mendelson, 1980, Dealership market: Market making with inventory, Journal of Financial Economics 8, 31–53.

Bank for International Settlements, 1990, BIS survey of foreign exchange market activity, Feb. (Monetary and Economic Department, BIS, Basel).

Bessembinder, H., 1994, Bid–ask spreads in the interbank foreign exchange markets, Journal of Financial Economics 35, 317–348.

Bollerslev, T. and I. Domowitz, 1993, Trading patterns and prices in the interbank foreign exchange market, Journal of Finance 48, 1421–1444.

Easley, D. and M. O'Hara, 1987, Price, quantity, and information in securities markets, Journal of Financial Economics 19, 60–90.

Easley, D. and M. O'Hara, 1992, Time and the process of security price adjustment, Journal of Finance 47, 577–605.

Flood, M., 1994, Market structure and inefficiency in the foreign exchange market, Journal of International Money and Finance 13, 131–158.

Foster, D. and S. Viswanathan, 1990, Variations in volumes, variances, and trading costs, Working paper no. 88-108 (Duke University, Durhan, NC).

Garman, M., 1976, Market microstructure, Journal of Financial Economics 3, 257–275.

Glosten, L. and L. Harris, 1988, Estimating the components of the bid–ask spread, Journal of Financial Economics 21, 123–142.

Glosten, L. and P. Milgrom, 1985, Bid, ask, and transaction prices in a specialist market with heterogeneously informed agents, Journal of Financial Economics 14, 71–100.

Goodhart, C. and L. Figliuoli, 1991, Every minute counts in financial markets, Journal of International Money and Finance 10, 23–52.

Goodhart, C., T. Ito, and R. Payne, 1994, One day in June 1993: A study of the working of Reuters' dealing 2000-2 electronic foreign exchange trading system, in: J. Frankel, ed., The microstructure of the foreign exchange market (University of Chicago Press, Chicago, IL) forthcoming.

Hasbrouck, J., 1988, Trades, quotes, inventories, and information, Journal of Financial Economics 22, 229–252.

Hasbrouck, J., 1991, Measuring the information content of stock trades, Journal of Finance 46, 179–208.

Hasbrouck, J. and G. Sofianos, 1993, The trades of market makers: An empirical analysis of NYSE specialists, Journal of Finance 48, 1565–1593.

Hausman, J., A. Lo, and C. MacKinlay, 1992, An ordered probit analysis of transaction stock prices, Journal of Financial Economics 31, 319–379.

Ho, T. and H. Stoll, 1983, The dynamics of dealer markets under competition, Journal of Finance 38, 1053–1074.

Kyle, A., 1985, Continuous auctions and insider trading, Econometrica 53, 1315–1335.

Kyle, A., 1989, Informed speculation with imperfect competition, Review of Economic Studies 56, 317–356.

Laux, P., 1993, Intraday price formation in the stock index futures market, Working paper (University of Texas, Austin, TX).

Lee, C. and M. Ready, 1991, Inferring trade direction from intradaily data, Journal of Finance 46, 733–746.

Lyons, R., 1994, Information externalities in the microstructure of the foreign exchange market, Manuscript, Oct., (Berkeley Business School, Berkeley, CA).

Madhavan, A. and S. Smidt, 1991, A Bayesian model of intraday specialist pricing, Journal of Financial Economics 30, 99–134.

Madhavan, A. and S. Smidt, 1993, An analysis of changes in specialist inventories and quotations, Journal of Finance 48, 1595–1628.

Manaster, S. and S. Mann, 1992, Life in the pits: competitive market making and inventory control, Working paper (University of Utah, Salt Lake City, UT).

New York Federal Reserve Bank, 1992, Summary of results of the U.S. foreign exchange market turnover survey conducted in April 1992, Mimeo. (Federal Reserve Bank, New York, NY).

O'Hara, M. and G. Oldfield, 1986, The microeconomics of market making, Journal of Financial and Quantitative Analysis 21, 361–376.

Reuters Ltd., 1990, The Reuters dealing 2000-1 service: User guide, Version 3 (Reuters Ltd., London).

Stoll, H., 1989, Inferring the components of the bid–ask spread: Theory and empirical tests, Journal of Finance 44, 115–134.

[15]

THE JOURNAL OF FINANCE • VOL. LII, NO. 4 • SEPTEMBER 1997

Informed Traders, Intervention, and Price Leadership: A Deeper View of the Microstructure of the Foreign Exchange Market

BETTINA PEIERS*

ABSTRACT

This article identifies price leadership patterns in foreign exchange trading, with a focus on central bank intervention as an informational trigger for leadership positioning. Granger causality tests applied to DM/US$ spot rate quotes reveal Deutsche Bank as a price leader up to 60 minutes prior to Bundesbank interventionary reports. By the minus 25-minute mark, interbank quote adjustments become two-way Granger-causal. These results suggest that central bank activity is revealed in stages: first to the price leader, then to competitors, and lastly to the general public.

INFORMATION-BASED MICROSTRUCTURE THEORY views the trading process for financial assets as a strategic game involving players who adjust order flows and prices based on asymmetric information regarding the underlying asset's true value. Unfortunately, we can only verify such theories empirically if we have access to high-frequency data. For this reason, empirical studies of information asymmetry have focused predominantly on the equity markets (see Hasbrouck (1991) and Easley, O'Hara, and Srinivas (1993) for recent examples). However, with the recent availability of continuous time spot rate data, it has now become possible to apply tests of microstructure trading theories to the foreign exchange market.

This study aims to shed light on strategic foreign exchange trader behavior by focusing on spot rate revisions around an exogenous news event. Specifically, we will show that central bank intervention establishes certain bank traders as price leaders because they are perceived to be better informed about future changes in the exchange rate than some other agents.

Charles Goodhart (1988) has asserted the importance of information asymmetries in short-term interactions among foreign exchange trading banks. From interviews with foreign exchange specialists in London, he concluded the following:

A further source of informational advantage to the traders is their access to, and trained interpretation of, the information contained in the order

* Department of Economics, Arizona State University, and American Express Company. I thank René Stulz, an anonymous referee, and participants at the HFDF-1 Conference in Zurich for valuable comments. Seung Ahn, Tim Bollerslev, and Michael Melvin provided useful suggestions on earlier drafts. I am grateful to Michel Dacorogna and the research team at Olsen & Associates for sharing their Reuters data.

> *flow . . . Some market actions may indicate central bank involvement. Each bank seeks to interpret the activity of other banks in the market; some have a reputation of being able to position themselves well in certain currencies, and their perceived operations* <u>*may cause others to follow their lead*</u> (emphasis added). *Each bank will also know what their own customer enquiries and orders have been in the course of the day, and will try to deduce from that the positions of others in the market, and overall market developments as they unfold* (p. 456).

Hence, if there is any evidence of information-based leadership in the foreign exchange market, it should be observable through systematic changes in order flows, i.e., quantities traded, around key market events—central bank intervention in particular. However, in the foreign exchange market, only indicative price quotes, and not positions, are publicly available. Since theory predicts information-based order flows to be reflected in price adjustments (see Kyle (1985) and Glosten and Milgrom (1985)),[1] we test Goodhart's (1988) leadership hypothesis from a "pricing" perspective by using a continuously sampled series of DM/US$ spot rate indications.[2] As in Goodhart (1988), the event focus is on central bank activity, or more specifically, reported Bundesbank interventions.

Granger-type regressions on a cross-section of individual bank quotes provide empirical evidence of Deutsche Bank price leadership between 60 and 25 minutes prior to Bundesbank intervention reports. Thereafter, strategic quote interactions prevail across banks, as evidenced by two-way Granger causalities. These preannouncement quote dynamics indicate the existence of information asymmetries in the foreign exchange market: Central bank activity is revealed to the market well before a public announcement, with Deutsche Bank perceived to be the early information insider to Bundesbank intervention. Once information is more broadly disseminated to the market, less informed banks learn from the informed trader's order flows and revise their prices for profit-taking. These results are in line with the market microstructure theory of pricing following Kyle (1985) and Glosten and Milgrom (1985).

The next section highlights the role of central bank intervention in a world of heterogeneously informed traders. Section II reviews the nature of high-frequency foreign exchange data and defines the sampling horizon within which we will examine intervention-dependent price leadership effects. Section III analyzes the cross-section of banks considered for price leadership analysis. Deutsche Bank's unique position in the DM/US$ market is discussed in Section IV. Section V identifies distinct subsamples of quoting patterns surrounding Bundesbank intervention reports. Section VI presents time-vary-

[1] There also exists empirical evidence that this relationship holds in the foreign exchange market. Refer to Lyons (1995), whose results are based on proprietary data of one trader's transactions prices.

[2] Although banks that post indicative quotes are not committed to trading them, reputational concerns ensure that foreign exchange transactions occur at prices close to those advertised (see Goodhart and Payne (1996) for details).

ing Granger-causality specifications to test the hypothesis of Deutsche Bank price leadership. Empirical results are reported in Section VII, with economic interpretations provided in Section VIII. Section IX concludes.

I. Informational Asymmetry and Intervention

In contrast to the rich equity market literature on informational asymmetry (see O'Hara (1995) for a literature review), foreign exchange market research has only recently developed theories of strategic trading behavior. While stock markets are centralized exchanges and based on specialist systems, foreign exchange trading is largely decentralized and organized around interbank direct dealer networks.[3] Decentralized trader interactions might impact the price discovery process, as shown by Wolinsky (1990). Furthermore, trading motives in the foreign exchange market are a bit different, as they involve both speculative and liquidity aspects.

According to Lyons (1997), "speculative" or informed traders can privately distinguish between own-customer orders that are liquidity-based and those that reflect superior information regarding the fundamental determinants of the spot exchange rate. Hence, informed agents are optimally qualified to take advantage of short-term profit opportunities. "Liquidity" or uninformed traders, on the other hand, are driven by customer needs for financing international trade and corporate transactions. Their strategies are designed to minimize losses when dealing with informed traders.

This study aims to examine how interactions between informed and uninformed foreign exchange traders give rise to short-term sole price leadership during periods of central bank intervention. In a modification to Kyle's (1985) model, suppose that central bank order flows provide an intermediary bank trader, y, with a one-time exogenous information advantage. Since y has private information regarding the authority's intended market correction, Δp, it will adjust order flows and prices first, thereby extracting positive economic rents from its insider information. Further suppose that uninformed competitor banks, x, view y's price adjustment as a signal that they are dealing with an informed trader. To minimize their losses, banks x follow bank y's price revision and adjust their positions accordingly. Based on this sequence of price reactions, trader y emerges as a Stackelberg-type price leader. Trader y's leadership status will persist until all central bank operations are revealed to follower banks, thereby resolving intervention-related informational differences between uninformed banks x and informed bank y.

One may question whether interventions are indeed newsworthy events to banks. Past empirical findings related to the effects of intervention on exchange rates have been inconclusive. Edison (1993) reviews this large literature and concludes

[3] Dealers can also trade through foreign exchange brokers. The brokers' market will be discussed in further detail in Section IV.

> *... as with any empirical work, existing models and the quality of the available data may not be sophisticated enough to resolve properly the questions asked. These qualifications seem consistent with the observation that exchange-market participants appear to believe that central-bank intervention is important and that they therefore react to news of intervention* (p. 55).

Until recently, intervention studies had to rely on lower-frequency data, defined in hours, days, or even weeks. There is only a brief literature that has analyzed intervention news in a very short-run context.[4] Goodhart and Hesse (1993) use three months of high-frequency Reuters quotes (April through June 1989 data) to assess exchange rate movements immediately following central bank intervention. In their case, "immediate" refers to half-hourly and one-hour mean returns following a Reuters report. Based on their small sample of intervention periods, they find that intervention has "no immediate, or short-term, systematic effect" (p. 384) on DM/US$ and ¥/US$ returns.

This article expands upon Goodhart and Hesse (1993) by evaluating high-frequency foreign exchange quotes for only a specific subgroup of traders and by using a more refined sampling methodology. Under the hypothesis that central bank interventions are newsworthy events to bank traders, this article will examine to-the-minute subsamples around reported intervention to discern information asymmetries in interbank quoting behavior.

II. The Data

The exchange rate data in this study are tick-by-tick DM/US$ spot quotes, as posted on the Reuters "FXFX" screen between October 1, 1992 and September 30, 1993 (a total of 1,466,946 observations). Each data record includes the date and time to the nearest second of quote recording (in Greenwich Mean Time (GMT)), the bid and the ask quote, as well as codes for the country/city branch location and the name of the quoting bank. For a summary of the stylized facts underlying continuous time quote characteristics, see Guillaume et al. (1994).

News on central bank intervention is gathered from the Reuters "AAMM" headline screen. A search was conducted for all reports of Bundesbank (BUBA) intervention over the 1992–1993 data period. Since each report also carries a date and time-per-second stamp, it can be easily matched to the Reuters FXFX quote records.

One may question whether reports of intervention closely follow actual intervention operations. Goodhart and Hesse (1993) claim that the announcement lag is no longer than 15 to 30 minutes, while conversations with other foreign exchange traders suggest a maximum lag of 10 to 15 minutes. To be thorough, we will trace "interventionary" activity up to one hour before a

[4] Bossaerts and Hillion (1991) were among the first to provide a microstructural perspective on intervention in the foreign exchange market. Their model focuses on movements in the spread as a function of asymmetric intervention information.

Reuters report. Furthermore, we will consider "preinterventionary" dynamics by defining a −120 to −60 minute window (see Section VII for details).

Our upper boundary for postrelease effects will be 60 minutes after a given report. Such a small time horizon is in line with the evidence that interventionary effects on exchange rates are short-lived. Hence, our overall intervention sample will extend from −120 to +60 minutes surrounding time-stamped Reuters announcements.

The conditions for including a given BUBA intervention headline in our event sample are as follows: First, the associated AAMM Reuters report may not refer to so-called daily "fixings" by the Bundesbank.[5] Second, a reported intervention, INT1, may not overlap with another reported intervention, INT2, for the −120 to +60 minute time window surrounding the announcement of INT1 at time 0. The latter condition is vital to ensure that more current intervention announcements do not interfere with the identification of interbank quote patterns associated with previous reports. Based on these two selection criteria, 14 BUBA intervention announcements, reported by Reuters between Oct. 1, 1992 and Sept. 30, 1993, were chosen as relevant event samples. See Table I for their original Reuters headline listings.

III. Top Quoting Banks in the DM/US$ Market

Table II lists the six commercial banks with the most bid/ask quotes posted in the DM/US$ market. For this study, the key period within which we expect intervention-related market activity is the −60/+60 minute time window mentioned above. In the empirical analysis to follow, the intervention sample will be further segmented into subperiods −60/−25, −25/0, 0/+25, and +25/+60 to account for potential structural breaks in quoting patterns.[6] Two broader horizons of interest are the entire one-year data period as well as European business hours (8:00–16:00 GMT), i.e., the time period during which most Bundesbank interventions occur.

Deutsche Bank (DB) is by far the most active contributor to Reuters DM/US$ quotations. This holds for the smallest to the broadest time horizons considered. Over the entire sample period, 121,055 quotes are attributable to DB, which constitutes almost one-tenth of total DM/US$ quoting volume. During the −60/+60 window around Reuters reports, DB's quote frequency is more than forty percent larger than that of the next most active bank, Chemical Bank (CH). The next four banks by number of quote indications are Societe

[5] Fixings are routine institutional transactions by some Western European central banks in which currencies are traded with commercial banks in order to meet small customer needs. Bundesbank fixings in the DM/US$ market are reported daily between 12:00 and 12:30 GMT (standard time). Only in rare cases do fixings coincide with small-scale interventionary activities. Bundesbank officials claim that fixings have little or no effect on exchange rate movements.

[6] At −60 and −25 minutes before a report, around the time of the report (time 0), and around +25 minutes after, we observe clear breaks in interbank quoting patterns. Details on the choice of subsample periods are provided in Section V.

Table I

14 Bundesbank Interventions Considered for Modeling: As Reported by Reuters Between 10-01-1992 and 09-30-1993

The following is a listing of Reuters AAMM screen headlines describing the 14 Bundesbank intervention reports considered for empirical analysis. Reuters clock times are in Greenwich Mean Time. Subsequent tables will index Reuters time stamps as time 0. Foreign currencies traded by the Bundesbank are underlined for emphasis. Note that the Bundesbank is referenced as BUBA in Reuters listings.

Event	Date	Time	Reuters Report
1.	12-02-1992	8:47:36	"BUBA buys FF for marks."
2.	12-15-1992	12:05:34	"Mark strength prompts BUBA intervention (in FF)."
3.	12-17-1992	12:01:18	"BUBA buys FF."
4.	01-04-1993	15:03:54	"BUBA says intervenes to buy FF."
5.	02-03-1993	15:48:46	"Denmark, BUBA support crown in intervention."
6.	02-17-1993	14:28:14	"Peseta falls below 72/DM; (German)[a] intervention rumored."
7.	02-18-1993	9:05:16	"Peseta gains at open; (German)[a] intervention suspected."
8.	04-23-1993	12:34:26	"EMS central banks, BUBA intervene to help peseta."
9.	04-23-1993	15:22:34	"BUBA says buying pesetas in second round."
10.	07-22-1993	10:05:26	"BUBA buys FF in open market."
11.	07-22-1993	12:36:28	"BUBA says still buying FF."
12.	07-23-1993	14:18:18	"(European) central banks selling marks at FF 3.418-dealers."
13.	07-29-1993	14:41:28	"BUBA confirms concerted action in support of FF."
14.	07-30-1993	11:18:30	"BUBA buying FF-dealers."

[a] Reuters intervention headlines for 02-17-1993 and 02-18-1993 did not indicate the central bank of origin. Through alternative sources it was confirmed that these interventions refer to the Bundesbank.

Generale (SG), Rabobank (RB), Berliner Handels-und Frankfurter Bank (BH), and Den Norske Bank (DN).

Note that market activity is most heavily skewed toward DB in the period immediately preceding Reuters reports: compared to the aggregate $-60/+60$ period, indications by other banks relative to DB, fall by up to nine percent in the $-25/0$ period. This unusual decline in quote frequency is a first indication of shifts in market signals around intervention. We will return to a further discussion of this issue in Section VIII.

IV. Deutsche Bank's Unique Market Position

DB's dominance in quoting activity should be expected in the DM/US$ market. For this currency pair, *Euromoney* Magazine (June 1994) has reported DB as holding the largest European customer base in 1993. In the same year, DB also ranked as the 13th largest bank in the world in terms of shareholder equity and asset value.

DB's customer depth enhances the bank's ability to gain early access to new information as well as to disseminate such information quickly. Additionally,

Table II

Top Banks by Number of DM/US$ Spot Rate Quotations Posted Between 10-01-1992 and 09-30-1993

This table presents the six commercial banks with the largest number of Reuters DM/US$ spot rate quotations posted over the 1992–1993 sample period. These banks are: Deutsche Bank (DB), Chemical Bank (CH), Societe Generale (SG), Rabobank (RB), BHF Bank (BH), and Den Norske Bank (DN). Columns two through six list each bank's quote frequencies within 60 minutes before (−) and after (+) reported Bundesbank interventions, with frequencies pooled across the 14 Reuters reports identified in Table I. −60/−25, −25/0, 0/+25, and +25/+60 are time intervals in minutes which define subsamples *within* the aggregate −60/+60 minute intervention period. Each interval is mutually exclusive from another and counts frequencies by the tick. For instance, the column labeled "−60/−25" indicates that across all 14 Bundesbank interventions, DB posted a total of 303 DM/US$ quotes between −60:00 minutes and −25:01 minutes prior to a Reuters report at time 0. Column seven reports the number of bank quotes occurring during European business hours (GMT), and the last column summarizes counts over the entire one-year sample period.

	14 Bundesbank Intervention Samples					European Hours 8:00:00–16:00:00 GMT	All Quotes 0:00:00–23:59:59
Banks	−60/−25	−25/0	0/+25	+25/+60	−60/+60 min.		
Deutsche Bank (DB)	303	238	210	253	1,004	74,216	121,055
Chemical Bank (CH)	190	143	147	184	690	43,772	67,554
Societe Generale (SG)	192	127	131	167	617	60,059	72,891
Rabobank (RB)	198	123	102	133	556	57,274	57,274
BHF Bank (BF)	176	95	97	127	495	38,138	70,227
Den Norske Bank (DN)	145	103	97	128	475	34,144	38,958

its size advantage allows DB to provide more rapid liquidity and volume turnover than most competitors in the DM/US$ market.

Since there are no public records on Bundesbank interventionary transactions, one can only speculate about the commercial agents through which the Bundesbank executes its foreign exchange trades. For political reasons, banks of German nationality are prime candidates. Furthermore, we would expect market share and liquidity to be of important concern to the central bank. Based on these criteria, DB is likely to be a key intermediary to BUBA intervention order placements. Therefore, empirical tests of price leadership will be stated specifically with respect to Deutsche Bank.

It should be noted that in executing an intervention, a central bank can deal either directly with commercial banks as counterparties or go through the brokers' market. In dealing directly with commercial banks, the central bank chooses a particular counterparty who may then be allowed to make the intervention information public. Brokers, on the other hand, act as intermediaries who bring market makers together by accumulating limit orders. They also provide anonymity to the trading counterparties until after a transaction is completed. So when dealing through the brokers' market, the central bank chooses not to target a particular bank for its order placement and can delay the market revelation of the intervention.

Officials in Frankfurt have claimed that the Bundesbank uses a mix of both broker and direct bank contacts to place intervention orders. However, independent research by Humpage (1994) and Dominguez and Frankel (1993) reveals that since the mid-1980s, most G-7 central banks deal directly with bank dealers to allow for a more rapid information flow about intervention activities. This institutional development makes it feasible that a bank can gain insider information from direct central bank contact—a key condition to the price leadership hypothesis examined here.

V. Identifying Relevant Time Segments Around Intervention Reports

Empirical analysis focuses on quote returns, defined as the percentage change in the midpoint of DM/US$ bid-ask quotes.[7] Descriptive statistics for the first four moments of the tick-by-tick returns are consistent with the high-frequency time-series properties documented by Goodhart and Figliouli (1991) and Bollerslev and Domowitz (1993).[8]

In Figure 1, we plot the market's return volatility around intervention, based on five-minute standard deviation averages over 14 BUBA intervention reports. The time period covered is −60 minutes before to +25 minutes after a given intervention report.[9]

Figure 1 indicates a distinct news effect. Of particular interest is the statistically significant one-basis point volatility increase at −5 minutes prior to BUBA intervention reports. This is consistent with the findings by Ederington and Lee (1993) and DeGennaro and Shrieves (1995) who have shown that private information leakages cause foreign exchange volatility to increase just prior to official news reports. A theoretical underpinning for this finding is provided in the information-asymmetry model by Ross (1989).

Following the peak observed at −5, market volatility tapers off quickly. This finding is consistent with the claim by Edison (1993) and Goodhart and Hesse (1993) that the news content of interventionary activities is transitory.

It should be noted that between October 1, 1992 and September 30, 1993, the European exchange markets were in the midst of a crisis that called into question the validity of the European Monetary System's (EMS) exchange rate bands. All 14 intervention reports used in the empirical portion of this article involve efforts to sell Deutsche Marks and buy European currencies. Most interventions were clustered around the new year 1992/1993 and again around July 1993, when the French Franc threatened to fall below the FF/DM ex-

[7] The bid and the ask may not move in unison since at a given point in time, a trader is interested in either buying or selling. To smooth these transactions-related biases in the data series, it is most appropriate to use the average of the bid and the ask.

[8] Results are available from the author upon request.

[9] In this graph and subsequent illustrations (see Figures 2 and 3), "time 0" refers to the precise time in seconds at which an intervention was reported on the Reuters screen. An extension of the plot to the +25/+60 time horizon following intervention reports did not add any new information to the stylized facts and was, therefore, omitted from this article.

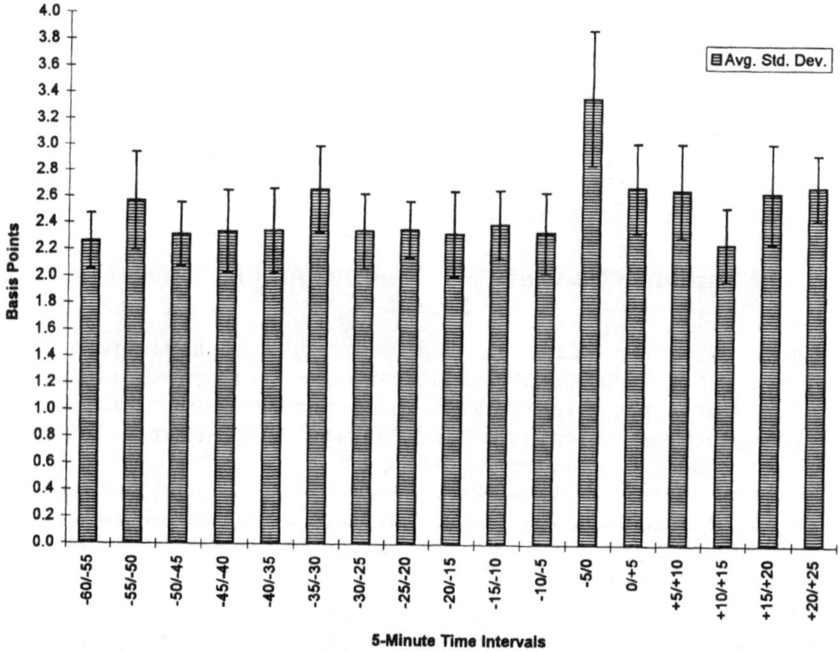

Figure 1. Mean DM/US$ quote volatility around Bundesbank intervention. This plot presents standard deviations of tick-by-tick DM/US$ quote revisions, averaged per five-minute interval across 14 pooled Bundesbank intervention periods. Quote revisions are based on percentage changes in bid-ask midpoint quotes across all Reuters FXFX screen entries between Oct. 1, 1992 and Sept. 30, 1993. Five-minute average standard deviations are in basis points and capture all quotes between −60 minutes before and +25 minutes after a given intervention report. The time stamp on Reuters intervention headlines is denoted as time 0. Lines at the top of each bar denote ± one standard error around the standard deviation means.

change rate level permitted under EMS rules. Between October 1, 1992 and September 30, 1993, no specific DM/US$ interventions were reported by Reuters. However, the European currency interventions clearly had a spillover effect on the U.S. Dollar, as evidenced by the volatility pattern in Figure 1.

This study is not as interested in intervention-linked market fluctuations as it is in evaluating the timing of quote revisions by individual players. Figures 2 and 3 focus on average quote changes by the six most frequently quoting banks identified in Section III.

As shown in Figure 2, the pattern of midpoint quote revisions for DB, CH, and SG does not suggest any clear correlation among these three banks. Prior to −25 minutes and again after time 0, DB, CH, and SG display divergent quote return patterns, with DB raising DM/US$ quotes and CH and SG

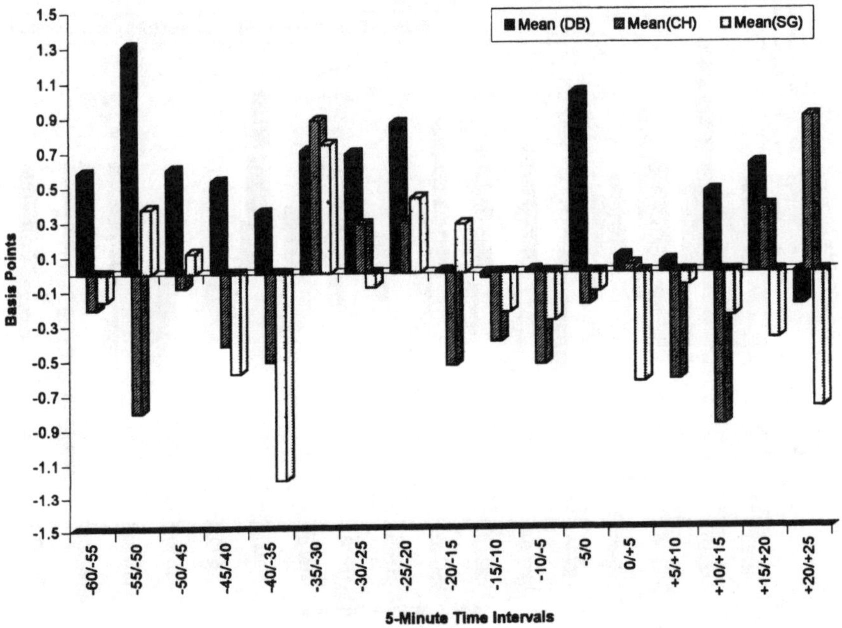

Figure 2. Mean DM/US$ quote revisions by Deutsche Bank, Chemical Bank, and Societe Generale around Bundesbank intervention. This plot depicts tick-by-tick DM/US$ quote revisions by Deutsche Bank (DB), Chemical Bank (CH), and Societe Generale (SG), averaged per five-minute interval across 14 pooled Bundesbank intervention periods. Five-minute bank averages are in basis points and reflect percentage changes in bid-ask midpoint quotes between −60 minutes before and +25 minutes after a given intervention report. Each intervention is identified based on Reuters headlines between Oct. 1, 1992 and Sept. 30, 1993. The time stamp on Reuters entries is denoted as time 0.

lowering their price indications.[10] Between −25 and −5 minutes prior to intervention reports, however, the dispersion among quote returns narrows as all three banks tend to lower their DM/US$ quotes.

Figure 3 displays markedly different inferences for the interrelations of DB with RB, DN, and BH. These three banks seem to follow DB over the entire −60/+25 minute time span. From −25 to −5, the overall convergence in quoting patterns is most pronounced. After time 0, the dispersion among quote returns reverts to initial levels, with DB leading RB, DN, and BH.

Figures 2 and 3 contain important information for the subsequent regression analysis: First, they provide cursory evidence of DB price leadership with

[10] The divergent quote patterns displayed in the figures should not be confused with arbitrage opportunities. Note that the data plots are based on midpoints of *indicative* bid/ask prices computed as *averages* over five-minute intervals. Furthermore, differences across banks are of such a small magnitude relative to the typical market spread that they are unlikely to exceed the transactions costs of arbitrage.

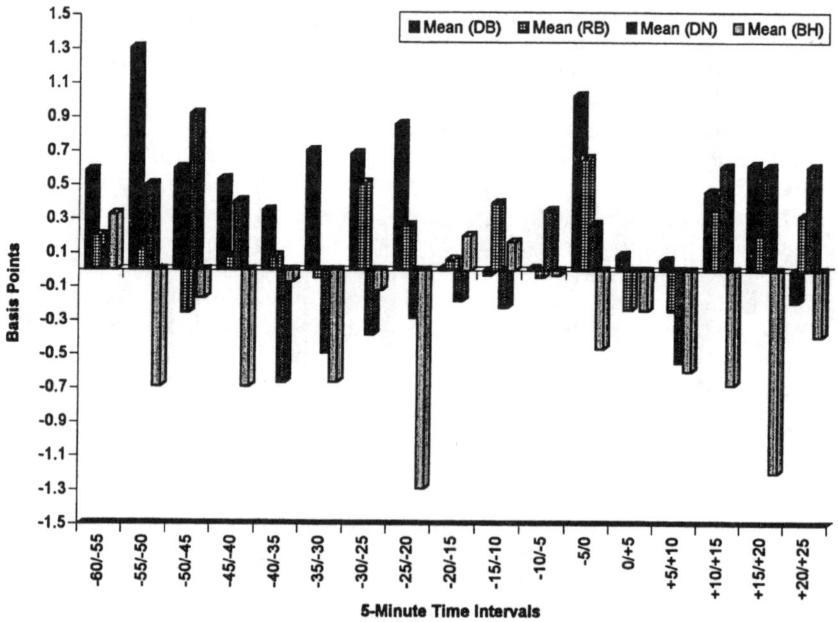

Figure 3. Mean DM/US$ quote revisions by Deutsche Bank, Rabobank, Den Norske Bank, and BHF Bank around Bundesbank intervention. This plot depicts tick-by-tick DM/US$ quote revisions by Deutsche Bank (DB), Rabobank (RB), Den Norske Bank (DN), and BHF Bank (BH), averaged per five-minute interval across 14 pooled Bundesbank intervention periods. Five-minute bank averages are in basis points and reflect percentage changes in bid-ask midpoint quotes between −60 minutes before and +25 minutes after a given intervention report. Each intervention is identified based on Reuters headlines between Oct. 1, 1992 and Sept. 30, 1993. The time stamp on Reuters entries is denoted as time 0.

respect to at least four other banks, in particular CH, RB, DN, and BH. Second, the charts identify distinct bandwagon effects of trading between −25 and −5 minutes prior to Reuters reports. These visually evident breaks in quoting patterns will form the basis for the sampling technique introduced in Section II and applied in the empirical analysis below.

VI. Granger-Causality Tests in a Time-Varying Framework

The empirical investigation of the price leadership hypothesis formulated in Section I is based on Granger-causality tests of quote return interrelations across banks. Following Granger (1969), a *necessary* condition for price leadership by a particular bank, y, involves the premise that its current return pattern, y_t, be uncorrelated to past revisions by other market participants, x_{t-i}. Banks x fail to "Granger-cause" bank y if past modifications that have altered the time-varying process of x_{t-i} do not affect the contemporaneous conditional distribution of y_t.

As a *sufficient* condition for price leadership, we might expect lagged observations y_{t-i} to have a positively significant effect on the contemporaneous series x_t. For our data, however, we need not impose a positive restriction on the coefficient sign for y_{t-i} to establish price leadership by bank y. This is due to the nature of interventions recorded over the 1992/1993 data period.

As mentioned in Section V and shown in Table I, the 14 Bundesbank interventions in our sample are exclusively in EMS currencies and not in the U.S. Dollar. Of those 14 interventions, nine are in support of the French Franc, four to help stabilize the Spanish Peseta, and one to promote the Danish Crown. This type of cross-currency intervention might result in follower banks selling a different currency than the leader bank, with one side selling Dollars and the other selling Marks. Therefore, the expected direction of DM/US$ quote adjustments by follower banks, x, in response to price leader, y, is ambiguous.[11] Econometrically, then, bank y meets the sufficient condition of price leadership as long as its past quote revisions, y_{t-i}, have a statistically significant impact on the contemporaneous bank series, x_t, regardless of sign.

A. Periodicity of Quote Indications

In this study, causality tests will be constructed for the six most active DM/US$ bank traders identified in Section III: DB, CH, SG, RB, DN, and BH. Before an empirical model can be defined, however, we need to address the issue of heterogeneous quote frequencies across banks. Tick-by-tick quote sampling is not driven by clock time, t, but rather by bank indications that are irregularly spaced in time, i.e., driven by "event time" τ. As shown in Table II, DB inputs quotes much more frequently than the other five banks in our sample. Hence, Granger-causality testing would likely skew predictive power in favor of DB.

Conventional time-series analysis requires equal periodicities across input observations. This is accomplished by standardizing all bank quote revision series by the length of the time interval between each bank's current and last

[11] As an illustration of how a negative, rather than a positive, sign might arise with regard to the leader's lagged quote changes, consider a case where the Bundesbank intervenes by buying French Francs with Marks. If bank y is the first to observe Bundesbank's order flow, it will exploit this temporary information advantage by taking a long position in the FF against the DM. To attract counterparties, bank y will therefore raise its DM/FF quote. Other things equal, this will be associated with a rise in bank y's DM/US$ quote. Now suppose that anticipation of further Franc weakening has led some other, uninformed, bank x to short the Franc against the Dollar. If this bank interprets bank y's quote adjustment as insider knowledge of Franc appreciation, it will react by covering its position through Franc purchases. This will be reflected in lower FF/US$ quotes and, other things equal, in lower DM/US$ quotes by bank x. Thus, intervention-induced information asymmetries will cause DM/US$ quote adjustments by bank x to follow bank y's DM/US$ quote adjustments. However, these quote adjustments will be negatively related due to differences in underlying cross-currency positions. Certainly, there exist cases where we would expect a positive sign on bank y's DM/US$ causality coefficient (such as banks x and y holding opposite positions in the same currency pair). Without knowing actual positions and trading volumes, however, we can only look for a nonzero coefficient, rather than any particular sign, as evidence of bank y's price leadership.

preceding quote entry. Let us define banks j = Deutsche Bank (DB), Societe Generale (SG), Chemical Bank (CH), Rabobank (RB), Den Norske Bank (DN), and Berliner Handels-und Frankfurter Bank (BH). If S^j_τ is the percentage change in bank j's midpoint DM/US\$ quote between indication time τ and $\tau - 1$ (measured in seconds), then each bank's smoothed return, QM^j_τ, is defined as:

$$QM^j_\tau = \frac{S^j_\tau}{[(\tau - (\tau - 1)^j)/60]}. \tag{1}$$

QM^j_τ reflects quote revisions on a per-minute basis—a standardized input measure for comparing bank series of different quoting periodicities.

B. Time-Varying Parameter Specification

The appropriate Granger-causality model for this study has to account for yet another timing feature governing bank indications. Consider the impact of varying time differences between Granger-causing bank observations, QM^k, where banks $k \neq j$, and the dependent variable bank's current observations, QM^j. We would expect "older" quote revisions by regressor banks, k, to have a smaller impact on the dependent variable bank's current quote revisions than more recent bank k quote adjustments. Accordingly, we propose the following model:

$$QM^j_\tau = a + \sum_{k=1}^{5} \sum_{i=1}^{2} b^k_i QM^k_{(\tau-i)^k} + \sum_{i=1}^{5} c^j_i QM^j_{(\tau-i)^j} \tag{2}$$

where the regressor coefficients vary linearly such that

$$b^k_i = e^k_i + \frac{f^k_i}{[(\tau - (\tau - i)^k)/60]} \tag{3}$$

$$c^i_j = g^j_i + \frac{h^j_i}{[(\tau - (\tau - i)^j)/60]} \tag{4}$$

In equations (2) through (4), we define subscripts i as lagged quote revisions. Superscripts denote bank affiliations. QM^j_τ measures the per-minute percentage change in bank j's DM/US\$ midpoint quotes between time $\tau - 1$ and τ; $QM^k_{(\tau-i)^k}$ denotes the ith preceding per-minute quote revisions by banks $k \neq j$, and $QM^j_{(\tau-i)^j}$ represents bank j's own lagged indications. f^k_i and h^j_i are coefficients that proxy the time lapse since the last quote revision by regressor bank k in relation to the dependent variable bank, j, at time τ.

Equation (2) serves to test the hypothesis that DB's current quote changes are not Granger-caused by lagged quote revisions of other banks, k, whereas DB's lagged adjustments Granger-cause current quote changes by banks $k \neq$ DB. As outlined in Section VI, the necessary condition for the hypothesis of sole price leadership by DB entails $\Sigma b_i^k = 0$ for dependent variable bank DB, with $\Sigma b_i^{DB} \neq 0$ for dependent variable banks $k \neq$ DB as the sufficient condition.

The time-varying coefficient effect of regressor banks, k, on dependent variable bank j can be illustrated by assuming that bank j's current quote revision follows bank $k = 1$'s previous quote change by 10 seconds but follows bank $k = 2$'s last revision by 100 seconds. If the time-varying model captures the passage of time since the last quote revision, then the combined marginal effect of bank $k = 2$ on j, indicated by parameter $b_i^{k=2}$ (see equation (3)), ought to be smaller than the marginal effect of bank $k = 1$ on j. On the other hand, if the age of quotes is irrelevant in establishing Granger-causality, then $f_i^k = 0$ such that $b_i^k = e_i^k$. Similarly, for the own lags of the dependent variable bank j, $h_i^j = 0$ so that $c_i^j = g_i^j$.[12]

VII. Empirical Results

It is commonly known that high-frequency financial data exhibit autoregressive conditional heteroskedasticity (ARCH)-type dynamics in the residuals (see Bollerslev, Chou and Kroner (1992)). Ljung-Box diagnostics on squared residuals show that time-dependent heteroscedasticity also underlies the quote revisions in equation (2). To obtain robust standard errors, the model is estimated using a Newey–West (1987) covariance adjustment.[13] Due to the complex parameterization of equation (2), it was found that this approach outperforms standard ARCH/GARCH models in goodness-of-fit.

The appropriate choice of lag length, i, was determined through experimentation with alternative lag structures. Based on under- and overfitting the model, we found that $i = 2$ for regressor banks, $k \neq j$, and $i = 5$ for dependent variable banks' own lags provide the best econometric fit.

Qualitative results of equation (2) are summarized in Tables III and IV. Due to space constraints, parameter estimates are reported only for Deutsche Bank as the hypothesized price leader (see Appendix Table A.I) and for Societe Generale as a representative follower bank (see Appendix Table A.II).[14]

Within the −60/+60 intervention period, we define four subsample horizons: −60/−25, −25/0, 0/+25, and +25/+60. These time windows are based on structural breaks in quoting patterns, as identified in Figures 2 and 3. Furthermore, a −120/−60 minute interval is constructed to identify interbank quoting patterns in a "preinterventionary" time period. This control sample is

[12] It is possible that differential quote frequencies across banks could lead to spurious Granger causality where the more frequently quoting bank—DB in our case—would naturally emerge as the price leader. Section VII will show that the banks' coefficient patterns fluctuate over different subsamples but the relative frequency of DB quotes vis-a-vis other banks does not (see Table II). This rules out spurious causality as an explanation for our empirical findings.

[13] I thank Tim Bollerslev for suggesting the Newey–West (1987) approach to attaining robust standard errors.

[14] Complete estimation results for all banks are available either from the author upon request or can be referenced on *The Journal of Finance* World Wide Web site.

Table III

Constant Coefficient Model: Summary of Granger-Causality Tests for Deutsche Bank Price Leadership

This table summarizes interbank dependencies in quoting patterns around Bundesbank intervention reports. Results are based on Granger-causality tests with constant coefficient specifications, as detailed in Appendix Tables A.I–A.VI. Per-minute DM/US$ quote revisions by banks j = Deutsche Bank (DB), Societe Generale (SG), Chemical Bank (CH), Rabobank (RB), Den Norske Bank (DN) and BHF Bank (BH) are regressed on two lagged per-minute quote revisions by banks $k \neq j$ and five own lags. No account is taken of the age of regressor banks' prior quote revisions. The sample comprises 14 pooled Bundesbank intervention periods between Oct. 1, 1992 and Sept. 30, 1993. −120/−60, −60/−25, −25/0, 0/+25 and +25/+60 are time intervals in minutes that define subsamples around Bundesbank intervention reports. The time stamp on intervention headline entries is denoted as time 0. L1 (L2) indicates that the first (second) lag of regressor bank $k \neq j$ Granger-causes time τ quote revisions by dependent variable bank j. * denotes statistically significant own first lags. In a given time period, bank j is not Granger-caused by other banks, k, if the associated regressor bank column is blank.

Bank	Granger-Causing Regressor Banks																													
	−120/−60 Minutes						−60/−25 Minutes						−25/0 Minutes						0/+25 Minutes						+25/+60 Minutes					
j	DB	SG	CH	RB	DN	BH	DB	SG	CH	RB	DN	BH	DB	SG	CH	RB	DN	BH	DB	SG	CH	RB	DN	BH	DB	SG	CH	RB	DN	BH
DB	*						*				L1		*	L2	L2		L1		*						*					
SG		*					L1	*					L1, L2	*	L1, L2		L1			*	L1					*				
CH			*				L1		*					L2	*		L2				*		L2				*		L2	
RB				*		L2	L2			*			L1			*			L1		L1, L	*						*		
DN	L2	L1		L2	*	L2	L1		L1		*		L2	L2	L1		*	L2			L2		*		L2				*	
BH					L1	*	L1, L					*	L1	L1, L2	L1		L1	*						*	L1					*

Table IV

Time-Varying Coefficient Model: Summary of Granger-Causality Tests for Deutsche Bank Price Leadership

This table summarizes interbank dependencies in quoting patterns around Bundesbank intervention reports. Results are based on Granger-causality tests with time-varying coefficient specifications, as detailed in Appendix Tables A.I through A.VI. Per-minute DM/US$ quote revisions by banks j = Deutsche Bank (DB), Societe Generale (SG), Chemical Bank (CH), Rabobank (RB), Den Norske Bank (DN), and BHF Bank (BH) are regressed on two lagged per-minute quote revisions by banks $k \neq j$ and five own lags. Coefficients are allowed to vary with the age of regressor banks' prior quote revisions. The sample comprises 14 pooled Bundesbank intervention periods between Oct. 1, 1992 and Sept. 30, 1993. −120/−60, −60/−25, −25/0, 0/+25, and +25/+60 are time intervals in minutes that define subsamples around Bundesbank intervention reports. The time stamp on intervention headline entries is denoted as time 0. L1 (L2) indicates that the first (second) lag of regressor bank $k \neq j$ Granger-causes time τ quote revisions by dependent variable bank j. * Denotes statistically significant own first lags. In a given time period, bank j is not Granger-caused by other banks, k, if the associated regressor bank column is blank.

Granger-Causing Regressor Banks

Bank	−120/−60 Minutes						−60/−25 Minutes						−25/0 Minutes						0/+25 Minutes						+25/+60 Minutes					
j	DB	SG	CH	RB	DN	BH	DB	SG	CH	RB	DN	BH	DB	SG	CH	RB	DN	BH	DB	SG	CH	RB	DN	BH	DB	SG	CH	RB	DN	BH
DB	*						*						*	L2	L2				*		L1				*					
SG		*					L1	*					L1, L2	*	L1, L2		L1			*	L1					*	L1		L2	
CH			*				L1		*				L2	L2	*		L2				*						*			
RB				*		L1, L2	L1, L2			*				L2	L1	*	L2		L1			*			L2			*		
DN	L2	L1		L2	*		L1, L2		L1		*				L1		*	L2	L1	L1	L2	L1	*		L2				*	
BH					L1	*	L2		L1	L1		*	L1	L2	L1	L1	L1	*	L1	L1	L1	L2		*	L1					*

preferred over sampling across nonintervention days since it contains no other news events of relevance that might affect quote dynamics. Note that the Appendix tables also report estimates for the *entire* −60/+60 minute sampling interval. The idea is to illustrate the potential for spurious inference when structural breaks are not accounted for.

A. Deutsche Bank as Dependent Variable

The first row of Tables III and IV summarizes the economic impact of competitor banks' quote revisions on DB. Underlying regressions are based on equation (2) with DB as the dependent variable. Detailed estimation results are presented in Appendix Table A.I, where adjusted R^2 statistics identify the time-varying model as the econometrically superior specification.

In the preinterventionary time period between −120 and −60, none of the competitor banks' quote revisions Granger-cause DB. Only DB's own first lag enters statistically significantly. Negative AR(1) processes are well-documented in high-frequency foreign exchange data and can be observed across all dependent variable banks and across all time periods considered in this study. Explanations for such systematic own quote reversals include order imbalances (see Bollerslev and Domowitz (1993)) and data noise (see Zhou (1996)).

Inferences over the −60 and −25 minute period are similar to the initial period. In the time-varying coefficient model (see Table IV), DB quote revisions remain empirically unexplained by competitors' quote adjustments. Only in the constant coefficient case (see Table III) do we find Den Norske's last lag as entering significantly.

Results for the period between −25 and the time of the announcement reflect a distinct structural break in DB quoting patterns. Over this time interval, DB quote revisions are Granger-caused by past returns of other banks, specifically by SG's and CH's two period lags. The fact that statistical significance occurs at the second, as opposed to the first, lag is of little economic relevance here. The explanation lies in the rapid frequency of quote entries: During turbulent market periods, such as during intervention, DB may not have observed the most recent indications by SG and CH as it updates its quotes at time τ.

Once Reuters announces a BUBA intervention at time 0, lagged quote revisions by SG and CH become statistically insignificant. Only in the time-varying model does the first lag of CH retain some predictive power. DB sensitivity to competitor quote revisions disappears altogether in the +25/+60 period. This result is identical to DB quoting behavior observed over the preinterventionary period.

Appendix Table A.I also presents results for the intervention period as a whole (−60/+60). These results would suggest that competitor banks are Granger-causing DB throughout. However, our *within-period* results contradict this finding, which reinforces the argument that high-frequency sampling should be used when analyzing interventionary dynamics.

B. Other Banks as Dependent Variables

The lack of Granger causality on DB prior to $t = -25$ is a necessary condition to establish DB as a price leader. It remains to show that other banks' quote adjustments are Granger-caused by DB to make the empirical case for price leadership.

Qualitative results for SG, CH, RB, DN, and BH are displayed in the lower rows of Tables III and IV. Based on regression diagnostics for the individual banks, the time-varying specification again proves to be statistically superior. For details on one bank's (SG) estimation results, refer to Appendix Table A.II.

In the preinterventionary period, −120/−60, previous competitor actions are insignificant in predicting dependent variable banks' quote patterns. The only exception is DN. These findings are consistent with the hypothesis of equalized information dissemination in the foreign exchange market. In a trading environment undisturbed by major news, there are no profit opportunities from tracking competitor moves.

Bank interactions change over the −60/−25 subsample, where DB is shown to Granger-cause quote revisions by SG, CH, RB, DN, and BH. Since no other bank Granger-causes DB over this time period (see first row of Table IV), DB meets the necessary and sufficient conditions to be considered a price leader from −60 to −25 minutes prior to a Reuters report.

Between −25 and the time of the news release, SG, CH, and BH continue to be affected by DB's past indications; but now a multitude of banks besides DB Granger-causes competitor banks' quote adjustments. Note that −25/0 is the same time period over which DB is Granger-caused by SG and CH (see first row of Table IV). Such "two-way" Granger-causality is consistent with the relative convergence of quote patterns seen in Figures 2 and 3.

Within 25 minutes after the intervention reports, bank traders resume quote patterns similar to those exhibited between −120 and −60 minutes. The speed of reversal appears most pronounced for CH (see Table IV). Implications for these distinct interbank behavioral shifts at −60, −25, and time 0 will be discussed next.

VIII. Implications of Empirical Results

Intervention is believed to move exchange rates, either by changing relative money supplies, as in the case of unsterilized intervention, or through signalling policy changes, as in the case of sterilized intervention. Note that this study considers a sample of Bundesbank interventions aimed at defending EMS cross-currencies. In the basic target zone literature, discussed by Svensson (1992), interventions are assumed to be unsterilized since target zone authorities use changes in fundamentals to keep exchange rates within bands.

In the case where a central bank prefers to keep fundamentals unchanged, "signaling" operates as the primary driver behind intervention-related foreign exchange dynamics. Further discussion of this issue is provided by Obstfeld (1990), Goodhart and Hesse (1993), and Dominguez and Frankel (1993). Under the signaling hypothesis, central banks intervene in order to communicate future policy information to the market.

This study does not seek to explain the channeling device by which intervention activity moves exchange rates. Rather, this study is concerned with the information asymmetries created through interventionary activity. To explore this issue, we require knowledge of the microstructure relations between the central bank and foreign exchange traders.

The empirical results of this article suggest that certain commercial bank dealers have privileged information regarding central bank activities. In the case of the Bundesbank, intervention orders might be funneled largely through DB's trading desk. From BUBA's perspective, such selective dealing appears rational: DB's strong market presence and liquidity provide the central bank with more efficient transactions turnover than independent brokers (see discussion in Section IV). Based on the shift in regression results, initial BUBA order placements with DB occur up to 60 minutes prior to public knowledge of the intervention—a longer lag than suggested by Goodhart and Hesse (1993).

Over the next 35 minutes, DB's efforts to profit from interventionary order flows provide a signal to uninformed traders that the central bank has entered the market. Thus, competitor bank dealers follow DB's superior information lead in quote adjustments, as indicated by the results for the −60/−25 time period. This pattern precisely confirms Goodhart's (1988) claim that there can be temporary price leadership in the foreign exchange market.

As we get closer to the public announcement, however, quoting behavior evolves away from price leadership. There are two explanations for the two-way Granger-causalities observed between −25 and time 0: Under the first scenario, traders might be jockeying for strategic positions. Since DB knows that its insider status is transitory, its trading desk begins to track competitors closely in order to position itself optimally for profit-taking. Note especially DB's relationship to the larger banks, SG and CH, as shown in the first row of Tables III and IV. As time passes, the probability of information leakages increases. Market participation, proxied by quoting frequency, declines as competitor banks carefully position themselves to discern the future direction of the market (see Table II). Once the extent of interventionary activities is leaked sufficiently, small and large traders will enter the race for any remaining profits. Hence, the two-way causalities in quote revisions observed between −25 to 0.

An alternative explanation for the estimated two-way Granger causalities draws from Montgomery and Popper (1995). Their model shows that *sharing* of intervention information can increase the welfare of all traders, informed and uninformed alike. Accordingly, DB would have an incentive to actively promote its insider information with others: DB's expected payoff would be higher than under a strategy of information concealment. Empirically, sharing of information is difficult to distinguish from information leakage. Both would be consistent with the observed alignment of quote revisions. However, when news is shared openly, we would expect subsequent profit-reaping activities to die out faster.

Table A.I

Deutsche Bank: Time-Varying Effect of Competitor Banks' Quote Revisions

This table estimates DM/US$ quote revisions by Deutsche Bank (DB) as a function of two lagged quote revisions by competitor banks and five own lags:

$$\mathrm{QM}_{\tau}^{\mathrm{DB}} = a + \sum_{k=1}^{5} \sum_{i=1}^{2} b_i^k \mathrm{QM}_{(\tau-i)^k}^{k} + \sum_{i=1}^{5} c_i^{\mathrm{DB}} \mathrm{QM}_{(\tau-i)^{\mathrm{DB}}}^{\mathrm{DB}}$$

$$\text{where} \quad b_i^k = e_i^k + \frac{f_i^k}{(\tau - (\tau - i)^k)/60}; \qquad c_i^{\mathrm{DB}} = g_i^{\mathrm{DB}} + \frac{h_i^{\mathrm{DB}}}{(\tau - (\tau - i)^{\mathrm{DB}})/60}.$$

$\mathrm{QM}_{\tau}^{\mathrm{DB}}$ is measured as the per-minute percentage change in DB's midpoint quotes between time $\tau - 1$ and τ, $\mathrm{QM}_{(\tau-i)^k}^{k}$ denotes the ith preceding per-minute quote change by competitor banks k = Societe Generale (SG), Chemical Bank (CH), Rabobank (RB), Den Norske Bank (DN), and BHF Bank (BH). $\mathrm{QM}_{(\tau-i)^{\mathrm{DB}}}^{\mathrm{DB}}$ represents DB's own lagged indications. f_i^k and h_i^{DB} are coefficients that capture the time lapse between regressor banks' lagged quote revisions and DB's adjustment at time τ. The sample comprises 14 pooled Bundesbank intervention periods between Oct. 1, 1992 and Sept. 30, 1993. −120/−60, −60/−25, −25/0, 0/+25, +25/+60 and −60/+60 are time intervals in minutes that define subsamples around Bundesbank intervention reports. The time stamp on intervention headline entries is denoted as time 0. Due to the time-varying nature of the model, marginal effects are reported in lieu of individual coefficient estimates. For instance, $\delta\mathrm{QM}^{\mathrm{DB}}/\delta\mathrm{QM}_{(\tau-1)^{\mathrm{SG}}}^{\mathrm{SG}}$ measures the incremental impact of SG's time $\tau - 1$ quote changes on DB's time τ quote revisions. DW is the Durbin–Watson measure. t-statistics are in parentheses. Statistical significance is denoted by * (**) at the 5 percent (1 percent) level using robust standard errors with Newey–West (1987) serial-correlation and heteroscedasticity correction.

continued overleaf

Marginal Effects	−120/−60 Minutes		−60/−25 Minutes		−25/0 Minutes		0/+25 Minutes		+25/+60 Minutes		−60/+60 Minutes	
	$f_i^k = h_i^{DB} = 0$	$f_i^k \neq h_i^{DB} \neq 0$	$f_i^k = h_i^{DB} = 0$	$f_i^k \neq h_i^{DB} \neq 0$	$f_i^k = h_i^{DB} = 0$	$f_i^k \neq h_i^{DB} \neq 0$	$f_i^k = h_i^{DB} = 0$	$f_i^k \neq h_i^{DB} \neq 0$	$f_i^k = h_i^{DB} = 0$	$f_i^k \neq h_i^{DB} \neq 0$	$f_i^k = h_i^{DB} = 0$	$f_i^k \neq h_i^{DB} \neq 0$
a	0.05	0.06	−0.70	−0.66	−0.65	−0.65	0.39	0.41	0.27	0.51	−0.23	−0.15
	(0.12)	(0.26)	(−1.29)	(−1.37)	(−1.46)	(−1.53)	(0.84)	(0.95)	(0.54)	(1.01)	(−0.95)	(−0.64)
$\delta QM^{DB}/\delta QM^{SG}_{(\tau-1)}$ SG	0.04	0.03	0.07	0.10	0.004	0.04	−0.008	0.0005	0.05	−0.03	−0.02	−0.02
	(0.80)	(0.61)	(1.09)	(1.20)	(0.05)	(0.48)	(−0.10)	(0.006)	(−1.06)	(−0.68)	(−0.49)	(−0.76)
$\delta QM^{DB}/\delta QM^{SG}_{(\tau-2)}$ SG	0.07	0.06	0.08	0.06	0.16*	0.05*	−0.02	0.02	−0.03	−0.11	0.04	0.02
	(1.69)	(1.29)	(1.36)	0.71)	(1.97)	(1.99)	(−0.42)	(0.35)	(−0.23)	(−1.25)	(0.93)	(0.58)
$\delta QM^{DB}/\delta QM^{CH}_{(\tau-1)}$ CH	0.10	0.03	0.09	0.23	−0.05	−0.03	0.16	0.27*	0.14	0.16	0.08	0.08
	(1.57)	(0.53)	(0.74)	(1.69)	(−0.40)	(−0.22)	(1.32)	(2.16)	(0.73)	(0.82)	(1.29)	(1.31)
$\delta QM^{DB}/\delta QM^{CH}_{(\tau-2)}$ CH	0.08	0.02	−0.19	−0.08	0.18*	0.20**	0.01	0.08	0.02	0.03	−0.003	0.03
	(1.43)	(0.26)	(−1.70)	(−0.57)	(2.48)	(3.04)	(0.20)	(0.92)	(0.18)	(0.30)	(−0.07)	(0.54)
$\delta QM^{DB}/\delta QM^{RB}_{(\tau-1)}$ RB	0.02	−0.003	0.10	0.11	0.02	0.005	−0.19	−0.02	0.06	−0.02	0.06*	0.06*
	(0.20)	(−0.04)	(1.53)	(1.68)	(0.33)	(0.07)	(−0.23)	(−0.17)	(1.40)	(−0.31)	(2.03)	(2.32)
$\delta QM^{DB}/\delta QM^{RB}_{(\tau-2)}$ RB	0.008	−0.007	−0.03	−0.05	0.03	0.006	0.03	0.05	0.05	0.03	−0.004	−0.18
	(0.26)	(−0.20)	(−0.49)	(−0.78)	(0.98)	(0.11)	(0.56)	(0.46)	(1.48)	(0.86)	(−0.13)	(−0.50)
$\delta QM^{DB}/\delta QM^{DN}_{(\tau-1)}$ DN	0.22	0.13	0.30**	0.16	0.23*	0.27	0.22	0.22	0.005	−0.04	0.17**	0.12*
	(1.85)	(1.71)	(2.64)	(1.39)	(2.12)	(1.03)	(1.39)	(1.41)	(0.06)	(−0.58)	(3.13)	(2.26)
$\delta QM^{DB}/\delta QM^{DN}_{(\tau-2)}$ DN	0.14	0.05	−0.002	−0.11	0.07	0.21	0.0001	0.0004	−0.11	−0.17	0.01	−0.003
	(1.83)	(0.57)	(−0.02)	(−0.95)	(0.69)	(1.28)	(0.001)	(0.002)	(−0.87)	(−1.44)	(0.26)	(−0.05)
$\delta QM^{DB}/\delta QM^{BH}_{(\tau-1)}$ BH	0.03	0.17	0.37	0.54	0.29	0.25	0.09	0.04	−0.03	0.09	0.16	0.20
	(1.59)	(1.75)	(1.10)	(1.48)	(1.13)	(0.99)	(0.20)	(0.09)	(−0.13)	(0.34)	(1.16)	(1.45)
$\delta QM^{DB}/\delta QM^{BH}_{(\tau-2)}$ BH	0.03	−0.04	0.45	0.40	0.20	0.18	0.34	0.27	0.14	0.06	0.28*	0.23
	(0.43)	(−0.53)	(1.44)	(1.30)	(1.13)	(1.20)	(0.85)	(0.83)	(0.80)	(0.33)	(2.05)	(1.71)
$\delta QM^{DB}/\delta QM^{DB}_{(\tau-1)}$ DB	−0.07*	−0.09*	−0.22**	−0.29**	−0.21**	−0.30**	−0.34*	−0.30*	−0.12**	−0.18**	−0.20**	−0.23**
	(−1.98)	(−2.47)	(−3.72)	(−4.74)	(−3.27)	(−3.12)	(−2.40)	(−2.11)	(−2.71)	(−3.30)	(−5.06)	(−5.82)
$\delta QM^{DB}/\delta QM^{DB}_{(\tau-2)}$ DB	0.005	−0.02	0.006	−0.05	−0.22	0.10	−0.19	−0.15	−0.003	0.005	−0.02	−0.03
	(0.13)	(−0.51)	(0.15)	(−0.94)	(−0.26)	(−1.07)	(−1.28)	(−0.13)	(−0.08)	(0.12)	(−0.41)	(−0.63)
$\delta QM^{DB}/\delta QM^{DB}_{(\tau-3)}$ DB	0.03	0.01	0.08	0.10	−0.10	−0.08	−0.09	−0.16	−0.13	−0.11*	−0.004	0.007
	(0.60).	(0.27)	(0.89)	(1.08)	(−0.97)	(−0.89)	(−1.28)	(−1.53)	(−1.86)	(−2.25)	(0.08)	(1.13)
$\delta QM^{DB}/\delta QM^{DB}_{(\tau-4)}$ DB	0.04	0.004	0.03	0.05	0.06	0.06	−0.19	−0.33	0.09*	0.06	0.03	0.03
	(0.87)	(0.10)	(0.76)	(1.27)	(1.10)	(1.25)	(−1.50)	(−1.66)	(2.08)	(1.31)	(0.87)	(0.91)
$\delta QM^{DB}/\delta QM^{DB}_{(\tau-5)}$ DB	0.11	0.06	−0.03	−0.006	0.05	0.05	0.007	−0.05	−0.03	0.004	0.004	0.004
	(1.82)	(0.91)	(−1.08)	(−0.17)	(1.10)	(0.68)	(0.11)	(−0.42)	(−1.02)	(0.13)	(0.23)	(0.26)
N	437		303		238		210		253		1004	
$\bar{R}^2$	0.02	0.07	0.03	0.15	0.05	0.12	0.07	0.05	0.03	0.04	0.03	0.07
DW	2.04	2.02	2.04	2.09	2.00	2.06	2.01	2.06	2.00	2.03	2.00	2.01

Table A.II

Societe Generale: Time-Varying Effect of Competitor Banks' Quote Revisions

This table estimates DM/US$ quote revisions by Societe Generale (SG) as a function of two lagged quote revisions by competitor banks and five own lags:

$$QM_{\tau}^{SG} = a + \sum_{k=1}^{5} \sum_{i=1}^{2} b_i^k QM_{(\tau-i)^k}^k + \sum_{i=1}^{5} c_i^{SG} QM_{(\tau-i)^{SG}}^{SG}$$

$$\text{where} \quad b_i^k = e_i^k + \frac{f_i^k}{(\tau-(\tau-1)^k)/60}; \qquad c_i^{SG} = g_i^{SG} + \frac{h_i^{SG}}{(\tau-(\tau-i)^{SG})/60}.$$

QM_{τ}^{SG} is measured as the per-minute percentage change in SG's midpoint quotes between time $\tau - 1$ and τ; $QM_{(\tau-i)^k}^k$ denotes the ith preceding per-minute quote change by competitor banks k = Deutsche Bank (DB), Chemical Bank (CH), Rabobank (RB), Den Norske Bank (DN), and BHF Bank (BH). $QM_{(\tau-i)^{SG}}^{SG}$ represents SG's own lagged indications. f_i^k and h_i^{SG} are coefficients that capture the time lapse between regressor banks' lagged quote revisions and SG's adjustment at time τ. The sample comprises 14 pooled Bundesbank intervention periods between Oct. 1, 1992 and Sept. 30, 1993. −120/−60, −60/−25, −25/0, 0/+25, +25/+60, and −60/+60 are time intervals in minutes that define subsamples around Bundesbank intervention reports. The time stamp on intervention headline entries is denoted as time 0. Due to the time-varying nature of the model, marginal effects are reported in lieu of individual coefficient estimates. For instance, $\delta QM^{SG}/\delta QM_{(\tau-1)^{DB}}^{DB}$ measures the incremental impact of DB's time $\tau - 1$ quote changes on SG's time τ quote revisions. DW is the Durbin–Watson measure. t-statistics are in parentheses. Statistical significance is denoted by * (**) at the 5 percent (1 percent) level using robust standard errors with Newey–West (1987) serial-correlation and heteroscedasticity correction.

continued overleaf

Marginal Effects	−120/−60 Minutes		−60/−25 Minutes		−25/0 Minutes		0/+25 Minutes		+25/+60 Minutes		−60/+60 Minutes	
	$f_i^k = h_i^{SG} = 0$	$f_i^k \neq h_i^{SG} \neq 0$	$f_i^k = h_i^{SG} = 0$	$f_i^k \neq h_i^{SG} \neq 0$	$f_i^k = h_i^{SG} = 0$	$f_i^k \neq h_i^{SG} \neq 0$	$f_i^k = h_i^{SG} = 0$	$f_i^k \neq h_i^{SG} \neq 0$	$f_i^k = h_i^{SG} = 0$	$f_i^k \neq h_i^{SG} \neq 0$	$f_i^k = h_i^{SG} = 0$	$f_i^k \neq h_i^{SG} \neq 0$
a	0.27 (0.85)	0.21 (0.57)	0.39 (0.50)	0.86 (1.26)	0.55 (1.28)	0.40 (0.85)	0.30 (0.55)	0.92 (1.40)	−0.60 (−1.04)	−0.66 (−1.15)	0.15 (0.50)	0.38 (1.06)
$\delta QM^{SG}/\delta QM^{DB}_{(\tau-1)}$ DB	0.03 (0.50)	0.03 (0.55)	0.05** (2.58)	0.01* (2.18)	−0.02* (−2.34)	0.004* (2.08)	−0.02 (−0.21)	0.009 (0.08)	−0.10 (−1.54)	−0.15 (−1.81)	0.002 (0.04)	0.01 (0.02)
$\delta QM^{SG}/\delta QM^{DB}_{(\tau-2)}$ DB	0.03 (0.50)	0.10 (1.32)	0.02 0.67)	0.03 (0.74)	0.12* (2.06)	0.08* (2.45)	0.07 (0.85)	0.12 (1.23)	0.06 (0.91)	−0.04 (−0.44)	0.07* (2.40)	0.06* (2.11)
$\delta QM^{SG}/\delta QM^{CH}_{(\tau-1)}$ CH	0.11 (1.35)	0.07 (0.83)	0.20 (1.79)	0.21 (1.32)	−0.02* (−2.30)	0.01* (2.16)	0.25** (3.35)	0.31** (2.94)	0.25 (1.10)	0.36* (2.00)	0.14** (3.27)	0.14** (3.36)
$\delta QM^{SG}/\delta QM^{CH}_{(\tau-2)}$ CH	−0.04 (−0.80)	−0.12 (−1.29)	0.17 (1.39)	0.40 (1.16)	0.08* (2.23)	−0.09* (−2.28)	0.04 (0.67)	0.18 (1.65)	−0.22 (−1.48)	−0.16 (−0.92)	−0.001 (−0.04)	0.02 (0.43)
$\delta QM^{SG}/\delta QM^{RB}_{(\tau-1)}$ RB	0.14 (1.38)	0.12 (1.13)	−0.14 (−0.81)	−0.06 (−0.48)	0.14 (0.82)	0.13 (1.23)	−0.07 (−1.26)	0.01 (0.19)	0.08 (0.66)	−0.05 (−0.37)	0.0001 (0.01)	0.008 (0.12)
$\delta QM^{SG}/\delta QM^{RB}_{(\tau-2)}$ RB	−0.04 (−0.62)	−0.057 (−0.59)	0.03 (0.58)	0.09 (0.72)	0.07 (1.02)	0.12 (1.07)	−0.03 (−0.68)	0.003 (0.06)	0.02 (0.38)	−0.007 (−0.14)	0.03 (1.10)	0.04 (0.87)
$\delta QM^{SG}/\delta QM^{DN}_{(\tau-1)}$ DN	0.25 (1.12)	0.18 (1.00)	−0.05 (−0.41)	0.01 (0.11)	0.16* (2.17)	−0.14* (−2.04)	−0.17 (−1.68)	−0.20 (−1.86)	−0.01 (−0.14)	−0.05 (−0.55)	−0.02 (−0.38)	−0.04 (−0.77)
$\delta QM^{SG}/\delta QM^{DN}_{(\tau-2)}$ DN	0.19 (1.79)	0.21 (1.52)	0.04 (0.35)	−0.14 (−0.77)	0.02 (0.09)	0.13 (0.42)	0.17 (1.36)	0.24 (1.59)	0.09 (0.69)	0.25* (2.16)	0.03 (0.40)	0.002 (0.03)
$\delta QM^{SG}/\delta QM^{BH}_{(\tau-1)}$ BH	−0.13 (−0.56)	0.03 (0.12)	−0.83 (−1.93)	−0.51 (−1.04)	0.13 (0.37)	0.14 (0.48)	−0.21 (−0.71)	−0.17 (−0.59)	−0.13 (−0.69)	0.05 (0.28)	−0.28 (−1.80)	−0.23 (−1.57)
$\delta QM^{SG}/\delta QM^{BH}_{(\tau-2)}$ BH	0.50 (1.34)	0.10 (0.33)	−1.09 (−0.84)	−1.06 (−0.69)	0.03 (0.06)	0.13 (0.23)	−0.30 (−0.61)	−0.50 (−1.02)	0.18 (0.24)	0.64 (1.12)	−0.32 (−0.77)	−0.33 (−0.75)
$\delta QM^{SG}/\delta QM^{SG}_{(\tau-1)}$ SG	−0.18 (−1.78)	−0.09* (−1.96)	−0.16** (−3.35)	−0.21* (−2.24)	−0.05 (−0.46)	−0.39** (−2.94)	−0.21** (−2.72)	−0.18* (−2.70)	−0.19 (−1.67)	−0.26** (−2.60)	−0.14** (−3.32)	−0.09** (−2.61)
$\delta QM^{SG}/\delta QM^{SG}_{(\tau-2)}$ SG	−0.09 (−0.77)	−0.20* (−2.27)	−0.06 (−1.10)	−0.02 (−0.22)	0.0003 (0.002)	−0.10 (−0.70)	−0.05 (−0.97)	−0.06 (−1.29)	−0.06 (−1.00)	−0.08 (−0.76)	−0.03 (−1.29)	−0.03 (−1.01)
$\delta QM^{SG}/\delta QM^{SG}_{(\tau-3)}$ SG	0.04 (0.61)	0.08 (1.38)	−0.04 (−0.61)	−0.04 (−0.65)	0.03 (0.23)	−0.06 (−0.54)	−0.20** (−2.63)	−0.18* (−2.44)	−0.09 (−1.63)	−0.05 (−0.85)	−0.07 (−1.66)	−0.05 (−1.48)
$\delta QM^{SG}/\delta QM^{SG}_{(\tau-4)}$ SG	−0.02 (−0.51)	0.01 (0.27)	0.20* (−2.52)	0.09* (−2.48)	−0.09 (−1.15)	−0.24** (−2.66)	0.10 (1.26)	0.12 (1.68)	0.03 (−0.34)	−0.04 (−0.72)	−0.08 (−1.50)	−0.06 (−1.42)
$\delta QM^{SG}/\delta QM^{SG}_{(\tau-5)}$ SG	0.008 (0.18)	0.04 (0.77)	−0.10 (−1.40)	−0.06 (−0.55)	0.01 (0.18)	−0.20* (−1.96)	0.20* (2.16)	0.18 (1.87)	0.0007 (0.01)	0.03 (0.42)	−0.01 (−0.27)	0.002 (0.05)
N	230		192		127		131		167		617	
$\bar{R}^2$	0.08	0.11	0.02	0.10	0.02	0.22	0.07	0.15	0.03	0.14	0.02	0.07
DW	2.05	2.12	2.08	2.11	2.06	2.12	2.12	2.11	2.01	2.02	2.01	2.00

Beyond the specific bank interrelations, our results establish quite powerfully that the trader community learns about interventionary activity *before* the public is informed. Foreign exchange volatility increases until information is fully shared among traders, which occurs around 5 minutes *prior to* Reuters reports (see Fig. 1). Thereafter, volatility tapers off. This finding suggests that Reuters intervention reports are not actual "news" to market participants but constitute redundant information that has already been discounted through trading activity.

IX. Conclusion

This article investigates Goodhart's (1988) hypothesis that short-run information asymmetries establish certain bank traders as price leaders in the foreign exchange market. The focal news events here are Bundesbank intervention reports as recorded on the Reuters headline screen between 10/1/1992 and 9/30/1993. We create within-the-hour subsamples around these reports to examine tick-by-tick quote revisions for the six banks that input the most DM/US$ quotes on the Reuters screen.

The empirical methodology involves Granger-causality tests that are conducted in a time-varying framework to account for the age of past quote entries. It is shown that competitive traders treat Deutsche Bank as a price leader up to 60 minutes prior to intervention reports. As the market moves closer to the public announcement, strategic positioning becomes the prevalent driver of quote adjustment patterns. By the time of the Reuters announcement, attention to competitors' quote adjustments tapers off, and traders resume their preinterventionary trading interactions.

Our findings confirm the hypothesis that official Bundesbank intervention is associated with asymmetric information flows and transitory price leadership by Deutsche Bank. More broadly, the results support microstructure theories emphasizing news being disseminated through trading among heterogeneously informed agents. Furthermore, this article shows a distinct lead of actual trader reactions to interventions relative to their public announcement. The existence and duration of such informational leads should be an important empirical concern for studying other classes of news effects besides intervention in the foreign exchange market.

Appendix

Appendix Tables A.I and A.II present estimation results for a subset of banks based on the Granger causality model specified in equation (2) of the text. Specifically, results are reported for bank j = DB as the hypothesized price leader and for bank j = SG as a representative price follower. Six subsamples are defined around Bundesbank intervention reports: −120/−60 (preintervention period), −60/−25, −25/0, 0/+25, +25/+60, and −60/+60 (aggregate intervention period). For each sample period, the marginal effects for both a constant coefficient model and one considering the age of regressor bank quotes are reported. Estimates are based on robust standard errors with Newey-West (1987) serial correlation and heteroscedasticity correction.

REFERENCES

Bollerslev, Tim, Ray. Y. Chou, and Kenneth F. Kroner, 1992, ARCH modeling in finance: A review of the theory and empirical evidence, *Journal of Econometrics* 52, 5–59.

Bollerslev, Tim, and Ian Domowitz, 1993, Trading patterns and prices in the interbank foreign exchange market, *Journal of Finance* 48, 1421–1443.

Bossaerts, Peter, and Pierre Hillion, 1991, Market microstructure effects of government intervention in the foreign exchange market, *Review of Financial Studies* 4, 513–541.

DeGennaro, Ramon P., and Ronald E. Shrieves, 1995, Public information releases, private information arrival, and volatility in the foreign exchange market, in *High-Frequency Data in Finance-1 Conference Proceedings,* Vol. 1.

Dominguez, Kathryn M., and Jeffrey A. Frankel, 1993. *Does Foreign Exchange Intervention Work?* (Institute for International Economics, Washington, D.C.).

Easley, David, Maureen O'Hara, and P. S. Srinivas, 1993, Option volume and stock prices: Evidence on where informed traders trade, Mimeo, Cornell University.

Ederington, Louis H., and Jae H. Lee, 1993, How markets process information: News releases and volatility, *Journal of Finance* 48, 1161–1191.

Edison, Hali J., 1993, The effectiveness of central-bank intervention: A survey of the literature after 1982, *Special Papers in International Economics* 18, Princeton University.

Euromoney Magazine, June, 1994.

Glosten, Lawrence R., and Paul L. Milgrom, 1985, Bid, ask, and transactions prices in a specialist market with heterogeneously informed traders, *Journal of Financial Economics* 14, 71–100.

Goodhart, Charles A. E., 1988, The foreign exchange market: A random walk with a dragging anchor, *Economica* 55, 437–460.

Goodhart, Charles A. E., and L. Figliuoli, 1991, Every minute counts in financial markets, *Journal of International Money and Finance* 10, 23–52.

Goodhart, Charles A. E., and Thomas Hesse, 1993, Central bank forex intervention assessed in continuous time, *Journal of International Money and Finance* 12, 368–389.

Goodhart, Charles A. E., and Richard Payne, 1996, Microstructural dynamics in a foreign exchange electronic broking system, *Journal of International Money and Finance* 15, 829–852.

Granger, Clive W. J., 1969, Investigating causal relations by econometric models and cross-spectral methods, *Econometrica* 37, 24–36.

Guillaume, Dominique M., Michel M. Dacorogna, Rakhal Dave, Ulrich A. Müller, Richard B. Olsen, and Olivier V. Pictet, 1994, From the bird's eye to the microscope, Mimeo, Olsen & Associates, Research Institute for Applied Economics.

Hasbrouck, Joel, 1991, Measuring the information content of stock trades, *Journal of Finance* 46, 179–208.

Humpage, Owen F., 1994, Institutional aspects of U.S. intervention, *Economic Review* 30, 2–19.

Kyle, Albert, 1985, Continuous auctions and insider trading, *Econometrica* 53, 1315–1335.

Lyons, Richard K., 1995, Tests of microstructural hypotheses in the foreign exchange market, *Journal of Financial Economics* 39, 321–351.

Lyons, Richard K., 1997, A simultaneous trade model of the foreign exchange hot potato, *Journal of International Economics*, Forthcoming.

Montgomery, John D., and Helen A. Popper, 1995, Information sharing and central bank intervention in the foreign exchange market, Mimeo, Santa Clara University.

Newey, Whitney, and Kenneth West, 1987, A simple positive semidefinite, heteroscedasticity and autocorrelation consistent covariance matrix, *Econometrica* 55, 703–708.

Obstfeld, Maurice, 1990, The effectiveness of foreign-exchange intervention: Recent experience, 1985–1988, in William H. Branson, Jacob A. Frenkel, and Morris Goldstein, Eds.: *International Policy Coordination and Exchange Rate Fluctuations* (University of Chicago Press, Chicago, Illinois).

O'Hara, Maureen, 1995. *Market Microstructure Theory* (Blackwell Publishers, Cambridge, Massachusetts).

Ross, Stephen A., 1989, Information and volatility: The no-arbitrage martingale approach to timing and resolution irrelevancy, *Journal of Finance* 44, 1–18.

Svensson, Lars E. O., 1992, An interpretation of recent research on exchange rate target zones, *Journal of Economic Perspectives* 6, 119–144.

Wolinsky, Asher, 1990, Information revelation in a market with pairwise meetings, *Econometrica* 58, 1–23.

Zhou, Bin, 1996, High-frequency data and volatility in foreign exchange rates, *Journal of Business and Economic Statistics* 14, 45–52.

[16]

ELSEVIER

Journal of Empirical Finance 9 (2002) 271–285

Journal of EMPIRICAL FINANCE

www.elsevier.com/locate/econbase

Asymmetric information and price discovery in the FX market: does Tokyo know more about the yen?☆

Vicentiu Covrig [a], Michael Melvin [b,*]

[a]Division of Banking and Finance, Nanyang Technological University, Singapore 639798
[b]Department of Economics, Arizona State University, Tempe, AZ 85287-3806, USA

Accepted 23 November 2001

Abstract

We identify a period with a high concentration of informed yen/dollar traders active in Tokyo. Findings include:

1. Japanese quotes lead the rest of the market when the informed are active. At other times, two-way causality is observed in quotes.
2. The contribution of Japanese quotes to yen/dollar price discovery relative to quotes of the rest-of-the-world is 5 to 12 percentage points higher when the informed are active compared to when they are absent.

Private information can, at times, be important, yet "normal" times are characterized as periods where public information results in a high contemporaneous correlation across quotes.

JEL classification: F31; G15
Keywords: Foreign exchange; Microstructure; Yen

☆ Helpful comments on an earlier draft were received from Jonathan Batten, Dan Bernhardt, JinWan Cho, Lutz Kilian, Mark Lundin, Lilian Ng, an anonymous referee and seminar participants at the City University of Hong Kong, Claremont, the Federal Reserve Bank of St. Louis, Nanyang Technological University, Oxford University, the University of Strathclyde, the HFDFII conference, the Econometric Society winter meetings and the Georgia Tech International Finance conference. We assume responsibility for any remaining errors.

* Corresponding author. Tel.: +1-480-965-6860; fax: +1-480-965-0748.
E-mail address: mmelvin@asu.edu (M. Melvin).

0927-5398/02/$ - see front matter
PII: S0927-5398(01)00056-1

1. Introduction

If we could identify periods where a financial market experienced a concentration of informed trading activity and then compared this to other periods where such informed trading was less pronounced, what would we expect to find? Theory suggests we should observe important differences. Specifically, microstructure models of financial markets suggest that market dynamics will be affected by the presence or absence of informed traders (see O'Hara, 1995 for a review). Empirical tests of such models are lacking due to the obvious problem of identifying an "informed" trader. We attempt to address this problem by focusing on a particular period of Asian yen/dollar trading when a compression of the time available for trading likely results in a high concentration of informed trading. By exploiting the information in yen/dollar quotes in this market interval, we have evidence supporting the hypothesis that there is, indeed, a high concentration of informed trading activity where the following empirical regularities are found. (1) The quotes of the informed traders tend to lead the quotes of the uninformed. (2) The contribution to price discovery of the quotes coming from the region where the informed are concentrated (Japan) is higher during times that are rich in informed trading than in other times.

The particular period of interest was identified in a recent paper by Ito et al. (1998), who studied a change in trading regime that occurred in the Tokyo foreign exchange market on December 22, 1994. On this day, Japan lifted a restriction against trading the yen over the lunch break from 12:00 to 1:30 (Tokyo time). Ito et al. analyzed foreign exchange market activity during Asian business hours for the periods before and after the lunchtime trading and found evidence consistent with the presence of significant private information in the foreign exchange market. A particularly important piece of evidence in their study was that there is a U-shape of volatility of yen/dollar exchange rate returns in the Tokyo morning when the lunchtime closing occurs that disappears once lunchtime trading begins. This is consistent with models of private information where the informed traders must exploit their informational advantage prior to the market closing so that a compressed trading time results in a faster revelation of the private information. A criticism of the Ito et al. paper was that change in the U-shape of volatility could also have been related to inventory control behavior so that the information story was not necessarily the only interpretation of the empirical findings. The evidence in the present paper, based on more direct tests of the informational asymmetries story, offers new support for the role of private information in foreign exchange markets.

For our purposes, the late morning period in the pre-December 22, 1994 era (which will henceforth be identified as the before period) is viewed to be relatively rich in informed trading compared to the post-December 22, 1994 era (which will henceforth be identified as the after period) when trading occurs through the midday lunchtime so no Tokyo market closing exists. In addition, we hypothesize that the Japanese traders have superior information on the yen/dollar exchange rate relative to non-Japanese traders.

A natural question at this point is to inquire about the source of this informational advantage. While one cannot offer any hard evidence on this question, there is wide recognition of some potential sources. One important source of private information in the foreign exchange market is the customer order flow. For instance, large Japanese banks will receive the foreign exchange business of the largest Japanese corporations and this proprietary information confers a temporary informational advantage on Japanese banks relative to non-Japanese banks in making a market in the yen/dollar. Another potential source of informational advantage is early knowledge of important government data releases or policy actions. Peiers (1997) presents evidence that Deutschebank acts as a price leader in the mark/dollar market around periods of Bundesbank intervention. The inference is that Deutschebank receives a significant portion of the intervention-related currency trades of Germany's central bank and this confers a temporary information advantage. This is but one possible example of how a large and important bank may have temporary sources of private information. In similar fashion, it may be the case that some Japanese banks have superior ability to anticipate policy movements of the Japanese authorities.[1]

We will focus on the pre-lunch before period as a useful sample for testing implications of microstructure theories regarding market dynamics in periods rich in informed trading. Section 2 will discuss empirically testable implications of informed trader concentration as suggested by the existing theoretical literature and present results for one hypothesis: If Japanese traders are believed to have superior information at certain times, then we would expect quotes from Japan to lead quotes from other areas during periods rich in informed trading. Section 2 provides evidence that Japanese quotes lead the rest of the market during the late morning before period. In other periods, two-way causality is observed. Section 3 provides another test of Japanese informed trader presence—is yen/dollar price discovery concentrated in Japan when the informed are active? It is shown that the relative share of information generated by Japanese quotes is higher in the period when the informed Japanese traders are believed to be active than in other periods. Finally, Section 4 provides a summary and conclusions. The battery of tests applied to the yen/dollar data go well beyond the investigation of the U-shape of volatility provided by Ito, Lyons, and Melvin. Such a U-shape might not only reflect private information but could also be a result of inventory rebalancing at the open and close of trading as discussed in Brock and Kleidon (1992) so that the volatility is simply volume induced rather than associated with privately informed trading. However, the following sections will present new evidence of price leadership and price discovery suggesting that Japanese banks are, indeed, better informed than the rest of the market. These new results cannot be explained by simple inventory rebalancing stories.

[1] An interesting and entertaining story told by one experienced trader is found in Niederhoffer's (1997) fable of "The Old Trader and the Yen." He asserts the informational advantage of the Japanese banks when he describes them in the following passage: "At 7:00 p.m. in New York, it is morning in Asia.... The banks will wait for their customers to sell the dollar to hedge their export earnings, and then they will buy it... They drink sake each night with their friends from school and the ministries, and they learn what is going to be announced and where they will be buying and selling." Whether truth or fiction, if non-Japanese traders believe that Japanese banks have superior information, then the dynamics investigated in the following sections will be expected. Recently, a *Wall Street Journal* article discussed Japanese government investigation of corruption at the Bank of Japan and stated that "Traders have long accused central bank officials of leaking the *tankan* survey, a closely watched quarterly poll of business sentiment that can often suggest when the bank will change interest rates" (Sapsford, 1998, p. A12).

2. Implications of informed trader concentration for Japanese and non-Japanese bank quotes

Due to the lunchtime shutdown of trading in Tokyo prior to December 22, 1994, we expect that there was an exogenous concentration of informed trading prior to the 1.5-h Tokyo market closure. What sort of market dynamics should result from this clustering of informed trading? The literature associated with papers such as Kyle (1985, 1989), Admati and Pfleiderer (1988) and Subrahmanyam (1991) suggests testable hypotheses related to informed trader presence. An Admati and Pfleiderer type model can be used to motivate the intradaily U-shape of volatility. More relevant to the empirical work in the current study is Subrahmanyam's model which indicates that the informational efficiency of price depends upon the number of informed traders. In the context of the problem under study, a greater concentration of informed traders prior to lunch in the pre-December 22, 1994 period should be associated with a faster speed of adjustment of the yen/dollar exchange rate to full-information levels.[2] The intuition behind this result is that the greater the number of informed traders, the more aggressively they trade. An increase in trading aggressiveness causes private information to be revealed in price faster. Therefore, prices are more informative (and will converge more quickly to full information levels), the greater the number of informed traders in the market.

During times of intense informed trader activity, the informed traders are revealing information to the rest of the market regarding unobservable fundamentals. In the case of the trading break during the Tokyo lunchtime, we believe that there should be a clustering of informed traders prior to the market closure as traders seek to exploit any informational advantages prior to the closure. This clustering of the informed has implications for quote dynamics between Japanese and non-Japanese banks.

As discussed in Section 1, it is commonly believed that Japanese banks have superior information regarding the yen. The source of this advantage is, presumably, the close links between banks and large non-bank corporate customers in Japan, who fill their currency needs through the Japanese banks. There may also be a closer relationship between Japanese governmental agencies and Japanese banks than foreign banks. Without being able to identify the source of informational advantage, if the rest of the market believes that Japanese banks are, at times, better informed on the yen/dollar exchange rate, we should expect to observe periods when the Japanese bank quotes *lead* the quotes of banks in other locations.

When the lunchtime closing occurred in Tokyo (the before period), we expect that the late morning pre-lunch period was a period of informed trading concentration, while the same time of day in the after period contained no such clustering of the informed. Therefore, if Japanese banks are believed to have superior information relative to non-Japanese banks, we hypothesize that the before pre-lunch period when informed trader

[2] None of the theoretical papers cited are aimed at the foreign exchange market. The varieties of models following Kyle assumes the one market-maker can observe total order flow. However, the foreign exchange market is a multiple dealer market with low transparency where no one market-maker can observe the market-wide order flow. As an appropriate theoretical model for currencies is still missing from the literature, we do not want to push any particular theory descendent from Kyle as being an accurate model of currency trading.

clustering occurs in Japan, should exhibit Japanese bank quotes causing non-Japanese quotes, but this one-way causality should not appear in the after pre-lunch period. This is, essentially, a test of whether the rest of the market believes that the informed yen traders are concentrated among the Japanese banks.

To test this hypothesis, we examine the evidence regarding causality between Japanese and non-Japanese quotes over the late morning (10:30 am–12:00 noon) in Tokyo for both the before and after periods and compare this evidence to other times of day. The data we use are based on quotes appearing on the Reuters FXFX screen during the period from November 1994 to January 1995.[3] We focus on this short period around the change in trading regime in order to concentrate on the effect of this one event rather than contaminate the sample with extraneous events that may enter in a longer time frame.

Since quotes from Japanese and non-Japanese banks arrive at different points in time and have a different number of observations in the sample we have a nonsynchronous quoting problem. Any approach to this problem requires some potentially controversial assumptions. Harris et al. (1995) chose to use observations only when all markets have quotes, so their sample is defined by the least-frequent quote source. De Jong et al. (1998) explicitly enter missing values for intervals when no new quote appears for a market and then develop an estimator which explicitly accounts for these missing observations. We will utilize two approaches. First, we will employ the methodology of De Jong et al. to utilize all quotes in inferring causality. Second, we will filter the data for quote revisions that would be noticed in the noise of intradaily trading and use these big quote revisions to investigate causality.

2.1. A model of nonsynchronous quoting and causality

The approach employed explicitly takes into account the irregular spacing of the data and uses all observations to investigate lead–lag relationships among Japanese and non-Japanese banks. There are two approaches to deal with irregularly spaced data: one which assumes that the most recent quote remains valid if the quote is not updated and another which explicitly puts a missing value at the intervals during which there is no new quote. We use the latter method with an estimator that takes these missing observations explicitly into account. This approach follows the contributions of Lo and MacKinlay (1990), De Jong and Nijman (1997) and De Jong et al. (1998). The method allows estimates of the cross-covariances between return series when the quotes are irregularly spaced in time. An important feature of the method is that time is measured as calendar (real) time and we assume that there exists a regular underlying unobserved discrete time process from which

[3] The data were obtained from Olsen and Associates Research Institute for Applied Economics in Zurich. The sample periods for analysis are before: November 24 to December 21 and after: January 4 to January 31. The holiday period is omitted from the early after sample as many traders take vacation and market activity is abnormally low. An outlier in the data on December 1, 1994 at 2:26:56 was discovered that had a reasonable bid quote but an ask quote a full yen higher than the bid. Rather than take the average of the bid and ask for this outlier, we use the bid quote in the work below.

observed quotes are drawn. The ultimate goal is to estimate the cross-correlations between these unobserved returns.

The first step in the derivation is to write the difference between two observed quotes as a sum of the price changes of the underlying unobservable quote process:

$$q_{t_{i+1}} - q_{t_i} = \sum_{t=t_i+1}^{t_{i+1}} \Delta q_t \tag{1}$$

where t_i denotes the clock time index of the ith observation. The unobserved quotes are sampled at the clock time frequency and the observed quotes are indexed by the quote time.

The expectation of the cross product of observed returns in the two markets can be written as:

$$E(y_{ij}) = E\left[\left(q^{\mathrm{J}}_{t_{i+1}} - q^{\mathrm{J}}_{t_i}\right)\left(q^{\mathrm{N}}_{t_{j+1}} - q^{\mathrm{N}}_{t_j}\right)\right] \tag{2}$$

One can prove that the expectation of this cross product, conditional on the observed quote times, is a linear combination of the cross covariances γ_k of the underlying returns:

$$E(y_{ij}) = \sum_{t=t_i+1}^{t_{i+1}} \sum_{k=t_j+1}^{t_{j+1}} \gamma_{t-k} \tag{3}$$

where k is the order of the cross covariances and

$$\gamma_k = \mathrm{cov}(r^{\mathrm{J}}_t, r^{\mathrm{NJ}}_{t-k}) \quad \text{where } r_t = q_t - q_{t-1} \tag{4}$$

Let $\chi_{ij}(k)$ be the number of times that γ_k appears in the right hand side of Eq. (3) and we can derive the following expression:

$$\chi_{ij}(k) = \max[0, \min(t_{i+1}, t_{j+1} + k) - \max(t_i, t_j + k)] \tag{5}$$

An important property of Eq. (5) is that $\chi_{ij}(k)$ are functions of the quote times t only, and not of the observed quotes. Substituting Eq. (5) on the right hand side of Eq. (3), we obtain:

$$E(y_{ij} \mid \chi_{ij}) = \sum_{k=-K}^{K} \chi_{ij}(k)\gamma_k \tag{6}$$

where we assume that all covariances of higher order than K are zero.

We can consider Eq. (6) as a regression with the unknown covariances γ_k as parameters and the coefficients $\chi_{ij}(k)$ as explanatory variables. In vector notation, the regression is:

$$y_{ij} = \chi'_{ij}\gamma + e_{ij} \tag{7}$$

Table 1
Wald tests for lead–lag correlations between Japanese and non-Japanese quotes

	Before	After
Japanese quotes lead Non-Japanese	16.2 (0.01)	12.6 (0.03)
Non-Japanese quotes lead Japanese	8.3 (0.14)	15.7 (0.01)

This table reports Wald tests for the joint significance of leads and lags of cross-correlations between Japanese and non-Japanese quotes on the yen/dollar for 20 days before and after the start of lunchtime trading in Tokyo. All data are used by employing an estimator that explicitly takes into account nonsynchronous quoting so that cross-covariances are estimated for quotes that are irregularly spaced in time. Before refers to the late morning period when lunchtime trading was prohibited and a concentration of informed Japanese traders is expected. After refers to the late-morning period after the lunchtime trading prohibition was lifted and informed trading is expected to be diffused throughout the day. We cannot reject the hypothesis that Japanese quotes lead non-Japanese in the before period. In the after period, the evidence suggests two-way causality. The table entries are *F*-statistics for the hypothesis that the lag or lead covariances are jointly equal to zero. This statistic has an asymptotic distribution of $\chi^2(5)$. *P*-values are in parentheses.

The regression (Eq. (7)) can be estimated by OLS. In principle, the regression equation involves all possible cross products in the observed quote changes. However, we can confine ourselves only to the adjacent quotes and we can ignore the observations that are more than K apart. De Jong and Nijman proved that the estimators of γ are consistent and they also provide a method to estimate the asymptotic standard errors of the estimators.

Estimates of the cross-correlations between Japanese and non-Japanese quotes are found as the estimated γ covariances from Eq. (7) divided by the standard deviation of the Japanese and non-Japanese returns over the same interval. Negative lags ($k>0$) represent the correlation between the current Japanese quote and non-Japanese quotes k periods ahead—so this tests whether Japanese quotes lead non-Japanese. Similarly, positive lags ($k<0$) test whether Japanese quotes lag non-Japanese. Wald tests for the joint significance of the leads and lags are reported in Table 1. The Wald tests send a clear signal: there is two-way causality in the after period, but in the before period there is one-way causality as Japanese quotes lead non-Japanese and the reverse causality is statistically insignificant.

2.2. Large quote revisions and causality

The evidence presented in the prior section is persuasive. Additional evidence is provided in this section via causality tests. A strong test of causality would be provided by filtering the quotes to identify relatively large changes that should be noticed in the noise of intradaily quoting. Specifically, we split the quotes into those originating in Japan and those originating elsewhere and filter the quote returns to establish a minimum threshold for size. We test for causality with the following regression:

$$r_t^d = a + br_{t-1}^i + cr_{t-1}^d + e_t \tag{8}$$

where d and i index the origin of quotes as either Japan or non-Japan and r is the exchange rate return. Therefore, r_t^d is the return from consecutive quotes of region d at time t. When

d is Japan and i is non-Japan, we test the null hypothesis that b=0, or non-Japanese returns do not cause Japanese returns. Similarly, when d is non-Japan and i is Japan, we test the null that Japanese returns do not cause non-Japanese returns. A lagged dependent variable is added to the equation to account for autocorrelation existing in the dependent variable series and guard against the independent variable return simply capturing the time-dependency that exists in high-frequency data. The model is estimated using a Newey–West adjustment.

The returns series are constructed from tick-by-tick data on the yen/dollar and are defined as the change in the log of the midpoint of the bid and ask quotes multiplied by 10,000 (so that the units are basis points). The data are constructed as follows.

Table 2
Causality tests of Japanese and non-Japanese bank quotes

	a	*b*	*c*	q(12)	Observations
(A) Non-Japanese dependent variable, Japanese independent variable					
Before 9:00–10:30	0.185 (0.23)	0.180 (0.00)	−0.258 (0.03)	11.7 (0.47)	270
Before 10:30–12:00	−0.432 (0.03)	0.157 (0.00)	−0.301 (0.00)	10.6 (0.56)	134
Before 1:30–3:00	0.211 (0.23)	0.088 (0.01)	−0.215 (0.02)	13.3 (0.28)	220
After 9:00–10:30	−0.130 (0.17)	0.112 (0.00)	−0.273 (0.00)	10.8 (0.54)	599
After 10:30–12:00	−0.006 (0.96)	0.219 (0.00)	−0.377 (0.00)	13.5 (0.33)	410
After 1:30–3:00	0.105 (0.26)	0.142 (0.00)	−0.241 (0.00)	17.3 (0.10)	462
(B) Japanese dependent variable, non-Japanese independent variable					
Before 9:00–10:30	0.002 (0.99)	0.097 (0.01)	−0.376 (0.00)	12.9 (0.30)	233
Before 10:30–12:00	0.062 (0.67)	0.041 (0.21)	−0.267 (0.00)	17.6 (0.13)	158
Before 1:30–3:00	−0.170 (0.19)	0.135 (0.00)	−0.267 (0.00)	10.0 (0.62)	212
After 9:00–10:30	−0.037 (0.71)	0.149 (0.00)	−0.386 (0.00)	15.9 (0.14)	512
After 10:30–12:00	−0.091 (0.42)	0.130 (0.00)	−0.214 (0.00)	9.2 (0.69)	364
After 1:30–3:00	0.068 (0.56)	0.099 (0.00)	−0.299 (0.00)	10.5 (0.57)	359

Returns, r, are created from tick-by-tick yen/dollar quotes for 20 days before and after the start of lunchtime trading in Tokyo. First, the change in the log of the midpoint of the bid and ask multiplied by 10,000 is created to have units of basis points. Then, in order to identify causality emanating from large quote revisions that should be noticeable in the noise of intradaily quoting, the data are filtered so that only returns greater than 2.5 basis points are retained. This gives the independent variable series, r_t^i. Dependent variable observations, r_t^d, are matched by taking the corresponding dependent variable quote return following the independent variable observations. Causality is then tested by estimating the following equation:

$$r_t^d = a + br_{t-1}^i + cr_{t-1}^d + e_t$$

When d is Japan (non-Japan) and i is non-Japan (Japan), we test the null hypothesis that b=0 or non-Japanese (Japanese) returns do not cause Japanese (non-Japanese) returns. The lagged dependent variable is included to account for autocorrelation existing in the dependent variable series and guard against the independent variable return capturing the time-dependency that exists in high-frequency data. Coefficient estimates and related t-statistics are reported in the table along with q-statistics on residual autocorrelation and the number of observations resulting from the filtering procedure for each time period. Moving average terms were estimated for the following four models where the q-statistics indicated autocorrelation problems: Part A—before 1:30–3:00, ma(6); after 1:30–3:00, ma(1). Part B—before 9:00–10:30, ma(10); after 9:00–10:30, ma(1). Estimation incorporates a Newey–West adjustment for heteroskedasticity. The results indicate two-way causality for every period except the late-morning before when Japanese quotes cause non-Japanese. This is consistent with the presence of a high concentration of informed Japanese traders in this period. p-values in parentheses.

(i) We begin by filtering the independent variable tick-by-tick returns so that only returns exceeding 2.5 basis points are kept.[4] This filter is intended to reduce the noise in the series and sharpen the test so that independent variable observations are measuring sizable exchange rate changes that would be noticed in the noise of intradaily trading.

(ii) For each observation on the independent variable return, we construct the corresponding dependent variable return by taking the change in the log of the midpoint observations based on the dependent variable quotes following the independent variable returns.[5]

The idea is to examine whether sizable changes in the quotes of one group have a significant effect on the quotes of the other group.[6]

Causality tests are performed separately for the before and after samples. Results are given in Table 2. Note that there is two-way causality for every period except the late morning before. In this period, Japanese quotes are seen to significantly cause non-Japanese quotes in Table 2A. However, in Table 2B, non-Japanese quotes do not significantly cause Japanese quotes for the same period. In every other period, both before and after, two-way causality exists. We interpret these results as supportive of a market-wide perception of a concentration of Japanese informed traders prior to the lunch break in the before period. In this particular period, the actions of the Japanese traders attract the attention of the rest of the market and generate the price leadership behavior found in the data.

Note that the finding of two-way causality is consistent with a market driven by public information arrival. Public information shared by all would result in a general price adjustment across the market that may be spread over a short time. This brief period of quotes adjusting to reflect the new information would generate the two-way causality found in most periods. This is not to say that important private information is not also present during these periods, but rather the private information is not as dominant a factor in "normal" times. The evidence suggests that the Tokyo lunchtime closing created an "abnormal" period of activity where private information revealed by the Tokyo traders dominated market dynamics in the period just prior to the lunch break in trading.

Whether we use only the observations involving large returns, as just reported, or all the data, as in Section 2.1, we find the same result. In the before period presumed to be rich in informed trading, there is one-way causality where Japanese quotes lead non-Japanese. In the after period, two-way causality exists regardless of which methodology is employed.

3. Price discovery in Japan and elsewhere

Having documented that non-Japanese quotes tended to lag behind Japanese quotes for the yen/dollar in the pre-lunch before period, we now want to conduct an analysis

[4] We choose 2.5 basis points on the basis of this equaling approximately 2 standard deviations for the morning data.

[5] For the before (after) sample, the average time between dependent and independent variable quotes was 33 (24) s.

[6] While we later discuss implications of cointegration between Japanese and non-Japanese quotes when observations are sampled at 1-min intervals, we point out that such cointegration issues are not relevant here since observations have been discarded through the filtering for large returns.

following Hasbrouck (1995) on the contribution of Japanese and non-Japanese quotes to yen/dollar price discovery. We begin by assuming that both Japanese (q_j) and non-Japanese (q_n) quotes contain a random-walk component (are $I(1)$) and the quote returns, i.e., the differences of logs of the q, are covariance stationary. These returns may be written in vector moving average form:

$$r_t = \Psi(L)e_t \tag{9}$$

where $\Psi(L)$ is a polynomial in the lag operator and e_t is a zero-mean vector of serially uncorrelated innovations with covariance matrix Ω. While each quote series is nonstationary, the difference between the two series is stationary or the quotes are cointegrated of order 1. Then $\beta' q_t$, where $\beta' = [1 -1]$, is a stationary series, implying that $\beta' \Psi(1)=0$, where $\Psi(1)$ is the sum of the moving-average coefficients. Similar to the Stock and Watson (1988) common trends representation of a cointegrated system, the rows of $\Psi(1)$ are identical. We denote ψ as the common row vector in $\Psi(1)$, and it can be shown that the elements of ψ sum to unity.

As shown in Hasbrouck, the system may be written in error correction form as:

$$r_t = \alpha(\beta' q_{t-1} - E\beta' q_t) + \Gamma_1 r_{t-1} + \Gamma_2 r_{t-2} + \ldots + \Gamma_{k-1} r_{t-k+1} + e_t \tag{10}$$

when there is a nonstationary autoregressive representation of order k for the quotes.[7] The $E\beta' q_t$ term reflects systematic differences in the two quote series. In order to estimate this model, we follow Hasbrouck in estimating this term by calculating the mean value over the sample so that $(\beta' q_{t-1} - E\beta' q_t)$ is a "demeaned" quote vector. Once this vector is created, the model is then estimable by linear least squares.

If the error covariance matrix Ω is diagonal, then it is possible to directly calculate the contribution of the innovations in one market, say Japan, to the total variance. This may be thought of as the "information share" of the Japanese quotes. If only private information was relevant, we might expect such a structure. However, the presence of public information, shared equally by all, should lead to the innovations being contemporaneously correlated across markets. In this case, Ω is not diagonal. Hasbrouck recommends a procedure to bound the information shares of each region through a triangularization of Ω. First, let the innovations in the two regions' quotes be given by $e_t = Fz_t$, where F is the Cholesky factorization of Ω and z is a vector of random variables with $Ez_t = 0$ and $\mathrm{Var}(z_t) = I$ (an identity matrix). Then the market share of the innovation attributable to a particular z_j is found as:

$$S_j = ([\psi F]_j)^2 / (\psi \Omega \psi') \tag{11}$$

where $[\psi F]_j$ is the jth element of the row matrix ψF. By permuting ψ and Ω, we get an upper (lower) bound on the information share of Japanese (non-Japanese) quotes by placing Japan

[7] De Jong et al. (2001) propose an alternative estimation strategy based upon a model developed in Harvey (1989). Their model imposes cointegration directly and offers a more parsimonious lag structure than the Hasbrouck method. This can often be important in high-frequency applications where long lags are sometimes needed and, consequently, parameter instability may result. However, in our case, we find that inference regarding information shares is unaffected after four lags, so the order of lags is not particularly high and inference is robust with regard to lag structure.

first. When non-Japanese quotes are placed first, we get an upper (lower) bound on non-Japanese (Japanese) quotes. The factorization imposes a structure that maximizes the information share on the first quote and minimizes the information share of the last quote. As Hasbrouck states, using the Cholesky factorization in this manner is analogous to allocating the explained variance in a multiple regression by considering the incremental improvement in the R^2 that occurs when variables are added in sequence. The information share is a measure of who moves first in adjusting quotes. The magnitude of the difference between the upper and lower bound reflects the importance of contemporaneous correlation between Japanese and non-Japanese quotes. With a diagonal Ω there is no such problem and unique values of the information shares may be estimated.

We estimate the information shares for the late-morning before and after periods. The quotes are sampled at 1-min frequency, where the prior quote to each minute is used. No overnight returns are included. The specific functional form of Eq. (10) uses four lags of

Table 3
Information shares of japanese and non-japanese quotes

(A) Japan and non-Japan quotes

Quote origin	Bounds for information shares (%)					
	Before			After		
	Upper	Lower	Mean	Upper	Lower	Mean
Japan	56	41	49	64	30	47
Non-Japan	58	44	51	70	36	53

t-statistic for difference of before and after means: 10.9

(B) Japan and Hong Kong quotes

Quote origin	Bounds for information shares (%)					
	Before			After		
	Upper	Lower	Mean	Upper	Lower	Mean
Japan	59	54	56	65	40	52
Hong Kong	46	41	44	60	35	48

t-statistic for difference of before and after means: 22.3

The information shares are based upon the innovations from a vector moving average model of quote returns on the yen/dollar exchange rate from banks in Japan and elsewhere during the late morning in Asia. The sample is split into 20 days prior to the beginning of lunchtime trading in Asia (the before period) and 20 days after the start of lunchtime trading (the after period). Specifically, the information shares are given by the equation:

$$S_j = ([\psi F]_j)^2/(\psi\Omega\psi')$$

where Ω is the error covariance matrix of the residuals from the quote returns model, ψ is the common row vector of coefficients from the moving average model and F is the Cholesky factorization of Ω. Permuting ψ and Ω, we get an upper (lower) bound on the information share of Japanese (non-Japanese) quotes by placing Japan first. When non-Japanese quotes are placed first, we get an upper (lower) bound on non-Japanese (Japanese) quotes. The distributions and related t-statistics are generated via bootstrap methods. The information share of Japanese quotes relative to non-Japanese or Hong Kong quotes is higher in the before period, when the prohibition of lunchtime trading leads to a concentration of informed Japanese trading prior to lunch, than in the after period when lunchtime trading is possible so there is no midday market closing inducing a clustering of informed, late-morning trading.

returns of each region. We experimented with alternative lags running from 2 to 12 and found that generally after four lags, the information shares are essentially unchanged. Table 3A. contains the estimated bounds for the Japanese and non-Japanese information shares. We disaggregate all quotes into those originating in Japan and those originating elsewhere. Comparing the information share of Japanese quotes to those of non-Japanese quotes, we see in the before period that the Japanese information share is 96% of the non-Japanese (49%/51%) at the mean, 97% at the upper bound, and 93% at the lower bound. In the after period, the information share of Japanese quotes falls to 89% of non-Japanese at the mean, 91% at the upper bound and 83% at the lower bound. These results indicate that the before period of heavy Japanese informed-trader concentration has a larger share of information for Japanese quotes than in the after period when the concentration of informed traders is absent. The distribution of the information shares was generated via a bootstrap on the estimates. Following Sapp (1999), we employ the method suggested by Li and Maddala (1997).[8] The associated t-statistic on the difference of means indicates that there is a statistically significant drop in the Japanese information share in the after period compared to the before. This result is consistent with the hypothesis that the rest of the market is looking to Japan for information during the before period as the concentration of the informed Japanese traders tend to lead the market.

The fact that the information share of Japan is estimated to be slightly below that of the rest of the market is an artifact of the comparison of only one country's quotes, Japan, against all the rest of the quotes in the market. The methodology is sensitive to the frequency of quote updating and will be biased in favor of large information shares for a region with more frequent quoting. This is, of course, due to the fact that the more frequently quotes are posted, the smaller the number of 1-min observations with zero returns entering into the calculations. For this reason, we believe the relative information shares between Japanese and non-Japanese quotes are more useful to examine than the absolute estimates of the information shares of a single region.

To illustrate this quote frequency sensitivity, we estimated information shares of Japan versus Hong Kong, with results reported in Table 3B. We now find that Japan's information share in the before period is 59% at the upper bound and 54% at the lower bound while Hong Kong's is 46% at the upper bound and 41% at the lower bound. The less frequent quoting of Hong Kong compared to the entire non-Japanese region results in a higher information share for Japan relative to Hong Kong than Japan relative to all non-Japanese quotes. Calculating the shares of information coming from Japan relative to Hong Kong, we find values of 128% at the upper bound and 131% at the lower bound in the before period. For the after period, the shares are 108% and 114%. Again we bootstrap distributions to generate a t-statistic for the difference of the mean information shares and find a statistically significant drop in the relative share of information coming from Japanese quotes in the after period compared to the before. In both cases of Table 3 we find that the relative share of information generated by Japanese quotes drops in the after period relative to the before. Once the informed trader concentration ends, the importance of Japanese quotes relative to the rest of the market falls.

[8] Sapp provides a good discussion of the bootstrap method in his Appendix.

4. Summary and conclusions

Microstructure models of financial markets have shown that we should expect markets to behave differently when there are many informed traders present than in times of informed trader absence. Empirical tests of the implications of these models have been hindered by the difficulty of identifying the informed traders. We have identified a period in the foreign exchange market where there should be a high concentration of informed trading. Following Ito et al., we look to the late-morning period of yen/dollar trading in Tokyo prior to December 22, 1994 (the before period) as a period where there is a concentration of informed Japanese traders relative to other times. This concentration of the informed arises from the lunchtime closing of yen/dollar trading that occurred in Tokyo until December 22, 1994. After that date (the after period), Tokyo trading at lunchtime was permitted.

We focus on the late-morning in Asian trading, hypothesizing that there should be different market dynamics in the before period compared to the after period that would allow tests of the implications of market microstructure models. To this end, we investigate hypotheses consistent with an informed trader concentration before that would disappear after. If the market believes that Japanese traders are better informed regarding the yen, then any time there is a perceived concentration of the Japanese informed traders, we should expect to see quotes from Japan leading quotes of other regions. We tested this hypothesis by performing causality tests of Japanese versus non-Japanese quotes. In general, there is two-way causality. This is consistent with a market driven by public information arrival shared equally by all so that following the arrival of news, there is a brief period of quotes adjusting across the market to the new information. The general finding of two-way causality is also consistent with a market where private information is always important, but the informed behave strategically and reveal their information slowly over time so that in normal periods one cannot detect a dominant presence of the informed. The Tokyo lunch closing compressed the time available for the informed Japanese traders to exploit their informational advantage so that the period prior to the lunch break finds the informed traders forced to reveal their information more quickly. As a result, in this one period—the late-morning before—we find one-way causality where Japanese quotes lead non-Japanese quotes. In the period leading up to the Tokyo lunchtime closing, the clustering of the informed Japanese traders seems to have created an environment where the rest of the market believed that the Japanese possessed superior information and were acting on that information so that Japanese quote leadership is observed.

A final examination of the implications of informed trader clustering was conducted by estimating the contribution of different trading centers to price discovery. Specifically, we estimate the shares of information that may be attributed to Japanese quotes versus non-Japanese quotes. Given the contemporaneous correlation between Japanese and non-Japanese quotes, we are unable to estimate unique values of the information shares but, instead, estimate upper and lower bounds for each region. We find that in the late-morning before period the information share of Japanese quotes is between 97% and 93% of the information share of the rest of the market. However, in the late-morning after period, the information share of the Japanese quotes is between 91% and 83% of the rest of the market, depending on whether we evaluate at the upper or lower bound of estimates. We find qualitatively similar results comparing Japan with Hong Kong. This drop in the information share of Japanese quotes in the after period is consistent with the dissipation of the informed trader clustering existing in the before period. It appears that the Japanese traders' contributions to yen/dollar price discovery are at a peak when the market perceives these traders to have private information.

Taken as a whole, we have provided evidence on the implications of informed trader clustering in the foreign exchange market. While we cannot make any claims to generality of findings, it would be surprising if such implications did not extend to other financial markets. Returning to the question incorporated in the title: "Does Tokyo Know More About the Yen?", it appears the answer is a qualified "yes." At times, Japanese traders appear to have superior information—or, at least, the rest of the market believes that they do. However, the normal state of the market is one where Japan does not dominate in setting yen/dollar quotes. This does not mean that private information is unimportant in "normal" times, but rather that the informed are able to slowly reveal their information. In this case, it may not be unreasonable to think of the market as largely being driven by public information.

References

Admati, A., Pfleiderer, P., 1988. A theory of intraday patterns: volume and price variability. Review of Financial Studies 1, 3–40.

Brock, W.A., Kleidon, A.W., 1992. Periodic market closure and trading volume. Journal of Economic Dynamics and Control 16, 451–489.

De Jong, F., Nijman, T., 1997. High frequency analysis of lead–lag relationships between financial markets. Journal of Empirical Finance 4, 259–277.

De Jong, F., Mahieu, R., Schotman, P., 1998. Price discovery in the foreign exchange market: an empirical analysis of the yen/dmark rate. Journal of International Money and Finance 17, 5–28.

De Jong, F., Mahieu, R., Schotman, P., van Leeuwen, I., 2001. Price discovery on foreign exchange markets with differentially informed traders. Working Paper, Limburg Institute of Financial Economics.

Harris, F.H.deB., McInish, T.H., Shoesmith, G.L., Wood, R.A., 1995. Cointegration, error correction, and price discovery on informationally linked security markets. Journal of Financial and Quantitative Analysis 30, 563–579.

Harvey, A.C., 1989. Forecasting, Structural Time Series Models and the Kalman Filter Cambridge Univ. Press, Cambridge.

Hasbrouck, J., 1995. One security, many markets: determining the contributions to price discovery. Journal of Finance 50, 1175–1199.

Ito, T., Lyons, R.K., Melvin, M., 1998. Is there private information in the FX market? The Tokyo experiment. Journal of Finance 53, 1111–1130.

Kyle, A.S., 1985. Continuous auctions and insider trading. Econometrica 53, 1315–1335.

Kyle, A.S., 1989. Informed speculation with imperfect competition. Review of Economic Studies 56, 317–356.

Li, H., Maddala, G.S., 1997. Bootstrapping cointegrating regressions. Journal of Econometrics 80, 297–318.

Lo, A., MacKinlay, A.C., 1990. An econometric analysis of infrequent trading. Journal of Econometrics 45, 181–211.

Niederhoffer, V., 1997. The Education of a Speculator Wiley, New York.

O'Hara, M., 1995. Market Microstructure Theory Blackwell, Cambridge, MA.

Peiers, B., 1997. Informed traders, intervention, and price leadership: a deeper view of the microstructure of the foreign exchange market. Journal of Finance 52, 1589–1614.

Sapp, S., 1999. Price leadership in the spot foreign exchange market. Working Paper, University of Western Ontario.

Sapsford, J., 1998. Japan's corruption scandal hits central bank. The Wall Street Journal 12, A12 March.

Stock, J.H., Watson, M.W., 1988. Testing for common trends. Journal of the American Statistical Association 83, 1097–1107.

Subrahmanyam, A., 1991. Risk aversion, market liquidity, and price efficiency. The Review of Financial Studies 4, 417–441.

[17]

Order Flow and Exchange Rate Dynamics

Martin D. D. Evans

Georgetown University and National Bureau of Economic Research

Richard K. Lyons

University of California, Berkeley and National Bureau of Economic Research

This paper presents an exchange rate model of a new kind. Instead of relying exclusively on macroeconomic determinants, the model includes a determinant from the field of microstructure finance—order flow. Order flow is a determinant because it conveys information. This is a radically different approach to exchange rates. It is also strikingly successful. Our model of daily deutsche mark/dollar log changes produces an R^2 statistic above 60 percent. For the deutsche mark/dollar spot market as a whole, we find that $1 billion of net dollar purchases increases the deutsche mark price of a dollar by 0.5 percent.

I. Introduction

Macroeconomic models of exchange rates perform poorly at frequencies higher than one year. Indeed, the explanatory power of these models is essentially zero (Meese and Rogoff 1983; Meese 1990). In the words of Frankel and Rose (1995, p. 1704), this negative result has had a "pessimistic effect on the field of empirical exchange rate modeling

We thank the following for valuable comments: three anonymous referees, Menzie Chinn, Peter DeMarzo, Frank Diebold, Petra Geraats, Robert Lucas (the editor), Richard Meese, Michael Melvin, Peter Reiss, Andrew Rose, Mark Taranto, Ingrid Werner, Alwyn Young, and seminar participants at Chicago, Wharton, Columbia, Massachusetts Institute of Technology, Iowa, Houston, Stanford, Berkeley, Princeton, the 1999 NBER Summer Institute, and the December 1999 NBER program meeting in microstructure. We thank the National Science Foundation for financial assistance.

[*Journal of Political Economy*, 2002, vol. 110, no. 1]

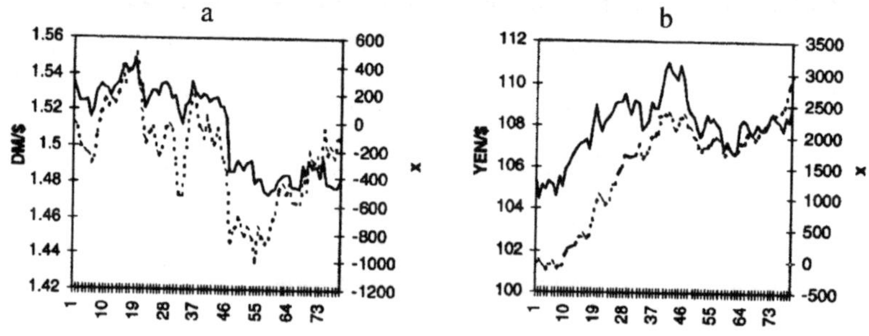

FIG. 1.—Four months of exchange rates (solid) and cumulative order flow (dashed), May 1–August 31, 1996: *a*, deutsche mark/dollar; *b*, yen/dollar.

in particular and international finance in general." The pessimistic effect has been with us 20 years.[1]

This paper moves in a new direction. We augment traditional macro analysis with some price determination microeconomics. This leads us to a class of models—from microstructure finance—that highlight new variables that macro models omit. The most important such variable is order flow. Order flow is defined as the net of buyer-initiated and seller-initiated orders; it is a measure of net buying pressure. Order flow is a proximate determinant of price in these models because it conveys information that currency markets need to aggregate.[2] This information includes anything pertaining to the realization of uncertain demands (differential interpretation of news, shocks to hedging demands, shocks to liquidity demands, etc.). When one maps information to price, order flow is essential to the transmission mechanism.

Figure 1 provides a first glimpse of order flow's role in this transmission mechanism. The solid lines are the spot rates of the deutsche mark and yen against the dollar over our four-month sample (May 1 to August 31, 1996). The dashed lines are worldwide order flow for the respective currencies. This order flow measure, denoted by x, is the sum

[1] Surveys of the literature include Frankel and Rose (1995), Isard (1995), and Taylor (1995). Alternatives to traditional models, such as the "new open-economy macro" approach (e.g., Obstfeld and Rogoff 1995), have yet to produce empirical exchange rate equations that alter the Meese-Rogoff conclusions.

[2] For evidence that foreign exchange order flow conveys information, see Lyons (1995), Covrig and Melvin (1998), Ito, Lyons, and Melvin (1998), Yao (1998), Payne (1999), Cheung and Wong (2000), Naranjo and Nimalendran (2000), and Evans (2002).

over time of signed interdealer trades.[3] Order flow and nominal exchange rates are strongly positively correlated, indicating that price increases with buying pressure. Though seemingly natural, a causal relation of this kind has conceptual implications: actual trades are neither necessary nor sufficient for price movements in traditional macro models.

We develop and estimate a model that specifies how interdealer order flow drives price determination via information aggregation. Our estimates verify the significance of this correlation. The model accounts for more than 60 percent of daily changes in the log deutsche mark/dollar exchange rate and more than 40 percent of daily changes in the log yen/dollar rate. This analysis fills the missing middle between past microstructure work using tick-by-tick data and macro work using monthly data. It helps to clarify how lower-frequency exchange rate dynamics emerge from the market's operation in real time.

This paper has four remaining sections. Section II develops a model with both micro and macro determinants. Section III describes our data. Section IV presents our results. Section V presents conclusions.

II. Portfolio Shifts Model

The model sketched in this section serves several purposes. First, it is designed to accommodate data at the daily frequency (unlike existing transaction frequency models). Second, the model provides a clear null under which causation runs from order flow to price, with interdealer flow serving as the means by which nonpublic information is learned. Third, the model shows why order flow's impact on price should persist using a familiar portfolio balance channel; this clarification is important for those who believe that trades can have only fleeting "indigestion" effects on price.

There are two basic types of information that order flow can convey. The first is information about the stream of future cash flows (i.e., numerators in a security valuation model). In foreign exchange, this stream takes the form of future interest differentials. The second is information about market-clearing discount rates (i.e., valuation denominators). The trading model we develop is based on the second type. It adopts a simultaneous-trade approach (see, e.g., the transaction frequency model of Lyons [1997]). Where applicable, we compress our

[3] For example, if a dealer initiates a trade against another dealer's deutsche mark/dollar quote and the trade is a dollar purchase (sale), then order flow is +1 (−1). These unit order flow values are cumulated across dealers over each 24-hour trading day (weekend trading—which is minimal—is included in Monday). In spot foreign exchange, roughly 75 percent of total volume occurs between dealers (25 percent occurs between dealers and nondealer customers).

presentation of the model below by using results established for other simultaneous-trade models.

The economic intuition behind our model is quite simple. Uncertain public demands for foreign exchange are realized at the start of each day. These demand realizations produce orders that are not publicly observed, so any information they convey needs to be aggregated in the trading process. Also, these demand realizations are, for simplicity, uncorrelated with future interest differentials, so any price impact operates through discount rates. (Demands of this type include liquidity demands, hedging demands, and, more subtly, speculative demands from varying risk tolerance.) These demands affect price because the rest of the market—being less than perfectly elastic—requires a price concession to absorb them.[4]

Consider a pure exchange economy with T trading periods (days) and two assets, one riskless (with gross return equal to one) and one risky. The $T+1$ payoff on the risky asset—foreign exchange—is denoted R, where R is composed of a series of increments:

$$R = \sum_{t=1}^{T+1} \Delta r_t. \tag{1}$$

The Δr_t increments are independently and identically distributed normal$(0, \sigma_r^2)$ and are observed publicly each day before trading. These realized increments represent innovations over time in public macroeconomic information (e.g., changes in interest rates). The foreign exchange market is organized as a dealership market with N dealers, indexed by i, and a continuum of nondealer customers (the public), indexed by $z \in [0, 1]$. The mass of customers on $[0, 1]$ is large (in a convergence sense) relative to the N dealers. Dealers and customers all have identical negative exponential utility defined over $T+1$ wealth.

The timing of the model is summarized in figure 2. Within each day there are three rounds of trading. In the first round, dealers trade with the public. In the second round, dealers trade among themselves (to share the resulting inventory risk). In the third round, dealers trade again with the public (to share inventory risk more broadly).

Each day begins with public observation of the day's payoff increment Δr_t. On the basis of this increment and other available information, each dealer simultaneously and independently quotes a scalar price to his

[4] For evidence that aggregate demand across stocks is less than perfectly elastic, see Scholes (1972), Shleifer (1986), Bagwell (1992), and Kaul, Mehrotra, and Morck (2000). The spot deutsche mark/dollar market needs to absorb much larger portfolio shifts than the market for a representative stock (the daily volume per stock on the New York Stock Exchange in 1998 averaged less than $10 million, whereas the daily volume in the spot deutsche mark/dollar market averaged about $300 billion).

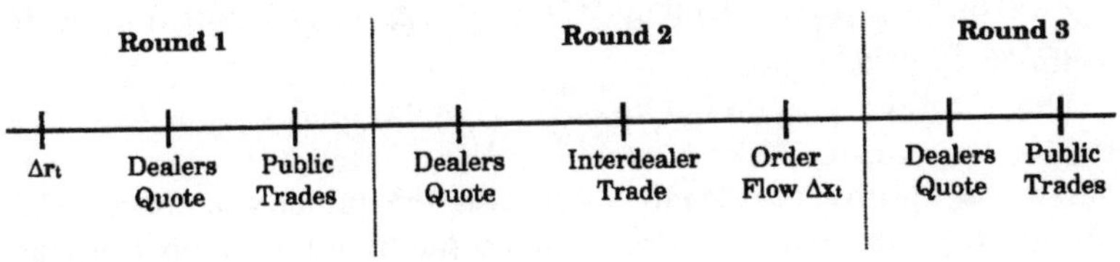

FIG. 2.—Daily timing

customers at which he agrees to buy and sell any amount.[5] We denote this round 1 price of dealer i on day t as P_{it}^1. Each dealer then receives a customer order realization C_{it}^1 that is executed at his quoted price P_{it}^1. Let $C_{it}^1 < 0$ denote net customer selling (dealer i buying). The individual C_{it}^1's are distributed normal$(0, \sigma_C^2)$; they are uncorrelated across dealers, are uncorrelated with the payoff increment Δr_t, and are not publicly observed. We refer to these orders as "portfolio shifts" of the nondealer public.

In round 2, each dealer simultaneously and independently quotes a scalar price to other dealers at which he agrees to buy and sell any amount. These interdealer quotes are observable and available to all dealers. Each dealer then simultaneously and independently trades on other dealers' quotes. (Orders at a given price are split evenly across dealers quoting that price.) Let T_{it} denote the (net) interdealer trade initiated by dealer i in round 2 (negative for dealer i net selling). At the close of round 2, all agents observe the interdealer order flow from that period:

$$\Delta x_t = \sum_{i=1}^{N} T_{it}. \tag{2}$$

In round 3 of each day, dealers share overnight risk with the nondealer public. In contrast to round 1, the public's motive for trading in round 3 is nonstochastic. Initially, each dealer simultaneously and independently quotes a scalar price P_{it}^3 at which he agrees to buy and sell any amount. These quotes are observable and available to the public. We assume that total public demand for the risky asset in round 3, denoted C_t^3, is less than infinitely elastic. With our earlier assumptions, this allows

[5] Introducing a bid-offer spread (or price schedule) in round 1 to endogenize the number of dealers is a straightforward—but distracting—extension.

us to write total public demand in round 3 as a linear function of the expected return:

$$C_t^3 = \gamma(E[P_{t+1}^3 \mid \Omega_3] - P_t^3), \qquad (3)$$

where the positive coefficient γ captures the public's aggregate risk-bearing capacity, and Ω_3 is the available public information (includes all payoff increments Δr_t and interdealer flows Δx_t through day t).

The equilibrium relation between interdealer order flow and price adjustment follows directly from results established for the simultaneous-trade model of Lyons (1997). First, propositions 1 and 2 of that paper show that within a given round, all dealers quote a common price (this is necessary for no arbitrage). It follows that this price is conditioned on common information only. Though each day's payoff increment Δr_t is common information at the beginning of round 1, order flow Δx_t is not observed until the end of round 2. The price for round 3 trading, P_t^3, reflects the information in both Δr_t and Δx_t.

The information in the payoff increment Δr_t is straightforward. The information in the order flow Δx_t relates to portfolio balance effects. To understand why, note first that in equilibrium each dealer's interdealer trade, T_{it}, will be proportional to the customer order C_{it}^1 he receives (see Lyons 1996, proposition 4). This implies that when dealers observe Δx_t at the end of round 2 (eq. [2]), they can infer the aggregate portfolio shift on the part of the public in round 1, $\Sigma_{i=1}^N C_{it}^1$ (henceforth denoted C_t^1). Dealers also know that, for a risk-averse public to reabsorb this portfolio shift in round 3, price must adjust. In particular, price adjusts in round 3 so that $C_t^1 + C_t^3 = 0$, where C_t^3 is given by equation (3). The resulting price change from the end of period $t-1$ to the end of period t can be written as

$$\Delta P_t = \Delta r_t + \lambda \Delta x_t, \qquad (4)$$

where λ is a positive constant that depends on γ and the variances σ_r^2 and σ_C^2 (see the working paper version of this article [Evans and Lyons 1999] for details).[6]

We make two changes to equation (4) for estimation purposes. First, we specialize the public information increment Δr_t to equal the change in the nominal interest differential, $\Delta(i_t - i_t^*)$, plus a white-noise error term, where i_t is the nominal dollar interest rate and i_t^* is the nominal nondollar interest rate (deutsche mark or yen). Although Δr_t could also

[6] For intuition on eq. (4), consider P_T, the final day's price. This is a one-period problem with Δr_{T+1} yet to be realized. The price P_T reflects all past payoff increments Δr_t, as well as all changes in risky asset "effective supply"—the sum of public portfolio shifts $(\Sigma_{t=1}^T C_t^1)$, the size of which is conveyed by past interdealer flow Δx_t. These effective-supply effects on price are no less fundamental than the Δr_t effects; this is how the market facilitates redistribution among risk-averse agents.

be correlated with other macro fundamentals, we use the interest differential because it is the main engine of exchange rate variation in macro models and is readily available daily. Second, we replace the dependent variable with the change in the log spot rate, Δp_t. This substitution makes our empirical specification comparable to standard macro models. Estimates using ΔP_t produce results nearly identical to those we report (R^2's, coefficient significance, lack of autocorrelation, etc.).

III. Data

Our data set includes all the deutsche mark/dollar and yen/dollar transactions that occurred from May 1 to August 31, 1996, on an interdealer trading system called Reuters Dealing 2000-1.[7] All trades on this system take the form of electronic bilateral conversations. A conversation is initiated when a dealer calls another dealer using the system to request a quote. If the calling dealer buys (sells) dollars, then order flow from that trade is +1 (−1).[8] A dealer who has been called is expected to provide a fast two-way quote with a tight spread. Quotes are take-it-or-leave-it, and if not dealt or declined quickly (i.e., within seconds), the quoting dealer retracts the quote, ending the conversation. To settle disputes, Reuters keeps a record of all bilateral conversations. This record is the source of our data. (For more detail on the Dealing 2000-1 system, see Lyons [1995] and Evans [1997].)

The three variables in our portfolio shifts model are measured as follows. The change in the spot rate (deutsche mark/dollar or yen/dollar), Δp_t, is the log change in the purchase transaction price between 4:00 P.M. (Greenwich mean time [GMT]) on day t and 4:00 P.M. on day $t-1$. When a purchase transaction does not occur precisely at 4:00 P.M., we use the subsequent purchase transaction (with roughly one million trades per day, the subsequent transaction is generally within a few seconds of 4:00 P.M.). When day t is a Monday, the day $t-1$ price is the previous Friday's price. The daily order flow, Δx_t, is the difference between the number of buyer-initiated trades and the number of seller-

[7] In 1996, interdealer transactions account for about 75 percent of total volume in major spot markets (see Bank for International Settlements 1996). This 75 percent from interdealer trading breaks into two transaction types, direct and brokered. Direct trading accounts for about 60 percent of interdealer volume, and brokered trading accounts for about 40 percent. Reuters Dealing 2000-1 is used for the direct portion. According to Reuters, over 90 percent of the world's direct interdealer transactions take place on this system (only dealers have access).

[8] Our data set does not identify the size of individual transactions. (See Jones, Kaul, and Lipson [1994] for evidence that trade size contains no information beyond that in the number of transactions.) Our data set does include total dollar volume over our sample, however, which allows us to calculate an average trade size; we use this below to interpret the estimated coefficients.

TABLE 1
MODEL ESTIMATES

Specification	$\Delta(i_t - i_t^*)$ (1)	Δx_t (2)	$i_{t-1} - i_{t-1}^*$ (3)	R^2 (4)	Diagnostics: Serial (5)	Diagnostics: Heteroskedasticity (6)
			Deutsche Mark/Dollar			
I	.51	2.14		.64	.77	.07
	(.26)	(.29)			.40	.02
II		2.15		.63	.73	.05
		(.29)			.45	.03
III	.62			.01	.78	.92
	(.77)				.77	.99
IV		2.15	.022	.64	.49	.17
		(.29)	(.013)		.43	.01
V			.022	.00	.04	.83
			(.022)		.24	.98
			Yen/Dollar			
I	2.47	2.86		.46	.06	.92
	(.92)	(.36)			.44	.74
II		2.61		.40	.19	.60
		(.36)			.33	.83
III	.57			.00	.85	.13
	(1.20)				.81	.67
IV		2.78	.016	.42	.00	.66
		(.38)	(.011)		.03	.72
V			−.009	.00	.12	.18
			(.014)		.46	.79

NOTE.—The table reports ordinary least squares estimates of the portfolio shifts model (specification I), $\Delta p_t = \beta_1\Delta(i_t - i_t^*) + \beta_2\Delta x_t + \eta_t$, and four alternatives (specifications II–V). The dependent variable Δp_t is the change in the log spot exchange rate from 4:00 P.M. (GMT) on day $t-1$ to 4:00 P.M. (GMT) on day t (deutsche mark/dollar or yen/dollar). The regressor $\Delta(i_t - i_t^*)$ is the change in the one-day interest differential from day $t-1$ to day t (an asterisk denotes deutsche mark or yen, annual basis). The regressor Δx_t is the interdealer order flow between 4:00 P.M. (GMT) on day $t-1$ and 4:00 P.M. (GMT) on day t (negative for net dollar sales, in thousands). Specifications IV and V replace $\Delta(i_t - i_t^*)$ with the interest differential at 4:00 P.M. on day $t-1$. Standard errors are shown in parentheses (corrected for heteroskedasticity in the case of the deutsche mark). The sample spans four months (May 1 to August 31, 1996). Col. 5 presents the p-value of Breusch-Godfrey Lagrange multiplier tests for residual serial correlation, first-order in the top row and fifth-order (one week) in the bottom row. Col. 6 presents the p-values of Engle (1982) Lagrange multiplier tests for autoregressive conditional heteroskedasticity in the residuals, first-order in the top row and fifth-order in the bottom row.

initiated trades (in thousands), also measured from 4:00 P.M. (GMT) on day $t-1$ to 4:00 P.M. on day t (a negative sign denotes net dollar sales). The change in interest differential, $\Delta(i_t - i_t^*)$, is calculated from the daily overnight interest rates for the dollar, the deutsche mark, and the yen (annual basis); the source is Datastream (typically measured at approximately 4:00 P.M. GMT).

IV. Empirical Results

Table 1 presents estimates of the portfolio shifts model (specification I) using daily data for the deutsche mark/dollar and yen/dollar. The coefficient on order flow Δx_t is correctly signed and significant, with t-

statistics above five for both currency pairs. The positive sign indicates that net dollar purchases—a positive Δx_t—lead to a higher deutsche mark price of dollars. The traditional macro fundamental—the interest differential—is correctly signed and significant. (The positive sign arises in the sticky-price monetary model, e.g., because an increase in the dollar interest rate i_t requires immediate dollar appreciation—increase in deutsche mark/dollar—to make room for dollar depreciation induced by uncovered interest parity.) The equation for the deutsche mark shows some evidence of heteroskedasticity, so we correct the standard errors in that case using a heteroskedasticity-consistent covariance matrix (White 1980).

The explanatory power of these regressions is due to order flow Δx_t: regressing Δp_t only on $\Delta(i_t - i_t^*)$ produces an R^2 statistic at 1 percent or lower for both currency pairs and coefficients on $\Delta(i_t - i_t^*)$ that are insignificant at the 5 percent level. (The same story emerges when the *level* of the interest differential is included rather than the change—specifications IV and V.) Adding order flow is what increases the fit so dramatically: R^2 statistics of 64 percent and 46 percent for the deutsche mark and yen equations (specification I), respectively.[9]

The size of the order flow coefficient is consistent with past estimates from single-dealer data. The coefficient of 2.1 in the deutsche mark equation implies that a day with 1,000 more dollar purchases than sales increases the deutsche mark price of a dollar by 2.1 percent. Given an average trade size in our sample of \$3.9 million, \$1 billion of net dollar purchases increases the deutsche mark price by 0.54 percent (= 2.1/3.9), or, at a spot rate of 1.5 deutsche mark/dollar, 0.8 pfennig. For comparison, at the single-dealer level, Lyons (1995) finds that information asymmetry induces the dealer he tracks to increase price by 0.01 of a pfennig (0.0001 deutsche mark) for every incoming buy order of \$10 million. That is 1 pfennig per \$1 billion, quite close to the 0.8 pfennig found here. (Though linearly extrapolating the single-dealer estimate is not an accurate description of individual dealers, it may be a good description of the market's aggregate elasticity.)

V. Conclusion

This paper presents a model of exchange rate determination of a new kind. Instead of relying exclusively on macroeconomic determinants, we draw on a determinant from the field of microstructure: order flow. Order flow is a determinant because it conveys information. This is a

[9] We refer readers to Evans and Lyons (1999) for results on robustness regarding (1) adding constants, insignificant in all equations, (2) direction of causality, (3) nonlinearities, (4) dependence on day of week and activity level, and (5) forecasting.

radical departure from traditional macro approaches, which—with their common-knowledge environments—admit no role for information aggregation. Our findings suggest instead that this market is indeed aggregating information.

Our portfolio shifts model provides explicit characterization of this information aggregation process. The model is also quite successful in that it accounts for more than 60 percent of daily changes in the deutsche mark/dollar rate and more than 40 percent of daily changes in the yen/dollar rate. Our estimates of the sensitivity of the spot rate to order flow are sensible as well and square with past estimates at the individual-dealer level.

Our objective in this paper is to clarify order flow's role in transmitting information to price. Pushing this line further, one may ask, What precisely is the information driving order flow? As noted, from a valuation perspective, there are two distinct views. The first view is that order flow reflects new information about valuation numerators (i.e., future interest differentials). The second view is that order flow reflects new information about valuation denominators (i.e., anything that affects discount rates). Our portfolio shifts model is an example of the latter: by assumption, order flow is unrelated to valuation numerators—the future Δr_t. Order flow of this type can result from, for example, shocks to liquidity demands, shocks to hedging demands, or time-varying risk tolerance. An example consistent with the valuation numerators view is that order flow proxies for changes in individuals' interest differential *expectations.* Future work can distinguish the two views, for example, by decomposing order flow to determine whether specific trader types produce higher-impact (i.e., more informative) orders, as opposed to the undifferentiated price impact of public orders in the portfolio shifts model.

References

Bagwell, Laurie S. "Dutch Auction Repurchases: An Analysis of Shareholder Heterogeneity." *J. Finance* 47 (March 1992): 71–105.

Bank for International Settlements. *Central Bank Survey of Foreign Exchange Market Activity in April 1995.* Basle: Bank Internat. Settlements, Monetary and Econ. Dept., 1996.

Cheung, Yin-Wong, and Wong, Clement Yuk-Pang. "A Survey of Market Practitioners' Views on Exchange Rate Dynamics." *J. Internat. Econ.* 51 (August 2000): 401–19.

Covrig, Vincentiu, and Melvin, Michael T. "Asymmetric Information and Price Discovery in the FX Market: Does Tokyo Know More about the Yen?" Manuscript. Tempe: Arizona State Univ., Dept. Econ., 1998.

Engle, Robert F. "Autoregressive Conditional Heteroscedasticity with Estimates of the Variance of United Kingdom Inflation." *Econometrica* 50 (July 1982): 987–1007.

Evans, Martin D. D. "The Microstructure of Foreign Exchange Dynamics." Manuscript. Washington: Georgetown Univ., Dept. Econ., 1997.

———. "FX Trading and Exchange Rate Dynamics." *J. Finance* (2002), in press.

Evans, Martin D. D., and Lyons, Richard K. "Order Flow and Exchange-Rate Dynamics." Manuscript. Berkeley: Univ. California, Haas School Bus., 1999. http://www.haas.berkeley.edu/~lyons.

Frankel, Jeffrey A., and Rose, Andrew K. "Empirical Research on Nominal Exchange Rates." In *Handbook of International Economics,* vol. 3, edited by Gene M. Grossman and Kenneth S. Rogoff. Amsterdam: Elsevier, 1995.

Isard, Peter. *Exchange Rate Economics.* Cambridge: Cambridge Univ. Press, 1995.

Ito, Takatoshi; Lyons, Richard K.; and Melvin, Michael T. "Is There Private Information in the FX Market? The Tokyo Experiment." *J. Finance* 53 (June 1998): 1111–30.

Jones, Charles M.; Kaul, Gautam; and Lipson, Marc L. "Transactions, Volume, and Volatility." *Rev. Financial Studies* 7 (Winter 1994): 631–51.

Kaul, Aditya; Mehrotra, Vikas; and Morck, Randall. "Demand Curves for Stock Do Slope Down: New Evidence from an Index Weights Adjustment." *J. Finance* 55 (April 2000): 893–912.

Lyons, Richard K. "Tests of Microstructural Hypotheses in the Foreign Exchange Market." *J. Financial Econ.* 39 (October 1995): 321–51.

———. "Optimal Transparency in a Dealer Market with an Application to Foreign Exchange." *J. Financial Intermediation* 5 (July 1996): 225–54.

———. "A Simultaneous Trade Model of the Foreign Exchange Hot Potato." *J. Internat. Econ.* 42 (May 1997): 275–98.

Meese, Richard A. "Currency Fluctuations in the Post–Bretton Woods Era." *J. Econ. Perspectives* 4 (Winter 1990): 117–34.

Meese, Richard A., and Rogoff, Kenneth S. "Empirical Exchange Rate Models of the Seventies: Do They Fit out of Sample?" *J. Internat. Econ.* 14 (February 1983): 3–24.

Naranjo, Andy, and Nimalendran, M. "Government Intervention and Adverse Selection Costs in Foreign Exchange Markets." *Rev. Financial Studies* 13 (Summer 2000): 453–77.

Obstfeld, Maurice, and Rogoff, Kenneth S. "Exchange Rate Dynamics Redux." *J.P.E.* 103 (June 1995): 624–60.

Payne, Richard. "Informed Trade in Spot Foreign Exchange Markets: An Empirical Investigation." Manuscript. London: London School Econ., 1999.

Scholes, Myron S. "The Market for Securities: Substitution versus Price Pressure and the Effects of Information on Share Prices." *J. Bus.* 45 (April 1972): 179–211.

Shleifer, Andrei. "Do Demand Curves for Stocks Slope Down?" *J. Finance* 41 (July 1986): 579–90.

Taylor, Mark P. "The Economics of Exchange Rates." *J. Econ. Literature* 33 (March 1995): 13–47.

White, Halbert. "A Heteroskedasticity-Consistent Covariance Matrix Estimator and a Direct Test for Heteroskedasticity." *Econometrica* 48 (May 1980): 817–38.

Yao, Jian. "Market Making in the Interbank Foreign Exchange Market." Working Paper no. S-98-3. New York: New York Univ., Salomon Center, 1998.

Name Index

The International Library of Critical Writings in Financial Economics

1. The Theory of Corporate Finance (Volumes I and II) *Michael J. Brennan*
2. Futures Markets (Volumes I, II and III) *A.G. Malliaris*
3. Market Efficiency: Stock Market Behaviour in Theory and Practice (Volumes I and II) *Andrew W. Lo*
4. Microstructure: The Organization of Trading and Short Term Price Behavior (Volumes I and II) *Hans R. Stoll*
5. The Debt Market (Volumes I, II and III) *Stephen A. Ross*
6. Options Markets (Volumes I, II and III) *George M. Constantinides and A.G. Malliaris*
7. Empirical Corporate Finance (Volumes I, II, III and IV) *Michael J. Brennan*
8. The Foundations of Continuous Time Finance *Stephen M. Schaefer*
9. International Securities (Volumes I and II) *George C. Philippatos and Gregory Koutmos*
10. Behavioral Finance (Volumes I, II and III) *Hersh Shefrin*
11. Asset Pricing Theory and Tests (Volumes I and II) *Robert R. Grauer*
12. International Capital Markets (Volumes I, II and III) *G. Andrew Karolyi and René M. Stulz*
13. Financial Forecasting (Volumes I and II) *Roy Batchelor and Pami Dua*
14. Emerging Markets *Geert Bekaert and Campbell R. Harvey*
15. Corporate Restructuring (Volumes I and II) *John J. McConnell and David J. Denis*
16. Recent Developments in Corporate Finance (Volumes I and II) *Jay R. Ritter*
17. Foreign Exchange Markets *Richard J. Sweeney*

Future titles will include:

Financial Markets and the Real Economy
John H. Cochrane